Mastering
Visual C#.NET

Mastering™
Visual C#™.NET

Jason Price

Mike Gunderloy

San Francisco   London

Associate Publisher: Richard Mills

Acquisitions Editor: Denise Santoro-Lincoln

Developmental Editor: Tom Cirtin

Editor: Kim Wimpsett

Production Editor: Erica Yee

Technical Editor: Gregory Beamer

Book Designer: Maureen Forys, Happenstance Type-O-Rama

Graphic Illustrator: Tony Jonick

Electronic Publishing Specialist: Jill Niles, Judy Fung, Scott Benoit

Proofreaders: Emily Hsuan, Nelson Kim, Laurie O'Connell, Yariv Rabinovitch, Nancy Riddiough

Indexer: Nancy Guenther

Cover Designer: Design Site

Cover Illustrator/Photographer: Sergie Loobkoff

This book is dedicated to my family. You're still in my heart, even though you are far away.
—Jason Price

This one's for Steve, who is long overdue for a dedication.
—Mike Gunderloy

Acknowledgments

MANY THANKS TO ALL the great, hard-working people at Sybex, including Tom Cirtin, Denise Santoro Lincoln, Kim Wimpsett, and Erica Yee. Thanks also to Gregory Beamer for his thorough technical review.

—Jason Price

As much as some authors (including myself) are solitary creatures, in this electronic age it's impossible to be truly isolated. This book is better for that lack of isolation because it allowed me to bother Ken Getz, Steve White, and Mary Chipman with questions. Mary was especially helpful as I tried to figure out .NET security. The remaining errors, of course, are entirely mine.

Thanks to the editorial staff at *MCP Magazine*—Di Schaffhauser, Keith Ward, Kristen McCarthy, and Michael Domingo—for understanding and for some slack as I tried to juggle book deadlines with magazine deadlines.

Thanks to Denise Santoro Lincoln and the lead author of this book, Jason Price, for bringing me into this project. And of course I'd like to add my thanks to Jason's for the great team at Sybex.

My online family was always there when I wanted to rant about failing code, impossible deadlines, or the general annoyances associated with developing software. Thanks, folks.

And special thanks, as always, to Dana and Adam, who put up with my late nights and distraction as this one went through the publishing process. Without a loving family, I wouldn't have the sanity to write a single word.

—Mike Gunderloy

Contents at a Glance

Contents

Introduction

WELCOME TO *MASTERING VISUAL C# .NET!* As you may already know, .NET is poised to become *the* hot platform for the next wave of technology deployment. .NET's strength is that it is built from the ground up to be used in a distributed environment—in other words, an environment that consists of computers and devices connected via a network.

Microsoft has pledged its commitment and resources to making .NET a pervasive component of life in our technological society—you ignore .NET at your own peril. The bottom line is you need to learn .NET if you want to remain competitive in today's—and tomorrow's—marketplace.

In a nutshell, .NET is a completely new framework for writing many types of applications. Some of the applications you can write using .NET include Windows applications and web-based applications. You can use .NET to develop systems composed of interconnected services that communicate with each other over the Internet.

In addition, you can use .NET to create applications that run on devices such as handheld computers and cellular phones. Although other languages allow you to develop such applications, .NET was designed with the interconnected network in mind.

The .NET Framework consists of the following three primary components:

Development Languages and Tools The development languages that enable you to write .NET programs include C#, Visual Basic .NET (VB .NET), and Managed C++. Microsoft also has a Rapid Application Development (RAD) tool called Visual Studio .NET (VS .NET) that allows you to develop programs in an integrated development environment (IDE). You'll learn how to use C# and VS .NET in this book.

Common Language Runtime The Common Language Runtime (CLR) manages your running code and provides services such as memory management, thread management (which allows you to perform multiple tasks in parallel), and remoting (which allows objects in one application to communicate with objects in another application). The CLR also enforces strict safety and accuracy of your executable code to ensure no tampering occurs.

Framework Base Class Library The Framework Base Class Library is an extensive collection of code written by Microsoft that you can use in your own programs. For example, the Framework Base Class Library contains code that allows you to develop Windows applications, access directories and files on disk, connect to databases and retrieve information, and send and receive data across a network, among many other functions. You'll use the most important classes in the Framework Base Class Library in this book.

C# is one of languages you can use to write .NET applications. C# owes its heritage to languages such as Java, C, and C++—and, of course, those languages arose from the development of earlier languages. If you've programmed in Java or C++, you'll find C# easy to learn. C# isn't the only language for writing .NET applications. It is our opinion, however, that C# will be the primary language of choice for .NET development.

You might be wondering if you should learn C# or Java. Our answer is that you should learn both. Just because .NET is hot, it doesn't mean Java will be displaced any time soon. Both languages will coexist and evolve together—until something better comes along.

Who Should Read This Book?

This book was written for budding C# programmers. This book contains everything you need to know to master C#. No prior programming experience is assumed, but if you already know a programming language such as Java, C++, or Visual Basic, you'll be off to a running start. You may even know C# already; if so, you'll find that this book delves deeper into the advanced C# and .NET topics than most other books.

If you're a novice, you'll find Part I of this book easy to follow, and you'll get up to speed on the fundamental programming concepts used in C#. If you're an intermediate to advanced programmer, you'll be able to skim through the first five chapters of Part I quickly. Once you've mastered the C# language covered in Part I, you'll find Parts II and III of this book ideal for understanding the more advanced aspects of C# and .NET.

How to Use This Book

This book is divided up into three parts.

Part 1: "Fundamental C# Programming"

In Part I of this book, "Fundamental C# Programming," you'll learn everything you need to know to write simple C# programs. Part I consists of 13 chapters.

In Chapter 1, "Introduction to Visual C# and the .NET Framework," you'll be introduced to the C# language. You also learn about Microsoft's RAD tool, Visual Studio .NET. Visual Studio .NET allows you to develop programs in an IDE. Finally, you'll see how to use the extensive documentation from Microsoft that comes with .NET.

In Chapter 2, "Basic C# Programming," you'll learn how to write simple programs, how to store information in memory, and how to handle keyboard input and format screen output.

In Chapter 3, "Expressions and Operators," you'll explore how to use expressions and operators. An *expression* is typically a statement that performs some kind of calculation—using an *operator*—and returns a value.

In Chapter 4, "Decisions, Loops, and Preprocessor Directives," you'll learn how to execute different branches of code based on decisions and how to repeat statements using loops. You'll also learn about the preprocessor, which is program that reads your program source files prior to compilation. You can give the preprocessor instructions, known as *directives*, which can affect what parts of your program are actually compiled.

In Chapter 5, "Object-Oriented Programming," and Chapter 6, "More about Classes and Objects," you'll explore how to define your own types using classes and structs—and how to use them in your programs. You'll see how you can create objects from classes. You'll also learn how you can use classes and objects to model things that exist in the real world and how they can simplify the task of writing programs to solve complex problems.

In Chapter 7, "Derived Classes," you'll learn how a class may be derived from another class. You'll also learn how you can overload an operator to perform your own code when a particular operator is used, rather than using the default provided by C#.

In Chapter 8, "Interfaces," you'll explore interfaces. An *interface* contains a list of declarations such as method and property declarations. You can then have your class implement a given interface; your class must then define the code for the declarations specified in that interface. By having your class implement an interface, you're guaranteeing that your class contains the code for the items declared in that interface.

In Chapter 9, "Strings, Dates, Times, and Time Spans," you'll examine the use of strings and how you manipulate strings in your programs. You'll also learn how to represent dates and times in your programs.

In Chapter 10, "Arrays and Indexers," you'll learn about *arrays*, which are sets of consecutive of storage compartments that can hold data elements of the same type. You use arrays to store multiple variables or objects.

In Chapter 11, "Collections," you'll explore collections. *Collections* are objects that store many elements and whose capacity you can change after you've created them. These objects offer flexible ways to access their elements. As you master C#, you'll find collections to be useful when you need to perform complex manipulation of data.

In Chapter 12, "Delegates and Events," you'll learn about delegates and events. A *delegate* acts like a pointer to a function, and you can use them to call different functions that you specify at run-time. Delegates are closely tied to events—*events* are in fact a special kind of delegate. You can use events to send notifications that something has occurred to a particular object.

In Chapter 13, "Exceptions and Debugging," you'll explore exceptions and debugging. When an error or abnormal condition occurs during your program's execution, an *exception* is thrown. An example of a program error, or *bug*, might be attempting to divide a number by zero. An example of an abnormal program condition might be running out of memory.

Part 2: "Advanced C# Programming"

In Part II of this book, "Advanced C# Programming," you'll learn about the more complex aspects of C# programming. Part II consists of 8 chapters.

In Chapter 14, "Threads," you'll learn how to use threads, which allow you to perform multiple tasks in parallel. You'll learn that there are some problems to consider when your application uses multiple threads. In particular, you need to worry about synchronizing threads and handling deadlocks that can arise when two threads are fighting for resources to do their work.

In Chapter 15, "Streams and Input/Output," you'll explore how to work with input/output streams. You'll look at basic file and directory operations, such as opening a file and examining the contents of a directory. You'll also learn how to read and write data in a variety of ways, including ways to use the network as a data transport.

In Chapter 16, "Assemblies," you'll examine how .NET groups code into units known as *assemblies*. .NET uses assemblies for version tracking, security, deployment, and type identity—among other things. You'll learn how to create assemblies and how to include more than one file in the same assembly.

In Chapter 17, "Attributes and Reflection," you'll learn about metadata, which describes the contents of assemblies. Metadata consists of attributes that describe types, members, modules, and assemblies. You'll explore intrinsic attributes that are provided by default and custom attributes; you'll see how to create of your own custom attributes to extend the metadata stored in assemblies.

In Chapter 18, "Remoting," you'll explore remoting, which allows objects in one application to communicate with objects in another application. Remoting allows you to develop distributed software components that interact with each other.

In Chapter 19, "Security," you'll learn about .NET's security system. You can use code-access security to specify exactly which operations an application is allowed to perform. Code-access security allows you to select individual permissions to apply to code based on the code's membership in code groups. A code group can be based on the publisher of the code, the identity of the code, the location from which the code was obtained, or other factors. .NET also includes a role-based security system that lets you determine whether a particular user should have access to a resource.

In Chapter 20, "XML," you'll explore how to use the Extensible Markup Language (XML) with .NET. .NET uses XML for many tasks, from storing configuration files to serializing objects for transmission to a remote application. You can read and write XML files, analyze their structure, transform XML files into new formats, or use them to work with data.

In Chapter 21, "Other Classes in the Base Class Library," you'll learn about some of the other .NET classes contained in the Framework Base Class Library. You'll explore the graphics classes that allow you to draw elements, globalization classes that allow your software to be used in other locales and other languages, debug and trace classes that allow you to see debugging information either at design-time or run-time, along with advanced classes that support the features of the .NET runtime itself.

Part 3: ".NET Programming with C#"

In Part III of this book, ".NET Programming with C#," you'll be introduced to databases, you'll learn how to access a database using a C# program, and you'll see how to program Windows and web applications. Part III consists of 5 chapters.

In Chapter 22, "Introduction to Databases," you'll learn the basics of databases and see how to use the Structured Query Language (SQL) to access a database. This chapter shows how to access a SQL Server database named Northwind. This database contains the information for the fictitious Northwind Company, which sells food products.

In Chapter 23, "Active Data Objects: ADO.NET," you'll explore how to access a database from a C# program using ADO.NET. ADO.NET is Active Data Objects for the .NET Framework. You'll learn how to connect to a database and issue SQL statements that retrieve and modify the information stored in a database.

In Chapter 24, "Introduction to Windows Applications," you'll learn about Windows programming. A Windows program takes advantage of the graphical environment for display and use of the mouse, as well as the keyboard, for input. Windows provides graphical items such as menus, text boxes, radio buttons, and text boxes that allow you to build a visual interface that is easy to use.

In Chapter 25, "Active Server Pages: ASP.NET," you'll explore Active Server Pages for .NET (ASP.NET). ASP.NET allows you to create web pages whose content may change at run-time and allows you to develop applications that are accessed using a web browser. For example, you could develop an application that allows users to order products over the Web, or you could create a stock-trading application that allows users to place trades for shares in companies.

In Chapter 26, "Web Services," you'll learn how to build a simple web service. A *web service* is a software component that delivers information over the Internet (or a private intranet) to fulfill a specific need. For example, you could build a web service that returns the current price of a company's stock.

Appendixes

This book also contains three appendixes for reference purposes.

Appendix A, "C# Keywords," summarizes the keywords used in the C# language.

Appendix B, "C# Compiler Options," lists the options used with the C# compiler, which enable you to compile your programs.

Appendix C, "Regular Expressions," summarizes the C# regular expressions, which allow you to search for a specified set of characters or pattern of characters.

Downloading the Example Programs

Throughout this book, you'll see many example programs that illustrate the concepts described in the text. These are marked with a listing number and title, such as the one shown here:

LISTING 1.1: THE "HELLO WORLD" PROGRAM

You can download a ZIP file containing these programs from the Sybex website at www.sybex.com. You can use a program such as WinZip to extract the contents of the ZIP file. The filenames will correspond to the listing numbers.

Part 1

Fundamental C# Programming

Chapter 1

Introduction to C#

IN THIS CHAPTER, YOU'LL be introduced to the C# language. You'll see a simple example program that displays the words *Hello World!* on your computer's screen, along with the current date and time.

You'll also learn about Microsoft's Rapid Application Development (RAD) tool, Visual Studio .NET. Visual Studio .NET enables you to develop and run programs in an integrated development environment. This environment uses all the great features of Windows, such as the mouse and intuitive menus, and increases your productivity as a programmer.

In the final sections of this chapter, you'll see how to use the extensive documentation from Microsoft that comes with the .NET Software Development Kit (SDK) and Visual Studio .NET. This documentation goes well beyond the text of this book, and you'll find it invaluable as you become an expert C# programmer.

NOTE *Before you can develop C# programs, you'll need to install the .NET SDK or Visual Studio .NET. You can download the .NET SDK at* http://msdn.microsoft.com/downloads. *Once you've downloaded the executable file, go ahead and run it. Follow the instructions on the screen to install the .NET SDK on your computer. You can also purchase a copy of Visual Studio .NET from Microsoft at their website.*

Featured in this chapter:

◆ Building Your First C# Program

◆ Learning about Visual Studio .NET

◆ Working with the .NET Documentation

Developing Your First C# Program

Learning a new programming language is sometimes a daunting task. To get you started, you'll begin with a variation on the classic "Hello World" program. This program traditionally starts all programming books—and who are we to argue with tradition?

THE ORIGINS OF THE "HELLO WORLD" PROGRAM

As far as we know, the tradition of the "Hello World" program being used to start programming books began in the seminal work *The C Programming Language* by Brian Kernighan and Dennis Ritchie (Prentice Hall PTR, 1988). Incidentally, C is one of the languages that C# owes its development to, along with Java and C++.

The following program displays the words *Hello World!* on your computer's screen. The program will also display the current date and time retrieved from your computer. This program, shown in Listing 1.1, illustrates a few simple tenets of the C# language.

LISTING 1.1: THE "HELLO WORLD" PROGRAM

```
/*
   Example1_1.cs: a variation on the classic "Hello World!" program.
   This program displays the words "Hello World!" on the screen,
   along with the current date and time
*/

class Example1_1
{

  public static void Main()
  {

    // display "Hello World!" on the screen
    System.Console.WriteLine("Hello World!");

    // display the current date and time
    System.Console.WriteLine("The current date and time is " +
      System.DateTime.Now);
  }

}
```

This program is contained in a text file named Example1_1.cs. This file is known as a *program source file*, or simply a *source file*, because it contains the lines that make up the program. You use a compiler to translate a source file into an executable file that a computer can run; you'll learn more about this later in the "Compiling a Program" section.

NOTE You can download all the source files for the programs featured in this book from the Sybex website at www.sybex.com. You'll find instructions on downloading these files in the introduction of this book. Once you've downloaded the files, you can follow along with the examples without having to type in the program listings.

The `Example1_1.cs` source file contains the lines that make up the "Hello World" program. You'll notice that the extension for the `Example1_1.cs` file is `.cs`—this is the recommended extension for C# source files. Because the file is a text file, you can open and view the `Example1_1.cs` file using a text editor such as Notepad. Go ahead and open the file if you want.

TIP *You can also edit and save source files using Notepad, although as you develop more complex programs you'll find that Visual Studio .NET is a much more efficient tool to use. You'll learn about Visual Studio .NET later in this chapter.*

Let's go through the lines in `Example1_1.cs`. The first four lines are as follows:

```
/*
  Example1_1.cs: a variation on the classic "Hello World!" program.
  This program displays the words "Hello World!" on the screen,
  along with the current date and time
*/
```

The compiler ignores anything placed between the `/*` and `*/` characters. They are comments that we've used to inform you what the program does. Later, you'll see the use of single-line comments that start with two forward slash characters (`//`).

The next two lines start a class using the `class` keyword:

```
class Example1_1
{
```

The open curly brace (`{`) marks the beginning of the `Example1_1` class. Similarly, the close curly brace (`}`), shown at the end of Listing 1.1, marks the end of the `Example1_1` class. As you'll learn in Chapter 5, "Object-Oriented Programming," you use a *class* to define a template that contains methods and fields—and you can use this template to create objects of that class.

Methods are self-contained units of code that carry out a specific task, and they typically consist of one or more program lines. *Fields* are named storage areas where you can store values. The `Example1_1` class doesn't contain any fields, but it does contain a method named `Main()`.

NOTE *Programs typically contain a `Main()` method. This method is run, or called, automatically when you run your program. The exception is a type library, which requires another program to call its functionality and therefore doesn't require a `Main()` method.*

In the next section, we'll take you through the lines in the `Main()` method.

Understanding the *Main()* Method

As mentioned, methods typically consist of one or more program lines that carry out the method's task. The program lines that make up a method begin and end with open and close curly braces, respectively. The `Main()` method in the example "Hello World" program is defined as follows:

```
public static void Main()
{

  // display "Hello World!" on the screen
  System.Console.WriteLine("Hello World!");
```

```
    // display the current date and time
    System.Console.WriteLine("The current date and time is " +
      System.DateTime.Now);

  }
```

The `public` keyword is an access modifier that specifies the level of availability of the method outside of the class; `public` specifies that the `Main()` method is available without restriction and may be called anywhere.

NOTE *You'll learn more about access modifiers in Chapter 5.*

As you'll learn in Chapter 6, "More about Classes and Objects," the `static` keyword indicates that the `Main()` method belongs to the class, rather than any particular object of the class. If we didn't use the `static` keyword when defining the method, we would have to first create an object of the class and then call the method. This may sound a little confusing, but you'll understand exactly what we mean after you've read Chapters 5 and 6.

Methods can return a value to the statement from which they are called. For example, you might want to perform some kind of calculation in a method and return the result of that calculation. However, you may not always want to return a value, and that's what the `void` keyword does. As you can see in the example program, the `void` keyword indicates that the `Main()` method doesn't return a value.

Let's take a look at the program lines contained within the open and close curly brackets; these lines carry out the tasks for the method and are run when the `Main()` method is called. The first program line is as follows:

```
    // display "Hello World!" on the screen
```

This line begins with two forward slash characters (`//`). These indicate that the line is a comment. As mentioned, the `/*` and `*/` characters also mark the beginning and end of comments. The difference between these two ways of marking lines as comments is that the `//` characters mark a single line as a comment, whereas the `/*` and `*/` characters mark multiple lines as comments. You'll learn more about comments in Chapter 2, "Basic C# Programming."

The second program line in the `Main()` method is as follows:

```
    System.Console.WriteLine("Hello World!");
```

This line calls the `WriteLine()` method. This method displays a line of output on your computer's screen. In the example program, the call to this method displays a line containing the words *Hello World!*

As you'll learn in Chapter 6, *namespaces* separate class declarations, and `System` is a namespace created by Microsoft. The `System` namespace contains a number of useful classes you can use in your programs, and you'll see some of them in this book. The `Console` class is one of the classes in the `System` namespace. The `Console` class contains methods you can use to display output on a computer's screen.

NOTE *The `Console` class also contains methods you can use to read input from the computer's keyboard, and you'll see how to do that in Chapter 2.*

As you can see from the previous line, a period (`.`) separates the `System` namespace, the `Console` class, and the `WriteLine()` method. The period is known as the *dot operator*, and it may be used to separate the namespace, class, and method parts of a program line. You'll learn more about the dot operator in Chapter 5.

The third line in the `Main()` method is another single line comment:

```
// display the current date and time
```

The fourth line in the `Main()` method displays the current date and time:

```
System.Console.WriteLine("The current date and time is " +
    System.DateTime.Now);
```

As you can see, this line uses `System.DateTime.Now` to display the current date and time. `Now` is a *property* of `DateTime` that returns the current date and time set for the computer on which the program is running. You'll learn all about properties in Chapter 6. In a nutshell, the `Now` property reads the current date and time from your computer. `Now` is a static property, which means you can call it without first creating a `DateTime` object.

The remaining lines in `Example1_1.cs` contain close curly braces that end the `Main()` method and the `Example1_1` class.

Compiling a Program

A program source file is written in text that you can read. Unfortunately, a computer cannot directly run the instructions contained in that source file, and you must first *compile* that file using a piece of software known as a *compiler.* The compiler reads your program source file and converts the instructions contained in that file into code that a computer may then run, or *execute.* The file produced by the compiler is known as an *executable file.* Once you've compiled your program, you can then run it.

You can compile a program using either the command-line compiler that comes with the .NET SDK, or you can use Visual Studio .NET. In this section, you'll see how to use the command-line version of the compiler to compile the `Example1_1.cs` program. Later in the "Introducing Visual Studio .NET" section you'll see how to use Visual Studio .NET to compile a program.

You run the command-line version of the compiler by entering `csc` in the Command Prompt tool, followed by the name of your program source file. For example, to compile `Example1_1.cs`, you would enter the following command in the Command Prompt tool:

```
csc Example1_1.cs
```

NOTE *You can also enter one or more options that are then passed to the compiler. These options control things like the name of the executable file produced by the compiler. You can see the full list of options in Appendix B, "C# Compiler Options." You can also view the compiler options by entering* `csc /help` *in the Command Prompt tool.*

If you want to follow along with the examples, go ahead and start the Command Prompt tool by selecting Start ➢ Programs ➢ Accessories ➢ Command Prompt.

NOTE *If you're using Windows XP rather than Windows 2000, you start the Command Prompt tool by selecting Start ➢ All Programs ➢ Accessories ➢ Command Prompt.*

Next, you need to change directories to where you copied the `Example1_1.cs` file. To do this, you first enter the partition on your hard disk where you saved the file. For example, let's say you saved the file in the C#\programs directory of the C partition of your hard disk. To access the C partition, you enter the following line into the Command Prompt tool, then you press the Enter key:

```
C:
```

Next, to move to the C#\programs directory, you enter cd followed by C#\programs:

```
cd C#\programs
```

To compile Example1_1.cs using csc, you enter the following command:

```
csc Example1_1.cs
```

Notice that the name of the program source file follows csc—it's Example1_1.cs in this case.

WARNING   If you get an error when running csc, you'll need to add the directory where you installed the SDK to your Path environment variable. The Path environment variable specifies a list of directories that contain executable programs. Whenever you run a program from the Command Prompt tool, the directories in the Path variable are searched for the program you want to run. Your current directory is also searched. To set your Path environment variable, select Start ➢ Settings ➢ Control Panel. Then double-click System and select the Advanced tab. Next, click the Environment Variables button and double-click Path from the system variables area at the bottom. Finally, add the directory where you installed the SDK to your Path environment variable. Click OK to save your change, and then click OK again on the next dialog box. Next, restart the Command Prompt tool so that your change is picked up. You should then be able to run csc successfully.

The compiler takes the Example1_1.cs file and compiles it into an executable file named Example1_1 .exe. The .exe file contains instructions that a computer can run—and the .exe file extension indicates the file is an executable file.

You run an executable file using the Command Prompt tool by entering the name of that executable file. For example, to run the Example1_1.exe file, you enter the following line in the Command Prompt tool and then you press the Enter key:

```
Example1_1
```

NOTE   You can omit the .exe extension when running a program. For example, you can use Example1_1 to run Example1_1.exe.

When you run the program, you should see the following text displayed in your Command Prompt window:

```
Hello World!
The current date and time is 8/1/2002 12:22:44 PM
```

Needless to say, your date and time will differ from that shown in the previous line. This date and time is read from your computer when you run the program.

Introducing the Microsoft Intermediate Language (MSIL)

When you compile a program, the .exe file produced by the compiler contains instructions written in Microsoft Intermediate Language (MSIL). MSIL is frequently abbreviated to IL. Now, a computer can only run programs written in their own native tongue: machine code. *Machine code* is a series of binary numbers (zeros and ones) that a computer can understand and run.

IL instructions are not written in machine code—and therefore an additional step is required to convert the IL into machine code before your program is run for the first time. This step is performed automatically by a piece of software known as the Just In Time (JIT) compiler.

When you run your program, the IL instructions in your `.exe` file are converted by the JIT compiler into machine code that the computer then runs. This is efficient because the JIT compiler detects the type of Central Processing Unit (CPU) in the computer and produces machine code specifically tailored to that CPU. This results in machine code that runs as fast as possible.

NOTE *When you distribute your programs, you can then be sure your program will run as fast as possible, regardless of the CPU used by the computer on which your program runs.*

JIT compilation is only performed the first time your program is run, and the resulting machine code is automatically stored. When your program runs again, the stored machine code is reused. That way, the computer doesn't need to keep re-compiling the IL instructions into machine code. Of course, when the computer is turned off or rebooted, the JIT will need to recompile your program into IL instructions when it is run again.

Introducing Visual Studio .NET

Visual Studio .NET (VS .NET) is Microsoft's Rapid Application Development (RAD) tool. VS .NET is an integrated development environment that you can use to create many types of .NET programs. VS .NET is a more productive tool than a simple text editor such as Notepad. This is because VS .NET allows you to enter your program, compile it, and run it—all within an easy to use graphical Windows environment.

VS .NET also enables you to step through each line in your program as it runs. This is useful when your program has errors, or *bugs*. The process of getting rid of bugs in your program is known as *debugging*—and you'll learn about this in Chapter 13, "Exceptions and Debugging." You'll also learn how to use VS .NET's *debugger* in that chapter. You use the debugger to step through each line in your program.

In the previous section, you saw a program that displayed the words *Hello World!* along with the current date and time on your computer's screen. This type of program is known as a *console application* because it displays output directly on the computer's screen on which the program is running.

You can use VS .NET to create console applications, as well as the following type of applications:

Windows Applications   Windows applications are programs that take advantage of the visual controls offered by the Windows operating system, such as menus, buttons, and editable text boxes. Windows Explorer, which you use to navigate the file system of your computer, is one example of a Windows application. You'll learn about Windows programming in Chapter 24, "Introduction to Windows Applications."

ASP.NET Applications   ASP.NET applications are programs that run over the Internet. You access an ASP.NET application using a web browser, such as Internet Explorer. Examples of ASP.NET applications would be online banking, stock trading, or auction systems. You'll learn about ASP.NET programming in Chapter 25, "Active Server Pages: ASP.NET."

ASP.NET Web Services   ASP.NET web services are also programs that run over the Internet. ASP.NET web services are also known as XML web services. The difference is that you can use them to offer a service that could be used in a distributed system of interconnected services. For example, Microsoft's Passport web service offers identification and authentication of web users you could then use in your own web application. You'll learn about web services in Chapter 26, "Web Services."

The previous list is not an exhaustive list of the types of applications you can develop with VS .NET, but it does give you flavor for the broad range of VS .NET's capabilities.

In the rest of this section, you'll see how to develop and run the "Hello World" program using VS .NET. If you've installed VS .NET on your computer, you'll be able to follow along with the example. If you don't have VS .NET, then don't worry—you'll be able to see what's going on from the figures provided.

Starting Visual Studio .NET and Creating a Project

All of your work in VS .NET is organized into *projects*. Projects contain the source and executable files for your program, among other items. If you have VS .NET installed, go ahead and start it by selecting Start ➢ Programs ➢ Microsoft Visual Studio .NET ➢ Microsoft Visual Studio .NET. Once VS .NET has started, you'll see the Start page (see Figure 1.1).

FIGURE 1.1

The Start page

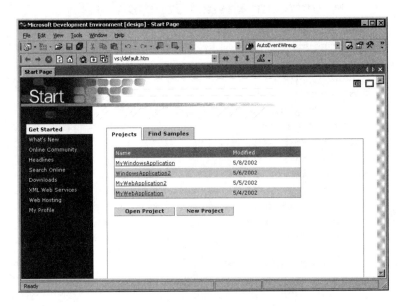

From the Start page, you can see any existing projects you've created. You can open and create projects using the Open Project and New Project buttons, respectively. You'll create a new project shortly.

USING THE VS .NET LINKS

As you can see from Figure 1.1, VS .NET contains a number of links on the left of the Start page. Some of these links provide access to useful information on the Internet about .NET; the links are as follows:

Get Started Opens the Start page. You can open and create projects from the Start page, and you saw an example Start page earlier in Figure 1.1.

What's New Use this link to view any updates for VS .NET or Windows. You can also view upcoming training events and conferences.

Online Community Get in touch with other members of the .NET community. Includes links to websites and newsgroups.

Headlines View the latest news on .NET.

Search Online Use this link to search the MSDN Online Library for technical material such as published articles on .NET.

Downloads Download trial applications and example programs from the websites featured here.

XML Web Services Find registered XML web services that you can then use in your own programs. XML web services are also known as ASP.NET web services. You'll learn more about web services in Chapter 26.

Web Hosting A web hosting company is an organization that can take your program and run it for you. They take care of the computers on which your program runs. You use the Web Hosting link to view companies that provide web hosting services to run your programs.

My Profile This link allows you to set items such as your required keyboard scheme and window layout.

Go ahead and click these links and explore the information provided. As you'll see, there's a huge amount of information about .NET on the Internet.

CREATING A NEW PROJECT

When you're finished examining the information in the previous links, go ahead and create a new project by clicking the New Project button on the Get Started page.

NOTE *You can also create a new project by selecting File ➤ New ➤ Project or by pressing Ctrl+Shift+N on your keyboard.*

When you create a new project, VS .NET displays the New Project dialog box that you use to select the type of project you want to create. You also enter the name and location of your new project; the location is the directory where you want to store the files for your project.

Because you're going to be creating a C# console application, select Visual C# Projects from the Project Types section on the left of the New Project dialog box, and select Console Application from the Templates section on the right. Enter **MyConsoleApplication** in the Name field, and keep the default directory in the Location field. Figure 1.2 shows the completed New Project dialog box with these settings.

FIGURE 1.2

The New Project dialog box with the appropriate settings for a C# console application

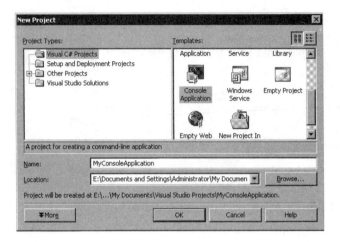

Click the OK button to create the new project.

WORKING IN THE VS .NET ENVIRONMENT

Once your new project has been created, the main development screen is displayed (see Figure 1.3). This screen is the environment in which you'll develop your project. As you can see, VS .NET has already created some starting code for you; this code is a skeleton for your program—you'll see how to modify it shortly. In this section, we'll give you a brief description of the different parts of the VS .NET environment.

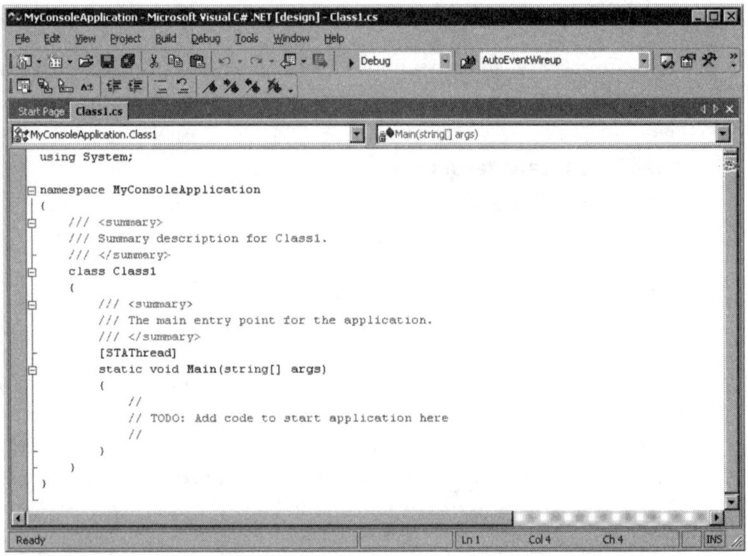

FIGURE 1.3

The VS .NET environment

```
using System;

namespace MyConsoleApplication
{
    /// <summary>
    /// Summary description for Class1.
    /// </summary>
    class Class1
    {
        /// <summary>
        /// The main entry point for the application.
        /// </summary>
        [STAThread]
        static void Main(string[] args)
        {
            //
            // TODO: Add code to start application here
            //
        }
    }
}
```

NOTE   *Depending on your settings for VS .NET, your screen may look slightly different from that shown in Figure 1.3.*

The VS .NET menu contains the following items:

File   From the File menu, you can open, close, and save project files.

Edit   From the Edit menu, you can cut, copy, and paste text from the Clipboard. The Clipboard is a temporary storage area.

View   From the View menu, you can hide and show different windows such as the Solution Explorer (which allows you to see the files that make up your project), Class View (which allows you to see the classes and objects in your project), Server Explorer (which allows you to explore items such as databases—you'll learn about databases and the use of Server Explorer in Part III of this book), and the Properties window (which allows you to set the properties of objects, such as the size of a button, for example), among others. You can also use the View menu to select the toolbars you want to display.

Project   From the Project menu, you can add class files to your project and add Windows forms and controls (you'll learn about Windows forms and controls in Part III).

Build   From the Build menu, you can compile the source files in your project.

Debug   From the Debug menu, you can start your program with or without debugging. Debugging enables you to step through your program line by line looking for errors. You'll learn about the debugger in Chapter 13.

Tools   From the Tools menu, you can connect to a database and customize your settings for VS .NET (for example, you can set the colors used for different parts of your program lines or set the initial page displayed by VS .NET when you start it).

Window   From the Window menu, you can like switch between files you've opened and hide windows.

Help   From the Help menu, you can open the documentation on .NET. You'll learn how to use this documentation later in this chapter in the "Using the .NET Documentation" section.

The VS .NET toolbar contains a series of buttons that act as shortcuts to some of the options in the menus. For example, you can save a file or all files, cut and paste text from the Clipboard, and start a program using the debugger. You'll learn how to use some of these features in this chapter.

The code shown in the window (below the toolbar) with the title `Class.1.cs` is code that is automatically generated by VS .NET, and in the next section you'll modify this code.

MODIFYING THE VS .NET–GENERATED CODE

Once VS .NET has created your project, it will display some starting code for the console application with a class name of `Class1.cs`. You can use this code as the beginning for your own program. Figure 1.3—shown earlier—shows the starting code created by VS .NET.

The Main() method created by VS .NET is as follows:

```
static void Main(string[] args)
{
  //
  // TODO: Add code to start application here
  //
}
```

As you can see, this code contains comments that indicate where you add your own code. Go ahead and replace the three lines in the Main() method with the lines shown in the following Main() method:

```
static void Main(string[] args)
{
  // display "Hello World!" on the screen
  System.Console.WriteLine("Hello World!");

  // display the current date and time
  System.Console.WriteLine("The current date and time is " +
    System.DateTime.Now);
}
```

As you can see, the new lines display the words *Hello World!* on the screen, along with the current date and time. Once you've replaced the code in the Main() method, the next steps are to compile and run your program.

Compiling and Running the Program

As always, you must first compile your program before you can run it. Because programs in VS .NET are organized into projects, you must compile the project—this is also known as *building* the project. To build your project, select Build ➢ Build Solution. This compiles the Class1.cs source file into an executable file.

TIP   You can also press Ctrl+Shift+B on your keyboard to build your project.

Finally, you can now run your program. To run your program, select Debug ➢ Start Without Debugging. When you select Start Without Debugging, the program will pause at the end allowing you to view the output.

TIP   You can also press Ctrl+F5 on your keyboard to run your program.

When you run your program, VS .NET will run the program in a new Command Prompt window, as shown in Figure 1.4. Your program is run in a Command Prompt window because it is a console application.

To end the program, go ahead and press any key. This will also close the Command Prompt window.

You've barely scratched the surface of VS .NET in this section. You'll explore some of the other features of VS .NET later in this book—including how to step through each line in a program using the debugger that is integrated with VS .NET. You typically use the debugger to find errors in your programs, and you'll see how to use the debugger in Chapter 13.

In the next section, you'll learn how to use the extensive documentation that comes with .NET.

FIGURE 1.4

The running program

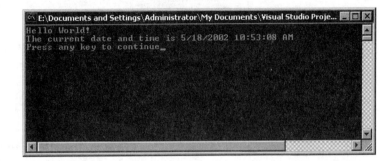

Using the .NET Documentation

Both the .NET SDK and VS .NET come with extensive documentation, including the full reference to all the classes in .NET. As you become proficient with C#, you'll find this reference documentation invaluable.

In the following sections, you'll see how to access the .NET documentation, see how to search the documentation, and view some of the contents of the documentation. Depending on whether you're using the .NET SDK or VS .NET, you access the documentation in a slightly different way. You'll see how to use both ways to access the documentation in this section.

NOTE *The documentation that comes with the .NET SDK is a subset of the documentation that comes with VS .NET.*

Accessing the Documentation Using the .NET SDK

If you're using the .NET SDK, you access the documentation by selecting Start ➢ Programs ➢ .NET Framework SDK ➢ Overview. Figure 1.5 shows the .NET Framework SDK Documentation home page—this is the starting page for the documentation.

On the left of the page, you can see the various sections that make up the contents of the documentation. You can view the index of the documentation by selecting the Index tab at the bottom of the page.

TIP *You can also view the Index window by selecting Help ➢ Index or by pressing Ctrl+Alt+F2 on your keyboard.*

You can search the index by entering a word in the Look For field of the Index tab. Figure 1.6 shows the results of searching for *Console*. Figure 1.6 also shows the overview for the Console class on the right. We opened this overview by double-clicking the About Console Class link in the Index window on the left of the screen.

FIGURE 1.5

The documentation
home page

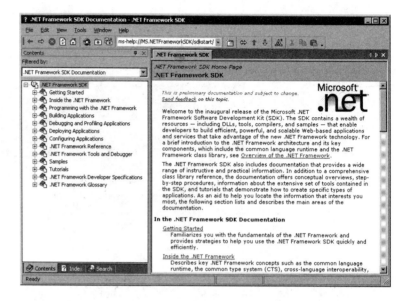

FIGURE 1.6

Searching the index
for the word
Console

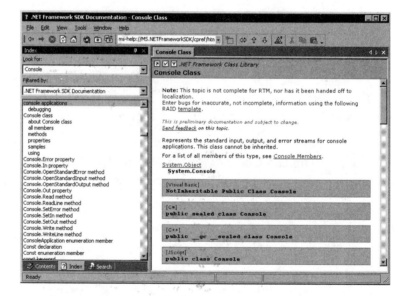

You can also search all pages in the documentation using the Search tab. You display the Search tab by selecting it from the bottom of the screen.

TIP   You can also view the Search window by selecting Help ➤ Search or by pressing Ctrl+Alt+F3 on your keyboard.

You enter the words you want to search for in the Look For field of the Search window. Figure 1.7 shows the Search tab and the search results returned by a search for *WriteLine*. When you run the search, the names of the pages that contain your required words are displayed in the Search Results window that appears at the bottom of the screen (you can see this window in Figure 1.7).

FIGURE 1.7

Searching all of the documentation for the word *WriteLine*

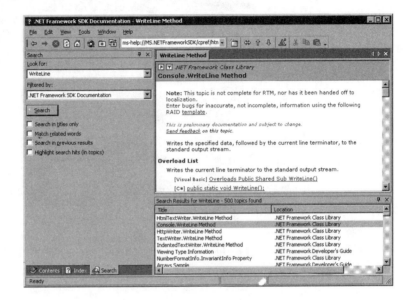

TIP   You can also view the Search Results window by selecting Help ➤ Search results or by pressing Shift+Alt+F3 on your keyboard.

You view the contents of a particular page shown in the Search Results window by double-clicking the appropriate line. For example, in Figure 1.7 shown earlier, we double-clicked the second line in the Search Results window. This line contained the "Console.WriteLine Method" page and as you can see, this page is displayed in the window above the search results in Figure 1.7.

In the next section, you'll see how to access the documentation using VS .NET.

Accessing the Documentation Using VS .NET

If you're using VS .NET, you access the documentation using the Help menu. To access the contents of the documentation, you select Help ➤ Contents. Figure 1.8 shows the contents displayed in VS .NET. Notice that the documentation is displayed directly in VS .NET, rather than in a separate window as is done when viewing documentation with the .NET SDK.

FIGURE 1.8

The documentation contents viewed in VS .NET

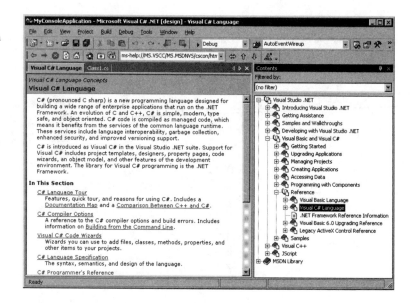

The Help menu also provides access to similar Index and Search windows as you saw in the previous section.

Summary

In this chapter, you were introduced to the C# language. You saw a simple example program that displayed the words *Hello World!* on your computer's screen, along with the current date and time. You also learned about the compiler.

You also learned about Microsoft's Rapid Application Development (RAD) tool, Visual Studio .NET. Visual Studio .NET allows you to develop, run, and debug programs in an integrated development environment.

In the final sections of this chapter, you saw how to use the extensive documentation from Microsoft that comes with the .NET SDK and Visual Studio .NET. As you become an expert C# programmer, you'll find this documentation invaluable.

In the next chapter, you'll learn more about the basics of C# programming.

Chapter 2

Basic C# Programming

THIS CHAPTER PROVIDES A foundation for writing simple C# programs. Later chapters will build on this foundation. You'll learn how to write simple programs, store information in memory, handle keyboard input, and format screen output.

Featured in this chapter:

◆ Understanding Statements, Whitespace, and Blocks

◆ Using Comments to Explain Your Code

◆ Understanding Data Types, Variables, and Constants

◆ Introducing Strings

◆ Understanding Enumerations

◆ Handling Input and Output

Using Statements, Whitespace, and Blocks

A C# program consists of a file that contains a series of instructions; each instruction is a *statement* that tells C# what to do. A statement terminates with a semicolon (;), which is what tells C# the end of the statement has been reached. The following are examples of statements:

```
int count = 1;
System.Console.WriteLine("count = " + count);
System.Console.WriteLine(
  "A multi-line statement"
);
```

The first statement is a *variable declaration*, which creates a variable named count. We will use this variable to store only integer values, so we declare its type to be int, and we assign it the integer value 1. (We'll talk more about types, variables, and variable assignments later in this chapter.) The second statement displays the value stored in the count variable using a call to the System.Console .WriteLine() method—a *method* is a group of statements that you can execute as one unit; you'll learn about methods in Chapter 5, "Object-Oriented Programming."

When you're coding statements, you'll often want to use spacing to make your code more readable. Adding blank lines between sections or indenting a series of related instructions, for example, can help show how your program is structured. In C#, these extra spaces, tabs, and blank lines are all known as *whitespace* because those characters are just extra "room" in the statements.

The following examples show the same statements as those shown previously, but with additional whitespace:

```
int count = 1;
System.Console.WriteLine( "count = " + count);
```

C# usually ignores the whitespace within code. In this example, the variable count is declared and assigned the value 1 without any problems; its value is also displayed correctly by the second statement. However, C# does not ignore whitespace when it forms part of a string. For example:

```
System.Console.WriteLine( "count   =   " + count);
```

In this case, the code in the quotes contains whitespace that forms part of the string and is therefore *not* ignored.

TIP   You need to use whitespace appropriately to make your program more readable. Too much or too little whitespace will make your program difficult to read. You'll see the appropriate use of whitespace throughout this book's examples.

You can use *blocks* to group statements together. A block begins with an open curly brace ({) and ends with a close curly brace (}). As this book progresses, you'll see how to use blocks to structure such items as if statements, loops, and methods. The following example shows a block; notice that the two statements within the block are indented using two spaces, which helps you to see that the statements are contained within the block:

```
{
  int count = 1;
  System.Console.WriteLine("count = " + count);
}
```

Listing 2.1 illustrates the use of statements, whitespace, and blocks.

LISTING 2.1: STATEMENTS, WHITESPACE, AND BLOCKS

```
class Example2_1
{

  public static void Main()
  {

    int count = 1;
    System.Console.WriteLine("count = " + count);

  }

}
```

You can compile this file using either the command-line version of the C# compiler (`csc`) or Visual Studio .NET, as you learned in Chapter 1, "Introduction to Visual C# and the .NET Framework." The following example uses `csc` to compile the `Example2_1.cs` file:

```
csc Example2_1.cs
```

Once you've compiled the program, go ahead and run it using the command line or Visual Studio .NET. The following example uses the command-line to run the `Example2_1` program:

```
Example2_1
```

The output from this program is as follows:

```
count = 1
```

Adding Comments

You can add *comments* to your programs to describe code, making it more understandable for both yourself and other programmers. You may think you understand your own programs inside out, but when you return to them for maintenance six months later, you might have forgotten the intricacies of your own creation! The point is that you should add comments to your code to aid understanding, but don't think you have to comment every line. You should use comments, like whitespace, judiciously.

C# ignores comments, but you need to mark them off with specific characters. C# provides two types of comments: a single-line comment and a multiline comment. A single-line comment uses two slashes (`//`) and may span only one line, as shown here:

```
// A single-line comment may only span one line.
```

The `//` tells C# to ignore everything up to the end of that line.

A multiline comment begins with an open comment mark (`/*`) and ends with a close comment mark (`*/`):

```
/* A multiline comment
   may span more than one
   line. */
```

The `/*` tells C# to ignore everything up to the next `*/` mark, no matter how many lines forward it is. If you were to use single-line comments in this example, you would have to add `//` characters at the beginning of every line that made up the comment.

Multiline comments can of course also span only one line:

```
/* Another comment */
```

Listing 2.2 shows a program with both single and multiline comments.

LISTING 2.2: COMMENTS

```
/*
  Example2_2.cs illustrates the use of comments
*/
```

```
class Example2_2
{

  public static void Main()
  {

    // display "Hello World!" on the screen
    System.Console.WriteLine("Hello World!");

  }

}
```

The output from this program is as follows:

```
Hello World!
```

Throughout this book you'll see comments used extensively—they explain what the programs are doing. Use them to supplement the book's text and explain the purpose of the code.

Using Data Types, Variables, and Constants

You've seen how statements give instructions to C#, but those instructions need data or values to work with—text to be displayed on the screen or ZIP codes to be sorted, for example. C# contains many *data types*, which indicate the kind of value you want to store—text or numbers, for example. You use data types when creating *variables* and *constants*, as well as other storage elements you'll see in later chapters. The value stored in a variable may be changed by setting it to another value later in the program; a constant, however, cannot be changed in your program once it has been set.

C# is a *strongly typed* language, which means you must assign a data type to every storage element you use in your program. Although this might appear restrictive, it helps you during program development because the C# compiler will check your program to make sure you use the correct types for your data. Essentially, this traps bugs in your program before you even run it.

In the following sections, you'll learn what the C# data types are and how to use them to create variables and constants.

Introducing Data Types

C# contains a number of built-in data types—you've already seen examples that use the int data type in the previous examples. Data types are also simply referred to as *types*. C# also enables you to create your own types, known as *user-defined* types. You'll learn how to create your own types in Chapter 5.

Both built-in and user-defined types come in three flavors:

Value Types   Value types store an actual value. For example, if you used the int value type to store 8, then an actual 8 would be stored.

Reference Types   Reference types store the address of an object. An object is an instance of a class, and you'll learn about them in Chapter 5.

Pointer Types   Pointer types are only for memory manipulation of unsafe code. You might write such code in C or C++, and it's called *unsafe* because using pointers to directly manipulate memory sometimes causes problems when the wrong memory address is accessed (that's not to say that unsafe code is always bad). In fact, a pointer is a kind of reference type.

Now, without further ado, let's take a look at the built-in types that come with C#.

Looking at C#'s Built-in Types

C#, being a modern language, has many built-in types that come ready for you to use in your own programs. As mentioned, these built-in types come as value types and reference types. The built-in value types represent actual values and are made up of types that enable you to represent integers, floating-point numbers, decimal numbers, Boolean values, and characters. The built-in reference types represent the address of an object. You'll learn about objects and object-oriented programming in Chapter 5.

In the following sections, you'll learn about the various built-in value types and see examples of them. You'll then learn how you can take a value stored using one built-in type and convert it to another type.

INTEGRAL TYPES

There are eight integral types you can use to represent whole, or *integer*, numbers. Table 2.1 lists these integral types. It also shows the C# type, the .NET type (this is the underlying type defined in the Common Language Specification, or CLS), the number of bytes used to store the type, and the range of values that may be stored for that type.

TABLE 2.1: INTEGRAL TYPES

C# TYPE	.NET TYPE	BYTES USED	VALUES
sbyte	SByte	1	−128 to 127 (signed)
byte	Byte	1	0 to 255 (unsigned)
short	Int16	2	−32,768 to 32,767 (signed)
ushort	UInt16	2	0 to 65,535 (unsigned)
int	Int32	4	−2,147,483,647 to 2,147,483,647 (signed)
uint	UInt32	4	0 to 4,294,967,295 (unsigned)
long	Int64	8	−9,223,372,036,854,775,808 to 9,223,372,036,854,775,807 (signed)
ulong	UInt64	8	0 to 18,446,744,073,709,551,615 (unsigned)

As you can see, each type has a signed and unsigned version of the type. The signed types can store signs with the number and can therefore store both positive and negative numbers. The unsigned types can only store positive numbers.

NOTE *Make sure you pick the appropriate type depending on whether your integer value is signed or unsigned and the range of values that you need to store.*

The following examples create variables using the int, long, and ulong types:

```
int myInt = 1;
long myLong = -1234;
ulong myUlong = 9;
```

You can assign a hexadecimal number by supplying a leading zero and x character to the literal number. For example:

```
int myInt2 = 0xf;  // f = 15 in base 10
```

NOTE *Hexadecimal numbers are base-16 numbers that use the digits 0 through 9 and the letters a through f (or A through F), with a (or A) representing the number 10 in base-10, and f (or F) representing the number 15 in base-10.*

FLOATING-POINT TYPES

There are three floating-point types you can use to represent floating-point numbers (see Table 2.2). Depending upon the values and number of significant figures you need to store for your floating-point number, you should pick the appropriate type.

TABLE 2.2: FLOATING-POINT TYPES

C# TYPE	.NET TYPE	BYTES USED	VALUES
float	Single	4	Approximately $+/-1.5 * 10^{-45}$ to approximately $+/-3.4 * 10^{38}$ with seven significant figures. Implements the IEEE 754 standard.
double	Double	8	Approximately $+/-5 * 10^{-324}$ to approximately $+/-1.7 * 10^{308}$ with 15 to 16 significant figures. Implements the IEEE 754 standard.
decimal	Decimal	12	$+/-1.0 * 10^{-28}$ to approximately $+/-7.9 * 10^{28}$ with 28 significant figures.

Although the decimal type supports a smaller range of numbers, it is preferable in some instances, as you will never encounter the rounding errors that may occur with the float and double types. A decimal number stores a number to an accuracy of 28 digits. You would use the decimal type if you needed to represent monetary values or for any other application that wouldn't tolerate the possibility of rounding errors.

When assigning a literal number to a `float`, you must supply an `f` or `F` character to the end. For example:

```
float myFloat1 = 1.2f;
```

When assigning a literal number to a `double`, you may choose to supply a `d` or `D` character to the end, but this is not required. For example:

```
double myDouble1 = 1234.5678;
double myDouble2 = 1234.5678d;
```

You can also use the exponential notation when assigning a literal to a `float` or `double`. For example:

```
double myDouble3 = 3.6e+5;  // = 360000
double myDouble4 = 1.2e-2;  // = 0.012
```

The number 3.6e+5 uses the exponential notation to specify the number $3.6*10^5$ and is the same as 360,000. Similarly, the number 1.2e-2 is $1.2*10^{-2}$ is the same as 0.012.

When using the `decimal` type, you must supply an `m` or `M` character at the end. For example:

```
decimal myDecimal1 = 34356.234567m;
```

NOTE *The* `float` *and* `double` *types implement the IEEE 754 standard—you can learn more about this standard at* www.ieee.org.

CHARACTER TYPE

The character `char` type represents 16-bit Unicode characters (see Table 2.3).

NOTE *Unicode is the standard for electronic encoding most of the world's written languages—you can find more details on Unicode at* www.unicode.org.

TABLE 2.3: CHARACTER TYPE

C# TYPE	.NET TYPE	BYTES USED	VALUES
char	Char	2	16-bit Unicode character

You can assign a character in single quotes to a `char`. For example:

```
char mySimpleChar = 'D';
```

You can also assign a Unicode character to a `char`. You specify a Unicode character using an escape sequence of the following format:

```
\uxxxx
```

where *xxxx* is a sequence of four hexadecimal digits. The following example assigns the D character using a Unicode escape sequence to `myUnicodeChar`:

```
char myUnicodeChar = '\u0044';
```

You can also assign an escape character to a char. An *escape character* is a character with a special meaning. Table 2.4 lists the escape characters allowed by C#, along with their meanings.

TABLE 2.4: ESCAPE CHARACTERS

ESCAPE CHARACTER	DESCRIPTION
\'	Single quote
\"	Double quote
\\	Backslash
\0	Null
\a	Alert
\b	Backspace
\f	Form feed
\n	Newline
\r	Carriage return
\t	Horizontal tab
\v	Vertical tab

The following example assigns a horizontal tab character to myEscapeChar:

```
char myEscapeChar = '\t';
```

Finally, you can also assign a hexadecimal number to a char. For example:

```
char myHexChar = '\x0f';
```

BOOLEAN TYPE

The bool type represents the Boolean logical values true or false (see Table 2.5).

TABLE 2.5: BOOLEAN TYPE

C# TYPE	.NET TYPE	BYTES USED	VALUES
bool	Boolean	1	Boolean true or false

The following example shows the use of the bool type:

```
bool myBool = true;
```

TYPE CONVERSION

A value stored using one type can sometimes be converted to another type. This conversion can take place *implicitly*, meaning that the compiler does the conversion automatically without you ever knowing about it.

Consider the following example:

```
short myShort = 1;
int myInt = myShort;
```

Now, a `short` uses 2 bytes, but an `int` uses 4 bytes, so the second statement that assigns `myShort` to `myInt` causes an implicit conversion to take place: The value in `myShort` is converted to a 4-byte value and then assigned to `myInt`.

An implicit conversion is only possible when no information would be lost; in the previous example, a 2-byte value is converted to a 4-byte value, and this never results in any information loss.

So, if you try to do the following:

```
myShort = myInt;
```

then the compiler will give you an error because you are trying to store a "bigger" value in a "smaller" value. In other words, you are trying to store a 4-byte value in a 2-byte value.

Cast Operator

You can force the conversion by doing an *explicit* conversion using the *cast operator*. The syntax for the cast operator is as follows:

```
(type)
```

where *type* is the name of the type to which you want to convert. You can place the cast operator in front of a variable, as shown in the following example:

```
myShort = (short) myInt;
```

In this example, the cast operator converts `myInt` to a `short`. You'll learn more about operators in Chapter 3, "Expressions and Operators."

You must be careful when using the cast operator to perform explicit conversions because you might unexpectedly lose information. Make sure you use the right types in your programs. To see the insidious problem of information loss in action, consider Listing 2.3.

LISTING 2.3: INFORMATION LOSS

```
/*
    Example2_3.cs shows the use of the cast operator,
    and how information loss can occur when explicitly
    converting a variable of one type to another

*/

class Example2_3
{
```

```
public static void Main()
{

  short myShort = 17000;
  System.Console.WriteLine("myShort = " + myShort);

  int myInt = myShort;
  System.Console.WriteLine("myInt = " + myInt);

  myShort = (short) (myInt * 2);
  System.Console.WriteLine("myShort = " + myShort);

}

}
```

This program declares a short variable named myShort and assigns the value 17,000 to myShort:

short myShort = 17000;

The value in myShort is then displayed, and the output from the program at this point is as follows:

myShort = 17000

Next, an int variable named myInt is declared and is assigned to the current value of myShort:

int myInt = myShort;

An implicit conversion changes the 2-byte myShort variable to the 4-byte myInt variable—there is no information loss because 4 bytes are greater than 2. Therefore, the value stored in myInt is now 17,000. This is verified by displaying the value stored in myInt, and the following line is displayed:

myInt = 17000

Finally, the variable myShort is then set to twice the value of myInt; this value is explicitly cast to a short before storing the value in myShort:

myShort = (short) (myInt * 2);

You might expect this to assign the value 34,000 to myShort (twice 17,000). However, the value actually assigned is −31,536! This is verified by the program output:

myShort = -31536

The reason for this is that a short only uses 2 bytes to store the value, and the cast operator causes 2 bytes to be lost—this is what causes the number to be different from what you might expect.

checked Operator

You can use the checked operator to catch the previous problem. The checked operator causes an *exception* to be thrown when a numeric variable is assigned a value beyond its supported range. As you'll learn in Chapter 13, "Exceptions and Debugging," exceptions are C#'s way of handling errors that may occur when you run your programs—such errors are known as *run-time* errors.

The following example shows the checked operator in action:

```
checked
{
  myShort = (short) (myInt * 2);
}
```

When the attempt to assign 34,000 to myShort is made, the following exception message is displayed:

```
Unhandled Exception: System.OverflowException: Exception of
 type System.OverflowException was thrown.
```

You can get the same effect by compiling Example2_3.cs with the /checked compiler option, as shown in the following command:

```
csc Example2_3.cs /checked
```

You can handle such an exception by placing the code in a try /catch block:

```
try
{
  checked
  {
    myShort = (short) (myInt * 2);
  }
} catch
{
  System.Console.WriteLine("Exception occurred");
}
```

The code that causes the exception is placed in the try block, and when the exception occurs, program flow moves to the catch block where a message is displayed. You'll learn more about exceptions in Chapter 13.

Understanding Variables

You've seen some examples of variables in the previous sections—this section formalizes the use of variables and goes deeper in the details of using variables in your programs. You use a variable to store a value in memory. You *declare* a variable by indicating its type and then assigning a name to the variable. You declare variables using the following simplified syntax:

```
data-type variable-name;
```

The syntax elements are as follows:

data-type   The data type for the variable.

variable-name   The name for the variable. By convention, the first character of a variable name is lowercase, and the first letter of a new word in the name is uppercase—myFirstVariable, for example. A variable name must begin with a letter or an underscore (_).

WARNING *A variable name shouldn't be the same as a C# keyword (the C# keywords are listed in Appendix A).*

The following example declares a variable of the int type and assigns it the name myValue:

```
int myValue;
```

You can also *initialize* a variable's value when you declare it—this assigns an initial value to the variable. The following example declares a char variable named myLetter and initializes it to 'A':

```
char myLetter = 'A';
```

DEFINITE ASSIGNMENT

In C#, you must assign a value to a variable before you attempt to reference that variable's value in your program—this is known as *definite assignment*. If you don't assign a value to a variable, and then you attempt to reference the value, then the compiler will give you an error. For example, let's say you tried doing the following:

```
int myValue;
System.Console.WriteLine(myValue);  // causes an error
```

The variable myValue has not been assigned a value before the second statements references it. Listing 2.4 contains a statement that attempts to actually do this.

LISTING 2.4: ATTEMPTING TO REFERENCE AN UNINITIALIZED VARIABLE

```
/*
  Example2_4.cs shows an attempt to reference an
  uninitialized variable
*/

class Example2_4
{

  public static void Main()
  {

    int myValue;
    System.Console.WriteLine(myValue);  // causes an error

  }

}
```

If you try to compile this code, the compiler will display the following error:

```
Example2_4.cs(11,30): error CS0165: Use of unassigned local
 variable 'myValue'
```

This error message tells you that an attempt was made to use the variable myValue, which has not been assigned a value. The two numbers in parentheses—(11,30)–in the message tell you the line number and column in the source file where the error occurred; in this case, line 11, column 30 is where myValue is used in the call to System.Console.WriteLine().

NOTE   *The errors produced when you compile your programs are known as compile-time or simply compilation errors. When you get them, you must go back and fix the error in your program reported by the compiler and then try compiling your program again.*

If the variable myValue is assigned a value before it is referenced, then the code will compile—this change is shown in Listing 2.5.

LISTING 2.5: ASSIGNING A VALUE BEFORE IT IS REFERENCED

```
/*
   Example2_5.cs is the same as Example2_4.cs, except
   myValue is assigned a value before it is referenced
*/

class Example2_5
{

   public static void Main()
   {

     int myValue = 2;
     System.Console.WriteLine(myValue);  // no error

   }

}
```

This program compiles because myValue is assigned a value before it is referenced.

You don't have to initialize all your variables when you declare them, however: You can also set a variable's value after it has been declared. For example:

```
int myValue;
myValue = 2;
System.Console.WriteLine(myValue);
```

NOTE   *The point is that you must assign a value to a variable before you reference it.*

SCOPE

Now that you know about variables and assignments, it's time to discuss scope. The *scope* of a variable is the block (or blocks) of code where that variable can be accessed. You can think of a variable's scope as the area where that variable exists. The following block declares a variable named myValue:

```
{
   int myValue = 1;
}
```

The curly brackets ({ and }) mark the beginning and the end of the block, respectively. The variable myValue may only be accessed within that block, and the scope of myValue is said to be limited to that block. If you tried to access myValue outside of this block, you will get a compilation error. Listing 2.6 illustrates the scope of a variable by attempting to access that variable outside of its block.

LISTING 2.6: ILLUSTRATING SCOPE

```
/*
   Example2_6.cs illustrates scope
*/

class Example2_6
{

  public static void Main()
  {

    {
      int myValue = 1;
    }

    myValue = 2;   // causes error

  }

}
```

If you try to compile this program, you will get the following compilation error:

```
Example2_6.cs(13,5): error CS0103: The name 'myValue' does
 not exist in the class or namespace 'Example2_9'
```

This error message tells you that the variable myValue doesn't exist. In other words, it is not in scope.

WARNING *To access a variable, that variable must be in scope. Scope also applies to constants, strings, and other items you declare in your program.*

The scope of a variable can be more than one block, as shown in the following example:

```
class MyClass
{

  public static void Main()
  {

    int myValue;
    {
      myValue = 1;
      {
        myValue = 2;
      }
    }
    myValue = 3;

  }

}
```

In this example, `myValue` is in scope for all the blocks.

Defining Constants

A *constant* is similar to a variable, except that the value stored in a constant cannot be changed and must be set when the constant is declared. Constants are useful because you can set their value and then reference that value in your program, knowing that the constant's value cannot be changed once you've set it. You could use a constant to store the value of the mathematical constant *pi*, for example.

Declaring a constant is similar to declaring a variable, except that you add the keyword `const` to the beginning of the declaration, and you must assign a value to the constant in the declaration. The following example declares an `int` constant named `Length`:

```
const int Length = 3;
```

Notice that the `const` keyword in this example is placed before the type of the constant. By convention, the first letter of the constant's name is in uppercase. Listing 2.7 illustrates the use of constants.

LISTING 2.7: USING CONSTANTS

```
/*
  Example2_7.cs illustrates the use of constants
*/

class Example2_7
{
```

```
public static void Main()
{

  const int Length = 3;

  // mathematical constant pi
  const double Pi = 3.14159;

  // speed of light in meters per second
  const double SpeedOfLight = 2.99792e8;

  System.Console.WriteLine(Length);
  System.Console.WriteLine(Pi);
  System.Console.WriteLine(SpeedOfLight);

}

}
```

The output from this program is as follows:

```
3
3.14159
299792000
```

Once you have declared a constant, you cannot change its value—attempting to do so will cause a compilation error, as shown in Listing 2.8.

LISTING 2.8: ATTEMPTING TO CHANGE A CONSTANT

```
/*
  Example2_8.cs tries to change a constant
*/

class Example2_8
{

  public static void Main()
  {

    const int Length = 3;
    Length = 4;  // causes an error

  }

}
```

If you try to compile this program, you will get the following error:

```
Example2_8.cs(10,5): error CS0131: The left-hand side of an
  assignment must be a variable, property or indexer
```

This tells you that you cannot assign a new value to a constant.

Introducing Strings

Strings are sequences of Unicode characters, and you declare them using the `string` type. One interesting point to note is that strings are actually objects and are therefore reference types—you'll learn about objects in Chapter 5.

The following example declares a `string` named `helloWorld` and sets it to `"Hello World!"`:

```
string helloWorld = "Hello World!";
```

The `helloWorld` string may then be displayed on the screen using the following call to the `System.Console.WriteLine()` method, which accepts a string as an input:

```
System.Console.WriteLine(helloWorld);
```

A string may also be built up from other smaller strings using the + operator (you'll learn more about operators in Chapter 3). For example:

```
helloWorld = "Hello World" + " from C#!";
```

This example set the `helloWorld` string to `"Hello World from C#!"`.
You can also embed escape characters in strings (discussed earlier in the "Character Type" section):

```
helloWorld = "Hello World" + "\n from C#!";
```

Because the `System.Console.WriteLine()` method accepts a `string`, you can also use the + operator to build up a string for display:

```
const double pi = 3.14159;
System.Console.WriteLine("pi = " + pi);
```

Listing 2.9 illustrates the use of strings.

LISTING 2.9: STRINGS

```
/*
  Example2_9.cs illustrates the use of strings
*/

class Example2_9
{

  public static void Main()
  {
```

```
    string helloWorld = "Hello World!";
    System.Console.WriteLine(helloWorld);

    helloWorld = "Hello World" + " from C#!";
    System.Console.WriteLine(helloWorld);

    helloWorld = "Hello World" + "\n from C#!";
    System.Console.WriteLine(helloWorld);

    const double Pi = 3.14159;
    System.Console.WriteLine("Pi = " + Pi);

  }

}
```

The output from this program is as follows:

```
Hello World!
Hello World from C#!
Hello World
 from C#!
pi = 3.14159
```

C# has a rich set of string manipulation functionality, but we'll defer discussion of it until Chapter 9, "Strings, Dates, Times, and Time Spans," because you'll need to understand object-oriented programming first. (We'll also discuss how you use dates in that chapter.)

Understanding Enumerations

Enumerations enable you to create a set of constants that you can reference in your program. An enumeration is a value type. Let's say you were writing a program to be used in an astronomy class, and your program had to reference the order of the planets in our solar system relative to the Sun—the order is Mercury, Venus, Earth, Mars, Jupiter, Saturn, Uranus, Neptune, and Pluto. You could create an int constant that represents the position for each planet. For example:

```
const int Mercury = 1;
const int Venus  = 2;
const int Earth = 3;
...
```

This works, but it's repetitive. A better approach is to use an enumeration, which lets you group common constants together. You declare an enumeration using enum. The following simplified syntax shows how to create an enumeration:

```
enum enum-name {constant-list}
```

The syntax elements are as follows:

enum-name   The name you assign to your enumeration. By convention, the first letter of an enumeration name is in uppercase.

constant-list   A list of constants contained in your enumeration.

The following example declares an enumeration named `Planets`:

```
enum Planets
{
  Mercury,
  Venus,
  Earth,
  Mars,
  Jupiter,
  Saturn,
  Uranus,
  Neptune,
  Pluto
}
```

As you can see, `Planets` defines nine constants, with each constant representing the planet's position from the Sun. The first constant, `Mercury`, has a default value of 0. The other constants are set to 1 plus the previous value, so `Venus` is set to 1, `Earth` to 2, and so on up to `Pluto`, which is set to 8. The default type for the constants in an enumeration is `int`.

You can also initialize a constant in an enumeration, as shown in the next example:

```
enum Planets
{
  Mercury = 1,
  Venus,
  Earth,
  Mars,
  Jupiter,
  Saturn,
  Uranus,
  Neptune,
  Pluto
}
```

The first entry sets `Mercury` equal to the value 1. As before, the other constants are set to 1 plus the previous value, so `Venus` is set to 2, `Earth` to 3, and so on up to `Pluto`, which is set to 9.

To access an element, you use the *dot notation*. For example, to access the `Earth` element, you would use `Planets.Earth`. The following example displays the position of Earth relative to the Sun:

```
System.Console.WriteLine("Position of Earth = " +
  (int) Planets.Earth);
```

Notice the use of the cast operator to get the value that `Earth` was set to in the enumeration. This statement displays the following output:

```
Position of Earth = 3
```

If you don't do the cast, then `Planets.Earth` returns the string `"Earth"` in the previous statement.

NOTE You use the cast operator to convert the value set in an enumeration constant to one of the integer types. (For more information, see the section "Cast Operator" earlier in this chapter.) We'll discuss more operators in Chapter 3.

Listing 2.10 illustrates the `Planets` enumeration.

LISTING 2.10: USING ENUMERATIONS

```
/*
  Example2_10.cs illustrates the use of an enumeration
  that defines the positions of the planets in
  the solar system relative to the Sun
*/

class Example2_10
{

  enum Planets
  {
    Mercury = 1,
    Venus,
    Earth,
    Mars,
    Jupiter,
    Saturn,
    Uranus,
    Neptune,
    Pluto
  }

  public static void Main()
  {

    System.Console.WriteLine("Position of Earth = " +
      (int) Planets.Earth);

    System.Console.WriteLine("Planets.Earth = " +
      Planets.Earth);

  }

}
```

The output from this program is as follows:

```
Position of Earth = 3
Planets.Earth = Earth
```

Specifying Values in an Enumeration

You can specify the values of the constants in an enumeration. For example, the following enumeration, named PlanetPeriods, defines the orbital periods (the time it takes for a planet to go around the Sun) for the first four planets; the orbital periods are specified in days:

```
enum PlanetPeriods
{
  Mercury = 88,
  Venus = 225,
  Earth = 365,
  Mars = 687
}
```

The following example displays the orbital period for Mars:

```
System.Console.WriteLine("Orbital period for Mars = " +
  (int) PlanetPeriods.Mars + " days");
```

This statement displays:

```
Orbital period for Mars = 687 days
```

Listing 2.11 illustrates the use of the PlanetPeriods enumeration that specifies values in an enumeration.

LISTING 2.11: SPECIFYING VALUES IN AN ENUMERATION

```
/*
  Example2_11.cs illustrates the use of an enumeration
  that defines the orbital periods of the first four
  planets in days
*/

class Example2_11
{

  enum PlanetPeriods
  {
    Mercury = 88,
    Venus = 225,
    Earth = 365,
    Mars = 687
  }
```

```
public static void Main()
{

  System.Console.WriteLine("Orbital period for Mars = " +
    (int) PlanetPeriods.Mars + " days");

}

}
```

The output from this program is as follows:

```
Orbital period for Mars = 687 days
```

Specifying an Enumeration Base Type

As mentioned earlier, the default type for an enumeration is int. The type used by an enumeration is known as its *base type*. You can in fact use any of the integer types as the base type for an enumeration. To set the base type, you put the type after the name of the enumeration, and add a colon to the front of the type. For example, the following enumeration uses the long type as its base type:

```
enum PlanetPeriods :long
{
  Mercury = 88,
  Venus = 225,
  Earth = 365,
  Mars = 687
}
```

Listing 2.12 illustrates the new PlanetPeriods enumeration that specifies the base type used by the enumeration.

LISTING 2.12: SPECIFYING AN ENUMERATION BASE TYPE

```
/*
  Example2_12.cs illustrates the use of an enumeration
  that defines the orbital periods of the first four
  planets in days, using a base type of long
*/

class Example2_12
{

  enum PlanetPeriods :long
  {
    Mercury = 88,
    Venus = 225,
```

```
   Earth = 365,
   Mars = 687
}

public static void Main()
{

   System.Console.WriteLine("Orbital period for Mars = " +
     (long) PlanetPeriods.Mars + " days");

}

}
```

Notice that the `long` type is used in the cast for this program. We didn't have to do this—we could have still used `int` as the base type of our enumeration because none of the constants exceed the maximum permissible range of numbers allowed by an `int`.

Handling Input and Output

So far, you've only seen programs that display output on the screen in the default format. There are occasions when you might need to get information from your program's users, and they can use the keyboard to enter that information. You might also need to format output on the screen; for example, you might need to display a financial report that contains formatted numbers. In this section, you'll learn how to read a single character and a string entered using the keyboard and how to format output displayed on the screen.

Reading a Single Character

You can read a single character from the keyboard using the `System.Console.Read()` method. This method returns an `int`, so you must cast the returned result to a `char` if you want to interpret the input as a character, as shown in the following example:

```
char myChar = (char) System.Console.Read();
```

Listing 2.13 illustrates reading a single character entered using the keyboard.

LISTING 2.13: READING A SINGLE CHARACTER ENTERED USING THE KEYBOARD

```
/*
   Example2_13.cs illustrates how to read
   a character entered using the keyboard
*/

class Example2_13
{
```

```
public static void Main()
{

  System.Console.Write("Enter a character: ");
  char myChar = (char) System.Console.Read();
  System.Console.WriteLine("You entered " + myChar);

}

}
```

Notice that this program uses the System.Console.Write() method to prompt you to enter a character; the method displays a line without a carriage return at the end. Let's say you run this program and enter the letter *a* on the keyboard; the output from this program would be:

```
Enter a character: a
You entered a
```

Reading a String of Characters

You can read a string of characters from the keyboard using the System.Console.ReadLine() method, as shown in the following example:

```
string myString = System.Console.ReadLine();
```

Listing 2.14 illustrates reading a string of characters entered using the keyboard.

LISTING 2.14: READING A STRING OF CHARACTERS ENTERED USING THE KEYBOARD

```
/*
  Example2_14.cs illustrates how to
  read a string entered using the keyboard
*/

class Example2_14
{

  public static void Main()
  {

    System.Console.Write("Enter a string: ");
    string myString = System.Console.ReadLine();
    System.Console.WriteLine("You entered " + myString);

  }

}
```

Let's say you run this program and enter the string *Hello there!* on the keyboard; the output from this program would be the following:

```
Enter a character: Hello there!
You entered Hello there!
```

Formatting Output

You can format the output displayed by the `System.Console.Write()` and `System.Console.Write-Line()` methods. This enables you to specify the format for integers, floating-point numbers, and even display numbers as currency values.

Let's say that you had an `int` variable named `myInt`:

```
int myInt = 12345;
```

Up until now, we've only shown you how to display such a variable as follows:

```
System.Console.WriteLine("myInt = " + myInt);
```

This displays the following:

```
myInt = 12345
```

This just displays the value for `myInt` "as is"—it doesn't do anything fancy, it just displays the value. This may not always be appropriate; for example, you may need to write a program that displays a specially formatted report. Fortunately, C# allows you to customize output.

You can display the `myInt` value using a total width of 6 using the following statement:

```
System.Console.WriteLine("myInt = {0, 6}", myInt);
```

Notice that {0, 6} formats the variable's value. The first number specifies the variable *number:* 0 corresponds to the first variable, `myInt` (the variables are specified after the comma in the call to the `System.Console.WriteLine()` method). The second number is the *width* for the display of that variable—6 in this case. When the variable is displayed, its value will be padded to this width, so 12345 will padded by one space in front to bring the total width up to 6 characters. Therefore, this statement displays the following:

```
myInt =  12345
```

There is an extra space in front of the value.

NOTE *If the width is less than the length of the actual value, then the value will be displayed as is.*

You can display more than one variable using braces:

```
int myInt2 = 67890;
System.Console.WriteLine("myInt = {0, 6}, myInt2 = {1, 5}",
 myInt, myInt2);
```

This displays the following:

```
myInt =  12345, myInt2 = 67890
```

Formatting floating-point numbers is a little more complex. Let's say you had a **double** variable named **myDouble**:

```
double myDouble = 1234.56789;
```

The following example displays the value for **myDouble** with a width of 10, and it rounds the value to three decimal places:

```
System.Console.WriteLine("myDouble = {0, 10:f3}", myDouble);
```

Notice the use of **f3** in this example; this means that the value is treated as a floating-point number, as indicated by the *format character* **f**, and that the value is to be rounded to three decimal places, as indicated by the 3 after the **f**.

You can use the same formatting technique with **float** and **decimal** variables. For example:

```
float myFloat = 1234.56789f;
System.Console.WriteLine("myFloat = {0, 10:f3}", myFloat);
decimal myDecimal = 1234.56789m;
System.Console.WriteLine("myDecimal = {0, 10:f3}", myDecimal);
```

These examples display the following:

```
myFloat =    1234.568
myDecimal =    1234.568
```

There are a total of eight format characters you can use to format a number, as shown in Table 2.6.

TABLE 2.6: FORMAT CHARACTERS

FORMAT CHARACTER	DESCRIPTION
f or F	Formats a floating-point number
e or E	Formats a number using exponential notation
p or P	Formats a percentage
n or N	Formats a number using comma separators
c or C	Formats a local currency number
d or D	Formats a decimal number
g or G	Formats a number using either the floating-point or exponential notation
x or X	Converts an integer to a hexadecimal number

Listing 2.15 shows how to use these characters to format the display of numbers.

LISTING 2.15: FORMATTING NUMBERS

```
/*
  Example2_15.cs illustrates formatting numbers
*/
```

```
class Example2_15
{

  public static void Main()
  {

    // formatting integers
    int myInt = 12345;
    int myInt2 = 67890;
    System.Console.WriteLine("myInt = {0, 6}, myInt2 = {1, 5}",
      myInt, myInt2);
    System.Console.WriteLine("myInt using 10:d = {0, 10:d}",
      myInt);
    System.Console.WriteLine("myInt using 10:x = {0, 10:x2}",
      myInt);

    // formatting floating-point numbers
    double myDouble = 1234.56789;
    System.Console.WriteLine("myDouble using 10:f3 = {0, 10:f3}",
      myDouble);
    float myFloat = 1234.56789f;
    System.Console.WriteLine("myFloat using 10:f3 = {0, 10:f3}",
      myFloat);
    decimal myDecimal = 1234.56789m;
    System.Console.WriteLine("myDecimal using 10:f3 = {0, 10:f3}",
      myDecimal);
    System.Console.WriteLine("myFloat using 10:e3 = {0, 10:e3}",
      myFloat);
    System.Console.WriteLine("myFloat using 10:p2 = {0, 10:p2}",
      myFloat);
    System.Console.WriteLine("myFloat using 10:n2 = {0, 10:n2}",
      myFloat);
    System.Console.WriteLine("myFloat using 10:g2 = {0, 10:g2}",
      myFloat);

    // formatting currency values
    decimal myMoney = 15123.45m;
    System.Console.WriteLine("myMoney using 10:c2 = {0, 10:c2}",
      myMoney);

  }

}
```

The output from this program is as follows:

```
myInt =  12345, myInt2 = 67890
myInt using 10:d =       12345
myInt using 10:x =        3039
myDouble using 10:f3 =    1234.568
myFloat using 10:f3 =    1234.568
myDecimal using 10:f3 =    1234.568
myFloat using 10:e3 = 1.235e+003
myFloat using 10:p2 = 123,456.79 %
myFloat using 10:n2 =    1,234.57
myFloat using 10:g2 =      1.2e+03
myMoney using 10:c2 = $15,123.45
```

Summary

This chapter has covered a lot of material, all of which lays the foundation for upcoming chapters. Those of you who are familiar with other programming languages probably found most of this material straightforward. You learned that C# programs are made up of *statements* that instruct C# what do, and statements are grouped into *blocks*. Statements and blocks form the core of any C# program. You can embed *comments* in your programs, and when they are used correctly they should help others understand your program. Comments should also help you understand your own program if you modify it later.

You also learned that programs use *variables* and *constants* to store values. A variable's value may be changed as a program runs, but a constant's value remains fixed after it has been declared. Constants are useful when you want to reference a fixed value in your programs.

Both variables and constants are declared using a particular *type*, which tells C# what kind of value you want to store. C# has many data types, including types that let you store integers, floating-point numbers, characters, and strings. All variables and constants have *scope*, which determines where they can be accessed within your program.

Further, you now know that *enumerations* allow you to group related constants of a particular type together as one self-contained unit. Once you've created an enumeration containing constant values, you can then use those constants in your program. You may also set the type used in an enumeration—known as the *base type*.

Finally, you can now read characters and strings entered using the keyboard, and you can format output sent to the screen. You can also display numbers on the screen in a wide variety of formats.

Chapter 3

Expressions and Operators

AN EXPRESSION IS TYPICALLY a statement that performs some kind of calculation—using an *operator*—and returns a value. You've already seen some examples of expressions and operators in the previous chapters; this chapter will formalize their definitions and show you the main operators available within C#. As this book progresses, you'll see the other operators.

Featured in this chapter:

◆ Writing Expressions

◆ Using Operators in Expressions

◆ Understanding Operator Precedence

Understanding Expressions and Operators

As mentioned, an expression is typically a statement that performs some kind of calculation and returns a value. An expression consists of one or more *operands*—which may be variables, constants, or literal values—along with one or more *operators*—the addition operator (+), for example. The following example shows an expression:

```
1 + 2
```

In this example, 1 and 2 are the operands, and + is the operator. This expression returns the value 3.

Here are some more examples of expressions:

```
1 * 3 + 2
1 / 4 - 3
myValue + 1
```

Each of these expressions is a calculation that returns a value. A variable assignment is also an example of an expression:

```
myValue = 1;
```

The equals sign (=) is also an operator, known as the *assignment operator*. Here's another example of an expression containing a variable assignment:

```
myValue = 2 * 3;
```

This example performs the calculation on the right side of the assignment operator (=), which returns 6, and assigns this result to myValue.

All of these examples have performed calculations. However, an expression doesn't necessarily require a calculation. For example, the following example uses strings instead:

```
string myString = "Hello" + " World!";
```

In this example, the strings on the right side are joined together into one string ("Hello World!"), and that string is assigned to myString.

Listing 3.1 illustrates an expression that calculates the circumference of a circle by multiplying pi by the circle's diameter.

LISTING 3.1: USING AN EXPRESSION TO PERFORM A CALCULATION

```
/*
  Example3_1.cs illustrates the use of
  expressions to calculate and display
  the circumference of a circle
*/

class Example3_1
{
  public static void Main()
  {

    const double Pi = 3.14159;
    double diameter = 2.5;

    // calculate the circumference
    double circumference = Pi * diameter;

    // display the circumference
    System.Console.WriteLine("Circumference = " +
      circumference);

  }
}
```

The output from this program is as follows:

```
Circumference = 7.853975
```

The following sections describe the various C# operators in detail, with examples showing how each one is used. This chapter ends with a discussion of the rules that determine the order in which C# evaluates operators.

Assignment Operator

The assignment operator sets a variable or constant to a value (see Table 3.1).

TABLE 3.1: ASSIGNMENT OPERATOR

OPERATOR	DESCRIPTION
=	Variable assignment

The following examples show how to use the assignment operator (=):

```
int myInt = 1;
myInt = 2;
```

The value on the right side of the assignment operator can itself be an expression. For example:

```
myInt = 1 + 5 - 2;
```

This statement assigns the value 4 to myInt.

Arithmetic Operators

The arithmetic operators perform arithmetic. There are five arithmetic operators (see Table 3.2).

TABLE 3.2: ARITHMETIC OPERATORS

OPERATOR	DESCRIPTION
+	Addition
–	Subtraction
*	Multiplication
/	Division
%	Modulus

The following expressions show the use of the addition (+), subtraction (-), multiplication (*), and division (/) operators, respectively:

```
1 + 2
3 - 2
2 * 5
10 / 3
```

When integers are used with the arithmetic operators, an integer is returned and any remainder is discarded after the division has been performed. In the example 10 / 3, the integer 10 is divided by

3—this returns 3, with the remainder of 1 being discarded. If you want to get the remainder, you can use the modulus operator (%); for example, the following expression returns the remainder of 1 after the integer division is performed:

```
10 % 3
```

When floating-point numbers are used with arithmetic expressions, a floating-point number is returned. For instance, the following example returns 3.333333:

```
10f / 3f
```

Also, you can use multiple arithmetic operators and operands together, as shown in the following example, which returns 6:

```
3 * 4 / 2
```

Listing 3.2 illustrates how to use the arithmetic operators.

LISTING 3.2: ARITHMETIC OPERATORS

```
/*
  Example3_2.cs illustrates the use of
  the arithmetic operators
*/

class Example3_2
{
  public static void Main()
  {

    // integers and arithmetic operators
    System.Console.WriteLine("10 / 3 = " + 10 / 3);
    System.Console.WriteLine("10 % 3 = " + 10 % 3);
    int intValue1 = 10;
    int intValue2 = 3;
    System.Console.WriteLine("intValue1 / intValue2 = " +
      intValue1 / intValue2);
    System.Console.WriteLine("intValue1 % intValue2 = " +
      intValue1 % intValue2);

    // floats and arithmetic operators
    System.Console.WriteLine("10f / 3f = " + 10f / 3f);
    float floatValue1 = 10f;
    float floatValue2 = 3f;
    System.Console.WriteLine("floatValue1 / floatValue2 = " +
      floatValue1 / floatValue2);

    // doubles and arithmetic operators
    System.Console.WriteLine("10d / 3d = " + 10d / 3d);
    System.Console.WriteLine("10.0 / 3.0 = " + 10.0 / 3.0);
```

```
        double doubleValue1 = 10;
        double doubleValue2 = 3;
        System.Console.WriteLine("doubleValue1 / doubleValue2 = " +
          doubleValue1 / doubleValue2);

        // decimals and arithmetic operators
        System.Console.WriteLine("10m / 3m = " + 10m / 3m);
        decimal decimalValue1 = 10;
        decimal decimalValue2 = 3;
        System.Console.WriteLine("decimalValue1 / decimalValue2 = " +
          decimalValue1 / decimalValue2);

        // multiple arithmetic operators
        System.Console.WriteLine("3 * 4 / 2 = " + 3 * 4 / 2);

    }
}
```

The output from this program is as follows:

```
10 / 3 = 3
10 % 3 = 1
intValue1 / intValue2 = 3
intValue1 % intValue2 = 1
10f / 3f = 3.333333
floatValue1 / floatValue2 = 3.333333
10d / 3d = 3.33333333333333
10.0 / 3.0 = 3.33333333333333
doubleValue1 / doubleValue2 = 3.33333333333333
10m / 3m = 3.3333333333333333333333333333
decimalValue1 / decimalValue2 = 3.3333333333333333333333333333
3 * 4 / 2 = 6
```

Notice that because 10.0 and 3.0 contain digits to the right of the decimal point, these numbers are treated as double precision floating-point numbers.

Comparison Operators

The comparison operators compare the relationship between values and return a Boolean `bool` value (`true` or `false`). There are six comparison operators (see Table 3.3).

The following expression returns `false`:

```
10 == 1
```

Because the value 10 is not equal to 1, this expression returns `false`.

WARNING   *Be careful to distinguish between the equal to operator (==), which compares two values, and the assignment operator (=), which sets a value.*

TABLE 3.3: COMPARISON OPERATORS

OPERATOR	DESCRIPTION
==	Equal to
!=	Not equal to
>	Greater than
<	Less than
>=	Greater than or equal to
<=	Less than or equal to

The following expressions also return `false`:

```
10 < 1
10 <= 1
```

On the other hand, the following expressions all return `true`:

```
10 != 1
10 > 1
10 >= 1
```

Of course, you can also use variables with a comparison operator:

```
int intValue1 = 10;
int intValue2 = 1;
bool result = intValue1 != intValue2;
```

In this example, the `bool` variable `result` is set to `true` because 10 is not equal to 1. Listing 3.3 uses the comparison operators shown in Table 3.3.

LISTING 3.3: COMPARISON OPERATORS

```
/*
   Example3_3.cs illustrates the use of
   the comparison operators
*/

class Example3_3
{
  public static void Main()
  {

    bool result;

    // false expressions
    result = 10 == 1;
```

```
System.Console.WriteLine("10 == 1 is " + result);
result = 10 < 1;
System.Console.WriteLine("10 < 1 is " + result);
result = 10 <= 1;
System.Console.WriteLine("10 <= 1 is " + result);

// true expressions
result = 10 != 1;
System.Console.WriteLine("10 != 1 is " + result);
result = 10 > 1;
System.Console.WriteLine("10 > 1 is " + result);
result = 10 >= 1;
System.Console.WriteLine("10 >= 1 is " + result);
int intValue1 = 10;
int intValue2 = 1;
result = intValue1 != intValue2;
System.Console.WriteLine("intValue1 != intValue2 is " + result);

    }
}
```

The output from this program is as follows:

```
10 == 1 is False
10 < 1 is False
10 <= 1 is False
10 != 1 is True
10 > 1 is True
10 >= 1 is True
intValue1 != intValue2 is True
```

Boolean Logical Operators

The Boolean logical operators perform logical comparisons that deal with Boolean true and false values. There are three Boolean logical operators (see Table 3.4).

TABLE 3.4: BOOLEAN LOGICAL OPERATORS

OPERATOR	DESCRIPTION
&&	Boolean logical AND
||	Boolean logical OR
!	Boolean logical NOT

The Boolean logical operators return true or false. The AND (&&) and OR (||) operators use two Boolean expressions as their operands, but the NOT operator (!) requires only one Boolean expression. The following sections cover the details of these operators.

Boolean Logical AND Operator

The Boolean logical AND operator (`&&`) returns `true` only if both expressions are `true`; otherwise it returns `false` (see Table 3.5). Table 3.5 is known as a *truth table* because it shows `true` and `false` values.

TABLE 3.5: Boolean Logical AND Operator Truth Table

Expression 1	Expression 2	Expression 1 && Expression 2
false	false	false
false	true	false
true	false	false
true	true	true

Let's take a look at a couple of examples that use the AND operator—the following example returns `true`:

```
(1 == 1) && (2 > 1)
```

This example returns `true` because both of the expressions used with the AND operator are `true`. In other words, 1 *is* equal to 1 (`1 == 1`), and 2 *is* greater than 1 (`2 > 1`).

On the other hand, the following example returns `false`:

```
(1 == 1) && (2 < 1)
```

This example returns `false` because the second expression is `false`. In other words, 2 *is not* less than 1: (`2 < 1`).

Boolean Logical OR Operator

The Boolean logical OR operator (`||`) returns `true` if either expression is `true` or both expressions are `true`, and it returns `false` if either expression is `false` (see Table 3.6).

TABLE 3.6: Boolean Logical OR Operator Truth Table

Expression 1	Expression 2	Expression 1 || Expression 2
false	false	false
false	true	true
true	false	true
true	true	true

Let's take a look at a couple of examples that use the OR operator—the following example returns `true`:

```
(1 == 1) || (1 == 0)
```

This example returns true because the first expression is true. In other words, 1 *is* equal to 1. It doesn't matter that the second expression is false because the first expression is true.

The following example returns false:

```
(1 == 0) || (1 == 0)
```

This example returns false because both of the expressions are false. In other words, 1 *is not* equal to 0 in either expression.

NOTE   *If the first expression is* false, *then the result of the second expression is irrelevant in the evaluation because the returned result will always be* false. *This is known as a short-circuit evaluation, and it saves some time during evaluations.*

BOOLEAN LOGICAL NOT OPERATOR

The Boolean logical NOT operator (!) returns the logical opposite of the supplied expression (see Table 3.7).

TABLE 3.7: BOOLEAN LOGICAL NOT OPERATOR TRUTH TABLE

EXPRESSION	!EXPRESSION
true	false
false	true

Let's take a look at a couple of examples that use the NOT operator. The following example returns true:

```
!(1 == 0)
```

This example returns true because the supplied expression is false. In other words, 1 *is not* equal to 0, so the logical opposite of false is true.

Conversely, the following example returns false:

```
!(1 == 1)
```

This example returns false because the supplied expression is true and the logical opposite of false is true.

Listing 3.4 illustrates the use of the three Boolean logical operators.

LISTING 3.4: BOOLEAN LOGICAL OPERATORS

```
/*
  Example3_4.cs illustrates the use of
  the Boolean logical operators
*/

class Example3_4
{
```

```
public static void Main()
{

  bool result;

  // use of the Boolean logical AND operator
  result = (1 == 1) && (2 > 1);
  System.Console.WriteLine("(1 == 1) && (2 > 1) is " + result);
  result = (1 == 1) && (2 < 1);
  System.Console.WriteLine("(1 == 1) && (2 < 1) is " + result);

  // use of the Boolean logical OR operator
  result = (1 == 1) || (1 == 0);
  System.Console.WriteLine("(1 == 1) || (1 == 0) is " + result);
  result = (1 == 0) || (1 == 0);
  System.Console.WriteLine("(1 == 0) || (1 == 0) is " + result);

  // use of the Boolean logical NOT operator
  result = !(1 == 0);
  System.Console.WriteLine("!(1 == 0) is " + result);
  result = !(1 == 1);
  System.Console.WriteLine("!(1 == 1) is " + result);

}

}
```

The output from this program is as follows:

```
(1 == 1) && (2 > 1) is True
(1 == 1) && (2 < 1) is False
(1 == 1) || (1 == 0) is True
(1 == 0) || (1 == 0) is False
!(1 == 0) is True
!(1 == 1) is False
```

Ternary Operator

The ternary operator returns one of two possible expressions based on the result of a Boolean expression. The ternary operator is so named because it uses *three* expressions; the syntax for the ternary operator is as follows:

```
condition ? expression1 : expression2
```

The `condition` expression is a Boolean expression that returns `true` or `false`. If `condition` is true, then *expression1* is evaluated and returned; otherwise *expression2* is evaluated and returned.

Let's look at an example that uses the ternary operator:

```
int result = 10 > 1 ? 20 : 10;
```

The condition expression is `10 > 1`. Because 10 is greater than 1 (in other words, the condition expression is `true`), the first expression is evaluated and returned. The first expression is 20, and therefore 20 is returned. This sets `result` to 20.

In the next example, the condition expression is changed to `10 < 1`:

```
int result = 10 < 1 ? 20 : 10;
```

Because the condition expression is `false` (10 is not less than 1), the second expression is evaluated and returned—in other words, the value 10 is returned, and `result` is set equal to 10.

Listing 3.5 shows the ternary operator in action.

LISTING 3.5: TERNARY OPERATOR

```
/*
  Example3_5.cs illustrates the use of
  the ternary operator
*/

class Example3_5
{

  public static void Main()
  {

    int result;

    result = 10 > 1 ? 20 : 10;
    System.Console.WriteLine("result = " + result);

    result = 10 < 1 ? 20 : 10;
    System.Console.WriteLine("result = " + result);

  }

}
```

The output from this program is as follows:

```
result = 20
result = 10
```

Bitwise Operators

The bitwise operators compare and manipulate bits—a *bit* being a single binary digit that may take one of two values: 0 or 1. There are six bitwise operators (see Table 3.8).

TABLE 3.8: BITWISE OPERATORS

OPERATOR	DESCRIPTION
&	Bitwise AND
|	Bitwise OR
^	Bitwise Exclusive OR
~	Bitwise NOT
<<	Left shift
>>	Right shift

The following sections describe these operators and use `byte` variables—which are made up of 8 bits—to illustrate the results returned by the bitwise operators.

The following example declares two `byte` variables, named `byte1` and `byte2`:

```
byte1 = 0x9a;  // binary 10011010, decimal 154
byte2 = 0xdb;  // binary 11011011, decimal 219
```

Notice that `byte1` is set to the hexadecimal number 9a (hexadecimal numbers are prefixed with `0x` in an assignment). In binary, 9a is 10011010, and in decimal, 9a is 154. Similarly, `byte2` is set to the hexadecimal number db, which is 11011011 in binary and 219 in decimal. These binary and decimal numbers are shown in the comments after the variable assignments for `byte1` and `byte2`.

NOTE *Groups of bits are sometimes referred to as bit patterns.*

The following example declares another `byte` variable, named `result`, which will be used to store the resulting values returned by the bitwise operators in the following sections:

```
byte result;
```

WARNING *Be careful to distinguish between the bitwise operators and the Boolean logical operators. For example, the bitwise AND operator uses a single ampersand (&), and the Boolean logical AND operator uses two ampersands (&&).*

BITWISE AND OPERATOR

The bitwise AND operator (&) compares two bits. If they are both 1, then 1 is returned; otherwise, 0 is returned (see Table 3.9).

TABLE 3.9: BITWISE AND OPERATOR RESULT TABLE

BIT 1	BIT 2	BIT 1 & BIT 2
0	0	0
0	1	0
1	0	0
1	1	1

The following example sets the `byte` variable `result` equal to the result returned by the bitwise AND operator with the values stored in the `byte1` and `byte2` variables:

```
result = (byte) (byte1 & byte2);
```

The result variable is set to 10011010 (decimal value 154). To see why this is so, let's take a look at the binary numbers:

```
  byte1 = 10011010 (154)
& byte2 = 11011011 (219)
-----------------------
 result = 10011010 (154)
```

Each bit in `byte1` and `byte2` is used with the bitwise AND operator, with the result of each operation shown below the corresponding bits. As you can see, the final result is the binary number 10011010, which is 154 in decimal.

BITWISE OR OPERATOR

The bitwise OR operator (|) compares two bits. If either bit is 1, then 1 is returned; otherwise 0 is returned (see Table 3.10).

TABLE 3.10: BITWISE OR OPERATOR RESULT TABLE

BIT 1	BIT 2	BIT 1 | BIT 2
0	0	0
0	1	1
1	0	1
1	1	1

The following example sets `result` equal to the result of using the bitwise OR operator with the values stored in the `byte1` and `byte2` variables:

```
result = (byte) (byte1 | byte2);
```

In this case, `result` is set to 10011010 (decimal value 219):

```
  byte1 = 10011010 (154)
| byte2 = 11011011 (219)
-----------------------
 result = 11011011 (219)
```

BITWISE EXCLUSIVE OR OPERATOR

The bitwise Exclusive OR operator (^) compares two bits. If either bit is 1, then 1 is returned; if both bits are 1 or 0, then 0 is returned (see Table 3.11).

TABLE 3.11: BITWISE EXCLUSIVE OR OPERATOR RESULT TABLE

BIT 1	BIT 2	BIT 1 ^ BIT 2
0	0	0
0	1	1
1	0	1
1	1	0

The following example sets `result` equal to the result of using the bitwise Exclusive OR operator with byte1 and byte2:

```
result = (byte) (byte1 ^ byte2);
```
In this case, `result` is set to 01000001 (decimal value 65):
```
  byte1 = 10011010 (154)
^ byte2 = 11011011 (219)
-----------------------
 result = 01000001  (65)
```

BITWISE NOT OPERATOR

The bitwise NOT operator (~) returns 1 if the bit is 0, and it returns 0 if the bit is 1 (see Table 3.12).

TABLE 3.12: BITWISE NOT OPERATOR RESULT TABLE

BIT 1	~BIT 1
0	1
1	0

The following example sets `result` equal to the result of using the bitwise NOT operator with byte1:

```
result = (byte) ~byte1;
```
In this case, `result` is set to 01100101 (decimal value 101):
```
  byte1 = 10011010 (154)
~ byte1 = 01100101 (101)
```

NOTE *The bitwise NOT operator is also known as the ones complement operator, or the invert operator, because it converts ones to zeros and zeros to ones.*

LEFT SHIFT OPERATOR

The left shift operator (<<) shifts the bits in a binary number to the left by a specified number of places. Any bits that are shifted off the left end are lost, and the new bits from the right are set to 0.

The following example shifts the bit pattern in byte1 one place to the left and stores the resulting bits in result:

```
result = (byte) (byte1 << 1);
```

The value 00110100 (decimal value 52) is stored in result. Let's take a look at the bits:

```
byte1     10011010 (154)
<< 1
----------------------
result = 00110100  (52)
```

As you can see, shifting the bit pattern 10011010 one place to the left gives the result 00110100, which has a decimal value of 52.

RIGHT SHIFT OPERATOR

The right shift operator (>>) shifts the bits in a binary number to the right by a specified number of places. Any bits that are shifted off the right end are lost, and the new bits from the left being set to are set to 0.

The following example shifts the bit pattern in byte1 one place to the right and stores the resulting bits in result:

```
result = (byte) (byte1 >> 1);
```

The value 01001101 (decimal value 77) is stored in result. Let's take a look at the bits:

```
byte1     10011010 (154)
>> 1
----------------------
result = 01001101  (77)
```

As you can see, shifting 10011010 one place to the right gives the result 01001101, which has a decimal value of 77.

Listing 3.6 shows how to use bitwise operators.

LISTING 3.6: BITWISE OPERATORS

```
/*
  Example3_6.cs illustrates the use of
  the bitwise operators
*/

class Example3_6
{

  public static void Main()
  {

    byte byte1 = 0x9a;  // binary 10011010, decimal 154
    byte byte2 = 0xdb;  // binary 11011011, decimal 219
    byte result;
```

```
System.Console.WriteLine("byte1 = " + byte1);
System.Console.WriteLine("byte2 = " + byte2);

// bitwise AND
result = (byte) (byte1 & byte2);
System.Console.WriteLine("byte1 & byte2 = " + result);

// bitwise OR
result = (byte) (byte1 | byte2);
System.Console.WriteLine("byte1 | byte2 = " + result);

// bitwise exclusive OR
result = (byte) (byte1 ^ byte2);
System.Console.WriteLine("byte1 ^ byte2 = " + result);

// bitwise NOT
result = (byte) ~byte1;
System.Console.WriteLine("~byte1 = " + result);

// left shift
result = (byte) (byte1 << 1);
System.Console.WriteLine("byte1 << 1 = " + result);

// right shift
result = (byte) (byte1 >> 1);
System.Console.WriteLine("byte1 >> 1 = " + result);

  }

}
```

The output from this program is as follows:

```
byte1 = 154
byte2 = 219
byte1 & byte2 = 154
byte1 | byte2 = 219
byte1 ^ byte2 = 65
~byte1 = 101
byte1 << 1 = 52
byte1 >> 1 = 77
```

Shortcut Operators

The shortcut operators assign a value to a variable and at the same time perform an operation on that value. There are 14 shortcut operators (see Table 3.13).

TABLE 3.13: SHORTCUT OPERATORS

OPERATOR	DESCRIPTION
+=	Addition
-=	Subtraction
*=	Multiplication
/=	Division
++x	Prefix increment
--x	Prefix decrement
x++	Postfix increment
x--	Postfix decrement
&=	Bitwise AND
|=	Bitwise OR
^=	Bitwise exclusive OR
~=	Bitwise NOT
<<=	Left shift
>>=	Right shift

These operators are useful because they act as shortcuts when you want to perform an addition or subtraction, for example, on the same variable. For example, let's assume you have an `int` variable named `length`, and you want to add 10 to that variable. You could do the following:

```
length = length + 10;
```

There's nothing wrong with this statement, but the `length` variable is repeated twice. By using the `+=` operator, you only need to use `length` once in the statement:

```
length += 10;
```

This adds 10 to `length` in one step.
Here are some other examples:

```
length *= 2;  // multiplies length by 2
length /= 3;  // divides length by 3
```

Listing 3.7 shows how to use the shortcut operators.

LISTING 3.7: SHORTCUT OPERATORS

```
/*
  Example3_7.cs illustrates the use of
```

```
   the shortcut operators
*/

class Example3_7
{

  public static void Main()
  {

    int length = 1;

    length += 10;
    System.Console.WriteLine("length = " + length);

    length *= 2;  // multiplies length by 2
    System.Console.WriteLine("length = " + length);

    length /= 3;  // divides length by 3
    System.Console.WriteLine("length = " + length);

  }

}
```

The output from this program is as follows:

```
length = 11
length = 22
length = 7
```

The other operators work in a similar way, but the prefix and postfix operators require some additional explanation.

PREFIX AND POSTFIX INCREMENT AND DECREMENT OPERATORS

The prefix and postfix versions of the increment (++) and decrement (--) operators enable you to add and subtract 1 from a value, respectively. The following example increments length by 1:

```
length++;
```

The following example decrements length by 1:

```
length--;
```

You can use the increment and decrement operators before or after a variable—this is where the *prefix* and *postfix* part comes into the picture. The two previous examples used the postfix versions of the operators; in other words, the operators were placed *after* the variable.

By placing the operator first, you use the prefix version. For example:

```
++length;
--length;
```

These examples, and the two earlier examples, are fairly simple to understand: The `length` variable is incremented or decremented by 1 immediately. The situation gets more complex if you use the increment and decrement operators in a statement that assigns a value to another variable. For example:

```
length = 3;
int newLength = length++;
```

In this case, `newLength` is *first* assigned the current value of `length` (3) and *then* `length` is incremented by 1 to 4 by the increment operator. Let's look at another example:

```
length = 3;
newLength = ++length;
```

This time, `length` is incremented *first* because the increment operator is placed before `length`. So `length` is incremented by 1 to 4 and *then* `newLength` is assigned the current value of `length` (4).

Listing 3.8 illustrates how to use the prefix and postfix increment and decrement operators.

LISTING 3.8: PREFIX AND POSTFIX INCREMENT AND DECREMENT OPERATORS

```
/*
   Example3_8.cs illustrates the use of
   prefix and postfix versions of the
   increment and decrement operators
*/

class Example3_8
{

   public static void Main()
   {

     // postfix increment
     int length = 3;
     int newLength = length++;
     System.Console.WriteLine("Postfix increment example");
     System.Console.WriteLine("length = " + length);
     System.Console.WriteLine("newLength = " + newLength);

     // prefix increment
     length = 3;
     newLength = ++length;
     System.Console.WriteLine("Prefix increment example");
     System.Console.WriteLine("length = " + length);
     System.Console.WriteLine("newLength = " + newLength);
```

```
// postfix decrement
length = 3;
newLength = length--;
System.Console.WriteLine("Postfix decrement example");
System.Console.WriteLine("length = " + length);
System.Console.WriteLine("newLength = " + newLength);

// prefix decrement
length = 3;
newLength = --length;
System.Console.WriteLine("Prefix decrement example");
System.Console.WriteLine("length = " + length);
System.Console.WriteLine("newLength = " + newLength);

   }

}
```

The output from this program is as follows:

```
Postfix increment example
length = 4
newLength = 3
Prefix increment example
length = 4
newLength = 4
Postfix decrement example
length = 2
newLength = 3
Prefix decrement example
length = 2
newLength = 2
```

is Operator

The is operator checks if a variable or constant (or more generally, an expression) is of a specified type. For example, let's assume you have an int variable named myInt:

```
int myInt = 0;
```

You can check if myInt is of the int type using the following statement:

```
bool compatible = myInt is int;
```

Notice that the is operator returns a Boolean value. In this example, myInt is an int, and therefore the is operator returns true.

In the following examples, the is operator returns false:

```
compatible = myInt is long;
compatible = myInt is float;
```

Because myInt is not of the long or float types, the is operator returns false.

NOTE   *The is operator is more useful to check if the class of an object is derived from a specified class or if the class of an object implements a specified interface. You'll learn about classes and objects in Chapter 5, "Object-Oriented Programming." You'll learn about derived classes in Chapter 7, "Derived Classes," and you'll learn about interfaces in Chapter 8, "Interfaces."*

Listing 3.9 illustrates the is operator.

LISTING 3.9: is OPERATOR

```
/*
  Example3_9.cs illustrates the use of
  the is operator
*/

class Example3_9
{

  public static void Main()
  {

    int myInt = 0;
    bool compatible = myInt is int;
    System.Console.WriteLine("myInt is int = " + compatible);

    compatible = myInt is long;
    System.Console.WriteLine("myInt is long = " + compatible);

    compatible = myInt is float;
    System.Console.WriteLine("myInt is float = " + compatible);

  }

}
```

The output from this program is as follows:

```
myInt is int = True
myInt is long = False
myInt is float = False
```

Operator Precedence

When you write an expression that contains more than one operator, the compiler uses a set of rules that determines which operator to evaluate first, second, third, and so on until the whole expression is evaluated. Each operator has a built-in priority, or *precedence*, which the compiler uses to determine the operator to evaluate next.

Let's take a look at an example that assigns a value to an `int` variable named `myInt`:

```
int myInt = 2 + 5 * 10;
```

Initially, you might think the value assigned to `myInt` is 70 because $2 + 5 = 7$, and $7 * 10 = 70$, right? Wrong! The multiplication operator (*) has a higher priority, or higher precedence, than the addition operator (+), so the right side of the expression is evaluated as follows: $5 * 10 = 50$, $2 + 50 = 52$. Therefore, `myInt` is assigned the value 52.

However, you can override the operator precedence using parentheses. For example:

```
myInt = (2 + 5) * 10;
```

Because $2 + 5$ is placed in parentheses, it is evaluated first. So, $2 + 5 = 7$, and $7 * 10 = 70$. Therefore, the value 70 is assigned to `myInt`.

Let's take a look at a different example:

```
myInt = 2 * 20 / 5;
```

The multiplication (*) and division (/) operators have the same precedence, so the operators are evaluated from left to right. So, $2 * 20 (= 40)$ is evaluated first, followed by $40 / 5 (= 8)$. Therefore, the value 8 is assigned to `myInt`.

Listing 3.10 illustrates operator precedence.

LISTING 3.10: OPERATOR PRECEDENCE

```
/*
  Example3_10.cs illustrates operator precedence
*/

class Example3_10
{

  public static void Main()
  {

    int myInt = 2 + 5 * 10;
    System.Console.WriteLine("2 + 5 * 10 = " + myInt);

    myInt = (2 + 5) * 10;
    System.Console.WriteLine("(2 + 5) * 10 = " + myInt);

    myInt = 2 * 20 / 5;
    System.Console.WriteLine("2 * 20 / 5 = " + myInt);

  }

}
```

The output from this program is as follows:

```
2 + 5 * 10 = 52
(2 + 5) * 10 = 70
2 * 20 / 5 = 8
```

You've already seen that C# has many operators, and you may group these operators into categories that have the same precedence. Table 3.14 shows the operator categories and the operators for each category in order of precedence—the highest precedence category is shown first.

TABLE 3.14: OPERATOR PRECEDENCE

CATEGORY	OPERATORS
Primary	Group: (x)
	Field access: x.y
	Method call: f(x)
	Index access: a[x]
	Postfix increment: x++
	Postfix decrement: x--
	New object: new
	Get type: typeof
	Get size: sizeof
	Use boundary check: checked
	No boundary check: unchecked
Unary	Positive value: +
	Negative value: -
	Boolean logical NOT: !
	Bitwise NOT: ~
	Prefix increment: ++x
	Prefix decrement: --x
	Cast: (type)
Multiplicative	Multiply: *
	Divide: /
	Modulus: %
Additive	Add: +
	Subtract: -
Bitwise shifts	Left shift: <<
	Right shift: >>
Relational	Less than: <
	Greater than: >
	Less than or equal to: <=
	Greater than or equal to: >=
	Type compatible: is
	Type compatible with cast: as
Equality	Equal to: ==
	Not equal to: !=

Continued on next page

TABLE 3.14: OPERATOR PRECEDENCE *(continued)*

CATEGORY	OPERATORS
Bitwise AND	&
Bitwise exclusive OR	^
Bitwise OR	|
Boolean logical AND	&&
Boolean logical OR	||
Ternary	?:
Assignment	= *= /= %= += -= <<= >>= &= ^= !=

When an operand is placed between two operators with the same precedence, the *associativity* of the operators determines the order that the operations are performed. With the exception of the assignment operators, the operators that use two operands (the addition operator, for example) are *left-associative*—which means that the operations are performed from the left to the right. The assignment operators and the ternary operator are *right-associative*—which means the operations are performed from right to left.

You saw how to use most of the operators in Table 3.14 in this chapter; you'll see the use of the other operators as this book progresses.

Summary

This chapter introduced you to expressions and operators. An *expression* is typically a statement that performs some kind of calculation and returns a value. An expression consists of one or more *operands*—which may be variables, constants, or literal values—along with one or more *operators*.

C# contains many operators that allow you to perform assignments, arithmetic, logical operations, and so on. For example, you use the addition operator (+) to add numbers, the multiplication operator (*) to multiply numbers, and the Boolean logical AND operator (&&) to compare two Boolean values. In the next chapter, you'll look at decisions, loops, and preprocessor directives.

Chapter 4

Decisions, Loops, and Preprocessor Directives

So FAR, ALL THE sample programs you've seen contain statements performed in sequence, one after another, until the program ends. In this chapter, you'll learn how to execute different branches of code based on decisions and how to repeat statements using loops.

You'll also learn about the *preprocessor*, which is program that reads your program source files prior to compilation—you can give the preprocessor instructions, known as *directives*, which can affect what parts of your program are actually compiled.

Featured in this chapter:

♦ Implementing the if and switch Statements

♦ Using Loop and Jump Statements

♦ Creating Preprocessor Directives

Using the *if* Statement

The if statement enables you to test for a Boolean logical condition in your program, and if that condition is true, execute some code contained in that branch. The syntax for the if statement is as follows:

```
if (condition)
  statement1
[else
  statement2]
```

If *condition* is true, then *statement1* will be executed. The optional else keyword allows your program to execute code if the condition is false. So, in the previous syntax, *statement2* will be executed if *condition* is false. Now, *condition* can be any expression that returns a Boolean true or false value.

Listing 4.1 illustrates how to use the if statement to compare two int variables.

LISTING 4.1: THE if STATEMENT

```
/*
  Example4_1.cs illustrates the use of the if statement
*/

class Example4_1
{

  public static void Main()
  {

    int smallNumber = 5;
    int bigNumber = 100;

    if (bigNumber > smallNumber)
      System.Console.WriteLine(bigNumber + " is greater than " +
        smallNumber);
    else
      System.Console.WriteLine(bigNumber + " is less than " +
        smallNumber);

  }

}
```

Because bigNumber is greater than smallNumber, the logical condition bigNumber > smallNumber used in the if statement is true and the output from this program is therefore:

```
100 is greater than 5
```

Replacing a Single Statement with a Block

In Chapter 2, "Basic C# Programming," we introduced the concept of *blocks*—a block consists of a group of statements surrounded by curly brackets ({ and }). You can replace a single statement with a block. For example, you may use the if statement to execute a block:

```
if (condition)
{
  statements1
} [else
{
  statements2
}]
```

If *condition* is true, then *statements1* are executed; if *condition* is false, then *statements2* are executed—*statements1* and *statements2* represent one or more statements.

TIP   *It is considered good programming practice to use blocks even when there is only one statement. That way, if you want to add another statement, your block is already in place—if you didn't have a block, you might make the mistake of adding a new statement but forgetting to add the block!*

The curly brackets that mark the beginning and the end of the block may also appear on their own lines:

```
if (condition)
{
  statements1
}
[else
{
  statement2
}]
```

In this book, we use the previous style: placing curly brackets on the same lines as the statements.

NOTE   *You can use whichever style you prefer as long as you use it consistently.*

Listing 4.2 illustrates using an if statement to execute a block.

LISTING 4.2: AN if STATEMENT THAT EXECUTES A BLOCK

```
/*
  Example4_2.cs illustrates the use of an if statement
  that executes a block
*/

class Example4_2
{

  public static void Main()
  {

    int smallNumber = 5;
    int bigNumber = 100;

    if (bigNumber < smallNumber)
    {
      System.Console.Write(bigNumber);
      System.Console.Write(" is less than ");
      System.Console.Write(smallNumber);
    } else
    {
      System.Console.Write(smallNumber);
      System.Console.Write(" is less than ");
```

```
        System.Console.Write(bigNumber);
     }

  }

}
```

Because `bigNumber` is not less than `smallNumber`, the logical condition used in the `if` statement is `false`, and so the statements in the `else` branch are executed. The output from this program is therefore:

```
5 is less than 100
```

Using Nested *if* Statements

You can place an `if` statement within another `if` statement—the inner `if` statement is said to be *nested* within the other. Nested `if` statements enable you to build up quite complicated logical conditions from simple `if` statements. The following syntax shows a nested `if` statement:

```
if (condition1)
{
  statements1
} else
{
  if (condition2)
  {  // nested if
    statements2
  } else
  {
    statements3
  }
}
```

If *condition1* is true, then *statements1* are executed. If *condition1* is false, and *condition2* is true, then *statements3* are executed. If *condition1* is false, and *condition2* is false, then *statements3* are executed.

Listing 4.3 illustrates the use of a nested `if` statement.

LISTING 4.3: A NESTED if STATEMENT

```
/*
  Example4_3.cs illustrates the use of
  a nested if statement
*/

class Example4_3
{
```

```
public static void Main()
{

  int reactorTemp = 1500;
  string emergencyValve = "closed";

  if (reactorTemp <= 1000)
  {
    System.Console.WriteLine("Reactor temperature normal");
  } else
  {
    System.Console.WriteLine("Reactor temperature too high!");
    if (emergencyValve == "closed")
    {
      System.Console.WriteLine("Reactor meltdown in progress!");
    }
  }

}

}
```

This program is a *very* simple nuclear reactor simulator. The reactor temperature is specified using the int variable reactorTemp, which is set to 1,500 degrees centigrade. If the reactor temperature goes higher than 1,000 degrees, then the emergency valve must be opened to prevent a meltdown—the status of the emergency valve is set using the string variable emergencyValve, which is set to "closed".

Because reactorTemp is greater than 1,000 and emergencyValve is not equal to "closed", the reactor melts down, as shown in the output of this program:

```
Reactor temperature too high!
Reactor meltdown in progress!
```

Using Logical Operators with the *if* Statement

In the previous chapter, you saw three logical operators: && (AND), || (OR), and ! (NOT). You may use these operators in the condition expression of an if statement, as shown in Listing 4.4.

LISTING 4.4: USING LOGICAL OPERATORS WITH AN if STATEMENT

```
/*
  Example4_4.cs illustrates the use of
  logical operators with an if statement
*/

class Example4_4
{
```

```
public static void Main()
{

  int reactorTemp = 1500;
  string emergencyValve = "closed";

  if ((reactorTemp > 1000) && (emergencyValve == "closed"))
  {
    System.Console.WriteLine("Reactor meltdown in progress!");
  }

}

}
```

The logical condition used in the if statement is (reactorTemp > 1000) && (emergencyValve == "closed"). This means that both the expression reactorTemp > 1000 and the expression emergencyValve == "closed" must be true for the reactor to meltdown—and because reactorTemp is set to 1500 and emergencyValve is set to "closed", the reactor does indeed meltdown again, as shown by the output of this program:

```
Reactor meltdown in progress!
```

With all these meltdowns, it looks like we need to get someone else to manage the reactor!

Implementing the *switch* Statement

The switch statement enables you to pick one branch of code for execution from a list of many options. The syntax for the switch statement is as follows:

```
switch (expression)
{
  case value1:
    statements1
    break;
  case value2:
    statements2
    break;
  ...
  [default:
    default-statements
    break;]
}
```

In the switch statement, the value returned by *expression* is compared to each value that follows the case keyword. If there is a match between any two values, then the statements for that case branch are executed. For example, if the value returned by *expression* matches *value2*, then *statements2* are executed. If no matches are found, and if the optional default branch is included, then *default-statements* are executed.

The break statement marks the end of each branch—break causes execution of the switch statement to end, and program flow continues from the statement that follows the switch.

Listing 4.5 illustrates the use of the switch statement—the program displays the name of the planet based on its specified position from the Sun.

LISTING 4.5: THE switch STATEMENT

```
/*
  Example4_5.cs illustrates the use of
  the switch statement
*/

class Example4_5
{

  public static void Main()
  {

    int planetPosition = 4;  // Mars
    switch (planetPosition)
    {
      case 1:  // Mercury
        System.Console.WriteLine("Mercury");
        break;
      case 2:  // Venus
        System.Console.WriteLine("Venus");
        break;
      case 3:  // Earth
        System.Console.WriteLine("Earth");
        break;
      case 4:  // Mars
        System.Console.WriteLine("Mars");
        break;
      case 5:  // Jupiter
        System.Console.WriteLine("Jupiter");
        break;
      case 6:  // Saturn
        System.Console.WriteLine("Saturn");
        break;
      case 7:  // Uranus
        System.Console.WriteLine("Uranus");
        break;
      case 8:  // Neptune
        System.Console.WriteLine("Neptune");
        break;
```

```
        case 9:  // Pluto
          System.Console.WriteLine("Pluto");
          break;
        default:  // Planet unknown
          System.Console.WriteLine("Planet unknown");
          break;
      }

    }

}
```

Because the fourth planet from the Sun is Mars, the switch statement matches the planetPosition variable's value of 4 with the case branch that has the value 4, and "Mars" is displayed on the screen:

Mars

When the break is executed, program control leaves the switch and the program ends.

Comparing String Values Using a *switch* Statement

You aren't limited to comparing integer values in a switch statement; you can also use a switch statement to compare string values. Listing 4.6 illustrates the use of a switch statement to compare string values, and it displays a planet's position based on that planet's name.

LISTING 4.6: THE switch STATEMENT COMPARING STRING VALUES

```
/*
  Example4_6.cs illustrates the use of
  the switch statement to compare string values
*/

class Example4_6
{

  public static void Main()
  {

    string planetName = "Saturn";  // sixth planet from the Sun
    switch (planetName)
    {
      case "Mercury":
        System.Console.WriteLine(1);
        break;
      case "Venus":
        System.Console.WriteLine(2);
        break;
```

```
        case "Earth":
          System.Console.WriteLine(3);
          break;
        case "Mars":
          System.Console.WriteLine(4);
          break;
        case "Jupiter":
          System.Console.WriteLine(5);
          break;
        case "Saturn":
          System.Console.WriteLine(6);
          break;
        case "Uranus":
          System.Console.WriteLine(7);
          break;
        case "Neptune":
          System.Console.WriteLine(8);
          break;
        case "Pluto":
          System.Console.WriteLine(9);
          break;
        default:
          System.Console.WriteLine("Planet unknown");
          break;
      }

    }

  }
```

The `planetName` string, which is set to `"Saturn"` matches the `case` branch for Saturn, and therefore the output from this program is this:

```
6
```

Introducing Fall-Through

If you don't include any statements for a particular `case` branch, then program control will continue on to the next `case` branch and execute any statements it finds until a `break` is reached. This is known as a *fall-through* because although a match was made for a particular `case` branch, program control went through it and into the next `case` branch.

Listing 4.7 illustrates a `switch` statement with a fall-though.

LISTING 4.7: A switch STATEMENT WITH A FALL-THROUGH

```
/*
  Example4_7.cs illustrates the use of
```

```
     the switch statement containing a branch
     with no statements: causes a "fall-through"
     to the next branch
*/

class Example4_7
{

  public static void Main()
  {

    int value = 1;
    switch (value)
    {
      case 0:
        System.Console.WriteLine("Zero");
        break;
      case 1:
      case 2:
        System.Console.WriteLine("One or two");
        break;
      case 3:
        System.Console.WriteLine("Three");
        break;
      default:
        System.Console.WriteLine("Other number");
        break;
    }

  }

}
```

The int variable value is set to 1, but because the branch for the case of 1 doesn't contain any statements, program control falls through to the next branch—the case for 2, which displays this value:

```
One or two
```

WARNING   *Make sure you don't accidentally have fall-throughs in your programs. There are in fact only a few cases where a fall-through is valid, and the compiler will report any invalid fall-throughs in your code. For example, if you comment out the* **break** *in the* **Case** 0 *branch of the previous program, you'll get a compilation error.*

Using Loop Statements

Sometimes you might need your program to run the same basic statements repeatedly, until a certain condition is satisfied. For example, you might need to add up a list of numbers or perform a complex calculation on a table of data. Loops allow you to do these kinds of tasks, and C# has a number of statements for writing loops.

The *while* Loop

You use a while loop when you want to repeat one or more statements while a specified logical condition is true. The syntax for the while loop statement is as follows:

```
while (condition)
    statement
```

The condition expression must return a Boolean true or false value; condition is tested before each iteration of the loop, and if true, the loop statement is executed—if condition is false, then the loop terminates. Because condition is checked at the start of the loop, this means that the code inside the while loop may never execute. The statement may be replaced with a block containing multiple statements.

Listing 4.8 illustrates using while loop to display the numbers 1 to 5.

LISTING 4.8: A while LOOP

```
/*
   Example4_8.cs illustrates the use of
   a while loop to display 1 to 5
*/

class Example4_8
{

  public static void Main()
  {

    int counter = 1;
    while (counter <= 5)
    {
      System.Console.WriteLine("counter = " + counter);
      counter++;
    }

  }

}
```

This program declares an `int` variable named `counter` and initializes its value to 1. Next, the program executes a `while` loop. The loop condition is `counter <= 5`, this means that the loop will repeat while `counter` is less than or equal to 5—when `counter` reaches 6, the loop condition is `false` and the loop terminates. The code in the loop block displays the current value for `counter` and then increments its value by 1.

The output from this program is as follows:

```
counter = 1
counter = 2
counter = 3
counter = 4
counter = 5
```

THE FIBONACCI SERIES

As slightly more complex example of a `while` loop, we're going to show you a program that calculates and displays the *Fibonacci series* of numbers. The Fibonacci series is a list of numbers originally used to model the population growth of rabbits.

The Fibonacci series starts with the numbers 1 and 1. These two numbers are then added together to produce the next number in the series—2. The rest of the series is produced by adding the last two numbers in the series together to produce the next number—so, the next number in the series is 3 (2 + 1), the next is 5 (3 + 2), and so on. The Fibonacci series continues into infinity.

Listing 4.9 illustrates using a `while` loop to calculate and display the Fibonacci series of numbers that are less than 50.

LISTING 4.9: THE FIBONACCI SERIES

```
/*
   Example4_9.cs illustrates the use of
   a while loop to calculate and display
   the Fibonacci numbers less than 50
*/

class Example4_9
{

  public static void Main()
  {

    // initialize the first two numbers in the sequence
    int oldNumber = 1;
    int currentNumber = 1;

    int nextNumber;
```

```
    System.Console.Write(currentNumber + " ");

    while (currentNumber < 50)
    {
      System.Console.Write(currentNumber + " ");

      // calculate the next number by adding the
      // current number to the old number
      nextNumber = currentNumber + oldNumber;

      oldNumber = currentNumber;
      currentNumber = nextNumber;
    }

  }

}
```

The output from this program is as follows:

```
1 1 2 3 5 8 13 21 34
```

The *do...while* Loop

A do...while loop is similar to a while loop, except the logical condition is checked at the end of the loop rather than at the beginning. This means that the statements in a do...while loop execute at least once, unlike the statements in a while loop, which may never execute.

NOTE *You should use a* do...while *loop if you want your loop statements to execute at least once.*

The syntax for the do...while loop statement is as follows:

```
do
  statement
while (condition);
```

The *statement* (or block of statements) executes with each iteration of the loop. The *condition* expression must return a Boolean true or false value and is tested at the end of each loop iteration—if true, the loop will be repeated; if false, the loop terminates.

Listing 4.10 illustrates using a do..while loop to display the number 1.

LISTING 4.10: THE do...while LOOP

```
/*
  Example4_10.cs illustrates the use of
  a do...while loop
*/
```

```
class Example4_10
{

  public static void Main()
  {

    int counter = 1;
    do
    {
      System.Console.WriteLine("counter = " + counter);
      counter--;
    } while (counter > 1);

  }

}
```

The `int` variable `counter` is initialized to 1. The statements in the do…while loop display the value of `counter` and then decrement its value by 1—so after the first iteration of the loop, `counter` is 0. Because `counter` is 0, the loop condition `counter > 1` returns `false` and the loop terminates. Thus, the statements in the loop are executed only once.

The output from this program is as follows:

```
counter = 1
```

The *for* Loop

The `for` loop is basically a shorthand way of writing a `while` loop that uses a variable value to determine when the loop is terminated, and in that loop the variable's value is incremented or decremented.

For example, the program shown in Listing 4.8 declared and initialized a variable named `counter` and used a `while` loop to check that the counter variable was less than or equal to 5—at the end of this loop, `counter` was incremented by 1:

```
int counter = 1;
while (counter <= 5)
{
  System.Console.WriteLine("counter = " + counter);
  counter++;
}
```

You may replace this with a `for` loop, which uses a more concise syntax:

```
for ([initializer]; [condition]; [iterator])
  statement
```

where the syntax elements are as follows:

initializer   An expression evaluated prior to the loop being executed. This is usually a variable declaration and initialization—int counter = 1, for example. The scope of a variable declared using the *initializer* is local to that loop; it may not be used outside of the loop. You can in fact use more than one initializer in a for loop, but it's rare that you'll want to do so.

condition   An expression evaluated at the start of each loop iteration; if it is true, then the loop statements are executed, and if false, the loop terminates. An example *condition* is counter <= 5.

iterator   An expression evaluated at the end of each loop iteration. This is usually an expression that increments or decrements the variable declared in the *initializer*. An example *iterator* is counter++.

The following for loop replaces the previous while loop:

```
for (int counter = 1; counter <= 5; counter++)
{
  System.Console.WriteLine("counter = " + counter);
}
```

The int variable counter is declared and initialized to 1. The loop condition counter <= 5 is checked at the start of each iteration. The counter variable is displayed by the statement contained in the loop. At the end of each iteration, counter is incremented by 1 using counter++.

WARNING   *The* counter *variable's scope is local to the loop—if you attempted to use this variable outside of the loop, you will get a compilation error.*

You can also use an existing variable in a for loop, for example:

```
int counter;
for (counter = 1; counter <= 5; counter++)
{
  System.Console.WriteLine("counter = " + counter);
}
```

When you use an existing variable in a for loop, the scope of that variable is, of course, not limited to the for loop because it was declared outside—but its scope must *include* the for loop.

Also, because the *initializer* expression is optional, you can even omit it altogether:

```
int counter = 1;
for (; counter <= 5; counter++)
{
  System.Console.WriteLine("counter = " + counter);
}
```

TIP   *Although you can omit any of the expressions in a* for *loop, if you do so, you might find it is better to use one of the other loops previously described.*

Listing 4.11 illustrates a for loop.

LISTING 4.11: THE for LOOP

```
/*
   Example4_11.cs illustrates the use of
   a for loop to display 1 to 5
*/

class Example4_11
{

  public static void Main()
  {

    for (int counter = 1; counter <= 5; counter++)
    {
      System.Console.WriteLine("counter = " + counter);
    }

  }

}
```

The output from this program is as follows:

```
counter = 1
counter = 2
counter = 3
counter = 4
counter = 5
```

The *foreach* Loop

The foreach loop enables you to iterate over a set of elements. The syntax for the foreach loop statement is as follows:

```
foreach (type variable-name in expression)
   statement
```

Now, variable-name is the name assigned to the variable that is used in the loop to access the set of elements specified in expression. A set of elements may be an array or collection, both of which will be covered later in this book. Also, the variable may be an object, a struct, or a collection—all of which will be covered in later chapters.

For now, we'll just introduce the basics of using the foreach statement—once you've seen the basics, you will easily see how to use the foreach statement in the more complex cases.

The following statement declares a set of int elements—known as an *array*—named myValues:

```
int [] myValues = {2, 4, 3, 5, 1};
```

The myValues array consists of five int elements that are set to 2, 4, 3, 5, and 1. Don't worry too much about the details of this statement—you'll learn the details of arrays in Chapter 10, "Arrays and Indexers."

The following foreach statement iterates over these int elements, using the int variable counter:

```
foreach (int counter in myValues)
{
   System.Console.WriteLine("counter = " + counter);
}
```

The counter variable is set to 2 in the first iteration of the loop, 4 in the second iteration, and so on through to 1 in the fifth iteration.

Listing 4.12 illustrates the use of this foreach loop.

LISTING 4.12: THE foreach LOOP

```
/*
   Example4_12.cs illustrates the use of
   a foreach loop
*/

class Example4_12
{

  public static void Main()
  {

    int [] myValues = {2, 4, 3, 5, 1};
    foreach (int counter in myValues)
    {
      System.Console.WriteLine("counter = " + counter);
    }

  }

}
```

The output from this program is as follows:

```
counter = 2
counter = 4
counter = 3
counter = 5
counter = 1
```

Understanding Jump Statements

You might need to terminate a loop before it has reached the end, or you might need to skip an iteration of a loop. The break statement allows you to accomplish the first action, and the continue statement allows you to do the second. You can also jump to a specific point in a program using the goto statement.

The *break* Statement

Sometimes you might want to terminate a loop prematurely. In the case of a while, do...while, or for loop, you might want to end the loop before the end condition is satisfied; and in the case of a foreach loop, you might want to end the loop before the end of the list of elements has been reached. You can terminate any type of loop using the break statement. We showed you one use for the break statement earlier in "The switch Statement" section, where it was used to end branches of the switch statement.

Listing 4.13 illustrates using the break statement to terminate a for loop.

LISTING 4.13: USING THE break STATEMENT TO TERMINATE A LOOP

```
/*
  Example4_13.cs illustrates the use of
  the break statement
*/

class Example4_13
{

  public static void Main()
  {

    int total = 0;

    for (int counter = 1; counter <= 10; counter++)
    {
      System.Console.WriteLine("counter = " + counter);
      total += counter;
      if (counter == 5)
      {
        System.Console.WriteLine("break from loop");
        break;
      }
    }

    System.Console.WriteLine("total = " + total);

  }

}
```

In the absence of the break statement, this for loop would run 10 times and terminate when the counter variable reaches 11. In this program, when counter reaches 5, the break statement in the if terminates the loop prematurely, and program control jumps to the next statement after the loop. The total variable is used to store a running total of the counter variable's values as the loop executes.

The output from this program is as follows:

```
counter = 1
counter = 2
counter = 3
counter = 4
counter = 5
break from loop
total = 15
```

Because the counter variable has the values 1, 2, 3, 4, and 5 during the execution of the loop, the total variable has a final value of 15, which is the sum of the counter variable's values.

The *continue* Statement

The continue statement allows you to start the next iteration of a loop immediately, skipping over any remaining code in the loop body. The continue statement causes program control to jump back to the start of the loop.

Listing 4.14 illustrates using the continue statement in a for loop.

LISTING 4.14: USING THE continue STATEMENT

```
/*
  Example4_14.cs illustrates the use of
  the continue statement
*/

class Example4_14
{

  public static void Main()
  {

    int total = 0;

    for (int counter = 1; counter <= 10; counter++)
    {
      if (counter == 6)
      {
        System.Console.WriteLine("continue from loop start");
        continue;
      }
```

```
        System.Console.WriteLine("counter = " + counter);
        total += counter;
    }

    System.Console.WriteLine("total = " + total);

  }

}
```

When the `counter` variable reaches 6, the `continue` statement in the `if` statement is executed—this causes the next iteration of the `for` loop to be started immediately, skipping the rest of the lines in the loop for that iteration. The `total` variable is used to store a running total of the `counter` variable's values (excluding 6).

The output from this program is as follows:

```
counter = 1
counter = 2
counter = 3
counter = 4
counter = 5
continue from loop start
counter = 7
counter = 8
counter = 9
counter = 10
total = 49
```

The `counter` value of 6 is not added to the `total` variable, which has a final value of 49.

The *goto* Statement

The `goto` statement allows you jump to a *label* that you define in the program. Before we show you the details of the `goto` statement, you should be aware that its use is considered poor programming practice, and you should avoid it if at all possible. It is generally possible to structure a program such that you shouldn't need to use the `goto` statement. Having said that, we've included it in this chapter for completeness.

As mentioned, the `goto` statement requires that you create a label in your program. You do this by placing an identifier containing the label name in your program, followed by a colon (:). The following example creates a label named `myLabel`:

```
myLabel:
```

You may then use the `goto` statement to jump to that label, for example:

```
goto myLabel;
```

Listing 4.15 shows a program that illustrates using the `goto` statement to perform a simple loop.

LISTING 4.15: USING THE goto STATEMENT

```
/*
  Example4_15.cs illustrates the use of
  the goto statement
*/

class Example4_15
{

  public static void Main()
  {

    int total = 0;
    int counter = 0;

    myLabel:
    counter++;
    total += counter;
    System.Console.WriteLine("counter = " + counter);
    if (counter < 5)
    {
      System.Console.WriteLine("goto myLabel");
      goto myLabel;
    }
    System.Console.WriteLine("total = " + total);

  }

}
```

The use of the goto statement in this program simulates the action of a simple loop. If the counter variable is less than 5, then the goto statement causes program control to jump to myLabel.

The output from this program is as follows:

```
counter = 1
goto myLabel
counter = 2
goto myLabel
counter = 3
goto myLabel
counter = 4
goto myLabel
counter = 5
total = 15
```

The actual outcome of this program is the same as the program previously shown in Listing 4.13—the `counter` variable is incremented by 1, and its value is added to a running total with a final value of 15. This reinforces what we said earlier about the `goto` statement: you can usually restructure your program such that you don't need to use a `goto`.

Creating Preprocessor Directives

As you already know, before you can run a program, you must first compile it. In all the sample programs you've seen so far, the code contained in the source files is included for compilation, and you must compile the source file before you can run the program.

Before the compiler actually compiles your program, it runs the preprocessor. The preprocessor prepares your program for submission to the compiler, and you can give the preprocessor instructions—known as *directives*. Before we get into the details of the preprocessor directives, we must give you some insight as to why you might want to use them in the first place.

All of the programs you've seen in this book have been small—fewer than 30 lines or so. In the real world, you might be writing programs containing many hundreds of lines of code, and you may include many statements that assist you in debugging your program. You may not want to include all of that debugging code in the compiled program that you release for use, and this is where preprocessor directives are useful—you can use them to indicate which parts of your program you actually want to compile.

You place preprocessor directives in your source file, beginning them with the pound character (#). When the preprocessor runs, it examines your source file and looks for any lines beginning with #.

Defining Symbols

Preprocessor actions are based on *symbols* that you define—and depending on whether a particular symbol is defined, you can tell the preprocessor which parts of your program to compile.

You define preprocessor symbols using the `#define` directive. The following example defines a symbol named `DEBUG`:

```
#define DEBUG
```

You can then test for the definition of the `DEBUG` symbol using the `#if` directive:

```
#if DEBUG
  System.Console.WriteLine("counter = " + counter);
#endif
```

If the `DEBUG` symbol is defined, then the C# code placed between the `#if` directive and the terminating `#endif` directive would be included by the preprocessor in the source code sent to the compiler. Therefore, in this example, your compiled program would contain the call to the `System.Console`.`WriteLine()` method. If the `DEBUG` symbol wasn't defined, then the call wouldn't be included in the complied program.

You can also "undefine" a symbol using the `#undef` directive. The following example undefines the `DEBUG` symbol:

```
#undef DEBUG
```

This has the same effect as not having defined the DEBUG symbol to begin with.

NOTE   *The* #define *and* #undef *directives must appear before any C# program lines—although they may appear after any initial program comments.*

Listing 4.16 illustrates the #define, #if, and #endif preprocessor directives.

LISTING 4.16: USING THE #define, #if, AND #endif PREPROCESSOR DIRECTIVES

```
/*
   Example4_16.cs illustrates the use of the
   #define, #if, and #endif preprocessor directives
*/

#define DEBUG

class Example4_16
{

   public static void Main()
   {

      int total = 0;
      int counter = 0;

      myLabel:
      counter++;
      total += counter;
      System.Console.WriteLine("counter = " + counter);
      if (counter < 5)
      {
#if DEBUG
         System.Console.WriteLine("goto myLabel");
#endif
         goto myLabel;
      }

      System.Console.WriteLine("total = " + total);

   }

}
```

Because the DEBUG symbol is defined by the #define directive at the start of the program, the call to the System.Console.WriteLine() method code in the #if directive is included in the compiled program.

The output from this program is as follows:

```
counter = 1
goto myLabel
counter = 2
goto myLabel
counter = 3
goto myLabel
counter = 4
goto myLabel
counter = 5
total = 15
```

Using the *#if*, *#elif*, and *#else* Directives

You can do some quite complicated tests for symbols using the following preprocessor directives: #if, #elif (else if), and #else. The following example shows how to use the #if and #else directives:

```
#undef DEBUG
/*
   ... C# code ...
*/
#if DEBUG
    System.Console.WriteLine("Reached end of program, total = " + total);
#else
    System.Console.WriteLine("total = " + total);
#endif
```

Because the DEBUG symbols is undefined, only the code after the #else directive is included. The following example shows how to use the #elif directive:

```
#undef DEBUG
#define PRODUCTION
/*
   ... C# code ...
*/
#if DEBUG
    System.Console.WriteLine("goto myLabel");
#elif PRODUCTION
    System.Console.WriteLine("counter < 5");
#else
    System.Console.WriteLine("goto myLabel, counter < 5");
#endif
```

Because only the PRODUCTION symbol is defined, only the code after the #elif directive is included. Listing 4.17 illustrates the use of the #undef, #elif, and #else preprocessor directives.

LISTING 4.17: USING THE #undef, #elif AND #else PREPROCESSOR DIRECTIVES

```csharp
/*
  Example4_17.cs illustrates the use of the
  #undef, #elif, and #else preprocessor directives
*/

#define DEBUG
#undef DEBUG
#define PRODUCTION

class Example4_17
{

  public static void Main()
  {

    int total = 0;
    int counter = 0;

    myLabel:
    counter++;
    total += counter;
    System.Console.WriteLine("counter = " + counter);
    if (counter < 5)
    {
#if DEBUG
      System.Console.WriteLine("goto myLabel");
#elif PRODUCTION
      System.Console.WriteLine("counter < 5");
#else
      System.Console.WriteLine("goto myLabel, counter < 5");
#endif
      goto myLabel;
    }

    System.Console.WriteLine("total = " + total);

  }

}
```

The output from this program is as follows:

```
counter = 1
counter < 5
counter = 2
counter < 5
counter = 3
counter < 5
counter = 4
counter < 5
counter = 5
total = 15
```

Summary

In this chapter you've seen how to use decisions, loops, and directives. Specifically, the `if` statement enables your program to test for a Boolean logical condition, and if that condition is `true`, execute some code contained in that branch. You can also add an `else` clause to execute some other code if the condition is `false`. You can embed a nested `if` statement within another to perform complex logic.

The `switch` statement allows your program to pick one branch of execution from a list of many options, and it may be used to replace long `if` statements.

Loops let you repeatedly execute statements. The `while`, `do...while`, and `for` loops enable you to execute statements until a specified condition is satisfied. A `foreach` loop allows you to iterate over a set of elements, such as array of numbers.

You can prematurely terminate a loop before it has reached the end using the `break` statement, and you can skip an iteration of a loop using the `continue` statement. You can also jump to a specific point in a program—identified using a label—using the `goto` statement, although its use is considered poor programming practice.

The *preprocessor* prepares your program for submission to the compiler, and you can give the preprocessor instructions—known as *directives*—that tell it what to do. You can use preprocessor directives to selectively include, or exclude, code in your source file for compilation. In the next chapter you'll see how Visual C# works as object-oriented programming.

Chapter 5

Object-Oriented Programming

IN CHAPTER 2, "BASIC C# Programming," you learned about the various C# built-in types and how to declare variables using those types. In this chapter, you'll learn how to define your own types using classes and structs—and how to use them in your programs. You'll see how you can create objects from classes. You'll also see how you can use classes and objects to model things that exist in the real world and how they can simplify the task of writing programs to solve complex problems.

Featured in this chapter:

◆ Introducing Classes and Objects

◆ Declaring a Class

◆ Creating and Destroying Objects

◆ Using Methods and Access Modifiers

◆ Learning about Structs

Introducing Classes and Objects

Our world is filled with objects. My car is an object, my bike is an object, and my house is an object—in fact, any tangible item is an object. Similar objects may be grouped together into a *class*. For example, my car is similar to other cars on the road: It has an engine and four wheels, and it's operated with pedals and a steering wheel. So, my car can be grouped into a generic class of cars, all of which have similar characteristics and behaviors. An object can also represent more abstract things—such as an electronic order, for example.

A class specifies the characteristics and behaviors shared by all members of that class. For example, all cars have the following characteristics: make, model, color, and year they were built. All cars also have the following behaviors: the ability to start, stop, and run at different speeds.

NOTE   *You can think of a class as a blueprint from which individual objects are created.*

An object has *individual* characteristics. For example, my car's make is Toyota, its model is MR2, its color is black, and it was built in 1995; my neighbor's car's make is Buick, its model is Century, its color is silver, and it was built in 1992—the point is that both cars have their own characteristics. Of course, some characteristics are common to both our cars—they both have four wheels, for example. In addition, some of the behaviors of our cars are common—for example, both our cars can be started and stopped.

NOTE   *An object has its own individual characteristics, but it has the same behaviors as other objects.*

Classes and objects can be modeled using a computer program. The ability to model classes and objects using a programming language is not new to C#—the idea was developed back in the 1970s at Xerox PARC, and many earlier programming languages have been able to model classes and objects, including Smalltalk, Eiffel, Object Pascal, C++, and more recently Java. These languages are known as *object-oriented programming* (OOP) languages.

Object-oriented programming is a powerful way of solving complex problems. The advantage of using classes and objects in a program is that you can use them to model objects in the real world, which can help reduce the complexity of creating a program to solve difficult problems. You can *encapsulate*, or group together, the characteristics and behaviors of a real object in a class and develop your program from those simple building blocks. For example, imagine writing a program to simulate a nuclear reactor—a complex piece of machinery—by using objects to model features such as the fuel rods, sensors, pumps, boilers, and heat exchangers. In other words, you can break the problem up into smaller components that mirror the real system you're trying to simulate.

Declaring a Class

A class defines the characteristics and behaviors for objects—you can think of a class as a template from which objects are created. In C#, the characteristics are stored in variables known as *fields*, and the behaviors are modeled by *methods*—which are groups of statements that perform a specific task and may return a value. Together, the fields and methods of a class are known as *class members*.

NOTE   *You've already seen an example of one method:* `Main()`. *In all the programs you've seen so far, the* `Main()` *method has performed all the actions of the program and is run—or called—automatically when you run the program.* `Main()` *is a special method that acts as a starting point for a program.*

You declare a class using the `class` keyword, which uses the following simplified syntax:

```
[access-modifier] class class-name {class-body}
```

The syntax elements are as follows:

access-modifier   The degree to which your class is available to the outside world.

class-name   The name you assign to your class.

class-body   The body of your class.

Classes are usually declared using the `public` access modifier, meaning that the class is available without restriction—you'll learn more about access modifiers later in this chapter (see "Using Access Modifiers"). The previous syntax has been simplified because we don't want to overload you with too much information at this stage. Don't worry, though, you'll see examples that use the full class syntax as this book progresses.

We talked a little bit about cars earlier in this chapter, so we'll continue with cars in the code examples. For instance, the following example declares a class named Car—you'll use this class to create objects later:

```
public class Car
{

    // declare the fields
    public string make;
    public string model;
    public string color;
    public int yearBuilt;

    // define the methods
    public void Start()
    {
        System.Console.WriteLine(model + " started");
    }

    public void Stop()
    {
        System.Console.WriteLine(model + " stopped");
    }

}
```

As you can see, the Car class declares four fields: make, model, color, and yearBuilt. The make, model, and color fields are strings that store the make, model, and color of a car, respectively; the yearBuilt field is an integer variable that stores the year a car was built. Each field also has an access modifier, and the four fields of this class are declared using the **public** access modifier—indicating that the fields are accessible without restriction.

The Car class also defines two methods—Start() and Stop()—that simulate the action of starting and stopping a car. When the Start() method is called, it displays a string containing the value for the model field followed by the word *started*; similarly, the Stop() method displays the model field followed by the word *stopped*. You'll notice that these methods are also **public**, indicating they can be called without restriction. These methods also use the **void** keyword—this indicates that the methods don't return a value. You'll learn more about methods, and how they may be used to return values, later in this chapter.

Creating Objects

As you now know, a class defines a template for creating objects. Once you've declared a class, you can then create objects of that class.

The following statements create a Car object:

```
Car myCar;
myCar = new Car();
```

The first statement declares a *reference* to a Car object, named myCar, and it is used to hold the memory location of an actual Car object. The second statement actually creates a Car object in the computer's memory. The new operator allocates the memory for the Car object, and the Car() method creates the object—the Car() method is known as a *constructor*, and you'll learn more about them later in this chapter. The memory location of the newly created Car object is assigned to myCar, and myCar is a reference through which you can access the actual Car object.

NOTE   *The new operator and the constructor are used to create an object. You access an object through an object reference, which holds the location of the actual object in memory.*

To access the fields and methods for an object, you use the *dot operator* (.) with an object reference. You can assign values to the fields of the new Car object through the myCar reference, as shown in the following statements:

```
myCar.make = "Toyota";
myCar.model = "MR2";
myCar.color = "black";
myCar.yearBuilt = 1995;
```

In these examples, the make, model, color, and yearBuilt fields for the Car object are set to "Toyota", "MR2", "black", and 1995, respectively. The following statement displays the value of the model field:

```
System.Console.WriteLine("myCar is an " + myCar.model);
```

This statement displays the following line of output:

```
myCar is an MR2
```

To call the methods, you also use the dot operator. The following statement calls the Start() method for the Car object using the myCar reference:

```
myCar.Start()
```

This runs the statements contained in the Start() method and displays the following line of output:

```
MR2 started
```

Similarly, calling the myCar.Stop() method displays the following line:

```
MR2 stopped
```

The following statement creates another Car object:

```
Car redPorsche = new Car();
```

Notice that the declaration of the object reference and the creation of the new object are combined into one statement. The redPorsche reference is used to access this new Car object.

NOTE   *Creating an object is also called instantiating an object, with the object being known as an instance of the class.*

Each `Car` object has its own copy of the fields declared in the class, and the following statements set its fields using `redPorsche`:

```
redPorsche.make = "Porsche";
redPorsche.model = "Boxster";
redPorsche.color = "red";
redPorsche.yearBuilt = 2000;
```

Because an object reference contains a location of an object in memory, you can change the object actually referenced. For example, let's say I traded in my MR2 for a Porsche (I wish!); then I could record this programmatically using the following statement:

```
myCar = redPorsche;
```

Now `myCar` references the same object referenced by `redPorsche`. This may be verified using the following statement:

```
System.Console.WriteLine("myCar is a " + myCar.model);
```

This statement displays the following line:

```
myCar is a Porsche
```

Null Values

When you declare an object reference, it is initially set to `null`—you can think of `null` as meaning "no reference." When you declare an object reference, it doesn't initially reference an actual object in memory. For example, the following statement declares an object reference named `myOtherCar`:

```
Car myOtherCar;
```

Here, `myOtherCar` is initially set to `null`, and it doesn't reference actual object. Because `myOtherCar` doesn't yet reference an object (or, is not assigned), the following line will not compile:

```
System.Console.WriteLine(myOtherCar.model);  // causes compilation error
```

Attempting to compile this line causes the following compilation error:

```
error CS0165: Use of unassigned local variable 'myOtherCar'
```

WARNING   *Before you attempt to access an object's fields or methods though an object reference, the object reference must reference an object. This is another example of definite assignment, described earlier in Chapter 2.*

You can also assign `null` to an object reference. For example:

```
myCar = null;
```

This means that `myCar` no longer references an object. Unless the `Car` object previously referenced by `myCar` is referenced elsewhere, then that `Car` object is no longer available to the program—as you'll see later, the object will be scheduled for removal from memory in a process known as *garbage collection*. Listing 5.1 illustrates the `Car` class and objects.

LISTING 5.1: A SIMPLE CLASS AND OBJECTS

```
/*
  Example5_1.cs illustrates how to declare
  classes, object references, and create objects
*/


// declare the Car class
public class Car
{

  // declare the fields
  public string make;
  public string model;
  public string color;
  public int yearBuilt;

  // define the methods
  public void Start()
  {
    System.Console.WriteLine(model + " started");
  }

  public void Stop()
  {
    System.Console.WriteLine(model + " stopped");
  }

}


class Example5_1
{

  public static void Main()
  {

    // declare a Car object reference named myCar
    Car myCar;

    // create a Car object, and assign its address to myCar
    System.Console.WriteLine("Creating a Car object and assigning " +
      "its memory location to myCar");
    myCar = new Car();

    // assign values to the Car object's fields using myCar
    myCar.make = "Toyota";
    myCar.model = "MR2";
```

```
myCar.color = "black";
myCar.yearBuilt = 1995;

// display the field values using myCar
System.Console.WriteLine("myCar details:");
System.Console.WriteLine("myCar.make = " + myCar.make);
System.Console.WriteLine("myCar.model = " + myCar.model);
System.Console.WriteLine("myCar.color = " + myCar.color);
System.Console.WriteLine("myCar.yearBuilt = " + myCar.yearBuilt);

// call the methods using myCar
myCar.Start();
myCar.Stop();

// declare another Car object reference and
// create another Car object
System.Console.WriteLine("Creating another Car object and " +
  "assigning its memory location to redPorsche");
Car redPorsche = new Car();
redPorsche.make = "Porsche";
redPorsche.model = "Boxster";
redPorsche.color = "red";
redPorsche.yearBuilt = 2000;
System.Console.WriteLine("redPorsche is a " + redPorsche.model);

// change the object referenced by the myCar object reference
// to the object referenced by redPorsche
System.Console.WriteLine("Assigning redPorsche to myCar");
myCar = redPorsche;
System.Console.WriteLine("myCar details:");
System.Console.WriteLine("myCar.make = " + myCar.make);
System.Console.WriteLine("myCar.model = " + myCar.model);
System.Console.WriteLine("myCar.color = " + myCar.color);
System.Console.WriteLine("myCar.yearBuilt = " + myCar.yearBuilt);

// assign null to myCar (myCar will no longer reference an object)
myCar = null;

  }

}
```

The output from this program is as follows:

```
Creating a Car object and assigning its memory location to myCar
myCar details:
myCar.make = Toyota
myCar.model = MR2
```

```
myCar.color = black
myCar.yearBuilt = 1995
MR2 started
MR2 stopped
Creating another Car object and assigning its memory location to redPorsche
redPorsche is a Boxster
Assigning redPorsche to myCar
myCar details:
myCar.make = Porsche
myCar.model = Boxster
myCar.color = red
myCar.yearBuilt = 2000
```

Default Field Values and Initializers

When an object is created from a class, the object will get its own copy of the fields declared in the class. Table 5.1 shows the default values taken by fields of various types.

TABLE 5.1: DEFAULT FIELD VALUES

TYPE	DEFAULT VALUE
All numeric types	0
bool	false
char	'\0'
string	null

You can set the default value for a field in a class using an *initializer*. Using an initializer is just like assigning a value to a variable, except that it is placed in the class declaration and it specifies a default value for a field.

The following Car class uses initializers to set default values for the make, model, and yearBuilt fields (we've not supplied an initializer for the color field, so it keeps its default of null because color is a string):

```
public class Car
{

    // declare the fields
    public string make = "Ford";
    public string model = "T";
    public string color;  // default value of null
    public int yearBuilt = 1910;

    // define the methods
    ...
}
```

When a Car object is created, its make, model, color, and yearBuilt fields have the default values of "Ford", "T", null, and 1910 respectively.

TIP   You should only use initializers when an object can be assumed to have certain characteristics.

Listing 5.2 illustrates how to assign default values to fields using initializers.

LISTING 5.2: USING INITIALIZERS

```
/*
  Example5_2.cs illustrates how to assign default values
  to fields using initializers
*/


// declare the Car class
public class Car
{

  // declare the fields
  public string make = "Ford";
  public string model = "T";
  public string color;  // default value of null
  public int yearBuilt = 1910;

  // define the methods
  public void Start()
  {
    System.Console.WriteLine(model + " started");
  }

  public void Stop()
  {
    System.Console.WriteLine(model + " stopped");
  }

}


class Example5_2
{

  public static void Main()
  {

    // create a Car object
    Car myCar = new Car();
```

```
                 // display the default values for the Car object fields
                 System.Console.WriteLine("myCar.make = " + myCar.make);
                 System.Console.WriteLine("myCar.model = " + myCar.model);
                 if (myCar.color == null)
                 {
                    System.Console.WriteLine("myCar.color is null");
                 }
                 System.Console.WriteLine("myCar.yearBuilt = " + myCar.yearBuilt);

          }

      }
```

The output from this program is as follows:

```
myCar.make = Ford
myCar.model = T
myCar.color is null
myCar.yearBuilt = 1910
```

Using Methods

A *method* is a group of declarations and other statements that perform a specific task—a method may be called repeatedly to perform that task. In the previous section, the Car class defined two simple methods, Start() and Stop(). These methods contained a single statement that displayed a line of output. When those methods were called using an object, the statement contained in the methods was run. In this section, you'll delve deeper into the details of methods.

Defining Methods

A method may return a value to the statement that called it, and a method may also accept values from the calling statement—these values are known as *parameters*. The simplified syntax for defining a method is as follows:

```
[access-modifier] return-type method-name(
   [parameter-type parameter-name[, ...]]
) {method-body}
```

The syntax elements are as follows:

access-modifier Determines the degree to which your method is accessible by other classes.

return-type The type of the variable returned by the method (a method can also return an object of a specified class). Your method must return a value using the return keyword, and it must return a value that matches *return-type*.

method-name The name you assign to your method.

parameter-type The type of the parameter passed to your method (a method can also accept objects of a specified class).

parameter-name The name of the parameter passed to your method.

method-body The statements that perform your method's task.

The following `Car` class defines two methods, named `Age()` and `Distance()`, along with a new field named `maximumSpeed`. The `Age()` method calculates and returns the age of the car in years, and the `Distance()` method calculates and returns the distance traveled by the car in miles. The `maximum-Speed` field stores the maximum speed of the car in miles per hour:

```
public class Car
{

  public int yearBuilt;
  public double maximumSpeed;

  // the Age() method calculates and returns the
  // age of the car in years
  public int Age(int currentYear)
  {
    int age = currentYear - yearBuilt;
    return age;
  }

  // the Distance() method calculates and returns the
  // distance traveled by the car, given its initial speed,
  // maximum speed, and time for the journey
  // (assuming constant acceleration of the car)
  public double Distance(double initialSpeed, double time)
  {
    return (initialSpeed + maximumSpeed) / 2 * time;
  }

}
```

The `Age()` method calculates and returns the age of the car in years. This method returns an `int` and accepts an `int` parameter named `currentYear`. The age of a car is calculated by subtracting the year the car was built (stored in the `yearBuilt` field) from the current year (passed as the `current-Year` parameter)—the result of this calculation is stored in an `int` variable named `age`. The `return` keyword is used to return the value stored in `age` to the statement that calls the method.

The `Distance()` method calculates and returns the distance traveled by the car in miles. This distance is calculated using the following formula (assuming constant acceleration for the car and that the car travels in a straight line):

```
(initial speed + maximum speed) / 2 * time
```

The initial speed of the car is passed to the `Distance()` method as the `initialSpeed` parameter; the maximum speed of a car is stored in the `maximumSpeed` field; and the time for the journey is also passed to the method as the `time` parameter. The speeds are specified in miles per hour, and the time is specified in hours. The `double` value returned by `Distance()` is the total distance traveled by the car in miles.

RETURNING A VALUE FROM A METHOD

Methods that return a value use the `return` keyword, followed by an expression. That expression may be just a literal value, it may be a variable, or it may even be a complete calculation. In fact, it can be any expression that evaluates to a matching return type for the method. For example, a method that returns an `int` could return the following literal value:

```
return 3;
```

The method could also return an `int` variable:

```
int intValue = 2;
return intValue;
```

The method could also evaluate and then return the result of a calculation:

```
return intValue * 4;
```

When a `return` statement is run, the expression is evaluated and the result is returned to the statement that called the method.

NOTE   *A method with a return type of* `void` *doesn't return a value and therefore doesn't require a return statement.*

LOCAL VARIABLES

In Chapter 2, you learned that the scope of a variable is the section of code where that variable exists. When a variable is declared in a method, then that variable only exists in that particular method, and its scope is limited to that method. These are known as *local variables* because their scope is local to the method.

In the `Age()` method shown earlier, `age` is a local variable and its scope is limited to that method. Therefore, the `age` variable may only be used within that method. Similarly, the parameter `currentYear` is also local to the `Age()` method. We'll talk more about parameters shortly.

Calling Methods

Let's take a look at examples of calling the `Age()` and `Distance()` methods defined in the previous section. First, the following statements create a `Car` object, store a reference to that object in `redPorsche`, and assign values to the object's fields:

```
Car redPorsche = new Car();
redPorsche.yearBuilt = 2000;
redPorsche.maximumSpeed = 150;
```

You call a method using an object reference and the name of the method, along with any values for the parameters. The following statement calls the `Age()` method using the `redPorsche` object reference and passes the value 2001 as the current year:

```
int age = redPorsche.Age(2001);
```

The `Age()` method calculates the age of the car by subtracting the value in the `yearBuilt` field for this `Car` object (2000) and by subtracting the `currentYear` parameter passed to it (2001)—therefore the value returned by the `Age()` method is 1.

Second, the following statement calls the `Distance()` method, which calculates and returns the distance traveled by the `Car` object; notice that the `double` value returned by this method is displayed directly in a call to the `System.Console.WriteLine()` method:

```
System.Console.WriteLine("redPorsche travels " +
  redPorsche.Distance(31, .25) + " miles.");
```

The first parameter passed to the `Distance()` method specifies the initial speed of the car in miles per hour (31), and the second parameter specifies the total time of the journey in hours (.25, or a quarter of an hour).

Listing 5.3 shows how the `Age()` and `Distance()` methods return values and accept parameters.

LISTING 5.3: METHODS THAT RETURN A VALUE AND ACCEPT PARAMETERS

```
/*
  Example5_3.cs illustrates how to define methods
  that return a value and accept parameters
*/


// declare the Car class
public class Car {

  public int yearBuilt;
  public double maximumSpeed;

  // the Age() method calculates and returns the
  // age of the car in years
  public int Age(int currentYear)
  {
    int age = currentYear - yearBuilt;
    return age;
  }

  // the Distance() method calculates and returns the
  // distance traveled by the car, given its initial speed,
  // maximum speed, and time for the journey
  // (assuming constant acceleration of the car)
  public double Distance(double initialSpeed, double time)
  {
    return (initialSpeed + maximumSpeed) / 2 * time;
  }

}


class Example5_3
{
```

```
public static void Main()
{

  // declare a Car object reference and
  // create a Car object
  System.Console.WriteLine("Creating a Car object and " +
    "assigning its memory location to redPorsche");
  Car redPorsche = new Car();

  // assign values to the fields
  redPorsche.yearBuilt = 2000;
  redPorsche.maximumSpeed = 150;

  // call the methods
  int age = redPorsche.Age(2001);
  System.Console.WriteLine("redPorsche is " + age + " year old.");
  System.Console.WriteLine("redPorsche travels " +
    redPorsche.Distance(31, .25) + " miles.");

}

}
```

The output from this program is as follows:

```
Creating a Car object and assigning its memory location to redPorsche
redPorsche is 1 year old.
redPorsche travels 22.625 miles.
```

Hiding

If you declare a local variable in a method that has the same name as a field, then the local variable *hides* the field. The following class illustrates this point, with the maximumSpeed field being hidden in the Age() method by a variable of the same name:

```
public class Car
{

  ...

  public double maximumSpeed;

  public int Age(int currentYear)
  {
    int maximumSpeed = 100;  // hides the field
    System.Console.WriteLine("In Age(): maximumSpeed = " +
      maximumSpeed);
    ...
  }
```

```
   public double Distance(double initialSpeed, double time)
   {
     System.Console.WriteLine("In Distance(): maximumSpeed = " +
       maximumSpeed);

     ...

   }


}
```

In this Car class, the Age() method declares its own local maximumSpeed variable, and sets it to 100. This maximumSpeed variable hides the maximumSpeed field of the class. Thus, when maximumSpeed is displayed in the Age() method, the value displayed is 100—the value assigned to the variable in the Age() method.

Now, in the Distance() method, the maximumSpeed field is not hidden, and when this field is displayed in the Distance() method, the value displayed is whatever the field was set to for the particular Car object for which the method was called.

Listing 5.4 illustrates hiding.

LISTING 5.4: HIDING

```
/*
   Example5_4.cs illustrates hiding
*/


// declare the Car class
public class Car
{

  public int yearBuilt;
  public double maximumSpeed;

  public int Age(int currentYear)
  {
    int maximumSpeed = 100;  // hides the field
    System.Console.WriteLine("In Age(): maximumSpeed = " +
      maximumSpeed);
    int age = currentYear - yearBuilt;
    return age;
  }

  public double Distance(double initialSpeed, double time)
  {
    System.Console.WriteLine("In Distance(): maximumSpeed = " +
```

```
        maximumSpeed);
      return (initialSpeed + maximumSpeed) / 2 * time;
  }

}


class Example5_4
{

  public static void Main()
  {

    // create a Car object
    Car redPorsche = new Car();
    redPorsche.yearBuilt = 2000;
    redPorsche.maximumSpeed = 150;

    int age = redPorsche.Age(2001);
    System.Console.WriteLine("redPorsche is " + age + " year old.");
    System.Console.WriteLine("redPorsche travels " +
      redPorsche.Distance(31, .25) + " miles.");

  }

}
```

The output from this program is as follows:

```
In Age(): maximumSpeed = 100
redPorsche is 1 year old.
In Distance(): maximumSpeed = 150
redPorsche travels 22.625 miles.
```

The *this* Object Reference

The this keyword is an object reference, and it references the *current* object in use. The this object reference is useful when you want to set the value for a field in a method but the field is hidden by a parameter. In the following class, the yearBuilt field is hidden in the SetYearBuilt() method:

```
public class Car
{

  public int yearBuilt;

  public void SetYearBuilt(int yearBuilt)
  {
    // the yearBuilt parameter hides the
```

```
      // the yearBuilt field
      this.yearBuilt = yearBuilt;
    }

  }
```

The SetYearBuilt() method sets the yearBuilt field to a value supplied in the yearBuilt parameter. Because the yearBuilt parameter is a local variable in this method, it hides the yearBuilt field. To get around this problem, the method uses the this object reference to access the current object, and this.yearBuilt refers to the yearBuilt field of the current object. Thus, the method can successfully use a parameter and field of the same name.

You're probably asking why we didn't simply use different names for the parameter and the field. Well, we could have done that, but then the names become a little contorted—for example, we might use builtYear or yearOfManufacture for the parameter name, but those names aren't very elegant. Using the this object reference is a much neater solution, and you'll see its use again later in the "Constructors" section.

Listing 5.5 illustrates the this object reference.

LISTING 5.5: USING THE this OBJECT REFERENCE

```
/*
  Example5_5.cs illustrates the use of the this
  object reference
*/


// declare the Car class
public class Car
{

  public int yearBuilt;

  public void SetYearBuilt(int yearBuilt)
  {
    // the yearBuilt parameter hides the
    // the yearBuilt field
    this.yearBuilt = yearBuilt;
  }

}


class Example5_5
{

  public static void Main()
  {
```

```
        // create a Car object
        Car myCar = new Car();

        myCar.SetYearBuilt(2000);
        System.Console.WriteLine("myCar.yearBuilt = " + myCar.yearBuilt);

    }

}
```

The output from this program is as follows:

```
myCar.yearBuilt = 2000
```

More on Parameters

You were introduced to method parameters earlier in the chapter. In this section, you'll learn about what happens when parameters are passed to a method.

PASSING PARAMETERS BY VALUE

In the methods you've seen so far, the parameters act as local variables to the method. Because of this, when you pass a variable to a method from a calling statement, the method makes a *copy* of the variable. Then, any changes made to the parameter inside the method are made to that copy—and not the actual variable in the calling statement. This is known as passing a parameter by *value*.

NOTE   *If you pass an object reference as a parameter to a method, no copy of the referenced object is made. You can modify the object directly in the method using the object reference parameter. The information in this section therefore applies only to value types—such as* int *parameters, for example.*

Passing parameters by value is best understood by looking at an example, as shown in Listing 5.6.

LISTING 5.6: PASSING PARAMETERS BY VALUE

```
/*
   Example5_6.cs illustrates passing parameters by value
*/


// declare the Swapper class
public class Swapper
{

   // the Swap() method swaps parameters passed by value
   public void Swap(int x, int y)
   {
```

```csharp
        // display the initial values
        System.Console.WriteLine("In Swap(): initial x = " + x +
          ", y = " + y);

        // swap x and y
        int temp = x;
        x = y;
        y = temp;

        // display the final values
        System.Console.WriteLine("In Swap(): final   x = " + x +
          ", y = " + y);
    }

}


class Example5_6
{

  public static void Main()
  {

      // declare x and y (the variables whose values
      // are to be swapped)
      int x = 2;
      int y = 5;

      // display the initial values
      System.Console.WriteLine("In Main(): initial x = " + x +
        ", y = " + y);

      // create a Swapper object
      Swapper mySwapper = new Swapper();

      // swap the values in x and y
      mySwapper.Swap(x, y);

      // display the final values
      System.Console.WriteLine("In Main(): final   x = " + x +
        ", y = " + y);

  }

}
```

The output from this program is as follows:

```
In Main(): initial x = 2, y = 5
In Swap(): initial x = 2, y = 5
In Swap(): final   x = 5, y = 2
In Main(): final   x = 2, y = 5
```

As you can see, the x and y variables are initially set to 2 and 5 (respectively) in the Main() method, which also displays the initial x and y values:

```
In Main(): initial x = 2, y = 5
```

The x and y variables are then passed as parameters to the Swap() method. Swap() then makes local copies of these variables and displays the initial values of the copies:

```
In Swap(): initial x = 2, y = 5
```

Next, Swap() swaps the values, but because *copies* of the variables were made, the values swapped are the copies—not the actual variables originally passed. The final values of these copies are displayed by Swap():

```
In Swap(): final   x = 5, y = 2
```

Program control returns to the calling statement in Main(), where the final values for x and y are displayed:

```
In Main(): final   x = 2, y = 5
```

Notice that the variables still have their original values. This is as expected because the values in x and y were *copied* and then swapped; the actual x and y variables that were passed as parameters remain unaffected.

PASSING PARAMETERS BY REFERENCE

If you want to change the value for a variable passed as a parameter, you must pass a reference to that variable—that way, the method will change the actual variable, not a copy of it. This is known as passing a parameter by *reference*.

WARNING *Only modify referenced parameters in your methods when you absolutely must. This practice is generally frowned upon because it can easily cause logical errors in your programs.*

To pass a parameter by reference, you use the ref keyword—this is placed in front of the parameter type in the method definition. The following example shows the use of the ref keyword to indicate that the x and y parameters are passed by reference:

```
public class Swapper
{

  public void Swap(ref int x, ref int y)
  {
    ...
  }
}
```

You also need to use the `ref` keyword in the calling statement. For example:

```
int x = 2;
int y = 5;
mySwapper.Swap(ref x, ref y);
```

This time, when the `Swap()` method is called, references to the x and y variables are passed. When the x and y parameters are changed by the method, then the underlying variables to which they refer are changed—not copies of them.

NOTE   *When passing parameters by value or by reference, the variables that are passed as parameters must be assigned a value before the method is called. This is another example of definite assignment, described in Chapter 2.*

Listing 5.7 illustrates passing parameters by reference.

LISTING 5.7: PASSING PARAMETERS BY REFERENCE

```
/*
  Example5_7.cs illustrates passing parameters by reference
*/


// declare the Swapper class
public class Swapper
{

  // the Swap() method swaps parameters passed by reference
  public void Swap(ref int x, ref int y)
  {

    // display the initial values
    System.Console.WriteLine("In Swap(): initial x = " + x +
      ", y = " + y);

    // swap x and y
    int temp = x;
    x = y;
    y = temp;

    // display the final values
    System.Console.WriteLine("In Swap(): final   x = " + x +
      ", y = " + y);
  }

}


class Example5_7
{
```

```
public static void Main()
{

  // declare x and y (the variables whose values
  // are to be swapped)
  int x = 2;
  int y = 5;

  // display the initial values
  System.Console.WriteLine("In Main(): initial x = " + x +
    ", y = " + y);

  // create a Swapper object
  Swapper mySwapper = new Swapper();

  // swap the values, passing a reference to the Swap() method
  mySwapper.Swap(ref x, ref y);

  // display the final values
  System.Console.WriteLine("In Main(): final   x = " + x +
    ", y = " + y);

}

}
```

The output from this program is as follows:

```
In Main(): initial x = 2, y = 5
In Swap():  initial x = 2, y = 5
In Swap():  final   x = 5, y = 2
In Main(): final    x = 5, y = 2
```

Notice that x and y are swapped.

OUT PARAMETERS

Methods can only return one value using a return statement. Sometimes you might need to return more than one value, and out parameters are useful for this purpose. An out parameter acts like a reference to a variable, except that you don't assign a value to the variable before passing it to the method—an out parameter is assigned a value inside the method. You can use more than one out parameter in a method.

WARNING   Typically, your methods should return only one value. This works for 90 percent or more of your programming needs, and it provides a good level of abstraction in your programs. Out parameters are useful, but they are an exception, rather than a rule.

Listing 5.8 illustrates passing parameters by reference, and it declares a class that defines a method named SinAndCos(); this method accepts a double parameter that contains an angle (specified in radians) and uses out parameters to return the sine and cosine values for that angle.

LISTING 5.8: USING OUT PARAMETERS

```csharp
/*
  Example5_8.cs illustrates the use of out parameters
*/


// declare the MyMath class
public class MyMath
{

  // the SinAndCos() method returns the sin and cos values for
  // a given angle (in radians)
  public void SinAndCos(double angle, out double sin, out double cos)
  {
    sin = System.Math.Sin(angle);
    cos = System.Math.Cos(angle);
  }

}


class Example5_8
{

  public static void Main()
  {

    // declare and set the angle in radians
    double angle = System.Math.PI / 2;

    // declare the variables that will be used as out paramters
    double sin;
    double cos;

    // create a MyMath object
    MyMath myMath = new MyMath();

    // get the sin and cos values from the SinAndCos() method
    myMath.SinAndCos(angle, out sin, out cos);

    // display sin and cos
    System.Console.WriteLine("sin = " + sin + ", cos = " + cos);


  }

}
```

You'll notice that this program uses the System.Math class—this class contains many mathematical methods and constants that you can use in your programs. In this program, the System.Math.Sin() and System.Math.Cos() methods get the sine and cosine values for an angle, and the System.Math.PI constant represents the value of the mathematical constant pi.

The output from this program is as follows:

```
sin = 1, cos = 6.12303176911189E-17
```

Method Overloading

With *method overloading*, you can define methods in a class that have the same name but use different parameters. An overloaded method may have a different number of parameters or the parameters may have different types. For example:

```
int DoComputation(int value1, int value2);
int DoComputation(int value1);
int DoComputation(int value1, float value2);
```

You can assume the DoComputation() method performs some kind of calculation and returns an int value. This method is overloaded and has three different lists of parameters—the first has two int parameters, the second has one int parameter, and the third has one int and one float parameter. When the method is called with a given list of parameters, the method with the matching list of parameters will be run.

WARNING *If you attempt to compile a program with a method call that doesn't match any of the methods, then the compiler will generate an error and your program won't compile. Also, if your overloaded method has different return types, but the list of parameters for those methods are the same, then your program won't compile. In addition, you cannot have a method that has the same parameter list but different output types.*

Let's consider an example. Earlier, you saw the Swap() method defined in the Swapper class—that method accepted two references to int parameters and swapped them. You might want to also swap float parameters using the same name of Swap() for the method.

Listing 5.9 illustrates a class that overloads the Swap() method to swap both int and float parameters.

LISTING 5.9: METHOD OVERLOADING

```
/*
   Example5_9.cs illustrates method overloading
*/


// declare the Swapper class
public class Swapper
{

   // this Swap() method swaps two int parameters
   public void Swap(ref int x, ref int y)
```

```
    {
      int temp = x;
      x = y;
      y = temp;
    }

    // this Swap() method swaps two float parameters
    public void Swap(ref float x, ref float y)
    {
      float temp = x;
      x = y;
      y = temp;
    }

}


class Example5_9
{

  public static void Main()
  {

    // create a Swapper object
    Swapper mySwapper = new Swapper();

    // declare two int variables
    int intValue1 = 2;
    int intValue2 = 5;
    System.Console.WriteLine("initial intValue1 = " + intValue1 +
      ", intValue2 = " + intValue2);

    // swap the two float two int variables
    // (uses the Swap() method that accepts int parameters)
    mySwapper.Swap(ref intValue1, ref intValue2);

    // display the final values
    System.Console.WriteLine("final    intValue1 = " + intValue1 +
      ", intValue2 = " + intValue2);

    // declare two float variables
    float floatValue1 = 2f;
    float floatValue2 = 5f;
    System.Console.WriteLine("initial floatValue1 = " + floatValue1 +
      ", floatValue2 = " + floatValue2);
```

```
        // swap the two float variables
        // (uses the Swap() method that accepts float parameters)
        mySwapper.Swap(ref floatValue1, ref floatValue2);

        // display the final values
        System.Console.WriteLine("final   floatValue1 = " + floatValue1 +
          ", floatValue2 = " + floatValue2);
        mySwapper.Swap(ref floatValue1, ref floatValue2);

    }

}
```

Based on the parameters to the Swap() method, the appropriate method is called. The output from this program is as follows:

```
initial intValue1 = 2, intValue2 = 5
final   intValue1 = 5, intValue2 = 2
initial floatValue1 = 2, floatValue2 = 5
final   floatValue1 = 5, floatValue2 = 2
```

Using Access Modifiers

Access modifiers enable you to specify the degree to which a class member is available outside of the class. You can also use an access modifier to specify the degree to which the class itself is available—although as mentioned, you'll usually declare your classes as being public.

Table 5.2 shows the access modifiers in decreasing order of availability: public is the most accessible, and private is the least accessible. Some of the access modifiers mention *derived classes* and *assemblies*—derived classes are covered in Chapter 7, "Derived Classes," and assemblies are covered in Chapter 16, "Assemblies."

TABLE 5.2: ACCESS MODIFIERS

ACCESS MODIFIER	ACCESSIBILITY
public	Member accessible without restriction.
protected internal	Member only accessible within the class, a derived class, or class in the same program (or assembly).
internal	Member only accessible within the class or class in the same program (or assembly).
protected	Member only accessible within the class or derived classes.
private	Member only accessible within the class. This is the default.

So far, you've only seen examples of members that use the `public` access modifier. The following `Car` class illustrates the use of the various access modifiers for the class members:

```
public class Car
{

    // declare the fields
    public             string make;
    protected internal string model;
    internal           string color;
    protected          int horsepower = 150;
    private            int yearBuilt;

    // define the methods
    public void SetYearBuilt(int yearBuilt)
    {
      this.yearBuilt = yearBuilt;
    }

    public int GetYearBuilt()
    {
      return yearBuilt;
    }

    public void Start()
    {
      System.Console.WriteLine("Starting car ...");
      TurnStarterMotor();
      System.Console.WriteLine("Car started");
    }

    private void TurnStarterMotor()
    {
      System.Console.WriteLine("Turning starter motor ...");
    }

}
```

TIP   You should include the access modifier when declaring class members, even for your private members (the `private` *access modifier is the default). This is just good programming practice, and by including the access modifiers, your classes will be easier to read.*

Because the `make`, `model`, and `color` fields respectively use the access modifiers `public`, `protected internal`, and `internal`, they are available to other classes in the same program. However, the horsepower and `yearBuilt` fields respectively use the `protected` and `private` access modifiers and are therefore not available to other classes in the same program (unless there is a derived class, in which case the protected members would be accessible within that class—you'll learn about derived classes in Chapter 7). The `horsepower` field uses an initializer to set it to 150.

The value for the yearBuilt field is set using the public SetYearBuilt() method, and its value is retrieved using the public GetYearBuilt() method. You'll see in Chapter 6, "More about Classes and Objects," how *properties* can be used to achieve similar functionality.

The public Start() method calls the private method TurnStarterMotor(); this closely models a real car, which uses a starter motor to start the car's engine. Think of a real car: As a driver, you don't directly use your car's starter motor to start your car—you just use your ignition key to start your car. Going back to the Car class that models a car, when the Start() method is called, it calls the TurnStarterMotor() method for you. You can't call the TurnStarterMotor() method directly—just as in the real world, you don't directly use your car's starter motor to start your car.

TIP   *This illustrates an important part of object-oriented programming: You should hide the internal details of how your class works from the outside world by using private members as much as possible.*

Let's take a look at some examples of accessing the members of this Car class. The following statement creates a Car object:

```
Car myCar = new Car();
```

You can access the make, model, and color fields of this Car object without any restriction, and the following statements assign values to these fields using the myCar object reference:

```
myCar.make = "Toyota";
myCar.model = "MR2";
myCar.color = "black";
```

You cannot access the horsepower or yearBuilt fields directly because these fields use the protected and private access modifiers respectively and are therefore only available within the code contained in the Car class itself. The horsepower field is set to 150 by an initializer in the Car class, and the yearBuilt field may be set using the SetYearBuilt() method—the following statement uses this method to set the yearBuilt field to 1995:

```
myCar.SetYearBuilt(1995);
```

To get the value for the yearBuilt field, you use the GetYearBuilt() method, as shown in the following statement:

```
System.Console.WriteLine("myCar.GetYearBuilt() = " + myCar.GetYearBuilt());
```

The following statement calls the Start() method, which then calls the private TurnStarterMotor() method:

```
myCar.Start();
```

Listing 5.10 illustrates the Car class and how the access modifiers affect accessibility to class members.

LISTING 5.10: USING ACCESS MODIFIERS

```csharp
/*
  Example5_10.cs illustrates the use of various
  access modifiers
*/


// declare the Car class
public class Car
{

  // declare the fields
  public            string make;
  protected internal string model;
  internal          string color;
  protected         int horsepower = 150;
  private           int yearBuilt;

  // define the methods
  public void SetYearBuilt(int yearBuilt)
  {
    this.yearBuilt = yearBuilt;
  }

  public int GetYearBuilt()
  {
    return yearBuilt;
  }

  public void Start()
  {
    System.Console.WriteLine("Starting car ...");
    TurnStarterMotor();
    System.Console.WriteLine("Car started");
  }

  private void TurnStarterMotor()
  {
    System.Console.WriteLine("Turning starter motor ...");
  }

}


class Example5_10
{
```

```
public static void Main()
{

  // create a Car object
  Car myCar = new Car();

  // assign values to the Car object fields
  myCar.make = "Toyota";
  myCar.model = "MR2";
  myCar.color = "black";
  // myCar.horsepower = 200;   // protected field not accessible
  // myCar.yearBuilt = 1995;   // private field not accessible

  // call the SetYearBuilt() method to set the private yearBuilt field
  myCar.SetYearBuilt(1995);

  // display the values for the Car object fields
  System.Console.WriteLine("myCar.make = " + myCar.make);
  System.Console.WriteLine("myCar.model = " + myCar.model);
  System.Console.WriteLine("myCar.color = " + myCar.color);

  // call the GetYearBuilt() method to get the private yearBuilt field
  System.Console.WriteLine("myCar.GetYearBuilt() = " + myCar.GetYearBuilt());

  // call the Start() method
  myCar.Start();
  // myCar.TurnStarterMotor();   // private method not accessible

}

}
```

The output from this program is as follows:

```
myCar.make = Toyota
myCar.model = MR2
myCar.color = black
myCar.GetYearBuilt() = 1995
Starting car ...
Turning starter motor ...
Car started
```

Creating and Destroying Objects

You've already seen examples of creating objects in C#. A *constructor* is a method that has the same name as the class. As you will see in this section, you can define your own constructors, so you can do things such as initialize fields using parameters. You can also define overloaded constructors that accept different parameters, and you can even define constructors that allow you copy the fields from one object to another.

One thing you haven't seen until this point is how C# manages objects and variables stored in the computer's memory. In Chapter 2, you saw that variables are declared using value types—`int`, `float`, and `char`, for example. Variables are stored in an area of memory known as the *stack*. You can think of the stack as a pile of dish plates—variables are be *pushed* onto the stack to store them and *popped* off of the stack to remove them. The reference types—objects and strings—are stored in a different area of memory known as the *heap*.

The stack is program-specific memory, and each program has its own stack. The heap, however, is universally accessible memory. Because value types are generally small, storing them on the stack is good. With objects, however, it's better to store them on the heap and create an object reference to them on the stack.

Variables, objects, and strings are removed from memory—or *destroyed*—by a process known as *garbage collection*. The object that does the garbage collection is known as the *garbage collector*. The garbage collector periodically cleans up the data stored in memory that is no longer used. When a variable goes out of scope it is scheduled for destruction by the garbage collector. An example of this is when a local variable is declared by a method: When the method is called, the local variable is pushed onto the stack, and when the method ends, the local variable goes out of scope and is scheduled for destruction— when the variable is destroyed it is popped of the stack. Similarly, when all references to an object are gone, then that object is scheduled for removal by the garbage collector.

Normally, you don't have to concern yourself with memory cleanup—you can just let the garbage collector take care of it. There are cases, however, when you might want to do some cleaning up of your own. For example, if you have an object that opens a file, then you might want to close that file gracefully before destroying your object. You can use *destructors* to do this, which you'll learn about shortly. Now, you'll learn about constructors.

Using Constructors

In the previous examples, you saw `Car` objects being created using statements similar to the following one:

```
Car myCar = new Car();
```

We mentioned earlier that the `Car()` method is a constructor, and it is used in conjunction with the **new** operator to create an object.

NOTE *A constructor has the same name as the class.*

You can define a constructor in your class, or you can use the default constructor that is always available; the default constructor doesn't take any parameters. The default constructor creates a new object for you, but it doesn't do anything else.

If you want to do something in addition to just creating a new object, then you must define your own constructor. The most common reason for defining your own constructor is to initialize the fields of the new object—passing the values for those fields as parameters to your constructor. The following class defines a constructor:

```
public class Car
{
```

```
// declare the fields
private string make;
private string model;
private string color;
private int yearBuilt;

// define the constructor
public Car(string make, string model, string color, int yearBuilt)
{
  System.Console.WriteLine("In Car() constructor");
  this.make = make;
  this.model = model;
  this.color = color;
  this.yearBuilt = yearBuilt;
}

...

}
```

Notice that the constructor accepts four parameters (one for each field) and sets the fields of the new object to the values provided using the parameters. You can see the usefulness of the this object reference in the constructor—as you saw earlier, this refers to the current object.

NOTE   You cannot use a constructor to return a value.

The following statement creates a Car object, passing parameter values to the constructor:

```
Car myCar = new Car("Toyota", "MR2", "black", 1995);
```

The constructor sets the make, model, color, and yearBuilt fields to "Toyota", "MR2", "black", and 1995 respectively.

Listing 5.11 illustrates the use of the constructor shown in this section.

LISTING 5.11: DEFINING A CONSTRUCTOR

```
/*
  Example5_11.cs illustrates how to define a constructor
*/


// declare the Car class
public class Car
{

  // declare the fields
  private string make;
  private string model;
```

```
  private string color;
  private int yearBuilt;

  // define the constructor
  public Car(string make, string model, string color, int yearBuilt)
  {
    System.Console.WriteLine("In Car() constructor");
    this.make = make;
    this.model = model;
    this.color = color;
    this.yearBuilt = yearBuilt;
  }

  // define a method to display the fields
  public void Display()
  {
    System.Console.WriteLine("Car details:");
    System.Console.WriteLine("make = " + make);
    System.Console.WriteLine("model = " + model);
    System.Console.WriteLine("color = " + color);
    System.Console.WriteLine("yearBuilt = " + yearBuilt);
  }

}


class Example5_11
{

  public static void Main()
  {

    // create a Car object using the constructor
    // defined in the class
    Car myCar = new Car("Toyota", "MR2", "black", 1995);

    // display the values for the Car object fields
    myCar.Display();

  }

}
```

The output from this program is as follows:

```
In Car() constructor
Car details:
```

```
make = Toyota
model = MR2
color = black
yearBuilt = 1995
```

OVERLOADED CONSTRUCTORS

Earlier, you saw how multiple methods can be overloaded—overloaded methods all have the same name as each other but a different list of parameters. Because a constructor is a method, you can overload them.

Now, with the Car class shown in the previous listing, you *cannot* create Car objects using the following statements:

```
Car myCar2 = new Car();   // causes compilation error
Car myCar3 = new Car("Chevrolet"); // causes compilation error
```

TIP   *When you define a constructor that accepts parameters, you should also define a default constructor with no parameters.*

The reason why these statements cause compilation errors is that there is no matching constructor in the Car class. Notice that there isn't even a default constructor. You must provide a constructor with a matching list of parameters using method overloading to get the two previous statements to compile. The following class shows the additional constructors required to handle the two previous statements:

```
public class Car
{

    ...

    // define the overloaded constructors
    public Car()
    {
      this.make = "Ford";
      this.model = "Mustang";
      this.color = "red";
      this.yearBuilt = 1970;
    }

    public Car(string make)
    {
      this.make = make;
      this.model = "Corvette";
      this.color = "silver";
      this.yearBuilt = 1969;
    }

    ...

}
```

Notice that initializers assign values to the fields whose values are not supplied using a parameter—we didn't have to do this, we could have just left those fields as the default, but we wanted to explicitly set them just to make the example more complete.

With this class, the two statements shown earlier will now compile:

```
Car myCar2 = new Car();
Car myCar3 = new Car("Chevrolet");
```

So, myCar2.make is "Ford", and myCar3.make is "Chevrolet". The rest of the fields are set to the other values shown in the class.

Listing 5.12 illustrates overloaded constructors.

LISTING 5.12: OVERLOADED CONSTRUCTORS

```csharp
/*
  Example5_12.cs illustrates overloaded constructors
*/


// declare the Car class
public class Car
{

  // declare the fields
  private string make;
  private string model;
  private string color;
  private int yearBuilt;

  // define the overloaded constructors
  public Car()
  {
    this.make = "Ford";
    this.model = "Mustang";
    this.color = "red";
    this.yearBuilt = 1970;
  }

  public Car(string make)
  {
    this.make = make;
    this.model = "Corvette";
    this.color = "silver";
    this.yearBuilt = 1969;
  }

  public Car(string make, string model, string color, int yearBuilt)
  {
    this.make = make;
```

```
            this.model = model;
            this.color = color;
            this.yearBuilt = yearBuilt;
          }

          // define method to display the fields
          public void Display()
          {
            System.Console.WriteLine("make = " + make);
            System.Console.WriteLine("model = " + model);
            System.Console.WriteLine("color = " + color);
            System.Console.WriteLine("yearBuilt = " + yearBuilt);
          }

        }


        class Example5_12
        {

          public static void Main()
          {

            // create three Car objects using the constructors
            // defined in the class
            Car myCar = new Car("Toyota", "MR2", "black", 1995);
            Car myCar2 = new Car();
            Car myCar3 = new Car("Chevrolet");

            // display the values for the Car object's fields
            System.Console.WriteLine("myCar details:");
            myCar.Display();
            System.Console.WriteLine("myCar2 details:");
            myCar2.Display();
            System.Console.WriteLine("myCar3 details:");
            myCar3.Display();

          }

        }
```

The output from this program is as follows:

```
myCar details:
make = Toyota
model = MR2
color = black
yearBuilt = 1995
```

```
myCar2 details:
make = Ford
model = Mustang
color = red
yearBuilt = 1970
myCar3 details:
make = Chevrolet
model = Corvette
color = silver
yearBuilt = 1969
```

COPY CONSTRUCTORS

C# doesn't provide a default way for you to copy one object's fields to another. To do this, you must write your own copy constructor. The following class shows a copy constructor—the constructor accepts a Car object reference as a parameter and copies the fields from the referenced object to the newly created Car object:

```csharp
public class Car
{

   ...

   // define the copy constructor
   public Car(Car car)
   {
     this.make = car.make;
     this.model = car.model;
     this.color = car.color;
     this.yearBuilt = car.yearBuilt;
   }

   ...

}
```

The following statement creates a Car object:

```csharp
Car myCar = new Car("Toyota", "MR2", "black", 1995);
```

In the next statement, the myCar object reference is then passed to the copy constructor, which copies the field values of the previous Car object to the new object:

```csharp
Car carCopy = new Car(myCar);
```

This Car object also has the same field values as the previous one: "Toyota", "MR2", "black", and 1995.

Listing 5.13 illustrates a copy constructor.

LISTING 5.13: A COPY CONSTRUCTOR

```
/*
  Example5_13.cs illustrates a copy constructor
*/


// declare the Car class
public class Car
{

  // declare the fields
  private string make;
  private string model;
  private string color;
  private int yearBuilt;

  // define the copy constructor
  public Car(Car car)
  {
    this.make = car.make;
    this.model = car.model;
    this.color = car.color;
    this.yearBuilt = car.yearBuilt;
  }

  public Car(string make, string model, string color, int yearBuilt)
  {
    this.make = make;
    this.model = model;
    this.color = color;
    this.yearBuilt = yearBuilt;
  }

  // define method to display the fields
  public void Display()
  {
    System.Console.WriteLine("make = " + make);
    System.Console.WriteLine("model = " + model);
    System.Console.WriteLine("color = " + color);
    System.Console.WriteLine("yearBuilt = " + yearBuilt);
  }

}


class Example5_13
{
```

```
    public static void Main()
    {

        // create a Car object
        Car myCar = new Car("Toyota", "MR2", "black", 1995);

        // create a copy of this Car object
        Car carCopy = new Car(myCar);

        // display the values for the Car object's fields
        System.Console.WriteLine("myCar details:");
        myCar.Display();
        System.Console.WriteLine("carCopy details:");
        carCopy.Display();

    }

}
```

The output from this program is as follows:

```
myCar details:
make = Toyota
model = MR2
color = black
yearBuilt = 1995
carCopy details:
make = Toyota
model = MR2
color = black
yearBuilt = 1995
```

Using Destructors

You can use a *destructor* to clean up after your objects before they're removed from memory by the garbage collector. You might want to use a destructor to close a file—you'll learn about opening and closing files in Chapter 15, "Streams and Input/Output."

Like a constructor, a destructor has the same name as the class, but it is preceded by a tilde (~). Destructors don't accept parameters and can't return a value. The following class shows a destructor:

```
public class Car
{

    ...

    // define the destructor
    ~Car()
    {
```

```
    // do any cleaning up here
    ...
  }

  ...

}
```

NOTE   *Prior to an object being destroyed by the garbage collector, the destructor is called and any code contained within it is run.*

Listing 5.14 illustrates a simple destructor for the Car class.

LISTING 5.14: A DESTRUCTOR

```
/*
  Example5_14.cs illustrates a destructor
*/


// declare the Car class
public class Car
{

  // define the destructor
  ~Car()
  {
    System.Console.WriteLine("In ~Car() destructor");
    // do any cleaning up here
  }

}


class Example5_14
{

  public static void Main()
  {

    // create a Car object
    Car myCar = new Car();

    System.Console.WriteLine("At the end of Main()");

  }

}
```

The output from this program is as follows:

```
At the end of Main()
In ~Car() destructor
```

Notice that the ~Car() destructor is run at the end of the program.

Introducing Structs

Structs are similar to classes, but they offer a somewhat "lighter" alternative to classes. Structs are treated as value types and are therefore stored on the stack—which means that when an instance of a struct goes out of scope it is immediately removed from memory. This is a fundamental difference of structs when compared to objects: Objects are stored on the heap and are only removed from memory when the garbage collector runs. Structs look like classes, but they are implemented differently.

TIP   *Structs are intended to be small. Consider using them when you have a few fields and methods.*

Just like classes, structs can have fields, methods, and constructors, but structs have some limitations when compared to classes:

- Structs don't support inheritance (you'll learn about inheritance in Chapter 7, "Derived Classes").

- You cannot define the default constructor for a struct.

- You cannot define a destructor for a struct.

- You cannot use an initializer to set a field to a value.

You declare structs using the **struct** keyword, and their declarations are similar to classes; the following example declares a struct named Rectangle, which represents a rectangular shape:

```
public struct Rectangle
{

  // declare the fields
  public int Width;
  public int Height;

  // define a constructor
  public Rectangle(int Width, int Height)
  {
    this.Width = Width;
    this.Height = Height;
  }

  // define the Area() method
  public int Area() {
    return Width * Height;
  }

}
```

Notice that this struct declares two fields, named `Width` and `Height`, which are used to store the width and height of a given rectangle. A constructor is provided to set these fields to values provided as parameters—a constructor isn't actually required because a default constructor is always supplied. The `Area()` method returns the area of the rectangle (this is calculated by multiplying the `Width` field by the `Height` field).

To create an instance of a struct, you should use the `new` keyword followed by a constructor. The following example creates an instance of the `Rectangle` struct named `myRectangle`:

```
Rectangle myRectangle = new Rectangle(2, 3);
```

Notice that the previous example uses the constructor defined in the `Rectangle` struct. C# also supplies a default constructor for a struct that you cannot redefine. The following example uses this default constructor to create another `Rectangle` instance and assigns values to its `Width` and `Height` fields:

```
Rectangle myRectangle2 = new Rectangle();
myRectangle2.Width = 3;
myRectangle2.Height = 4;
```

When you use the `new` keyword to create an instance of a struct using the default constructor, the fields will be assigned to default values for the field type—`int` fields will be set to 0, for example. So, in the previous example, if the last statement that assigned the value of 4 to `Height` was left out, then `Height` would have a default value of 0.

Because structs are value types, you don't even need to use `new` to create an instance—although we recommend you always do use `new`. The following example shows an example that doesn't use `new`:

```
Rectangle myRectangle3;
myRectangle3.Width = 1;
myRectangle3.Height = 2;
```

NOTE   *If you don't use* new *when creating an instance of a struct, then its fields will be unassigned—they won't even be set to a default value. You therefore need to assign a value to a field before using it. We recommend you always use* new.

You can also copy one struct to another. For example:

```
Rectangle myRectangle4 = myRectangle3;
```

This copies the field values from `myRectangle3` to `myRectangle4`. Listing 5.15 illustrates a struct.

LISTING 5.15: A STRUCT

```
/*
  Example5_15.cs illustrates the use of a struct
*/


// declare the Rectangle struct
public struct Rectangle
{
```

```
  // declare the fields
  public int Width;
  public int Height;

  // define a constructor
  public Rectangle(int Width, int Height)
  {
    this.Width = Width;
    this.Height = Height;
  }

  // define the Area() method
  public int Area()
  {
    return Width * Height;
  }

}


class Example5_15
{

  public static void Main()
  {

    // create an instance of a Rectangle
    System.Console.WriteLine("Creating a Rectangle instance");
    Rectangle myRectangle = new Rectangle(2, 3);

    // display the values for the Rectangle instance
    System.Console.WriteLine("myRectangle.Width = " + myRectangle.Width);
    System.Console.WriteLine("myRectangle.Height = " + myRectangle.Height);

    // call the Area() method of the Rectangle instance
    System.Console.WriteLine("myRectangle.Area() = " + myRectangle.Area());

  }

}
```

The output from this program is as follows:

```
Creating a Rectangle instance
myRectangle.Width = 2
myRectangle.Height = 3
myRectangle.Area() = 6
```

Summary

In this chapter, you learned that you can use classes and objects to model the real world. In fact, they can help simplify the task of writing programs to solve complex problems. C# builds on the seminal research work done by Xerox PARC in the 1970s and the other object-oriented languages developed since then.

A *class* is a template from which individual *objects* are created. A class contains fields and methods. A *field* is a variable or object, and a *method* is a group of declarations and other statements that perform a specific task. Fields and methods are collectively known as *members*.

A method may return a value to the statement that called it, and a method may also accept *parameters* from the calling statement. *Overloaded methods* have the same name but have different parameters. An *access modifier* allows you to specify the degree to which a class member is available outside of the class. The default access modifier is `private`.

An object is created from the class and has its own copy of the fields declared in the class. The `this` keyword accesses the current object.

A *constructor* method is called when an object is created. You can define your own constructors, through which you can do things such as initialize an object's fields using parameters. You can use a *destructor* to clean up after your objects before they're removed from memory by the *garbage collector*.

Structs are similar to classes, but they offer a "lighter" alternative to classes. Structs are treated as value types and are therefore stored on the *stack*, unlike objects that are stored on the *heap*. Structs are intended to be small, and you should consider using them when you have a few fields and methods.

Chapter 6

More about Classes and Objects

IN THIS CHAPTER, YOU'LL learn about static members, fields, and methods. *Static members* belong to the class itself, and not to any object. *Static fields* are useful for keeping track of things such as the number of objects of the class that have been created. *Static methods* are often used to access private static fields.

You'll also learn about properties. *Properties* allow you to set and get fields using methods. Properties allow you to hide your fields from your class users by making them private, while still providing an easy way to get at those fields. Objects in the real world often contain other objects. You'll learn how you can model this using a *"has a"* relationship, in which a field in a class is declared using another class.

Finally, you'll look at how you use *namespaces* to avoid conflicts of class names in your programs. Namespaces isolate your class declarations to a specific region of code.

Featured in this chapter:

◆ Introducing and Using Static Members and Readonly Fields

◆ Defining Properties

◆ Looking at the "Has a" Relationship

◆ Introducing Namespaces

Introducing Static Members

As you know, objects have their own copies of the fields declared in their class. These are known as *instance fields* because they belong to an instance of the class—an *instance* is just another name for a specific object. You access an instance field of an object using an object reference. You've already seen many examples of this—myCar.make, for example. Similarly, the methods you've seen so far have all been *instance methods*, and they are also called using object references—myCar.Start(), for example. Collectively, fields and methods are called *members*, so instance fields and methods are called *instance members*.

Static members (fields and methods) belong to the class itself, and not to any object. Static members are shared by all objects of a class. You use the `static` keyword to indicate that a member is static.

Static fields are useful for keeping track of things such as the number of objects of the class that have been created. We said earlier that you should keep your member fields private as much as possible, and you can often use *static methods* to access private static fields. Of course, these aren't the only uses for static members. In Listing 5.8, you saw a program that used the `System.Math.Sin()` and `System.Math`
`.Cos()` methods—these are static methods, which are used to get the sine and cosine values for an angle; that listing also used the `System.Math.PI` constant. The point is that the `System.Math` class contains a number of static members that are useful for mathematical programs. C# contains many other classes that have static members, and as you become more proficient in C# you'll probably find yourself writing your own classes containing useful static members.

Using Static Members

Let's consider an example class that contains a static field named `numberOfCars`, which keeps track of the number of `Car` objects created, and a static method named `getNumberOfCars()`, which returns the `value` of `numberOfCars`:

```
public class Car
{

  // declare a static field,
  // numberOfCars stores the number of Car objects
  private static int numberOfCars = 0;

  // define the constructor
  public Car()
  {
    System.Console.WriteLine("Creating a Car object");
    numberOfCars++;  // increment numberOfCars
  }

  // define the destructor
  ~Car()
  {
    System.Console.WriteLine("Destroying a Car object");
    numberOfCars--;  // decrement numberOfCars
  }

  // define a static method that returns numberOfCars
  public static int GetNumberOfCars()
  {
    return numberOfCars;
  }

}
```

There are a few things to notice about this class:

◆ The `numberOfCars` field is both static and private, and it is initialized to 0.

◆ The constructor for this class increments `numberOfCars` using the increment operator (++)—this adds 1 to `numberOfCars` when a new `Car` object is created.

◆ The destructor for this class decrements `numberOfCars` using the decrement operator (--), which subtracts 1 from `numberOfCars` when a `Car` object is destroyed.

◆ The `GetNumberOfCars()` static method returns the value of `numberOfCars`.

Because static members belong to the class, you access them using the name of the class—and not through an object reference. For example, you use `Car.GetNumberOfCars()` to call the static method to get the `numberOfCars` field. In fact, you don't even need to create an object to use the static members of a class—for example, if `Car.GetNumberOfCars()` is called prior to any objects being created, then this method returns 0 (the value that `numberOfCars` is initialized to in the class).

Before seeing a complete example program, you should be aware of the following issues when using static methods:

◆ Static methods cannot use the `this` object reference. This is because static methods belong to the class, and they are always called using the class name and never using an object—therefore the `this` object reference has no meaning.

◆ Static methods cannot directly access any of the instance members. This is because static methods are called using the class name, and there is no object to access.

Listing 6.1 illustrates the use of static members.

LISTING 6.1: STATIC MEMBERS

```
/*
  Example6_1.cs illustrates the use of static members
*/


// declare the Car class
public class Car
{

  // declare a static field,
  // numberOfCars stores the number of Car objects
  private static int numberOfCars = 0;

  // define the constructor
  public Car()
  {
    System.Console.WriteLine("Creating a Car object");
    numberOfCars++;  // increment numberOfCars
  }
```

```
    // define the destructor
    ~Car()
    {
      System.Console.WriteLine("Destroying a Car object");
      numberOfCars--;  // decrement numberOfCars
    }

    // declare a static method that returns numberOfCars
    public static int GetNumberOfCars()
    {
      return numberOfCars;
    }

  }


class Example6_1
{

  public static void Main()
  {

    // display numberOfCars
    System.Console.WriteLine("Car.GetNumberOfCars() = " +
      Car.GetNumberOfCars());

    // create a Car object
    Car myCar = new Car();
    System.Console.WriteLine("Car.GetNumberOfCars() = " +
      Car.GetNumberOfCars());

    // create another Car object
    Car myCar2 = new Car();
    System.Console.WriteLine("Car.GetNumberOfCars() = " +
      Car.GetNumberOfCars());

  }


}
```

The output from this program is as follows:

```
Car.GetNumberOfCars() = 0
Creating a Car object
Car.GetNumberOfCars() = 1
Creating a Car object
Car.GetNumberOfCars() = 2
```

```
Destroying a Car object
Destroying a Car object
```

Using Constant Fields

In Chapter 2, "Basic C# Programming," you saw that the const keyword declares constants. You can also declare *constant fields* using the const keyword—these fields are implicitly static and belong to the class, and you must set them using an initializer.

WARNING *Once the value for a constant field has been set, it may not be changed. Attempting to do so will cause a compilation error.*

The following class declares a constant field named wheels, whose value is set to 4 using an initializer:

```
public class Car
{

  // declare a const field
  public const int wheels = 4;

}
```

Notice that you don't use the static keyword; const fields are implicitly static. The wheels field is set to 4 and cannot be changed. Just as with any other static field, you use the class name to get the value of a const field—Car.wheels, for example.

Listing 6.2 illustrates a const field.

LISTING 6.2: A CONSTANT FIELD

```
/*
  Example6_2.cs illustrates the use of a const field
*/


// declare the Car class
public class Car
{

  // declare a const field
  public const int wheels = 4;

}


class Example6_2 {

  public static void Main()
  {
```

```
      System.Console.WriteLine("Car.wheels = " + Car.wheels);
      // Car.wheels = 5;  // causes compilation error

  }

}
```

The output from this program is as follows:

```
Car.wheels = 4
```

Using Readonly Fields

Readonly fields store set values and can belong to an instance *or* a class—if the field belongs to the class, then the field must be explicitly declared as static using the `static` keyword.

In the case of a readonly instance field, each object gets its own copy of the field (just like any other instance field) and you set its value in a constructor. In the case of a static readonly field, the field belongs to the class (just like any other static field), and you set its value using an initializer.

WARNING   *Once you have set the value for a readonly field, you cannot change it. Attempting to do so will cause a compilation error.*

The following class declares a readonly field named `make`, whose value is set in the constructor; and a static readonly field named `wheels`, whose value is set to 4 using an initializer:

```
public class Car
{

  // declare a readonly field
  public readonly string make;

  // declare a static readonly field
  public static readonly int wheels = 4;

  // define a constructor
  public Car(string make)
  {
    System.Console.WriteLine("Creating a Car object");
    this.make = make;
  }

}
```

Just as with any other static field, you use the class name to get the value of a static readonly field; and just as with any other instance field, you must use an object to get the value of a readonly instance field.

Listing 6.3 illustrates readonly fields.

LISTING 6.3: READONLY FIELDS

```csharp
/*
  Example6_3.cs illustrates the use of readonly fields
*/


// declare the Car class
public class Car
{

  // declare a readonly field
  public readonly string make;

  // declare a static readonly field
  public static readonly int wheels = 4;

  // define a constructor
  public Car(string make)
  {
    System.Console.WriteLine("Creating a Car object");
    this.make = make;
  }

}


class Example6_3
{

  public static void Main()
  {

    System.Console.WriteLine("Car.wheels = " + Car.wheels);
    // Car.wheels = 5;  // causes compilation error

    // create a Car object
    Car myCar = new Car("Toyota");

    System.Console.WriteLine("myCar.make = " + myCar.make);
    // myCar.make = "Porsche";  // causes compilation error

  }

}
```

The output from this program is as follows:

```
Car.wheels = 4
Creating a Car object
myCar.make = Toyota
```

Defining Properties

Properties allow you to set and get fields using methods. Properties are a great feature of C# because they enable you to hide your fields from your class users by making them private, while still providing those users an easy way to get at those fields. You can think of a property as a wrapper around a private field, through which the field is accessed.

TIP *Private fields and properties promote encapsulation. You should always try to use private fields and provide access to those fields using properties, rather than using public fields. For brevity, this book doesn't always follow this rule, but you should in your own programs.*

A property may define two methods, named get and set (brackets are omitted from these method definitions). The get method returns the value of the field, and the set method sets the value of the field. The following class declares a private field named make and a property named Make; notice the get method that returns the value for the make field, and the set method that assigns a value to the make field:

```
public class Car
{

  // declare a private field
  private string make;

  // declare a property
  public string Make
  {
    get
    {
      return make;
    }
    set
    {
      make = value;
    }
  }

}
```

The value keyword in the set method is an implicit parameter supplied to this method, and it contains the value to be assigned to the field. Instead of accessing the field directly, you use the property, and depending on the context either the get or set method will be used to actually access the underlying field.

Let's look at an example; the following statement creates a Car object:

```
Car myCar = new Car();
```

To set the value for the make field, you assign a value to the Make property. The following statement assigns the value of "Porsche" to myCar.Make:

```
myCar.Make = "Porsche";
```

Here, the context is an assignment and therefore the set method assigns the value to the make field. The value implicit parameter is set to "Porsche", and therefore the make field is set to "Porsche". The following statement displays the value of myCar.Make:

```
System.Console.WriteLine("myCar.Make = " + myCar.Make);
```

This time, because the context is retrieval, the get method of the Make property is called, which returns the value of the make field.

NOTE *You don't have to provide both a* get *and* set *method. If you just provide a* get *method, then you can only read from the property. If you just provide a* set *method, then you can only write to the property.*

Listing 6.4 illustrates a property.

LISTING 6.4: USING A PROPERTY

```
/*
  Example6_4.cs illustrates the use of a property
*/


// declare the Car class
public class Car
{

  // declare a private field
  private string make;

  // declare a property
  public string Make
  {
    get
    {
      return make;
    }
    set
    {
```

```
      make = value;
    }
  }

}


class Example6_4
{

  public static void Main()
  {

    // create a Car object
    System.Console.WriteLine("Creating a Car object");
    Car myCar = new Car();

    // set the Car Make
    System.Console.WriteLine("Setting the Car object's Make property to Porsche");
    myCar.Make = "Porsche";

    System.Console.WriteLine("myCar.Make = " + myCar.Make);

  }

}
```

The output from this program is as follows:

```
Creating a Car object
Setting the Car object's Make property to Porsche
myCar.Make = Porsche
```

Introducing the "Has a" Relationship

Objects in the real world often contain other objects. For example, a car has an engine, and an engine is itself an object. You can model this using a *"has a"* relationship, in which the field of a class is declared using another class. In this way, you can model complex classes made up of simpler classes. You can use "has a" relationships to an arbitrary level of detail—for example, an engine itself has pistons, fuel injectors, spark plugs, and so on, and each of these components has other smaller components.

TIP   The key to successful object-oriented programming is to model a real-world system to an appropriate level of detail for the task. For example, if you only need to model the overall behavior of a car, then there's no need to model how the engine's spark plugs work.

Using the "Has a" Relationship

Going back to the example of a car that has an engine, the following class represents engines:

```
public class Engine
{

  // declare the fields
  public int cylinders;
  public int horsepower;

  // define the method
  public void Start()
  {
    System.Console.WriteLine("Engine started");
  }

}
```

The cylinders field stores the number of cylinders in the engine, and the horsepower field stores the power of the engine. The Start() method models starting the engine.

Next, the following class represents cars, which declares a field named engine (of the Engine class):

```
public class Car
{

  // declare the fields
  public string make;
  public Engine engine;   // Car has an Engine

  // define the method
  public void Start()
  {
    engine.Start();
  }

}
```

This class uses a "has a" relationship: A Car object has an Engine object. As you can see, the Start() method for this class just calls the engine.Start() method. The engine field is just a reference to an Engine object, which is created separately from the associated Car object to which it belongs.

The following statement creates a Car object and an Engine object for that Car:

```
Car myCar = new Car();
myCar.engine = new Engine();
```

The fields for the Engine object are set using the engine object reference contained in the Car object, as shown in the following statements:

```
myCar.engine.cylinders = 4;
myCar.engine.horsepower = 180;
```

Listing 6.5 illustrates the "has a" relationship.

LISTING 6.5: "HAS A" RELATIONSHIP

```
/*
  Example6_5.cs illustrates how to use a "has a"
  relationship
*/


// declare the Engine class
public class Engine
{

  // declare the fields
  public int cylinders;
  public int horsepower;

  // define the method
  public void Start()
  {
    System.Console.WriteLine("Engine started");
  }

}


// declare the Car class
public class Car
{

  // declare the fields
  public string make;
  public Engine engine;   // Car has an Engine

  // define the method
  public void Start()
  {
    engine.Start();
  }

}


class Example6_5
{
```

```
public static void Main()
{

  // declare a Car object reference named myCar
  System.Console.WriteLine("Creating a Car object");
  Car myCar = new Car();
  myCar.make = "Toyota";

  // Car objects have an Engine object
  System.Console.WriteLine("Creating an Engine object");
  myCar.engine = new Engine();
  myCar.engine.cylinders = 4;
  myCar.engine.horsepower = 180;

  // display the values for the Car and Engine object fields
  System.Console.WriteLine("myCar.make = " + myCar.make);
  System.Console.WriteLine("myCar.engine.cylinders = " +
    myCar.engine.cylinders);
  System.Console.WriteLine("myCar.engine.horsepower = " +
    myCar.engine.horsepower);

  // call the Car object's Start() method
  myCar.Start();

}

}
```

The output from this program is as follows:

```
Creating a Car object
Creating an Engine object
myCar.make = Toyota
myCar.engine.cylinders = 4
myCar.engine.horsepower = 180
Engine started
```

Nesting Classes

You can declare, or *nest*, one class inside another. If you only use a class with one other class, then nesting the first class within the other class might make a lot of sense. The nested class is known as the *inner class*, and the class in which it is nested is known as the *outer class*. You could also make the inner class private, which would limit access to this class to the outer class.

One good use for nested classes is when using the "has a" relationship. For example, Listing 6.6 rewrites the Car class shown in Listing 6.5 to contain a nested Engine class. In this example, the Engine class is the inner class and the Car class is the outer class.

LISTING 6.6: NESTING CLASSES

```csharp
/*
  Example6_6.cs illustrates nested classes
*/


// declare the Car class
public class Car
{

  // declare the Engine class
  public class Engine
  {

    // declare the Engine fields
    public int cylinders;
    public int horsepower;

    // define the Engine method
    public void Start()
    {
      System.Console.WriteLine("Engine started");
    }

  }

  // declare the Car fields
  public string make;
  public Engine engine;  // Car has an Engine

  // define the Car method
  public void Start()
  {
    engine.Start();
  }

}


class Example6_6
{

  public static void Main()
  {

    // declare a Car object reference named myCar
    System.Console.WriteLine("Creating a Car object");
```

```
    Car myCar = new Car();
    myCar.make = "Toyota";

    // Car objects have an Engine object
    System.Console.WriteLine("Creating an Engine object");
    myCar.engine = new Car.Engine();
    myCar.engine.cylinders = 4;
    myCar.engine.horsepower = 180;

    // display the values for the Car and Engine object fields
    System.Console.WriteLine("myCar.make = " + myCar.make);
    System.Console.WriteLine("myCar.engine.cylinders = " +
      myCar.engine.cylinders);
    System.Console.WriteLine("myCar.engine.horsepower = " +
      myCar.engine.horsepower);

    // call the Car object's Start() method
    myCar.Start();

  }

}
```

The output from this program is as follows:

```
Creating a Car object
Creating an Engine object
myCar.make = Toyota
myCar.engine.cylinders = 4
myCar.engine.horsepower = 180
Engine started
```

Learning about Namespaces

Namespaces allow you to avoid conflicts of class names in your programs. For example, say you were working as a programmer in a team developing an application to model cars, and you are using classes developed by another company. For your program, you might want to write your own class named Car, but if a programmer in that other company has already used that class name, then you must choose another name for your class. Namespaces provide a solution to this problem by isolating the class declarations to a specific region of code.

TIP   By using namespaces in your own organization's code, you promote code reuse because another organization may also potentially use your code in their programs.

In fact, you've already seen the use of one namespace: the System namespace. The System namespace contains many class declarations, including the Console class, which defines the WriteLine() method.

You declare a namespace using the `namespace` keyword, followed by the name you want to assign to your namespace. You then place your classes within that namespace. The following example declares a namespace named `Sybex`:

```
namespace Sybex
{

  // declare the Car class
  public class Car
  {
    public string make;
  }

}
```

Notice that the `Car` class is declared inside the `Sybex` namespace. This means that another `Car` class in a different namespace can be declared, and it won't interfere with the first. For example:

```
namespace DifferentCompany
{

  // declare the Car class
  public class Car
  {
    public string make;
  }

}
```

The `Car` class declaration in this namespace doesn't clash with the other `Car` class in the previous `Sybex` namespace, and each `Car` class could contain different fields and methods. By using namespaces you can potentially use code written by another person in your own programs. Of course, you must use a different name for your namespaces because you cannot use a name already used by an existing namespace.

To create a `Car` object using the `Car` class declared in the `Sybex` namespace, you can use the following statement:

```
Sybex.Car myCar = new Sybex.Car();
```

Notice that the name of the namespace precedes the class name. Later in this section, you'll see how to use the `using` statement to specify the namespace to use.

Similarly, the following example creates a `Car` object using the `Car` class declared in the `Different-Company` namespace:

```
DifferentCompany.Car myOtherCar = new DifferentCompany.Car();
```

Listing 6.7 illustrates two namespaces.

LISTING 6.7: TWO NAMESPACES

```
/*
  Example6_7.cs illustrates the use of two namespaces
*/


// create the Sybex namespace
namespace Sybex
{

  // declare the Car class
  public class Car
  {
    public string make;
  }

}


// create the DifferentCompany namespace
namespace DifferentCompany
{

  // declare the Car class
  public class Car
  {
    public string make;
  }

}


class Example6_7
{

  public static void Main()
  {

    // create a Sybex.Car object
    System.Console.WriteLine("Creating a Sybex.Car object");
    Sybex.Car myCar = new Sybex.Car();
    myCar.make = "Toyota";
    System.Console.WriteLine("myCar.make = " + myCar.make);

    // create a DifferentCompany.Car object
    System.Console.WriteLine("Creating a DifferentCompany.Car object");
    DifferentCompany.Car myOtherCar = new DifferentCompany.Car();
```

```
        myOtherCar.make = "Porsche";
        System.Console.WriteLine("myOtherCar.make = " + myOtherCar.make);

    }

}
```

The output from this program is as follows:

```
Creating a Sybex.Car object
myCar.make = Toyota
Creating a DifferentCompany.Car object
myOtherCar.make = Porsche
```

Nesting Namespaces into Hierarchies

You can nest namespaces into a *hierarchy*. You might want to do this if your company has many programming teams, and each team needs to declare many classes of their own. For example, let's say **Sybex** has two programming teams working together to create a graphical program that accesses and displays information stored in a database. This program may be structured into two major pieces: the user interface code and the database access code. The first team works on the user interface code, and the second team works on the back-end database access code; let's say Sybex has decided to use two nested namespaces for this:

```
namespace Sybex
{

    namespace UserInterface
    {
      // … classes …
    }

    namespace DatabaseAccess
    {
      // … classes …
    }

}
```

The user interface classes are declared in the `UserInterface` namespace, and the database access classes are declared in the `DatabaseAccess` namespace. Both of these namespaces are nested within the `Sybex` namespace.

Nested namespaces can themselves contain nested namespaces. The following example shows a namespace called `WelcomeScreen` nested within the `UserInterface` namespace:

```
namespace Sybex
{
```

```
namespace UserInterface
{

  namespace WelcomeScreen
  {
    // … classes …
  }

}

  …

}
```

You can also separate namespaces using a dot (.). For example:

```
namespace Sybex.UserInterface
{
  // … classes …
}

namespace Sybex.DatabaseAccess
{
  // … classes …
}
```

You can also use namespace hierarchies in different files. By doing this, different teams can work on their own separate files and then compile them together. Listings 6.8 and 6.9 illustrate this.

LISTING 6.8: NESTED NAMESPACES ACROSS FILES, PART 1

```
/*
  Example6_8.cs illustrates the use of namespace
  hierarchies (part 1)
*/


namespace Sybex
{
  namespace UserInterface
  { // nested namespace
    public class MyClass
    {
      public void Test()
      {
        System.Console.WriteLine("UserInterface Test()");
      }
    }
  }
}
```

```csharp
namespace Sybex.DatabaseAccess {  // nested namespace using dot
  public class MyClass
  {
    public void Test()
    {
      System.Console.WriteLine("DatabaseAccess Test()");
    }
  }
}


class Example6_8
{
  public static void Main()
  {
    Sybex.UserInterface.MyClass myUI =
      new Sybex.UserInterface.MyClass();
    Sybex.DatabaseAccess.MyClass myDB =
      new Sybex.DatabaseAccess.MyClass();

    // uses class in MiddleTier namespace in Example6_9
    Sybex.MiddleTier.MyClass myMT =
      new Sybex.MiddleTier.MyClass();

    // call the Test() methods
    myUI.Test();
    myDB.Test();
    myMT.Test();
  }
}
```

Notice that the class declared in the MiddleTier namespace is used in this program. The MiddleTier namespace is contained in a separate file and is shown in Listing 6.9.

LISTING 6.9: NESTED NAMESPACES ACROSS FILES, PART 2

```csharp
/*
  Example6_9.cs illustrates the use of namespace
  hierarchies (part 2)
*/


namespace Sybex
{  // use the Sybex namespace
  namespace MiddleTier
  {  // another namespace
```

```
  public class MyClass
  {
    public void Test()
    {
      System.Console.WriteLine("MiddleTier Test()");
    }
  }
 }
}
```

To compile the entire program that is made up of both files, you may enter the following command:

```
csc Example6_8.cs Example6_9.cs
```

Because `Example6_8.cs` contains the `Main()` method, you run `Example6_8`. The output from this program is as follows:

```
UserInterface Test()
DatabaseAccess Test()
MiddleTier Test()
```

The *using* Statement

In the previous examples, the classes in the namespaces were referenced by placing the namespace in front of the class name. When your namespaces become long or deeply nested, including the namespace can become tedious. This is where the `using` statement comes in handy.

The `using` statement allows you to specify the namespace (or namespaces) used in the code. You must include any `using` statements at the beginning of a source file, but you may place them after any initial comments.

The following example shows a `using` statement:

```
// initial comments
using System;
...
class MyClass
{
  Console.WriteLine("Hello World!");
}
```

Notice that the `System` namespace is specified by the `using` statement, so `System` may be omitted from the call to the `Console.WriteLine()` method.

NOTE   *If two namespaces contain a class of the same name, then you must include the namespace when referencing that class; otherwise the compiler won't know which class you meant.*

You can also specify namespaces before they are declared in your program. For example:

```
using Sybex;
namespace Sybex
```

```
    {
      ...
    }
    ...
```

Listing 6.10 illustrates the using statement.

LISTING 6.10: THE using STATEMENT

```csharp
/*
  Example6_10.cs illustrates how the using
  statement is used to specify namespaces
*/

using Sybex;
using System;

namespace Sybex
{

  // declare the Car class
  public class Car
  {
    public string make;
  }

}


class Example6_10
{

  public static void Main()
  {

    // the Console.WriteLine() call uses the System namespace
    Console.WriteLine("Creating a Sybex.Car object");

    // create a Car object (uses the Sybex namespace)
    Car myCar = new Car();

    myCar.make = "Toyota";
    Console.WriteLine("myCar.make = " + myCar.make);

  }

}
```

The output from this program is as follows:

```
Creating a Sybex.Car object
myCar.make = Toyota
```

Summary

In this chapter, you added to the knowledge you already had about classes and objects. Specifically, you learned about static members, fields, and methods. *Static members* belong to the class itself, and not to any object. *Static fields* are useful for keeping track of things such as the number of objects of the class that have been created. *Static methods* are often used to access private static fields. Constant fields are static and belong to the class, and they are set using an *initializer*. *Readonly fields* are used to store set values, but they can belong to an instance or a class.

You also learned about properties. *Properties* allow you to set and get fields using methods. Properties allow you to hide your fields from your class users by making them private, while still providing an easy way to get at those fields. You can think of a property as a wrapper around a private field, through which the field is accessed.

Objects in the real world often contain other objects. You can model this using a *"has a"* relationship, in which a field in a class is declared using another class.

Finally, you looked at how you use *namespaces* to avoid conflicts of class names in your programs. Namespaces isolate the class declarations to a specific region of code. You can nest namespaces into a hierarchy. The `using` statement allows you to specify the namespaces used in your code.

Chapter 7

Derived Classes

IN THE PREVIOUS TWO chapters, you learned how to define classes and create objects from those classes. In this chapter, you'll learn how a class can be *derived* from another class. You'll also learn how you can overload an operator to perform your own code when a particular operator is used, rather than using the default provided by C#.

Featured in this chapter:

◆ Understanding Inheritance and Polymorphism

◆ Using Member Accessibility, Member Hiding, and Versioning

◆ Learning to Hide Members

◆ Using the `System.Object` Class

◆ Declaring Abstract Classes and Methods

◆ Marking Classes and Methods as Sealed

◆ Overloading Operators

Introducing Inheritance

The examples in the previous chapter featured a class named `Car`. Cars aren't the only type of motor vehicle—there are also motorcycles, trucks, and sports-utility vehicles on the road today. All of these forms of transportation are kinds of motor vehicles, and you can use the *"is a"* relationship to model this. For example, a car *"is a"* motor vehicle, a motorcycle *"is a"* motor vehicle, and so on. The *"is a"* relationship is different from the *"has a"* relationship described in the previous chapter.

TIP *By building a hierarchy of classes, you can potentially simplify the task of modeling complex systems by creating a tree of classes.*

You model the "is a" relationship in C# using *inheritance*. With inheritance, one class is the parent of another class. The parent class is the *base class*, and the child class is the *derived class*. Derived classes inherit the members of their base class.

Going back to the vehicle example, the class that represents motor vehicles would be the base class, and the classes that represent cars and motorcycles would then be derived classes. Let's take a look at some code to clarify these ideas. The following class, named `MotorVehicle`, represents motor vehicles:

```
public class MotorVehicle
{

  // declare the fields
  public string make;
  public string model;

  // define a constructor
  public MotorVehicle(string make, string model)
  {
    this.make = make;
    this.model = model;
  }

  // define a method
  public void Start()
  {
    Console.WriteLine(model + " started");
  }

}
```

The `MotorVehicle` class declares two public fields: `make` and `model`. This class defines a constructor to set the `make` and `model` fields, and it also defines a method named `Start()`. Both the constructor and the `Start()` method are public.

To derive a class from a base class, you place a colon (:) after the derived class name, followed by the name of the base class. For example, the following `Car` class is derived from the previous `MotorVehicle` class:

```
public class Car : MotorVehicle
{

  // declare an additional field
  public bool convertible;

  // define a constructor
  public Car(string make, string model, bool convertible) :
  base(make, model)  // calls the base class constructor
  {
    this.convertible = convertible;
  }

}
```

Now, a derived class inherits the members of its base class; because the Car class is derived from the MotorVehicle class, the Car class inherits the members of the MotorVehicle class. This means that the Car class inherits the make and model fields, along with the Start() method of the Motor-Vehicle class.

The Car class also declares an additional field named convertible; this field indicates if a car's roof may be put down. When a Car object is created from this class, it will have three fields: make, model, and convertible.

NOTE   *Derived classes do not inherit base class constructors. If you define a constructor in your base class, then you must also define a constructor in your derived class. If you want to call the base class constructor, your derived class constructor must explicitly call it.*

The Car class defines a constructor that accepts three parameters: make, model, and convertible. The make and model fields are passed to the constructor of the MotorVehicle class using the base keyword. The base keyword refers to the base class, and whenever C# sees this keyword, it will search the base class for the specified member. In the constructor defined in the Car class, base(make, model) refers to the constructor in the MotorVehicle class. You'll notice that the base(make, model) call goes after a colon (:).

The following statement creates a Car object:

```
Car myCar = new Car("Toyota", "MR2", true);
```

This example calls the Car constructor, which in turn calls the MotorVehicle constructor to set the make and model fields to "Toyota" and "MR2", respectively. The Car constructor then sets the convertible field of the new Car object to true.

Of course, you can derive more than one class from the same base class. The following code defines a class named Motorcycle that is also derived from the MotorVehicle class:

```
public class Motorcycle : MotorVehicle
{

  // declare an additional field
  public bool sidecar;

  // define a constructor
  public Motorcycle(string make, string model, bool sidecar) :
  base(make, model)  // calls the base class constructor
  {
    this.sidecar = sidecar;
  }

  // define an additional method
  public void PullWheelie()
  {
    Console.WriteLine(model + " pulling a wheelie!");
  }

}
```

The Motorcycle class declares an additional field named sidecar, which represents whether the motorcycle has an attached sidecar for passengers. Motorcycle objects will therefore get three fields: make, model, and sidecar.

The Motorcycle class also defines an additional method named PullWheelie(). For those of you who are unfamiliar with motorcycles, a motorcyclist "pulls a wheelie" when the front wheel of their motorcycle leaves the ground.

Listing 7.1 shows these classes and illustrates inheritance.

LISTING 7.1: INHERITANCE

```
/*
  Example7_1.cs illustrates inheritance
*/

using System;


// declare the MotorVehicle class (the base class)
public class MotorVehicle
{

  // declare the fields
  public string make;
  public string model;

  // define a constructor
  public MotorVehicle(string make, string model)
  {
    this.make = make;
    this.model = model;
  }

  // define a method
  public void Start()
  {
    Console.WriteLine(model + " started");
  }

}


// declare the Car class (derived from the MotorVehicle base class)
public class Car : MotorVehicle
{

  // declare an additional field
  public bool convertible;
```

```
  // define a constructor
  public Car(string make, string model, bool convertible) :
  base(make, model)  // calls the base class constructor
  {
    this.convertible = convertible;
  }

}


// declare the Motorcycle class (derived from the MotorVehicle base class)
public class Motorcycle : MotorVehicle
{

  // declare an additional field
  public bool sidecar;

  // define a constructor
  public Motorcycle(string make, string model, bool sidecar) :
  base(make, model)  // calls the base class constructor
  {
    this.sidecar = sidecar;
  }

  // define an additional method
  public void PullWheelie()
  {
    Console.WriteLine(model + " pulling a wheelie!");
  }

}


class Example7_1
{

  public static void Main()
  {

    // declare a Car object, display the object's fields, and call the
    // Start() method
    Car myCar = new Car("Toyota", "MR2", true);
    Console.WriteLine("myCar.make = " + myCar.make);
    Console.WriteLine("myCar.model = " + myCar.model);
    Console.WriteLine("myCar.convertible = " + myCar.convertible);
    myCar.Start();
```

```
// declare a Motorcycle object, display the object's fields, and call the
// Start() method
Motorcycle myMotorcycle = new Motorcycle("Harley-Davidson", "V-Rod", false);
Console.WriteLine("myMotorcycle.make = " + myMotorcycle.make);
Console.WriteLine("myMotorcycle.model = " + myMotorcycle.model);
Console.WriteLine("myMotorcycle.sidecar = " + myMotorcycle.sidecar);
myMotorcycle.Start();
myMotorcycle.PullWheelie();

  }

}
```

The output from this program is as follows:

```
myCar.make = Toyota
myCar.model = MR2
myCar.convertible = True
MR2 started
myMotorcycle.make = Harley-Davidson
myMotorcycle.model = V-Rod
myMotorcycle.sidecar = False
V-Rod started
V-Rod pulling a wheelie!
```

Learning about Polymorphism

Polymorphism comes from the Greek words *poly*, meaning many, and *morph*, meaning form. Therefore, *polymorphism* means many forms. In an object-oriented programming language, polymorphism refers to the fact that a method in a derived class may contain a different set of statements from the method in the base class; the method in the derived class is said to *override* the method in the base class.

To best understand polymorphism, let's return to the vehicle example. Now, to accelerate a car you must push the gas pedal, but to accelerate a motorcycle you must twist the throttle. The actual mechanism involved in acceleration isn't of much interest to you; you simply want the vehicle to move faster.

Polymorphism allows you to take account of the different ways that a car and a motorcycle accelerate. The MotorVehicle class should have a method, so let's call it Accelerate(), which should contain the actions common to all accelerating motor vehicles. This Accelerate() method should be overridden in the derived Car and Motorcycle classes to account for the differences between accelerating cars and motorcycles.

To allow a method to be overridden, you use the virtual keyword in the method definition contained in the base class. For example, the following MotorVehicle class uses the virtual keyword in the Accelerate() method definition:

```
public class MotorVehicle
{
    ...
```

```
  // define the Accelerate() method (may be overridden in a
  // derived class)
  public virtual void Accelerate()
  {
    Console.WriteLine(model + " accelerating");
  }

}
```

The `virtual` keyword indicates that the `Accelerate()` method may be overridden in a derived class. This `Accelerate()` method displays a single line of text, indicating that a particular `MotorVehicle` object is accelerating.

Next, to override a base method in a derived class, you use the `override` keyword in the method definition contained in the derived class. The following `Car` class overrides the previous `Accelerate()` method defined in the `MotorVehicle` class:

```
public class Car : MotorVehicle
{

  ...

  // override the base class Accelerate() method
  public override void Accelerate()
  {
    Console.WriteLine("Pushing gas pedal of " + model);
    base.Accelerate();  // calls the base class Accelerate() method
  }

}
```

This time, the `Accelerate()` method displays a line of text indicating that a particular `Car` object's gas pedal is being pushed and then calls the `base.Accelerate()` method—which calls the `Accelerate()` method in the `MotorVehicle` class.

NOTE *When you override a method, the method in the derived class must contain the same parameter list as the method in the base class.*

Now, in the case of a motorcycle, the throttle is twisted to accelerate it. This is modeled in the following `Motorcycle` class, which also overrides the `Accelerate()` method previously defined in the `MotorVehicle` class:

```
public class Motorcycle : MotorVehicle
{

  ...

  // override the base class Accelerate() method
  public override void Accelerate()
  {
```

```
    Console.WriteLine("Twisting throttle of " + model);
    base.Accelerate();  // calls the Accelerate() method in the base class
  }

}
```

Listing 7.2 shows these classes and illustrates polymorphism.

```
/*
  Example7_2.cs illustrates polymorphism
*/

using System;


// declare the MotorVehicle class
public class MotorVehicle
{

  // declare the fields
  public string make;
  public string model;

  // define a constructor
  public MotorVehicle(string make, string model)
  {
    this.make = make;
    this.model = model;
  }

  // define the Accelerate() method (may be overridden in a
  // derived class)
  public virtual void Accelerate()
  {
    Console.WriteLine(model + " accelerating");
  }

}


// declare the Car class (derived from MotorVehicle)
public class Car : MotorVehicle
{

  // define a constructor
  public Car(string make, string model) :
```

```
    base(make, model)
    {
      // do nothing
    }

    // override the base class Accelerate() method
    public override void Accelerate()
    {
      Console.WriteLine("Pushing gas pedal of " + model);
      base.Accelerate();  // calls the Accelerate() method in the base class
    }

  }


// declare the Motorcycle class (derived from MotorVehicle)
public class Motorcycle : MotorVehicle
{

  // define a constructor
  public Motorcycle(string make, string model) :
  base(make, model)
  {
    // do nothing
  }

  // override the base class Accelerate() method
  public override void Accelerate()
  {
    Console.WriteLine("Twisting throttle of " + model);
    base.Accelerate();  // calls the Accelerate() method in the base class
  }

}


class Example7_2
{

  public static void Main()
  {

    // create a Car object and call the object's Accelerate() method
    Car myCar = new Car("Toyota", "MR2");
    myCar.Accelerate();

    // create a Motorcycle object and call the object's Accelerate() method
    Motorcycle myMotorcycle = new Motorcycle("Harley-Davidson", "V-Rod");
```

```
    myMotorcycle.Accelerate();

  }

}
```

Notice that the Car and Motorcycle classes don't add any fields to the base class, and therefore the Car and Motorcycle constructors just call the base class constructor.

The output from this program is as follows:

```
Pushing gas pedal of MR2
MR2 accelerating
Twisting throttle of V-Rod
V-Rod accelerating
```

Specifying Member Accessibility

In the previous chapter, you saw how the various access modifiers—such as public and private—specify the degree to which a class member is available outside of the class (Table 5.2 lists the access modifiers in Chapter 5, "Object-Oriented Programming"). In this section, you'll see how the access modifiers affect member accessibility in derived classes.

The following MotorVehicle class uses the public, private, and protected access modifiers:

```
public class MotorVehicle
{

  // declare the fields
  private   string make;
  protected string model;

  // define a constructor
  public MotorVehicle(string make, string model)
  {
    this.make = make;
    this.model = model;
  }

  // define the Start() method (may be overridden in a
  // derived class)
  public virtual void Start()
  {
    TurnStarterMotor();
    System.Console.WriteLine("Vehicle started");
  }

  // define the TurnStarterMotor() method
  private void TurnStarterMotor()
```

```
  {
    System.Console.WriteLine("Turning starter motor...");
  }

}
```

The `make` field is private and is therefore only accessible within the `MotorVehicle` class. The `model` field is protected, meaning it is accessible within the `MotorVehicle` class and any derived classes. The constructor and the `Start()` method are public and are therefore accessible without restriction. The `Start()` method may be overridden in a derived class; this method calls the `TurnStarterMotor()` method, which is private and therefore only accessible within the `MotorVehicle` class.

Next, the following `Car` class is derived from this `MotorVehicle` class:

```
public class Car : MotorVehicle
{

  // define a constructor
  public Car(string make, string model) :
  base(make, model)
  {
    // do nothing
  }

  // override the base class Start() method
  public override void Start()
  {
    Console.WriteLine("Starting " + model);  // model accessible
    base.Start();  // calls the Start() method in the base class
    // Console.WriteLine("make = " + make);  // make is not accessible
  }

}
```

The `Car` constructor calls the base class constructor. The `Start()` method overrides the base class `Start()` method and displays a string containing the `model` field; because the `model` field is protected, this field is accessible within the `Car` class. The `make` field is not accessible because it is private to the `MotorVehicle` class, and therefore the statement that attempts to access the `make` field is commented out so that the code will compile.

Listing 7.3 uses these classes and illustrates member accessibility.

LISTING 7.3: MEMBER ACCESSIBILITY

```
/*
  Example7_3.cs illustrates member accessibility
*/

using System;
```

```csharp
// declare the MotorVehicle class
public class MotorVehicle
{

  // declare the fields
  private   string make;
  protected string model;

  // define a constructor
  public MotorVehicle(string make, string model)
  {
    this.make = make;
    this.model = model;
  }

  // define the Start() method (may be overridden in a
  // derived class)
  public virtual void Start()
  {
    TurnStarterMotor();
    System.Console.WriteLine("Vehicle started");
  }

  // define the TurnStarterMotor() method
  private void TurnStarterMotor()
  {
    System.Console.WriteLine("Turning starter motor...");
  }

}


// declare the Car class (derived from MotorVehicle)
public class Car : MotorVehicle
{

  // define a constructor
  public Car(string make, string model) :
  base(make, model)
  {
    // do nothing
  }

  // override the base class Start() method
  public override void Start()
  {
    Console.WriteLine("Starting " + model);  // model accessible
```

```
      base.Start();  // calls the Start() method in the base class
      // Console.WriteLine("make = " + make);  // make is not accessible
   }

}


class Example7_3
{

   public static void Main()
   {

      // create a Car object and call the object's Accelerate() method
      Car myCar = new Car("Toyota", "MR2");
      myCar.Start();

      // make and model are not accessible, so the following two lines
      // are commented out
      // Console.WriteLine("myCar.make = " + myCar.make);
      // Console.WriteLine("myCar.model = " + myCar.model);

   }

}
```

Notice that neither the make nor the model field is accessible to the Example7_3 class, and therefore the statements that attempt to access these fields are commented out so that the code will compile. The make field is not accessible because this field is private to the MotorVehicle class and the field is therefore only available within that class. The model field is not accessible because this field is protected and is therefore only available within the MotorVehicle and Car classes.

The output from this program is as follows:

```
Starting MR2
Turning starter motor...
Vehicle started
```

Hiding Members

Members of a derived class may *hide* members of a base class using the new keyword, which defines a new member in the derived class, separate from the member in the base class. Because the member in the derived class has the same name as the member in the base class, the member in the base class is hidden by the derived class. This might seem like a useless feature, but you'll see how using the new keyword to hide a method can be useful (see the "Versioning" section).

NOTE *By using the* new *keyword, you're telling the compiler that you've intentionally used the same name for the method.*

Let's take a look at some examples that make member hiding clearer. The following MotorVehicle class declares two public fields named make and model, along with a constructor that sets these fields and a DisplayModel() method to display the value of the model field:

```
public class MotorVehicle
{

  // declare the fields
  public string make;
  public string model;

  // define a constructor
  public MotorVehicle(string make, string model)
  {
    Console.WriteLine("In MotorVehicle constructor");
    this.make = make;
    this.model = model;
    Console.WriteLine("this.make = " + this.make);
    Console.WriteLine("this.model = " + this.model);
  }

  // define the DisplayModel() method
  public void DisplayModel()
  {
    Console.WriteLine("In MotorVehicle DisplayModel() method");
    Console.WriteLine("model = " + model);
  }

}
```

Next, the following Car class hides the model field and the DisplayModel() method previously defined in the MotorVehicle class by defining new members of the same name (notice that the constructor in this class calls the base constructor with a dummy value of "Test" for the model field—you'll see why this is important shortly):

```
public class Car : MotorVehicle
{

  // hide the base class model field
  public new string model;

  // define a constructor
  public Car(string make, string model) :
  base(make, "Test")
  {
```

```
      Console.WriteLine("In Car constructor");
      this.model = model;
      Console.WriteLine("this.model = " + this.model);
    }

    // hide the base class DisplayModel() method
    public new void DisplayModel()
    {
      Console.WriteLine("In Car DisplayModel() method");
      Console.WriteLine("model = " + model);
      base.DisplayModel();  // calls the DisplayModel() method in the base class
    }

  }
```

Because the new keyword defines new model and DisplayModel() members in this Car class, these members hide the member of the same name previously defined in the base class. Let's consider what happens when a Car object is created, as shown in the following statement:

```
Car myCar = new Car("Toyota", "MR2");
```

The Car constructor is called with the make and model parameters being set to "Toyota" and "MR2", respectively. The Car constructor then calls the MotorVehicle base class constructor with this setting for the make parameter ("Toyota"), but with the model parameter set to "Test". So, in the MotorVehicle constructor, the make field is set to "Toyota" and the model field is set to "Test"—these settings are confirmed in the MotorVehicle constructor by displaying the values of the make and model fields for the current object. After the MotorVehicle constructor has displayed the field values, program control returns to the Car constructor. In this constructor, the model field (which hides the base model field) is set to "MR2"—this is the original value set in the statement that created the Car object.

Next, the following statement calls the Car object's DisplayModel() method:

```
myCar.DisplayModel();
```

The DisplayModel() method in the Car class displays a string containing the model field value—this is set to "MR2" for the current Car object. The DisplayModel() method in the Car class then calls the base DisplayModel() method that displays the hidden model field, whose value is "Test".

Listing 7.4 shows these classes and illustrates member hiding.

LISTING 7.4: MEMBER HIDING

```
/*
  Example7_4.cs illustrates member hiding
*/

using System;


// declare the MotorVehicle class
```

```csharp
public class MotorVehicle
{

  // declare the fields
  public string make;
  public string model;

  // define a constructor
  public MotorVehicle(string make, string model)
  {
    Console.WriteLine("In MotorVehicle constructor");
    this.make = make;
    this.model = model;
    Console.WriteLine("this.make = " + this.make);
    Console.WriteLine("this.model = " + this.model);
  }

  // define the DisplayModel() method
  public void DisplayModel()
  {
    Console.WriteLine("In MotorVehicle DisplayModel() method");
    Console.WriteLine("model = " + model);
  }

}


// declare the Car class (derived from MotorVehicle)
public class Car : MotorVehicle
{

  // hide the base class model field
  public new string model;

  // define a constructor
  public Car(string make, string model) :
  base(make, "Test")
  {
    Console.WriteLine("In Car constructor");
    this.model = model;
    Console.WriteLine("this.model = " + this.model);
  }

  // hide the base class DisplayModel() method
  public new void DisplayModel()
  {
    Console.WriteLine("In Car DisplayModel() method");
    Console.WriteLine("model = " + model);
```

```
      base.DisplayModel();  // calls DisplayModel() in the base class
    }

}


class Example7_4
{

  public static void Main()
  {

    // create a Car object
    Console.WriteLine("Creating a Car object");
    Car myCar = new Car("Toyota", "MR2");

    Console.WriteLine("Back in Main() method");
    Console.WriteLine("myCar.make = " + myCar.make);
    Console.WriteLine("myCar.model = " + myCar.model);

    // call the Car object's DisplayModel() method
    Console.WriteLine("Calling myCar.DisplayModel()");
    myCar.DisplayModel();

  }

}
```

The output from this program is as follows:

```
Creating a Car object
In MotorVehicle constructor
this.make = Toyota
this.model = Test
In Car constructor
this.model = MR2
Back in Main() method
myCar.make = Toyota
myCar.model = MR2
Calling myCar.DisplayModel()
In Car DisplayModel() method
model = MR2
In MotorVehicle DisplayModel() method
model = Test
```

Versioning

At first glance, you may think that method hiding doesn't appear particularly useful. There is a situation where you might need to use it, however. Let's say you want to use a class named MotorVehicle that was written by another programmer, and you want to use this class to derive your own class. Further, let's also assume you want to define an Accelerate() method in your derived class. For example:

```
public class Car : MotorVehicle
{

  ...

  // define the Accelerate() method
  public void Accelerate()
  {
    Console.WriteLine("In Car Accelerate() method");
    Console.WriteLine(model + " accelerating");
  }

}
```

Next, let's suppose that the other programmer later modifies the MotorVehicle class and decides to add her own virtual Accelerate() method:

```
public class MotorVehicle
{

  ...

  // define the Accelerate() method
  public virtual void Accelerate()
  {
    Console.WriteLine("In MotorVehicle Accelerate() method");
    Console.WriteLine(model + " accelerating");
  }

}
```

The addition of this Accelerate() method by the other programmer causes a problem: The Accelerate() method in your Car class hides the inherited Accelerate() method now defined in their MotorVehicle class. Later, when you come to compile your Car class, it isn't clear to the compiler whether you actually intended your method to hide the inherited method. Because of this, the compiler reports the following warning when you try to compile your Car class:

```
warning CS0114: 'Car.Accelerate()' hides inherited member
'MotorVehicle.Accelerate()'. To make the current member override that
implementation, add the override keyword. Otherwise add the new keyword.
```

By adding the new keyword to your Accelerate() method definition, you make it clear to the compiler that you intend your method to hide the inherited method (see Listing 7.5).

NOTE *The important difference between* new *and* overrides *is the ability to call the parent method. When you use* overrides, *you are stuck with the new implementation, with no way to call the base class method. There are exceptions, of course, but generally this is true.*

LISTING 7.5: VERSIONING

```
/*
  Example7_5.cs illustrates versioning
*/

using System;


// declare the MotorVehicle class
public class MotorVehicle
{

  // declare the fields
  public string make;
  public string model;

  // define a constructor
  public MotorVehicle(string make, string model)
  {
    this.make = make;
    this.model = model;
  }

  // define the Accelerate() method
  public virtual void Accelerate()
  {
    Console.WriteLine("In MotorVehicle Accelerate() method");
    Console.WriteLine(model + " accelerating");
  }

}


// declare the Car class (derived from MotorVehicle)
public class Car : MotorVehicle
{

  // define a constructor
  public Car(string make, string model) :
  base(make, model)
  {
```

```
      // do nothing
    }

    // define the Accelerate() method (uses the new keyword to
    // tell the compiler a new method is to be defined)
    public new void Accelerate()
    {
      Console.WriteLine("In Car Accelerate() method");
      Console.WriteLine(model + " accelerating");
    }

}


class Example7_5
{

  public static void Main()
  {

    // create a Car object
    Console.WriteLine("Creating a Car object");
    Car myCar = new Car("Toyota", "MR2");

    // call the Car object's Accelerate() method
    Console.WriteLine("Calling myCar.Accelerate()");
    myCar.Accelerate();

  }

}
```

The output from this program is as follows:

```
Creating a Car object
Calling myCar.DisplayModel()
In Car Accelerate() method
MR2 accelerating
```

Using the *System.Object* Class

The System.Object class acts as the base class for all classes; in other words, all classes are ultimately derived from the System.Object class. This derivation of classes from the System.Object class is implicit—C# does it behind the scenes. Because this derivation is implicit, you don't explicitly indicate that your classes are derived from the System.Object class.

The System.Object class provides a number of useful methods, shown in Table 7.1.

TABLE 7.1: System.Object CLASS METHODS

METHOD	DESCRIPTION
public virtual string ToString()	Returns a string that is, by default, equal to the name of the object's class.
public virtual int GetHashCode()	Returns a hash value for a particular type; suitable for use in hashing algorithms and data structures such as hash tables.
public virtual bool Equals(*object*)	Returns true if two objects are equal; this method is an instance method and is overloaded with the Equals() class method described in the following line.
public static bool Equals(*object*, *object*)	Returns true if two objects are equal. This method is a class method and is overloaded with the Equals() instance method described in the previous line.
public static bool ReferenceEquals(*object*, *object*)	Returns true if two object references are equal—in other words, they reference the same object.
public Type GetType()	Returns the class (or type) of the object (or variable).
protected virtual void Finalize()	Allows an object to perform any cleaning up before the garbage collector removes the object from memory. The Finalize() method is basically the same as a destructor (described in Chapter 5).
protected object MemberwiseClone()	Creates a copy of the object.

Because all classes are derived from the System.Object class, any object may use these methods. Listing 7.6 declares a Car class and creates two Car objects; these objects then use some of the System.Object methods.

LISTING 7.6: OBJECT CLASS METHODS

```
/*
  Example7_6.cs illustrates some of the System.Object
  class methods
*/

using System;


// declare the Car class
public class Car
{

  // declare the fields
  public string make;
  public string model;
```

```csharp
    // define a constructor
    public Car(string make, string model)
    {
      this.make = make;
      this.model = model;
    }

    // define the Display() method
    public void Display()
    {
      Console.WriteLine("make = " + make);
      Console.WriteLine("model = " + model);
    }

    // define the Copy() method
    public static Car Copy(Car car)
    {
      // perform memberwise clone
      return (Car) car.MemberwiseClone();
    }

  }


class Example7_6
{

  public static void Main()
  {

    // create Car objects
    Console.WriteLine("Creating Car objects");
    Car myCar = new Car("Toyota", "MR2");
    Car myOtherCar = new Car("Porsche", "Boxter");
    Console.WriteLine("myCar details:");
    myCar.Display();
    Console.WriteLine("myOtherCar details:");
    myOtherCar.Display();

    // call some of the methods inherited from the System.Object class
    Console.WriteLine("myCar.ToString() = " + myCar.ToString());
    Console.WriteLine("myCar.GetType() = " + myCar.GetType());
    Console.WriteLine("myCar.GetHashCode() = " + myCar.GetHashCode());
    Console.WriteLine("Car.Equals(myCar, myOtherCar) = " +
      Car.Equals(myCar, myOtherCar));
    Console.WriteLine("Car.ReferenceEquals(myCar, myOtherCar) = " +
      Car.ReferenceEquals(myCar, myOtherCar));
```

```
// set the myCar object reference equal to myOtherCar
Console.WriteLine("Setting myCar equal to myOtherCar");
myCar = myOtherCar;

// check for equality
Console.WriteLine("Car.Equals(myCar, myOtherCar) = " +
  Car.Equals(myCar, myOtherCar));
Console.WriteLine("Car.ReferenceEquals(myCar, myOtherCar) = " +
  Car.ReferenceEquals(myCar, myOtherCar));

// perform a memberwise clone of myCar using the Car.Copy() method
Console.WriteLine("Performing a memberwise clone of myCar to myOldCar");
Car myOldCar = Car.Copy(myCar);
Console.WriteLine("myOldCar details:");
myOldCar.Display();

    }

}
```

Notice that the Car class defines a static method named Copy(); this method uses the Memberwise-Clone() method to perform a copy of the Car object passed to it.

The output from this program is as follows:

```
Creating Car objects
myCar details:
make = Toyota
model = MR2
myOtherCar details:
make = Porsche
model = Boxter
myCar.ToString() = Car
myCar.GetType() = Car
myCar.GetHashCode() = 65
Car.Equals(myCar, myOtherCar) = False
Car.ReferenceEquals(myCar, myOtherCar) = False
Setting myCar equal to myOtherCar
Car.Equals(myCar, myOtherCar) = True
Car.ReferenceEquals(myCar, myOtherCar) = True
Performing a memberwise clone of myCar to myOldCar
myOldCar details:
make = Porsche
model = Boxter
```

Overriding the *System.Object* Class Methods

The virtual methods of the System.Object class may be overridden in any of your classes. A common method to override in your classes is the ToString() method. As you saw in the previous example, the ToString() method returns the name of the class by default—which isn't particularly useful (but depends on the object, of course).

In this section, you'll see a program that causes the ToString() method to return a string containing the make and model fields of a Car object (see Listing 7.7). In the "Operator Overloading" section of this chapter, you'll see a program that overrides the Equals() method.

LISTING 7.7: OVERRIDING THE ToString() METHOD

```
/*
  Example7_7.cs illustrates how to override the ToString() method
*/

using System;


// declare the Car class
public class Car
{

  // declare the fields
  public string make;
  public string model;

  // define a constructor
  public Car(string make, string model)
  {
    this.make = make;
    this.model = model;
  }

  // override the ToString() method
  public override string ToString()
  {
    return make + " " + model;
  }

}


class Example7_7
{

  public static void Main()
  {
```

```
// create Car objects
Console.WriteLine("Creating Car objects");
Car myCar = new Car("Toyota", "MR2");
Car myOtherCar = new Car("Porsche", "Boxter");

// call the ToString() method for the Car objects
Console.WriteLine("myCar.ToString() = " +
  myCar.ToString());
Console.WriteLine("myOtherCar.ToString() = " +
  myOtherCar.ToString());

  }

}
```

The output from this program is as follows:

```
Creating Car objects
myCar.ToString() = Toyota MR2
myOtherCar.ToString() = Porsche Boxter
```

Boxing and Unboxing

You've now seen that all classes are derived from the System.Object class. In fact, even value types such as int and char are derived from the System.Object type and may therefore use the methods defined in the System.Object class. For example, the following statements declare an int variable and then call the ToString() and GetType() methods using this int variable:

```
int myInt1 = 10;
Console.WriteLine("myInt1.ToString() = " +
  myInt1.ToString());
Console.WriteLine("myInt1.GetType() = " +
  myInt1.GetType());
```

The last two statements display the following:

```
myInt1.ToString() = 10
myInt1.GetType() = System.Int32
```

This is at first glance a somewhat surprising result: How can a variable act like an object? The answer is that at run-time, the variable is first implicitly converted to an object of the System.Object class—this process is known as *boxing*.

In the following example, an int variable is explicitly assigned to a System.Object object:

```
int myInt2 = 10;
object myObject = myInt2;  // myInt2 is boxed
```

Here, myInt2 is first boxed and then assigned to myObject.

NOTE System.Object *and* object *mean the same thing: They both refer to* System.Object. *Therefore, in the example,* myObject *is an object of the* System.Object *class.*

On the other side of the coin, an object of the System.Object class may be converted to a value type—this process is known as *unboxing*. In the following example, myObject is unboxed to an int variable:

```
int myInt3 = (int) myObject;   // myObject is unboxed
```

Notice that myObject is cast to an int.
Listing 7.8 illustrates boxing and unboxing.

LISTING 7.8: BOXING AND UNBOXING

```
/*
   Example7_8.cs illustrates boxing and unboxing
*/

using System;

class Example7_8
{

  public static void Main()
  {

    // implicit boxing of an int
    int myInt1 = 10;
    Console.WriteLine("myInt1.ToString() = " + myInt1.ToString());
    Console.WriteLine("myInt1.GetType() = " + myInt1.GetType());

    // explicit boxing of an int to an object
    int myInt2 = 10;
    object myObject = myInt2;   // myInt2 is boxed
    Console.WriteLine("myInt2 = " + myInt2);
    Console.WriteLine("myObject = " + myObject);

    // explicit unboxing of an object to an int
    int myInt3 = (int) myObject;   // myObject is unboxed
    Console.WriteLine("myInt3 = " + myInt3);

  }

}
```

The output from this program is as follows:

```
myInt1.ToString() = 10
myInt1.GetType() = System.Int32
myInt2 = 10
myObject = 10
myInt3 = 10
```

Using Abstract Classes and Methods

Abstract classes enable you to define classes that represent abstract concepts. For example, you can consider a motor vehicle an abstract concept, and you could define an abstract MotorVehicle class to represent the concept of a motor vehicle. You could then use the MotorVehicle class to derive a Car class to represent actual cars—you'll see an example of this shortly. You use the abstract keyword to specify that a class is abstract.

You can also declare *abstract methods* using the abstract keyword, which specifies that the method must be overridden in a derived class. An abstract method may not contain any code; the code for the method must be implemented in the derived class.

You can declare the following MotorVehicle class as abstract using the abstract keyword; this class also declares an abstract Accelerate() method:

```
abstract public class MotorVehicle
{

    ...


    // declare the abstract Accelerate() method (no code)
    abstract public void Accelerate();

}
```

Notice that the abstract Accelerate() method doesn't contain any code; the code must be implemented in the derived class.

There are a few points to note about abstract classes and methods:

◆ You *cannot* create objects of an abstract class.

◆ You *cannot* mark a constructor as abstract.

◆ You may use an abstract class to derive other classes, including other abstract classes.

◆ You must override any abstract methods in a base class with methods that contain code in a derived class.

You derive classes from an abstract base class using the usual colon (:) between the base and derived class names. The following `Car` class is derived from the `MotorVehicle` class, and it overrides the `Accelerate()` method with a method containing code:

```
public class Car : MotorVehicle
{

  ...


  // override the Accelerate() method (contains code)
  public override void Accelerate()
  {
    Console.WriteLine("In Car Accelerate() method");
    Console.WriteLine(model + " accelerating");
  }

}
```

Listing 7.9 shows abstract classes and methods.

LISTING 7.9: ABSTRACT CLASSES AND METHODS

```
/*
  Example7_9.cs illustrates abstract classes and methods
*/

using System;


// declare the abstract MotorVehicle class
abstract public class MotorVehicle
{

  // declare the fields
  public string make;
  public string model;

  // define a constructor
  public MotorVehicle(string make, string model)
  {
    this.make = make;
    this.model = model;
  }

  // declare the abstract Accelerate() method (no code)
  abstract public void Accelerate();

}
```

```csharp
// declare the Car class (derived from MotorVehicle)
public class Car : MotorVehicle
{

  // define a constructor
  public Car(string make, string model) :
  base(make, model)
  {
    // do nothing
  }

  // override the Accelerate() method (contains code)
  public override void Accelerate()
  {
    Console.WriteLine("In Car Accelerate() method");
    Console.WriteLine(model + " accelerating");
  }

}


class Example7_9
{

  public static void Main()
  {

    // create a Car object
    Console.WriteLine("Creating a Car object");
    Car myCar = new Car("Toyota", "MR2");

    // call the Car object's Accelerate() method
    Console.WriteLine("Calling myCar.Accelerate()");
    myCar.Accelerate();

  }

}
```

The output from this program is as follows:

```
Creating a Car object
Calling myCar.Accelerate()
In Car Accelerate() method
MR2 accelerating
```

Declaring Sealed Classes and Methods

Sealed classes and methods restrict inheritance and polymorphism. You might want to use sealed classes and methods in code that you are going to sell, when you don't want someone attempting to alter your code.

Sealed Classes

You cannot use a sealed class to derive a class. You mark a class or method as sealed using the `sealed` keyword. The following example declares a sealed class:

```
sealed public class MotorVehicle
{

  …

}
```

You cannot derive a class from this sealed `MotorVehicle` class.

Sealed Methods

You cannot override a sealed method in a derived class. You may declare a sealed method in a non-sealed class, but that sealed method cannot be overridden in a derived class. The following example declares a non-sealed `MotorVehicle` class that defines a virtual `Accelerate()` method:

```
public class MotorVehicle
{

  …

  // define the Accelerate() method
  public virtual void Accelerate()
  {
    Console.WriteLine("In MotorVehicle Accelerate() method");
    Console.WriteLine(model + " accelerating");
  }

}
```

Next, the following `Car` class (derived from the `MotorVehicle` class) overrides the `Accelerate()` method with a sealed method:

```
public class Car : MotorVehicle
{

  …

  // override the Accelerate() method (sealed)
  sealed public override void Accelerate()
  {
```

```
    Console.WriteLine("In Car Accelerate() method");
    Console.WriteLine(model + " accelerating");
  }

}
```

Because this `Accelerate()` method is sealed, any classes derived from the `Car` class cannot override this method.

Listing 7.10 shows these classes and illustrates sealed methods.

LISTING 7.10: SEALED METHODS

```csharp
/*
  Example7_10.cs illustrates sealed methods
*/

using System;


// declare the MotorVehicle class
public class MotorVehicle
{

  // declare the fields
  public string make;
  public string model;

  // define a constructor
  public MotorVehicle(string make, string model)
  {
    this.make = make;
    this.model = model;
  }

  // define the Accelerate() method
  public virtual void Accelerate()
  {
    Console.WriteLine("In MotorVehicle Accelerate() method");
    Console.WriteLine(model + " accelerating");
  }

}


// declare the Car class (derived from MotorVehicle)
public class Car : MotorVehicle
{
```

```
    // define a constructor
    public Car(string make, string model) :
    base(make, model)
    {
      // do nothing
    }

    // override the Accelerate() method (sealed)
    sealed public override void Accelerate()
    {
      Console.WriteLine("In Car Accelerate() method");
      Console.WriteLine(model + " accelerating");
    }

}


class Example7_10
{

  public static void Main()
  {

    // create a Car object
    Console.WriteLine("Creating a Car object");
    Car myCar = new Car("Toyota", "MR2");

    // call the Car object's Accelerate() method
    Console.WriteLine("Calling myCar.Accelerate()");
    myCar.Accelerate();

  }

}
```

The output from this program is as follows:

```
Creating a Car object
Calling myCar.Accelerate()
In Car Accelerate() method
MR2 accelerating
```

Casting Objects

You can cast an object of a derived class to the base class (known as an *upcast*) and vice versa (known as a *downcast*). Because all classes are derived from the System.Object class, you can always upcast an object to this class.

You can only cast an object to a class when that class is compatible with the object's class. What do we mean by *compatible*? A derived class is compatible with its base class. For example, say class C was derived from class B, and class B was derived from class A; then C is compatible with B and A. You can therefore cast objects between A, B, and C. When you cast an object to a class, you only have access to the members of that class (you'll see an example of this shortly).

A class that is not derived from another class is not compatible. For example, say class B1 is derived from A, and B2 is also derived from A; then B1 and B2 are not compatible. Therefore, you cannot cast objects between B1 and B2.

The examples in the rest of this section use three classes, named `MotorVehicle`, `Car`, and `Motorcycle`. The `Car` and `Motorcycle` classes are both derived from a `MotorVehicle` class. The `MotorVehicle` class is as follows:

```
public class MotorVehicle
{

  public string model;

  public MotorVehicle(string model)
  {
    this.model = model;
  }

  public void Start()
  {
    Console.WriteLine(model + " started");
  }

}
```

The `Car` class is as follows:

```
public class Car : MotorVehicle
{

  public bool convertible;

  public Car(string model, bool convertible) :
  base(model)
  {
    this.convertible = convertible;
  }

}
```

The `Motorcycle` class is as follows:

```
public class Motorcycle : MotorVehicle
{
```

```
    public bool sidecar;

    // define a constructor
    public Motorcycle(string model, bool sidecar) :
    base(model)
    {
      this.sidecar = sidecar;
    }

    public void PullWheelie()
    {
      Console.WriteLine(model + " pulling a wheelie!");
    }

  }
```

The following sections describe upcasts and downcasts using these classes.

Upcasting

An upcast occurs when an object of a derived class is cast to its base class. For example, an object of either the Car or Motorcycle class could be upcast to the MotorVehicle class. The following statement creates a Car object:

```
Car myCar = new Car("MR2", true);
```

Next, the following statement performs an upcast of this object to the MotorVehicle class:

```
MotorVehicle myMotorVehicle = (MotorVehicle) myCar;
```

Now, because the MotorVehicle class only contains the model field and the Start() method, myMotorVehicle only has access to these members; myMotorVehicle doesn't have access to the additional member defined in the Car class, so it cannot access the convertible field (attempting to access this field will cause a compilation error).

Similarly, the following statements create a Motorcycle object and then cast that object to the MotorVehicle class:

```
Motorcycle myMotorcycle = new Motorcycle("V-Rod", true);
MotorVehicle myMotorVehicle2 = (MotorVehicle) myMotorcycle;
```

Now, myMotorVehicle2 only has access to the members of the MotorVehicle class and cannot access the sidecar field or PullWheelie() method.

Downcasting

A downcast occurs when an object of the base class is cast to a derived class. The following statement downcasts myMotorVehicle2 (created in the previous section) to the Motorcycle class:

```
Motorcycle myMotorcycle2 = (Motorcycle) myMotorVehicle2;
```

Because myMotorcycle2 is of the Motorcycle class, it now has access to all the members of the Motorcycle class, and therefore the sidecar field and PullWheelie() methods are also now available.

One thing you cannot do is downcast myMotorVehicle2 to the Car class. This is because myMotorVehicle2 was obtained (in the previous section) by upcasting myMotorcycle (a Motorcycle object), and you cannot cast a Motorcycle object to a Car object because the Motorcycle and Car classes are incompatible.

Listing 7.11 illustrates casting objects.

LISTING 7.11: CASTING OBJECTS

```csharp
/*
  Example7_11.cs illustrates casting objects
*/

using System;


// declare the MotorVehicle class (the base class)
public class MotorVehicle
{

  public string model;

  public MotorVehicle(string model)
  {
    this.model = model;
  }

  public void Start()
  {
    Console.WriteLine(model + " started");
  }

}


// declare the Car class
public class Car : MotorVehicle
{

  public bool convertible;

  public Car(string model, bool convertible) :
  base(model)
  {
```

```
      this.convertible = convertible;
    }

  }


  // declare the Motorcycle class
  public class Motorcycle : MotorVehicle
  {

    public bool sidecar;

    // define a constructor
    public Motorcycle(string model, bool sidecar) :
    base(model)
    {
      this.sidecar = sidecar;
    }

    public void PullWheelie()
    {
      Console.WriteLine(model + " pulling a wheelie!");
    }

  }


  class Example7_11
  {

    public static void Main()
    {

      // create a Car object
      Car myCar = new Car("MR2", true);

      // cast myCar to MotorVehicle (upcast)
      MotorVehicle myMotorVehicle = (MotorVehicle) myCar;

      // myMotorVehicle only has a model field and Start() method
      // (no convertible field)
      Console.WriteLine("myMotorVehicle.model = " + myMotorVehicle.model);
      myMotorVehicle.Start();
      // Console.WriteLine("myMotorVehicle.convertible = " +
      //   myMotorVehicle.convertible);

      // create a Motorcycle object
      Motorcycle myMotorcycle = new Motorcycle("V-Rod", true);
```

```
    // cast myMotorcycle to MotorVehicle (upcast)
    MotorVehicle myMotorVehicle2 = (MotorVehicle) myMotorcycle;

    // myMotorVehicle only has a model field and Start() method
    // (no sidecar field or PullWheelie() method)
    Console.WriteLine("myMotorVehicle2.model = " + myMotorVehicle2.model);
    myMotorVehicle2.Start();
    // Console.WriteLine("myMotorVehicle2.sidecar = " +
    //   myMotorVehicle2.sidecar);
    // myMotorVehicle2.PullWheelie();

    // cast myMotorVehicle2 to Motorcycle (downcast)
    Motorcycle myMotorcycle2 = (Motorcycle) myMotorVehicle2;

    // myMotorCycle2 has access to all members of the Motorcycle class
    Console.WriteLine("myMotorcycle2.model = " + myMotorcycle2.model);
    Console.WriteLine("myMotorcycle2.sidecar = " + myMotorcycle2.sidecar);
    myMotorcycle2.Start();
    myMotorcycle2.PullWheelie();

    // cannot cast a Motorcyle object to the Car class because
    // their classes are not compatible
    // Car myCar2 = (Car) myMotorVehicle2;

  }

}
```

The output from this program is as follows:

```
myMotorVehicle.model = MR2
MR2 started
myMotorVehicle2.model = V-Rod
V-Rod started
myMotorcycle2.model = V-Rod
myMotorcycle2.sidecar = True
V-Rod started
V-Rod pulling a wheelie!
```

Operator Overloading

Operator overloading enables you to write your own code to handle the operation performed by an operator, instead of just using the default operation. In Chapter 3, "Expressions and Operators," you learned that operators perform arithmetic, compare values, and so on. If you have written your own classes, then you might want an operator to do something different from the default operation.

For example, say you have a class named `Rectangle` that declares two fields named `width` and `height`:

```
public class Rectangle
{

  // declare the fields
  public int width;
  public int height;

  // define constructor
  public Rectangle(int width, int height)
  {
    this.width = width;
    this.height = height;
  }

}
```

You also create two `Rectangle` objects with the same values for their `width` and `height` fields:

```
Rectangle myRectangle = new Rectangle(1, 4);
Rectangle myRectangle2 = new Rectangle(1, 4);
```

Next, the following `if` statement uses the equal operator (`==`):

```
if (myRectangle == myRectangle2)
{
  Console.WriteLine("myRectangle is equal to myRectangle2");
}
else
{
  Console.WriteLine("myRectangle is not equal to myRectangle2");
}
```

In this case, the `==` operator compares the object references, and because `myRectangle` and `myRectangle2` reference different objects, this `if` statement always displays the text indicating that `myRectangle` and `myRectangle2` are not equal. You might want to overload the equal operator (`==`) to compare the `width` and `height` of the two rectangles instead; if they are the same, then the two objects are *identical*.

Also, the following statement attempts to use the addition operator (`+`) to add the two rectangles:

```
Rectangle myRectangle3 = myRectangle + myRectangle2;
```

This statement causes a compilation error because the addition operator (`+`) expects two numeric values. Therefore, you might also want to overload the addition operator, which would then add the `width` and `height` fields of both objects and return a new `Rectangle` object with these field values.

In the following sections, you'll see how to overload the equal operator and the addition operator. You'll also learn about the other operators you can overload.

Overloading the Equal Operator

You overload an operator using the `operator` keyword in a method for your class. For example, the following method overloads the equal operator (`==`); notice that the `operator` keyword follows the return type of the method (`bool`), and the operator to be overloaded (`==`) goes after the `operator` keyword:

```
public static bool operator ==(Rectangle lhs, Rectangle rhs)
{
  Console.WriteLine("In operator ==");
  if (lhs.width == rhs.width && lhs.height == rhs.height)
  {
    return true;
  }
  else
  {
    return false;
  }
}
```

NOTE Overloaded operator methods are always static because they belong to the class.

This method accepts two `Rectangle` parameters named `lhs` and `rhs`; these correspond to the two objects on the left and right sides of the `==` operator. For example, when `myRectangle == myRectangle2` is evaluated, `myRectangle` is passed into the method as the `lhs` parameter, and `myRectangle2` is passed in as the `rhs` parameter. The method returns `true` if `lhs` and `rhs` have the same values for their `width` and `height` fields; otherwise it returns `false`.

WARNING If you overload the equal operator, you should also overload the opposite not equal operator (`!=`); if you don't, then you'll get a compilation warning.

The following method overloads the not equal (`!=`) operator:

```
public static bool operator !=(Rectangle lhs, Rectangle rhs)
{
  Console.WriteLine("In operator !=");
  return !(lhs==rhs);
}
```

Notice that this simply invokes the equal operator (`==`) to check if `lhs` is equal to `rhs` and returns the logical opposite of this result—this saves you from writing similar code to what you previously wrote for the equal operator.

Finally, because you are overloading the equal operator, you should also override the `Equals()` method inherited from the `System.Object` class (described earlier in this chapter in the "Using the *System.Object* Class" section):

```
public override bool Equals(object obj)
{
  Console.WriteLine("In Equals()");
```

```
    if (!(obj is Rectangle))
    {
      return false;
    }
    else
    {
      return this == (Rectangle) obj;
    }
  }
```

If the object is not a Rectangle, then you simply return false. If the object is a Rectangle, then you invoke the equal operator (==) to perform the comparison.

Overloading the Addition Operator

You also want to overload the addition operator (+) for the Rectangle class so that the following statement will work:

```
Rectangle myRectangle3 = myRectangle + myRectangle2;
```

This statement will create a new Rectangle object whose width and height fields are set to the sum of those fields from myRectangle and myRectangle2.

The following method shows the required overload of the addition operator (+):

```
public static Rectangle operator +(Rectangle lhs, Rectangle rhs)
{
  Console.WriteLine("In operator +");
  return new Rectangle(lhs.width + rhs.width, lhs.height + rhs.height);
}
```

Listing 7.12 illustrates operator overloading.

LISTING 7.12: OPERATOR OVERLOADING

```
/*
  Example7_12.cs illustrates operator overloading
*/

using System;


// declare the Rectangle class
public class Rectangle
{

  // declare the fields
  public int width;
  public int height;
```

```csharp
// define constructor
public Rectangle(int width, int height)
{
  this.width = width;
  this.height = height;
}

// override the ToString() method
public override string ToString()
{
  return "width = " + width + ", height = " + height;
}

// overload the == operator
public static bool operator ==(Rectangle lhs, Rectangle rhs)
{
  Console.WriteLine("In operator ==");
  if (lhs.width == rhs.width && lhs.height == rhs.height)
  {
    return true;
  }
  else
  {
    return false;
  }
}

// overload the != operator
public static bool operator !=(Rectangle lhs, Rectangle rhs)
{
  Console.WriteLine("In operator !=");
  return !(lhs==rhs);
}

// override the Equals() method
public override bool Equals(object obj)
{
  Console.WriteLine("In Equals()");
  if (!(obj is Rectangle))
  {
    return false;
  }
  else
  {
    return this == (Rectangle) obj;
  }
}
```

```csharp
    // overload the + operator
    public static Rectangle operator +(Rectangle lhs, Rectangle rhs)
    {
      Console.WriteLine("In operator +");
      return new Rectangle(lhs.width + rhs.width, lhs.height + rhs.height);
    }

}


class Example7_12
{

  public static void Main()
  {

    // create Rectangle objects
    Rectangle myRectangle = new Rectangle(1, 4);
    Console.WriteLine("myRectangle: " + myRectangle);
    Rectangle myRectangle2 = new Rectangle(1, 4);
    Console.WriteLine("myRectangle2: " + myRectangle2);

    if (myRectangle == myRectangle2)
    {
      Console.WriteLine("myRectangle is equal to myRectangle2");
    }
    else
    {
      Console.WriteLine("myRectangle is not equal to myRectangle2");
    }

    Rectangle myRectangle3 = myRectangle + myRectangle2;
    Console.WriteLine("myRectangle3: " + myRectangle3);

  }

}
```

The output from this program is as follows:

```
myRectangle: width = 1, height = 4
myRectangle2: width = 1, height = 4
In operator ==
myRectangle is equal to myRectangle2
In operator +
myRectangle3: width = 2, height = 8
```

Overloading Other Operators

You can overload many operators, but you should only overload an operator if it makes sense to do so. For example, the previous example overloaded the addition operator, along with the equal and not equal operators—but there was no need to overload the multiplication operator. You shouldn't typically overload every operator you possibly can in your classes, as this may lead to confusing code. Table 7.2 lists the operators that may be overloaded.

TABLE 7.2: OVERLOADABLE OPERATORS

OPERATOR CATEGORY	OPERATORS
Unary	+, -, ++, --, !, ~, `true`, and `false`
Multiplicative	*, /, and %
Additive	+ and -
Bitwise shifts	<< and >>
Relational	<, >, <=, and >=
Equality	==, and !=
Bitwise AND	&
Bitwise exclusive OR	^
Bitwise OR	|

As mentioned earlier, if you overload one of the relational or equality operators, you should also overload the opposite operator. For example, if you overload the equal operator (==), then you should also overload the not equal operator (!=). Similarly, if you overload the less than operator (<), you should also overload the greater than operator (>).

Summary

In this chapter, you learned all about derived classes. Specifically, with *inheritance*, one class is used as the parent of another class. The parent class is known as the *base class*, and the child class is known as the *derived class*. Derived classes inherit the members of their base class. A class is derived from a base class by placing the name of the base class after a colon (:).

In an object-oriented programming language, *polymorphism* means a method in a derived class may contain a different set of statements from the method in the base class; the method in the derived class is said to *override* the method in the base class. A method that may be overridden in a derived class is declared using the `virtual` keyword in the base class and is overridden in the derived class using the `override` keyword.

Depending on the access modifier used with a member in a base class, that member may or may not be accessible to a derived class. In addition, members of a base class may be hidden by members of a derived class using the `new` keyword. This technique is useful when you want to define your own version of a method that has been previously defined as virtual in the base class.

The System.Object class acts as the base class for all classes: All classes are ultimately derived from the System.Object class, including the value types such as int and char. The System.Object class provides a number of useful methods, some of which may be overridden in a class—a common method to override is the ToString() method. Value types may be implicitly converted to objects of the System.Object class using a process known as *boxing*; similarly, objects may be converted to value types using *unboxing*.

You also learned about declaring abstract classes and sealed classes. *Abstract classes* allow you to define classes that represent abstract concepts. *Abstract methods* must be overridden in a derived class, which must also implement the code for the method. You declare a class or method to be abstract using the **abstract** keyword. You use *sealed* classes and methods to restrict inheritance and polymorphism. You might want to use sealed classes and methods in code that you are going to sell, and you don't want someone attempting to add to your code. You declare a class or method as sealed using the **sealed** keyword.

Finally, *operator overloading* allows you to write your own code to handle the operation performed by an operator, instead of just using the default operation. In the next chapter, you'll learn all about interfaces.

Chapter 8

Interfaces

AN *INTERFACE* CONTAINS A list of declarations such as method and property declarations. You can then have your class *implement* a given interface; your class must then define the code for the declarations specified in that interface. By having your class implement an interface, you're guaranteeing that your class contains the code for the items declared in that interface. A struct may also implement an interface, and anything that applies to a class in this chapter also applies to a struct.

This ability to guarantee that a class does something is comparable to a contract in the legal world. For example, when a business accepts a contract for a piece of work, then that business agrees to perform the tasks listed in the contract. Similarly, when a class implements an interface, that class "agrees" to provide the items listed in the interface.

Classes can implement multiple interfaces. This is useful when your class must provide functionality listed in many interfaces.

Featured in this chapter:

- ◆ Defining and Implementing Interfaces
- ◆ Casting Objects to an Interface
- ◆ Using Derived Interfaces
- ◆ Implementing Explicit Interface Members

Defining an Interface

You define an interface using the `interface` keyword, which uses the following simplified syntax:

```
[access-modifier] interface interface-name
{
interface-body
}
```

The syntax elements are as follows:

access-modifier The degree to which the interface is available. The appropriate access modifiers for interfaces are `public` or `internal`. Chapter 5, "Object-Oriented Programming," covered access modifiers, and you can see the list of access modifiers and their descriptions in Table 5.2 of that chapter.

interface-name   The name you assign to your interface. By convention, interface names start with a capital *I*, and the character that follows the *I* is also capitalized—IDrivable, for example.

interface-body   The body of your interface. The body declares the various items for which an implementing class must provide code. An interface can declare methods, properties, indexers, and events, but *not* fields. You'll learn about indexers in Chapter 10, "Arrays and Indexers," and events in Chapter 12, "Delegates and Events." An interface body *only* contains declarations.

Let's consider an example using the familiar car theme. You know a car may be started and stopped, and all cars must "implement" these behaviors. You can model these behaviors using two methods, named Start() and Stop(), respectively. You'll also want to use a property to indicate whether a particular car is currently started; call this property Started. The following IDrivable interface declares these methods and the property (notice that none of the methods contain code):

```
public interface IDrivable
{

  // method declarations
  void Start();
  void Stop();

  // property declaration
  bool Started
  {
    get;
  }

}
```

All of the items declared in an interface are implicitly public, and you mustn't explicitly indicate an access modifier—if you do, you'll get a compilation error. The reason why the items in an interface are public is that the interface is just a list of declarations—the actual code must be defined in a class or struct that implements the interface.

WARNING   *Interfaces cannot declare fields, and you cannot create an instance of an interface. If you attempt to do either, you'll get a compilation error.*

The declarations in an interface don't contain the actual code for the methods or properties; the code is supplied by a class that implements the interface. So, for the IDrivable interface, you can see that the Start() and Stop() methods don't contain any code, and the Started property just indicates that a get method is required. In this example, a set method declaration has been omitted because the underlying field will be set by the Start() and Stop() methods instead—you'll see this in the next section.

Implementing an Interface Using a Class

Once you have an interface, you can implement that interface using a class. You indicate that a class implements an interface by placing a colon (:) after your class name, followed by the name of the interface. Your class must supply all the code for the items declared in the interface.

For example, a class that implements the IDrivable interface must supply code for the Start() and Stop() methods, and the Started property—along with an underlying field named started for this property. The following Car class implements the IDrivable interface, and this class therefore supplies the actual code for the required methods and the property:

```
public class Car : IDrivable
{

  // declare the underlying field used by the Started property
  private bool started = false;

  // implement the Start() method
  public void Start()
  {
    Console.WriteLine("car started");
    started = true;
  }

  // implement the Stop() method
  public void Stop()
  {
    Console.WriteLine("car stopped");
    started = false;
  }

  // implement the Started property
  public bool Started
  {
    get
    {
      return started;
    }
  }

}
```

You can then define a Car object with the usual syntax. For example:

```
Car myCar = new Car();
```

You also use the methods and properties of this Car object in the usual manner. For example:

```
myCar.Start();
Console.WriteLine("myCar.Started = " + myCar.Started);
```

Listing 8.1 illustrates interfaces using these examples.

LISTING 8.1: INTERFACES

```csharp
/*
  Example8_1.cs illustrates interfaces
*/

using System;


// define the IDrivable interface
public interface IDrivable
{

  // method declarations
  void Start();
  void Stop();

  // property declaration
  bool Started
  {
    get;
  }

}


// Car class implements the IDrivable interface
public class Car : IDrivable
{

  // declare the underlying field used by the Started property
  private bool started = false;

  // implement the Start() method
  public void Start()
  {
    Console.WriteLine("car started");
    started = true;
  }

  // implement the Stop() method
  public void Stop()
  {
    Console.WriteLine("car stopped");
    started = false;
  }
```

```
  // implement the Started property
  public bool Started
  {
    get
    {
      return started;
    }
  }

}


class Example8_1
{

  public static void Main()
  {

    // create a Car object
    Car myCar = new Car();

    // call myCar.Start()
    myCar.Start();
    Console.WriteLine("myCar.Started = " + myCar.Started);

    // call myCar.Stop()
    myCar.Stop();
    Console.WriteLine("myCar.Started = " + myCar.Started);

  }

}
```

The output from this program is as follows:

```
car started
myCar.Started = True
car stopped
myCar.Started = False
```

Implementing Multiple Interfaces

A class can implement multiple interfaces. When a class implements multiple interfaces, the class must implement the items declared in all of the interfaces. For example, let's say you have another interface named ISteerable, which declares two methods named TurnRight() and TurnLeft():

```
public interface ISteerable
{
```

```
  // method declarations
  void TurnLeft();
  void TurnRight();

}
```

You can have the Car class implement both the IDrivable and ISteerable interfaces by specifying both interfaces when defining the Car class, separating these interfaces by a comma (,) like so:

```
public class Car : IDrivable, ISteerable
{
  ...
}
```

By indicating that the Car class implements both the IDrivable and ISteerable interfaces, the Car class must implement all of the items declared in these interfaces. The following Car class shows the implementation of the TurnLeft() and TurnRight() methods of the ISteerable interface (the implementation of the Start() and Stop() methods and the Started property of the IDrivable interface are assumed to be the same as before and are therefore omitted):

```
public class Car : IDrivable, ISteerable
{

  // ... implementation of IDrivable interface ...

  // implement the TurnLeft() method of the ISteerable interface
  public void TurnLeft()
  {
    Console.WriteLine("car turning left");
  }

  // implement the TurnRight() method of the ISteerable interface
  public void TurnRight()
  {
    Console.WriteLine("car turning right");
  }

}
```

You can then create a Car object and call the methods for either of the interfaces implemented by the Car class, as shown in Listing 8.2.

LISTING 8.2: IMPLEMENTING MULTIPLE INTERFACES

```
/*
  Example8_2.cs illustrates implementing multiple interfaces
*/
```

```csharp
using System;


// define the IDrivable interface
public interface IDrivable
{

  // method declarations
  void Start();
  void Stop();

  // property declaration
  bool Started
  {
    get;
  }

}


// define the ISteerable interface
public interface ISteerable
{

  // method declarations
  void TurnLeft();
  void TurnRight();

}


// Car class implements the IMovable interface
public class Car : IDrivable, ISteerable
{

  // declare the underlying field used by the
  // Started property of the IDrivable interface
  private bool started = false;

  // implement the Start() method of the IDrivable interface
  public void Start()
  {
    Console.WriteLine("car started");
    started = true;
  }

  // implement the Stop() methodof the IDrivable interface
  public void Stop()
  {
```

```
      Console.WriteLine("car stopped");
      started = false;
    }

    // implement the Started property of the IDrivable interface
    public bool Started
    {
      get
      {
        return started;
      }
    }

    // implement the TurnLeft() method of the ISteerable interface
    public void TurnLeft()
    {
      Console.WriteLine("car turning left");
    }

    // implement the TurnRight() method of the ISteerable interface
    public void TurnRight()
    {
      Console.WriteLine("car turning right");
    }

}


class Example8_2
{

  public static void Main()
  {

    // create a Car object
    Car myCar = new Car();

    // call myCar.Start()
    Console.WriteLine("Calling myCar.Start()");
    myCar.Start();

    // call myCar.TurnLeft()
    Console.WriteLine("Calling myCar.TurnLeft()");
    myCar.TurnLeft();

  }

}
```

The output from this program is as follows:

```
Calling myCar.Start()
car started
Calling myCar.TurnLeft()
car turning left
```

Inheriting from a Class and Implementing Interfaces

You can also write a class that is derived from a base class and that implements one or more interfaces.
For example, you could write a Car class that is derived from a base class named MotorVehicle and
that implements the IDrivable and ISteerable interfaces (see Listing 8.3).

LISTING 8.3: INHERITING FROM A CLASS AND IMPLEMENTING INTERFACES

```
/*
   Example8_3.cs illustrates inheriting from a class and
   implementing multiple interfaces
*/

using System;


public interface IDrivable
{

  // method declarations
  void Start();
  void Stop();

  // property declaration
  bool Started
  {
    get;
  }

}


public interface ISteerable
{

  // method declarations
  void TurnLeft();
  void TurnRight();

}
```

```
public class MotorVehicle
{

  // declare the field
  private string model;

  // define a constructor
  public MotorVehicle(string model)
  {
    this.model = model;
  }

  // declare a property
  public string Model
  {
    get
    {
      return model;
    }
    set
    {
      model = value;
    }
  }

}


// Car class inherits from the MotorVehicle class and
// implements the IDrivable and ISteerable interfaces
public class Car : MotorVehicle, IDrivable, ISteerable
{

  // declare the underlying field used by the
  // Started property of the IDrivable interface
  private bool started = false;

  // define a constructor
  public Car(string model) :
  base(model)  // calls the base class constructor
  {
    // do nothing
  }

  // implement the Start() method of the IDrivable interface
  public void Start()
  {
    Console.WriteLine("car started");
```

```csharp
      started = true;
    }

    // implement the Stop() methodof the IDrivable interface
    public void Stop()
    {
      Console.WriteLine("car stopped");
      started = false;
    }

    // implement the Started property of the IDrivable interface
    public bool Started
    {
      get
      {
        return started;
      }
    }

    // implement the TurnLeft() method of the ISteerable interface
    public void TurnLeft()
    {
      Console.WriteLine("car turning left");
    }

    // implement the TurnRight() method of the ISteerable interface
    public void TurnRight()
    {
      Console.WriteLine("car turning right");
    }

}


class Example8_3
{

  public static void Main()
  {

    // create a Car object
    Car myCar = new Car("MR2");

    Console.WriteLine("myCar.Model = " + myCar.Model);

    // call myCar.Start()
    Console.WriteLine("Calling myCar.Start()");
    myCar.Start();
```

```
    // call myCar.TurnLeft()
    Console.WriteLine("Calling myCar.TurnLeft()");
    myCar.TurnLeft();

  }

}
```

The output from this program is as follows:

```
myCar.Model = MR2
Calling myCar.Start()
car started
Calling myCar.TurnLeft()
car turning left
```

Casting an Object to an Interface

Although you can't create a new object from an interface, you can cast an existing object to an interface. To do this, the class of that object must implement the specified interface—or in technical terms, the object must *support* that interface. The following statement casts the Car object referenced by myCar to IDrivable, and it stores the result in myDrivable:

```
IDrivable myDrivable = (IDrivable) myCar;
```

You can then use myDrivable to call the Start() and Stop() methods and access the Started property. For example:

```
myDrivable.Start();
myDrivable.Stop();
Console.WriteLine("myDrivable.Started = " + myDrivable.Started);
```

Now, before you cast an object to an interface, you must first check whether the object actually supports that interface. You'll see why this is important later in the "Deriving an Interface from Multiple Interfaces" section. You can check whether an object supports an interface using the is operator or the as operator—as shown in the following two sections.

The *is* Operator and Interfaces

You can check if an object supports a specified interface using the is operator. For example, myCar is IDrivable will return true if myCar supports the IDrivable interface; otherwise, false will be returned. The following if statement shows how to use the is operator:

```
if (myCar is IDrivable)
{
  Console.WriteLine("myCar supports IDrivable");
}
```

Because myCar supports the IDrivable interface, the statement contained in the body of this if statement will be executed.

The *as* Operator and Interfaces

The as operator first checks whether an object supports a specified interface. If it does, the as operator then performs the cast and returns the result; if it does not, then the as operator returns null. The following statement uses the as operator to cast myCar to IDrivable, and it stores the result in myDrivable2:

```
IDrivable myDrivable2 = myCar as IDrivable;
```

Because myCar supports the IDrivable interface, the cast is performed successfully. The following if statement checks that myDrivable2 is not null:

```
if (myDrivable2 != null)
{
  myDrivable2.Start();
  myDrivable2.Stop();
  Console.WriteLine("myDrivable2.Started = " + myDrivable2.Started);
}
```

Because myDrivable2 is not null (it contains the result of casting myCar to IDrivable), the if statement block is executed. This block calls the Start() and Stop() methods and displays the Started property for myDrivable2.

Listing 8.4 illustrates casting an object to an interface, along with the is and as operators.

LISTING 8.4: CASTING AN OBJECT TO AN INTERFACE

```
/*
  Example8_4.cs illustrates casting an object
  to an interface
*/

using System;


// define the IDrivable interface
public interface IDrivable
{

  // method declarations
  void Start();
  void Stop();

  // property declaration
  bool Started
```

```csharp
    {
      get;
    }

  }


  // Car class implements the IDrivable interface
  public class Car : IDrivable
  {

    // declare the underlying field used by the Started property
    private bool started = false;

    // implement the Start() method
    public void Start()
    {
      Console.WriteLine("car started");
      started = true;
    }

    // implement the Stop() method
    public void Stop()
    {
      Console.WriteLine("car stopped");
      started = false;
    }

    // implement the Started property
    public bool Started
    {
      get
      {
        return started;
      }
    }

  }


  class Example8_4
  {

    public static void Main()
    {

      // create a Car object
      Car myCar = new Car();
```

```
    // use the is operator to check that myCar supports the
    // IDrivable interface
    if (myCar is IDrivable)
    {
      Console.WriteLine("myCar supports IDrivable");
    }

    // cast the Car object to IDrivable
    IDrivable myDrivable = (IDrivable) myCar;

    // call myDrivable.Start()
    Console.WriteLine("Calling myDrivable.Start()");
    myDrivable.Start();
    Console.WriteLine("myDrivable.Started = " +
      myDrivable.Started);

    // call myDrivable.Stop()
    Console.WriteLine("Calling myDrivable.Stop()");
    myDrivable.Stop();
    Console.WriteLine("myDrivable.Started = " +
      myDrivable.Started);

    // cast the Car object to IDrivable using the as operator
    IDrivable myDrivable2 = myCar as IDrivable;
    if (myDrivable2 != null)
    {
      Console.WriteLine("Calling myDrivable2.Start()");
      myDrivable2.Start();
      Console.WriteLine("Calling myDrivable2.Stop()");
      myDrivable2.Stop();
      Console.WriteLine("myDrivable2.Started = " +
        myDrivable2.Started);
    }

  }

}
```

The output from this program is as follows:

```
myCar supports IDrivable
Calling myDrivable.Start()
car started
myDrivable.Started = True
Calling myDrivable.Stop()
car stopped
myDrivable.Started = False
```

```
Calling myDrivable2.Start()
car started
Calling myDrivable2.Stop()
car stopped
myDrivable2.Started = False
```

Using Derived Interfaces

In the previous chapter, you saw that a class may be derived from a base class—and the derived class inherits the members of the base class. Interfaces may also be derived from one another. One key difference is that an interface can be derived from one *or more* interfaces (a class can only be derived from one class). You'll learn how to derive interfaces from a single interface and multiple interfaces in this section.

Deriving an Interface from One Interface

To derive an interface from a base interface, you place a colon (:) after the derived interface name, followed by the name of the base interface. For example, the following IMovable interface is derived from the IDrivable interface shown earlier:

```
public interface IMovable : IDrivable
{

  // method declarations
  void Accelerate();
  void Brake();

}
```

IMovable inherits the declarations of IDrivable, and it adds two new method declarations: Accelerate() and Brake(). If a class implements the IMovable interface, then it must define the items declared in the IMovable interface. And because IMovable is derived from IDrivable, the class must also define the items listed in IDrivable.

Listing 8.5 illustrates how to derive an interface from one interface.

LISTING 8.5: DERIVING AN INTERFACE FROM ONE INTERFACE

```
/*
  Example8_5.cs illustrates deriving an
  interface from one interface
*/

using System;


// define the IDrivable interface
public interface IDrivable
{
```

```csharp
    // method declarations
    void Start();
    void Stop();

    // property declaration
    bool Started
    {
      get;
    }

}


// define the IMovable interface (derived from IDrivable)
public interface IMovable : IDrivable
{

  // method declarations
  void Accelerate();
  void Brake();

}


// Car class implements the IMovable interface
public class Car : IMovable
{

  // declare the underlying field used by the
  // Started property of the IDrivable interface
  private bool started = false;

  // implement the Start() method of the IDrivable interface
  public void Start()
  {
    Console.WriteLine("car started");
    started = true;
  }

  // implement the Stop() methodof the IDrivable interface
  public void Stop()
  {
    Console.WriteLine("car stopped");
    started = false;
  }
```

```csharp
    // implement the Started property of the IDrivable interface
    public bool Started
    {
      get
      {
        return started;
      }
    }

    // implement the Accelerate() method of the IMovable interface
    public void Accelerate()
    {
      Console.WriteLine("car accelerating");
    }

    // implement the Brake() method of the IMovable interface
    public void Brake()
    {
      Console.WriteLine("car braking");
    }

}


class Example8_5
{

  public static void Main()
  {

    // create a Car object
    Car myCar = new Car();

    // call myCar.Start()
    Console.WriteLine("Calling myCar.Start()");
    myCar.Start();

    // call myCar.Accelerate()
    Console.WriteLine("Calling myCar.Accelerate()");
    myCar.Accelerate();

  }

}
```

The output from this program is as follows:

```
Calling myCar.Start()
car started
Calling myCar.Accelerate()
car accelerating
```

Deriving an Interface from Multiple Interfaces

To derive an interface from multiple base interfaces, you place a colon (:) after the derived interface name, followed by the names of the base interfaces—with each separated by comma (,). For example, the following IMovable interface is derived from both the IDrivable and ISteerable interfaces shown earlier:

```
public interface IMovable : IDrivable, ISteerable
{

  // method declarations
  void Accelerate();
  void Brake();

}
```

This time, IMovable inherits the declarations of IDrivable and ISteerable, and it adds two method declarations: Accelerate() and Brake(). If a class implements the IMovable interface, then it must define the items declared in the IMovable and ISteerable interfaces, as well as the Accelerate() and Brake() methods.

Listing 8.6 illustrates how to derive an interface from multiple interfaces.

LISTING 8.6: DERIVING AN INTERFACE FROM MULTIPLE INTERFACES

```
/*
  Example8_6.cs illustrates deriving an
  interface from multiple interfaces
*/

using System;


// define the IDrivable interface
public interface IDrivable
{

  // method declarations
  void Start();
  void Stop();

  // property declaration
  bool Started
```

```csharp
    {
      get;
    }

}


// define the ISteerable interface
public interface ISteerable
{

  // method declarations
  void TurnLeft();
  void TurnRight();

}


// define the IMovable interface (derived from IDrivable and ISteerable)
public interface IMovable : IDrivable, ISteerable
{

  // method declarations
  void Accelerate();
  void Brake();

}


// Car class implements the IMovable interface
public class Car : IMovable
{

  // declare the underlying field used by the
  // Started property of the IDrivable interface
  private bool started = false;

  // implement the Start() method of the IDrivable interface
  public void Start()
  {
    Console.WriteLine("car started");
    started = true;
  }

  // implement the Stop() methodof the IDrivable interface
  public void Stop()
  {
    Console.WriteLine("car stopped");
```

```csharp
      started = false;
    }

    // implement the Started property of the IDrivable interface
    public bool Started
    {
      get
      {
        return started;
      }
    }

    // implement the TurnLeft() method of the ISteerable interface
    public void TurnLeft()
    {
      Console.WriteLine("car turning left");
    }

    // implement the TurnRight() method of the ISteerable interface
    public void TurnRight()
    {
      Console.WriteLine("car turning right");
    }

    // implement the Accelerate() method of the IMovable interface
    public void Accelerate()
    {
      Console.WriteLine("car accelerating");
    }

    // implement the Brake() method of the IMovable interface
    public void Brake()
    {
      Console.WriteLine("car braking");
    }

}


class Example8_6
{

  public static void Main()
  {

    // create a Car object
    Car myCar = new Car();
```

```
    // call myCar.Start()
    Console.WriteLine("Calling myCar.Start()");
    myCar.Start();

    // call myCar.TurnLeft()
    Console.WriteLine("Calling myCar.TurnLeft()");
    myCar.TurnLeft();

    // call myCar.Accelerate()
    Console.WriteLine("Calling myCar.Accelerate()");
    myCar.Accelerate();

  }

}
```

The output from this program is as follows:

```
Calling myCar.Start()
car started
Calling myCar.TurnLeft()
car turning left
Calling myCar.Accelerate()
car accelerating
```

Understanding Explicit Interface Members

Earlier in this chapter, you saw that a class can implement multiple interfaces. This gives rise to a potential problem when two interfaces declare the same members and a class implements both those interfaces. How do you differentiate between the two identical members?

Implementing Explicit Interface Members

Let's consider an example. The following IDrivable and ISteerable interfaces both declare a method named TurnLeft():

```
public interface IDrivable
{
  void TurnLeft();
}

public interface ISteerable
{
  void TurnLeft();
}
```

If you then declare a class that implements these two interfaces, then both `TurnLeft()` methods must be defined in your class. Because both method declarations are the same, how do you differentiate between the two identical method declarations in your class? The answer is that for one of the methods you must explicitly indicate the interface for which it applies. For example, the following statement specifies that this `TurnLeft()` method implementation is for the `IDrivable` interface:

```
void IDrivable.TurnLeft()
{
   Console.WriteLine("IDrivable implementation of TurnLeft()");
}
```

This is known as an *explicit interface member implementation* because you've explicitly specified the interface for which the member applies—in this case, the member is the `TurnLeft()` method of the `IDrivable` interface. Notice that there's no access modifier for the method—the method is implicitly public and may not be changed.

For the `ISteerable` implementation of `TurnLeft()`, you use the usual syntax for the method implementation. You don't explicitly specify the interface for which the method applies—because the previous statement already did that—and the method implementation is automatically assumed to be for the `ISteerable` interface. The following statement shows the implementation of `TurnLeft()` for the `ISteerable` interface:

```
public void TurnLeft()
{
   Console.WriteLine("ISteerable implementation of TurnLeft()");
}
```

The following `Car` class implements both the `IDrivable` and `ISteerable` interfaces, and it shows both `TurnLeft()` method implementations:

```
public class Car : IDrivable, ISteerable
{

   // explicitly implement the TurnLeft() method of the IDrivable interface
   void IDrivable.TurnLeft()
   {
      Console.WriteLine("IDrivable implementation of TurnLeft()");
   }

   // implement the TurnLeft() method of the ISteerable interface
   public void TurnLeft()
   {
      Console.WriteLine("ISteerable implementation of TurnLeft()");
   }

}
```

Let's take a look at how you call each of the `TurnLeft()` methods implemented by this `Car` class. First, the following statement creates a `Car` object:

```
Car myCar = new Car();
```

Next, the following statement calls the `myCar.TurnLeft()` method:

```
myCar.TurnLeft();
```

This statement calls the `ISteerable` implementation of `TurnLeft()`. To call the `IDrivable` implementation of `TurnLeft()`—the explicitly implemented method—you must first cast `myCar` to `IDrivable` and then call `TurnLeft()`:

```
IDrivable myDrivable = myCar as IDrivable;
myDrivable.TurnLeft();
```

Now, if you had instead explicitly implemented `TurnLeft()` for the `ISteerable` interface, then calling `myCar.TurnLeft()` would call the `IDrivable` implementation of `TurnLeft()`.

If you wanted, you could also cast `myCar` to `ISteerable` and call `TurnLeft()`:

```
ISteerable mySteerable = myCar as ISteerable;
mySteerable.TurnLeft();
```

This has the same effect as calling `myCar.TurnLeft()`.

NOTE   *It is more common that you'll run into the problem of identical members when you write a class derived from two interfaces that are themselves derived from the same base interface. This is an unfortunate side effect of interface inheritance. It can also plague classes but only from the single base class because a derived class cannot inherit from multiple base classes.*

Listing 8.7 illustrates the examples shown in this section.

LISTING 8.7: IMPLEMENTING AN EXPLICIT INTERFACE MEMBER

```
/*
  Example8_7.cs illustrates an explicit interface member
  implementation
*/

using System;


// define the IDrivable interface
public interface IDrivable
{
  void TurnLeft();
}


// define the ISteerable interface
public interface ISteerable
```

```
{
  void TurnLeft();
}

// Car class implements the IMovable interface
public class Car : IDrivable, ISteerable
{

  // explicitly implement the TurnLeft() method of the IDrivable interface
  void IDrivable.TurnLeft()
  {
    Console.WriteLine("IDrivable implementation of TurnLeft()");
  }

  // implement the TurnLeft() method of the ISteerable interface
  public void TurnLeft()
  {
    Console.WriteLine("ISteerable implementation of TurnLeft()");
  }

}


class Example8_7
{

  public static void Main()
  {

    // create a Car object
    Car myCar = new Car();

    // call myCar.TurnLeft()
    Console.WriteLine("Calling myCar.TurnLeft()");
    myCar.TurnLeft();

    // cast myCar to IDrivable
    IDrivable myDrivable = myCar as IDrivable;
    Console.WriteLine("Calling myDrivable.TurnLeft()");
    myDrivable.TurnLeft();

    // cast myCar to ISteerable
    ISteerable mySteerable = myCar as ISteerable;
    Console.WriteLine("Calling mySteerable.TurnLeft()");
    mySteerable.TurnLeft();

  }

}
```

The output from this program is as follows:

```
Calling myCar.TurnLeft()
ISteerable implementation of TurnLeft()
Calling myDrivable.TurnLeft()
IDrivable implementation of TurnLeft()
Calling mySteerable.TurnLeft()
ISteerable implementation of TurnLeft()
```

Hiding Interface Members

In the previous chapter, you saw how derived classes can hide a member of its base class by using the new keyword—this causes a new member to be defined in the derived class and hides the member in its base class. Similarly, a member in a derived interface can hide a member of its base interface.

Let's take a look at an example. The following IDrivable interface declares a method named TurnLeft():

```
public interface IDrivable
{
  void TurnLeft();
}
```

Next, the following ISteerable interface is derived from IDrivable; ISteerable declares a new TurnLeft() method that hides the method in IDrivable:

```
public interface ISteerable : IDrivable
{
  new void TurnLeft();  // hides TurnLeft() in IDrivable
}
```

If you then declare a class that implements ISteerable, then you must explicitly implement one of the TurnLeft() methods in either the IDrivable or ISteerable interface—you can pick either one. For example, the following Car class explicitly implements the TurnLeft() method of the ISteerable interface:

```
public class Car : ISteerable
{

  // explicitly implement the TurnLeft() method of the ISteerable interface
  void ISteerable.TurnLeft()
  {
    Console.WriteLine("ISteerable implementation of TurnLeft()");
  }

  // implement the TurnLeft() method of the IDrivable interface
  public void TurnLeft()
  {
    Console.WriteLine("IDrivable implementation of TurnLeft()");
  }

}
```

Let's take a look at how you call each of the TurnLeft() methods implemented by this Car class. First, the following statement creates a Car object:

```
Car myCar = new Car();
```

Next, the following statement calls the myCar.TurnLeft() method:

```
myCar.TurnLeft();
```

This statement calls the IDrivable implementation of TurnLeft(). To call the ISteerable implementation of TurnLeft()—the explicitly implemented method—you must first cast myCar to ISteerable and then call TurnLeft():

```
ISteerable mySteerable = myCar as ISteerable;
mySteerable.TurnLeft();
```

Now, if you had instead explicitly implemented TurnLeft() for the IDrivable interface, then calling myCar.TurnLeft() would call the ISteerable implementation of TurnLeft().

Listing 8.8 illustrates these examples.

LISTING 8.8: INTERFACE MEMBER HIDING

```csharp
/*
  Example8_8.cs illustrates interface member hiding
*/

using System;


// define the IDrivable interface
public interface IDrivable
{
  void TurnLeft();
}


// define the ISteerable interface (derived from IDrivable)
public interface ISteerable : IDrivable
{
  new void TurnLeft();  // hides TurnLeft() in IDrivable
}

// Car class implements the IMovable interface
public class Car : ISteerable
{

  // explicitly implement the TurnLeft() method of the ISteerable interface
  void ISteerable.TurnLeft()
```

```
    {
      Console.WriteLine("ISteerable implementation of TurnLeft()");
    }

    // implement the TurnLeft() method of the IDrivable interface
    public void TurnLeft()
    {
      Console.WriteLine("IDrivable implementation of TurnLeft()");
    }

  }


  class Example8_8
  {

    public static void Main()
    {

      // create a Car object
      Car myCar = new Car();

      // call myCar.TurnLeft()
      Console.WriteLine("Calling myCar.TurnLeft()");
      myCar.TurnLeft();

      // cast myCar to ISteerable
      ISteerable mySteerable = myCar as ISteerable;
      Console.WriteLine("Calling mySteerable.TurnLeft()");
      mySteerable.TurnLeft();

      // cast myCar to IDrivable
      IDrivable myDrivable = myCar as IDrivable;
      Console.WriteLine("Calling myDrivable.TurnLeft()");
      myDrivable.TurnLeft();

    }

  }
```

The output from this program is as follows:

```
Calling myCar.TurnLeft()
IDrivable implementation of TurnLeft()
Calling mySteerable.TurnLeft()
ISteerable implementation of TurnLeft()
Calling myDrivable.TurnLeft()
IDrivable implementation of TurnLeft()
```

Summary

In this chapter, you learned about *interfaces*. An interface contains a list of declarations such as method and property declarations. You can then have your class *implement* a given interface; your class must then define the code for the declarations specified in that interface. By having your class implement an interface, you're guaranteeing that your class contains the code for the items declared in that interface. You define an interface using the `interface` keyword.

Once you have an interface, you can implement that interface using a class or a struct. You indicate that a class implements an interface by placing a colon (:) after your class name, followed by the name of the interface. Your class must supply all the code for the items declared in the interface.

A class can implement multiple interfaces. When a class implements multiple interfaces, the class must implement the items declared in all of the interfaces. Now, although you can't create a new object from an interface, you can cast an existing object to an interface. To do this, the object must *support* that interface. Interfaces may also be derived from one another. One key difference from a class is that an interface be derived from one *or more* interfaces (a class can only be derived from one class).

Finally, because a class can implement multiple interfaces, this can give rise to a potential problem when two interfaces declare the same member. To differentiate between the two, you must mark one member as *explicitly* implementing one of the identical members. In the next chapter, you'll learn about strings, dates, and times.

Chapter 9

Strings, Dates, Times, and Time Spans

You've already seen examples of strings in earlier chapters. In this chapter, you'll delve deeper into the use of strings and how you manipulate strings in your programs. You'll also see how you can create dynamic strings, which have efficient manipulation methods.

In addition to strings and the other built-in types, you can also represent dates and times in your programs. Examples of using a date and time would be to store a person's birthdate and to record when a financial transaction took place.

You can also represent time intervals in your programs—these are known as *time spans*. An example of a time span is 4 days, 12 minutes, and 10 seconds.

Featured in this chapter:

◆ Introducing String Properties and Methods

◆ Using Dynamic Strings

◆ Representing Dates and Times

◆ Representing Time Spans

Using Strings

You often need to store a series of characters in your programs. For this purpose, you use a string to represent characters, which are stored as *Unicode*. Unicode is the standard for encoding most of the world's written languages, and it uses 16 bits to represent each letter. Although you've already seen examples of creating strings in previous chapters, you'll see more examples in this section to formalize their treatment. Later, you'll see the various methods you can use to manipulate strings.

Creating Strings

The following example creates a string named myString:

```
string myString = "To be or not to be";
```

You can embed escape characters in your strings (Table 2.4 in Chapter 2, "Basic C# Programming," lists the escape characters). For example, the following string contains a tab character, which is specified using the \t escape character:

```
string myString2 = "...\t that is the question";
```

When this string is displayed, a tab character will appear after the ellipsis:

```
...    that is the question
```

You can also create *verbatim* strings, meaning that your string's characters are to be treated "as is." In a verbatim string, characters that make up an escape character are treated as regular characters. Verbatim strings may also be split over multiple lines. You indicate that your string is to be treated verbatim by placing an at sign (@) at the start of the string. In the following example, the verbatim string contains \t and is split across multiple lines:

```
string myString3 = @"\t Friends, Romans, countrymen,
lend me your ears";
```

When this string is displayed, it will appear as follows:

```
\t Friends, Romans, countrymen,
lend me your ears
```

Using *String* Properties and Methods

Strings are actually objects of the System.String class; this class contains properties and a rich set of methods you can use in your programs to manipulate strings.

NOTE   *In fact, all the built-in types are represented using classes or structs, and they therefore have properties and methods you can use. For example, the* int *type is represented using the* System.Int32 *struct, the* double *type is represented using the* System.Double *struct, and* bool *is represented using the* System.Boolean *struct. You can view the properties and methods for all the types in the .NET reference documentation.*

Table 9.1 lists the Length public property of the String class.

TABLE 9.1: String Length PROPERTY

PROPERTY	TYPE	DESCRIPTION
Length	int	Gets the number of characters in the string

The String class also contains a number of public methods, as shown in Table 9.2.

TABLE 9.2: String Methods

Method	Return Type	Description
Compare() (static)	int	Overloaded. Compares the characters stored in two strings, taking into account the national language or culture.
CompareOrdinal() (static)	int	Overloaded. Compares the characters stored in two strings, without taking into account the national language or culture.
Concat() (static)	string	Overloaded. Returns the result of concatenating one or more strings. The returned string is built up by adding each string to the end of the previous string. The overloaded addition operator (+) also concatenates strings.
Copy() (static)	string	Returns a new string that is a copy of the supplied string. The overloaded assignment operator (=) also copies a string.
Equals() (static and instance versions)	bool	Overloaded. Returns a bool that specifies whether two strings are equal. The overloaded equal to operator (==) also checks whether two strings are equal.
Format() (static)	string	Overloaded. Returns a string formatted according to a supplied format.
Intern() (static)	string	Returns a system reference to the supplied string.
IsInterned() (static)	string	Returns a reference to the supplied string.
Join() (static)	string	Overloaded. Returns a string that is built up by taking the elements from an array of strings, along with a separator string. The separator is inserted between each string element in the returned string. Chapter 10, "Arrays and Indexers," covers arrays.
Clone()	Object	Returns a reference to the string.
CompareTo()	int	Overloaded. Compares the string with a supplied string.
CopyTo()	void	Copies a specified number of characters from the string to a specified position in an array of characters.
EndsWith()	bool	Returns a bool indicating whether the string has a supplied string at the end.
GetEnumerator()	CharEnumerator	Returns an enumerator that can iterate through the characters stored in the string. Enumerators are covered in Chapter 11, "Collections."
GetHashCode()	int	Returns a hash code for the string.
GetType() (inherited from Object)	Type	Returns the type of the current instance.

Continued on next page

TABLE 9.2: String METHODS *(continued)*

METHOD	RETURN TYPE	DESCRIPTION
GetTypeCode()	TypeCode	Returns the type code for the string.
IndexOf()	int	Overloaded. Returns the index of the first occurrence of a specified substring or characters within the string. Indexes start at zero. A *substring* is a portion of the original string.
IndexOfAny()	int	Overloaded. Returns the index of the first occurrence of any character in a supplied array of characters.
Insert()	string	Inserts a supplied string into the string at a specified index.
LastIndexOf()	int	Overloaded. Returns the index of the last occurrence of a supplied substring or character in the string.
LastIndexOfAny()	int	Overloaded. Returns the index of the last occurrence of any character in a supplied array of characters.
PadLeft()	string	Overloaded. Right-aligns the characters in the string, padding to the left with spaces or a specified character for a specified total length for the new string.
PadRight()	string	Overloaded. Left-aligns the characters in the string, padding to the right with spaces or a specified character for a specified total length for the new string.
Remove()	string	Removes a specified number of characters from the string, starting at a specified index in the string.
Replace()	string	Overloaded. Replaces all occurrences of a supplied substring or character with another substring or character.
Split()	string[]	Overloaded. Splits up the string into an array of strings using a supplied separator. The array of strings is then returned.
StartsWith()	bool	Returns a bool indicating whether the string has a supplied string at the start.
Substring()	string	Overloaded. Returns a substring from the string.
ToCharArray()	char[]	Overloaded. Copies the characters from the string to a supplied character array.
ToLower()	string	Overloaded. Returns a copy of the string with all the characters converted to lowercase.
ToString()	string	Overloaded. Returns the value of the string.
ToUpper()	string	Overloaded. Returns a copy of the string with all the characters converted to uppercase.

Continued on next page

TABLE 9.2: String METHODS *(continued)*

METHOD	RETURN TYPE	DESCRIPTION
Trim()	string	Overloaded. Removes spaces or specified characters from the beginning and end of the string.
TrimEnd()	string	Removes the specified characters (or spaces) from the end of the string.
TrimStart()	string	Removes the specified characters (or spaces) from the beginning of the string.

The following sections illustrate the Length property and some of the methods shown in Table 9.2.

READING INDIVIDUAL CHARACTERS FROM A STRING USING THE *LENGTH* PROPERTY

You can use the Length property to get the number of characters in a string. The Length property returns an int value. In the following example, myString.Length is displayed:

```
Console.WriteLine(myString.Length);
```

This example displays the following:

```
18
```

This result is the total number of characters in myString, which is set to "To be or not to be".

You can read the individual characters from your string by specifying the position index of the character in the string (the first characters has an index of zero). For example, myString is set to "To be or not to be", and myString[0] is T.

You can use the Length property in a for loop to read all the characters in a string. For example, the following for loop displays all the characters in myString:

```
for (int count = 0; count < myString.Length; count++)
{
  Console.WriteLine("myString[" + count + "] = " +
    myString[count]);
}
```

This example displays the following:

```
myString[0] = T
myString[1] = o
myString[2] =
myString[3] = b
myString[4] = e
myString[5] =
myString[6] = o
myString[7] = r
myString[8] =
myString[9] = n
myString[10] = o
```

```
myString[11] = t
myString[12] =
myString[13] = t
myString[14] = o
myString[15] =
myString[16] = b
myString[17] = e
```

COMPARING TWO STRINGS USING THE *COMPARE()* METHOD

You can use the Compare() method to compare the characters stored in two strings, taking into account the national language or culture. The Compare() method returns an int that specifies whether the first string is greater than, equal to, or less than the second string.

The comparison is performed alphabetically on letters and numerically on any numbers that appear in the strings. The Compare() method uses the following rules to determine the int value returned:

◆ If the first string is greater than the second string, then 1 is returned.

◆ If the first string is equal to the second string, then 0 is returned.

◆ If the first string is less than the second string, then −1 is returned.

The Compare() method is overloaded and therefore contains several versions you can call, each with different parameters (method overloading was covered in Chapter 5, "Object-Oriented Programming"). Also, because the Compare() method is static, this method belongs to the String class; therefore, you call the Compare() method using the String class, rather than an actual string object. The simplest version of Compare() accepts two string parameters and uses the following syntax:

```
String.Compare(string1, string2)
```

where *string1* and *string2* are the strings you want to compare.

The following example shows the use of this version of Compare():

```
int result = String.Compare("bbc", "abc");
```

Because "bbc" is alphabetically greater than "abc", Compare() returns 1, which is then stored in the int variable result.

In the next example, the two strings are switched in the call to Compare() and therefore Compare() returns −1:

```
result = String.Compare("abc", "bbc");
```

Next, two identical strings are compared—and therefore Compare() returns 0:

```
result = String.Compare("bbc", "bbc");
```

Using the Case of Strings in the Comparison

Another version of Compare() accepts a bool parameter that specifies whether you want to also use the case of the two supplied strings in the comparison. This version of Compare() uses the following syntax:

```
String.Compare(string1, string2, ignoreCase)
```

where *ignoreCase* is a `bool` that specifies whether you want to use the case of *string1* and *string2* in the comparison. If you set *ignoreCase* to `true`, then the case of the two strings is not considered in the comparison (this is the default). If you set *ignoreCase* to `false`, then the case of the strings is considered in the comparison.

In the following example, `Compare()` returns 0 because case is ignored when comparing `"bbc"` and `"BBC"`:

```
result = String.Compare("bbc", "BBC", true);
```

But `Compare()` returns −1 in the next example because `"bbc"` is less than `"BBC"` when case isn't ignored:

```
result = String.Compare("bbc", "BBC", false);
```

Comparing Parts of Strings

You can also compare parts of strings, known as *substrings*, by specifying the indexes to start comparison and the maximum number of characters to compare in each string passed to `Compare()`. This version of `Compare()` uses the following syntax:

```
String.Compare(string1, index1, string2, index2, numberOfChars)
```

where *index1* and *index2* are `int` parameters that specify the indexes to start at in *string1* and *string2*, respectively, and *numberOfChars* is an `int` parameter that specifies the maximum number of characters to compare in each string.

In the following example, the `"World"` parts of two strings are compared, and `Compare()` returns 0 because both parts of the strings are equal:

```
result = String.Compare("Hello World", 6, "Goodbye World", 8, 5);
```

Other overloaded versions of `Compare()` enable you to use a `System.Globalization.CultureInfo` object in the comparison. The `CultureInfo` class represents information about a specific culture, such as the language, the writing system, and the calendar used by a culture. You'll learn more about the `CultureInfo` class in Chapter 21, "Other Classes in the Base Class Library."

CONCATENATING STRINGS USING THE *CONCAT()* METHOD

You can use the static `Concat()` method to concatenate strings together. The `Concat()` method returns a new string that is built up by adding each supplied string to the end of the previous one. `Concat()` is overloaded, and the simplest version accepts two strings using the following syntax:

```
String.Concat(string1, string2)
```

where *string1* and *string2* are the strings you want to concatenate.

The following example uses this version of `Concat()` to concatenate two strings, `"Friends, "` and `"Romans"`, storing the returned string in `myString4`:

```
string myString4 = String.Concat("Friends, ", "Romans");
```

The string `"Friends, Romans"` will be stored in `myString4`.

You can pass any number of strings to Concat(), and the following example passes three strings to Concat():

```
string myString5 = String.Concat("Friends, ", "Romans, ", "and countrymen");
```

The string "Friends, Romans, and countrymen" will be stored in myString5.

NOTE *As you'll see later in the "Creating Dynamic Strings" section, the* StringBuilder *class is more efficient when you have to concatenate a lot of strings.*

CONCATENATING STRINGS USING THE OVERLOADED ADDITION OPERATOR

You can also use the overloaded addition operator (+) to concatenate strings. For example:

```
string myString6 = "To be, " + "or not to be";
```

The string "To be, or not to be" will be stored in myString6.

COPYING STRINGS USING THE *COPY()* METHOD

You can use the static Copy() method to copy a specified string. The Copy() method uses the following syntax:

```
String.Copy(string1)
```

where *string1* is the string you want to copy.

The following example shows the use of the Copy() method to copy myString4 to myString7:

```
string myString7 = String.Copy(myString4);
```

COPYING STRINGS USING THE OVERLOADED ASSIGNMENT OPERATOR

You can also copy strings using the overloaded assignment operator (=) to copy one string to another. For example:

```
myString7 = myString4;
```

CHECKING IF TWO STRINGS ARE EQUAL USING THE *EQUALS()* METHOD

You can use the Equals() method to check whether two strings are equal. The Equals() method returns a bool and has a static version as well as an instance version. You call the static version of Equals() through the String class, and it accepts two string parameters that are checked to see if they are the same. The syntax for the static version of Equals() is:

```
String.Equals(string1, string2)
```

where *string1* and *string2* are the two strings you want to compare.

In the following example, Equals() returns true because the two strings are equal:

```
bool boolResult = String.Equals("bbc", "bbc");
```

You call the instance version of Equals() using an actual string, and it compares that string to the supplied string parameter. The syntax for this version of Equals() is:

```
string1.Equals(string2)
```

where *string1* and *string2* are the two strings you want to compare.

In the following example, Equals() returns false because the contents of myString and myString2 are different:

```
boolResult = myString.Equals(myString2);
```

CHECKING IF TWO STRINGS ARE EQUAL USING THE OVERLOADED EQUAL TO OPERATOR

You can also use the overloaded equal to operator (==) to check if two strings are equal. In the following example, boolResult is set to false because the contents of myString and myString2 are different:

```
boolResult = myString == myString2;
```

FORMATTING STRINGS USING THE *FORMAT()* METHOD

You can use the overloaded static Format() method to return a string formatted according to a specified format. One use for the Format() method is to format a string containing a floating-point number, as shown in the following example:

```
float myFloat = 1234.56789f;
string myString8 = String.Format("{0, 10:f3}", myFloat);
```

The format is "{0, 10:f3}", meaning that the string containing myFloat is to be formatted with a width of 10, and myFloat is to be rounded to 3 decimal places; myString8 will be set to "   1234.568" (with two spaces in front).

NOTE   *Refer to Chapter 2 for details on format strings.*

JOINING MULTIPLE STRINGS TOGETHER USING THE *JOIN()* METHOD

You can use the static Join() method to build up a new string by joining the elements from an array of strings, along with a separator string. The separator is inserted between each string element in the new string.

Although the details of arrays are covered in Chapter 10, the basics are easy to understand. The following example creates an array of strings:

```
string[] myStrings = {"To", "be", "or", "not", "to", "be"};
```

There are six string elements in myStrings, with myStrings[0] set to "To", myStrings[1] set to "be", and so on up to myStrings[5] that is also set to "be".

The Join() method is overloaded, and its simplest version accepts a string containing your separator and an array of strings using the following syntax:

```
String.Join(separator, stringArray)
```

where *separator* is the string used to separate the strings contained in *stringArray*.

In the following example, `Join()` returns a string containing all the strings in `myStrings`, with each string separated by a period (`.`):

```
string myString9 = String.Join(".", myStrings);
```

After this statement is run, `myString9` will contain `"To.be.or.not.to.be"`.

SPLITTING STRINGS USING THE *SPLIT()* METHOD

You can use the `Split()` method to split up a string into an array of strings, using a separator to identify where your original string is to be split. The array of strings is then returned by `Split()`. The `Split()` method is overloaded, and its simplest version uses the following syntax:

```
originalString.Split(separator)
```

where *separator* is the string used to separate the strings contained in *originalString*.

In the following example, the `Split()` method splits `myString9` up into an array of strings using a period (`.`) as the separator:

```
myStrings = myString9.Split('.');
```

You can then use the following `foreach` loop to display the strings in the `myStrings` array:

```
foreach (string mySplitString in myStrings)
{
  Console.WriteLine("mySplitString = " + mySplitString);
}
```

This displays the following:
```
mySplitString = To
mySplitString = be
mySplitString = or
mySplitString = not
mySplitString = to
mySplitString = be
```

CHECKING THE START AND END OF A STRING USING THE *STARTSWITH()* AND *ENDSWITH()* METHODS

You can use the `StartsWith()` and `EndsWith()` methods to check whether a string contains a specified substring at its start or end. The `StartsWith()` and `EndsWith()` methods both return a `bool`. The syntax for these methods is:

```
string1.StartsWith(substring)
string1.EndsWith(substring)
```

where *substring* is the string to search for in *string1*.

Let's consider an example. Earlier, `myString` was set to `"To be or not to be"`, and the following examples use `StartsWith()` and `EndsWith()` to check if `myString` starts with `"To"` and ends with `"be"`:

```
if (myString.StartsWith("To"))
{
  Console.WriteLine("myString starts with \"To\"");
}
```

```
if (myString.EndsWith("be"))
{
  Console.WriteLine("myString ends with \"be\"");
}
```

Because myString does start with "To" and end with "be", the StartsWith() and EndsWith() methods both return true.

TIP   *To add quotes within a string, you put a backslash (\\) in front of the quotes. That way, the string contains the actual quotes, rather than terminating the string. You can see this in the previous example that displays strings with quotes. You can also use the backslash character to specify escape characters. You can see the list of escape characters in Table 2.4 of Chapter 2.*

FINDING SUBSTRINGS AND CHARACTERS IN A STRING USING THE *INDEXOF()* AND *LASTINDEXOF()* METHODS

You can use IndexOf() and LastIndexOf() methods to get the index of a supplied substring or a character within a string. The IndexOf() method finds the first occurrence of the substring or character, and LastIndexOf() finds the last occurrence. Both methods return an int index, starting at 0. If the substring or character isn't found in the string, then the methods return −1.

The IndexOf() and LastIndexOf() methods are overloaded, and the simplest versions accept a substring or character value using the following syntax:

```
string1.IndexOf(value)
string1.LastIndexOf(value)
```

where *value* is the substring or character for which to search *string1*.

The following examples show these versions of IndexOf() and LastIndexOf() to search for "be" in myString:

```
int index1 = myString.IndexOf("be");
int index2 = myString.LastIndexOf("be");
```

Because myString contains "To be or not to be", index1 is set to 3 because "be" first occurs at index 3 (remember that indexes start at 0). Similarly, index2 is set to 16 because "be" last occurs at index 16.

The following examples use IndexOf() and LastIndexOf() to search for 'b' in myString:

```
index1 = myString.IndexOf('b');
index2 = myString.LastIndexOf('b');
```

Because 'b' first occurs at index 3, and last occurs at index 16, index1 and index2 are set to 3 and 16, respectively.

Another version of IndexOf() and LastIndexOf() allows you to start searching at a specified index of a string:

```
string1.IndexOf(value, startIndex)
string1.LastIndexOf(value, startIndex)
```

where *startIndex* is the index to start searching *string1* for *value*.

You can also specify the number of characters in the string to search using the following syntax:

```
string1.IndexOf(value, startIndex, numberOfChars)
string1.LastIndexOf(value, startIndex numberOfChars)
```

where *numberOfChars* is the number of characters in *string1* to search for *value*, starting at *startIndex* of *string1*.

FINDING CHARACTERS USING THE *INDEXOFANY()* AND *LASTINDEXOFANY()* METHODS

You can use the IndexOfAny() and LastIndexOfAny() methods to get the index of the first and last occurrence of any character in a supplied array of characters. Both methods are overloaded and return an int index.

The simplest versions of IndexOfAny() and LastIndexOfAny() use the following syntax:

```
string1.IndexOfAny(charArray)
string1.LastIndexOfAny(charArray)
```

where *charArray* is an array of characters to search for in *string1*.

The following example shows this version of IndexOf() and LastIndexOf():

```
char[] myChars = {'b', 'e'};
int index1 = myString.IndexOfAny(myChars);
int index2 = myString.LastIndexOfAny(myChars);
```

Because myString contains "To be or not to be", index1 is set to 3 because 'b' first occurs at index 3. Similarly, index2 is set to 17 because 'b' last occurs at index 17.

Another version of IndexOfAny() and LastIndexOfAny() allows you to start searching from a specified index of a string; this version of these methods use the following syntax:

```
string1.IndexOfAny(charArray, startIndex)
string1.LastIndexOfAny(charArray, startIndex)
```

where *startIndex* is the index to start searching *string1* for the characters in *charArray*.

You can also specify the number of characters in the string to search using the following syntax:

```
string1.IndexOfAny(charArray, startIndex, numberOfChars)
string1.LastIndexOfAny(charArray, startIndex numberOfChars)
```

where *numberOfChars* is the number of characters in *string1* to search for the characters in *charArray*, starting at *startIndex* of *string1*.

NOTE   *In Appendix C, "Regular Expressions," you'll see how you can perform complex searches of strings.*

INSERTING A SUBSTRING INTO A STRING USING THE *INSERT()* METHOD

You can use the Insert() method to insert a supplied substring into a string at a specified index. The Insert() method returns a new string and uses the following syntax:

```
string1.Insert(index, substring)
```

where *substring* is the string to be inserted into *string1*, and *index* is the position in *string1* to insert *substring*.

The following example shows the use of the Insert() method:

```
string myString10 = myString.Insert(6, "friends, ");
```

Because myString contains "To be or not to be", myString10 is set to "To be friends, or not to be". Notice that the substring "friends" is inserted at index 6.

REMOVING CHARACTERS FROM A STRING USING THE *REMOVE()* METHOD

You can use the Remove() method to remove a specified number of characters from a string starting at specified index. This method returns a new string and has the following syntax:

```
string1.Remove(startIndex, numberOfChars)
```

where *startIndex* is the index in *string1* to start removing characters, and *numberOfChars* is the number of characters to remove.

The following example shows the use of the Remove() method:

```
string myString11 = myString10.Remove(14, 7);
```

Now, myString10 contains "To be friends, or not to be"; and so myString11 is set to "To be friends, to be". Notice that " or not" has been removed (these are the seven characters that start at index 14).

REPLACING CHARACTERS IN A STRING USING THE *REPLACE()* METHOD

You can use the Replace() method to replace all occurrences of a supplied substring or character with another substring or character. The Replace() method returns a new string and is overloaded. When replacing characters, the syntax of the Replace() method is:

```
string1.Replace(oldChar, newChar)
```

where *string1* is the string to be modified, and *oldChar* is the character to be replaced by *newChar*.

The following example uses this version of the Replace() method to replace any commas (,) in myString11 with question marks (?):

```
string myString12 = myString11.Replace(',', '?');
```

Because myString11 contains "To be friends, to be", and the comma is replaced by a question mark, myString12 is set to "To be friends? to be". Notice the comma has been replaced by a question mark.

The other version of Replace() replaces one substring with another and uses the following syntax:

```
string1.Replace(oldSubstring, newSubstring)
```

where *string1* is the string to be modified, and *oldSubstring* is the substring to be replaced by *newSubstring*.

The following example uses this version of the Replace() method to replace "to be" in myString12 with "Or not to be friends":

```
string myString13 = myString12.Replace("to be", "Or not to be friends");
```

Because myString12 contains "To be friends? to be", myString13 is set to "To be friends? Or not to be friends".

RIGHT-ALIGNING STRINGS USING THE *PADLEFT()* METHOD

You can use the PadLeft() method to right-align the characters in a string, padding the string with specified characters or spaces on the left. The PadLeft() method returns a new string, and this method is overloaded. The simplest version of PadLeft() pads a string with spaces for a specified total length and uses the following syntax:

```
string1.PadLeft(length)
```

where *string1* is the string to be padded with spaces, and *length* is an int that specifies the total length for the returned string.

The following example uses PadLeft() to right-align myString with spaces for a total length of 20 characters:

```
string myString14 = '(' + myString.PadLeft(20) + ')';
```

Because myString contains "To be or not to be", myString14 is set to "(To be or not to be)" (with two spaces after the open bracket).

The other version of PadLeft() pads a string with specified characters for a total length and uses the following syntax:

```
string1.PadLeft(length, padChar)
```

where *string1* is the string to be padded with *padChar* characters, and *length* is an int that specifies the total length for the returned string.

The following example uses this version of PadLeft() to right-align myString with periods for a total length of 20 characters:

```
string myString15 = '(' + myString.PadLeft(20, '.') + ')';
```

Because myString contains "To be or not to be", myString15 is set to "(..To be or not to be)".

LEFT-ALIGNING STRINGS USING THE *PADRIGHT()* METHOD

The PadRight() method works in the opposite manner to PadLeft(), and you use it to left-align the characters in a string. Like PadLeft(), PadRight() also has two versions, and the following examples illustrate their use:

```
string myString16 = '(' + myString.PadRight(20) + ')';
string myString17 = '(' + myString.PadRight(20, '.') + ')';
```

This results in myString16 and myString17 being set to the following respective strings:

```
"(To be or not to be  )"
"(To be or not to be..)"
```

TRIMMING THE START AND END OF A STRING USING THE *TRIM()* METHOD

You can use the Trim() method to remove spaces or specified characters from the beginning and end of a string. This method returns a string and is overloaded. The simplest version of Trim() removes spaces from the string and uses the following syntax:

```
string1.Trim()
```

where *string1* is the string to be trimmed.

The following example uses this version of Trim() to remove spaces from a string:

```
string myString18 = '(' + "  Whitespace  ".Trim() + ')';
```

In this example, myString18 is set to "(Whitespace)".

TRIMMING THE START OF A STRING USING THE *TRIMSTART()* METHOD

The TrimStart() method operates in the same manner as Trim(), except that it removes characters or spaces from the start of a string. For example:

```
string myString19 = '(' + "  Whitespace  ".TrimStart() + ')';
```

Here, myString19 is set to "(Whitespace)".

TRIMMING THE END OF A STRING USING THE *TRIMEND()* METHOD

The TrimEnd() method removes characters or spaces from the end of a string. For example:

```
string myString20 = '(' + "  Whitespace  ".TrimEnd() + ')';
```

Here, myString20 is set to "(Whitespace)".

RETRIEVING SUBSTRINGS FROM A STRING USING THE *SUBSTRING()* METHOD

You can use the Substring() method to retrieve a substring from a string. The Substring() method returns a string and is overloaded. The simplest version of Substring() returns the substring starting at a specified index and uses the following syntax:

```
string1.Substring(index)
```

where *index* is an int that specifies the character position to start reading from *string1*.

The following example uses this version of Substring() to retrieve a substring from myString, starting at index 3:

```
string myString21 = myString.Substring(3);
```

Because myString is set to "To be or not to be", myString21 is set to "be or not to be".

The other version of Substring() uses a second int parameter to specify the number of characters to read and uses the following syntax:

```
string1.Substring(index, numberOfChars)
```

The following example uses this version of Substring():

```
string myString22 = myString.Substring(3, 2);
```

Here, myString22 is set to "be".

CONVERTING THE CASE OF A STRING USING THE *TOUPPER()* AND *TOLOWER()* METHODS

You can use the ToUpper() and ToLower() methods to convert the case of a string. ToUpper() returns the string's characters in uppercase, and ToLower() returns the string's characters in lowercase. Both methods return a new string and are overloaded. The simplest versions of these methods use the following syntax:

```
string1.ToUpper();
string1.ToLower();
```

The following examples use the ToUpper() and ToLower() methods:

```
string myString23 = myString.ToUpper();
string myString24 = myString.ToLower();
```

This results in myString23 and myString24 being set to the following respective strings:

```
"TO BE OR NOT TO BE"
"to be or not to be"
```

Listing 9.1 illustrates the use of strings.

LISTING 9.1: STRINGS

```
/*
  Example9_1.cs illustrates the use of strings
*/

using System;

class Example9_1
{

  public static void Main()
  {

    // create some strings
    string myString = "To be or not to be";
    string myString2 = "...\t that is the question";
    string myString3 = @"\t Friends, Romans, countrymen,
lend me your ears";

    // display the strings and their Length properties
    Console.WriteLine("myString = " + myString);
    Console.WriteLine("myString.Length = " + myString.Length);
```

```
Console.WriteLine("myString2 = " + myString2);
Console.WriteLine("myString2.Length = " + myString2.Length);
Console.WriteLine("myString3 = " + myString3);
Console.WriteLine("myString3.Length = " + myString3.Length);

// display all the characters in myString using a for loop
for (int count = 0; count < myString.Length; count++)
{
  Console.WriteLine("myString[" + count + "] = " + myString[count]);
}

// use the Compare() method to compare strings
int result;
result = String.Compare("bbc", "abc");
Console.WriteLine("String.Compare(\"bbc\", \"abc\") = " + result);
result = String.Compare("abc", "bbc");
Console.WriteLine("String.Compare(\"abc\", \"bbc\") = " + result);
result = String.Compare("bbc", "bbc");
Console.WriteLine("String.Compare(\"bbc\", \"bbc\") = " + result);
result = String.Compare("bbc", "BBC", true);
Console.WriteLine("String.Compare(\"bbc\", \"BBC\", true) = " + result);
result = String.Compare("bbc", "BBC", false);
Console.WriteLine("String.Compare(\"bbc\", \"BBC\", false) = " + result);
result = String.Compare("Hello World", 6, "Goodbye World", 8, 5);
Console.WriteLine("String.Compare(\"Hello World\", 6, " +
  "\"Goodbye World\", 8, 5) = " + result);

// use the Concat() method to concatenate strings
string myString4 = String.Concat("Friends, ", "Romans");
Console.WriteLine("String.Concat(\"Friends, \", \"Romans\") = "
  + myString4);
string myString5 = String.Concat("Friends, ", "Romans, ", "and countrymen");
Console.WriteLine("String.Concat(\"Friends, \", \"Romans, \", " +
  "\"and countrymen\") = " + myString5);

// use the addition operator (+) to concatenate strings
string myString6 = "To be, " + "or not to be";
Console.WriteLine("\"To be, \" + \"or not to be\" = " + myString6);

// use the Copy() method to copy a string
Console.WriteLine("myString4 = " + myString4);
Console.WriteLine("Copying myString4 to myString7 using Copy()");
string myString7 = String.Copy(myString4);
Console.WriteLine("myString7 = " + myString7);

// use the Equals() method and equality operator to check if
// two strings are equal
bool boolResult;
```

```
boolResult = String.Equals("bbc", "bbc");
Console.WriteLine("String.Equals(\"bbc\", \"bbc\") is " + boolResult);
boolResult = myString.Equals(myString2);
Console.WriteLine("myString.Equals(myString2) is " + boolResult);
boolResult = myString == myString2;
Console.WriteLine("myString == myString2 is " + boolResult);

// use the Format() method to format a string
float myFloat = 1234.56789f;
string myString8 = String.Format("{0, 10:f3}", myFloat);
Console.WriteLine("String.Format(\"{0, 10:f3}\", myFloat) = " +
  myString8);

// use the Join() method to join strings
string[] myStrings = {"To", "be", "or", "not", "to", "be"};
string myString9 = String.Join(".", myStrings);
Console.WriteLine("myString9 = " + myString9);

// use the Split() method to split strings
myStrings = myString9.Split('.');
foreach (string mySplitString in myStrings)
{
  Console.WriteLine("mySplitString = " + mySplitString);
}

// use the StartsWith() and EndsWith() methods to check if
// a string contains a specified substring at the start and end
Console.WriteLine("myString = " + myString);
if (myString.StartsWith("To"))
{
  Console.WriteLine("myString starts with \"To\"");
}
if (myString.EndsWith("be"))
{
  Console.WriteLine("myString ends with \"be\"");
}

// use the IndexOf() and LastIndexOf() methods to search
// for substrings and characters; IndexOf() returns the first
// occurrence of a substring or character, and LastIndexOf()
// returns the last occurrence of a substring or character
int index = myString.IndexOf("be");
Console.WriteLine("\"be\" first occurs at index "
  + index + " of myString");
index = myString.LastIndexOf("be");
Console.WriteLine("\"be\" last occurs at index "
  + index + " of myString");
index = myString.IndexOf('b');
```

```
Console.WriteLine("'b' first occurs at index "
  + index + " of myString");
index = myString.LastIndexOf('b');
Console.WriteLine("'b' last occurs at index "
  + index + " of myString");

// use the IndexOfAny() and LastIndexOfAny() methods to search
// for character arrays in a string
char[] myChars = {'b', 'e'};
index = myString.IndexOfAny(myChars);
Console.WriteLine("'b' and 'e' occur at index "
  + index + " of myString");
index = myString.LastIndexOfAny(myChars);
Console.WriteLine("'b' and 'e' last occur at index "
  + index + " of myString");

// use the Insert(), Remove(), and Replace() methods to
// modify strings
string myString10 = myString.Insert(6, "friends, ");
Console.WriteLine("myString.Insert(6, \"friends, \") = " +
  myString10);
string myString11 = myString10.Remove(14, 7);
Console.WriteLine("myString10.Remove(14, 7) = " +
  myString11);
string myString12 = myString11.Replace(',', '?');
Console.WriteLine("myString11.Replace(',', '?') = " +
  myString12);
string myString13 =
  myString12.Replace("to be", "Or not to be friends");
Console.WriteLine(
  "myString12.Replace(\"to be\", \"Or not to be friends\") = " +
  myString13
);

// use the PadLeft() and PadRight() methods to align strings
string myString14 = '(' + myString.PadLeft(20) + ')';
Console.WriteLine("'(' + myString.PadLeft(20) + ')' = " +
  myString14);
string myString15 = '(' + myString.PadLeft(20, '.') + ')';
Console.WriteLine("'(' + myString.PadLeft(20, '.') = " +
  myString15);
string myString16 = '(' + myString.PadRight(20) + ')';
Console.WriteLine("'(' + myString.PadRight(20) + ')' = " +
  myString16);
string myString17 = '(' + myString.PadRight(20, '.') + ')';
Console.WriteLine("'(' + myString.PadRight(20, '.') + ')' = " +
  myString17);
```

```
// use the Trim(), TrimStart(), and TrimEnd() methods to
// trim strings
string myString18 = '(' + "  Whitespace  ".Trim() + ')';
Console.WriteLine("'(' + \"  Whitespace  \".Trim() + ')' = " +
  myString18);
string myString19 = '(' + "  Whitespace  ".TrimStart() + ')';
Console.WriteLine("'(' + \"  Whitespace  \".TrimStart() + ')' = " +
  myString19);
string myString20 = '(' + "  Whitespace  ".TrimEnd() + ')';
Console.WriteLine("'(' + \"  Whitespace  \".TrimEnd() + ')' = " +
  myString20);

// use the Substring() method to retrieve substrings
string myString21 = myString.Substring(3);
Console.WriteLine("myString.Substring(3) = " + myString21);
string myString22 = myString.Substring(3, 2);
Console.WriteLine("myString.Substring(3, 2) = " + myString22);

// use the ToUpper() and ToLower() methods to convert the
// case of a string
string myString23 = myString.ToUpper();
Console.WriteLine("myString.ToUpper() = " + myString23);
string myString24 = myString.ToLower();
Console.WriteLine("myString.ToLower() = " + myString24);

    }

}
```

The output from this program is as follows:

```
myString = To be or not to be
myString.Length = 18
myString2 = ...  that is the question
myString2.Length = 25
myString3 = \t Friends, Romans, countrymen,
lend me your ears
myString3.Length = 50
myString[0] = T
myString[1] = o
myString[2] =
myString[3] = b
myString[4] = e
myString[5] =
myString[6] = o
myString[7] = r
myString[8] =
```

```
myString[9] = n
myString[10] = o
myString[11] = t
myString[12] =
myString[13] = t
myString[14] = o
myString[15] =
myString[16] = b
myString[17] = e
String.Compare("bbc", "abc") = 1
String.Compare("abc", "bbc") = -1
String.Compare("bbc", "bbc") = 0
String.Compare("bbc", "BBC", true) = 0
String.Compare("bbc", "BBC", false) = -1
String.Compare("Hello World", 6, "Goodbye World", 8, 5) = 0
String.Concat("Friends, ", "Romans") = Friends, Romans
String.Concat("Friends, ", "Romans, ", "and countrymen") =
 Friends, Romans, and countrymen
"To be, " + "or not to be" = To be, or not to be
myString4 = Friends, Romans
Copying myString4 to myString7 using Copy()
myString7 = Friends, Romans
String.Equals("bbc", "bbc") is True
myString.Equals(myString2) is False
myString == myString2 is False
String.Format("{0, 10:f3}", myFloat) =   1234.568
myString9 = To.be.or.not.to.be
mySplitString = To
mySplitString = be
mySplitString = or
mySplitString = not
mySplitString = to
mySplitString = be
myString = To be or not to be
myString starts with "To"
myString ends with "be"
"be" first occurs at index 3 of myString
"be" last occurs at index 16 of myString
'b' first occurs at index 3 of myString
'b' last occurs at index 16 of myString
'b' and 'e' occur at index 3 of myString
'b' and 'e' last occur at index 17 of myString
myString.Insert(6, "friends, ") = To be friends, or not to be
myString10.Remove(14, 7) = To be friends, to be
myString11.Replace(',', '?') = To be friends? to be
myString12.Replace("to be", "Or not to be friends") =
 To be friends? Or not to be friends
'(' + myString.PadLeft(20) + ')' = (  To be or not to be)
```

```
'(' + myString.PadLeft(20, '.') = (..To be or not to be)
'(' + myString.PadRight(20) + ')' = (To be or not to be  )
'(' + myString.PadRight(20, '.') + ')' = (To be or not to be..)
'(' + "  Whitespace  ".Trim() + ')' = (Whitespace)
'(' + "  Whitespace  ".TrimStart() + ')' = (Whitespace  )
'(' + "  Whitespace  ".TrimEnd() + ')' = (  Whitespace)
myString.Substring(3) = be or not to be
myString.Substring(3, 2) = be
myString.ToUpper() = TO BE OR NOT TO BE
myString.ToLower() = to be or not to be
```

Creating Dynamic Strings

The `System.Text.StringBuilder` class allows you to create *dynamic strings*. Unlike a regular string of the `String` class, a dynamic string's characters may be modified directly; with a regular string, you always modify a copy of the string. In addition, the `StringBuilder` methods are fast and provide efficient string manipulation capabilities.

However, as you'll see, the methods provided by the `StringBuilder` class are not as comprehensive as those provided by the `String` class. The `StringBuilder` class does provide a `ToString()` method that converts a `StringBuilder` object to a string, and you can use this method if you need to use the additional `String` methods.

In this section, you'll learn how to create `StringBuilder` objects, and then you'll see the various `StringBuilder` properties and methods.

TIP If speed is your priority, then you should use the `StringBuilder` class to create and manipulate strings because the `StringBuilder` manipulation methods are faster. This is because when you manipulate a regular string, a whole new string has to be created and this takes time, whereas when you manipulate a `StringBuilder` object, no new object is created.

Creating *StringBuilder* Objects

The `StringBuilder` constructor is overloaded, and you can therefore create a `StringBuilder` object using a variety of techniques. The following example creates a `StringBuilder` object named `myStringBuilder`:

```
StringBuilder myStringBuilder = new StringBuilder();
```

NOTE This section's examples assume that the `System.Text` class is imported with the `using System.Text` statement. You can also use the fully qualified namespace and class name when creating a `StringBuilder` object.

By default a `StringBuilder` object can initially store up to 16 characters, but as you add to the object, its capacity will automatically increase. You can also specify the initial capacity of a `String-Builder` object by supplying an `int` parameter to the constructor. For example:

```
int capacity = 50;
StringBuilder myStringBuilder2 = new StringBuilder(capacity);
```

You can set the maximum capacity for a StringBuilder object by passing a second int parameter to the constructor. For example:

```
int maxCapacity = 100;
StringBuilder myStringBuilder3 = new StringBuilder(capacity, maxCapacity);
```

The maximum capacity for a StringBuilder object is 2147483647 (this is also the default capacity for StringBuilder objects).

You can also set the initial string stored in a StringBuilder object by passing as string to its constructor:

```
string myString = "To be or not to be";
StringBuilder myStringBuilder4 = new StringBuilder(myString);
```

Lastly, you can pass a string, the index of the string to start copying from, the number of characters to copy from the string, and the capacity to the StringBuilder constructor. For example:

```
int startIndex = 0;
int stringLength = myString.Length;
StringBuilder myStringBuilder5 =
   new StringBuilder(myString, startIndex, stringLength, capacity);
```

In the next section, you'll see some of the StringBuilder properties and methods.

Using *StringBuilder* Properties and Methods

The StringBuilder class provides a number of properties and methods you can use in your programs. Table 9.3 lists some of the public properties of the StringBuilder class.

TABLE 9.3: StringBuilder PROPERTIES

PROPERTY	TYPE	DESCRIPTION
Capacity	int	Gets or sets the maximum number of characters that can be stored in the StringBuilder object.
Length	int	Gets or sets the number of characters in the StringBuilder object.
MaxCapacity	int	Gets the maximum capacity of the StringBuilder object.

Table 9.4 shows the StringBuilder public methods.

TABLE 9.4: StringBuilder METHODS

METHOD	RETURN TYPE	DESCRIPTION
Append()	StringBuilder	Overloaded. Appends the string representation of a specified object to the end of the StringBuilder object.
AppendFormat()	StringBuilder	Overloaded. Appends a formatted string to the end of the StringBuilder object.

Continued on next page

TABLE 9.4: StringBuilder METHODS *(continued)*

METHOD	RETURN TYPE	DESCRIPTION
EnsureCapacity()	int	Ensures that the current capacity of the StringBuilder object is at least equal to a specified value and returns an int containing the current capacity of the StringBuilder object.
Equals()	bool	Overloaded. Returns a bool that specifies whether the StringBuilder object is equal to a specified object.
GetHashCode()	int	Returns an int hash code for the type.
GetType() (inherited from Object)	Type	Returns the type of the current object.
Insert()	StringBuilder	Overloaded. Inserts the string representation of a specified object into the StringBuilder object at a specified index.
Remove()	StringBuilder	Removes a specified number of characters from the StringBuilder object, starting at a specified index.
Replace()	StringBuilder	Overloaded. Replaces all occurrences of a specified string or character with another string or character in the StringBuilder object.
ToString()	string	Overloaded. Converts the StringBuilder object to a string.

As you can see, there are fewer methods for manipulating a dynamic string than for regular strings (the string methods were shown earlier in Table 9.2). The following sections illustrate some of the StringBuilder methods.

APPENDING TO A *STRINGBUILDER* OBJECT USING THE *APPEND()* AND *APPENDFORMAT()* METHODS

You can use the Append() method to append the string representation of a specified object to the end of a StringBuilder object. The Append() method, like many of the other StringBuilder methods, modifies the StringBuilder object directly.

The Append() method is overloaded, allowing you to pass a variable or object of the various built-in types, each of which is converted to a string and then appended to the StringBuilder object. The simplest version of Append() uses the following syntax:

```
stringBuilder.Append(value)
```

where *stringBuilder* is the StringBuilder object, and *value* is the item to be appended to *stringBuilder*.

The following example uses the Append() method to append two strings, an int, and a bool to myStringBuilder (which was created in the previous section):

```
string myString = "To be or not to be";
myStringBuilder.Append(myString);
myStringBuilder.Append(", that is the question ... ");
```

```
int myInt = 1234;
myStringBuilder.Append(myInt);
bool myBool = true;
myStringBuilder.Append(myBool);
```

Another version of `Append()` enables you to repeatedly append a character to a `StringBuilder` object. This version of `Append()` uses the following syntax:

```
stringBuilder.Append(appendChar, repeat)
```

where *appendChar* is the character to append to *stringBuilder*, and *repeat* is the number of times to perform the append.

The following example appends `'z'` fives times to `myStringBuilder`:

```
myStringBuilder.Append('z', 5);
```

You can also append a substring to a `StringBuilder` object using the following syntax:

```
stringBuilder.Append(appendString, startIndex, numberOfChars)
```

where *appendString* is a string, *startIndex* is the index from which to start reading from *appendString*, and *numberOfChars* is the number of characters to read from *appendString*.

In the following example, the substring `"Here"` is appended to `myStringBuilder`:

```
myStringBuilder.Append("Here's another string", 0, 4);
```

At this point, `myStringBuilder` contains the following:

```
To be or not to be, that is the question ... 1234TruezzzzHere
```

You can use the `AppendFormat()` method to append a formatted string to a `StringBuilder` object. For example:

```
float myFloat = 1234.56789f;
myStringBuilder.AppendFormat("{0, 10:f3}", myFloat);
```

Now `myStringBuilder` contains the following:

```
To be or not to be, that is the question ... 1234TruezzzzHere   1234.568
```

INSERTING A STRING INTO A *STRINGBUILDER* OBJECT USING THE *INSERT()* METHOD

You can use the `Insert()` method to append the string representation of a specified object into a `StringBuilder` object at a specified index. Like the `Append()` method, `Insert()` is also overloaded, allowing you to pass a variable or object of the various built-in types to this method.

The simplest version of `Insert()` uses the following syntax:

```
stringBuilder.Insert(index, value)
```

where *index* is the index at which the string representation of *value* is to be inserted into *stringBuilder*.

The following example uses the `Insert()` method to insert the string `"friends, "` at index 6 of `myStringBuilder`:

```
myStringBuilder.Insert(6, "friends, ");
```

You can also insert multiple copies of a string into a `StringBuilder` object using the following syntax:

```
stringBuilder.Insert(index, string, repeat)
```

The following example inserts three copies of the string `"Romans, "` at index 22 of `myStringBuilder`:

```
myStringBuilder.Insert(22, "Romans, ", 3);
```

REMOVING CHARACTERS FROM A *STRINGBUILDER* OBJECT USING THE *REMOVE()* METHOD

You can use the `Remove()` method to remove a specified number of characters from a `StringBuilder` object, starting at a specified index. The `Remove()` method uses the following syntax:

```
stringBuilder.Remove(index, numberOfChars)
```

where *index* is the index at which the removal is to start, and *numberOfChars* is the number of characters to remove from *stringBuilder*.

The following example uses the `Remove()` method to remove seven characters from `myStringBuilder`, starting at index 14:

```
myStringBuilder.Remove(14, 7);
```

REPLACING CHARACTERS IN A *STRINGBUILDER* OBJECT USING THE *REPLACE()* METHOD

You can use the `Replace()` method to replace all occurrences of a specified string or character with another string or character in a `StringBuilder` object. The `Replace()` method uses the following syntax:

```
stringBuilder.Replace(oldValue, newValue)
```

where *oldValue* is the string or character to replace, and *newValue* is the string or character to replace *oldValue* with in *stringBuilder*.

The following example uses the `Replace()` method to replace all occurrences of commas (,) with question marks (?) in `myStringBuilder`:

```
myStringBuilder.Replace(',', '?');
```

CONVERTING A *STRINGBUILDER* OBJECT TO A STRING USING THE *TOSTRING()* METHOD

You can use the `ToString()` method to convert a `StringBuilder` object to a string. The `ToString()` method uses the following syntax:

```
stringBuilder.ToString()
```

where *stringBuilder* is the `StringBuilder` object to convert to a string.

The following example uses the `ToString()` method to convert `myStringBuilder` to a string, storing the returned string in `myString2`:

```
string myString2 = myStringBuilder.ToString();
```
Listing 9.2 illustrates the use of `StringBuilder` objects.

LISTING 9.2: StringBuilder **OBJECTS**

```
/*
  Example9_2.cs illustrates the use of StringBuilder objects
*/

using System;
using System.Text;

class Example9_2
{

  public static void DisplayProperties(
    string name,
    StringBuilder myStringBuilder
  )
  {

    // display the properties for the StringBuilder object
    Console.WriteLine(name + ".Length = " +
      myStringBuilder.Length);
    Console.WriteLine(name + ".Capacity = " +
      myStringBuilder.Capacity);
    Console.WriteLine(name + ".MaxCapacity = " +
      myStringBuilder.MaxCapacity);

  }


  public static void Main()
  {

    // create some StringBuilder objects
    StringBuilder myStringBuilder = new StringBuilder();
    int capacity = 50;
    StringBuilder myStringBuilder2 = new StringBuilder(capacity);
    int maxCapacity = 100;
    StringBuilder myStringBuilder3 =
      new StringBuilder(capacity, maxCapacity);
    string myString = "To be or not to be";
    StringBuilder myStringBuilder4 = new StringBuilder(myString);
    int startIndex = 0;
    int stringLength = myString.Length;
    StringBuilder myStringBuilder5 =
      new StringBuilder(myString, startIndex, stringLength, capacity);
```

```
// display the StringBuilder objects' properties
DisplayProperties("myStringBuilder", myStringBuilder);
DisplayProperties("myStringBuilder2", myStringBuilder2);
DisplayProperties("myStringBuilder3", myStringBuilder3);
DisplayProperties("myStringBuilder4", myStringBuilder4);
DisplayProperties("myStringBuilder5", myStringBuilder5);

// use the Append() method to append two strings, an int, and a bool
// to myStringBuilder
myStringBuilder.Append(myString);
myStringBuilder.Append(", that is the question ... ");
int myInt = 1234;
myStringBuilder.Append(myInt);
bool myBool = true;
myStringBuilder.Append(myBool);

// use the Append() method to append a character to myStringBuilder
myStringBuilder.Append('z', 5);

// use the Append() method to append a substring to myStringBuilder
myStringBuilder.Append("Here's another string", 0, 4);

// display the contents of myStringBuilder
Console.WriteLine("myStringBuilder = " + myStringBuilder);

// use the AppendFormat() method to add a formatted
// string containing a floating point number to myStringBuilder
float myFloat = 1234.56789f;
myStringBuilder.AppendFormat("{0, 10:f3}", myFloat);
Console.WriteLine("myStringBuilder = " + myStringBuilder);

// use the Insert() method to insert strings into myStringBuilder
myStringBuilder.Insert(6, "friends, ");
myStringBuilder.Insert(22, "Romans, ", 3);
Console.WriteLine("myStringBuilder = " + myStringBuilder);

// use the Remove() method to remove part of myStringBuilder
myStringBuilder.Remove(14, 7);
Console.WriteLine("myStringBuilder = " + myStringBuilder);

// use the Replace() method to replace part of myStringBuilder
myStringBuilder.Replace(',', '?');
Console.WriteLine("myStringBuilder = " + myStringBuilder);

// use the ToString() method to convert myStringBuilder
// to a string
```

```
        string myString2 = myStringBuilder.ToString();
        Console.WriteLine("myString2 = " + myString2);

    }

}
```

The output from this program is as follows:

```
myStringBuilder.Length = 0
myStringBuilder.Capacity = 16
myStringBuilder.MaxCapacity = 2147483647
myStringBuilder2.Length = 0
myStringBuilder2.Capacity = 50
myStringBuilder2.MaxCapacity = 2147483647
myStringBuilder3.Length = 0
myStringBuilder3.Capacity = 50
myStringBuilder3.MaxCapacity = 100
myStringBuilder4.Length = 18
myStringBuilder4.Capacity = 32
myStringBuilder4.MaxCapacity = 2147483647
myStringBuilder5.Length = 18
myStringBuilder5.Capacity = 50
myStringBuilder5.MaxCapacity = 2147483647
myStringBuilder = To be or not to be, that is the question ... 1234TruezzzzHere
myStringBuilder = To be or not to be, that is the question
 ... 1234TruezzzzHere   1234.568
myStringBuilder = To be friends, or not Romans, Romans,
Romans, to be, that is the question ... 1234TruezzzzHere   1234.568
myStringBuilder = To be friends, Romans, Romans, Romans, to
 be, that is the question ... 1234TruezzzzHere   1234.568
myStringBuilder = To be friends? Romans? Romans? Romans? To
 be? that is the question ... 1234TruezzzzHere   1234.568
myString2 = To be friends? Romans? Romans? Romans? to be?
 that is the question ... 1234TruezzzzHere   1234.568
```

Representing Dates and Times

In addition to strings and the other built-in types, you can also represent dates and times in your programs. Examples of using a date and time would be to store a person's birthdate or to record when a financial transaction took place. You can represent dates and times in your programs using the System.DateTime struct.

In this section, you'll learn how to create DateTime instances and use the various DateTime properties and methods. You'll also be introduced to time spans, which represent time intervals.

NOTE *As mentioned in Chapter 5, a* struct *is a value type and is typically used as a lightweight alternative to a class.*

Creating *DateTime* Instances

The constructor for the DateTime struct is overloaded, and therefore there are several ways to create an instance of a DateTime. For example, you can create a DateTime instance with a specified year, month, and day, passing these int values to the DateTime constructor:

```
int year = 2002;
int month = 12;
int day = 25;
DateTime myDateTime = new DateTime(year, month, day);
```

You can also supply the hour (in 24-hour format), minute, second, and optional millisecond when creating a DateTime instance. For example:

```
int hour = 23;
int minute = 30;
int second = 12;
int millisecond = 5;
DateTime myDateTime2 =
  new DateTime(year, month, day, hour, minute, second, millisecond);
```

You can also supply an object of the System.Globalization.Calendar class as the last parameter to the DateTime constructor. The Calendar class represents time in divisions, such as weeks, months, and years. There are a number of classes that implement the Calendar class, including GregorianCalendar (the default for the United States), HebrewCalendar, HijriCalendar, JapaneseCalendar, and Julian-Calendar. The following example specifies the year, month, and day, along with a JulianCalendar object:

```
System.Globalization.JulianCalendar myCalendar =
  new System.Globalization.JulianCalendar();
DateTime myDateTime3 =
  new DateTime(year, month, day, myCalendar);
```

Finally, you can supply a long value to the DateTime constructor; this value is the number of *ticks*, measured in 100-nanosecond intervals after January 1 of the year 1 at 12 A.M. For example:

```
DateTime myDateTime4 = new DateTime(0);
```

You can view the date and time settings for a DateTime instance using the Year, Month, Day, Hour, Minute, Second, Millisecond, and Ticks properties. For example:

```
Console.WriteLine(myDateTime.Year);
Console.WriteLine(myDateTime.Month);
Console.WriteLine(myDateTime.Day);
Console.WriteLine(myDateTime.Hour);
Console.WriteLine(myDateTime.Minute);
Console.WriteLine(myDateTime.Second);
Console.WriteLine(myDateTime.Millisecond);
Console.WriteLine(myDateTime.Ticks);
```

You'll learn more about the other properties and the methods in the DateTime struct shortly; but before doing that, you'll look at time spans.

Introducing Time Spans

In addition to representing dates and times, you can also represent time intervals in your programs—these are known as *time spans*. An example of a time span is 4 hours, 12 minutes, and 10 seconds. You use the System.TimeSpan class to represent a time span. The following example creates a TimeSpan instance that represents an interval of 4 hours, 12 minutes, and 10 seconds:

```
TimeSpan myTimeSpan = new TimeSpan(4, 12, 10);
```
You can add a TimeSpan to a DateTime. The following example adds myTimeSpan to myDateTime4:
```
myDateTime4 += myTimeSpan;
```

Before this statement is run, the time part of myDateTime4 is set to 12:00:00 A.M., and after, it is set to 4:12:10 A.M. You'll learn more about the TimeSpan class shortly in the section "Using Time Spans." Listing 9.3 shows a complete program that uses DateTime and TimeSpan instances.

LISTING 9.3: DateTime **AND** TimeSpan **INSTANCES**

```
/*
  Example9_3.cs illustrates the use of DateTime and TimeSpan instances
*/

using System;

class Example9_3
{

  public static void DisplayDateTime(
    string name, DateTime myDateTime
  )
  {

    Console.WriteLine(name + " = " + myDateTime);

    // display the DateTime's properties
    Console.WriteLine(name + ".Year = " + myDateTime.Year);
    Console.WriteLine(name + ".Month = " + myDateTime.Month);
    Console.WriteLine(name + ".Day = " + myDateTime.Day);
    Console.WriteLine(name + ".Hour = " + myDateTime.Hour);
    Console.WriteLine(name + ".Minute = " + myDateTime.Minute);
    Console.WriteLine(name + ".Second = " + myDateTime.Second);
    Console.WriteLine(name + ".Millisecond = " +
      myDateTime.Millisecond);
    Console.WriteLine(name + ".Ticks = " +
      myDateTime.Ticks);

  }
```

```
public static void Main()
{

  // create a DateTime instance, specifying the year,
  // month, and day
  int year = 2002;
  int month = 12;
  int day = 25;
  DateTime myDateTime = new DateTime(year, month, day);

  // create a DateTime instance, specifying the year,
  // month, day, hour, minute, second, and millisecond
  int hour = 23;
  int minute = 30;
  int second = 12;
  int millisecond = 5;
  DateTime myDateTime2 =
    new DateTime(year, month, day, hour, minute, second, millisecond);

  // create a DateTime instance, specifying the year,
  // month, day, and JulianCalendar object
  System.Globalization.JulianCalendar myCalendar =
    new System.Globalization.JulianCalendar();
  DateTime myDateTime3 =
    new DateTime(year, month, day, myCalendar);

  // create a DateTime instance, specifying the number of ticks
  DateTime myDateTime4 = new DateTime(0);

  // display the various DateTime instances
  DisplayDateTime("myDateTime", myDateTime);
  DisplayDateTime("myDateTime2", myDateTime2);
  DisplayDateTime("myDateTime3", myDateTime3);
  DisplayDateTime("myDateTime4", myDateTime4);

  // create a TimeSpan instance, and add it to myDateTime4
  TimeSpan myTimeSpan = new TimeSpan(4, 12, 10);
  myDateTime4 += myTimeSpan;
  DisplayDateTime("myDateTime4", myDateTime4);

}

}
```

The output from this program is as follows:

```
myDateTime = 12/25/2002 12:00:00 AM
myDateTime.Year = 2002
myDateTime.Month = 12
myDateTime.Day = 25
myDateTime.Hour = 0
myDateTime.Minute = 0
myDateTime.Second = 0
myDateTime.Millisecond = 0
myDateTime.Ticks = 631763712000000000
myDateTime2 = 12/25/2002 11:30:12 PM
myDateTime2.Year = 2002
myDateTime2.Month = 12
myDateTime2.Day = 25
myDateTime2.Hour = 23
myDateTime2.Minute = 30
myDateTime2.Second = 12
myDateTime2.Millisecond = 5
myDateTime2.Ticks = 631764558120050000
myDateTime3 = 1/7/2003 12:00:00 AM
myDateTime3.Year = 2003
myDateTime3.Month = 1
myDateTime3.Day = 7
myDateTime3.Hour = 0
myDateTime3.Minute = 0
myDateTime3.Second = 0
myDateTime3.Millisecond = 0
myDateTime3.Ticks = 631774944000000000
myDateTime4 = 1/1/0001 12:00:00 AM
myDateTime4.Year = 1
myDateTime4.Month = 1
myDateTime4.Day = 1
myDateTime4.Hour = 0
myDateTime4.Minute = 0
myDateTime4.Second = 0
myDateTime4.Millisecond = 0
myDateTime4.Ticks = 0
myDateTime4 = 1/1/0001 4:12:10 AM
myDateTime4.Year = 1
myDateTime4.Month = 1
myDateTime4.Day = 1
myDateTime4.Hour = 4
myDateTime4.Minute = 12
myDateTime4.Second = 10
myDateTime4.Millisecond = 0
myDateTime4.Ticks = 151300000000
```

Using *DateTime* Properties and Methods

Now that you've been introduced to DateTime and TimeSpans, you can learn the various properties and methods offered by the DateTime struct. Table 9.5 lists the public properties of the DateTime struct.

TABLE 9.5: DateTime PROPERTIES

PROPERTY	TYPE	DESCRIPTION
Now (static)	DateTime	Gets the current date and time from the computer.
Today (static)	DateTime	Gets the current date from the computer, with the time set to 12 A.M. (12:00:00).
UtcNow() (static)	DateTime	Gets the current date and time from the computer expressed as *Universal Coordinated Time* (UTC). It is abbreviated UTC, rather than UCT, because the initials are based on the French words. UTC used to be known as *Greenwich Mean Time* (GMT) and is based on the time zone in Greenwich, England. UTC is 8 hours ahead of *Pacific Standard Time* (PST).
Date	DateTime	Gets the date part of the DateTime, with the time set to 12 A.M.
Day	int	Gets the day part of the DateTime. This value is between 1 and 31.
DayOfWeek	DayOfWeek	Gets the day of the week of the DateTime. This value is between 0 (Sunday) and 6 (Saturday).
DayOfYear	int	Gets the day of the year of the DateTime. This value is between 1 and 366.
Hour	int	Gets the hour part of the DateTime. This value is between 0 and 23.
Millisecond	int	Gets the millisecond part of the DateTime. This value is between 0 and 999.
Minute	int	Gets the minute part of the DateTime. This value is between 0 and 59.
Month	int	Gets the month part of the DateTime. This value is between 1 and 12.
Second	int	Gets the second part of the DateTime. This value is between 0 and 59.
Ticks	long	Gets the number of ticks (100-nanosecond intervals) for the DateTime that have elapsed since 12 A.M on January 1, 0001 (1/1/0001 12:00:00).
TimeOfDay	TimeSpan	Gets the time of day of the DateTime. This value is a TimeSpan that contains the time interval that has elapsed since 12 A.M of that day.
Year	int	Gets the year part of the DateTime. This value is between 1 and 9999.

Table 9.6 shows the DateTime public methods.

TABLE 9.6: DateTime METHODS

METHOD	RETURN TYPE	DESCRIPTION
Compare() (static)	int	Compares two DateTime instances and returns an indication of their relative values.
DaysInMonth() (static)	int	Returns the number of days in the specified month and year.
Equals() (static and instance versions)	bool	Overloaded. Returns a bool that indicates whether two DateTime instances are equal. The overloaded equal to operator (==) also does this.
FromFileTime() (static)	DateTime	Returns a DateTime equivalent to the specified operating system file timestamp, passed as a long parameter.
FromOADate() (static)	DateTime	Returns a DateTime equivalent to the specified OLE Automation date, passed as a double parameter. OLE stands for *Object Linking and Embedding*.
IsLeapYear() (static)	bool	Indicates whether the specified year is a leap year.
Parse() (static)	DateTime	Overloaded. Converts the specified string representation of a date and time to its equivalent DateTime.
ParseExact() (static)	DateTime	Overloaded. Converts the specified string representation of a date and time to an equivalent DateTime. The format of the string must match the specified format exactly.
Add()	DateTime	Adds the specified TimeSpan to the DateTime. The overloaded addition operator (+) also does this.
AddDays()	DateTime	Adds the specified number of days to the DateTime.
AddHours()	DateTime	Adds the specified number of hours to the DateTime.
AddMilliseconds()	DateTime	Adds the specified number of milliseconds to the DateTime.
AddMinutes()	DateTime	Adds the specified number of minutes to the DateTime.
AddMonths()	DateTime	Adds the specified number of months to the DateTime.
AddSeconds()	DateTime	Adds the specified number of seconds to the to the DateTime.
AddTicks()	DateTime	Adds the specified number of ticks to the to the DateTime.
AddYears()	DateTime	Adds the specified number of years to the to the DateTime.
CompareTo()	int	Compares the DateTime to a specified object and returns an indication of their relative values.
GetDateTimeFormats()	string[]	Overloaded. Converts the value of the DateTime to an array of strings containing all the formats supported by DateTime.
GetHashCode()	int	Returns the hash code for the DateTime.

Continued on next page

TABLE 9.6: DateTime METHODS *(continued)*

METHOD	RETURN TYPE	DESCRIPTION
GetType() (inherited from Object)	Type	Returns the type of the current instance.
Subtract()	TimeSpan	Overloaded. Subtracts the specified DateTime or TimeSpan from the DateTime. You can also use the overloaded subtraction operator (–) for this purpose.
ToFileTime()	long	Converts the value of the DateTime to an operating system file timestamp.
ToLocalTime()	DateTime	Converts the current Universal Coordinated Time (UTC) to local time.
ToLongDateString()	string	Converts the date part of the DateTime to the equivalent long date string. For example: "Thursday, January 15, 2004".
ToLongTimeString()	string	Converts the time part of the DateTime to the equivalent long time string. For example: "11:02:05 PM".
ToOADate()	double	Converts the DateTime to the equivalent OLE Automation date.
ToShortDateString()	string	Converts the DateTime to the equivalent short date string representation. For example: "1/15/2004".
ToShortTimeString()	string	Converts the DateTime to the equivalent short time string representation. For example: "11:02 PM".
ToString()	string	Overloaded. Converts the DateTime to the equivalent string representation.
ToUniversalTime()	DateTime	Converts the current local time to Universal Coordinated Time (UTC).

The following sections illustrate some of these properties and methods.

NOW AND *UTCNOW* PROPERTIES

You use the static Now property to get the current date and time from your computer. Similarly, you use the static UtcNow property to get the current date and time in *Universal Coordinated Time* (UTC). UTC used to be known as *Greenwich Mean Time* (GMT) and is based on the time zone in Greenwich, England. UTC is 8 hours ahead of *Pacific Standard Time* (PST).

Because both the Now and UtcNow properties are static, you access them using the DateTime struct. For example:

```
DateTime myDateTime = DateTime.Now;
DateTime myDateTime2 = DateTime.UtcNow;
```

Assuming the computer is in California (or, uses PST), `myDateTime` and `myDateTime2` will be set to something like this:

```
myDateTime = 3/24/2002 10:40:28 AM
myDateTime2 = 3/24/2002 6:40:28 PM
```

Notice that `myDateTime2` is 8 hours behind `myDateTime`. This is because `UtcNow` was used to set `myDateTime2`, and `UtcNow` is 8 hours behind PST.

DATE PROPERTY

You use the `Date` property to get the date part of a `DateTime` instance (the time will be returned as 12 A.M.). For example:

```
Console.WriteLine("myDateTime.Date = " + myDateTime.Date);
```

Because `myDateTime` is set to 3/34/2002 10:40:28 A.M., this example displays the following:

```
myDateTime.Date = 3/24/2002 12:00:00 AM
```

DAY PROPERTY

You use the `Day` property to get the numeric day of the month of a `DateTime` instance. For example:

```
Console.WriteLine("myDateTime.Day = " + myDateTime.Day);
```

This example displays the following:

```
myDateTime.Day = 24
```

DAYOFWEEK PROPERTY

You use the `DayOfWeek` property to get the day of the week of a `DateTime` instance. For example:

```
Console.WriteLine("myDateTime.DayOfWeek = " + myDateTime.DayOfWeek);
```

This example displays the following:

```
myDateTime.DayOfWeek = Sunday
```

DAYOFYEAR PROPERTY

You use the `DayOfYear` property to get the numeric day of the year of a `DateTime` instance. For example:

```
Console.WriteLine("myDateTime.DayOfYear = " + myDateTime.DayOfYear);
```

Because 3/34/2002 is the 83rd day of the year, this example displays the following:

```
myDateTime.DayOfYear = 83
```

TICKS PROPERTY

You use the `Ticks` property to get the number of ticks (100-nanosecond intervals) for a `DateTime` instance that have elapsed since 12 A.M. on January 1, 0001. For example:

```
Console.WriteLine("myDateTime.Ticks = " + myDateTime.Ticks);
```

This example displays the following:

```
myDateTime.Ticks = 631526496292475040
```

TimeOfDay Property

You use the `TimeOfDay` property to get the time of day of a `DateTime` instance. This value is a `TimeSpan` that contains the time interval that has elapsed since 12 A.M. of that day. For example:

```
Console.WriteLine("myDateTime.TimeOfDay = " + myDateTime.TimeOfDay);
```

This example displays the following:

```
myDateTime.TimeOfDay = 10:40:29.2475040
```

Comparing Two *DateTime* Instances Using the *Compare()* Method

You can use the static `Compare()` method to compare two `DateTime` instances. This method returns an `int`, which is determined using the following rules:

- ◆ If the first `DateTime` is greater than the second `DateTime`, then 1 is returned.
- ◆ If the first `DateTime` is equal to the second `DateTime`, then 0 is returned.
- ◆ If the first `DateTime` is less than the second `DateTime`, then −1 is returned.

Because the `Compare()` method is static, you call it using the `DateTime` struct. The `Compare()` method uses the following syntax:

```
DateTime.Compare(dateTime1, dateTime2)
```

where *dateTime1* and *dateTime2* are the two `DateTime` instances you want to compare.

The following example creates two `DateTime` instances and compares them using the `Compare()` method:

```
DateTime myDateTime3 = new DateTime(2004, 1, 13);
DateTime myDateTime4 = new DateTime(2004, 1, 14);
int intResult = DateTime.Compare(myDateTime3, myDateTime4);
```

Because `myDateTime3` is less than `myDateTime4`, `Compare()` returns −1, which is stored in `intResult`.

Comparing *DateTime* Instances Using Overloaded Operators

You can also use the following overloaded operators to compare the following `DateTime` instances: greater than (>), greater than or equal to (>=), less than (<), less than or equal to (<=), equal to (==), and not equal to (!=). For example:

```
bool boolResult = myDateTime3 < myDateTime4;
```

Because `myDateTime3` is less than `myDateTime4`, `boolResult` is set to `true`.

CHECKING IF TWO *DATETIME* INSTANCES ARE EQUAL USING THE *EQUALS()* METHOD

You can use the `Equals()` method to check if two `DateTime` instances are equal. This method returns a `bool` and has a static version and an instance version. The static version is called using the `DateTime` struct and accepts two `DateTime` instances as parameters. It uses the following syntax:

```
DateTime.Equals(dateTime1, dateTime2)
```

where *dateTime1* and *dateTime2* are the two `DateTime` instances you want to compare.

In the following example, `Equals()` returns `false` because `myDateTime3` and `myDateTime4` are different; this result is stored in `boolResult`:

```
bool boolResult = DateTime.Equals(myDateTime3, myDateTime4);
```

The instance version of `Equals()` is called using a `DateTime` instance and uses the following syntax:

```
dateTime1.Equals(dateTime2)
```

where *dateTime1* and *dateTime2* are once again the two `DateTime` instances you want to compare.

In the following example, `Equals()` returns `false` because `myDateTime3` and `myDateTime4` are different:

```
boolResult = myDateTime3.Equals(myDateTime4);
```

OBTAINING THE NUMBER OF DAYS IN A MONTH USING THE *DAYSINMONTH()* METHOD

You use the static `DaysInMonth()` method to obtain the number of days in a particular month and year. This method returns an `int` and its syntax is:

```
DateTime.DaysInMonth(year, month)
```

where *year* and *month* are the year and month for which you want the number of days in.

The following example uses the `DaysInMonth()` method to get the number of days in January 2004:

```
int days = DateTime.DaysInMonth(2004, 1);
```

Because there are 31 days in January, `DaysInMonth()` returns 31, which is stored in `days`.

DETERMINING IF A YEAR IS A LEAP YEAR USING THE *ISLEAPYEAR()* METHOD

You can use the static `IsLeapYear()` method to determine if a year is a leap year. This method returns a `bool` and uses the following syntax:

```
DateTime.IsLeapYear(year)
```

The following example uses the `IsLeapYear()` method to determine if 2004 is a leap year:

```
boolResult = DateTime.IsLeapYear(2004);
```

Because 2004 is a leap year, `IsLeapYear()` returns `true`, which is stored in `boolResult`.

CONVERTING A STRING TO A *DATETIME* INSTANCE USING THE *PARSE()* METHOD

You can use the static Parse() method to convert a specified string representing a date and time to an equivalent DateTime instance. The Parse() method is overloaded and returns a DateTime. The simplest version of Parse() accepts a string parameter and uses the following syntax:

```
DateTime.Parse(string1)
```

where *string1* is the string you want to convert to a DateTime.

The date part of the string passed to Parse() may be formatted as MM/dd/yyyy, where MM is the month, dd is the day, and yyyy is the year. The time part, if you supply one, may be formatted as HH:mm:ss, where HH is the hour (from 0 to 23), mm is the minute (from 0 to 59), and ss is the second (from 0 to 59). For example:

```
DateTime myDateTime5 = DateTime.Parse("1/13/2004");
DateTime myDateTime6 = DateTime.Parse("1/13/2004 23:10:30");
```

By default, when these DateTime instances are displayed, they appear as:

```
myDateTime5 = 1/13/2004 12:00:00 AM
myDateTime6 = 1/13/2004 11:10:30 PM
```

You'll see how to display DateTime instances in different formats shortly.

Other versions of Parse() allow you to specify a culture-specific format when parsing the supplied string. You'll learn about globalization in Chapter 21.

ADDING TO AND SUBTRACTING FROM *DATETIME* INSTANCES USING THE *ADD()* AND *SUBTRACT()* METHODS

You can use the Add() method to add a TimeSpan to a DateTime. Similarly, you can use the Subtract() method to subtract a TimeSpan from a DateTime. Both these methods return a new DateTime and use the following syntax:

```
dateTime.Add(timeSpan)
dateTime.Subtract(timeSpan)
```

where *dateTime* is the DateTime you want to add to or subtract from, and *timeSpan* is the TimeSpan to be added or subtracted.

The following example creates a TimeSpan of 1 day, 2 hours, 4 minutes, and 10 seconds and adds this TimeSpan to myDateTime6 using the Add() method:

```
TimeSpan myTimeSpan = new TimeSpan(1, 2, 4, 10);
DateTime myDateTime7 = myDateTime6.Add(myTimeSpan);
```

This sets myDateTime7 to the following:

```
1/15/2004 1:14:40 AM
```

The next example subtracts myTimeSpan from myDateTime6 using the Subtract() method:

```
myDateTime7 = myDateTime6.Subtract(myTimeSpan);
```

This sets myDateTime7 to the following:

```
1/12/2004 9:06:20 PM
```

USING THE OVERLOADED ADDITION AND SUBTRACTION OPERATORS WITH *DATETIME* AND *TIMESPAN* INSTANCES

You can also add or subtract a TimeSpan from a DateTime using the overloaded addition and subtraction operators (+ and -). For example:

```
DateTime myDateTime8 = myDateTime6 + myTimeSpan;
myDateTime8 = myDateTime6 - myTimeSpan;
```

ADDING PERIODS TO A *DATETIME* USING THE *ADDYEARS()*, *ADDMONTHS()*, *ADDDAYS()*, *ADDHOURS()*, AND *ADDMINUTES()* METHODS

You can add different periods to a DateTime using the AddYears(), AddMonths(), AddDays(), AddHours(), and AddMinutes() methods. Each of these methods accepts a double parameter, which specifies a whole or fractional period. For example:

```
DateTime myDateTime9 = new DateTime(2004, 1, 1);
myDateTime9 = myDateTime9.AddYears(1);
myDateTime9 = myDateTime9.AddMonths(5);
myDateTime9 = myDateTime9.AddDays(3);
myDateTime9 = myDateTime9.AddMinutes(30);
myDateTime9 = myDateTime9.AddSeconds(15);
```

The initial and final settings of myDateTime9 are as follows:

```
1/1/2004 12:00:00 AM
6/4/2005 12:30:15 AM
```

NOTE   You can also pass a negative number to each method, in which case the period is subtracted from the DateTime.

CONVERTING *DATETIME* INSTANCES TO AND FROM TIMESTAMPS USING THE *TOFILETIME()* AND *FROMFILETIME()* METHODS

You can use the ToFileTime() method to convert the value of a DateTime to an operating system file *timestamp*. A timestamp is a long value containing the number of 100-nanosecond intervals between 12 A.M. on January 1, 1601 and the DateTime used with the ToFileTime() method.

The syntax for the ToFileTime() method is as follows:

```
dateTime.ToFileTime()
```

where *dateTime* is the DateTime to be converted to a timestamp.

The following example creates a DateTime and converts it to a timestamp using the ToFileTime() method:

```
DateTime myDateTime10 = new DateTime(2004, 1, 15, 23, 2, 5);
long myFileTime = myDateTime10.ToFileTime();
```

This sets myFileTime to 127187101250000000, which is the number of 100-nanosecond intervals between 12 A.M. on January 1, 1601 and myDateTime10.

Similarly, the static `FromFileTime()` method converts a `long` value to a `DateTime` and has the following syntax:

```
DateTime.FromFileTime(fileTime)
```

where `fileTime` is the `long` value to be converted to a `DateTime`.

The following example converts `myFileTime` to a `DateTime` using the `FromFileTime()` method:

```
DateTime myDateTime11 = DateTime.FromFileTime(myFileTime);
```

This sets `myDateTime11` to the following:

```
1/15/2004 11:02:05 PM
```

Notice that this is the same as `myDateTime10`, which was used earlier when generating `myFileTime`.

CONVERTING DATES TO LONG AND SHORT STRINGS USING THE *TOLONGDATESTRING()* AND *TOSHORTDATESTRING()* METHODS

You can use the `ToLongDateString()` method to convert the date part of a `DateTime` to the equivalent long date string. This string contains the name of the day and month, along with the numerical year.

In the following example, the `ToLongDateString()` method is called using `myDateTime11` (created in the previous section):

```
Console.WriteLine(myDateTime11.ToLongDateString());
```

This example displays the following:

```
Thursday, January 15, 2004
```

Similarly, you use the `ToShortDateString()` method to convert the date part of `DateTime` to the equivalent short date string. This string contains the numerical month, day, and year. For example:

```
Console.WriteLine(myDateTime11.ToShortDateString());
```

This example displays the following:

```
1/15/2004
```

CONVERTING TIMES TO LONG AND SHORT STRINGS USING THE *TOLONGTIMESTRING()* AND *TOSHORTTIMESTRING()* METHODS

You can use the `ToLongTimeString()` method to convert the time part of a `DateTime` to the equivalent long time string. This string contains the numerical hour, minute, and second, along with an A.M./P.M. indicator. For example:

```
Console.WriteLine(myDateTime11.ToLongTimeString());
```

This example displays the following:

```
11:02:05 PM
```

Similarly, you use the `ToShortTimeString()` method to convert the time part of `DateTime` to the equivalent short time string. This string contains the numerical hour and minute, along with an A.M./P.M. indicator. For example:

```
Console.WriteLine(myDateTime11.ToShortTimeString());
```

This example displays the following:

```
11:02 PM
```

CONVERTING A *DATETIME* TO A STRING USING THE *TOSTRING()* METHOD

You can use the overloaded `ToString()` method to convert a `DateTime` to an equivalent string. The simplest version of the `ToString()` method accepts zero parameters, as shown in the following example:

```
DateTime myDateTime12 = new DateTime(2004, 1, 12, 22, 2, 10);
Console.WriteLine(myDateTime12.ToString());
```

This example displays the following:

```
01/12/2004 10:02:10 PM
```

You can also pass a string to `ToString()`, which specifies the format for the converted `DateTime`. This version of `ToString()` uses the following syntax:

```
dateTime.ToString(format)
```

where *dateTime* is the `DateTime` to convert, and *format* is the string containing the format for the conversion.

You'll be pleased to know you can use a variety of formats for the conversion. Before getting into some of the formats you can use, you need to understand the components that make up a format. Table 9.7 shows the various format components, along with a description and an example.

TABLE 9.7: DATE AND TIME FORMAT COMPONENTS

FORMAT COMPONENT	DESCRIPTION	EXAMPLE
d	The day of the month, *without* a leading zero for single-digit days.	2
dd	The day of the month, *with* a leading zero for single-digit days.	02
ddd	The abbreviated name for the day of the week.	Mon
dddd	The full name for the day of the week.	Monday
f	The fraction of a second with a precision of one digit. You can use up to seven f characters to increase the precision up to seven digits. Any remaining digits are truncated.	2
M	The month number, *without* a leading zero for single-digit months.	1
MM	The month number, *with* a leading zero for single-digit months.	01
MMM	The abbreviated name of the month.	Jan

Continued on next page

TABLE 9.7: DATE AND TIME FORMAT COMPONENTS *(continued)*

FORMAT COMPONENT	DESCRIPTION	EXAMPLE
MMMM	The full name of the month.	January
y	The year without the century. Values less than 10 are displayed *without* a leading zero.	4
yy	The year without the century. Values less than 10 are displayed *with* a leading zero.	04
yyyy	The full four-digit year.	2004
gg	The period or era. This is ignored if the date doesn't have a period or era.	A.D.
H	The hour in 12-hour format, *without* a leading zero for single-digit hours.	5
Hh	The hour in 12-hour format, *with* a leading zero for single-digit hours.	05
H	The hour in 24-hour format, *without* a leading zero for single-digit hours.	22
HH	The hour in 24-hour format, *without* a leading zero for single-digit hours.	22
m	The minute, *without* a leading zero for single-digit minutes.	7
mm	The minute, *with* a leading zero for single-digit minutes.	07
s	The second, *without* a leading zero for single-digit seconds.	9
ss	The minute, *with* a leading zero for single-digit minutes.	09
t	The first character in the A.M./P.M. designator.	AM
tt	The A.M./P.M. designator.	A
z	The time zone offset for the hour, *without* a leading zero for single-digit hours.	−8
zz	The time zone offset for the hour, *with* a leading zero for single-digit hours.	−08
zzz	The full time zone offset including the hour and minutes, *with* leading zeros for single-digit hours and minutes.	−08:00

You can use the format components shown in Table 9.7 to build up your own format. For example:

```
Console.WriteLine(myDateTime12.ToString("MMMM dd, yyyy"));
```

This example displays the following:

```
January 12, 2004
```

In addition, the format characters are also used in various built-in formats that you can pass to the `ToString()` method. For example, if you pass `"f"` to `ToString()`, your `DateTime` is formatted as `dddd, MMMM dd, yyyy HH:mm:ss`:

```
Console.WriteLine(myDateTime12.ToString("f"));
```

This example displays the following:

```
Monday, January 12, 2004 10:02 PM
```

Of course, "f" is only one of the built-in formats you can use. Table 9.8 shows the other characters and the format they represent. This table also shows example output from ToString() when the format is applied to a DateTime.

TABLE 9.8: BUILT-IN DATE AND TIME FORMATS

CHARACTER	FORMAT	EXAMPLE
d	MM/dd/yyyy	01/12/2004
D	dddd, MMMM dd, yyyy	Monday, January 12, 2004
f	dddd, MMMM dd, yyyy HH:mm	Monday, January 12, 2004 10:02 PM
F	dddd, MMMM dd, yyyy HH:mm:ss	Monday, January 12, 2004 10:02:10 PM
g	MM/dd/yyyy HH:mm	01/12/2004 10:02 PM
G	MM/dd/yyyy HH:mm:ss	01/12/2004 10:02:10 PM
m, M	MMMM dd	January 12
r, R	ddd, dd MMM yyyy HH':'mm':'ss 'GMT'	Mon, 12 Jan 2004 22:02:10 GMT
s	yyyy'-'MM'-'dd'T'HH':'mm':'ss	2004-01-12T22:02:10
t	HH:mm	10:02 PM
T	HH:mm:ss	10:02:10 PM
u	yyyy'-'MM'-'dd HH':'mm':'ss'Z'	2004-01-12 22:02:10Z
U	dddd, MMMM dd, yyyy HH:mm:ss	Tuesday, January 13, 2004 06:02:10 AM
y, Y	yyyy, MMMM	January, 2004

Listing 9.4 shows the various DateTime properties and methods described in this section, including some of the formats described in Table 9.8.

LISTING 9.4: DateTime **PROPERTIES AND METHODS**

```
/*
  Example9_4.cs illustrates the use of DateTime properties and methods
*/

using System;
```

```csharp
class Example9_4
{

  public static void Main()
  {

    // use the Now and UtcNow properties to get the currrent
    // date and time
    Console.WriteLine("DateTime.Now = " + DateTime.Now);
    Console.WriteLine("DateTime.UtcNow = " + DateTime.UtcNow);
    DateTime myDateTime = DateTime.Now;
    Console.WriteLine("myDateTime = " + myDateTime);
    DateTime myDateTime2 = DateTime.UtcNow;
    Console.WriteLine("myDateTime = " + myDateTime);

    // display the Date, Day, DayOfWeek, DayOfYear, Ticks, and
    // TimeOfDayProperties of myDateTime
    Console.WriteLine("myDateTime.Date = " + myDateTime.Date);
    Console.WriteLine("myDateTime.Day = " + myDateTime.Day);
    Console.WriteLine("myDateTime.DayOfWeek = " + myDateTime.DayOfWeek);
    Console.WriteLine("myDateTime.DayOfYear = " + myDateTime.DayOfYear);
    Console.WriteLine("myDateTime.Ticks = " + myDateTime.Ticks);
    Console.WriteLine("myDateTime.TimeOfDay = " + myDateTime.TimeOfDay);

    // use the Compare() method to compare DateTime instances
    DateTime myDateTime3 = new DateTime(2004, 1, 13);
    DateTime myDateTime4 = new DateTime(2004, 1, 14);
    Console.WriteLine("myDateTime3 = " + myDateTime3);
    Console.WriteLine("myDateTime4 = " + myDateTime4);
    int intResult = DateTime.Compare(myDateTime3, myDateTime4);
    Console.WriteLine("DateTime.Compare(myDateTime3, myDateTime4) = " +
      DateTime.Compare(myDateTime, myDateTime2));

    // use the overloaded less than operator (<) to compare two
    // DateTime instances
    bool boolResult = myDateTime3 < myDateTime4;
    Console.WriteLine("myDateTime3 < myDateTime4 is " +
      boolResult);

    // use the Equals() method to compare DateTime instances
    boolResult = DateTime.Equals(myDateTime3, myDateTime4);
    Console.WriteLine("DateTime.Equals(myDateTime3, myDateTime4) = " +
      boolResult);
    boolResult = myDateTime3.Equals(myDateTime4);
    Console.WriteLine("myDateTime3.Equals(myDateTime4) is " +
      boolResult);
```

```
// use the DaysInMonth() method to retrieve the number of days
// in a particular month and year
int days = DateTime.DaysInMonth(2004, 1);
Console.WriteLine("DateTime.DaysInMonth(2004, 1) = " +
  days);

// use the IsLeapYear() method to determine if a particular
// year is a leap year
boolResult = DateTime.IsLeapYear(2004);
Console.WriteLine("DateTime.IsLeapYear(2004) = " +
  boolResult);

// use the Parse() method to convert strings to DateTime instances
DateTime myDateTime5 = DateTime.Parse("1/13/2004");
DateTime myDateTime6 = DateTime.Parse("1/13/2004 23:10:30");
Console.WriteLine("myDateTime5 = " + myDateTime5);
Console.WriteLine("myDateTime6 = " + myDateTime6);

// use the Add() method to add a TimeSpan to a DateTime
TimeSpan myTimeSpan = new TimeSpan(1, 2, 4, 10);
DateTime myDateTime7 = myDateTime6.Add(myTimeSpan);
Console.WriteLine("myTimeSpan = " + myTimeSpan);
Console.WriteLine("myDateTime6.Add(myTimeSpan) = " +
  myDateTime7);

// use the Subtract() method to subtract a TimeSpan from a DateTime
myDateTime7 = myDateTime6.Subtract(myTimeSpan);
Console.WriteLine("myDateTime6.Subtract(myTimeSpan) = " +
  myDateTime7);

// use the overloaded addition operator (+) to add a TimeSpan
// to a DateTime
DateTime myDateTime8 = myDateTime6 + myTimeSpan;
Console.WriteLine("myDateTime6 + myTimeSpan = " + myDateTime8);

// use the overloaded subtraction operator (-) to subtract
// a TimeSpan from a DateTime
myDateTime8 = myDateTime6 - myTimeSpan;
Console.WriteLine("myDateTime6 - myTimeSpan = " + myDateTime8);

// use the AddYears(), AddMonths(), AddDays(), AddMinutes(), and
// AddSeconds() methods to add periods to a DateTime
DateTime myDateTime9 = new DateTime(2004, 1, 1);
Console.WriteLine("Initial myDateTime9 = " + myDateTime9);
myDateTime9 = myDateTime9.AddYears(1);
myDateTime9 = myDateTime9.AddMonths(5);
myDateTime9 = myDateTime9.AddDays(3);
myDateTime9 = myDateTime9.AddMinutes(30);
```

```
myDateTime9 = myDateTime9.AddSeconds(15);
Console.WriteLine("Final myDateTime9 = " + myDateTime9);

// use the ToFileTime() method to convert a DateTime to
// an operating system file timestamp
DateTime myDateTime10 = new DateTime(2004, 1, 15, 23, 2, 5);
long myFileTime = myDateTime10.ToFileTime();
Console.WriteLine("myDateTime10.ToFileTime() = " +
  myDateTime10.ToFileTime());

// use the FromFileTime() method to convert
// an operating system file timestamp to a DateTime
DateTime myDateTime11 = DateTime.FromFileTime(myFileTime);
Console.WriteLine("DateTime.FromFileTime() = " +
  myDateTime11);

// use the ToLongDateString() and ToShortDateString() methods
// to convert the date parts of a DateTime to long and short
// date strings
Console.WriteLine("myDateTime11 = " + myDateTime11);
Console.WriteLine("myDateTime11.ToLongDateString() = " +
  myDateTime11.ToLongDateString());
Console.WriteLine("myDateTime11.ToShortDateString() = " +
  myDateTime11.ToShortDateString());

// use the ToLongTimeString() and ToShortTimeString() methods
// to convert the time parts of a DateTime to long and short
// time strings
Console.WriteLine("myDateTime11.ToLongTimeString() = " +
  myDateTime11.ToLongTimeString());
Console.WriteLine("myDateTime11.ToShortTimeString() = " +
  myDateTime11.ToShortTimeString());

// use the ToString() method to convert a DateTime
// to a string
DateTime myDateTime12 = new DateTime(2004, 1, 12, 22, 2, 10);
Console.WriteLine("myDateTime12.ToString() = " +
  myDateTime12.ToString());
Console.WriteLine("myDateTime12.ToString(\"MMMM dd, yyyy\") = " +
  myDateTime12.ToString("MMMM dd, yyyy"));
Console.WriteLine("myDateTime12.ToString(\"d\") = " +
  myDateTime12.ToString("d"));
Console.WriteLine("myDateTime12.ToString(\"D\") = " +
  myDateTime12.ToString("D"));
Console.WriteLine("myDateTime12.ToString(\"f\") = " +
  myDateTime12.ToString("f"));
Console.WriteLine("myDateTime12.ToString(\"F\") = " +
  myDateTime12.ToString("F"));
```

```
Console.WriteLine("myDateTime12.ToString(\"g\") = " +
    myDateTime12.ToString("g"));
Console.WriteLine("myDateTime12.ToString(\"G\") = " +
    myDateTime12.ToString("G"));
Console.WriteLine("myDateTime12.ToString(\"m\") = " +
    myDateTime12.ToString("m"));
Console.WriteLine("myDateTime12.ToString(\"r\") = " +
    myDateTime12.ToString("r"));
Console.WriteLine("myDateTime12.ToString(\"s\") = " +
    myDateTime12.ToString("s"));
Console.WriteLine("myDateTime12.ToString(\"t\") = " +
    myDateTime12.ToString("t"));
Console.WriteLine("myDateTime12.ToString(\"T\") = " +
    myDateTime12.ToString("T"));
Console.WriteLine("myDateTime12.ToString(\"u\") = " +
    myDateTime12.ToString("u"));
Console.WriteLine("myDateTime12.ToString(\"U\") = " +
    myDateTime12.ToString("U"));
Console.WriteLine("myDateTime12.ToString(\"y\") = " +
    myDateTime12.ToString("y"));

    }


}
```

The output from this program is as follows:

```
DateTime.Now = 3/31/2002 4:34:12 PM
DateTime.UtcNow = 4/1/2002 12:34:12 AM
myDateTime = 3/31/2002 4:34:12 PM
myDateTime = 3/31/2002 4:34:12 PM
myDateTime.Date = 3/31/2002 12:00:00 AM
myDateTime.Day = 31
myDateTime.DayOfWeek = Sunday
myDateTime.DayOfYear = 90
myDateTime.Ticks = 631531892524029264
myDateTime.TimeOfDay = 16:34:12.4029264
myDateTime3 = 1/13/2004 12:00:00 AM
myDateTime4 = 1/14/2004 12:00:00 AM
DateTime.Compare(myDateTime3, myDateTime4) = -1
myDateTime3 < myDateTime4 is True
DateTime.Equals(myDateTime3, myDateTime4) = False
myDateTime3.Equals(myDateTime4) is False
DateTime.DaysInMonth(2004, 1) = 31
DateTime.IsLeapYear(2004) = True
myDateTime5 = 1/13/2004 12:00:00 AM
myDateTime6 = 1/13/2004 11:10:30 PM
```

```
myTimeSpan = 1.02:04:10
myDateTime6.Add(myTimeSpan) = 1/15/2004 1:14:40 AM
myDateTime6.Subtract(myTimeSpan) = 1/12/2004 9:06:20 PM
myDateTime6 + myTimeSpan = 1/15/2004 1:14:40 AM
myDateTime6 - myTimeSpan = 1/12/2004 9:06:20 PM
Initial myDateTime9 = 1/1/2004 12:00:00 AM
Final myDateTime9 = 6/4/2005 12:30:15 AM
myDateTime10.ToFileTime() = 127187101250000000
DateTime.FromFileTime() = 1/15/2004 11:02:05 PM
myDateTime11 = 1/15/2004 11:02:05 PM
myDateTime11.ToLongDateString() = Thursday, January 15, 2004
myDateTime11.ToShortDateString() = 1/15/2004
myDateTime11.ToLongTimeString() = 11:02:05 PM
myDateTime11.ToShortTimeString() = 11:02 PM
myDateTime12.ToString() = 1/12/2004 10:02:10 PM
myDateTime12.ToString("MMMM dd, yyyy") = January 12, 2004
myDateTime12.ToString("d") = 1/12/2004
myDateTime12.ToString("D") = Monday, January 12, 2004
myDateTime12.ToString("f") = Monday, January 12, 2004 10:02 PM
myDateTime12.ToString("F") = Monday, January 12, 2004 10:02:10 PM
myDateTime12.ToString("g") = 1/12/2004 10:02 PM
myDateTime12.ToString("G") = 1/12/2004 10:02:10 PM
myDateTime12.ToString("m") = January 12
myDateTime12.ToString("r") = Mon, 12 Jan 2004 22:02:10 GMT
myDateTime12.ToString("s") = 2004-01-12T22:02:10
myDateTime12.ToString("t") = 10:02 PM
myDateTime12.ToString("T") = 10:02:10 PM
myDateTime12.ToString("u") = 2004-01-12 22:02:10Z
myDateTime12.ToString("U") = Tuesday, January 13, 2004 6:02:10 AM
myDateTime12.ToString("y") = January, 2004
```

Using Time Spans

As you saw earlier, a TimeSpan instance represents an interval of time—4 days, 12 minutes, and 10 seconds, for example. This section will go deeper into the details of how to create TimeSpan instance, and you'll see the various properties and methods of the TimeSpan class.

Creating *TimeSpan* Instances

The constructor for the TimeSpan class is overloaded, and there are several ways you can create a TimeSpan instance. You can create a TimeSpan instance with a specified number of hours, minutes, and seconds, passing these int values to the TimeSpan constructor. For example:

```
int hours = 4;
int minutes = 12;
int seconds = 10;
TimeSpan myTimeSpan =
  new TimeSpan(hours, minutes, seconds);
```

You can also create a TimeSpan instance with a specified number of days:

```
int days = 1;
TimeSpan myTimeSpan2 = new TimeSpan(days, hours, minutes, seconds);
```

You can also supply the number of milliseconds when creating a TimeSpan instance:

```
int milliseconds = 20;
TimeSpan myTimeSpan3 =
  new TimeSpan(days, hours, minutes, seconds, milliseconds);
```

Finally, you can also create a TimeSpan instance with a specified number of ticks:

```
long ticks = 300;
TimeSpan myTimeSpan4 = new TimeSpan(ticks);
```

In the next section, you'll see the various TimeSpan properties and methods.

Using *TimeSpan* Properties and Methods

The TimeSpan class provides a number of properties and methods you can use in your programs. Table 9.9 lists the public properties of the TimeSpan class.

TABLE 9.9: TimeSpan PROPERTIES

PROPERTY	TYPE	DESCRIPTION
Days	int	Gets the number of days from the TimeSpan
Hours	int	Gets the number of hours from the TimeSpan
Milliseconds	int	Gets the number of milliseconds from the TimeSpan
Minutes	int	Gets the number of minutes from the TimeSpan
Seconds	int	Gets the number of seconds from the TimeSpan
Ticks	long	Gets the value of the TimeSpan in ticks
TotalDays	double	Gets the value the TimeSpan as days
TotalHours	double	Gets the value the TimeSpan as hours
TotalMilliseconds	double	Gets the value the TimeSpan as milliseconds
TotalMinutes	double	Gets the value the TimeSpan as minutes
TotalSeconds	double	Gets the value the TimeSpan as seconds

Table 9.10 shows the TimeSpan public methods.

TABLE 9.10: TimeSpan METHODS

METHOD	RETURN TYPE	DESCRIPTION
Compare() (static)	int	Compares two TimeSpan instances and returns an indication of their relative values.
Equals() (static and instance versions)	bool	Overloaded. Returns a bool that indicates whether DateTimeSpan instances are equal. The overloaded equal to operator (==) also does this.
FromDays() (static)	TimeSpan	Returns a TimeSpan containing the specified number of days.
FromHours() (static)	TimeSpan	Returns a TimeSpan containing the specified number of hours (a double value).
FromMilliseconds() (static)	TimeSpan	Returns a TimeSpan containing the specified number of milliseconds (a double value).
FromMinutes() (static)	TimeSpan	Returns a TimeSpan containing the specified number of minutes (a double value).
FromSeconds() (static)	TimeSpan	Returns a TimeSpan containing the specified number of seconds (a double value).
FromTicks() (static)	TimeSpan	Returns a TimeSpan containing the specified number of ticks (a long value).
Parse() (static)	TimeSpan	Converts the specified string representation of a time period to the equivalent TimeSpan.
Add()	TimeSpan	Adds the specified TimeSpan to the current TimeSpan. The overloaded addition operator (+) also does this.
CompareTo()	int	Compares two TimeSpan instances and returns an indication of their relative values.
Duration()	TimeSpan	Returns a TimeSpan whose value is the absolute value of this instance.
GetHashCode()	int	Returns the hash code for the TimeSpan.
GetType() (inherited from Object)	Type	Returns the type of the current instance.
Negate()	TimeSpan	Returns a TimeSpan whose value is the negative value of the current TimeSpan.
Subtract()	TimeSpan	Subtracts the specified TimeSpan from the current TimeSpan. You can also use the overloaded subtraction operator (−) for this purpose.
ToString()	string	Converts the TimeSpan to the equivalent string representation.

The following sections illustrate some of these properties and methods.

Days, Hours, Minutes, Seconds, and Milliseconds Properties

You get the various parts of a `TimeSpan` using the `Days`, `Hours`, `Minutes`, `Seconds`, and `Milliseconds` properties. These properties all return `int` values. The following example shows the use of these properties:

```
Console.WriteLine("myTimeSpan.Days = " + myTimeSpan.Days);
Console.WriteLine("myTimeSpan.Hours = " + myTimeSpan.Hours);
Console.WriteLine("myTimeSpan.Minutes = " + myTimeSpan.Minutes);
Console.WriteLine("myTimeSpan.Seconds = " + myTimeSpan.Seconds);
Console.WriteLine("myTimeSpan.Milliseconds = " + myTimeSpan.Milliseconds);
```

Because `myTimeSpan` was created earlier as a period of 4 hours, 12 minutes, and 10 seconds, the previous examples display the following:

```
myTimeSpan.Days = 0
myTimeSpan.Hours = 4
myTimeSpan.Minutes = 12
myTimeSpan.Seconds = 10
myTimeSpan.Milliseconds = 0
```

Notice that `Days` and `Milliseconds` are zero. This is because `myTimeSpan` didn't have settings for these parts.

Ticks Property

You get the value of a `TimeSpan` in ticks using the `Ticks` property, which returns a `long` value. As mentioned earlier, a tick is a 100-nanosecond interval. The following example shows the use of the `Ticks` property:

```
Console.WriteLine("myTimeSpan.Ticks = " + myTimeSpan.Ticks);
```

This example displays the following:

```
myTimeSpan.Ticks = 151300000000
```

TotalDays, TotalHours, TotalMinutes, TotalSeconds, and TotalMilliseconds Properties

You can get the total length of a `TimeSpan` in different periods using the `TotalDays`, `TotalHours`, `TotalMinutes`, `TotalSeconds`, and `TotalMilliseconds` properties. Each of these properties returns a double value. For example, `TotalDays` returns the value of a `TimeSpan` in days, and `TotalHours` returns the value in hours, and so on.

Now, `myTimeSpan` was created earlier as a period of 4 hours, 12 minutes, and 10 seconds; the following example shows the use of these properties of `myTimeSpan`:

```
Console.WriteLine("myTimeSpan.TotalDays = " +
  myTimeSpan.TotalDays);
Console.WriteLine("myTimeSpan.TotalHours = " +
  myTimeSpan.TotalHours);
```

```
Console.WriteLine("myTimeSpan.TotalMinutes = " +
  myTimeSpan.TotalMinutes);
Console.WriteLine("myTimeSpan.TotalSeconds = " +
  myTimeSpan.TotalSeconds);
Console.WriteLine("myTimeSpan.TotalMilliseconds = " +
  myTimeSpan.TotalMilliseconds);
```

These examples display the following:

```
myTimeSpan.TotalDays = 0.175115740740741
myTimeSpan.TotalHours = 4.20277777777778
myTimeSpan.TotalMinutes = 252.166666666667
myTimeSpan.TotalSeconds = 15130
myTimeSpan.TotalMilliseconds = 15130000
```

CREATING *TIMESPAN* INSTANCES USING THE *FROMDAYS()*, *FROMHOURS()*, *FROMMINUTES()*, *FROMSECONDS()*, AND *FROMMILLISECONDS()* METHODS

You can create new TimeSpan instances using the static FromDays(), FromHours(), FromMinutes(), FromSeconds(), and FromMilliseconds() methods. Each of these methods accept a **double** parameter that specifies the period (days, hours, and so on) and return a new TimeSpan instance for that period.

For example, passing 5 to FromDays() returns a TimeSpan of 5 days. Similarly, passing 10 to FromHours() returns a TimeSpan of 10 hours. Because each method accepts a **double** value, you can pass fractional periods to each method. For example, passing 2.5 to FromDays() returns a TimeSpan of 2.5 days.

The following examples show the various methods in action:

```
TimeSpan myTimeSpan5 = TimeSpan.FromDays(5);
TimeSpan myTimeSpan6 = TimeSpan.FromHours(10);
TimeSpan myTimeSpan7 = TimeSpan.FromMinutes(30);
TimeSpan myTimeSpan8 = TimeSpan.FromSeconds(15);
TimeSpan myTimeSpan9 = TimeSpan.FromMilliseconds(200);
```

CREATING *TIMESPAN* INSTANCES USING THE *FROMTICKS()* METHOD

You can also create TimeSpan instances using the static FromTicks() method. This method accepts a long value that specifies the number of ticks and returns a new TimeSpan instance. For example:

```
TimeSpan myTimeSpan10 = TimeSpan.FromTicks(500);
```

CONVERTING STRINGS TO *TIMESPAN* INSTANCES USING THE *PARSE()* METHOD

You can use the Parse() method to convert a specified string representation of a time period to the equivalent TimeSpan. The string passed to Parse() uses the following format:

```
[ws][-][d.]hh:mm:ss[.ff][ws]
```

The elements in the square brackets ([and]) are optional. Table 9.11 describes the other elements.

TABLE 9.11: PARSE FORMAT ELEMENTS

ELEMENT	DESCRIPTION
ws	Optional white space
–	Optional sign that indicates the time interval is negative
D	Optional days
hh	The hours in 24-hour format
mm	The minutes
ss	The seconds
ff	Optional fraction of a second specified using one to seven digits

The following example uses the `Parse()` method to create a new `TimeSpan` of 8 hours, 10 minutes, and 30 seconds:

```
TimeSpan myTimeSpan11 = TimeSpan.Parse("8:10:30");
```

The next example creates a new `TimeSpan` of 1 day, 8 hours, 10 minutes, and 30.1234567 seconds:

```
TimeSpan myTimeSpan12 = TimeSpan.Parse("1.8:10:30.1234567");
```

ADDING TO AND SUBTRACTING FROM A *TIMESPAN* INSTANCE USING THE *ADD()* AND *SUBTRACT()* METHODS

You can use the `Add()` method to add a `TimeSpan` to the current `TimeSpan`. Similarly, you can use the `Subtract()` method to subtract a `TimeSpan` from the current `TimeSpan`. These methods both return a new `TimeSpan` instance.

The following example creates two `TimeSpan` instances named `myTimeSpan13` and `myTimeSpan14`, and then uses the `Add()` method to add `myTimeSpan14` to `myTimeSpan13`, assigning the returned result to `myTimeSpan15`:

```
TimeSpan myTimeSpan13 = new TimeSpan(1, 10, 13);
TimeSpan myTimeSpan14 = new TimeSpan(2, 6, 10);
TimeSpan myTimeSpan15 = myTimeSpan13.Add(myTimeSpan14);
```

The result assigned to `myTimeSpan15` is 3 hours, 16 minutes, and 23 seconds, which is the sum of the components of `myTimeSpan13` and `myTimeSpan14`.

The next example subtracts `myTimeSpan14` from `myTimeSpan13`, assigning the result to `myTimeSpan15`:

```
myTimeSpan15 = myTimeSpan13.Subtract(myTimeSpan14);
```

The result assigned to `myTime15` is a period of –55 minutes and –57 seconds, which is a negative period. The following example displays `myTimeSpan15`:

```
Console.WriteLine(myTimeSpan15);
```

This example displays the following:

```
-00:55:57
```

NOTE   *It is perfectly legal to assign a negative period to a* TimeSpan.

OBTAINING THE ABSOLUTE VALUE OF A *TIMESPAN* INSTANCE USING THE *DURATION()* METHOD

You can use the Duration() method to get the absolute value of a TimeSpan instance. In the case when you have a negative period stored in a TimeSpan, Duration() will return the positive value.

For example, myTimeSpan15 was set to –55 minutes and –57 seconds in the previous example, and myTimeSpan15.Duration() returns a TimeSpan of 55 minutes and 57 seconds—a positive value:

```
Console.WriteLine(myTimeSpan15.Duration());
```

This example displays the following:

```
00:55:57
```

NEGATING A *TIMESPAN* INSTANCE USING THE *NEGATE()* METHOD

You can use the Negate() method to return a TimeSpan whose value is the negative of the current TimeSpan. Components of a TimeSpan that are negative are returned as positive, and vice versa.

For example, myTimeSpan15.Negate() returns a positive TimeSpan of 55 minutes and 57 seconds:

```
Console.WriteLine(myTimeSpan15.Negate());
```

This example displays the following:

```
00:55:57
```

Now, myTimeSpan14 was set to 2 hours, 6 minutes, and 10 seconds earlier, so myTimeSpan14.Negate() returns a negative TimeSpan of –2 hours, –6 minutes, and –10 seconds. For example:

```
Console.WriteLine(myTimeSpan14.Negate());
```

This example displays the following:

```
-02:06:10
```

Listing 9.5 shows the use of the various TimeSpan properties and methods described in this section.

LISTING 9.5: TimeSpan PROPERTIES AND METHODS

```
/*
  Example9_5.cs illustrates the use of TimeSpan properties and methods
*/

using System;

class Example9_5
{
```

```
public static void DisplayTimeSpan(
  string name, TimeSpan myTimeSpan
)
{

  Console.WriteLine(name + " = " + myTimeSpan);

  // display the TimeSpan's properties
  Console.WriteLine(name + ".Days = " + myTimeSpan.Days);
  Console.WriteLine(name + ".Hours = " + myTimeSpan.Hours);
  Console.WriteLine(name + ".Minutes = " + myTimeSpan.Minutes);
  Console.WriteLine(name + ".Seconds = " + myTimeSpan.Seconds);
  Console.WriteLine(name + ".Milliseconds = " +
    myTimeSpan.Milliseconds);
  Console.WriteLine(name + ".Ticks = " + myTimeSpan.Ticks);

}


public static void Main()
{

  // create a TimeSpan instance, specifying the hours, minutes,
  // and seconds
  int hours = 4;
  int minutes = 12;
  int seconds = 10;
  TimeSpan myTimeSpan = new TimeSpan(hours, minutes, seconds);
  Console.WriteLine("myTimeSpan = " + myTimeSpan);

  // create a TimeSpan instance, specifying the days, hours, minutes,
  // and seconds
  int days = 1;
  TimeSpan myTimeSpan2 = new TimeSpan(days, hours, minutes, seconds);
  Console.WriteLine("myTimeSpan2 = " + myTimeSpan2);

  // create a TimeSpan instance, specifying the days, hours, minutes,
  // seconds, and milliseconds
  int milliseconds = 20;
  TimeSpan myTimeSpan3 =
    new TimeSpan(days, hours, minutes, seconds, milliseconds);
  Console.WriteLine("myTimeSpan3 = " + myTimeSpan3);

  // create a TimeSpan instance, specifying the number of ticks
  long ticks = 300;
  TimeSpan myTimeSpan4 = new TimeSpan(ticks);
  Console.WriteLine("myTimeSpan4 = " + myTimeSpan4);
```

```
// display the properties for myTimeSpan
Console.WriteLine("myTimeSpan.Days = " +
  myTimeSpan.Days);
Console.WriteLine("myTimeSpan.Hours = " +
  myTimeSpan.Hours);
Console.WriteLine("myTimeSpan.Minutes = " +
  myTimeSpan.Minutes);
Console.WriteLine("myTimeSpan.Seconds = " +
  myTimeSpan.Seconds);
Console.WriteLine("myTimeSpan.Milliseconds = " +
  myTimeSpan.Milliseconds);
Console.WriteLine("myTimeSpan.Ticks = " +
  myTimeSpan.Ticks);
Console.WriteLine("myTimeSpan.TotalDays = " +
  myTimeSpan.TotalDays);
Console.WriteLine("myTimeSpan.TotalHours = " +
  myTimeSpan.TotalHours);
Console.WriteLine("myTimeSpan.TotalMinutes = " +
  myTimeSpan.TotalMinutes);
Console.WriteLine("myTimeSpan.TotalSeconds = " +
  myTimeSpan.TotalSeconds);
Console.WriteLine("myTimeSpan.TotalMilliseconds = " +
  myTimeSpan.TotalMilliseconds);

// use the FromDays(), FromHours(), FromMinutes(), FromSeconds(),
// FromMilliseconds(), and FromTicks() methods to create new
// TimeSpan instances
TimeSpan myTimeSpan5 = TimeSpan.FromDays(5);
Console.WriteLine("TimeSpan.FromDays(5) = " +
  myTimeSpan5);
TimeSpan myTimeSpan6 = TimeSpan.FromHours(10);
Console.WriteLine("TimeSpan.FromHours(10) = " +
  myTimeSpan6);
TimeSpan myTimeSpan7 = TimeSpan.FromMinutes(30);
Console.WriteLine("TimeSpan.FromMinutes(30) = " +
  myTimeSpan7);
TimeSpan myTimeSpan8 = TimeSpan.FromSeconds(15);
Console.WriteLine("TimeSpan.FromSeconds(15) = " +
  myTimeSpan8);
TimeSpan myTimeSpan9 = TimeSpan.FromMilliseconds(200);
Console.WriteLine("TimeSpan.FromMilliseconds(200) = " +
  myTimeSpan9);
TimeSpan myTimeSpan10 = TimeSpan.FromTicks(500);
Console.WriteLine("TimeSpan.FromTicks(500) = " +
  myTimeSpan10);

// use the Parse() method to convert strings to TimeSpan instances
TimeSpan myTimeSpan11 = TimeSpan.Parse("8:10:30");
```

```
Console.WriteLine("TimeSpan.Parse(\"8:10:30\") = " +
  myTimeSpan11);
TimeSpan myTimeSpan12 = TimeSpan.Parse("1.8:10:30.1234567");

Console.WriteLine("TimeSpan.Parse(\"1.8:10:30.1234567\") = " +
  myTimeSpan12);

// use the Add() method to add a TimeSpan instance to another
TimeSpan myTimeSpan13 = new TimeSpan(1, 10, 13);
TimeSpan myTimeSpan14 = new TimeSpan(2, 6, 10);
TimeSpan myTimeSpan15 = myTimeSpan13.Add(myTimeSpan14);
Console.WriteLine("myTimeSpan13 = " + myTimeSpan13);
Console.WriteLine("myTimeSpan14 = " + myTimeSpan14);
Console.WriteLine("myTimeSpan15 = " + myTimeSpan15);

// use the Subtract() method to subtract a TimeSpan instance
// from another
myTimeSpan15 = myTimeSpan13.Subtract(myTimeSpan14);
Console.WriteLine("myTimeSpan15 = " + myTimeSpan15);

// use the Duration() method to add two TimeSpan instances
Console.WriteLine("myTimeSpan15.Duration() = " +
  myTimeSpan15.Duration());

// use the Negate() method to add two TimeSpan instances
Console.WriteLine("myTimeSpan15.Negate() = " +
  myTimeSpan15.Negate());
Console.WriteLine("myTimeSpan14.Negate() = " +
  myTimeSpan14.Negate());

  }

}
```

The output from this program is as follows:

```
myTimeSpan = 04:12:10
myTimeSpan2 = 1.04:12:10
myTimeSpan3 = 1.04:12:10.0200000
myTimeSpan4 = 00:00:00.0000300
myTimeSpan.Days = 0
myTimeSpan.Hours = 4
myTimeSpan.Minutes = 12
myTimeSpan.Seconds = 10
myTimeSpan.Milliseconds = 0
myTimeSpan.Ticks = 151300000000
myTimeSpan.TotalDays = 0.175115740740741
```

```
myTimeSpan.TotalHours = 4.20277777777778
myTimeSpan.TotalMinutes = 252.166666666667
myTimeSpan.TotalSeconds = 15130
myTimeSpan.TotalMilliseconds = 15130000
TimeSpan.FromDays(5) = 5.00:00:00
TimeSpan.FromHours(10) = 10:00:00
TimeSpan.FromMinutes(30) = 00:30:00
TimeSpan.FromSeconds(15) = 00:00:15
TimeSpan.FromMilliseconds(200) = 00:00:00.2000000
TimeSpan.FromTicks(500) = 00:00:00.0000500
TimeSpan.Parse("8:10:30") = 08:10:30
TimeSpan.Parse("1.8:10:30.1234567") = 1.08:10:30.1234567
myTimeSpan13 = 01:10:13
myTimeSpan14 = 02:06:10
myTimeSpan15 = 03:16:23
myTimeSpan15 = -00:55:57
myTimeSpan15.Duration() = 00:55:57
myTimeSpan15.Negate() = 00:55:57
myTimeSpan14.Negate() = -02:06:10
```

Listing 9.6 shows another program, which measures the time taken to add some numbers.

LISTING 9.6: MEASURING THE TIME TAKEN TO ADD SOME NUMBERS

```csharp
/*
  Example9_6.cs measures the time taken to add some numbers
*/

using System;

class Example9_6
{

  public static void Main()
  {

    // create a DateTime object and set it to the
    // current date and time
    DateTime start = DateTime.Now;

    // add numbers using a for loop
    long total = 0;
    for (int count = 0; count < 1000000; count++)
    {
      total += count;
    }
```

```
    // subtract the current date and time from the start,
    // storing the difference in a TimeSpan
    TimeSpan timeTaken = DateTime.Now - start;

    // display the number of milliseconds taken to add the numbers
    Console.WriteLine("Milliseconds = " + timeTaken.Milliseconds);

    // display the total of the added numbers
    Console.WriteLine("total = " + total);

  }

}
```

The output from this program is as follows:

```
Milliseconds = 10
total = 499999500000
```

Summary

In this chapter, you learned about strings, dates, times, and time spans. Specifically, you use a string to represent a series of characters, which is stored as Unicode. Strings are actually objects of the `System.String` class. This class contains properties and a rich set of methods you can use in your programs to manipulate strings.

The `System.Text.StringBuilder` class allows you to create *dynamic strings*. Unlike a regular string of the `String` class, a dynamic string's characters may be modified directly; with a regular string, you always modify a copy of the string. In addition, the `StringBuilder` methods are fast and provide you with efficient string manipulation capabilities.

In addition to strings and the other built-in types, you can also represent dates and times in your programs. Examples of using a date and time would be to store a person's date-of-birth, or to record when a financial transaction took place. You can represent dates and times in your programs using the `System.DateTime` struct. The `DateTime` struct contains many properties and methods that allow you manipulate dates and times.

Finally, you also learned you can represent time intervals in your programs—these are known as *time spans*. An example of a time span is 4 days, 12 minutes, and 10 seconds. You use the `System.TimeSpan` class to represent a time span. The `TimeSpan` class contains many properties and methods that allow you manipulate time periods. In the next chapter you'll learn about arrays and indexers.

Chapter 10

Arrays and Indexers

IN THE PREVIOUS CHAPTERS, you saw how to declare single variables and objects. In this chapter you'll learn about *arrays*, which are sets of consecutive storage compartments that can hold data elements of the same type. You use arrays to store multiple variables or objects.

Featured in this chapter:

◆ Declaring, Creating, and Using Arrays

◆ Initializing Arrays

◆ Understanding Command-Line Arguments

◆ Understanding Array Properties and Methods

◆ Introducing Multidimensional Arrays

◆ Using Arrays of Objects

◆ Introducing Indexers

Declaring and Creating Arrays

You declare an array using the following syntax:

```
type[] array-name;
```

where *type* is the data type for the array elements and *array-name* is the name you want to assign to your array. The square brackets ([]) after *type* indicate that you've declared an array, rather than just a single variable or object.

The following example declares an array of int types named intArray:

```
int[] intArray;
```

All we have done in this statement is declare an array—we haven't as yet told C# to create an array with a specific number of elements. The following example tells C# to create an array of 10 int variables:

```
intArray = new int[10];
```

In this example, the `new` operator tells C# to create 10 `int` variables and allow `intArray` to access them. You can think of `intArray` as consisting of 10 consecutive elements that you can use to store `int` values.

You can specify the number of elements to create in an array using an expression that returns an integer value, including a constant or variable. The following example uses an `int` variable, named `arrayLength`, to specify the number of array elements:

```
int arrayLength = 10;
int[] intArray = new int[arrayLength]
```

You don't have to use two separate statements to declare and create an array; you can do both using only one statement. The following example shows this:

```
int[] intArray = new int[10];
```

You are not limited to arrays of numbers—you can use any type with an array. The following examples create an array of characters and an array of strings:

```
char[] stringArray = new char[5];
string[] stringArray = new string[2];
```

As you'll see later in this chapter, you can also create arrays of objects.

In Chapter 3, "Expressions and Operators," you saw that when a variable is declared it has an initial default value. The variable will keep this default value until you change it. Similarly, in an array of variables, each variable in the array will also have the same default value as a single variable. In the case of an array of any numeric variables (`int`, `long`, `float`, and so on), each variable will have a default value of 0. So, for `intArray`, each one of the 10 variables will have a default value of 0. For `charArray`, each of the five `char` variables will be set to \0. Finally, for `stringArray`, each of the two string variables will be set to `null`.

Using Arrays

As you now know, an array is a sequential set of elements all of the same type. To access an array element, you use the *index operator* (`[]`). The syntax for using the index operator with an array is as follows:

```
array-name[index]
```

where *array-name* is the name of the array and *index* is the number of the element in the array you want to access—*index* may be an expression that returns an integer value.

Array elements are numbered starting at zero. So, using the `intArray` created earlier that contains 10 `int` variables, `intArray[0]` accesses the first element, `intArray[1]` accesses the second element, and so on up to `intArray[9]`, which accessed the last element in the array.

The following examples assign the values 10 and 20 to the first and second elements of `intArray`:

```
intArray[0] = 10;
intArray[1] = 20;
```

Next, the following examples read those values:

```
int value1 = intArray[0];
int value2 = intArray[1];
```

Because `intArray[0]` and `intArray[1]` were set to 10 and 20, `value1` and `value2` will be set to 10 and 20, respectively.

An array is actually an object of the `System.Array` class, which provides a number of useful properties and methods you can use with your arrays. For example, you can get the number of elements in an array using the `Length` property. The following example gets the `Length` property of `intArray` and stores it in `arrayLength`:

```
int arrayLength = intArray.Length;
```

Because `intArray` contains 10 elements, the `Length` property returns the value 10. You'll learn about some of the other array properties and methods later in this chapter.

NOTE   *Array elements are consecutively numbered starting at zero and ending at (`Length - 1`).*

Accessing an Array Using a Loop

Using the array length, you can construct a `for` loop to access each element in the array. The following loop sets and displays the value of each element in `intArray`:

```
for (int counter = 0; counter < arrayLength; counter++)
{
  intArray[counter] = counter;
  Console.WriteLine(intArray[counter]);
}
```

This loop declares an `int` variable named `counter` and initializes it to 0—the loop performs 10 iterations, with `counter` being incremented by one until it reaches 10. In the loop body, the array element `intArray[counter]` is set to the same value as `counter`, and its value is then displayed.

You can also use the `foreach` statement to iterate over the elements in an array. The following example sets the first and second elements of `stringArray` to `"Hello"` and `"World"`, then iterates over those elements using a `foreach` statement:

```
stringArray[0] = "Hello";
stringArray[1] = "World";
foreach (string myString in stringArray)
{
  Console.WriteLine("myString = " + myString);
}
```

This loop will perform two iterations—one for each element in `stringArray`—and sets `myString` to `"Hello"` in the first iteration and `"World"` in the second.

NOTE   *In a `foreach` loop, you cannot modify the values. For example, you cannot modify `myString` in the previous `foreach` loop.*

Listing 10.1 illustrates the arrays shown in this section, along with an array of characters.

```
/*
  Example10_1.cs illustrates how to use arrays
*/

using System;

class Example10_1
{

  public static void Main()
  {

    // int arrays
    int[] intArray = new int[10];
    int arrayLength = intArray.Length;
    Console.WriteLine("arrayLength = " + arrayLength);
    for (int counter = 0; counter < arrayLength; counter++)
    {
      intArray[counter] = counter;
      Console.WriteLine("intArray[" + counter + "] = " +
        intArray[counter]);
    }

    // char arrays
    char[] charArray = new char[5];
    Console.WriteLine("charArray[0] = " + charArray[0]);
    charArray[0] = 'h';
    charArray[1] = 'e';
    charArray[2] = 'l';
    charArray[3] = 'l';
    charArray[4] = 'o';
    for (int counter = 0; counter < charArray.Length; counter++)
    {
      Console.WriteLine("charArray[" + counter + "] = " +
        charArray[counter]);
    }

    // string arrays
    string[] stringArray = new string[2];
    Console.WriteLine("stringArray[0] = " + stringArray[0]);
    stringArray[0] = "Hello";
    stringArray[1] = "World";
    foreach (string myString in stringArray)
    {
      Console.WriteLine("myString = " + myString);
    }
```

```
    }

}
```

The output from this program is as follows:

```
arrayLength = 10
intArray[0] = 0
intArray[1] = 1
intArray[2] = 2
intArray[3] = 3
intArray[4] = 4
intArray[5] = 5
intArray[6] = 6
intArray[7] = 7
intArray[8] = 8
intArray[9] = 9
charArray[0] = h
charArray[1] = e
charArray[2] = l
charArray[3] = l
charArray[4] = o
myString = Hello
myString = World
```

Attempting to Access a Nonexistent Array Element

It is common for new programmers to forget that array elements are numbered starting at zero and ending at (Length - 1). For example, let's assume we are working with the following array:

```
int[] intArray = new int[5];
```

There are five elements in this array, with the indexes numbered from 0 to 4. Often, a mistaken attempt is made to access the element with an index equal to the length of the array—5, in this example.

WARNING *If you attempt to access a nonexistent element of an array, C# will throw an exception. Exceptions allow you to catch error conditions in your code. You'll learn about exceptions in Chapter 13, "Exceptions and Debugging." Specifically, when you attempt to access a nonexistent element, C# will throw an exception of the* IndexOutOfRange-Exception *class.*

The following **for** loop shows this mistake:

```
for (int counter = 0; counter <= intArray.Length; counter++)
{
  intArray[counter] = counter;
  Console.WriteLine("intArray[" + counter + "] = " +
    intArray[counter]);
}
```

Can you see the problem? Look carefully at the loop condition—the loop uses the <= operator to loop, and the counter variable is less than *or equal to* the array length (counter <= intArray.Length). Thus, counter will be set to 0, 1, 2, 3, 4, and 5 in the loop. When counter gets to 5, the loop attempts to access the element intArray[5] and an exception is thrown. The loop should use the < operator, with the loop condition being counter < intArray.Length.

Listing 10.2 illustrates this bug.

LISTING 10.2: ATTEMPTING TO ACCESS A NONEXISTENT ARRAY ELEMENT

```
/*
  Example10_2.cs illustrates an attempt to write to
  a nonexistent array element
*/

using System;

class Example10_2
{

  public static void Main()
  {

    try
    {
      int[] intArray = new int[5];
      for (int counter = 0; counter <= intArray.Length; counter++)
      {
        intArray[counter] = counter;
        Console.WriteLine("intArray[" + counter + "] = " +
          intArray[counter]);
      }
    } catch (IndexOutOfRangeException e)
    {
      Console.WriteLine("IndexOutOfRangeException occurred");
      Console.WriteLine("Message = " + e.Message);
      Console.WriteLine("Stack trace = " + e.StackTrace);
    }

  }

}
```

Because the offending code is in the **try** block of a **try/catch** statement, when the exception occurs, program control passes to the **catch** block where the exception message and stack trace are displayed.

TIP *As you'll learn in Chapter 13, you should typically use exception handling to catch conditions beyond your control. In the previous example, we used an exception only to show you what happens when you attempt to access a nonexistent array element. In real code, this would never happen in the sample* for *loop by checking the condition* counter < intArray.Length.

The output from this program is as follows:

```
intArray[0] = 0
intArray[1] = 1
intArray[2] = 2
intArray[3] = 3
intArray[4] = 4
IndexOutOfRangeException occurred
Message = Exception of type System.IndexOutOfRangeException
 was thrown.
Stack trace =    at Example9_3.Main()
```

Initializing Arrays

You can initialize all the array elements in one statement when you create the array, rather than individually as shown in the previous section. To initialize all the elements, you specify the values using a comma-separated list contained in curly brackets ({}).

The following example creates an array, named intArray, and initializes all of its elements using a comma-separated list of values:

```
int[] intArray = new int[5] {10, 20, 30, 40, 50};
```

This sets intArray[0] to 10, intArray[1] to 20, and so on up to intArray[4], which is set to 50.

You can leave out the number of elements for the array when creating it, and the array will be automatically made large enough to store all of the elements in the list. The following example creates an array, named charArray, which contains five characters:

```
char[] charArray = new char[] {'h', 'e', 'l', 'l', 'o'};
```

This will automatically size charArray to five elements and set charArray[0] to 'h', charArray[1] to 'e', and so on up to charArray[4], which is set to 'o'.

You can leave out the new operator altogether when creating an array, and both the element types and size of the array will be set appropriately. The following example omits the new operator when creating an array:

```
string[] stringArray = {"Hello", "World!"};
```

This creates an array of two strings, with stringArray[0] set to "Hello" and stringArray[1] set to "World".

NOTE *When you initialize an array using a list, you must supply values for all the elements.*

Listing 10.3 illustrates how to initialize arrays.

LISTING 10.3: INITIALIZING ARRAYS

```
/*
   Example10_3.cs illustrates how to initialize arrays
*/

using System;

class Example10_3
{

  public static void Main()
  {

    // int arrays
    int[] intArray = new int[5] {10, 20, 30, 40, 50};
    for (int counter = 0; counter < intArray.Length; counter++)
    {
      Console.WriteLine("intArray[" + counter + "] = " +
        intArray[counter]);
    }

    // char arrays
    char[] charArray = new char[] {'h', 'e', 'l', 'l', 'o'};
    for (int counter = 0; counter < charArray.Length; counter++)
    {
      Console.WriteLine("charArray[" + counter + "] = " +
        charArray[counter]);
    }

    // string arrays
    string[] stringArray = {"Hello", "World"};
    foreach (string myString in stringArray)
    {
      Console.WriteLine("myString = " + myString);
    }

  }

}
```

The output from this program is as follows:

```
intArray[0] = 10
intArray[1] = 20
intArray[2] = 30
intArray[3] = 40
```

```
intArray[4] = 50
charArray[0] = h
charArray[1] = e
charArray[2] = l
charArray[3] = l
charArray[4] = o
myString = Hello
myString = World
```

Reading Command-Line Arguments

In all the programs you've seen so far, you can run them from the command line by entering the name of the program and then pressing Enter. Some programs can also accept arguments from the command line. *Arguments* are parameters placed on the command line after the program name. For example, MS-DOS comes with a tool named `diskcopy` that is used to copy the contents of one drive to another. `diskcopy` accepts two arguments: the drive to copy from and the drive to which to copy. The following example uses `diskcopy` to copy the contents of the A drive to the B drive:

```
diskcopy a: b:
```

In this example, the arguments passed to `diskcopy` are `a:` and `b:`.

You can also pass arguments to your C# programs—you do this by passing an array of strings to the `Main()` method of your program. In all the programs you've seen so far, `Main()` has always been declared as follows:

```
public static void Main()
{
  /*
    … some code …
  */
}
```

In the following declaration, `Main()` accepts an array of strings:

```
public static void Main(string[] arguments)
{
  /*
    … some code …
  */
}
```

In this example, the array of strings is named `arguments`—you can choose your own name for the array, as long as the name doesn't conflict with a C# keyword or another object in your program.

You may use this array to read the arguments entered on the command line when your program is run. For example, let's assume you had a program named `Example10_4`, and you ran this program using the following command:

```
Example10_4 Hello World 1 2 3
```

The arguments are placed after the program name, and in this example the `arguments` array would contain the following strings:

```
arguments[0] = Hello
arguments[1] = World
arguments[2] = 1
arguments[3] = 2
arguments[4] = 3.141
```

TIP *Arguments are useful for getting information from your program's users. For example, you might want to write your own* `diskcopy` *tool.*

Listing 10.4 illustrates how to read command-line arguments.

LISTING 10.4: READING COMMAND-LINE ARGUMENTS

```
/*
  Example10_4.cs illustrates how to read
  command-line arguments
*/

using System;

class Example10_4
{

  public static void Main(string[] arguments)
  {

    for (int counter = 0; counter < arguments.Length; counter++)
    {
      Console.WriteLine("arguments[" + counter + "] = " +
        arguments[counter]);
    }

  }

}
```

An example run of this program is as follows:

```
D:\jmp\C#\programs>Example9_4 Hello World 1 2 3.141
arguments[0] = Hello
arguments[1] = World
arguments[2] = 1
arguments[3] = 2
arguments[4] = 3.141
```

Introducing Array Properties and Methods

Arrays are objects of the System.Array class, and this class provides a number of useful properties and methods you can use with your arrays. Table 10.1 shows two of the public properties of the System.Array class.

TABLE 10.1: ARRAY PROPERTIES

PROPERTY	TYPE	DESCRIPTION
Length	int	Gets the number of elements in the array
Rank	int	Gets the number of dimensions of the array

You've already seen examples that use the Length property, and you'll explore the Rank property later in the "Using Multidimensional Arrays" section—these are arrays that have more than one dimension.

Array methods enable you to do tasks such as sort and search the elements in your arrays. Table 10.2 shows the public methods of the System.Array class.

TABLE 10.2: ARRAY METHODS

METHOD	RETURN TYPE	DESCRIPTION
BinarySearch() (static)	int	Overloaded. Searches a one-dimensional array that has been sorted.
Clear() (static)	void	Clears a range of elements by setting its values to either 0 or null.
Copy() (static)	void	Overloaded. Copies a range of elements from one array to another.
CreateInstance() (static)	Array	Overloaded. Creates a new instance of an array.
IndexOf() (static)	int	Overloaded. Finds the first matching value in a one-dimensional array and returns its index.
LastIndexOf() (static)	int	Overloaded. Finds the last matching value in a one-dimensional array and returns its index.
Reverse() (static)	void	Overloaded. Reverses the order of the elements in a one-dimensional array.
Sort() (static)	void	Overloaded. Sorts the values (in ascending order) of a one-dimensional array.
Equals() (inherited from Object)	bool	Overloaded. Returns a bool that specifies whether two Object instances are equal.

Continued on next page

TABLE 10.2: ARRAY METHODS *(continued)*

METHOD	RETURN TYPE	DESCRIPTION
GetEnumerator()	IEnumerator	Returns an IEnumerator instance that can iterate through the elements stored in the array. Enumerators are covered in Chapter 11, "Collections."
GetHashCode() (inherited from Object)	int	Returns a hash code for the array.
GetLength()	int	Returns the number of elements in the specified dimension of an array.
GetLowerBound()	int	Returns the lower bound of a specified dimension of an array.
GetType() (inherited from Object)	Type	Returns the type of the current instance.
GetUpperBound()	int	Returns the upper bound of a specified dimension of an array.
GetValue()	object	Overloaded. Returns the element at the specified index in a one-dimensional array.
GetUpperBound()	int	Returns the upper bound of a specified dimension of an array.
Initialize()	void	Initializes every element in a value type array by calling the default constructor of the value type.
SetValue()	void	Overloaded. Sets the specified array elements to a value.
ToString() (inherited from Object)	string	Returns a string that represents the current object.

The following sections illustrate some of these methods.

Sorting Array Elements Using the *Sort()* Method

You can use the static Sort() method to sort the elements in an array. If your array contains numbers, then the elements are sorted in ascending numeric order. If your array contains letters, then the elements are sorted in ascending alphabetical order. If your array contains a combination of letters and numbers, then the elements are sorted in alphabetical and numeric order. The Sort() method is overloaded, and the simplest version uses the following syntax:

```
Array.Sort(array1)
```

where *array1* is the array you want to sort. Because the Sort() method is static, you call it using the Array class.

NOTE *The examples in this section assume that* using System *has already been performed so that we don't have to add* System *when using the* Array *class.*

The following example creates an array of int elements named intArray and sorts this array using the Sort() method:

```
int[] intArray = {5, 2, 3, 1, 6, 9, 7, 14, 25};
Array.Sort(intArray);
```

This sorts the elements in intArray into ascending order as follows:

```
intArray[0] = 1
intArray[1] = 2
intArray[2] = 3
intArray[3] = 5
intArray[4] = 6
intArray[5] = 7
intArray[6] = 9
intArray[7] = 14
intArray[8] = 25
```

The next example creates an array of strings named stringArray and sorts the array using the Sort() method:

```
string[] stringArray = {"this", "is", "a", "test", "abc123", "abc345"};
Array.Sort(stringArray);
```

This sorts the elements in stringArray into ascending order as follows:

```
stringArray[0] = a
stringArray[1] = abc123
stringArray[2] = abc345
stringArray[3] = is
stringArray[4] = test
stringArray[5] = this
```

The final example creates an array of char elements named charArray and sorts the array using the Sort() method:

```
char[] charArray = {'w', 'e', 'l', 'c', 'o', 'm', 'e'};
Array.Sort(charArray);
```

The elements in charArray are sorted as follows:

```
charArray[0] = c
charArray[1] = e
charArray[2] = e
charArray[3] = l
charArray[4] = m
charArray[5] = o
charArray[6] = w
```

TIP   Sorting an array consumes a lot of computing resources. Therefore, you should only sort an array when you absolutely must.

Searching for an Array Element Using the *BinarySearch()* Method

You can use the static BinarySearch() method to search for an element in a sorted array. If the element is found in the array, BinarySearch() returns an int value containing the index of the element. If the element was not found, BinarySearch() returns a negative value, which is the index of the next largest element in the array minus 1.

WARNING *BinarySearch() requires you to first sort the elements in your array. As mentioned in the previous section, sorting an array consumes a lot of computing resources. If you don't want to sort your array, you can also search for elements using the* IndexOf() *and* LastIndexOf() *methods, which you'll learn about shortly.*

The BinarySearch() method is overloaded, and the simplest version uses the following syntax:

```
Array.BinarySearch(array1, value)
```

where *array1* is the array to be searched and *value* is the value for which you want to search.

The following example uses the BinarySearch() method to search intArray for the number 5, which is at index 3:

```
int index = Array.BinarySearch(intArray, 5);
```

HOW DOES *BINARYSEARCH()* WORK?

The BinarySearch() method searches for the value using the following steps:

1. Start at the middle of the elements.
2. If the value is found, then return the index.
3. If the value is not found, then divide the array into two. If the value is less than the middle value, then reject the upper half of the array. If value is higher, then reject the lower half of the array. Repeat step 1.

Because the BinarySearch() method expects the array to be sorted, you must ensure that your array is sorted before calling BinarySearch().

The next example searches intArray for the number 4, which isn't in intArray:

```
index = Array.BinarySearch(intArray, 4);
```

Because 4 isn't in intArray, BinarySearch() returns the negative of the index of the next largest element in intArray minus 1. The next largest element is 5, which is at index 3. Taking the negative of 3 gives –3, minus 1 gives –4. Therefore, BinarySearch() returns –4.

The next example searches stringArray for "abc345", which is at index 2:

```
index = Array.BinarySearch(stringArray, "abc345");
```

The final example searches charArray for 'o', which is at index 5:

```
index = Array.BinarySearch(charArray, 'o');
```

Reversing the Elements of an Array Using the *Reverse()* Method

You can use the static `Reverse()` method to reverse the order of the elements in an array. The `Reverse()` method is overloaded, and the simplest version uses the following syntax:

```
Array.Reverse(array1)
```

where *array1* is the array whose elements you want to reverse.

The following example reverses the elements in `intArray`:

```
Array.Reverse(intArray);
```

This sets the elements in `intArray` to the following:

```
intArray[0] = 25
intArray[1] = 14
intArray[2] = 9
intArray[3] = 7
intArray[4] = 6
intArray[5] = 5
intArray[6] = 3
intArray[7] = 2
intArray[8] = 1
```

The next example reverses the elements in `stringArray` and `charArray`:

```
Array.Reverse(stringArray);
Array.Reverse(charArray);
```

Searching for Array Elements Using the *IndexOf()* and *LastIndexOf()* Methods

You can use the static `IndexOf()` and `LastIndexOf()` methods to search for an element in an array. The `IndexOf()` method returns the index of the first element that matches a specified value. Similarly, the `LastIndexOf()` method returns the index of the last element that matches a specified value. The `IndexOf()` and `LastIndexOf()` methods are overloaded, and the simplest versions use the following syntax:

```
Array.IndexOf(array1, value)
Array.LastIndexOf(array1, value)
```

where *array1* is the array to be searched and *value* is the value for which you want to search.

In the following example, an array of `int` values named `intArray2` is first created, and then the `IndexOf()` and `LastIndexOf()` methods search `intArray2` for the number 1:

```
int[] intArray2 = {1, 2, 1, 3};
index = Array.IndexOf(intArray2, 1);
Console.WriteLine("Array.IndexOf(intArray2, 1) = " + index);
index = Array.LastIndexOf(intArray2, 1);
Console.WriteLine("Array.LastIndexOf(intArray2, 1) = " + index);
```

Because 1 first occurs at index 0 and last occurs at index 2, this example displays the following:

```
Array.IndexOf(intArray2, 1) = 0
Array.LastIndexOf(intArray2, 1) = 2
```

The next example searches an array of strings for "Hello":

```
string[] stringArray2 = {"Hello", "to", "everyone", "Hello", "all"};
index = Array.IndexOf(stringArray2, "Hello");
Console.WriteLine("Array.IndexOf(stringArray2, \"Hello\") = " + index);
index = Array.LastIndexOf(stringArray2, "Hello");
Console.WriteLine("Array.LastIndexOf(stringArray2, \"Hello\") = " + index);
```

Because "Hello" first occurs at index 0 and last occurs at index 3, this example displays the following:

```
Array.IndexOf(stringArray2, "Hello") = 0
Array.LastIndexOf(stringArray2, "Hello") = 3
```

Listing 10.5 illustrates some of the array properties and methods.

LISTING 10.5: ARRAY PROPERTIES AND METHODS

```
/*
  Example10_5.cs illustrates how to use array properties
  and methods
*/

using System;

class Example10_5
{

  public static void Main()
  {

    // use the Sort() method to sort the elements in an int array
    int[] intArray = {5, 2, 3, 1, 6, 9, 7, 14, 25};
    Array.Sort(intArray);  // sort the elements
    Console.WriteLine("Sorted intArray:");
    for (int counter = 0; counter < intArray.Length; counter++)
    {
      Console.WriteLine("intArray[" + counter + "] = " +
        intArray[counter]);
    }

    // use the Sort() method to sort the elements in a string array
    string[] stringArray = {"this", "is", "a", "test", "abc123", "abc345"};
    Array.Sort(stringArray);  // sort the elements
    Console.WriteLine("Sorted stringArray:");
    for (int counter = 0; counter < stringArray.Length; counter++)
    {
      Console.WriteLine("stringArray[" + counter + "] = " +
        stringArray[counter]);
    }
```

```
// use the Sort() method to sort the elements in a char array
char[] charArray = {'w', 'e', 'l', 'c', 'o', 'm', 'e'};
Array.Sort(charArray);  // sort the elements
Console.WriteLine("Sorted charArray:");
for (int counter = 0; counter < charArray.Length; counter++)
{
  Console.WriteLine("charArray[" + counter + "] = " +
    charArray[counter]);
}

// use the BinarySearch() method to search intArray for the number 5
int index = Array.BinarySearch(intArray, 5);
Console.WriteLine("Array.BinarySearch(intArray, 5) = " + index);

// use the BinarySearch() method to search intArray for the number 4
// (this number doesn't exist in intArray, and therefore BinarySearch()
// returns a negative value)
index = Array.BinarySearch(intArray, 4);
Console.WriteLine("Array.BinarySearch(intArray, 4) = " + index);

// use the BinarySearch() method to search stringArray for "abc345"
index = Array.BinarySearch(stringArray, "abc345");
Console.WriteLine("Array.BinarySearch(stringArray, \"abc345\") = " + index);

// use the BinarySearch() method to search charArray for 'o'
index = Array.BinarySearch(charArray, 'o');
Console.WriteLine("Array.BinarySearch(charArray, 'o') = " + index);

// use the Reverse() method to reverse the elements in intArray
Array.Reverse(intArray);
Console.WriteLine("Reversed intArray:");
for (int counter = 0; counter < intArray.Length; counter++)
{
  Console.WriteLine("intArray[" + counter + "] = " +
    intArray[counter]);
}

// use the Reverse() method to reverse the elements in stringArray
Array.Reverse(stringArray);
Console.WriteLine("Reversed stringArray:");
for (int counter = 0; counter < stringArray.Length; counter++)
{
  Console.WriteLine("stringArray[" + counter + "] = " +
    stringArray[counter]);
}

// use the Reverse() method to reverse the elements in charArray
Array.Reverse(charArray);
```

```csharp
      Console.WriteLine("Reversed charArray:");
      for (int counter = 0; counter < charArray.Length; counter++)
      {
        Console.WriteLine("charArray[" + counter + "] = " +
          charArray[counter]);
      }

      // create another array of int values named intArray2
      int[] intArray2 = {1, 2, 1, 3};
      Console.WriteLine("intArray2:");
      for (int counter = 0; counter < intArray2.Length; counter++)
      {
        Console.WriteLine("intArray2[" + counter + "] = " +
          intArray2[counter]);
      }

      // use the IndexOf() and LastIndexOf() methods to find the value 1
      // in intArray2
      index = Array.IndexOf(intArray2, 1);
      Console.WriteLine("Array.IndexOf(intArray2, 1) = " + index);
      index = Array.LastIndexOf(intArray2, 1);
      Console.WriteLine("Array.LastIndexOf(intArray2, 1) = " + index);

      // create another array of strings named stringArray2
      string[] stringArray2 = {"Hello", "to", "everyone", "Hello", "all"};
      Console.WriteLine("stringArray2:");
      for (int counter = 0; counter < stringArray2.Length; counter++)
      {
        Console.WriteLine("stringArray2[" + counter + "] = " +
          stringArray2[counter]);
      }

      // use the IndexOf() and LastIndexOf() methods to find the string "Hello"
      // in intArray2
      index = Array.IndexOf(stringArray2, "Hello");
      Console.WriteLine("Array.IndexOf(stringArray2, \"Hello\") = " + index);
      index = Array.LastIndexOf(stringArray2, "Hello");
      Console.WriteLine("Array.LastIndexOf(stringArray2, \"Hello\") = " + index);

    }

  }
```

The output of this program is as follows:

```
Sorted intArray:
intArray[0] = 1
intArray[1] = 2
```

```
intArray[2] = 3
intArray[3] = 5
intArray[4] = 6
intArray[5] = 7
intArray[6] = 9
intArray[7] = 14
intArray[8] = 25
Sorted stringArray:
stringArray[0] = a
stringArray[1] = abc123
stringArray[2] = abc345
stringArray[3] = is
stringArray[4] = test
stringArray[5] = this
Sorted charArray:
charArray[0] = c
charArray[1] = e
charArray[2] = e
charArray[3] = l
charArray[4] = m
charArray[5] = o
charArray[6] = w
Array.BinarySearch(intArray, 5) = 3
Array.BinarySearch(intArray, 4) = -4
Array.BinarySearch(stringArray, "abc345") = 2
Array.BinarySearch(charArray, 'o') = 5
Reversed intArray:
intArray[0] = 25
intArray[1] = 14
intArray[2] = 9
intArray[3] = 7
intArray[4] = 6
intArray[5] = 5
intArray[6] = 3
intArray[7] = 2
intArray[8] = 1
Reversed stringArray:
stringArray[0] = this
stringArray[1] = test
stringArray[2] = is
stringArray[3] = abc345
stringArray[4] = abc123
stringArray[5] = a
Reversed charArray:
charArray[0] = w
charArray[1] = o
charArray[2] = m
charArray[3] = l
```

```
charArray[4] = e
charArray[5] = e
charArray[6] = c
intArray2:
intArray2[0] = 1
intArray2[1] = 2
intArray2[2] = 1
intArray2[3] = 3
Array.IndexOf(intArray2, 1) = 0
Array.LastIndexOf(intArray2, 1) = 2
stringArray2:
stringArray2[0] = Hello
stringArray2[1] = to
stringArray2[2] = everyone
stringArray2[3] = Hello
stringArray2[4] = all
Array.IndexOf(stringArray2, "Hello") = 0
Array.LastIndexOf(stringArray2, "Hello") = 3
```

Using Multidimensional Arrays

You can visualize an array as a row of elements into which you can place a value. So far, all the arrays you've seen have used only one dimension. In other words, they use a single row of elements. You can access an element in a one-dimensional array using a single index—you can imagine this index as the number of "steps" you must take along the "width" of the row to get to the element you want.

You can also create *two-dimensional arrays*, and you can imagine these as consisting of a grid of elements like a chessboard. In this case, you need two values to access an element; you must specify the "width" and the "height" of the element in the grid.

In a *three-dimensional array*, you can think of the array as a cube of elements. To access an element, you must specify three values: the "width," "height," and "depth" of the element in the cube.

NOTE *You can create arrays of any dimension in C#.*

There are two kinds of multidimensional arrays in C#: rectangular and jagged. A *rectangular array* is one whose rows all have the same number of elements. A *jagged array* has rows that are themselves arrays—and these arrays may have different numbers of elements.

In the following sections, you'll see examples of a two-dimensional rectangular array, a three-dimensional rectangular array, and a two-dimensional jagged array.

Two-Dimensional Rectangular Arrays

You declare a two-dimensional rectangular array using the following syntax:

type[,] *array-name*;

where *type* is the data type for the array elements and *array-name* is the name you assign to the array. The square brackets and comma [,] after *type* indicate that a two-dimensional array is being declared.

DECLARING A TWO-DIMENSIONAL RECTANGULAR ARRAY

The following example creates a two-dimensional rectangular array named chessboard:

```
const int rows = 8;
const int columns = 8;
string[,] chessboard = new string[rows, columns];
```

As you can see, the chessboard array has eight rows and columns—because of this, it is said to be an 8×8 array (the number of rows are specified first, followed by the number of columns).

You can access an element in this array by specifying the row and column values using the index operator—for example, chessboard[0, 0] specifies the first row and column in the array. The following examples show how to set three of the chessboard array elements (assuming that a chess game is underway and the pieces have moved from their initial starting points):

```
chessboard[0, 0] = "White Rook";
chessboard[1, 0] = "White Pawn";
chessboard[4, 4] = "Black Pawn";
```

To display the all the values in the chessboard array, you can use the following loop:

```
for (int row = 0; row < rows; row++)
{
  for (int column = 0; column < columns; column++)
  {
    Console.WriteLine("chessboard[" + row + ", " + column + "] = " +
      chessboard[row, column]);
  }
}
```

Notice that this example contains two for loops: the outer loop iterates over the rows, and the inner loop iterates over the columns. The inner loop performs eight iterations for every iteration of the outer loop. In the first iteration of the outer loop, row is set to 0. The inner loop is then run, which then performs eight iterations for each row, setting column to the values between 0 and 7. The inner loop displays the value of the element specified by chessboard[row, column]. In this way, every element in the chessboard array is displayed—and because this is an 8×8 array, there are 64 lines of output produced by the inner loop.

Listing 10.6 illustrates this array.

LISTING 10.6: TWO-DIMENSIONAL RECTANGULAR ARRAY

```
/*
  Example10_6.cs illustrates the use of a two-dimensional
  rectangular array
*/

using System;

class Example10_6
{
```

```
public static void Main()
{

  // create the array
  const int rows = 8;
  const int columns = 8;
  string[,] chessboard = new string[rows, columns];

  // set some of the array elements to a value
  chessboard[0, 0] = "White Rook";
  chessboard[1, 0] = "White Pawn";
  chessboard[2, 3] = "White King";
  chessboard[3, 5] = "Black Bishop";
  chessboard[4, 4] = "Black Pawn";
  chessboard[5, 3] = "Black King";

  // display the array elements
  for (int row = 0; row < rows; row++)
  {
    for (int column = 0; column < columns; column++)
    {
      Console.WriteLine("chessboard[" + row + ", " + column + "] = " +
        chessboard[row, column]);
    }
  }

}
```

In this program output, only the lines that show the element values set by the program are listed:

```
chessboard[0, 0] = White Rook
chessboard[1, 0] = White Pawn
chessboard[2, 3] = White King
chessboard[3, 5] = Black Bishop
chessboard[4, 4] = Black Pawn
chessboard[5, 3] = Black King
```

INITIALIZING A TWO-DIMENSIONAL RECTANGULAR ARRAY

You can initialize a rectangular array using comma-separated lists of values. The following example creates and initializes a two-dimensional array of strings, called names:

```
string[,] names =
{
  {"Jason", "Marcus", "Price"},
  {"Steve", "Edward", "Smith"},
```

```
  {"Cynthia", "Ann", "Williams"},
  {"Gail", "Patricia", "Jones"},
};
```

The number of rows and columns for the array are implied by the values. In this example, it's easy to see the number of rows and columns for this array because each name in the array is on its own line in the code. Each row contains a name, with each name being broken down into the first, middle, and last name. This array has four rows (one for each name), with each row having three columns (one for each component of the name)—the array is therefore a 4×3 array.

Earlier, you saw examples of the properties and methods provided by the System.Array class when using a single-dimensional array—you can also use those properties and methods with a multidimensional array. The Rank property contains the number of dimensions for the array—because the names array has two dimensions, the Rank property is set to 2.

The Length property contains the total number of elements in the array. Because the names array has four rows and three columns, this is set to 12.

The GetLength() method returns the number of elements in the specified dimension of an array. The array dimension is specified using an integer, starting at 0 for the first dimension. Because the names array is a 4×3 array, names.GetLength(0) returns 4, and names.GetLength(1) returns 3. For example:

```
int numberOfRows = names.GetLength(0);
int numberOfColumns = names.GetLength(1);
```

To display the values in the names array, you can use the following loop:

```
for (int row = 0; row < numberOfRows; row++)
{
  for (int column = 0; column < numberOfColumns; column++)
  {
    Console.WriteLine("names[" + row + ", " + column + "] = " +
      names[row, column]);
  }
}
```

Listing 10.7 illustrates the names array and the array properties and methods.

LISTING 10.7: INITIALIZING A TWO-DIMENSIONAL RECTANGULAR ARRAY

```
/*
  Example10_7.cs illustrates how to initialize
  a two-dimensional rectangular array, and use the
  array properties and methods
*/

using System;

class Example10_7
{
```

```csharp
public static void Main()
{

  // create and initialize the names array
  string[,] names =
  {
    {"Jason", "Marcus", "Price"},
    {"Steve", "Edward", "Smith"},
    {"Cynthia", "Ann", "Williams"},
    {"Gail", "Patricia", "Jones"},
  };

  // display the Rank and Length properties of the names array
  Console.WriteLine("names.Rank (number of dimensions) = " + names.Rank);
  Console.WriteLine("names.Length (number of elements) = " + names.Length);

  // use the GetLength() method to get number of elements
  // in each dimension of the names array
  int numberOfRows = names.GetLength(0);
  int numberOfColumns = names.GetLength(1);
  Console.WriteLine("Number of rows = " + numberOfRows);
  Console.WriteLine("Number of columns = " + numberOfColumns);

  // display the elements of the names array
  for (int row = 0; row < numberOfRows; row++)
  {
    for (int column = 0; column < numberOfColumns; column++)
    {
      Console.WriteLine("names[" + row + ", " + column + "] = " +
        names[row, column]);
    }
  }

}

}
```

The output from this program is as follows:

```
names.Rank (number of dimensions) = 2
names.Length (number of elements) = 12
Number of rows = 4
Number of columns = 3
names[0, 0] = Jason
names[0, 1] = Marcus
names[0, 2] = Price
names[1, 0] = Steve
```

```
names[1, 1] = Edward
names[1, 2] = Smith
names[2, 0] = Cynthia
names[2, 1] = Ann
names[2, 2] = Williams
names[3, 0] = Gail
names[3, 1] = Patricia
names[3, 2] = Jones
```

Three-Dimensional Rectangular Arrays

You declare a three-dimensional rectangular array using the following syntax:

```
type[,,] array-name;
```

The two commas and brackets ([,,]) after *type* indicate that you are declaring a three-dimensional rectangular array.

NOTE   *An n-dimension rectangular array uses* (n - 1) *commas in the declaration: a two-dimensional array uses one comma, a three-dimensional array uses two commas, and so on.*

The following example creates a three-dimensional rectangular array named `galaxy`:

```
int[,,] galaxy = new int[10, 5, 3];
```

This array models a simple galaxy that is a box and has 10×5×3 elements that can contain a star. Because the `galaxy` array is a 10×5×3 array, the total number of elements in this array is therefore 150.

A star is represented by an `int` variable, whose value indicates the star's relative brightness from 1 to 10 (with 10 being the brightest); the absence of a value in an array element means that there is no star at that position.

The following statements add two stars to the `galaxy` array:

```
galaxy[1, 3, 2] = 3;
galaxy[4, 1, 2] = 9;
```

The following loop displays only the elements in the `galaxy` array that have been set to a value; notice the use of the `GetLength()` method to get the number of elements in each dimension:

```
for (int x = 0; x < galaxy.GetLength(0); x++)
{
  for (int y = 0; y < galaxy.GetLength(1); y++)
  {
    for (int z = 0; z < galaxy.GetLength(2); z++)
    {
      if (galaxy[x, y, z] != 0) {
        Console.WriteLine("galaxy[" + x + ", " + y + ", " + z +"] = " +
          galaxy[x, y, z]);
      }
    }
  }
}
```

Listing 10.8 illustrates the galaxy array.

```
/*
  Example10_8.cs illustrates the use of
  a three-dimensional rectangular array
*/

using System;

class Example10_8
{

  public static void Main()
  {

    // create the galaxy array
    int[,,] galaxy = new int [10, 5, 3];

    // set two galaxy array elements to the star's brightness
    galaxy[1, 3, 2] = 3;
    galaxy[4, 1, 2] = 9;

    // display the Rank and Length properties of the galaxy array
    Console.WriteLine("galaxy.Rank (number of dimensions) = " + galaxy.Rank);
    Console.WriteLine("galaxy.Length (number of elements) = " + galaxy.Length);

    // display the galaxy array elements, but only display elements that
    // have actually been set to a value (or "contain stars")
    for (int x = 0; x < galaxy.GetLength(0); x++)
    {
      for (int y = 0; y < galaxy.GetLength(1); y++)
      {
        for (int z = 0; z < galaxy.GetLength(2); z++)
        {
          if (galaxy[x, y, z] != 0) {
            Console.WriteLine("galaxy[" + x + ", " + y + ", " + z +"] = " +
              galaxy[x, y, z]);
          }
        }
      }
    }

  }

}
```

The output from this program is as follows:

```
galaxy.Rank (number of dimensions) = 3
galaxy.Length (number of elements) = 150
galaxy[1, 3, 2] = 3
galaxy[4, 1, 2] = 9
```

Jagged Arrays

A jagged array is an array whose rows are also arrays—and the number of elements in the row arrays can be different. This may sound confusing, but once you see the example in this section, it should make sense.

You declare a jagged two-dimensional array using the following syntax:

```
type[][] array-name;
```

NOTE   *A series of square brackets ([]) in an array declaration specify that the array is jagged, and the number of sets of brackets indicate the array's dimension.*

The following example declares a two-dimensional jagged array of strings, called `names`:

```
string[][] names;
```

Next, four arrays are created in `names`, whose elements are arrays of strings:

```
names = new string[4][];
```

You can think of `names` as being an array of four rows, and each one of these rows is a slot for an array of strings. To complete the `names` array, you must create an array of strings for each of the four rows. The following statement creates an array of three strings for the first row:

```
names[0] = new string[3];
```

Next, these three strings are assigned a value:

```
names[0][0] = "Jason";
names[0][1] = "Marcus";
names[0][2] = "Price";
```

That takes care of the first row. The arrays in each row can be of different lengths, and the second row is set to an array of two strings:

```
names[1] = new string[2];
names[1][0] = "Steve";
names[1][1] = "Smith";
```

See how the rows in this array are "jagged"? The first row has three strings, but this second row only has two. The elements in the array don't line up in a grid like a rectangular array would.

The third row is initialized to an array of four strings:

```
names[2] = new string[] {"Cynthia", "Ann", "Jane", "Williams"};
```

Finally, the fourth row is initialized to an array of two strings:

```
names[3] = new string[] {"Gail", "Jones"};
```

To sum up, the names array consists of four rows of string arrays. The first row has three strings, the second row has two, the third has four, and the fourth has two.

The Rank property for the names array is 1, and the Length property is 4—the reason for this is that only the outer array of rows are counted. Each of the four rows contains another inner array, and you can get the individual Rank and Length properties for those arrays separately. For example, names[0].Rank is 1, and names[0].Length is 3—corresponding to the three strings in the first row of the names array.

You can navigate the rows in the names array and display the strings in each row array using the following loop; notice the use of the Length property to get the number of elements in each row:

```
for (int row = 0; row < names.Length; row++)
{
  for (int element = 0; element < names[row].Length; element++)
  {
    Console.WriteLine("names[" + row + "][" + element + "] = " +
      names[row][element]);
  }
}
```

Listing 10.9 illustrates the names array.

LISTING 10.9: A JAGGED ARRAY

```
/*
  Example10_9.cs illustrates the use of a jagged array
*/

using System;

class Example10_9
{

  public static void Main()
  {

    // declare a jagged array of four rows,
    // with each row consisting of a string array
    string[][] names = new string[4][];

    // the first row is an array of three strings
    names[0] = new string[3];
    names[0][0] = "Jason";
    names[0][1] = "Marcus";
    names[0][2] = "Price";
```

```
    // the second row is an array of two strings
    names[1] = new string[2];
    names[1][0] = "Steve";
    names[1][1] = "Smith";

    // the third row is an array of four strings
    names[2] = new string[] {"Cynthia", "Ann", "Jane", "Williams"};
    names[3] = new string[] {"Gail", "Jones"};

    // display the Rank and Length properties for the names array
    Console.WriteLine("names.Rank = " + names.Rank);
    Console.WriteLine("names.Length = " + names.Length);

    // display the Rank and Length properties for the arrays
    // in each row of the names array
    for (int row = 0; row < names.Length; row++)
    {
      Console.WriteLine("names[" + row + "].Rank = " + names[row].Rank);
      Console.WriteLine("names[" + row + "].Length = " + names[row].Length);
    }

    // display the array elements for each row in the names array
    for (int row = 0; row < names.Length; row++)
    {
      for (int element = 0; element < names[row].Length; element++)
      {
        Console.WriteLine("names[" + row + "][" + element + "] = " +
          names[row][element]);
      }
    }

  }

}
```

The output from this program is as follows:

```
names.Rank = 1
names.Length = 4
names[0].Rank = 1
names[0].Length = 3
names[1].Rank = 1
names[1].Length = 2
names[2].Rank = 1
names[2].Length = 4
names[3].Rank = 1
names[3].Length = 2
```

```
names[0][0] = Jason
names[0][1] = Marcus
names[0][2] = Price
names[1][0] = Steve
names[1][1] = Smith
names[2][0] = Cynthia
names[2][1] = Ann
names[2][2] = Jane
names[2][3] = Williams
names[3][0] = Gail
names[3][1] = Jones
```

Creating Arrays of Objects

In this section, you'll see how to create arrays of objects. You can also create arrays of structures (with the struct keyword); the process for creating them is basically the same. (Chapter 5, "Object-Oriented Programming," covered objects and structures.)

Earlier, you saw a three-dimensional array named galaxy—that array used int variables to represent stars in a simple model of a galaxy. This section creates another three-dimensional array to model a galaxy, but this time the stars will be represented using objects of the following class:

```
public class Star
{

  // declare two fields
  public string name;
  public int brightness;

  // declare a constructor
  public Star(
    string name,
    int brightness
  ) {
    this.name = name;
    this.brightness = brightness;
  }

}
```

As you can see, the Star class contains the fields name and brightness. The name field will store the star's name, and the brightness field will store the relative brightness of the star. The constructor for the Star class sets name and brightness to the parameters passed to the constructor.

The following example declares a three-dimensional array of Star objects, named galaxy:

```
Star[,,] galaxy = new Star[10, 5, 3];
```

The galaxy array is a 10×5×3 array, and the total number of array elements in this array is therefore 150. The default value for an object is null, so each element in the galaxy array is initially set to null.

The following statements add two Star objects to the galaxy array:

```
galaxy[1, 3, 2] = new Star("Sun", 3);
galaxy[4, 1, 2] = new Star("Alpha Centuri", 9);
```

Listing 10.10 illustrates the galaxy array.

LISTING 10.10: A THREE-DIMENSIONAL RECTANGULAR ARRAY CONTAINING OBJECTS

```
/*
  Example10_10.cs illustrates the use of
  an array of objects
*/

using System;


public class Star
{

  // declare two fields
  public string name;
  public int brightness;

  // declare a constructor
  public Star(
    string name,
    int brightness
  ) {
    this.name = name;
    this.brightness = brightness;
  }

}


class Example10_10
{

  public static void Main()
  {

    // create the galaxy array of Star objects
    Star[,,] galaxy = new Star[10, 5, 3];

    // create two Star objects in the galaxy array
    galaxy[1, 3, 2] = new Star("Sun", 3);
    galaxy[4, 1, 2] = new Star("Alpha Centuri", 9);
```

```
      // display the Rank and Length properties of the galaxy array
      Console.WriteLine("galaxy.Rank (number of dimensions) = " + galaxy.Rank);
      Console.WriteLine("galaxy.Length (number of elements) = " + galaxy.Length);

      // display the galaxy array elements
      for (int x = 0; x < galaxy.GetLength(0); x++)
      {
        for (int y = 0; y < galaxy.GetLength(1); y++)
        {
          for (int z = 0; z < galaxy.GetLength(2); z++)
          {
            if (galaxy[x, y, z] != null)
            {
              Console.WriteLine("galaxy[" + x + ", " + y + ", " + z +"].name = " +
                galaxy[x, y, z].name);
              Console.WriteLine("galaxy[" + x + ", " + y +
                ", " + z +"].brightness = " +
                galaxy[x, y, z].brightness);
            }
          }
        }
      }

    }

  }
```

Notice that the loop only displays objects that are not null (the default value for an object). The output from this program is as follows:

```
galaxy.Rank (number of dimensions) = 3
galaxy.Length (number of elements) = 150
galaxy[1, 3, 2].name = Sun
galaxy[1, 3, 2].brightness = 3
galaxy[4, 1, 2].name = Alpha Centuri
galaxy[4, 1, 2].brightness = 9
```

Introducing Indexers

You can treat the fields of an object as array elements by defining an *indexer* for your class. You probably won't need to use indexers often, but you may find them useful occasionally. For example, you might want to use them when you already have an array of objects and you want to also use array access syntax to access the fields in your objects. In this section, you'll see a simple indexer that accesses the make and model fields of a Car object.

Defining an Indexer

You define an indexer using the following simplified syntax:

[*access-modifier*] *return-type* this[*parameter-type parameter-name*] {*indexer-body*}

The this keyword references the current object. The other syntax elements are as follows:

access-modifier   The degree to which your indexer is available (public, private, and so on).

return-type   The type of the field returned by your indexer.

parameter-type   The type of the parameter used by your indexer to access a field. Typically, *parameter-type* will be an int, but you can use any type.

parameter-name   The name of the parameter used by your indexer.

indexer-body   The body of your indexer where you can define a get and a set method to read from and write to the fields of an object. The get and set methods for an indexer operate in the same way as get and set methods for a property (properties were covered in Chapter 6, "More about Classes and Objects"). As with properties, you can make an indexer readonly by only defining a get method, and you can make an indexer write-only by defining only a set method.

The following Car class defines an indexer that reads and writes to two fields named make and model. Notice that the get method returns the make or the model field depending on the index parameter, and the set method sets the make or the model field (don't worry about the details of the indexer, as we'll cover that shortly):

```
public class Car
{

  // declare two fields
  private string make;
  private string model;

  // define a constructor
  public Car(string make, string model)
  {
    this.make = make;
    this.model = model;
  }

  // define the indexer
  public string this[int index]
  {
    get
    {
      switch (index)
      {
        case 0:
          return make;
```

```
        case 1:
          return model;
        default:
          throw new IndexOutOfRangeException();
    }
  }
  set
  {
    switch (index)
    {
      case 0:
        this.make = value;
        break;
      case 1:
        this.model = value;
        break;
      default:
        throw new IndexOutOfRangeException();
    }
  }
}

}
```

Let's examine the details of the indexer. The first line is as follows:

```
public string this[int index]
{
```

This indicates that the indexer returns a `string` and accepts an `int` parameter named `index`. The `this` keyword references the current object.

The `get` method for the indexer is as follows:

```
get
{
  switch (index)
  {
    case 0:
      return make;
    case 1:
      return model;
    default:
      throw new IndexOutOfRangeException();
  }
}
```

As you can see, if `index` is 0, then the `make` field for the current `Car` object is returned. If `index` is 1, then the `model` field is returned. If `index` is any other value, then an object of the `IndexOutOfRange-Exception` class is thrown—this is one way to handle invalid index values. You'll learn more about exceptions in Chapter 13.

NOTE *Notice that there's no* **break** *statement in each* **case** *branch of the* **switch**. *This is intentional because the* **return** *and* **throw** *statements immediately exit the switch and therefore* **break** *isn't necessary. In fact, providing one will cause a compilation warning.*

The `set` method for the indexer is as follows:

```
set
{
  switch (index)
  {
    case 0:
      this.make = value;
      break;
    case 1:
      this.model = value;
      break;
    default:
      throw new IndexOutOfRangeException();
  }
}
```

If `index` is 0, then the `make` field for the current object is set to `value`, which is implicitly passed to the `set` method—you'll see an example of this shortly. If `index` is 1, then the `model` field is set to `value`. If `index` is any other value than 0 or 1, then an object of the `IndexOutOfRangeException` class is thrown.

The following example creates a `Car` object and passes `"Toyota"` and `"MR2"` to the constructor, which sets the `make` and `model` field for the `Car` object to those values, respectively:

```
Car myCar = new Car("Toyota", "MR2");
```

Because an indexer has been defined in the `Car` class, the fields of a `Car` object can be accessed like the elements of an array. For example, the `make` field of `myCar` can be accessed using `myCar[0]`, and the `model` field can be accessed using `myCar[1]`. The integer specified in the brackets is supplied to the indexer through the `index` parameter. As you'll see in the following sections, depending on whether you are reading from or writing to the fields of `Car` object, either the `get` or `set` method will be implicitly called.

Reading from the Fields of an Object Using an Indexer

When reading from the fields of `myCar` using the indexer, the `get` method is implicitly called. The following statements display the values of `myCar[0]` and `myCar[1]`:

```
Console.WriteLine("myCar[0] = " + myCar[0]);
Console.WriteLine("myCar[1] = " + myCar[1]);
```

Because the `make` and `model` fields for `myCar` were set to `"Toyota"` and `"MR2"` earlier, these statements display the following:

```
myCar[0] = Toyota
myCar[1] = MR2
```

TIP   You should document your own classes with comments that state which fields are accessed by each index for your indexer. That way, the users of your class will know how to use your indexer. For example, index 0 accesses the make *field, and index 1 accesses the* model *field.*

Writing to the Fields of an Object Using an Indexer

When writing to the fields of myCar using the indexer, the set method is implicitly called. In the following example, myCar[0] is set to "Porsche" and myCar[1] is set to "Boxster":

```
myCar[0] = "Porsche";
myCar[1] = "Boxster";
```

The value variable used in the set method is implicitly set to the value on the right side of the previous statements, and therefore myCar.make is set to "Porsche" and myCar.model is set to "Boxster".

The following example attempts to access an invalid index and causes an IndexOutOfRangeException to be thrown:

```
myCar[2] = "Test";
```

Listing 10.11 illustrates an indexer.

LISTING 10.11: AN INDEXER

```
/*
  Example10_11.cs illustrates the use of an indexer
*/

using System;


// declare the Car class
public class Car
{

  // declare two fields
  private string make;
  private string model;

  // define a constructor
  public Car(string make, string model)
  {
    this.make = make;
    this.model = model;
  }

  // define the indexer
  public string this[int index]
```

```
    {
      get
      {
        switch (index)
        {
          case 0:
            return make;
          case 1:
            return model;
          default:
            throw new IndexOutOfRangeException();
        }
      }
      set
      {
        switch (index)
        {
          case 0:
            this.make = value;
            break;
          case 1:
            this.model = value;
            break;
          default:
            throw new IndexOutOfRangeException();
        }
      }
    }
}


class Example10_11
{

  public static void Main()
  {

    // create a Car object
    Car myCar = new Car("Toyota", "MR2");

    // display myCar[0] and myCar[1]
    Console.WriteLine("myCar[0] = " + myCar[0]);
    Console.WriteLine("myCar[1] = " + myCar[1]);

    // set myCar[0] to "Porsche" and myCar[1] to "Boxster"
    Console.WriteLine("Setting myCar[0] to \"Porsche\" " +
      "and myCar[1] to \"Boxster\"");
```

```
        myCar[0] = "Porsche";
        myCar[1] = "Boxster";
        // myCar[2] = "Test";  // causes IndeXOutOfRangeException to be thrown

        // display myCar[0] and myCar[1] again
        Console.WriteLine("myCar[0] = " + myCar[0]);
        Console.WriteLine("myCar[1] = " + myCar[1]);

    }

}
```

The output from this program is as follows:

```
myCar[0] = Toyota
myCar[1] = MR2
Setting myCar[0] to "Porsche" and myCar[1] to "Boxster"
myCar[0] = Porsche
myCar[1] = Boxster
```

Summary

In this chapter, you learned all about arrays and indexers. Specifically, an *array* is a set of consecutive storage compartments that can hold data elements of the same type—including objects and structures. An array is actually an object of the System.Array class, which provides a number of useful properties and methods you can use with your arrays.

You access the elements in an array using the *index operator* ([]). You can initialize all the array elements in one statement when you create the array using a comma-separated list contained in curly brackets ({}).

Arguments are parameters placed on the command line after the program name. You can pass arguments from the command line to your programs by passing an array of strings to the Main() method.

You also learned about several different types of arrays: A *multidimensional array* is one that has more than one dimension, a two-dimensional array is like a grid, and a three-dimensional array is like a cube. A *rectangular array* is one whose rows all have the same number of elements. A *jagged array* has rows that are themselves arrays—these arrays may have different numbers of elements.

Finally, you learned that you can treat the fields of an object as array elements by defining an *indexer* for your class. In the next chapter, you'll learn about collections.

Chapter 11

Collections

IN THE PREVIOUS CHAPTER, you saw how arrays can store many elements. Although arrays are powerful, they have a number of limitations:

◆ You can't change the number of elements that an array can store after you've created the array. So, your array might be too big or too small.

◆ You can't directly insert or delete array elements.

◆ You can only access an array element using a numeric index.

The System.Collections namespace contains a number of classes you can use to create objects that store many elements and whose capacity you can change after you've created them. Further, these objects offer flexible ways to access their elements. As you master C#, you'll find collections to be useful when you need to perform complex manipulation of data.

Featured in this chapter:

◆ Understanding Array Lists

◆ Using Bit Arrays

◆ Introducing Hash Tables

◆ Using Sorted Lists

◆ Introducing Queues

◆ Exploring Stacks

Introducing Array Lists

An *array list* is similar to an array, but it will automatically expand as you add elements—unlike an array, which has a fixed size. The ArrayList class contains the definition for an array list. The ArrayList class, like all the collection classes, is part of the System.Collections namespace. The ArrayList class contains a rich set of methods you can use to manipulate the elements; for example, you can insert and remove elements at any point in an ArrayList.

In this section, you'll first see a simple example of how to create and use an `ArrayList` object; then you'll see all the public properties and methods of the `ArrayList` class as well as a more complex example.

Creating and Using an *ArrayList*

The first step is to create an `ArrayList` object, as shown in the following example:

```
ArrayList myArrayList = new ArrayList();
```

Notice that you don't specify the capacity of the `ArrayList`. The initial capacity of an `ArrayList` is 16, meaning that it can initially store up to 16 elements. The capacity will automatically increase if you add more than 16 elements to the `ArrayList`. You can get or set the capacity of an `ArrayList` using the `Capacity` property, and the following example displays the `Capacity` property for `myArrayList`:

```
Console.WriteLine(myArrayList.Capacity);
```

You add an element to the `ArrayList` using the `Add()` method; the following examples add four `strings` to `myArrayList`:

```
myArrayList.Add("This");
myArrayList.Add("is");
myArrayList.Add("a");
myArrayList.Add("test");
```

The parameter to the `Add()` method can be of any type because the `ArrayList`—like all the collections described in this chapter—store elements as objects of the `System.Object` class. This is the class from which all classes are derived (see Chapter 7, "Derived Classes," for further details).

Each call to the `Add()` method appends the supplied object to the end of the `ArrayList`. You'll see the other methods (and properties) of the `ArrayList` class in the next section.

You can get the number of elements stored in the `ArrayList` using the `Count` property. For `myArrayList`, the `Count` property will be 4 because four elements were added to `myArrayList` earlier. You can use the `Count` property in a `for` loop that accesses the elements in an `ArrayList`. For example, the following `for` loop uses the `Count` property of `myArrayList` and displays the elements stored in `myArrayList`:

```
for (int counter = 0; counter < myArrayList.Count; counter++) {
  Console.WriteLine(myArrayList[counter]);
}
```

You can also create new collections by passing in an existing collection to the constructor; this copies the elements from the existing collection to the new collection. For example, the following statement creates a second `ArrayList`, passing `myArrayList` to the constructor of the new `ArrayList`:

```
ArrayList anotherArrayList = new ArrayList(myArrayList);
```

In this example, the elements from `myArrayList` are copied to `anotherArrayList`.
Listing 11.1 illustrates the `ArrayList` objects shown in this section.

LISTING 11.1: ArrayList OBJECTS

```
/*
  Example11_1.cs illustrates the use of ArrayLists
*/

using System;
using System.Collections;

class Example11_1
{

  // the DisplayArrayList() method displays the elements in the
  // ArrayList that is supplied as a parameter
  public static void DisplayArrayList(
    string arrayListName, ArrayList myArrayList
  ) {
    for (int counter = 0; counter < myArrayList.Count; counter++)
    {
      Console.WriteLine(arrayListName + "[" + counter + "] = " +
        myArrayList[counter]);
    }
  }

  public static void Main()
  {

    // create an ArrayList object
    ArrayList myArrayList = new ArrayList();

    // display the Capacity property
    Console.WriteLine("myArrayList.Capacity = " +
      myArrayList.Capacity);

    // add four strings to myArrayList using the Add() method
    myArrayList.Add("This");
    myArrayList.Add("is");
    myArrayList.Add("a");
    myArrayList.Add("test");

    // display the contents of myArrayList using DisplayArrayList()
    DisplayArrayList("myArrayList", myArrayList);

    // create another ArrayList, passing myArrayList to the
    // constructor of the new ArrayList
    ArrayList anotherArrayList = new ArrayList(myArrayList);
```

```
        // display the contents of anotherArrayList
        DisplayArrayList("anotherArrayList", anotherArrayList);

    }

}
```

Notice that this program defines a method named `DisplayArrayList()`. This method displays all the elements in the `ArrayList` that is supplied as a parameter to the method.

The output from this program is as follows:

```
myArrayList.Capacity = 16
myArrayList[0] = This
myArrayList[1] = is
myArrayList[2] = a
myArrayList[3] = test
anotherArrayList[0] = This
anotherArrayList[1] = is
anotherArrayList[2] = a
anotherArrayList[3] = test
```

ArrayList Properties and Methods

The `ArrayList` class provides a number of useful properties and methods that you can use in your programs. Table 11.1 shows the public `ArrayList` properties.

TABLE 11.1: `ArrayList` PROPERTIES

PROPERTY	TYPE	DESCRIPTION
Capacity	int	Gets or sets the capacity of the `ArrayList`. The capacity is the number of elements that can be stored in the `ArrayList`.
Count	int	Gets the number of elements actually stored in the `ArrayList`.
IsFixedSize	bool	Checks whether the `ArrayList` is of a fixed size.
IsReadOnly	bool	Checks whether the `ArrayList` is readonly.
IsSynchronized	bool	Checks whether access to the `ArrayList` is synchronized (thread-safe). Chapter 14, "Threads," covers synchronization and threading.
Item	object	Gets or sets the element at a specified index. This is the indexer for the `ArrayList` class. Chapter 10, "Arrays and Indexers," covered indexers.
SyncRoot	object	Gets an `object` that can be used to synchronize access to the `ArrayList`.

You've already seen examples that use the `Capacity` and `Count` properties, and you'll see a program at the end of this section that illustrates some of the other properties Table 11.1.

Table 11.2 shows the public `ArrayList` methods.

TABLE 11.2: ArrayList METHODS

METHOD	RETURN TYPE	DESCRIPTION
Adapter() (static)	ArrayList	Creates a wrapper for an ArrayList.
FixedSize() (static)	ArrayList	Overloaded. Returns an ArrayList wrapper with a fixed size. This wrapper contains the same elements as the original ArrayList. The elements of the ArrayList wrapper can be modified, but no elements can be added or removed.
ReadOnly() (static)	ArrayList	Overloaded. Returns an ArrayList wrapper that may only be read from.
Repeat() (static)	ArrayList	Returns a new ArrayList whose elements are copies of the specified value.
Synchronized() (static)	ArrayList	Overloaded. Returns an ArrayList wrapper that is synchronized (thread-safe).
Add()	int	Adds an object to the end of the ArrayList.
AddRange()	void	Adds the elements from another collection (such as an array) to the end of the ArrayList.
BinarySearch()	int	Overloaded. Performs a binary search to find a specific element in the sorted ArrayList.
Clear()	void	Removes all the elements from the ArrayList.
Clone()	object	Creates a shallow copy of the ArrayList. If the ArrayList contains object references, then those references are copied instead of the actual object.
Contains()	bool	Determines if a specified element is in the ArrayList.
CopyTo()	void	Overloaded. Copies elements from the ArrayList to a one-dimensional array.
Equals() (inherited from Object)	bool	Overloaded. Determines whether two object instances are equal.
GetEnumerator()	IEnumerator	Overloaded. Returns an enumerator that can iterate through the ArrayList. Enumerators are covered later in this chapter.
GetHashCode() (inherited from Object)	int	Returns a hash code for a particular type.
GetRange()	ArrayList	Returns a new ArrayList containing a range of elements from the original ArrayList.
GetType() (inherited from Object)	Type	Returns the type of the current instance.

Continued on next page

TABLE 11.2: ArrayList METHODS *(continued)*

METHOD	RETURN TYPE	DESCRIPTION
IndexOf()	int	Overloaded. Returns the index of the first occurrence of a specified element in the ArrayList. Indexes start at zero.
Insert()	void	Inserts an element into the ArrayList at a specified index.
InsertRange()	void	Inserts the elements from a collection into the ArrayList, starting at a specified index of the ArrayList.
LastIndexOf()	int	Overloaded. Returns the index of the last occurrence of a specified element in the ArrayList.
Remove()	void	Removes the first occurrence of a specified element from the ArrayList.
RemoveAt()	void	Removes the element at a specified index from the ArrayList.
RemoveRange()	void	Removes a range of elements from the ArrayList, starting and ending at specified indexes.
Reverse()	void	Overloaded. Reverses the order of the elements, or a range of elements, in the ArrayList.
SetRange()	void	Inserts the elements from a collection into a specified range of elements in the ArrayList, overwriting the existing elements.
Sort()	void	Overloaded. Sorts the elements, or a range of elements, in an ArrayList.
ToArray()	object[]	Copies the elements from an ArrayList to an array.
ToString() (inherited from Object)	string	Returns a string that represents the current object.
TrimToSize()	void	Reduces the capacity of the ArrayList to the actual number of elements stored in the ArrayList.

The following sections illustrate some of these methods.

ADDING AND INSERTING ELEMENTS USING THE *ADD()*, *INSERT()*, *ADDRANGE()*, *INSERTRANGE()*, AND *SETRANGE()* METHODS

Let's take a look at some examples of adding and inserting elements into an ArrayList. First, an ArrayList is needed:

```
ArrayList myArrayList = new ArrayList();
```

The Add() Method

You can use the Add() method to add an element to the end of an ArrayList. The Add() method accepts an object parameter, and this method uses the following syntax:

```
arrayList.Add(value)
```

where *value* is the value to be added to the end of *arrayList*.

The following example uses the Add() method to add the string "This" to myArrayList:

```
myArrayList.Add("This");
```

The Insert() Method

You can use the Insert() method to insert an element into an ArrayList at a specified index. The Insert() method accepts an int and an object parameter, and this method uses the following syntax:

```
arrayList.Insert(index, value)
```

where *value* is the value to be added to *arrayList* at the index specified by *index*.

NOTE   *The elements in an ArrayList start at index zero.*

The following example inserts the string "is" into myArrayList at index 1 using the Insert() method:

```
myArrayList.Insert(1, "is");
```

The AddRange() Method

You can use the AddRange() method to add a range of elements to the end of an ArrayList. The AddRange() method accepts a collection object (such as an array, for example), and this method uses the following syntax:

```
arrayList.AddRange(collection)
```

where *collection* is the collection to be added to the end of *arrayList*.

The following example adds an array of strings to the end of myArrayList using the AddRange() method:

```
string[] myStringArray = {"a", "test"};
myArrayList.AddRange(myStringArray);
```

The InsertRange() Method

You can use the InsertRange() method to insert elements at a specified index of an ArrayList. The InsertRange() method accepts an int and a collection parameter, and this method uses the following syntax:

```
arrayList.InsertRange(index, collection)
```

where *collection* is the collection object to be added to *arrayList* at the index specified by *index*.

The following example uses the InsertRange() method to add an array of strings to the end of myArrayList; notice the use of the Count property of myArrayList to specify the index:

```
string[] anotherStringArray = {"Here's", "some", "more", "text"};
myArrayList.InsertRange(myArrayList.Count, anotherStringArray);
```

The **SetRange()** *Method*

You can use the SetRange() method to replace elements in an ArrayList, starting at a specified index, with the elements from a collection (an array, for example). The SetRange() method accepts an int and a collection parameter, and this method uses the following syntax:

```
arrayList.SetRange(index, collection)
```

where *collection* is the collection object whose elements are to replace the elements in *arrayList*, starting at the index specified by *index* of *arrayList*.

The following example uses the SetRange() method to replace the first four elements in myArrayList with the four strings from anotherStringArray, starting at index 0 in myArrayList:

```
myArrayList.SetRange(0, anotherStringArray);
```

Because the replacement starts at index 0, this example replaces the first four strings in myArrayList with the strings from anotherStringArray.

After the statements shown in this section and the previous sections have been executed, myArrayList will contain the following eight elements:

```
myArrayList[0] = Here's
myArrayList[1] = some
myArrayList[2] = more
myArrayList[3] = text
myArrayList[4] = Here's
myArrayList[5] = some
myArrayList[6] = more
myArrayList[7] = text
```

FINDING ELEMENTS USING THE *CONTAINS()*, *INDEXOF()*, AND *LASTINDEXOF()* METHODS

You can use the Contains() method to determine if an ArrayList contains a specified element. You can use the IndexOf() and LastIndexOf() methods to get the index of the first and last occurrence of a specified element. These three methods return a bool and accept an object parameter that specifies the value to find in the ArrayList. These methods use the following syntax:

```
arrayList.Contains(value)
arrayList.IndexOf(value)
arrayList.LastIndexOf(value)
```

where *value* is the value to find in *arrayList*. If *value* is found, the methods return true; otherwise they return false.

The following if statement uses the Contains() method to determine if the string "text" is in myArrayList; if so, the IndexOf() and LastIndexOf() methods display the indexes of the first and last occurrence of "text":

```
if (myArrayList.Contains("text"))
{
  int index = myArrayList.IndexOf("text");
  Console.WriteLine("'text' first occurs at index " + index);
```

```
    index = myArrayList.LastIndexOf("text");
    Console.WriteLine("'text' last occurs at index " + index);
}
```

Because `myArrayList` contains `"text"` at index 3 and again at index 7, this example displays 3 and 7 for the index values.

REMOVING ELEMENTS USING THE *REMOVEAT()*, *REMOVE()*, AND *REMOVERANGE()* METHODS

You can use the `RemoveAt()`, `Remove()`, and `RemoveRange()` methods to remove elements from an `ArrayList`.

The RemoveAt() Method

You can use the `RemoveAt()` method to remove an element at a specified index. The `RemoveAt()` method accepts an `int` parameter, and this method uses the following syntax:

```
arrayList.RemoveAt(index)
```

where *index* is the index of the element to remove from *arrayList*.

The following example uses the `RemoveAt()` method to remove the element at index 0 from `myArrayList`:

```
myArrayList.RemoveAt(0);
```

The Remove() Method

You can use the `Remove()` method to remove a specified element. The `Remove()` method accepts an `object` parameter, and this method uses the following syntax:

```
arrayList.Remove(value)
```

where *value* is the value of the element to remove from *arrayList*. The first element whose value matches *value* is removed from *arrayList*.

The following example uses the `Remove()` method to remove the first occurrence of `"text"` from `myArrayList`:

```
myArrayList.Remove("text");
```

The RemoveRange() Method

You can use the `RemoveRange()` method to remove a range of elements. The `RemoveRange()` method accepts two `int` parameters, and this method uses the following syntax:

```
arrayList.RemoveRange(startIndex, numberOfElements)
```

where *startIndex* is the index to start removing elements from *arrayList* and *numberOfElements* is the number of elements to remove.

The following example uses the `RemoveRange()` method to remove two elements from `myArrayList`, starting at index 3:

```
myArrayList.RemoveRange(3, 2);
```

After the statements shown in this section and the previous sections have been executed, `myArrayList` will contain the following four elements:

```
myArrayList[0] = some
myArrayList[1] = more
myArrayList[2] = Here's
myArrayList[3] = text
```

SORTING, SEARCHING, AND REVERSING ELEMENTS USING THE *SORT()*, *BINARYSEARCH()*, AND *REVERSE()* METHODS

You can use the `Sort()`, `BinarySearch()`, and `Reverse()` methods to sort, search, and reverse elements in an `ArrayList`.

The Sort() Method

You can use the `Sort()` method to sort the elements in an `ArrayList`. Numbers are sorted in ascending numeric order, and letters are sorted in ascending alphabetical order. The `Sort()` method is overloaded, and the simplest version of this method uses the following syntax:

```
arrayList.Sort()
```

where *arrayList* is the ArrayList whose elements you want to sort.

The following example sorts the elements in `myArrayList` using the `Sort()` method:

```
myArrayList.Sort();
```

Because `myArrayList` contains `string` elements, the four elements will be sorted alphabetically into the following order:

```
myArrayList[0] = Here's
myArrayList[1] = more
myArrayList[2] = some
myArrayList[3] = text
```

The BinarySearch() Method

You can use the `BinarySearch()` method to search a sorted `ArrayList`. The `BinarySeach()` method works in the same manner as described in Chapter 10 for searching arrays. The `BinarySearch()` method is overloaded, and the simplest version of this method uses the following syntax:

```
arrayList.BinarySearch(value)
```

where *value* is the value you want to search for in *arrayList*.

The following example uses the `BinarySearch()` method to search `myArrayList` for the word "some", which occurs at index 2:

```
int index2 = myArrayList.BinarySearch("some");
```

The **Reverse()** *Method*

You can use the Reverse() method to reverse the order of elements in an ArrayList. The Reverse() method is overloaded, and the simplest version of this method uses the following syntax:

```
arrayList.Reverse()
```

where *arrayList* is the ArrayList whose elements you want to reverse.

The following example uses the Reverse() method to reverse the elements in myArrayList:

```
myArrayList.Reverse();
```

Once reversed, the elements in myArrayList will appear in the following order:

```
myArrayList[0] = text
myArrayList[1] = some
myArrayList[2] = more
myArrayList[3] = Here's
```

REDUCING CAPACITY USING THE *TRIMTOSIZE()* METHOD

You can use the TrimToSize() method to reduce the capacity of an ArrayList to the number of elements actually stored in the ArrayList. The TrimToSize() method doesn't accept any parameters, and this method use the following syntax:

```
arrayList.TrimToSize()
```

where *arrayList* is the ArrayList you want to trim.

The following example uses the TrimToSize() method to trim the elements in myArrayList:

```
myArrayList.TrimToSize();
```

Because myArrayList contains four elements, this example reduces the capacity of myArrayList to 4. If you later add another element to myArrayList, then its capacity will automatically increase to accommodate the new element.

GETTING A RANGE OF ELEMENTS USING THE *GETRANGE()* METHOD

You can use the GetRange() method to get a range of elements from an ArrayList. The GetRange() method returns a new ArrayList object containing the requested range of elements from your original ArrayList object. The GetRange() method accepts two int parameters, and this method uses the following syntax:

```
arrayList.GetRange(startIndex, numberOfElements)
```

where *startIndex* is the index to start reading elements from *arrayList* and *numberOfElements* is the number of elements to read.

The following example uses the GetRange() method to get two elements from myArrayList, starting at index 1:

```
ArrayList anotherArrayList = myArrayList.GetRange(1, 2);
```

The new ArrayList, named anotherArrayList, stores the returned ArrayList from GetRange(). The new ArrayList contains the following two elements:

```
anotherArrayList[0] = some
anotherArrayList[1] = more
```

USING AN ENUMERATOR TO READ AN *ARRAYLIST*

Like all collection classes, the ArrayList class implements the IEnumerable interface (interfaces were covered in Chapter 8, "Interfaces"). The IEnumerable interface specifies that the implementing class must provide code for the GetEnumerator() method, which returns an enumerator you can use to access each element in a collection. This is also known as *iterating* over a collection. An *enumerator* is an object of the IEnumurator interface—you'll learn more about its methods and properties shortly.

The GetEnumerator() method is overloaded, and the simplest version of this method uses the following syntax:

```
arrayList.GetEnumerator()
```

where *arrayList* is the ArrayList for which you want to get the enumerator.

The other version of GetEnumerator() accepts two int parameters and uses the following syntax:

```
arrayList.GetEnumerator(startIndex, numberOfElements)
```

where *startIndex* is the index to start reading elements from *arrayList* and *numberOfElements* is the number of elements to read.

The following example uses the GetEnumerator() method for myArrayList:

```
IEnumerator myEnumerator = myArrayList.GetEnumerator();
```

The IEnumerator interface has one property named Current; which enables you to read the current element in the collection. In addition, IEnumerator provides two methods:

◆ The MoveNext() method advances the enumerator to the next element in the collection and returns true if there is another element in the collection to read. MoveNext() returns false when the end of the elements has been reached.

◆ The Reset() method resets the enumerator back to its initial position, which is before the first element in the collection.

Before you can read an element, you must call MoveNext() to move to the first element in your collection. Once you've done that, you can read the element using the Current property. In the following example, a while loop iterates over all the elements using myEnumerator, which was declared earlier. Notice that the MoveNext() method moves to each successive element, and while the MoveNext() method returns true, each element is displayed using the Current property within the loop:

```
while (myEnumerator.MoveNext()) {
  Console.WriteLine(myEnumerator.Current);
}
```

As mentioned, the Reset() method sets the enumerator back to before the first element. In the following example, the Reset() method resets the position of myEnumerator, then the MoveNext() method advances to the first element, and finally the Current property displays the first element:

```
myEnumerator.Reset();
myEnumerator.MoveNext();
Console.WriteLine(myEnumerator.Current);
```

You can also use a foreach statement to iterate over a collection. The foreach statement uses an implicit enumerator to iterate over the elements, as shown in the following example that displays the elements in myArrayList:

```
foreach (string myString in myArrayList)
{
  System.Console.WriteLine("myString = " + myString);
}
```

Listing 11.2 illustrates the ArrayList properties and methods shown in this section.

LISTING 11.2: ArrayList PROPERTIES AND METHODS

```
/*
  Example11_2.cs illustrates the use of ArrayList properties
  and methods
*/

using System;
using System.Collections;

class Example11_2
{

  // the DisplayArrayList() method displays the elements in the
  // ArrayList that is supplied as a parameter
  public static void DisplayArrayList(
    string arrayListName, ArrayList myArrayList
  ) {
    for (int counter = 0; counter < myArrayList.Count; counter++)
    {
      Console.WriteLine(arrayListName + "[" + counter + "] = " +
        myArrayList[counter]);
    }
  }

  public static void Main()
  {

    // create an ArrayList object
    ArrayList myArrayList = new ArrayList();
```

```csharp
// set and display the Capacity property
myArrayList.Capacity = 10;
Console.WriteLine("myArrayList.Capacity = " +
    myArrayList.Capacity);

// display the IsFixedSize and IsReadOnly properties
Console.WriteLine("myArrayList.IsFixedSize = " +
    myArrayList.IsFixedSize);
Console.WriteLine("myArrayList.IsReadOnly = " +
    myArrayList.IsReadOnly);

// add eight string elements to myArrayList using the Add(),
// Insert(), AddRange(), and InsertRange() methods
Console.WriteLine("Adding eight string elements to myArrayList");
myArrayList.Add("This");
myArrayList.Insert(1, "is");
string[] myStringArray = {"a", "test"};
myArrayList.AddRange(myStringArray);
string[] anotherStringArray = {"Here's", "some", "more", "text"};
myArrayList.InsertRange(myArrayList.Count, anotherStringArray);

// display the elements in myArrayList using the
// DisplayArrayList() method defined earlier
DisplayArrayList("myArrayList", myArrayList);

// use the SetRange() method to copy the elements from
// anotherStringArray to myArrayList, starting at index 0
Console.WriteLine("Using the SetRange() method to copy the\n" +
    "elements from anotherStringArray to myArrayList,\n" +
    "starting at index 0");
myArrayList.SetRange(0, anotherStringArray);
DisplayArrayList("myArrayList", myArrayList);

// use the Contains() method to determine if the string "text"
// is in the ArrayList; if it is, then use the IndexOf() and
// LastIndexOf() methods to display the first and last occurrence
if (myArrayList.Contains("text"))
{
  int index = myArrayList.IndexOf("text");
  Console.WriteLine("myArrayList does contain the word 'text'");
  Console.WriteLine("'text' first occurs at index " + index);
  index = myArrayList.LastIndexOf("text");
  Console.WriteLine("'text' last occurs at index " + index);
}

// remove element 0, first "text" element, and two
// elements starting at index 3
Console.WriteLine("Removing elements from myArrayList");
```

```
myArrayList.RemoveAt(0);
myArrayList.Remove("text");
myArrayList.RemoveRange(3, 2);
DisplayArrayList("myArrayList", myArrayList);

// use the Sort() method to sort myArrayList
Console.WriteLine("Using the Sort() method to sort myArrayList");
myArrayList.Sort();
DisplayArrayList("myArrayList", myArrayList);

// use the BinarySearch() method to search myArrayList
Console.WriteLine("Using the BinarySearch() method to search myArrayList");
int index2 = myArrayList.BinarySearch("some");
Console.WriteLine("Found 'some' at index " + index2);

// use the Reverse() method to reverse myArrayList
Console.WriteLine("Using the Reverse() method");
myArrayList.Reverse();
DisplayArrayList("myArrayList", myArrayList);

// use the TrimToSize() method to reduce the capacity of
// myArrayList to the actual number of elements in myArrayList
Console.WriteLine("Using the TrimToSize() method to reduce the\n" +
  "capacity of myArrayList");
myArrayList.TrimToSize();
Console.WriteLine("myArrayList.Capacity = " +
    myArrayList.Capacity);

// use the GetRange() method to get a range of elements
// from myArrayList
Console.WriteLine("Using the GetRange() method to get two\n" +
  "elements from myArrayList, starting at index 1");
ArrayList anotherArrayList = myArrayList.GetRange(1, 2);
DisplayArrayList("anotherArrayList", anotherArrayList);

// get an enumerator using the GetEnumerator() method
// and use it to read the elements in myArrayList
Console.WriteLine("Using the GetEnumerator() method to get an enumerator");
IEnumerator myEnumerator = myArrayList.GetEnumerator();
while (myEnumerator.MoveNext())
{
  Console.WriteLine("myEnumerator.Current = " + myEnumerator.Current);
}

// use the Reset() method and access the first row again using MoveNext()
Console.WriteLine("Using the Reset() method and accessing\n" +
  " the first row again using MoveNext()");
myEnumerator.Reset();
```

```
        myEnumerator.MoveNext();
        Console.WriteLine("myEnumerator.Current = " + myEnumerator.Current);

        // Use a foreach statement to read the contents of myArrayList
        Console.WriteLine("Using a foreach statement to read " +
          "the contents of myArrayList");
        foreach (string myString in myArrayList)
        {
          System.Console.WriteLine("myString = " + myString);
        }

      }

  }
```

The output from this program is as follows:

```
myArrayList.Capacity = 10
myArrayList.IsFixedSize = False
myArrayList.IsReadOnly = False
Adding eight string elements to myArrayList
myArrayList[0] = This
myArrayList[1] = is
myArrayList[2] = a
myArrayList[3] = test
myArrayList[4] = Here's
myArrayList[5] = some
myArrayList[6] = more
myArrayList[7] = text
Using the SetRange() method to copy the
elements from anotherStringArray to myArrayList,
starting at index 0
myArrayList[0] = Here's
myArrayList[1] = some
myArrayList[2] = more
myArrayList[3] = text
myArrayList[4] = Here's
myArrayList[5] = some
myArrayList[6] = more
myArrayList[7] = text
myArrayList does contain the word 'text'
'text' first occurs at index 3
'text' last occurs at index 7
Removing elements from myArrayList
myArrayList[0] = some
myArrayList[1] = more
myArrayList[2] = Here's
myArrayList[3] = text
```

```
Using the Sort() method to sort myArrayList
myArrayList[0] = Here's
myArrayList[1] = more
myArrayList[2] = some
myArrayList[3] = text
Using the BinarySearch() method to search myArrayList
Found 'some' at index 2
Using the Reverse() method
myArrayList[0] = text
myArrayList[1] = some
myArrayList[2] = more
myArrayList[3] = Here's
Using the TrimToSize() method to reduce the
capacity of myArrayList
myArrayList.Capacity = 4
Using the GetRange() method to get two
elements from myArrayList, starting at index 1
anotherArrayList[0] = some
anotherArrayList[1] = more
Using the GetEnumerator() method to get an enumerator
myEnumerator.Current = text
myEnumerator.Current = some
myEnumerator.Current = more
myEnumerator.Current = Here's
Using the Reset() method and accessing
  the first row again using MoveNext()
myEnumerator.Current = text
Using a foreach statement to read the contents of myArrayList
myString = text
myString = some
myString = more
myString = Here's
```

Adding Objects to an *ArrayList*

The previous examples showed an ArrayList containing string elements. As you'll see in this section, you can also add objects of your own classes to an ArrayList. You'll see an ArrayList containing Car objects in these examples—you've seen similar Car classes in Chapter 5, "Object-Oriented Programming."

When you create an ArrayList consisting of elements that are objects of your own class—and you want to be able to sort those elements—then your class must implement the IComparable interface. The IComparable interface specifies that your class must implement the CompareTo() method. In addition, your class must implement the Compare() method of IComparer. By having your class implement these two methods, you enable an ArrayList to sort your objects. This may sound a little confusing, but it will make sense once you look at an example.

The following Car class implements the IComparable interface—which means we'll be able to sort an ArrayList of Car objects later. The Car class implements the CompareTo() method of the IComparable interface; in addition, the Car class implements the Compare() method of IComparer. Notice that the yearBuilt field sorts the Car objects (we didn't have to use the yearBuilt field to sort the objects; we could have picked the model field, but we picked the yearBuilt field to show you how to sort objects based on a number):

```
public class Car : IComparable
{

  // declare the fields
  public string model;
  public int yearBuilt;

  // define the constructor
  public Car(string model, int yearBuilt)
  {
    this.model = model;
    this.yearBuilt = yearBuilt;
  }

  // override the ToString() method
  public override string ToString()
  {
    return "model is " + model + ", yearBuilt is " + yearBuilt;
  }

  // implement the Compare() method of IComparer
  public int Compare(Object lhs, Object rhs)
  {
    Car lhsCar = (Car) lhs;
    Car rhsCar = (Car) rhs;
    if (lhsCar.yearBuilt < rhsCar.yearBuilt)
    {
      return -1;
    } else if (lhsCar.yearBuilt > rhsCar.yearBuilt)
    {
      return 1;
    } else
    {
      return 0;
    }
  }

  // implement the CompareTo() method of IComparable
  public int CompareTo(Object rhs)
  {
    return Compare(this, rhs);
  }

}
```

In the following sections you'll see how to add, find, remove, sort, and search elements in an ArrayList of Car objects.

ADDING ELEMENTS USING THE *ADD()* METHOD

You can use the Add() method to add an element to an ArrayList. First, we need to create a new ArrayList object:

```
ArrayList myArrayList = new ArrayList();
```

Second, we need to create some Car objects that we'll show you how to add later to myArrayList; the following statements create four Car objects:

```
Car myMR2 = new Car("MR2", 2001);
Car myBoxster = new Car("Boxster", 2001);
Car myCorvette = new Car("Corvette", 1999);
Car myThunderbird = new Car("Thunderbird", 1979);
```

The following examples add these Car objects to myArrayList using the Add() method; notice that the reference to each Car object is supplied as the parameter to the Add() method:

```
myArrayList.Add(myMR2);
myArrayList.Add(myBoxster);
myArrayList.Add(myCorvette);
myArrayList.Add(myThunderbird);
```

The other ArrayList methods for adding and inserting elements also accept object references. You saw examples of those methods earlier, so similar ones won't be repeated here.

FINDING ELEMENTS USING THE *CONTAINS()* AND *INDEXOF()* METHODS

You can use the Contains() method to find out if an element is contained in an ArrayList, and you can use the IndexOf() method to get the index of an element. The following if statement uses the Contains() method to determine if myBoxster is in myArrayList; if so, the IndexOf() method gets the index where myBoxster occurs:

```
if (myArrayList.Contains(myBoxster))
{
  int index = myArrayList.IndexOf(myBoxster);
  Console.WriteLine("myBoxster occurs at index " + index);
}
```

Because myArrayList contains myBoxster at index 1, this example displays 1 for the index value.

REMOVING ELEMENTS USING THE *REMOVE()* METHOD

You can use the Remove() method to remove elements from an ArrayList. The following example uses the Remove() method to remove myBoxster from myArrayList:

```
myArrayList.Remove(myBoxster);
```

Notice that the myBoxster object reference is passed to the Remove() method.

SORTING ELEMENTS USING THE *SORT()* METHOD

You can use the Sort() method to sort elements in an ArrayList. If your ArrayList contains any of the base types such as numbers or strings, then the elements are sorted in ascending numeric or alphabetical order. If, however, your ArrayList contains objects, then you must indicate how the objects are to be sorted. This is where the CompareTo() and Compare() methods mentioned earlier come in.

Before getting into these methods, we just want to say that you still call the Sort() method in the usual way. For example, the following statement calls the Sort() method for myArrayList:

```
myArrayList.Sort();
```

To sort the objects in your ArrayList, your class must implement the CompareTo() method of the IComparable interface, and it can also implement the Compare() method of the IComparer interface.

Implementing the CompareTo() Method

The CompareTo() method is invoked automatically when you call the Sort() method for your ArrayList. The CompareTo() method compares the current object with another object of the same class and returns an int. The value of this int decides whether the current object appears before the other object in the sorted list:

- ◆ If the int is negative, then the current object is less than the other object, and the current object will appear first.

- ◆ If the int is positive, then the current object is greater than the other object, and the current object will appear second.

- ◆ If the int is zero, then the current object is equal to the other object, and the position of the current object is unchanged.

Precisely what is meant by *less than*, *equal to*, or *greater than* for your objects is for you to decide. In our example, it depends on the value of the yearBuilt field of each Car object.

Getting back to the code, the CompareTo() method is called repeatedly until all the objects in your ArrayList are sorted. The CompareTo() method for the Car class is defined as follows:

```
public int CompareTo(object rhs) {
    return Compare(this, rhs);
}
```

Because each element in an ArrayList is stored as an object, the parameter to the CompareTo() method is an object. You can think of the two elements that are to be ordered as being on the left and right side (*lhs* and *rhs*). As you can see from the definition of the CompareTo() method, it accepts an object parameter named rhs; rhs represents the object on the right side. The this object reference refers to the current object, which corresponds to the object on the left side. The CompareTo() method then calls the Compare() method to perform the comparison, passing the this object reference and rhs as parameters to Compare().

Implementing the Compare() Method

The Compare() method actually compares the two objects, and it returns the int that indicates whether the object on the left side is less than, equal to, or greater than the object on the right side. The Compare() method for the Car class is as follows:

```
public int Compare(object lhs, object rhs)
{
  Car lhsCar = (Car) lhs;
  Car rhsCar = (Car) rhs;
  if (lhsCar.yearBuilt < rhsCar.yearBuilt)
  {
    return -1;
  } else if (lhsCar.yearBuilt > rhsCar.yearBuilt)
  {
    return 1;
  } else
  {
    return 0;
  }
}
```

The Compare() method accepts two object parameters named lhs and rhs—these are the objects on the left and right side, respectively. These parameters are then cast to Car objects named lhsCar and rhsCar. As mentioned earlier, the yearBuilt field orders the objects, so the yearBuilt fields of lhsCar and rhsCar are compared using if statements:

- If lhsCar.yearBuilt is less than rhsCar.yearBuilt, then −1 is returned.

- If lhsCar.yearBuilt is greater than rhsCar.yearBuilt, then 1 is returned.

- If lhsCar.yearBuilt is equal to rhsCar.yearBuilt, then 0 is returned.

The returned value is passed back to CompareTo(), which originally called Compare().

Now that you've seen the long way to do comparisons, we can tell you about a shortcut: We didn't have to implement the Compare() method at all. We could have simply called the CompareTo() method for the int type using the yearBuilt field. For example, the original CompareTo() method could have simply been as follows:

```
public int CompareTo(object rhs)
{
  Car rhsCar = (Car) rhs;
  return this.yearBuilt.CompareTo(rhsCar.yearBuilt);
}
```

As you can see, in this example, we didn't call a Compare() method. We just called the CompareTo() method using the yearBuilt field. The CompareTo() method called comes with the int type, and you can use this method as is, instead of writing your own Compare() method. Why then—you cry—did we go into so much detail before? The answer is that you should understand how to write your own Compare() method—eventually you'll need to do so when developing your own complex classes.

SEARCHING ELEMENTS USING THE *BINARYSEARCH()* METHOD

You can use the BinarySearch() method to search for elements in a sorted ArrayList. Once your ArrayList is sorted, you can use the BinarySearch() method to search for a specified object. For example, the following statement uses the BinarySearch() method to search myArrayList for myCorvette:

```
int index2 = myArrayList.BinarySearch(myCorvette);
```

Listing 11.3 illustrates an ArrayList containing Car objects.

LISTING 11.3: AN ArrayList CONTAINING CAR OBJECTS

```csharp
/*
  Example11_3.cs illustrates the use of an ArrayList that contains
  objects of the Car class
*/

using System;
using System.Collections;


// declare the Car class
public class Car : IComparable
{

  // declare the fields
  public string model;
  public int yearBuilt;

  // define the constructor
  public Car(string model, int yearBuilt)
  {
    this.model = model;
    this.yearBuilt = yearBuilt;
  }

  // override the ToString() method
  public override string ToString()
  {
    return "model is " + model + ", yearBuilt is " + yearBuilt;
  }

  // implement the Compare() method of IComparer
  public int Compare(object lhs, object rhs)
  {
    Car lhsCar = (Car) lhs;
    Car rhsCar = (Car) rhs;
```

```csharp
    if (lhsCar.yearBuilt < rhsCar.yearBuilt)
    {
      return -1;
    } else if (lhsCar.yearBuilt > rhsCar.yearBuilt)
    {
      return 1;
    } else
    {
      return 0;
    }
  }

  // implement the CompareTo() method of IComparable
  public int CompareTo(object rhs)
  {
    return Compare(this, rhs);
  }

  // alternative CompareTo() method that simply calls the
  // CompareTo() method that comes with the int type
  // (currently commented out)
  /* public int CompareTo(object rhs)
  {
    Car rhsCar = (Car) rhs;
    return this.yearBuilt.CompareTo(rhsCar.yearBuilt);
  }*/

}


class Example11_3
{

  // the DisplayArrayList() method displays the elements in the
  // supplied ArrayList
  public static void DisplayArrayList(
    string arrayListName, ArrayList myArrayList
  ) {
    for (int counter = 0; counter < myArrayList.Count; counter++)
    {
      Console.WriteLine(arrayListName + "[" + counter + "] = " +
        myArrayList[counter]);
    }
  }

  public static void Main()
  {
```

```
// create an ArrayList object
ArrayList myArrayList = new ArrayList();

// add four Car objects to myArrayList using the Add() method
Console.WriteLine("Adding four Car objects to myArrayList");
Car myMR2 = new Car("MR2", 2001);
Car myBoxster = new Car("Boxster", 2001);
Car myCorvette = new Car("Corvette", 1999);
Car myThunderbird = new Car("Thunderbird", 1979);
myArrayList.Add(myMR2);
myArrayList.Add(myBoxster);
myArrayList.Add(myCorvette);
myArrayList.Add(myThunderbird);
DisplayArrayList("myArrayList", myArrayList);

// use the Contains() method to determine if myBoxster
// is in the ArrayList; if it is, then use the IndexOf()
// method to display the index
if (myArrayList.Contains(myBoxster))
{
  Console.WriteLine("myArrayList does contain myBoxster");
  int index = myArrayList.IndexOf(myBoxster);
  Console.WriteLine("myBoxster occurs at index " + index);
}

// remove myBoxster from myArrayList
Console.WriteLine("Removing myBoxster from myArrayList");
myArrayList.Remove(myBoxster);
DisplayArrayList("myArrayList", myArrayList);

// use the Sort() method to sort myArrayList
Console.WriteLine("Using the Sort() method to sort myArrayList");
myArrayList.Sort();
DisplayArrayList("myArrayList", myArrayList);

// use the BinarySearch() method to search myArrayList for
// myCorvette
Console.WriteLine("Using the BinarySearch() method to " +
  "search myArrayList\n" +
  " for myCorvette");
int index2 = myArrayList.BinarySearch(myCorvette);
Console.WriteLine("Found myCorvette at index " + index2);

// use the GetRange() method to get a range of elements
// from myArrayList
Console.WriteLine("Using the GetRange() method to get two\n" +
  " elements from myArrayList, starting at index 1");
```

```
        ArrayList anotherArrayList = myArrayList.GetRange(1, 2);
        DisplayArrayList("anotherArrayList", anotherArrayList);

        // get an enumerator using the GetEnumerator() method
        // and use it to read the elements in myArrayList
        Console.WriteLine("Using the GetEnumerator() method to get an enumerator");
        IEnumerator myEnumerator = myArrayList.GetEnumerator();
        while (myEnumerator.MoveNext())
        {
          Console.WriteLine("myEnumerator.Current = " + myEnumerator.Current);
        }

        // use the Reset() method and access the first row again using MoveNext()
        Console.WriteLine("Using the Reset() method and accessing\n" +
          " the first row again using MoveNext()");
        myEnumerator.Reset();
        myEnumerator.MoveNext();
        Console.WriteLine("myEnumerator.Current = " + myEnumerator.Current);

        // Use a foreach statement to read the contents of myArrayList
        Console.WriteLine("Using a foreach statement to read " +
          "the contents of myArrayList");
        foreach (Car myCar in myArrayList)
        {
          System.Console.WriteLine("myCar = " + myCar);
        }

    }

}
```

Notice the simplified CompareTo() method in the Car class; it is commented out so that you can see the use of the Compare() method.

The output from this program is as follows:

```
Adding four Car objects to myArrayList
myArrayList[0] = model is MR2, yearBuilt is 2001
myArrayList[1] = model is Boxster, yearBuilt is 2001
myArrayList[2] = model is Corvette, yearBuilt is 1999
myArrayList[3] = model is Thunderbird, yearBuilt is 1979
myArrayList does contain myBoxster
myBoxster occurs at index 1
Removing myBoxster from myArrayList
myArrayList[0] = model is MR2, yearBuilt is 2001
myArrayList[1] = model is Corvette, yearBuilt is 1999
myArrayList[2] = model is Thunderbird, yearBuilt is 1979
Using the Sort() method to sort myArrayList
```

```
myArrayList[0] = model is Thunderbird, yearBuilt is 1979
myArrayList[1] = model is Corvette, yearBuilt is 1999
myArrayList[2] = model is MR2, yearBuilt is 2001
Using the BinarySearch() method to search myArrayList
  for myCorvette
Found myCorvette at index 1
Using the GetRange() method to get two
  elements from myArrayList, starting at index 1
anotherArrayList[0] = model is Corvette, yearBuilt is 1999
anotherArrayList[1] = model is MR2, yearBuilt is 2001
Using the GetEnumerator() method to get an enumerator
myEnumerator.Current = model is Thunderbird, yearBuilt is 1979
myEnumerator.Current = model is Corvette, yearBuilt is 1999
myEnumerator.Current = model is MR2, yearBuilt is 2001
Using the Reset() method and accessing
  the first row again using MoveNext()
myEnumerator.Current = model is Thunderbird, yearBuilt is 1979
Using a foreach statement to read the contents of myArrayList
myCar = model is Thunderbird, yearBuilt is 1979
myCar = model is Corvette, yearBuilt is 1999
myCar = model is MR2, yearBuilt is 2001
```

Understanding Bit Arrays

A *bit array* is an array of Boolean values. Each Boolean value in the array is represented using a single bit (0 or 1). Using a bit to store each Boolean value requires less memory than a `bool`, and therefore a bit array uses less memory than an array of `bool` elements. Like the other collections, the number of elements stored in a bit array is dynamic.

The `BitArray` class contains the definition for a bit array. The `BitArray` class also contains a rich set of methods you can use to manipulate the bit elements. For example, you can perform AND, OR, and exclusive OR operations on corresponding bits stored in two separate bit arrays.

You'll first examine a simple example of how to create and use a `BitArray` object; then you'll see all the public properties and methods of the `BitArray` class and examine a more complex example.

Creating and Using a *BitArray*

The first step is to create a `BitArray` object, as shown in the following example:

```
BitArray myBitArray = new BitArray(4);
```

As you can see, you can specify the initial number of array elements in the constructor. In this example, `myBitArray` has four elements. You can get or set the number of array elements using the `Length` property; the following example displays the `Length` property for `myBitArray`:

```
Console.WriteLine(myBitArray.Length);
```

As with a regular array, you set an element in a `BitArray` by specifying its index placed within square brackets. The following examples set the four elements in `myBitArray` to Boolean values:

```
myBitArray[0] = false;
myBitArray[1] = true;
myBitArray[2] = true;
myBitArray[3] = false;
```

You get the actual number of elements stored in a `BitArray` using the `Count` property. The `Count` property for `myBitArray` is 4 because there are four elements in this `BitArray`. The following `for` loop uses the `Count` property and displays the four elements in `myBitArray`:

```
for (int counter = 0; counter < myBitArray.Count; counter++) {
  Console.WriteLine(myBitArray[counter]);
}
```

Listing 11.4 illustrates the use of this `BitArray`.

LISTING 11.4: A BitArray

```
/*
  Example11_4.cs illustrates the use of a BitArray
*/

using System;
using System.Collections;

class Example11_4
{

  public static void Main()
  {

    // create a BitArray object
    BitArray myBitArray = new BitArray(4);

    // display the Length property
    Console.WriteLine("myBitArray.Length = " +
      myBitArray.Length);

    // set the four elements of the BitArray
    myBitArray[0] = false;
    myBitArray[1] = true;
    myBitArray[2] = true;
    myBitArray[3] = false;

    // display the elements of the BitArray
    for (int counter = 0; counter < myBitArray.Count; counter++)
    {
```

```
        Console.WriteLine("myBitArray[" + counter + "] = " +
            myBitArray[counter]);
    }

  }

}
```

The output from this program is as follows:

```
myBitArray.Length = 4
myBitArray[0] = False
myBitArray[1] = True
myBitArray[2] = True
myBitArray[3] = False
```

BitArray Properties and Methods

The BitArray class provides a number of useful properties and methods you can use in your programs. Table 11.3 shows the public BitArray properties.

TABLE 11.3: BitArray PROPERTIES

PROPERTY	TYPE	DESCRIPTION
Count	int	Gets the number of elements actually stored in the BitArray.
IsReadOnly	bool	Checks whether the BitArray is readonly.
IsSynchronized	bool	Checks whether access to the BitArray is synchronized (thread-safe).
Item	object	Gets or sets the element at the specified index. This is the indexer for the BitArray class.
Length	object	Gets or sets the number of elements that can be stored in the BitArray.
SyncRoot	object	Gets an object that can be used to synchronize access to the BitArray.

Table 11.4 shows the public BitArray methods.

TABLE 11.4: BitArray METHODS

METHOD	RETURN TYPE	DESCRIPTION
And()	BitArray	Performs an AND operation on the elements in the current BitArray with the corresponding elements in a BitArray supplied as a parameter.
Clone()	object	Creates a shallow copy of the BitArray.

Continued on next page

TABLE 11.4: BitArray METHODS *(continued)*

METHOD	RETURN TYPE	DESCRIPTION
CopyTo()	void	Copies elements from the BitArray to a one-dimensional array.
Equals() (inherited from Object)	bool	Overloaded. Determines whether two object instances are equal.
Get()	bool	Returns the value of the bit at a specified position in the BitArray.
GetEnumerator()	IEnumerator	Returns an enumerator that can iterate through the BitArray.
GetHashCode() (inherited from Object)	int	Returns a hash code for a particular type.
GetType() (inherited from Object)	Type	Returns the type of the current instance.
Not()	BitArray	Inverts all the element values in the BitArray: Elements that are set to true are changed to false, and elements that are set to false are changed to true.
Or()	BitArray	Performs an OR operation on the elements in the current BitArray with the corresponding elements in a BitArray supplied as a parameter.
Set()	void	Sets the element at a specified position in the BitArray to a supplied value.
SetAll()	void	Sets all the elements in the BitArray to the specified value.
ToString() (inherited from Object)	string	Returns a string that represents the current object.
Xor()	BitArray	Performs an exclusive OR operation on the elements in the current BitArray with the corresponding elements in a BitArray supplied as a value.

The following sections illustrate some of these methods.

INVERTING THE ELEMENTS VALUES USING THE *NOT()* METHOD

You can use the Not() method to invert the element values in a BitArray. Elements that are set to true are changed to false, and elements that are set to false are changed to true. The Not() method doesn't accept any parameters, and this method uses the following syntax:

```
bitArray.Not()
```

where *bitArray* is the BitArray whose elements you want to invert.

The following example uses the Not() method to invert the element values set earlier for myBitArray:

```
myBitArray.Not();
```

The elements in myBitArray will be changed to the following:

```
myBitArray[0] = true
myBitArray[1] = false
myBitArray[2] = false
myBitArray[3] = true
```

Notice that the element values are inverted.

PERFORMING AN OR OPERATION USING THE *OR()* METHOD

You can use the Or() method to perform an OR operation on the elements in the current BitArray with the corresponding elements in a BitArray supplied as a parameter to the Or() method. The Or() method accepts a BitArray object, and this method uses the following syntax:

```
bitArray1.Or(bitArray2)
```

where *bitArray1* and *bitArray2* are the BitArray objects whose elements you want to perform an OR operation on. The result of the OR operation is stored in *bitArray1*.

Assume you have two BitArray objects, named myBitArray and anotherBitArray, with four elements each:

```
myBitArray[0] = true
myBitArray[1] = false
myBitArray[2] = false
myBitArray[3] = true
anotherBitArray[0] = false
anotherBitArray[1] = true
anotherBitArray[2] = true
anotherBitArray[3] = false
```

The following example uses the Or() method to perform an OR operation on each corresponding element in myBitArray and anotherBitArray (the results of the OR operation are stored in myBitArray):

```
myBitArray.Or(anotherBitArray);
```

Because myBitArray[0] is true and anotherBitArray[0] is false, the result of the OR operation for these two elements is true—which is the result assigned to myBitArray[0]. Similarly, because myBitArray[1] is false and anotherBitArray[1] is false, the result assigned to myBitArray[1] is true. The OR operation is repeated for the remaining elements in the two BitArray objects, and at the end of the OR operations myBitArray will be set to the following:

```
myBitArray[0] = true
myBitArray[1] = true
myBitArray[2] = true
myBitArray[3] = true
```

Listing 11.5 illustrates the Not() and Or() methods for the two BitArray objects shown in these examples.

LISTING 11.5: BitArray **METHODS**

```
/*
  Example11_5.cs illustrates the use of BitArray methods
*/

using System;
using System.Collections;

class Example11_5
{

  // the DisplayBitArray() method displays the elements in the
  // supplied BitArray
  public static void DisplayBitArray(
    string arrayListName, BitArray myBitArray
  ) {
    for (int counter = 0; counter < myBitArray.Count; counter++)
    {
      Console.WriteLine(arrayListName + "[" + counter + "] = " +
        myBitArray[counter]);
    }
  }

  public static void Main()
  {

    // create a BitArray object
    BitArray myBitArray = new BitArray(4);
    myBitArray[0] = false;
    myBitArray[1] = true;
    myBitArray[2] = true;
    myBitArray[3] = false;
    DisplayBitArray("myBitArray", myBitArray);

    // create another BitArray object, passing myBitArray to
    // the constructor
    BitArray anotherBitArray = new BitArray(myBitArray);
    DisplayBitArray("anotherBitArray", myBitArray);

    // use the Not() method to reverse the elements in myBitArray
    Console.WriteLine("Using the Not() method to reverse the element\n" +
      " values in myBitArray");
    myBitArray.Not();
    DisplayBitArray("myBitArray", myBitArray);

    // use the Or() method to perform an OR operation on the elements
    // in myBitArray and anotherBitArray
```

```
        Console.WriteLine("Using the Or() method to perform an OR operation on\n" +
            " the elements in myBitArray and anotherBitArray");
        myBitArray.Or(anotherBitArray);
        DisplayBitArray("myBitArray", myBitArray);

    }

}
```

The output from this program is as follows:

```
myBitArray[0] = False
myBitArray[1] = True
myBitArray[2] = True
myBitArray[3] = False
anotherBitArray[0] = False
anotherBitArray[1] = True
anotherBitArray[2] = True
anotherBitArray[3] = False
Using the Not() method to reverse the element
 values in myBitArray
myBitArray[0] = True
myBitArray[1] = False
myBitArray[2] = False
myBitArray[3] = True
Using the Or() method to perform an OR operation on
 the elements in myBitArray and anotherBitArray
myBitArray[0] = True
myBitArray[1] = True
myBitArray[2] = True
myBitArray[3] = True
```

Understanding Hash Tables

A *hash table* allows you to store a *key* along with a *value*. You can then use this key to later look up the value in the hash table. Conceptually, you can think of a hash table as being similar to a dictionary. In a dictionary, you can look up the definition of word; the word acts as the key, and the word definition is the value.

One use of a hash table is to store a list of U.S. state abbreviations along with the corresponding state name. The state abbreviation would be the key (`"CA"`, for example), and the state name would be the value (`"California"`).

The `Hashtable` class contains the definition for a hash table. In the following sections, you'll examine a simple example of how to create and use a `Hashtable` object; then you'll see all the public properties and methods of the `Hashtable` class and examine a more complex example.

Creating and Using a *Hashtable*

The first step is to create a Hashtable object, as shown in the following example:

```
Hashtable myHashtable = new Hashtable();
```

You use the Add() method to add an element to a Hashtable. The following statements add some state abbreviations and their corresponding names to myHashtable using the Add() method:

```
myHashtable.Add("AL", "Alabama");
myHashtable.Add("CA", "California");
myHashtable.Add("FL", "Florida");
myHashtable.Add("NY", "New York");
myHashtable.Add("WY", "Wyoming");
```

The first parameter to the Add() method is the key, and the second parameter is the value.

NOTE *The keys and values are stored in a* Hashtable *as objects of the* System.Object *class. You can therefore provide any type for the key and the value—although you'll typically use a string for the key.*

To look up a value for a given key, you supply the key in square brackets to your Hashtable. For example, the following statement looks up the state name for the key "CA" in myHashtable:

```
string myState = (string) myHashtable["CA"];
```

The value returned by the lookup is an object, and therefore we cast it to a string before storing it in myState.

You can use the Keys property of a Hashtable to get all the keys. For example, the following foreach loop uses the Keys property of myHashtable to display all the keys:

```
foreach (string myKey in myHashtable.Keys) \
{
  Console.WriteLine("myKey = " + myKey);
}
```

Similarly, you can use the Values property of a Hashtable to get all the values:

```
foreach(string myValue in myHashtable.Values)
{
  Console.WriteLine("myValue = " + myValue);
}
```

As with other collections, the Count property returns the number of elements in the Hashtable. Because myHashtable contains five elements, the Count property is set to 5. The following example displays the Count property for myHashtable:

```
Console.WriteLine(myHashtable.Count);
```

Listing 11.6 illustrates the Hashtable shown in this section.

LISTING 11.6: A Hashtable

```
/*
  Example11_6.cs illustrates the use of a Hashtable
*/

using System;
using System.Collections;

class Example11_6
{

  public static void Main()
  {

    // create a Hashtable object
    Hashtable myHashtable = new Hashtable();

    // add elements containing US state abbreviations and state
    // names to myHashtable using the Add() method
    myHashtable.Add("AL", "Alabama");
    myHashtable.Add("CA", "California");
    myHashtable.Add("FL", "Florida");
    myHashtable.Add("NY", "New York");
    myHashtable.Add("WY", "Wyoming");

    // display the Count property
    Console.WriteLine("myHashtable.Count = " + myHashtable.Count);

    // lookup the state name for "CA"
    string myState = (string) myHashtable["CA"];
    Console.WriteLine("myState = " + myState);

    // display the keys for myHashtable using the Keys property
    foreach (string myKey in myHashtable.Keys)
    {
      Console.WriteLine("myKey = " + myKey);
    }

    // display the values for myHashtable using the Values property
    foreach(string myValue in myHashtable.Values)
    {
      Console.WriteLine("myValue = " + myValue);
    }

  }

}
```

The output from this program is as follows:

```
myHashtable.Count = 5
myState = California
myKey = CA
myKey = NY
myKey = AL
myKey = FL
myKey = WY
myValue = California
myValue = New York
myValue = Alabama
myValue = Florida
myValue = Wyoming
```

Hashtable **Properties and Methods**

The Hashtable class provides a number of useful properties and methods you can use in your programs. Table 11.5 shows the public Hashtable properties.

TABLE 11.5: Hashtable PROPERTIES

PROPERTY	TYPE	DESCRIPTION
Count	int	Gets the number of elements actually stored in the Hashtable.
IsFixedSize	bool	Checks whether the Hashtable is of a fixed size.
IsReadOnly	bool	Checks whether the Hashtable is readonly.
IsSynchronized	bool	Checks whether access to the Hashtable is synchronized (thread-safe).
Item	object	Gets or sets the element with a specified key. This is the indexer for the Hashtable class.
Keys	ICollection	Gets a collection containing the keys in the Hashtable. The ICollection interface defines the size, enumerators, and synchronization methods for all collections.
SyncRoot	object	Gets an object that can be used to synchronize access to the Hashtable.
Values	ICollection	Gets a collection containing the values in the Hashtable.

Table 11.6 shows the public Hashtable methods.

TABLE 11.6: Hashtable METHODS

METHOD	RETURN TYPE	DESCRIPTION
Synchronized() (static)	Hashtable	Returns a Hashtable wrapper that is synchronized (thread-safe).
Add()	void	Adds an element with a specified key and value to the Hashtable.
Clear()	void	Removes all the elements from the Hashtable.
Clone()	object	Creates a shallow copy of the Hashtable.
Contains()	bool	Determines if a specified key is in the Hashtable.
ContainsKey()	bool	Determines if a specified key is in the Hashtable.
ContainsValue()	bool	Determines if a specified value is in the Hashtable.
CopyTo()	void	Copies the keys or values from the Hashtable to a one-dimensional array.
Equals() (inherited from Object)	bool	Determines whether two object instances are equal.
GetEnumerator()	IEnumerator	Overloaded. Returns an enumerator that can iterate through the Hashtable.
GetHashCode() (inherited from Object)	int	Returns a hash code for a particular type.
GetObjectData()	void	Returns the data required to serialize a Hashtable. See Chapter 15, "Streams and Input/Output," for details on serialization.
GetType() (inherited from Object)	Type	Returns the type of the current instance.
OnDeserialization()	void	Implements the ISerializable interface and raises the deserialization event when the deserialization is complete. See Chapter 12, "Delegates and Events," for details on events.
Remove()	void	Removes an element with a specified key from the Hashtable.
ToString() (inherited from Object)	string	Returns a string that represents the current object.

The following sections illustrate some of these methods.

CHECKING FOR A KEY USING THE *CONTAINSKEY()* METHOD

You can use the Contains() or ContainsKey() methods to check if a Hashtable contains a specified key. Both of these methods return a bool value that indicates if the key was found; both methods accept an object parameter and use the following syntax:

```
hashtable.Contains(value)
hashtable.ContainsKey(value)
```

where *value* is the value you want to find in *hashtable*. If *value* is found, then the methods return true; otherwise they return false.

The following example checks if myHashtable contains the key "FL" using the ContainsKey() method:

```
if (myHastable.ContainsKey("FL"))
{
   Console.WriteLine("myHashtable contains the key FL");
}
```

Because myHashtable does contain the key "FL", ContainsKey() returns true and therefore Console.WriteLine() will be called to display the message.

CHECKING FOR A VALUE USING THE *CONTAINSVALUE()* METHOD

You can use the ContainsValue() method to check if a Hashtable contains a specified value. The ContainsValue() method accepts an object parameter, and this method uses the following syntax:

```
hashtable.ContainsValue(value)
```

where *value* is the value you want to find in *hashtable*. If *value* is found, then ContainsValue() returns true; otherwise it returns false.

The following example uses the ContainsValue() method to check if myHashtable contains the value "Florida":

```
if (myHashtable.ContainsValue("Florida"))
{
   Console.WriteLine("myHashtable contains the value Florida");
}
```

Because myHashtable does contain the value "Florida", ContainsValue() returns true and Console.WriteLine() will be called to display the message.

REMOVING AN ELEMENT USING THE *REMOVE()* METHOD

You can use the Remove() method to remove an element with a specified key from a Hashtable. The Remove() method accepts an object parameter, and this method uses the following syntax:

```
hashtable.Remove(value)
```

where *value* is the value you want to remove from *hashtable*.

The following example uses the Remove() method to remove the element with the key "FL" from myHashtable:

```
myHashtable.Remove("FL");
```

COPYING KEYS AND VALUES TO AN ARRAY USING THE *COPYTO()* METHOD

You can use the CopyTo() method to copy keys and values from a Hashtable to a one-dimensional array. The CopyTo() method accepts an array and an int parameter, and this method uses the following syntax:

```
hashtable.CopyTo(array, index)
```

where *array* is the one-dimensional array to copy elements from *hashtable* and *index* is the index to start reading elements from *hashtable*.

In the examples, we'll show you how to copy the keys and values from myHashtable. Now, although the keys and values are stored as objects of the System.Object class in a Hashtable, the keys in myHashtable are actually strings—therefore, we'll create an array of strings in preparation for storing the keys:

```
string[] myKeys = new string[myHashtable.Count];
```

Notice that the Count property of myHashtable is used to set the size of the array (the Count property contains the number of elements in a Hashtable).

The next statement calls the CopyTo() method to copy the keys from myHashtable to the myKeys array, starting at index 0; notice that the CopyTo() method is called via the Keys property:

```
myHashtable.Keys.CopyTo(myKeys, 0);
```

The next example copies the values from myHashtable into a new array named myValues; notice that CopyTo() is called via the Values property:

```
string[] myValues = new string[myHashtable.Count];
myHashtable.Values.CopyTo(myValues, 0);
```

Listing 11.7 illustrates the Hashtable methods.

LISTING 11.7: Hashtable METHODS

```
/*
  Example11_7.cs illustrates the use of the Hashtable methods
*/

using System;
using System.Collections;

class Example11_7
{

  public static void Main()
  {
```

```csharp
// create a Hashtable object
Hashtable myHashtable = new Hashtable();

// add elements containing US state abbreviations and state
// names to myHashtable using the Add() method
myHashtable.Add("AL", "Alabama");
myHashtable.Add("CA", "California");
myHashtable.Add("FL", "Florida");
myHashtable.Add("NY", "New York");
myHashtable.Add("WY", "Wyoming");

// display the keys for myHashtable using the Keys property
foreach (string myKey in myHashtable.Keys)
{
  Console.WriteLine("myKey = " + myKey);
}

// display the values for myHashtable using the Values property
foreach(string myValue in myHashtable.Values)
{
  Console.WriteLine("myValue = " + myValue);
}

// use the ContainsKey() method to check if myHashtable
// contains the key "FL"
if (myHashtable.ContainsKey("FL"))
{
  Console.WriteLine("myHashtable contains the key FL");
}

// use the ContainsValue() method to check if myHashtable
// contains the value "Florida"
if (myHashtable.ContainsValue("Florida"))
{
  Console.WriteLine("myHashtable contains the value Florida");
}

// use the Remove() method to remove FL from myHashtable
Console.WriteLine("Removing FL from myHashtable");
myHashtable.Remove("FL");

// get the number of elements in myHashtable using the Count
// property
int count = myHashtable.Count;

// copy the keys from myHashtable into an array using
// the CopyTo() method and then display the array contents
Console.WriteLine("Copying keys to myKeys array");
```

```
      string[] myKeys = new string[count];
      myHashtable.Keys.CopyTo(myKeys, 0);
      for (int counter = 0; counter < myKeys.Length; counter++)
      {
        Console.WriteLine("myKeys[" + counter + "] = " +
          myKeys[counter]);
      }

      // copy the values from myHashtable into an array using
      // the CopyTo() method and then display the array contents
      Console.WriteLine("Copying values to myValues array");
      string[] myValues = new string[count];
      myHashtable.Values.CopyTo(myValues, 0);
      for (int counter = 0; counter < myValues.Length; counter++)
      {
        Console.WriteLine("myValues[" + counter + "] = " +
          myValues[counter]);
      }

    }

  }
```

The output from this program is as follows:

```
myKey = CA
myKey = NY
myKey = AL
myKey = FL
myKey = WY
myValue = California
myValue = New York
myValue = Alabama
myValue = Florida
myValue = Wyoming
myHashtable contains the key FL
myHashtable contains the value Florida
Removing FL from myHashtable
Copying keys to myKeys array
myKeys[0] = CA
myKeys[1] = NY
myKeys[2] = AL
myKeys[3] = WY
Copying values to myValues array
myValues[0] = California
myValues[1] = New York
myValues[2] = Alabama
myValues[3] = Wyoming
```

Understanding Sorted Lists

A *sorted list* is a combination of an array list and a hash table. Like an array list, the elements in a sorted list can be accessed using an index. Like a hash table, each element in a sorted list contains both a key and a value, and each element can also be accessed using the key.

Each element in a sorted list is sorted according to the key, and in the case of a `string` key, the keys will be sorted in alphabetical order. In other words, when you add a new element to a sorted list, the element will automatically be inserted into the sorted list at the appropriate point to maintain the sorted order in the list.

The `SortedList` class contains the definition for a sorted list. You'll first examine a simple example of how to create and use a `SortedList` object; then you'll see all the public properties and methods of the `SortedList` class and examine a more complex example.

Creating and Using a *SortedList*

The first step is to create a `SortedList` object, as shown in the following example:

```
SortedList mySortedList = new SortedList();
```

You can add an element to a `SortedList` using the `Add()` method. Like a `Hashtable`, the first parameter to the `Add()` method for a `SortedList` is the key, and the second parameter is the value. The following statements add some state abbreviations and their corresponding names to `mySortedList` using the `Add()` method:

```
mySortedList.Add("NY", "New York");
mySortedList.Add("FL", "Florida");
mySortedList.Add("AL", "Alabama");
mySortedList.Add("WY", "Wyoming");
mySortedList.Add("CA", "California");
```

As each element is added, it is automatically inserted at the appropriate point to maintain the ordering of the keys. In the example, the ordering of the keys will be `"AL"`, `"CA"`, `"FL"`, `"NY"`, and `"WY"`, and the elements in `mySortedList` will be ordered accordingly.

To get the state name value for `"CA"`, you can pass the key `"CA"` in square brackets to `mySortedList`. For example:

```
string myState = (string) mySortedList["CA"];
```

In this example, the value returned by the lookup is a `System.Object`, and we therefore cast that value to a `string` before storing it in `myState`.

You can also get the state name value for an element at a specified index using the `GetByIndex()` method. The following example gets the state name value for the element at index 3 from `mySortedList` using the `GetByIndex()` method:

```
string anotherState = (string) mySortedList.GetByIndex(3);
```

In this example, `GetByIndex()` returns `"New York"`.

You can use the Keys property of a SortedList to get all the keys. For example, the following foreach loop uses the Keys property and displays all the keys in mySortedList:

```
foreach (string myKey in mySortedList.Keys)
{
  Console.WriteLine("myKey = " + myKey);
}
```

Similarly, you can use the Values property of a SortedList to get all the values:

```
foreach(string myValue in mySortedList.Values)
{
  Console.WriteLine("myValue = " + myValue);
}
```

Listing 11.8 illustrates this SortedList.

LISTING 11.8: A SortedList

```
/*
  Example11_8.cs illustrates the use of a SortedList
*/

using System;
using System.Collections;

class Example11_8
{

  public static void Main()
  {

    // create a SortedList object
    SortedList mySortedList = new SortedList();

    // add elements containing US state abbreviations and state
    // names to mySortedList using the Add() method
    mySortedList.Add("NY", "New York");
    mySortedList.Add("FL", "Florida");
    mySortedList.Add("AL", "Alabama");
    mySortedList.Add("WY", "Wyoming");
    mySortedList.Add("CA", "California");

    // get the state name value for "CA"
    string myState = (string) mySortedList["CA"];
    Console.WriteLine("myState = " + myState);

    // get the state name value at index 3 using the GetByIndex() method
    string anotherState = (string) mySortedList.GetByIndex(3);
    Console.WriteLine("anotherState = " + anotherState);
```

```
    // display the keys for mySortedList using the Keys property
    foreach (string myKey in mySortedList.Keys)
    {
      Console.WriteLine("myKey = " + myKey);
    }

    // display the values for mySortedList using the Values property
    foreach(string myValue in mySortedList.Values)
    {
      Console.WriteLine("myValue = " + myValue);
    }

  }

}
```

The output from this program is as follows:

```
myState = California
anotherState = New York
myKey = AL
myKey = CA
myKey = FL
myKey = NY
myKey = WY
myValue = Alabama
myValue = California
myValue = Florida
myValue = New York
myValue = Wyoming
```

SortedList Properties and Methods

The SortedList class provides a number of useful properties and methods you can use in your programs. Table 11.7 shows the public SortedList properties.

TABLE 11.7: SortedList PROPERTIES

PROPERTY	TYPE	DESCRIPTION
Capacity	int	Gets or sets the capacity of the SortedList.
Count	int	Gets the number of elements actually stored in the SortedList.
IsFixedSize	bool	Checks whether the SortedList is of a fixed size.
IsReadOnly	bool	Checks whether the SortedList is read only.
IsSynchronized	bool	Checks whether access to the SortedList is synchronized (thread-safe).

Continued on next page

TABLE 11.7: SortedList PROPERTIES *(continued)*

PROPERTY	TYPE	DESCRIPTION
Item	object	Gets or sets the element with a specified key. This is the indexer for the SortedList class.
Keys	ICollection	Gets a collection containing the keys in the SortedList.
SyncRoot	object	Gets an object that can be used to synchronize access to the SortedList.
Values	ICollection	Gets a collection containing the values in the SortedList.

Table 11.8 shows the public SortedList methods.

TABLE 11.8: SortedList METHODS

METHOD	RETURN TYPE	DESCRIPTION
Synchronized() (static)	SortedList	Returns a synchronized (thread-safe) wrapper for the SortedList.
Add()	void	Adds an element with a specified key and value to the SortedList.
Clear()	void	Removes all the elements from the SortedList.
Clone()	object	Creates a shallow copy of the SortedList.
Contains()	bool	Determines if a specified key is in the SortedList.
ContainsKey()	bool	Determines if a specified key is in the SortedList.
ContainsValue()	bool	Determines if a specified value is in the SortedList.
CopyTo()	void	Copies the keys or values from the SortedList to a one-dimensional array.
Equals() (inherited from Object)	bool	Overloaded. Determines whether two object instances are equal.
GetByIndex()	object	Returns the value at the specified index of the SortedList.
GetEnumerator()	IDictionaryEnumerator	Returns an enumerator that can iterate through the SortedList.
GetHashCode() (inherited from Object)	int	Returns a hash code for a particular type.

Continued on next page

TABLE 11.8: SortedList METHODS *(continued)*

METHOD	RETURN TYPE	DESCRIPTION
GetKey()	object	Returns the key at the specified index of the SortedList.
GetKeyList()	IList	Returns the keys in the SortedList.
GetType() (inherited from Object)	Type	Returns the type of the current instance.
GetValueList()	IList	Returns the values in the SortedList.
IndexOfKey()	int	Returns the index of a specified key in the SortedList.
IndexOfValue()	int	Returns the index of a specified value in the SortedList.
Remove()	void	Removes the element with a specified key from the SortedList.
RemoveAt()	void	Removes the element at a specified index from the SortedList.
SetByIndex()	void	Replaces the value at a specified index in the SortedList.
ToString() (inherited from Object)	string	Returns a string that represents the current object.
TrimToSize()	void	Reduces the capacity of the SortedList to the actual number of elements stored in the SortedList.

The following sections illustrate some of these methods.

CHECKING FOR A KEY USING THE *CONTAINSKEY()* METHOD

You can use the Contains() method or the ContainsKey() method to check if a SortedList contains a specified key. These methods return true if the SortedList contains the key. The following example checks if mySortedList contains the key "FL" using the ContainsKey() method:

```
if (mySortedList.ContainsKey("FL"))
{
  Console.WriteLine("mySortedList contains the key FL");
}
```

Because mySortedList does contain the key "FL", the Console.WriteLine() method will be called to display the message.

CHECKING FOR A VALUE USING THE *CONTAINSVALUE()* METHOD

You can use the ContainsValue() method to check if a SortedList contains a specified value. This method returns true if the SortedList contains the value. The following example checks if mySorted-List contains the value "Florida" using the ContainsValue() method:

```
if (mySortedList.ContainsValue("Florida"))
{
  Console.WriteLine("mySortedList contains the value Florida");
}
```

Because mySortedList does contain the value "Florida", ContainsValue() returns true and therefore Console.WriteLine()will be called to display the message.

REMOVING AN ELEMENT USING THE *REMOVE()* METHOD

You can use the Remove() method to remove an element with a specified key from a SortedList. The following example removes the element with the key "FL" from mySortedList using Remove():

```
mySortedList.Remove("FL");
```

GETTING A KEY USING THE *GETKEY()* METHOD

You can use the GetKey() method to get the key at a specified index in a SortedList. The following example gets the key at index 3 from mySortedList using GetKey():

```
string keyAtIndex3 = (string) mySortedList.GetKey(3);
```

GETTING AN INDEX USING THE *INDEXOFKEY()* AND *INDEXOFVALUE()* METHODS

You can use the IndexOfKey() method to get the index of an element with a specified key from a SortedList. The following example gets the index of element with the key "NY" from mySortedList using IndexOfKey():

```
int myIndex = mySortedList.IndexOfKey("NY");
```

Similarly, you get the index of an element with a specified value using the IndexOfValue() method:

```
myIndex = mySortedList.IndexOfValue("New York");
```

NOTE IndexOfKey() *will return −1 if the key cannot be found. Similarly,* IndexOfValue() *will return −1 if the value cannot be found.*

REPLACING A VALUE USING THE *SETBYINDEX()* METHOD

You can use the SetByIndex() method to replace the value for an existing element in a SortedList. In the previous example, myIndex was set to the index of the element containing the value "New York"; the following example replaces the value for that element with "New York State":

```
mySortedList.SetByIndex(myIndex, "New York State");
```

GETTING THE KEY LIST USING THE *GETKEYLIST()* METHOD

You can use the GetKeyList() method to get the key list from a SortedList. This method returns an object of the IList interface. The IList interface represents a collection of objects that you can then read, and the IList object returned by GetKeyList() contains the keys from the SortedList.

The following example gets the key list from mySortedList using the GetKeyList() method and then uses a foreach loop to display each key in the list:

```
IList myKeyList = mySortedList.GetKeyList();
foreach(string myKey in myKeyList)
{
  Console.WriteLine("myKey = " + myKey);
}
```

GETTING THE VALUE LIST USING THE *GETVALUELIST()* METHOD

In a similar manner to the GetKeyList() method, the GetValueList() method returns an IList object containing the values from a SortedList. For example:

```
IList myValueList = mySortedList.GetValueList();
foreach(string myValue in myValueList)
{
  Console.WriteLine("myValue = " + myValue);
}
```

Listing 11.9 illustrates these methods.

LISTING 11.9: SortedList METHODS

```
/*
  Example11_9.cs illustrates the use of the SortedList methods
*/

using System;
using System.Collections;

class Example11_9
{

  public static void Main()
  {

    // create a SortedList object
    SortedList mySortedList = new SortedList();

    // add elements containing US state abbreviations and state
    // names to mySortedList using the Add() method
    mySortedList.Add("NY", "New York");
    mySortedList.Add("FL", "Florida");
```

```
mySortedList.Add("AL", "Alabama");
mySortedList.Add("WY", "Wyoming");
mySortedList.Add("CA", "California");

// display the keys for mySortedList using the Keys property
foreach (string myKey in mySortedList.Keys)
{
  Console.WriteLine("myKey = " + myKey);
}

// display the values for mySortedList using the Values property
foreach(string myValue in mySortedList.Values)
{
  Console.WriteLine("myValue = " + myValue);
}

// use the ContainsKey() method to check if mySortedList
// contains the key "FL"
if (mySortedList.ContainsKey("FL"))
{
  Console.WriteLine("mySortedList contains the key FL");
}

// use the ContainsValue() method to check if mySortedList
// contains the value "Florida"
if (mySortedList.ContainsValue("Florida"))
{
  Console.WriteLine("mySortedList contains the value Florida");
}

// use the Remove() method to remove FL from mySortedList
Console.WriteLine("Removing FL from mySortedList");
mySortedList.Remove("FL");

// get the key at index 3 using the GetKey() method
string keyAtIndex3 = (string) mySortedList.GetKey(3);
Console.WriteLine("The key at index 3 is " + keyAtIndex3);

// get the index of the element with the key "NY"
// using the IndexOfKey() method
int myIndex = mySortedList.IndexOfKey("NY");
Console.WriteLine("The index of NY is " + myIndex);

// get the index of the element with the value "New York"
// using the IndexOfValue() method
myIndex = mySortedList.IndexOfValue("New York");
Console.WriteLine("The index of New York is " + myIndex);
```

```
    // replace the value of the element at myIndex with "New York State"
    // using the SetByIndex() method
    Console.WriteLine("Replacing the value New York with New York State");
    mySortedList.SetByIndex(myIndex, "New York State");

    // get the key list using the GetKeyList() method
    Console.WriteLine("Getting the key list");
    IList myKeyList = mySortedList.GetKeyList();
    foreach(string myKey in myKeyList)
    {
      Console.WriteLine("myKey = " + myKey);
    }

    // get the value list using the GetValueList() method
    Console.WriteLine("Getting the value list");
    IList myValueList = mySortedList.GetValueList();
    foreach(string myValue in myValueList)
    {
      Console.WriteLine("myValue = " + myValue);
    }

  }

}
```

The output from this program is as follows:

```
myKey = CA
myKey = NY
myKey = AL
myKey = FL
myKey = WY
myValue = California
myValue = New York
myValue = Alabama
myValue = Florida
myValue = Wyoming
myHashtable contains the key FL
myHashtable contains the value Florida
Removing FL from myHashtable
Copying keys to myKeys array
myKeys[0] = CA
myKeys[1] = NY
myKeys[2] = AL
myKeys[3] = WY
Copying values to myValues array
myValues[0] = California
```

```
myValues[1] = New York
myValues[2] = Alabama
myValues[3] = Wyoming
```

Understanding Queues

A *queue* allows you to store elements on a first-in, first-out basis (FIFO). A C# queue operates in the same manner as a queue in the real world. For example, when you go to your local bank, you join a queue and wait for a bank employee to talk with you; the teller deals with the people in front of you first, and after a person is dealt with, that person leaves the queue.

The Queue class contains the definition for a queue; you'll see the use of a Queue object in this section.

Creating and Using a *Queue*

The first step is to create a Queue object, as shown in the following example:

```
Queue myQueue = new Queue();
```

You add an element to the end of a Queue using the Enqueue() method. The following example adds four elements to myQueue using the Enqueue() method:

```
myQueue.Enqueue("This");
myQueue.Enqueue("is");
myQueue.Enqueue("a");
myQueue.Enqueue("test");
```

The order of these elements in myQueue is "This", "is", "a", and "Test".

You remove an element from the front of a Queue using the Dequeue() method. This method both returns the element and removes it from the Queue. For example:

```
Console.WriteLine(myQueue.Dequeue());
```

This example will display "This". "This" will also be removed from myQueue. Calling myQueue .Dequeue() again will return and remove "is" from myQueue.

You can read the element at the front of a Queue using the Peek() method. This method returns the element but doesn't remove it from the Queue. The following example shows the use of the Peek() method:

```
Console.WriteLine(myQueue.Peek());
```

This example will display "is"—the element currently at the front of myQueue (assuming that "This" is the only element that has been removed from myQueue).

Listing 11.10 illustrates this Queue.

LISTING 11.10: A Queue

```
/*
  Example11_10.cs illustrates the use of a Queue
*/
```

```
using System;
using System.Collections;

class Example11_10
{

  public static void Main()
  {

    // create a Queue object
    Queue myQueue = new Queue();

    // add elements to myQueue using the Enqueue() method
    myQueue.Enqueue("This");
    myQueue.Enqueue("is");
    myQueue.Enqueue("a");
    myQueue.Enqueue("test");

    // display the elements in myQueue
    foreach (string myString in myQueue)
    {
      Console.WriteLine("myString = " + myString);
    }

    // get the number of elements in myQueue using the
    // Count property
    int numElements = myQueue.Count;

    for (int count = 0; count < numElements; count++)
    {

      // examine an element in myQueue using Peek()
      Console.WriteLine("myQueue.Peek() = " +
        myQueue.Peek());

      // remove an element from myQueue using Dequeue()
      Console.WriteLine("myQueue.Dequeue() = " +
        myQueue.Dequeue());

    }

  }

}
```

The output from this program is as follows:

```
myString = This
myString = is
myString = a
myString = test
myQueue.Peek() = This
myQueue.Dequeue() = This
myQueue.Peek() = is
myQueue.Dequeue() = is
myQueue.Peek() = a
myQueue.Dequeue() = a
myQueue.Peek() = test
myQueue.Dequeue() = test
```

Queue Properties and Methods

The Queue class provides a number of useful properties and methods you can use in your programs. Table 11.9 shows the public Queue properties.

TABLE 11.9: Queue PROPERTIES

PROPERTY	TYPE	DESCRIPTION
Count	int	Gets the number of elements actually stored in the Queue
IsReadOnly	bool	Checks whether the Queue is readonly
IsSynchronized	bool	Checks whether access to the Queue is synchronized (thread-safe)
SyncRoot	object	Gets an object that can be used to synchronize access to the Queue

Table 11.10 shows the public Queue methods.

TABLE 11.10: Queue METHODS

METHOD	RETURN TYPE	DESCRIPTION
Synchronized() (static)	Queue	Returns a Queue wrapper that is synchronized (thread-safe).
Clear()	void	Removes all the elements from the Queue.
Clone()	object	Creates a shallow copy of the Queue.
Contains()	bool	Determines if a specified key is in the Queue.
CopyTo()	void	Copies the elements from the Queue to a one-dimensional array.
Dequeue()	object	Removes and returns the element from the beginning of the Queue.

Continued on next page

TABLE 11.10: Queue METHODS *(continued)*

METHOD	RETURN TYPE	DESCRIPTION
Enqueue()	void	Adds an element to the beginning of the Queue.
Equals() (inherited from Object)	bool	Overloaded. Determines whether two object instances are equal.
GetEnumerator()	IEnumerator	Returns an enumerator that can iterate through the Queue.
GetHashCode() (inherited from Object)	int	Returns a hash code for a particular type.
GetType() (inherited from Object)	Type	Returns the type of the current instance.
Peek()	object	Returns the element from the beginning of the Queue but doesn't remove it.
ToArray()	object[]	Copies the elements in the Queue to an array.
ToString() (inherited from Object)	string	Returns a string that represents the current object.

The previous program shown in Listing 11.10 already illustrated the use of the main property and methods.

Understanding Stacks

A *stack* allows you to store elements on a last-in, first-out basis (LIFO). You can think of a stack as a pile of plates: You add and remove plates from the top of the pile. A C# stack operates in a similar manner: Elements are added and removed from the top of a stack.

The Stack class contains the definition for a stack; you'll see the use of a Stack object in this section.

Creating and Using a *Stack*

The first step is to create a Stack object, as shown in the following example:

```
Stack myStack = new Stack();
```

You add an element to the top of a Stack using the Push() method. The following example adds four elements to myStack using the Push() method:

```
myStack.Push("This");
myStack.Push("is");
myStack.Push("a");
myStack.Push("test");
```

From top to bottom, the order of these elements in myStack is "test", "a", "is", and "This".

You remove an element from the top of a Stack using the Pop() method. This method both returns the element and removes it from the Stack. For example:

```
Console.WriteLine(myStack.Pop());
```

This example will display "test"—which is the element at the top of myStack. "test" will also be removed from myStack. Calling myStack.Pop() again will return and remove "a" from myStack.

You can read the element at the front of a Stack using the Peek() method. This method returns the element but doesn't remove it from the Stack. The following example shows the use of the Peek() method:

```
Console.WriteLine(myStack.Peek());
```

This example will display "a"—the element currently at the top of myStack (assuming that "test" is the only element that has been removed from myStack).

Listing 11.11 illustrates this Stack.

LISTING 11.11: A Stack

```
/*
  Example11_11.cs illustrates the use of a Stack
*/

using System;
using System.Collections;

class Example11_11
{

  public static void Main()
  {

    // create a Stack object
    Stack myStack = new Stack();

    // add four elements to myStack using the Push() method
    myStack.Push("This");
    myStack.Push("is");
    myStack.Push("a");
    myStack.Push("test");

    // display the elements in myStack
    foreach (string myString in myStack)
    {
      Console.WriteLine("myString = " + myString);
    }

    // get the number of elements in myStack using the
    // Count property
```

```
    int numElements = myStack.Count;
    for (int count = 0; count < numElements; count++)
    {

      // examine an element in myStack using Peek()
      Console.WriteLine("myStack.Peek() = " +
        myStack.Peek());

      // remove an element from myStack using Pop()
      Console.WriteLine("myStack.Pop() = " +
        myStack.Pop());

    }

  }

}
```

The output from this program is as follows:

```
myString = test
myString = a
myString = is
myString = This
myStack.Peek() = test
myStack.Pop() = test
myStack.Peek() = a
myStack.Pop() = a
myStack.Peek() = is
myStack.Pop() = is
myStack.Peek() = This
myStack.Pop() = This
```

Stack **Properties and Methods**

The Stack class provides a number of useful properties and methods that you can use in your programs. Table 11.11 shows the public Stack properties.

TABLE 11.11: Stack PROPERTIES

PROPERTY	TYPE	DESCRIPTION
Count	int	Gets the number of elements actually stored in the Stack
IsReadOnly	bool	Checks whether the Stack is read only
IsSynchronized	bool	Checks whether access to the Stack is synchronized (thread-safe)
SyncRoot	object	Gets an object that can be used to synchronize access to the Stack

Table 11.12 shows the public Stack methods.

TABLE 11.12: Stack METHODS

METHOD	RETURN TYPE	DESCRIPTION
Synchronized() (static)	Stack	Returns a Stack wrapper that is synchronized (thread-safe).
Clear()	void	Removes all the elements from the Stack.
Clone()	object	Creates a shallow copy of the Stack.
Contains()	bool	Determines if a specified element is in the Stack.
CopyTo()	void	Copies the elements from the Stack to a one-dimensional array.
Equals() (inherited from Object)	bool	Overloaded. Determines whether two object instances are equal.
GetEnumerator()	IEnumerator	Returns an enumerator that can iterate through the Stack.
GetHashCode() (inherited from Object)	int	Returns a hash code for a particular type.
GetType() (inherited from Object)	Type	Returns the type of the current instance.
Peek()	object	Returns the element from the top of the Stack, but doesn't remove it.
Pop()	object	Returns and removes the element from the top of the Stack.
Push()	void	Adds an element to the top of the Stack.
ToArray()	object[]	Copies the elements in the Stack to an array.
ToString() (inherited from Object)	string	Returns a string that represents the current object.

The previous program shown in Listing 11.11 illustrated the use of the main property and methods.

Summary

In this chapter, you learned all about collections. Specifically, the System.Collections namespace contains a number of classes you can use to create objects that store many elements and whose capacity can be changed after they've been created. Collections also offer flexible ways to access their elements. As you master C#, you'll find the Collections objects to be useful when you need to perform complex manipulation of data.

An *array list* is similar to an array, but it will automatically expand as you add elements—unlike an array with a fixed size. The `ArrayList` class contains the definition for an array list. The `ArrayList` class contains a rich set of methods that you can use to manipulate the elements; for example, you can insert and remove elements at any point in an `ArrayList`.

A *bit array* is an array of Boolean values. Each Boolean value in the array is represented using a single bit (0 or 1). Using a bit to store each Boolean value requires less memory than a `bool`, and therefore a bit array uses less memory than an array of `bool` elements. The `BitArray` class contains the definition for a bit array. The `BitArray` class contains a rich set of methods you can use to manipulate the bit elements; for example, you can perform AND, OR, and exclusive OR operations on corresponding bits stored in two separate bit arrays.

A *hash table* allows you to store a key along with a value. You can then use this key to later look up the value in the hash table. A *sorted list* is a combination of an array list and a hash table. Like an array list, the elements in a sorted list can be accessed using an index. Like a hash table, each element in a sorted list contains both a key and a value, and each element can also be accessed using the key. Each element in a sorted list is sorted according to the key, and in the case of a `string` key, the keys will be sorted in alphabetical order. The `SortedList` class contains the definition for a sorted list.

A *queue* allows you to store elements on a first-in, first-out basis (FIFO). A C# queue operates in the same manner as a queue in the real world. The `Queue` class contains the definition for a queue. A *stack* allows you to store elements on a last-in, first-out basis (LIFO). The `Stack` class contains the definition for a stack. In the next chapter you'll learn about delegates and events.

Chapter 12

Delegates and Events

A DELEGATE ACTS LIKE a pointer to a function, and you can use them to call different functions that you specify at run-time. You can use delegates in any situation where you don't know up front which method to call.

Delegates are closely tied to events—events are in fact a special kind of delegate. You can use events to send notifications that something has occurred to a particular object. Examples of events are the pressing of a mouse button or the selecting of a menu option in a Windows program. You'll learn about Windows programming in Chapter 24, "Introduction to Windows Applications." Events don't have to be related to Windows programming; for example, you could use an event to indicate that a meltdown of a nuclear reactor has occurred in a computer simulation.

Featured in this chapter:

◆ Understanding and Declaring Delegates

◆ Understanding and Declaring Events

Understanding Delegates

A *delegate* acts like a pointer to a function, and you can use them to call different functions that you specify at run-time. A delegate stores a method name, along with a return type and parameter list. There are two parts to a delegate: the delegate class and a delegate object of that class. Once you've declared a delegate class, you can then create a delegate object and use it to store and call a method with a specific method signature (a method signature is the return type and parameter list for that method).

In this section, you'll see a delegate used to call two different methods that calculate the final speed and distance traveled by a physical object—a car, for example. You can use delegates in any situation where you don't know up front which method to call.

Declaring a Delegate Class

You declare a delegate class using the `delegate` keyword, which uses the following simplified syntax:

```
[access-modifier] delegate delegate-class-name return-type
([parameter-type parameter-name[, ...]]);
```

The syntax elements are as follows:

access-modifier   The degree to which your delegate class is available to the outside world. This can be `public`, `protected`, and so on.

delegate-class-name   The name you assign to your delegate class.

return-type   The type or class of the value returned by your delegate.

parameter-type   The type or class of the parameter passed to your delegate.

parameter-name   The name of the parameter passed to your delegate.

The following example declares a delegate class named `DelegateCalculation`:

```
public delegate double DelegateCalculation(
  double acceleration, double time
);
```

You can use `DelegateCalculation` to delegate methods that return a `double` value and accept two `double` parameters named `acceleration` and `time`. In the next section, you'll see a class that contains two methods that satisfy this method specification, and you'll learn how to create and use objects of a delegate class.

Creating and Using Delegate Objects

In this section you'll see the declaration for a class named `MotionCalculations`, which contains two static methods named `FinalSpeed()` and `Distance()`. Both of these methods return a `double` value and accept two `double` parameters named `acceleration` and `time`. You'll then see how to create a delegate object and then use that object to call the `FinalSpeed()` and `Distance()` methods.

The `FinalSpeed()` method calculates the final speed of any physical object (a car, for example) that undergoes a constant acceleration for a specified period of time from a standing start. The final speed is calculated by multiplying the acceleration by the time.

The `Distance()` method calculates the total distance traveled by the physical object by multiplying the acceleration by the square of the time (raising the time to the power of 2), and then dividing that result by 2.

RAISING NUMBERS TO POWERS USING THE *SYSTEM.MATH.POW()* METHOD

You can get the value of a number raised to a specified power using the `System.Math.Pow()` method. This method accepts two `double` values and returns a `double` value that is the result of raising the first value to the power specified by the second value. For example, `System.Math.Pow(3, 2)` returns the value of 3 raised to the power 2, which is 9 (3 * 3).

The `MotionCalculations` class is as follows; notice the use of `Math.Pow()` in the `Distance()` method (this assumes `using System` has already been done earlier so that the `System` part can be omitted when calling the `Math.Pow()` method):

```
public class MotionCalculations
{
```

```
// FinalSpeed() calculates the final speed
public static double FinalSpeed(
  double acceleration, double time
)
{
  double finalSpeed = acceleration * time;
  return finalSpeed;
}

// Distance() calculates the distance traveled
public static double Distance(
  double acceleration, double time
)
{

  double distance = acceleration * Math.Pow(time, 2) / 2;
  return distance;
}

}
```

Next, in the `Main()` method for example, you can create a delegate object, passing in the name of the method to be delegated using the constructor. In the following example, a `DelegateCalculation` object named `myDelegateCalculation` is created, passing `MotionCalculations.FinalSpeed` to the constructor:

```
DelegateCalculation myDelegateCalculation =
  new DelegateCalculation(MotionCalculations.FinalSpeed);
```

You can then call the `FinalSpeed()` method through `myDelegateCalculation`. For example:

```
double acceleration = 10;  // meters per second per second
double time = 5;  // seconds
double finalSpeed = myDelegateCalculation(acceleration, time);
```

You'll notice that the `acceleration` and `time` parameters are passed to `myDelegateCalculation`, which then calls the `FinalSpeed()` method with these parameters. The result calculated by `Final-Speed()` is then returned and stored in the `finalSpeed` variable. In this example, `finalSpeed` is set to 50 (in units of meters per second).

You can also assign a different method to `myDelegateCalculation`. In the following example, `MotionCalculations.Distance` is passed to `myDelegateCalculation`:

```
myDelegateCalculation =
  new DelegateCalculation(MotionCalculations.Distance);
```

You can then call the `Distance()` method using `myDelegateCalculation`. For example:

```
double distance = myDelegateCalculation(acceleration, time);
```

Once again, the `acceleration` and `time` parameters are passed to `myDelegateCalculation`, which then calls the `Distance()` method with these parameters. The result calculated by `Distance()` is then returned and stored in the `distance` variable; in this example, distance is set to 125 (meters).

NOTE *You should be starting to see the power of delegates: You can use them to call any method that has the same method signature as the delegate class.*

Listing 12.1 illustrates the use of a delegate.

LISTING 12.1: A DELEGATE

```
/*
  Example12_1.cs illustrates the use of a delegate
*/

using System;


// declare the DelegateCalculation delegate class
public delegate double DelegateCalculation(
  double acceleration, double time
);


// declare the MotionCalculations class
public class MotionCalculations
{

  // FinalSpeed() calculates the final speed
  public static double FinalSpeed(
    double acceleration, double time
  )
  {
    double finalSpeed = acceleration * time;
    return finalSpeed;
  }

  // Distance() calculates the distance traveled
  public static double Distance(
    double acceleration, double time
  )
  {
    double distance = acceleration * Math.Pow(time, 2) / 2;
    return distance;
  }

}


class Example12_1
{
```

```
public static void Main()
{

   // declare and initialize the acceleration and time
   double acceleration = 10;   // meters per second per second
   double time = 5;   // seconds
   Console.WriteLine("acceleration = " + acceleration +
     " meters per second per second");
   Console.WriteLine("time = " + time + " seconds");

   // create a delegate object that calls
   // MotionCalculations.FinalSpeed
   DelegateCalculation myDelegateCalculation =
     new
   DelegateCalculation(MotionCalculations.FinalSpeed);

   // calculate and display the final speed
   double finalSpeed = myDelegateCalculation(acceleration, time);
   Console.WriteLine("finalSpeed = " + finalSpeed +
     " meters per second");

   // set the delegate method to MotionCalculations.Distance
   myDelegateCalculation =
     new DelegateCalculation(MotionCalculations.Distance);

   // calculate and display the distance traveled
   double distance = myDelegateCalculation(acceleration, time);
   Console.WriteLine("distance = " + distance + " meters");

}

}
```

The output from this program is as follows:

```
acceleration = 10 meters per second per second
time = 5 seconds
finalSpeed = 50 meters per second
distance = 125 meters
```

Delegate Multicasting

You can call multiple methods using a delegate. There is a limitation imposed on the delegate and the methods: The delegate and the methods must return void. The reason for this is that there's no way to store a returned value from multiple methods in a delegate.

Let's consider a couple of examples when you might want to use delegate multicasting. Let's say you were developing a program to calculate and display the final speed and total distance traveled by a car. You may assume that the final speed and distance are calculated using two methods, and these methods simply display the computed values rather than returning them. You could use a multicast delegate to call each of these methods in turn. Delegate multicasting is also useful with event processing. You might need to call multiple methods when the user performs a certain action and an event occurs. For example, your program might need to call multiple methods as a result of the user selecting a menu option in a Windows program.

In this section, you'll see a simple example of delegate multicasting.

The following example declares a delegate class named `DelegateCalculation` that returns `void`:

```
public delegate void DelegateCalculation(
  double acceleration, double time
);
```

Next, the following `MotionCalculations` class defines two methods named `FinalSpeed()` and `Distance()`, which return `void`; notice that the final speed and distance are displayed by the actual methods, rather than returning values as was done earlier:

```
public class MotionCalculations
{

  // FinalSpeed() calculates the final speed
  public static void FinalSpeed(
    double acceleration, double time
  )
  {
    double finalSpeed = acceleration * time;
    Console.WriteLine("finalSpeed = " + finalSpeed +
      " meters per second");
  }

  // Distance() calculates the distance traveled
  public static void Distance(
    double acceleration, double time
  )
  {
    double distance = acceleration * Math.Pow(time, 2) / 2;
    Console.WriteLine("distance = " + distance + " meters");
  }

}
```

Next, two delegate objects are created, passing `MotionCalculations.FinalSpeed` and `Motion-Calculations.Distance` to the constructors:

```
DelegateCalculation myDelegateCalculation1 =
  new DelegateCalculation(MotionCalculations.FinalSpeed);
DelegateCalculation myDelegateCalculation2 =
  new DelegateCalculation(MotionCalculations.Distance);
```

These two delegates can be added together using the overloaded addition operator (+). For example:

```
DelegateCalculation myDelegateCalculations =
  myDelegateCalculation1 + myDelegateCalculation2;
```

NOTE   *You can also add a delegate object using the shortcut addition operator (+=), and you can subtract a delegate object using the subtraction (-) or shortcut subtraction (-=) operators.*

Next, the following example calls the `FinalSpeed()` and `Distance()` methods through `myDelegateCalculations`:

```
double acceleration = 10;  // meters per second per second
double time = 5;  // seconds
myDelegateCalculations(acceleration, time);
```

This example displays the following:

```
finalSpeed = 50 meters per second
distance = 125 meters
```

Listing 12.2 illustrates the use of delegate multicasting.

LISTING 12.2: DELEGATE MULTICASTING

```
/*
  Example12_2.cs illustrates the use of a multicast delegate
*/

using System;


// declare the DelegateCalculation delegate class
public delegate void DelegateCalculation(
  double acceleration, double time
);


// declare the MotionCalculations class
public class MotionCalculations
{

  // FinalSpeed() calculates the final speed
  public static void FinalSpeed(
    double acceleration, double time
  )
  {
    double finalSpeed = acceleration * time;
    Console.WriteLine("finalSpeed = " + finalSpeed +
      " meters per second");
  }
```

```
    // Distance() calculates the distance traveled
    public static void Distance(
      double acceleration, double time
    )
    {
      double distance = acceleration * Math.Pow(time, 2) / 2;
      Console.WriteLine("distance = " + distance + " meters");
    }

}


class Example12_2
{

  public static void Main()
  {

    // declare and initialize the acceleration and time
    double acceleration = 10;   // meters per second per second
    double time = 5;  // seconds
    Console.WriteLine("acceleration = " + acceleration +
      " meters per second per second");
    Console.WriteLine("time = " + time + " seconds");

    // create delegate object that call the
    // MotionCalculations.FinalSpeed() and
    // MotionCalculations.Distance() methods
    DelegateCalculation myDelegateCalculation1 =
      new
    DelegateCalculation(MotionCalculations.FinalSpeed);
    DelegateCalculation myDelegateCalculation2 =
      new DelegateCalculation(MotionCalculations.Distance);

    // create a multicast delegate object from
    // myDelegateCalculation1 and
    // myDelegateCalculation2
    DelegateCalculation myDelegateCalculations =
      myDelegateCalculation1 + myDelegateCalculation2;

    // calculate and display the final speed and distance
    // using myDelegateCalculations
    myDelegateCalculations(acceleration, time);

  }

}
```

The output from this program is as follows:

```
acceleration = 10 meters per second per second
time = 5 seconds
finalSpeed = 50 meters per second
distance = 125 meters
```

Calling Object Methods Using a Delegate

In the previous sections, you saw how to call static class methods using a delegate. You can also call object methods using a delegate. The following example declares a delegate class named `Delegate-Description` that returns a string:

```
public delegate string DelegateDescription();
```

Next, we'll declare two classes. The first class will be used to represent a car and is named `Car`. The second method will be used to represent a person and is named `Person`. Each class will declare a method that returns string that describes an object of the class. Later, we'll create objects of the `Car` and `Person` class and call the object's method using a delegate object.

The following `Car` class declares two private fields to store a car's model and top speed, whose values are returned in a string using a method named `MakeAndTopSpeed()`:

```
public class Car
{

  // declare two private fields
  private string model;
  private int topSpeed;

  // define a constructor
  public Car(string model, int topSpeed)
  {
    this.model = model;
    this.topSpeed = topSpeed;
  }

  // define a method that returns a string containing
  // the car's model and top speed
  public string MakeAndTopSpeed()
  {
    return("The top speed of the " + model + " is " +
      topSpeed + " mph");
  }

}
```

The following `Person` class declares two private fields to store a person's name and age, whose values are returned in a string using a method named `NameAndAge()`:

```
public class Person
{
```

```
// declare two private fields
private string name;
private int age;

// define a constructor
public Person(string name, int age)
{
  this.name = name;
  this.age = age;
}

// define a method that returns a string containing
// the person's name and age
public string NameAndAge()
{
  return(name + " is " + age + " years old");
}

}
```

Next, in the `Main()` method, for example, the following statement creates a `Person` object:

```
Person myPerson = new Person("Jason Price", 32);
```

We can create a delegate object and pass the object method `myPerson.NameAndAge()` to the constructor:

```
DelegateDescription myDelegateDescription =
  new DelegateDescription(myPerson.NameAndAge);
```

Finally, we call `myPerson.NameAndAge()` through `myDelegateDescription`:

```
string personDescription = myDelegateDescription();
Console.WriteLine("personDescription = " + personDescription);
```

This example displays this:

```
personDescription = Jason Price is 32 years old
```

We can call any method that returns a string and accepts no parameters using `myDelegate`. The following example creates a `Car` object named `myCar` and then calls `myCar.MakeAndTopSpeed()` through `myDelegateDescription`:

```
Car myCar = new Car("MR2", 140);
myDelegateDescription =
  new DelegateDescription(myCar.MakeAndTopSpeed);
string carDescription = myDelegateDescription();
Console.WriteLine("carDescription = " + carDescription);
```

This example displays the following:

```
carDescription = The top speed of the MR2 is 140 mph
```

Listing 12.3 illustrates how to call object methods using a delegate.

```
/*
  Example12_3.cs illustrates the use of a delegate
  that calls object methods
*/

using System;


// declare the DelegateCalculation delegate class
public delegate string DelegateDescription();


// declare the Person class
public class Person
{

  // declare two private fields
  private string name;
  private int age;

  // define a constructor
  public Person(string name, int age)
  {
    this.name = name;
    this.age = age;
  }

  // define a method that returns a string containing
  // the person's name and age
  public string NameAndAge()
  {
    return(name + " is " + age + " years old");
  }

}


// declare the Car class
public class Car
{

  // declare two private fields
  private string model;
  private int topSpeed;
```

```
    // define a constructor
    public Car(string model, int topSpeed)
    {
      this.model = model;
      this.topSpeed = topSpeed;
    }

    // define a method that returns a string containing
    // the car's model and top speed
    public string MakeAndTopSpeed()
    {
      return("The top speed of the " + model + " is " +
        topSpeed + " mph");
    }

  }


class Example12_3
{

  public static void Main()
  {

    // create a Person object named myPerson
    Person myPerson = new Person("Jason Price", 32);

    // create a delegate object that calls myPerson.NameAndAge()
    DelegateDescription myDelegateDescription =
      new DelegateDescription(myPerson.NameAndAge);

    // call myPerson.NameAndAge() through myDelegateDescription
    string personDescription = myDelegateDescription();
    Console.WriteLine("personDescription = " + personDescription);

    // create a Car object named myCar
    Car myCar = new Car("MR2", 140);

    // set myDelegateDescription to call myCar.MakeAndTopSpeed()
    myDelegateDescription =
      new DelegateDescription(myCar.MakeAndTopSpeed);

    // call myCar.MakeAndTopSpeed() through myDelegateDescription
    string carDescription = myDelegateDescription();
    Console.WriteLine("carDescription = " + carDescription);

  }

}
```

The output from this program is as follows:

```
personDescription = Jason Price is 32 years old
carDescription = The top speed of the MR2 is 140 mph
```

Understanding Events

Events allow one object to notify another object that something has occurred. For example, when you click a mouse button in a Windows application, an event occurs, or is *raised*. Depending on which button you pressed and in what position in the application you clicked it, the application may take a different action when handling the event. The piece of code that handles the event is known as an *event handler*. For example, if you clicked the right mouse button in an application, the application might handle the event by displaying a pop-up context sensitive menu; if you clicked the left mouse button on the application's minimize button, the application will handle the event by minimizing the application. Just moving the mouse raises many events, which Windows handles by moving the pointer on the screen.

NOTE   *Events are a special kind of delegate, and you can write your own events and event handlers.*

In the next section, you'll see an example of a simple nuclear reactor simulator. The reactor will raise an event when the reactor core temperature is set too high and the core melts down. The event handler will display a message stating that a reactor meltdown is in progress. You'll also see how to create an object to monitor the reactor for the meltdown event. Later in Chapter 24, you'll learn how to handle Windows events like the clicking of a button.

Declaring an Event

You declare an event using the **event** keyword, which uses the following simplified syntax:

```
[access-modifier] event delegate-class-name event-name;
```

The syntax elements are as follows:

access-modifier   The degree to which your event is available to the outside world. This can be **public**, **protected**, and so on.

delegate-class-name   The delegate class to use with your event. This delegate class represents the method that handles the event—this method is called when the event is raised.

event-name   The name you want to assign to your event. By convention, event names begin with the word *On*—**OnClick**, **OnDisplay**, **OnMeltdown**, for example.

The following example declares an event named **OnMeltdown** that uses the **MeltdownHandler** delegate class:

```
public event MeltdownHandler OnMeltdown;
```

This event will be raised when the temperature of the nuclear reactor core is set too high. You'll learn about the **MeltdownHandler** delegate class in the next section.

Declaring the Delegate Class Used with an Event

You must declare the delegate class used with your event. In the previous example, the OnMeltdown event uses a delegate class named MeltdownHandler. MeltdownHandler represents the method that is called when the OnMeltdown event is raised. The MeltdownHandler delegate class is declared as follows:

```
public delegate void MeltdownHandler(
  object reactor,
  MeltdownEventArgs myMEA
);
```

All event handler delegates must return void and accept two parameters. The first parameter is an object, and it represents the object that raises the event—and in the example, this is a reactor that may melt down. The second parameter is an object of a class that is derived from the System.EventArgs class. The EventArgs class is the base class for event data and represents the details of the event. In the example, the second parameter is of the class MeltdownEventArgs, which is declared as follows:

```
public class MeltdownEventArgs : EventArgs
{

  // declare a private field named message
  private string message;

  // define a constructor
  public MeltdownEventArgs(string message)
  {
    this.message = message;
  }

  // define a property to get the message
  public string Message
  {
    get
    {
      return message;
    }
  }

}
```

The MeltdownEventArgs class declares a private field named message, which as you'll see shortly, stores a message describing that a reactor meltdown is in progress. The message field is set using the constructor for the MeltdownEventArgs class and may be read using the Message property that defines a get method.

Declaring the Reactor Class

The next step is to declare a class to represent a reactor, and we'll name this class Reactor. The Reactor class will contain the declaration for the OnMeltdown event and the MeltdownHandler delegate class shown in the previous section. The Reactor class is declared as follows:

```
public class Reactor
{

  // declare a private field named temperature
  private int temperature;

  // declare a delegate class named MeltdownHandler
  public delegate void MeltdownHandler(
    object reactor,
    MeltdownEventArgs myMEA
  );

  // declare an event named OnMeltdown
  public event MeltdownHandler OnMeltdown;

  // define a property to set the temperature
  public int Temperature
  {
    set
    {
      temperature = value;

      // if the temperature is too high, the reactor melts down
      if (temperature > 1000)
      {
        MeltdownEventArgs myMEA =
          new MeltdownEventArgs("Reactor meltdown in progress!");
          OnMeltdown(this, myMEA);
      }
    }
  }

}
```

As you can see, the Reactor class declares a private field named temperature, which is set using the set method of the Temperature property. If the setting for temperature is too high (greater than 1,000 degrees Centigrade), then a reactor meltdown occurs. Let's take a closer look at the if statement that checks temperature:

```
if (temperature > 1000)
{
  MeltdownEventArgs myMEA =
```

```
      new MeltdownEventArgs("Reactor meltdown in progress!");
      OnMeltdown(this, myMEA);
  }
```

The first line after the if creates a MeltdownEventArgs object named myMEA, passing the string "Reactor meltdown in progress!" to the constructor. This sets the message field of myMEA to that string. The second line raises the OnMeltdown event, passing the current Reactor object (using the this object reference), and myMEA as parameters to OnMeltdown.

Declaring the ReactorMonitor Class

The OnMeltdown event can be monitored by another object, and for this purpose, we'll declare a ReactorMonitor class that will be used to create an object to monitor a Reactor object. The Reactor-Monitor class is declared as follows:

```
public class ReactorMonitor
{

  // define a constructor
  public ReactorMonitor(Reactor myReactor)
  {
    myReactor.OnMeltdown +=
      new Reactor.MeltdownHandler(DisplayMessage);
  }

  // define the DisplayMessage() method
  public void DisplayMessage(
    object myReactor, MeltdownEventArgs myMEA
  )
  {
    Console.WriteLine(myMEA.Message);
  }

}
```

The constructor for ReactorMonitor accepts a Reactor parameter named myReactor and monitors that object for the OnMeltdown event. You do this using the following statement; notice the use of the shortcut addition operator (+=):

```
myReactor.OnMeltdown +=
  new Reactor.MeltdownHandler(DisplayMessage);
```

This statement indicates that when myReactor raises the OnMeltdown event, the DisplayMessage() method is called to handle the event. Earlier, you saw that MeltdownHandler is a delegate that may be set to a method that returns void and accepts two parameters: an object and a MeltdownEventArgs object. This is exactly the method signature for DisplayMessage().

DisplayMessage() simply displays the Message property for the Reactor object. Therefore, when the Reactor object raises the OnMeltdown event, the string "Reactor meltdown in progress!" is displayed. You'll see an example of this in the next section.

Creating and Using a Reactor and ReactorMonitor Object

We're now ready to create and use a Reactor and ReactorMonitor objects. The examples shown in this section could be placed in the Main() method of a program. The following example creates a Reactor object and a ReactorMonitor object, passing the Reactor object to the ReactorMonitor constructor:

```
Reactor myReactor = new Reactor();
ReactorMonitor myReactorMonitor = new ReactorMonitor(myReactor);
```

Next, the Temperature property of myReactor is set to 100 degrees Centigrade—well within the safety limit of 1,000:

```
myReactor.Temperature = 100;
```

Finally, the Temperature property is set to 2,000 degrees Centigrade—this causes myReactor to meltdown, and therefore myReactor raises the OnMeltdown event:

```
myReactor.Temperature = 2000;
```

When myReactor raises the OnMeltdown event, myReactorMonitor notices the event and calls DisplayMessage(), which displays this:

```
Reactor meltdown in progress!
```

Listing 12.4 illustrates this example event.

LISTING 12.4: AN EVENT

```
/*
  Example12_4.cs illustrates the use of an event
*/

using System;


// declare the MeltdownEventArgs class (implements EventArgs)
public class MeltdownEventArgs : EventArgs
{

  // declare a private field named message
  private string message;

  // define a constructor
  public MeltdownEventArgs(string message)
  {
    this.message = message;
  }

  // define a property to get the message
  public string Message
  {
```

```
    get
    {
      return message;
    }
  }

}


// declare the Reactor class
public class Reactor
{

  // declare a private field named temperature
  private int temperature;

  // declare a delegate class named MeltdownHandler
  public delegate void MeltdownHandler(
    object reactor,
    MeltdownEventArgs myMEA
  );

  // declare an event named OnMeltdown
  public event MeltdownHandler OnMeltdown;

  // define a property to set the temperature
  public int Temperature
  {
    set
    {
      temperature = value;

      // if the temperature is too high, the reactor melts down
      if (temperature > 1000)
      {
        MeltdownEventArgs myMEA =
          new MeltdownEventArgs("Reactor meltdown in progress!");
          OnMeltdown(this, myMEA);
      }
    }
  }

}


// declare the ReactorMonitor class
public class ReactorMonitor
{
```

```
  // define a constructor
  public ReactorMonitor(Reactor myReactor)
  {
    myReactor.OnMeltdown +=
      new Reactor.MeltdownHandler(DisplayMessage);
  }

  // define the DisplayMessage() method
  public void DisplayMessage(
    object myReactor, MeltdownEventArgs myMEA
  )
  {
    Console.WriteLine(myMEA.Message);
  }

}


class Example12_4
{

  public static void Main()
  {

    // create a Reactor object
    Reactor myReactor = new Reactor();

    // create a ReactorMonitor object
    ReactorMonitor myReactorMonitor = new ReactorMonitor(myReactor);

    // set myReactor.Temperature to 100 degrees Centigrade
    Console.WriteLine("Setting reactor temperature to 100 degrees Centigrade");
    myReactor.Temperature = 100;

    // set myReactor.Temperature to 500 degrees Centigrade
    Console.WriteLine("Setting reactor temperature to 500 degrees Centigrade");
    myReactor.Temperature = 500;

    // set myReactor.Temperature to 2000 degrees Centigrade
    // (this causes the reactor to meltdown)
    Console.WriteLine("Setting reactor temperature to 2000 degrees Centigrade");
    myReactor.Temperature = 2000;

  }

}
```

The output from this program is as follows:

```
Setting reactor temperature to 100 degrees Centigrade
Setting reactor temperature to 500 degrees Centigrade
Setting reactor temperature to 2000 degrees Centigrade
Reactor meltdown in progress!
```

Summary

In this chapter, you learned about delegates and events. A *delegate* acts like a pointer to a function, and you can use them to call different functions that you specify at run-time. A delegate stores a method name, along with a return type and parameter list. There are two parts to a delegate: the delegate class and a delegate object of that class. Once you've declared a delegate class, you can then create a delegate object and use it to store and call a method with a specific method signature (a method signature is the return type and parameter list for that method).

Events allow one object to notify another object that something has occurred. For example, when you click a mouse button in a Windows application, an event is raised. Depending on which button you pressed and in what position in the application you clicked it, the application may take a different action when handling the event. The piece of code that handles the event is known as an *event handler*.

In the next chapter, you'll learn about exceptions and debugging.

Chapter 13

Exceptions and Debugging

In this final chapter of Part I, you'll learn about exceptions and debugging. When an error or abnormal condition occurs during your program's execution, an *exception* is thrown. An example of a program error, or *bug*, might be attempting to divide a number by zero. An example of an abnormal program condition might be running out of memory.

An exception contains detailed information about the error or condition; you can then catch these exceptions in your program and take some kind of action—for example, displaying a friendly message to your program's user.

Closely coupled with the subject of exceptions is program *debugging*. Debugging a program involves removing bugs from your program. You'll see how you can use Visual Studio .NET to track down bugs in your program by setting pauses, or *breakpoints*, in your program and inspecting variable values.

Even after you've removed all bugs from your program, your program might still encounter abnormal conditions, such as running out of memory. You can't do anything to prevent these circumstances, but you can at least catch them and take action.

Featured in this chapter:

♦ Handling Generic Exceptions and Specific Exceptions

♦ Learning about Exception Objects

♦ Propagating Exceptions

♦ Creating and Throwing Exception Objects

♦ Understanding Custom Exceptions

♦ Debugging Your Programs

Handling Exceptions

To handle an exception, you must divide your code block into a `try` block and a `catch` block. The `try` block contains the code that might throw an exception, and the `catch` block contains the code to handle the exception. The following example illustrates how to structure a `try`/`catch` block:

```
try
{
```

```
    // code that might throw an exception

} catch
{

    // code that handles the exception

}
```

Using *Try/Catch* Blocks

Let's consider an example. Say you're dividing one integer variable by a second integer variable. If that second variable is zero, then your division will throw an exception because dividing by zero has no meaning. To handle this exception, you place the division in the try block and add a catch block to handle the exception. For example:

```
try
{

    // code that throws an exception
    int zero = 0;
    Console.WriteLine("Attempting division by zero");
    int myInt = 1 / zero;   // throws the exception
    Console.WriteLine("You never see this message!");

} catch
{

    // code that handles the exception
    Console.WriteLine("In catch block: an exception was thrown");

}
```

When the division is attempted in the try block, an exception is thrown, and program control immediately passes to the catch block, where the code in this block is run. You never see the message that would otherwise be displayed at the end of the try block because program control has already passed to the catch block.

Using *Finally* Blocks

You can supply an optional finally block to do any cleaning up. For example, you might want to close any files that your program previously opened (you'll learn about opening files later in Chapter 15, "Streams and Input/Output"). Any code in your finally block is guaranteed to run, even if no exception is thrown.

You add the optional finally block after the catch block. The following example illustrates how to structure try, catch, and finally blocks:

```
try
{
```

```
  // code that might throw an exception

} catch
{

  // code that handles the exception

} finally
{

  // code that does any cleaning up; this code is always
  // run at the end, even if no exception is thrown

}
```

Once program control has reached the end of the `try` or the `catch` block, program control passes to the `finally` block where any cleaning up will be performed.

Listing 13.1 illustrates a `try`, `catch`, and `finally` block.

LISTING 13.1: A try, catch, AND finally BLOCK

```
/*
   Example13_1.cs illustrates a try, catch, and finally block
*/

using System;

class Example13_1
{

  public static void Main()
  {

    try
    {

      // code that throws an exception
      int zero = 0;
      Console.WriteLine("In try block: attempting division by zero");
      int myInt = 1 / zero;   // throws the exception
      Console.WriteLine("You never see this message!");

    } catch
    {

      // code that handles the exception
      Console.WriteLine("In catch block: an exception was thrown");
```

```
        } finally
        {

            // code that does any cleaning up
            Console.WriteLine("In finally block: do any cleaning up here");

        }

    }

}
```

The output from this program is as follows:

```
In try block: attempting division by zero
In catch block: an exception was thrown
In finally block: do any cleaning up here
```

Notice that when the exception is thrown, program control immediately passes to the catch block—and you never see the message at the end of the try block. The code in the catch block is then run. At the end, the code in the finally block is run (this code is always run, regardless of whether an exception is thrown in the try block).

Understanding Exception Objects

An exception is actually an object. When a generic exception is thrown, a System.Exception object is passed to the catch block (later, you'll see there are other specific exceptions derived from this base class). The System.Exception class provides a number of useful properties you may use to get detailed information about the exception. Table 13.1 shows these properties.

TABLE 13.1: System.Exception PROPERTIES

PROPERTY	TYPE	DESCRIPTION
HelpLink	string	You can set this property to the name of a file or web address containing more information about the exception.
InnerException	Exception	Contains a reference to an inner exception.
Message	string	Contains a description of the exception.
Source	string	Contains the name of the program that caused the exception.
StackTrace	string	Contains the name of the class and method from which the exception was thrown.
TargetSite	MethodBase	Contains the method name from which the exception was thrown.

You can access these properties for the System.Exception object that is passed to your catch block. The following example displays the properties of such an object; notice that this object is declared within the parentheses for the catch block:

```
try
{

    ...

} catch (System.Exception myException)
{

    // display the exception object's properties
    Console.WriteLine(myException.HelpLink);
    Console.WriteLine(myException.Message);
    Console.WriteLine(myException.Source);
    Console.WriteLine(myException.StackTrace);
    Console.WriteLine(myException.TargetSite);

}
```

When an exception is thrown in the try block, control passes to the catch block where the exception object's properties are displayed.

Listing 13.2 illustrates a System.Exception object and displays its properties.

LISTING 13.2: AN EXCEPTION OBJECT

```
/*
  Example13_2.cs illustrates the use of a
  System.Exception object
*/

using System;

class Example13_2
{

  public static void Main()
  {

    try
    {

      int zero = 0;
      Console.WriteLine("In try block: attempting division by zero");
      int myInt = 1 / zero;  // throws the exception
```

```
    } catch (System.Exception myException)
    {

      // display the exception object's properties
      Console.WriteLine("HelpLink = " + myException.HelpLink);
      Console.WriteLine("Message = " + myException.Message);
      Console.WriteLine("Source = " + myException.Source);
      Console.WriteLine("StackTrace = " + myException.StackTrace);
      Console.WriteLine("TargetSite = " + myException.TargetSite);

    }

  }

}
```

The output from this program is as follows:

```
In try block: attempting division by zero
HelpLink =
Message = Attempted to divide by zero.
Source = Example13_2
StackTrace =     at Example13_2.Main()
TargetSite = Void Main()
```

Notice that the HelpLink property is null. You'll see how you can set this property later in this chapter. As you can see from the other properties, an attempt to divide by zero was made in the Main() method of Example13_2.

TIP *If you add the* using System *statement to the start of your program, then you can simply reference* Exception *in your program, rather than* System.Exception. *All the examples from this point onward will assume that this is the case. We'll also drop the* System *part in the discussion and programs in rest of this chapter; we'll refer to* System.Exception *simply as* Exception.

Handling Specific Exceptions

So far, you've seen how to handle a generic exception object of the Exception class. In the previous examples, when *any* exception occurs, program control passes to the catch block where the generic Exception object is handled.

There are in fact many different exception classes, all of which are derived from the Exception base class. You can use these classes to catch specific exceptions, rather than just catching the generic Exception class; you'll do this when you want to use specific code to handle a specified exception. Table 13.2 lists the derived classes for the most commonly thrown exceptions.

TABLE 13.2: COMMONLY THROWN EXCEPTION CLASSES

DERIVED CLASS	DESCRIPTION
ArithmeticException	The base class for exceptions thrown by arithmetic operations—such as DivideByZero and OverflowException. These classes are derived from ArithmeticException.
ArrayTypeMismatchException	Thrown when an attempt is made to store an incompatible variable or object type into an array of a certain type.
DivideByZeroException	Thrown when an attempt is made to divide a number by zero.
IndexOutOfRangeException	Thrown when an attempt is made to access an invalid array element.
InvalidCastException	Thrown when a failed attempt is made to explicitly cast an object of a base or interface class to a derived class; the cast isn't possible.
MulticastNotSupportedException	Thrown when a failed attempt is made to combine two null delegates because the delegate type doesn't support a void return type.
NullReferenceException	Thrown when an attempt is made to use a null reference when a reference to an actual object was required.
OutOfMemoryException	Thrown when a failed attempt is made to allocate memory using the new operator.
OverflowException	Thrown when an arithmetic operation overflows and the checked operator is used to surround that operation.
StackOverflowException	Thrown when the execution stack has too many method calls that have yet to be completed.
TypeInitializationException	Thrown when a static constructor throws an exception and there's no catch block for that exception.

Using One *catch* Block

You can handle a specific exception in a catch block. You do this by specifying the name of the derived class in your catch block. For example, say you wanted to handle a DivideByZeroException (thrown when an attempt is made to divide a number by zero). Then your try/catch block would be as follows:

```
try
{

  // code that might throw a DivideByZeroException

} catch (DivideByZeroException myException)
{

  // code that handles a DivideByZeroException

}
```

In this example, the catch block only handles a DivideByZeroException. If any other exception is thrown in the try block, then it will not be handled by this particular catch block. You can also add multiple catch blocks to handle more than one type of exception—you'll see how to do that in the next section.

Listing 13.3 illustrates the specific handling of a DivideByZeroException.

LISTING 13.3: HANDLING A SPECIFIC EXCEPTION

```
/*
  Example13_3.cs illustrates how to handle a specific exception
*/

using System;

class Example13_3
{

  public static void Main()
  {

    try
    {

      int zero = 0;
      Console.WriteLine("In try block: attempting division by zero");
      int myInt = 1 / zero;  // throws the exception

    } catch (DivideByZeroException myException)
    {

      // code that handles a DivideByZeroException
      Console.WriteLine("Message = " + myException.Message);
      Console.WriteLine("StackTrace = " + myException.StackTrace);

    }

  }

}
```

The output from this program is as follows:

```
In try block: attempting division by zero
Message = Attempted to divide by zero.
StackTrace =    at Example13_3.Main()
```

Using Multiple *catch* Blocks

You can add multiple catch blocks after a try block to provide different code to handle each type of exception. For example, let's say you wanted to provide catch blocks to handle the following two exceptions:

♦ DivideByZeroException—thrown when an attempt is made to divide a number by zero.

♦ IndexOutOfRangeException—thrown when an attempt is made to access an invalid array element.

The following example shows the two required catch blocks to handle these two exceptions, plus a generic catch block to handle all other exceptions:

```
try
{

  // code that might throw an exception

} catch (DivideByZeroException e)
{

  // code that handles a DivideByZeroException

} catch (IndexOutOfRangeException e)
{

  // code that handles an IndexOutOfRangeException

} catch (Exception e)
{

  // code that handles a generic Exception: all other exceptions

}
```

If an attempt to divide a number by zero is made in the try block, then program control passes to the catch block for the DivideByZeroException. Similarly, if an attempt to access an invalid array element is made, then program control passes to the catch block for the IndexOutOfRangeException. Finally, if any other type of exception is thrown, then program control passes to the catch block for the generic Exception.

WARNING *If you have a series of* catch *blocks that handle specific exceptions plus the generic* catch *block for* Exception *objects, then you must place the generic* catch *block at the end. If you didn't do this—for example, if you placed the generic* catch *block first—then that* catch *block would handle all the exceptions, and any specific exceptions wouldn't reach your other* catch *blocks.*

You could, of course, only provide the generic catch block, which would then handle all exceptions—this is the technique shown in Listings 13.1 and 13.2. That's fine if you want to handle every exception in the same way, but if you want to handle each exception using different code, then you must provide a different catch block for each exception.

Listing 13.4 illustrates multiple catch blocks.

```
/*
  Example13_4.cs illustrates multiple catch blocks
*/

using System;

class Example13_4
{

  public static void Main()
  {

    try
    {

      int[] myArray = new int[2];
      Console.WriteLine("Attempting to access an invalid array element");
      myArray[2] = 1;

    } catch (DivideByZeroException e)
    {

      // code that handles a DivideByZeroException
      Console.WriteLine("Handling a System.DivideByZeroException object");
      Console.WriteLine("Message = " + e.Message);
      Console.WriteLine("StackTrace = " + e.StackTrace);

    } catch (IndexOutOfRangeException e)
    {

      // code that handles an IndexOutOfRangeException
      Console.WriteLine("Handling a System.IndexOutOfRangeException object");
      Console.WriteLine("Message = " + e.Message);
      Console.WriteLine("StackTrace = " + e.StackTrace);

    } catch (Exception e)
    {

      // code that handles a generic Exception: all other exceptions
      Console.WriteLine("Handling a System.Exception object");
      Console.WriteLine("Message = " + e.Message);
      Console.WriteLine("StackTrace = " + e.StackTrace);
```

```
        }

    }

}
```

When an attempt to access the invalid array element is made in the `try` block, program control passes to the `catch` block that handles the `IndexOutOfRangeException`.

The output from this program is as follows:

```
Attempting to access an invalid array element
Handling a System.IndexOutOfRangeException object
Message = Exception of type System.IndexOutOfRangeException was thrown.
StackTrace =    at Example13_4.Main()
```

Exploring Exception Propagation

When an exception is thrown, program control searches for a `catch` block to handle the exception. For example, when the `IndexOutOfRangeException` was thrown in Listing 13.4, program control searches the `catch` blocks for an appropriate handler for this exception. If an appropriate `catch` block cannot be found locally, then the exception is *propagated* upward, and the search then continues for an appropriate `catch` block. If no appropriate `catch` block is found in your program, then the Common Language Runtime (CLR) handles the exception. You'll see an example of this shortly.

In this section, you'll see how exceptions are propagated upward by a nested `try`/`catch` block and a method in a class. You'll also see how the CLR deals with exceptions that aren't handled in your code. Before getting into these details, we'll explain why you might not want to handle exceptions locally—and therefore let them propagate upward:

◆ You might be writing a library of classes, and you might want the methods in those classes to propagate exceptions upward. The user of your classes would then handle those exceptions in their code. This is in fact the way some of the base classes work: When you call methods in those classes, they expect your code to handle any of the exceptions.

◆ You might want to centralize exception handling in one place in your program. Handling all of your exceptions in one place may help you uniformly handle each exception.

Exception Propagation with a Nested *try/catch* Block

The following example shows a nested `try`/`catch` block placed within another `try`/`catch` block:

```
try
{

    try
    {

        // code that throws an IndexOutOfRangeException
```

```
        } catch (DivideByZeroException e)
        {

          // code that handles a DivideByZeroException

        }

    } catch (IndexOutOfRangeException e)
    {

      // code that handles an IndexOutOfRangeException

    }
```

The nested try block throws an IndexOutOfRangeException, but the catch block immediately following this try block only handles a DivideByZeroException. The IndexOutOfRangeException is therefore propagated to the outer catch block, which then handles the exception.

Listing 13.5 illustrates a nested try/catch block.

LISTING 13.5: EXCEPTION PROPAGTION WITH A NESTED try/catch BLOCK

```
/*
  Example13_5.cs illustrates a nested try/catch block;
  the nested if throws an exception that is propagated to the
  outer exception
*/

using System;

class Example13_5
{

  public static void Main()
  {

    try
    {

      // a nested try and catch block
      try
      {

        int[] myArray = new int[2];
        Console.WriteLine("Attempting to access an invalid array element");
        myArray[2] = 1;  // throws the exception

      } catch (DivideByZeroException e)
      {
```

```
    // code that handles a DivideByZeroException
    Console.WriteLine("Handling a DivideByZeroException");
    Console.WriteLine("Message = " + e.Message);
    Console.WriteLine("StackTrace = " + e.StackTrace);

  }

} catch (IndexOutOfRangeException e)
{

  // code that handles an IndexOutOfRangeException
  Console.WriteLine("Handling an IndexOutOfRangeException");
  Console.WriteLine("Message = " + e.Message);
  Console.WriteLine("StackTrace = " + e.StackTrace);

}

}

}
```

The output from this program is as follows:

```
Attempting to access an invalid array element
Handling an IndexOutOfRangeException
Message = Exception of type System.IndexOutOfRangeException was thrown.
StackTrace =    at Example13_5.Main()
```

Exception Propagation with Methods

In a method, either you can add a try/catch block to that method or you can simply let any exceptions be propagated up to the code where your method was called. Unless you are writing a class library or handling exceptions in one place in your program, you should handle any exceptions locally in your methods.

You'll see two example methods in this section: The first method contains a try/catch block, but the second method does not. Any exceptions that are thrown in the second method are therefore propagated up to the calling statement.

The following method has a try/catch block; the IndexOutOfRangeException thrown by the try block is handled locally in this method's catch block:

```
public void AccessInvalidArrayElement()
{
  int[] myArray = new int[2];
  try
  {
    Console.WriteLine("Attempting to access an invalid array element");
    myArray[2] = 1;
  } catch (IndexOutOfRangeException e)
```

```
      {
        Console.WriteLine("Handling an IndexOutOfRangeException");
        Console.WriteLine("Message = " + e.Message);
        Console.WriteLine("StackTrace = " + e.StackTrace);
      }
    }
```

TIP *When the* `StackTrace` *property is displayed in a method, it will display the name of the class and the method name. This helps you when tracking down where the exception was thrown.*

If you don't include a `try`/`catch` block in your method, then any exceptions thrown by your method will be propagated up to the calling statement. For example, the following method throws a `DivideByZeroException`:

```
public void DivideByZero()
{
  int zero = 0;
  Console.WriteLine("Attempting division by zero");
  int myInt = 1 / zero;
}
```

When this method is called, the `DivideByZeroException` will be propagated up to the calling statement.

Listing 13.6 illustrates these two methods.

LISTING 13.6: EXCEPTION PROPAGTION WITH METHODS

```
/*
  Example13_6.cs illustrates exception propagation
  with methods
*/

using System;


// declare the ExceptionsTest class
public class ExceptionsTest
{

  public void AccessInvalidArrayElement()
  {
    int[] myArray = new int[2];
    try {
      Console.WriteLine("Attempting to access an invalid array element");
      myArray[2] = 1;
    } catch (IndexOutOfRangeException e)
    {
      Console.WriteLine("Handling an IndexOutOfRangeException");
      Console.WriteLine("Message = " + e.Message);
```

```csharp
      Console.WriteLine("StackTrace = " + e.StackTrace);
    }
  }

  public void DivideByZero()
  {
    int zero = 0;
    Console.WriteLine("Attempting division by zero");
    int myInt = 1 / zero;
  }

}


class Example13_6
{

  public static void Main()
  {

    ExceptionsTest myExceptionsTest = new ExceptionsTest();

    // call the AccessInvalidArrayElement() method,
    // this method handles the exception locally
    Console.WriteLine("Calling AccessInvalidArrayElement()");
    myExceptionsTest.AccessInvalidArrayElement();

    try
    {

      // call the DivideByZero() method,
      // this method doesn't handle the exception locally and
      // so it must be handled here
      Console.WriteLine("Calling DivideByZero()");
      myExceptionsTest.DivideByZero();

    } catch (DivideByZeroException e)
    {

      Console.WriteLine("Handling an IndexOutOfRangeException");
      Console.WriteLine("Message = " + e.Message);
      Console.WriteLine("StackTrace = " + e.StackTrace);

    }

  }

}
```

The output from this program is as follows:

```
Calling AccessInvalidArrayElement()
Attempting to access an invalid array element
Handling an IndexOutOfRangeException
Message = Exception of type System.IndexOutOfRangeException was thrown.
StackTrace =    at ExceptionsTest.AccessInvalidArrayElement()
Calling DivideByZero()
Attempting division by zero
Handling an IndexOutOfRangeException
Message = Attempted to divide by zero.
StackTrace =    at Example13_6.Main()
```

Notice that when the `AccessInvalidArrayElement()` method is called, the `StackTrace` property contains the name of the class and the method name. When the `DivideByZero()` method is called, the `DivideByZeroException` is propagated up to the calling statement in the `Main()` method; this exception is then handled by the `catch` block of the `Main()` method.

Unhandled Exceptions

If your program throws an exception but you don't provide an appropriate `catch` block anywhere in your code to handle that exception, then the CLR handles the exception.

For example, Listing 13.7 shows a program that throws an `IndexOutOfRangeException`; this exception is not handled in that program. Therefore, when you run this program, the exception is propagated up to the CLR, which then handles the exception for you.

LISTING 13.7: UNHANDLED EXCEPTIONS

```csharp
/*
  Example13_7.cs illustrates an unhandled exception
*/

using System;

class Example13_7
{

  public static void Main()
  {

    int[] myArray = new int[2];
    Console.WriteLine("Attempting to access an invalid array element");
    myArray[2] = 1;

  }

}
```

The output from this program is as follows:

```
Attempting to access an invalid array element
```

```
Unhandled Exception: System.IndexOutOfRangeException:
 Exception of type System.IndexOutOfRangeException was thrown.
   at Example13_7.Main()
```

Notice that this output indicates that the exception was not handled in the program.

Creating and Throwing Exception Objects

You can create your own exception objects and then throw them using the `throw` statement. You might want to do this if you want to handle an exception and then throw another exception to handle a related exception. For example, when a `DivideByZeroException` is thrown and caught, you might want to handle that exception and throw a different exception. For example, you might want to throw a custom exception—you'll learn how to do that shortly.

By creating and throwing your own exception object, you can also set the properties of that object (listed earlier in Table 3.1). For example, you could set the `HelpLink` property of that object prior to throwing it, which allows you to specify a filename or web address that provides additional information about the exception.

The `HelpLink` property is just a string, so you can set it to whatever you want; you could use it to supply a phone number where you can be contacted in the event of a problem, but you should typically stick with a filename or web address. You can even set your string for the `Message` and `Source` properties of your exception object if you wanted.

Let's take a look at an example of creating an `Exception` object and setting the `Message`, `HelpLink`, and `Source` properties. The following statement creates an `Exception` object, passing a string to the constructor (this string will be used to set the object's `Message` property):

```
Exception myException = new Exception("myException");
```

Next, the following statements set the `HelpLink` and `Source` properties for this `Exception` object:

```
myException.HelpLink = "See the Readme.txt file";
myException.Source = "My Example13_8 Program";
```

Finally, the following statement throws this `Exception` object using the `throw` statement:

```
throw myException;
```

This throws an exception in the same manner as any other exception—and you can handle it using a `catch` block.

Listing 13.8 creates and throws an `Exception` object.

LISTING 13.8: CREATING AND THROWING AN EXCEPTION OBJECT

```
/*
  Example13_8.cs illustrates creating and
  throwing an exception object
*/
```

```
using System;

class Example13_8
{

  public static void Main()
  {

    try
    {

      // create a new Exception object, passing a string
      // for the Message property to the constructor
      Exception myException = new Exception("myException");

      // set the HelpLink and Source properties
      myException.HelpLink = "See the Readme.txt file";
      myException.Source = "My Example13_8 Program";

      // throw the Exception object
      throw myException;

    } catch (Exception e)
    {

      // display the exception object's properties
      Console.WriteLine("HelpLink = " + e.HelpLink);
      Console.WriteLine("Message = " + e.Message);
      Console.WriteLine("Source = " + e.Source);
      Console.WriteLine("StackTrace = " + e.StackTrace);
      Console.WriteLine("TargetSite = " + e.TargetSite);

    }

  }

}
```

The output from this program is as follows:

```
HelpLink = See the Readme.txt file
Message = myException
Source = My Example13_8 Program
StackTrace =     at Example13_8.Main()
TargetSite = Void Main()
```

Notice that the HelpLink, Message, and Source properties use the strings set for the Exception object.

Declaring Custom Exceptions

You can declare your own custom exception classes. You can use custom exceptions to set your own HelpLink and Source properties, and you don't have to keep setting them for every exception of this class that is thrown. You could even add your own methods and properties to your custom exception class to add additional functionality.

Declaring your own custom exception class is straightforward. Your class must be derived from the System.ApplicationException class, and your class must call the base constructor for that class.

NOTE   *Your custom exception class is derived from the* System.ApplicationException *class—and not the* System .Exception *class. Microsoft has reserved the* System.Exception *class, so you shouldn't derive your custom exception classes from it.*

The following example declares a custom exception class named CustomException:

```
public class CustomException : System.ApplicationException
{

  public CustomException(string Message) : base(Message)
  {

    // set the HelpLink and Source properties
    this.HelpLink = "See the Readme.txt file";
    this.Source = "My Example13_9 Program";

  }

}
```

To throw an exception object of this class, you use the throw statement. For example:

```
throw new CustomException("My CustomException message");
```

This example creates a new exception object and then throws it. You could, of course, create the object separately and then throw it. The string passed to the constructor in the example sets the Message property of the CustomException object. This string is then passed to the base class constructor.

To handle this exception, you just provide a catch block to handle the CustomException object. For example:

```
try
{

  throw new CustomException("My CustomException message");

} catch (CustomException e)
{

  // code that handles a CustomException

}
```

Listing 13.9 uses this custom exception.

LISTING 13.9: A CUSTOM EXCEPTION

```
/*
  Example13_9.cs illustrates a custom exception
*/

using System;


// declare the CustomException class
public class CustomException : ApplicationException
{

  public CustomException(string Message) : base(Message)
  {

    // set the HelpLink and Source properties
    this.HelpLink = "See the Readme.txt file";
    this.Source = "My Example13_9 Program";

  }

}


class Example13_9
{

  public static void Main()
  {

    try
    {

      // throw a new CustomException object
      Console.WriteLine("Throwing a new CustomException object");
      throw new CustomException("My CustomException message");

    } catch (CustomException e)
    {

      // display the CustomException object's properties
      Console.WriteLine("HelpLink = " + e.HelpLink);
      Console.WriteLine("Message = " + e.Message);
      Console.WriteLine("Source = " + e.Source);
```

```
        Console.WriteLine("StackTrace = " + e.StackTrace);
        Console.WriteLine("TargetSite = " + e.TargetSite);

    }

  }

}
```

The output from this program is as follows:

```
Throwing a new CustomException object
HelpLink = See the Readme.txt file
Message = My CustomException message
Source = My Example13_9 Program
StackTrace =     at Example13_9.Main()
TargetSite = Void Main()
```

Debugging

In this section, you'll learn how to debug a program. As you saw in Chapter 1, "Introduction to Visual C# and the .NET Framework," VS .NET is a graphical Integrated Development Environment (IDE) that enables you to develop and run programs. VS .NET also contains a debugger that enables you to do things such as step through your program statements and examine variable values; you can use these features to discover why a program is not behaving as expected.

As you'll see, the VS .NET debugger is quite easy to learn and use. In the following sections, you'll see a program containing a bug, then you'll go through the steps of creating a new VS .NET project for the program, and finally you'll see how to debug the program.

Creating the Program

First, you need a program containing a bug. Listing 13.10 shows a program that attempts to access an invalid array element. Take a look at this program and see if you can spot the bug before we show you how to debug it using VS .NET.

LISTING 13.10: A PROGRAM CONTAINING A BUG

```
/*
  Example13_10.cs is used to illustrate the use of the debugger;
  this program attempts to access an invalid array element
*/

using System;
```

```
class Example13_10
{
  public static void Main()
  {
    try
    {
      const int ArraySize = 5;

      // create an array
      int[] myArray = new int[ArraySize];

      // set the elements of the array using a for loop
      for (int count = 0; count <= ArraySize; count++)
      {
        myArray[count] = count;
        Console.WriteLine("myArray[" + count + "] = " +
          myArray[count]);
      }
    } catch (System.IndexOutOfRangeException e)
    {
      Console.WriteLine("Message = " + e.Message);
      Console.WriteLine("StackTrace = " + e.StackTrace);
    }
  }
}
```

Creating the New VS .NET Project

Second, you'll create a new VS .NET project, and then you'll cut and paste the code from
Example13_10.cs into that project. Go ahead and start VS .NET. Your screen should display the
Start page (see Figure 13.1).

From this page you can open an existing project or create a new one. You're going to create a new
project, so go ahead and press the New Project button.

This will open the New Project dialog box, which shows the various project types and templates,
along with the name and location for your new project. Select Visual C# Projects from Project Types,
select Console Application from Templates, and then enter **MyDebugApplication** as the name of the
project (see Figure 13.2). You can leave the other fields in this dialog box in their default state. Click
OK to proceed.

FIGURE 13.1

The VS .NET
Start page

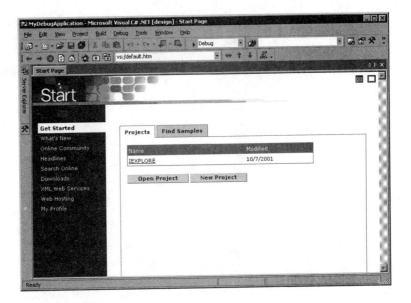

FIGURE 13.2

The New Project
dialog box

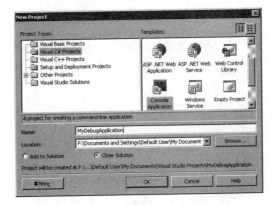

Next, replace the code for `Class1.cs` by cutting and pasting the code from `Example13_10.cs` into
the `Class1.cs` tab (see Figure 13.3).

FIGURE 13.3

The new code

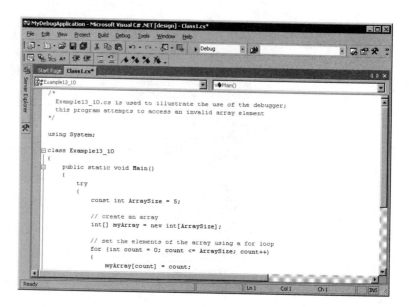

Save the new code by selecting File ➢ Save Class1.cs As. This will open the Save File As dialog box; enter **Example13_10.cs** in the File Name field (see Figure 13.4).

FIGURE 13.4

The Save File As
dialog box

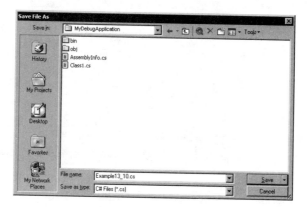

Click the Save button to save Example13_10.cs. Your screen should now look like Figure 13.5.

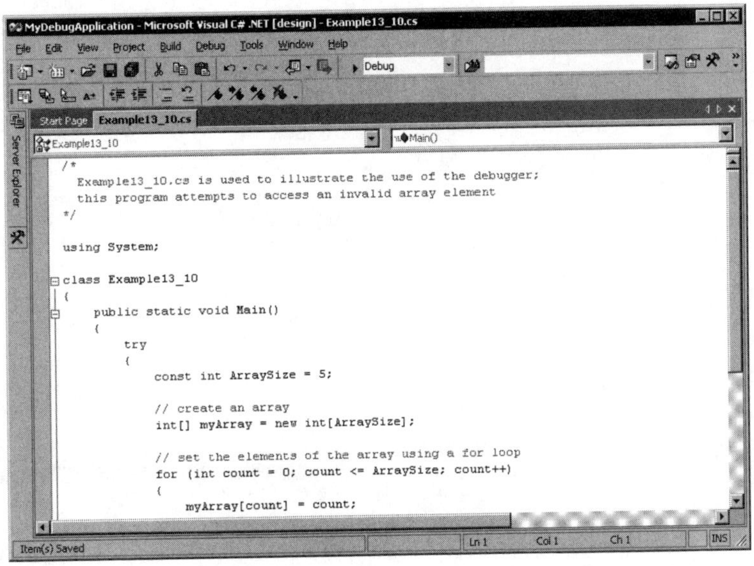

FIGURE 13.5

The
Example13_10.cs
code

You're now ready to begin debugging this code.

Debugging the Program

The first step in debugging a program is to add a *breakpoint* to one of your statements. When the VS .NET debugger encounters a breakpoint, it pauses the execution of your program at that point and turns program control back to you. You can then step through your program and examine your variable's values; by stepping through your program, you can find bugs in your program. In this section, you'll see how to set a breakpoint in Example13_10.cs, step through the program, and examine its variables.

SETTING A BREAKPOINT

You set a breakpoint for a particular statement, and you can set as many as you'd like in your programs. To set a breakpoint, you click in the left margin for the particular statement. Go ahead and set a breakpoint for the for loop (see Figure 13.6).

FIGURE 13.6

Setting a breakpoint

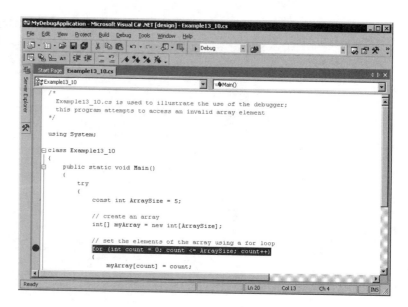

TIP *You can also set a breakpoint by pressing the F9 key. This sets a breakpoint for the line on which the cursor is currently located.*

You can remove a breakpoint by clicking it in the left margin. You can set additional properties for a new breakpoint by selecting Debug ➤ New Breakpoint. One example of a property you can set for a breakpoint is a condition that will be tested before the program pauses at the breakpoint; if that condition is true, then the program pauses at the breakpoint.

STARTING THE DEBUGGER

Once you've set a breakpoint, the next step is run the program using the debugger. To do this, select Debug ➤ Start.

TIP *You can also start the debugger by pressing the F5 key.*

Because you haven't yet compiled `Example13_10.cs`, VS .NET will first compile this program for you. Once compilation is completed, the debugger will start running your program. You'll see an external program window being started by the debugger—this is where the results of the calls to the `Console.WriteLine()` method will go.

TIP *You can run a program without debugging by pressing Ctrl+F5.*

VIEWING VARIABLE VALUES

The statements leading up to your breakpoint will be executed; when your breakpoint is encountered, the debugger suspends program execution and returns control of the program to you. The program statement at which the debugger stopped is indicated by an arrow in the left margin (see Figure 13.7).

FIGURE 13.7

The current statement

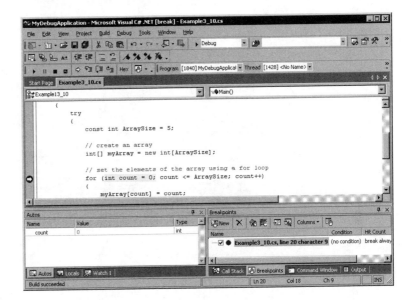

The current statement has not yet been run; the debugger is waiting for you to take action. You can now examine the variables' contents.

The Autos Window

The Autos window at the bottom of the debugger shows the variables—and their values—that are used in the current statement and the previous statement. As you can see from Figure 13.7, the only variable shown in the Autos window at this point in program execution is the count variable, which has a value of 0.

TIP   If the Autos window is not visible, you can show it by selecting Debug ➤ Windows ➤ Autos.

You can also view the contents of a variable by moving the mouse over the variable in the code.

The Locals Window

When you click the Locals tab at the bottom of the debugger, you'll see the Locals window (see Figure 13.8). This window shows the variables currently in scope. (Variable scope was discussed in Chapter 2, "Basic C# Programming," but just as a reminder, the scope of a variable is the block of code where that variable can be accessed.)

FIGURE 13.8

The Locals window

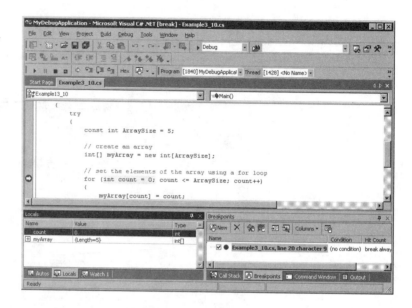

As you can see from Figure 13.8, both the `count` variable and `myArray` are currently in scope. You can view an array's elements by clicking the box containing the plus (+)—this expands the array to show the elements.

TIP   If the Locals window is not visible, you can show it by selecting Debug ➤ Windows ➤ Locals.

The Watch Window

Click the Watch tab at the bottom of the debugger, and you'll see the Watch window. The Watch window allows you to specifically view a variable, which is useful when you have a lot of variables in scope but you're only interested in a subset of them. You add a watch for a variable by right-clicking a variable and selecting Add Watch from the context-sensitive pop-up window. Go ahead and add a watch for the `count` variable. Figure 13.9 shows the resulting Watch window.

FIGURE 13.9

The Watch window

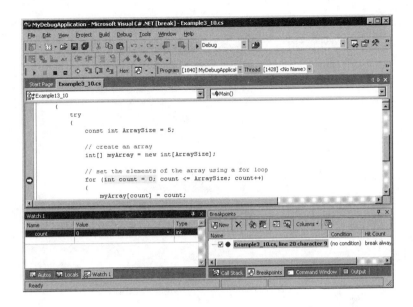

As you can see from Figure 13.9, the count variable is shown.

TIP   If the Watch window is not visible, you can show it by selecting Debug ➤ Windows ➤ Watch ➤ Watch 1.

STEPPING THROUGH A PROGRAM

Debugging a program is a combination of examining variable values and stepping through each statement in your program. The debugger is stopped at the current statement. You can execute the current statement by selecting Debug ➤ Step Over. You can also step into and out of any methods by selecting Debug ➤ Step Into and Debug ➤ Step Out. Stepping into a method takes you into the code for that method. This allows you to step through the code for that method using the debugger. Stepping out of a method takes you out of the code for the current method.

TIP   You can also step over, step into, and step out by pressing the F10, F11, and Shift+F11 keys, respectively.

Keep stepping through the statements in the for loop. As you go through each iteration of the loop, notice how the count variable increases and how the elements of myArray are set. You can also see the console output going to the external program window.

When the count variable reaches 5, an attempt to set an invalid array element is made inside the for loop. This is the bug, and it's caused by the condition in the for loop; the condition should be count < ArraySize and not count <= ArraySize. This causes an IndexOutOfRangeException to be thrown, and program control passes to the catch block (see Figure 13.10).

FIGURE 13.10

The catch block

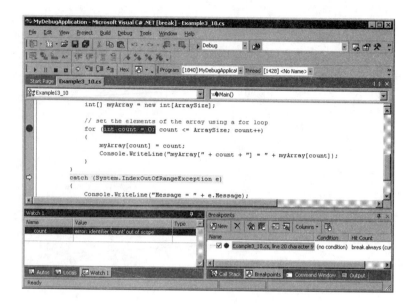

Notice that the Watch window indicates that the count variable is no longer in scope. Continue to step over the remaining program statements in the catch block until the program terminates.

This section has given you a brief introduction of the VS .NET debugger. You should feel free to run the program again and investigate the other features of the VS .NET debugger.

Summary

In this chapter, you learned about exceptions and debugging. Specifically, when an error or abnormal condition occurs during the execution of your program, an *exception* is thrown. An exception contains detailed information about the error or condition; you can then catch these exceptions in your program.

To handle an exception, you must divide your code block into a try block and a catch block. The try block contains the code that might throw an exception, and the catch block contains the code to handle the exception.

You then learned that you can supply an optional finally block to do any cleaning up; for example, you might want to close any files or database connections that were previously opened. Any code in your finally block is guaranteed to be run, even if no exception is thrown. You add the optional finally block after the catch block.

Moreover, you learned that an exception is actually an object. When a generic exception is thrown, a System.Exception object is passed to the catch block. The Exception class provides a number of useful properties you may use to get detailed information about the exception. In fact, there are many different exception classes, all of which are derived from the Exception class. You can use these classes to catch specific exceptions, rather than just catching the generic Exception class. You can add multiple catch blocks after a try block. This allows you to provide different code to handle each type of exception.

When an exception is thrown, program control searches for a `catch` block to handle the exception. If an appropriate `catch` block cannot be found locally, then the exception is propagated upward. If no appropriate `catch` block is found in your program, then the Common Language Runtime (CLR) handles the exception.

Further, you can create your own exception objects and then throw them using the `throw` statement. You can also derive your own custom exception classes from the `System.ApplicationException` base class.

This chapter concludes Part I. In Part II, you'll learn about advanced C# programming. You'll start off by learning about threads.

Part 2

Advanced C# Programming

In this section you will find:

Chapter 14

Threads

By now, you've seen nearly all of the C# language itself. But you still have many things to learn to be an effective C# developer. That's because computer languages are only part of the .NET platform. Perhaps equally important is the .NET Framework Class Library, often just called the *base class library* or *class library*.

The class library is a collection of classes, interfaces, and types that provide useful services to your applications. These services range from opening a file and reading its contents to interacting with Extensible Markup Language (XML), SQL databases, message queues, and other system services. The class library groups these classes into a set of *namespaces*, each of which provides support for particular activities. For example, the `System.Globalization` namespace contains classes that are useful in preparing your application for an international market.

In Part II of this book, we'll drill into some of the most useful classes from the class library to show you how you can apply the C# language to particular tasks. We won't try to cover every class in the library, but we will show you how to handle such problems as managing security, reading and writing to files, and using XML.

In this chapter, we'll show you the `System.Threading` namespace. This namespace includes classes that enable *multithreaded* programming. That is, a C# program that uses threads can perform multiple tasks in parallel. You'll see that there are some problems to consider when your application uses multiple threads. In particular, you need to worry about synchronizing threads and handling deadlocks that can arise when two threads are fighting for resources to do their work.

Featured in this chapter:

- All about the .NET Framework Class Library

- Using and Managing Threads

- Handling Thread Problems

- Using Thread Pooling

Understanding the .NET Framework Class Library

You learned about namespaces and namespace hierarchies in Chapter 6, "More about Classes and Objects." But what that chapter didn't discuss was the rich set of namespaces that the .NET Framework provides for your use. These namespaces collectively make up the .NET Framework Class Library (sometimes referred to as the *base class library* or just the *class library*).

Introducing the Namespaces in the Class Library

In its first release, the class library contains roughly 100 namespaces and thousands of classes, interfaces, and enumerations.

Clearly, in a book this size, we can't cover the class library exhaustively. Instead, we'll dig into some of the most useful and interesting namespaces to give you an idea of what you can do using C# and the .NET Framework together. Any time you need a common system service, though, you should investigate the class library. If Microsoft has already supplied an applicable base class, you can avoid writing your own code.

Table 14.1 lists the namespaces that ship with the .NET Framework.

TABLE 14.1: THE .NET FRAMEWORK CLASS LIBRARY NAMESPACES

NAMESPACE	CHILD NAMESPACES	DESCRIPTION
Microsoft.CSharp		Compilation and code-generation functions for C#.
Microsoft.Jscript		The JScript runtime.
Microsoft.VisualBasic		The VB .NET runtime.
Microsoft.Vsa		Support for scripting engines.
Microsoft.Win32		Operating system event and Registry support.
System	All the namespaces in the following rows of this table	The root namespace for most of the class library. Also contains commonly used data types and base classes.
System.CodeDom	System.CodeDom.Compiler	Represents the structure of a source code document.
System.Collections	System.Collections .Specialized	Data structures such as hash tables, dictionaries, and queues. Chapter 11, "Collections," covered this namespace.
System.ComponentModel	System.ComponentModel.Design, System.ComponentModel.Design .Serialization	Implements the run-time and design-time behavior of components and controls.

Continued on next page

TABLE 14.1: THE .NET FRAMEWORK CLASS LIBRARY NAMESPACES *(continued)*

NAMESPACE	CHILD NAMESPACES	DESCRIPTION
System.Configuration	System.Configuration.Assemblies, System.Configuration.Install	Programmatic access for .config files.
System.Data	System.Data.Common, System.Data.OleDb, System.Data.SqlClient, System.Data.SqlTypes	Classes that implement ADO.NET. Chapter 23, "Active Data Objects: ADO.NET," covers this namespace.
System.Diagnostics	System.Diagnostics.SymbolStore	Supports interaction with the event log, system processes, and performance counters. Chapter 21, "Other Classes in the Base Class Library," covers this namespace.
System.Directory-Services		Access to Active Directory information.
System.Drawing	System.Drawing.Design, System.Drawing.Drawing2D, System.Drawing.Imaging, System.Drawing.Printing, System.Drawing.Text	Classes that implement GDI+ graphics capabilities. Chapter 21 covers this namespace.
System.Enterprise-Services	System.EnterpriseServices.CompensatingResourceManager	Access to COM+ services. Chapter 21 covers this namespace.
System.Globalization		Support for internationalizing applications. Chapter 21 covers this namespace.
System.IO	System.IO.IsolatedStorage	Input and output for streams and files. Chapter 15, "Streams and Input/Output," covers this namespace.
System.Management, System.Management.Instrumentation		Access to WMI.
System.Messaging		Support for message queues.
System.Net, System.Net.Sockets		Support for network protocols.
System.Reflection, System.Reflection.Emit		Access to metadata contained within .NET applications. Chapter 17, "Attributes and Reflection," covers this namespace.
System.Resources		Creation and management of culture-specific resources.

Continued on next page

TABLE 14.1: THE .NET FRAMEWORK CLASS LIBRARY NAMESPACES *(continued)*

NAMESPACE	CHILD NAMESPACES	DESCRIPTION
System.Runtime	System.Runtime.CompilerServices, System.Runtime.InteropServices, System.Runtime.InteropServices .CustomMarshalers, System.Runtime .InteropServices.Expando, System .Runtime.Remoting, System.Runtime .Remoting.Activation, System.Runtime.Remoting .Channels, System.Runtime .Remoting.Channels.Http, System .Runtime.Remoting.Channels.Tcp, System.Runtime.Remoting .Contexts, System.Runtime .Remoting.Lifetime, System .Runtime.Remoting.Messaging, System.Runtime.Remoting .Metadata, System.Runtime .Remoting.Metadata.W3cXsd2001, System.Runtime.Remoting .MetadataServices, System.Runtime .Remoting.Proxies, System.Runtime .Remoting.Services, System .Runtime.Serialization, System.Runtime.Serialization .Formatters, System.Runtime .Serialization.Formatters .Binary, System.Runtime .Serialization.Formatters.Soap	Support for various features of the Common Language Runtime (CLR). Chapter 18, "Remoting," covers the remoting features of .NET.
System.Security	System.Security.Crytography, System.Security.Crytography.X50 9Certificates, System.Security.Crytography.Xml , System.Security.Permissions, System.Security.Policy, System.Security.Principal	The CLR security system. Chapter 19, "Security," covers this namespace.
System.ServiceProcess		Creation and control of Windows services.
System.Text	System.Text.RegularExpressions	Support for working with text and strings.
System.Threading		Support for threads. We'll cover this namespace in the rest of this chapter.

Continued on next page

TABLE 14.1: THE .NET FRAMEWORK CLASS LIBRARY NAMESPACES *(continued)*

NAMESPACE	CHILD NAMESPACES	DESCRIPTION
System.Timers		Server-based timer support.
System.Web	System.Web.Caching, System.Web .Configuration, System.Web .Hosting, System.Web.Mail, System .Web.Security, System.Web .Services, System.Web.Services .Configuration, System.Web .Services.Description, System.Web.Services.Discovery, System.Web.Services.Protocol, System.Web.SessionState, System .Web.UI, System.Web.UI.Design, System.Web.UI.Design.WebControls , System.Web.UI.HtmlConttrols, System.Web.UI.WebControls	Support for browser-based communication, ASP.NET, and Web Services. See Chapter 24, "Introduction to Windows Applications," and Chapter 25, "Web Services," for more information.
System.Windows.Forms	System.Windows.Forms.Design	User interface for Windows applications.
System.Xml	System.Xml.Schema, System .Xml.Serialization, System .Xml.XPath, System.Xml.Xsl	XML and related standards. Chapter 20, "XML," covers this namespace.

Exploring Namespaces

If you'd like to know more about a particular namespace in the class library, there are several tools available to help you:

◆ The Microsoft .NET Framework documentation

◆ The Object Browser

◆ The Windows Forms Class Viewer

THE MICROSOFT .NET FRAMEWORK DOCUMENTATION

Full documentation for the .NET Framework Class Library ships as part of the .NET Framework Software Development Kit (SDK) and as part of the Visual Studio .NET documentation. Whether you've downloaded the SDK to get the .NET Framework for free or paid for it as part of Visual Studio .NET, the help files are the same (though you'll find the class library documentation at different locations within the respective help files). Figure 14.1 shows part of the documentation for the class library—in this case, a small portion of the documentation for the Hashtable class in the System .Collections namespace.

FIGURE 14.1

Browsing the
Framework
documentation

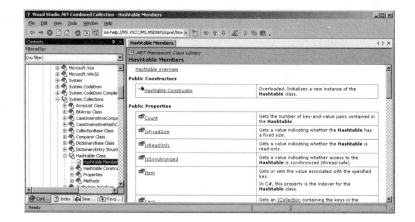

OBJECT BROWSER

The Object Browser is a tool built into the Visual Studio .NET Integrated Development Environment
(IDE). To launch the Object Browser, you can select View ➢ Other Windows ➢ Object Browser or
press F2. Figure 14.2 shows the Object Browser viewing the Hashtable class.

FIGURE 14.2

Using the Object
Browser

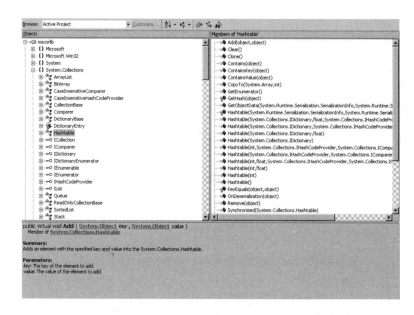

As you can see, there are three panels in the Object Browser:

The Objects Panel   The Objects panel, in the upper-left portion of the Object Browser, provides
a hierarchical view of all projects, namespaces, classes, and interfaces accessible to your project. This
includes classes in the .NET Framework, classes in your application, and classes in any referenced
assemblies.

The Members Panel The Members panel, in the upper-right portion of the Object Browser, shows the details of the object that's currently selected in the Objects panel. This includes constructors, methods, properties, and events for the selected item.

The Help Panel The Help panel, at the bottom of the Object Browser, provides additional information on the selected object or member. This includes prototypes and documentation. Objects and members in this panel are hyperlinked to their place in the upper panels.

The Find Symbol button at the right side of the Object Browser's toolbar lets you search across all loaded namespaces for a particular item. After you've found the item that you're looking for, you can press F1 to load the full documentation for that item directly into the Visual Studio .NET IDE.

WINDOWS FORMS CLASS VIEWER

If you're working outside of the Visual Studio .NET IDE, you may find the Windows Forms Class Viewer to be a more convenient way than the Object Browser to view a quick summary of a class and its members because it doesn't require you to launch the IDE. To launch the Windows Forms Class Viewer, select Start ➤ Programs ➤ Microsoft Visual Studio .NET ➤ Visual Studio .NET Tools ➤ Visual Studio .NET Command Prompt from the Windows Start menu. This will open a command prompt with environment variables set to run the Visual Studio .NET tools. Next, type **wincv**. Figure 14.3 shows the Windows Forms Class Viewer.

TIP *If you haven't installed Visual Studio .NET, you'll still find the Windows Forms Class Viewer as part of the .NET Framework SDK. The default location for this utility is* `C:\Program Files\Microsoft Visual Studio .NET\ FrameworkSDK\Bin\WinCV.exe`.

FIGURE 14.3

The WindowsForms Class Viewer

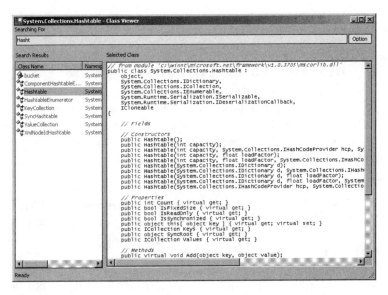

To use the Class Viewer after you've launched it, type any portion of the class or member that you're searching for in the box at the top of the viewer. As you type, the list of available classes will automatically narrow to ones that contain the text you're entering. When you locate the class of interest, click it in the Search Results window to see the details in the Selected Class window. You'll notice that the object interfaces are shown in code with this tool. It doesn't have some of the graphical features of the Object Browser.

By default, the Class Viewer opens with the classes from the .NET Framework itself loaded. However, there is a set of command-line switches you can use to modify its operation. Table 14.2 lists these switches.

TABLE 14.2: COMMAND-LINE SWITCHES FOR WINDOWS FORMS CLASS VIEWER

SWITCH	DESCRIPTION
/h or /?	Displays help information on these options.
/hide:*type*	Hides the specified type. The type to hide can be protected, private, internal, or inherited. By default, protected, private, and internal types are hidden.
/nostdlib-	Loads the default assemblies containing the .NET Framework Class Library.
/nostdlib+	Does not load the default assemblies containing the .NET Framework Class Library.
/r:*assemblyfile*	Loads the specified file so that you can browse its classes.
/show:*type*	Displays the specified type. The type to show can be protected, private, internal, or inherited. By default, inherited types are shown.
@*filename*	Reads command-line options from the specified file.

Understanding Threads

We'll start our tour of the class library with the System.Threading namespace. This namespace contains 18 classes, as well as assorted delegates, types, and enumerations. Rather than dig into all of these in detail (that's what the product documentation is for), we'll demonstrate some of these classes in code, starting with the Thread class itself. But first, we need to answer a fundamental question: What is a *thread*?

If you look at your computer right now, you'll probably see multiple programs running. Perhaps you have a document open in Word, a C# project open in Visual Studio .NET, and your e-mail arriving to your Outlook inbox. Each of these programs is represented by Windows as a single *process*. The Central Processing Unit (CPU) in your computer is responsible for executing all of the code for every process that's running at the time.

Of course, a single CPU can't really execute code for three processes at the same time. The fact that Word, Visual Studio .NET, and Outlook all appear to be running simultaneously is an optical illusion, caused by the fact that the CPU can switch very quickly between multiple processes. It does a little work in Word, then a little work in Visual Studio .NET, then a little work in Outlook, and so on. The result is that it looks to you like everything is running at once. Inside, though, the CPU is switching back and forth between processes as dictated by a sophisticated scheduling algorithm.

Threads take the notion of processes one step further. A single process can have one thread or many threads (each process always has at least one thread). The threads all share some resources. For example, each thread has access to all of the memory allocated to the process. The CPU switches between threads just as it does between processes, according to its own scheduler.

Threads don't increase the amount of work your computer can do in a given time, but they can help the computer *appear* more responsive. The classic example is background printing. When you tell Word to print a document, it doesn't do so on the main thread of the Word process. Instead, it launches another thread and lets that thread handle the printing. The original thread can then continue to handle user input and display tasks. The CPU switches between the two threads, giving the illusion that printing is happening at the same time as the rest of its work.

Of course, some computers have more than one CPU. But having a dual- or quad-processor computer doesn't change the basic way that threads work. It just means that each CPU executes some of the threads.

Creating Threads

In the .NET Framework, you can create a thread by instantiating the `Thread` class. The constructor for the `Thread` class takes a single parameter, an instance of the `ThreadStart` delegate. A `ThreadStart` delegate represents a method that will be called to do the work of the thread. In skeleton form, the declaration of a thread looks something like this:

```
public static void AMethod()
{
  {
    // Method body here
  }
}
public static void Main()
{
    Thread t2 = new Thread(new ThreadStart(AMethod));
```

This code creates a thread named `t2`. When the thread is started, it begins executing the `AMethod` method. You can start a thread by calling its `Start` method.

Listing 14.1 illustrates the `Thread` class.

LISTING 14.1: LAUNCHING A SECOND THREAD

```
/*
  Example14_1.cs illustrates the creation of threads
*/

using System;
using System.Threading;
```

```
class Example14_1
{

    // the Countdown method counts down from 1000 to 1
    public static void Countdown()
    {
     for (int counter = 1000; counter > 0; counter--)
     {
       Console.Write(counter.ToString() + " ");
     }
    }

    public static void Main()
    {

      // create a second thread
      Thread t2 = new Thread(new ThreadStart(Countdown));

      // launch the second thread
      t2.Start();

      // and meanwhile call the Countdown method from the first thread
      Countdown();

    }

}
```

This code creates a thread named t2 and then calls its Start method. When the thread's Start method is called, it begins executing the Countdown method. Meanwhile, the main thread also calls Countdown. The net effect is to have two copies of the Countdown method running "at the same time." Figure 14.4 shows the results of running this example, which you may find rather surprising.

FIGURE 14.4

Threads in contention

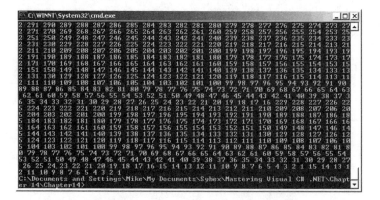

If you inspect the figure, you'll see that the output from the two threads is interspersed. That's because even though the threads are executed separately by the CPU, they share common resources (in this case, the console). You can see where one of the threads counts down to 16, only to be interrupted by the other thread counting down from 229 to 1 before the first thread can resume its work and count down from 15 to 1.

If you run this code several times, you'll probably see several different results. Exactly when the CPU switches from one thread to another is unpredictable. In the "Managing Threads" section later in this chapter you'll learn about techniques for synchronizing threads, which can help you get this sort of resource contention under control.

Setting Thread Properties and Methods

The Thread class has an assortment of methods and properties. Table 14.3 shows the public Thread properties.

TABLE 14.3: Thread PROPERTIES

PROPERTY	TYPE	DESCRIPTION
ApartmentState	ApartmentState	Whether the Thread object runs in a single-threaded or multithreaded apartment.
CurrentContext	Context	Undocumented property used internally by the .NET Framework.
CurrentCulture	CultureInfo	Gets or sets the culture (combination of language and other local settings) for the Thread object.
CurrentPrincipal	IPrincipal	Gets or sets the security context of the Thread object.
CurrentThread	Thread	Gets the currently executing Thread object.
CurrentUICulture	CultureInfo	Gets or sets the culture (combination of language and other local settings) for the user interface of the Thread object.
IsAlive	bool	Returns true if the Thread object has been started and not terminated.
IsBackground	bool	Gets or sets the background status of the Thread object.
IsThreadPoolThread	bool	Returns true if the Thread object is a member of a thread pool.
Name	string	Gets or sets the name of the Thread object. The name will be null if you don't explicitly set it.
Priority	ThreadPriority	Gets or sets the priority of the Thread object.
ThreadState	ThreadState	Gets the state of the Thread object.

Table 14.4 shows the public Thread methods.

TABLE 14.4: Thread METHODS

METHOD	STATIC?	DESCRIPTION
Abort()	No	Raises a ThreadAbortException to begin the process of terminating the Thread object.
AllocateDataSlot()	Yes	Allocates an unnamed data slot on all Thread objects.
AllocateNamedDataSlot()	Yes	Allocates a named data slot on all Thread objects.
Equals() (inherited from Object)	No	Determines whether two Object instances are equal.
FreeNamedDataSlot	Yes	Frees a previously allocated named data slot.
GetData	Yes	Retrieves a value from a data slot.
GetDomain	Yes	Returns the domain in which the Thread object is running.
GetDomainID	Yes	Returns the domain identifier for the domain in which the Thread object is running.
GetHashCode() (inherited from Object)	No	Returns a hash code for a particular type.
GetNamedDataSlot	Yes	Looks up a named data slot.
GetType() (inherited from Object)	No	Returns the type of the current instance.
Interrupt()	No	Interrupts a Thread object.
Join	No	Blocks the calling Thread object until another Thread object terminates.
ResetAbort	Yes	Cancels an abort request for the current Thread object.
Resume	No	Resumes a Thread object that has been suspended.
SetData	Yes	Sets data in a data slot.
Sleep	No	Blocks the current Thread object for a specified amount of time.
SpinWait	Yes	Causes the Thread object to wait a specified number of times.
Start	No	Starts the Thread object.
Suspend	No	Suspends the Thread object.
ToString() (inherited from Object)	No	Returns a string that represents the current Object.

In the remainder of this section, we'll use some of these properties and methods to customize the behavior of Thread objects.

Setting Thread Priorities

One of the basic principles of threads is that not all threads are created equal. Or rather, they're all created equal, but they don't have to stay that way. Think again about the example of printing in the background while you continue to work on a document in the foreground. You probably wouldn't want to devote half of the CPU time to printing. It would be better for the foreground application to get more than its fair share so that it could remain responsive. The printing will finish eventually.

Making these trade-offs is the job of the `Priority` property of the `Thread` object. There are five values for this property, which are listed in the `ThreadPriority` enumeration:

- ◆ Lowest
- ◆ BelowNormal
- ◆ Normal
- ◆ AboveNormal
- ◆ Highest

All threads are originally created with the `Normal` priority, but you can adjust this in code.

NOTE *Because the .NET Framework is designed to be explicitly cross-platform, these priority values may not match all of the thread priorities that can be used by any particular operating system. Windows 2000, for example, has six main priority classes, and Windows CE 3.0 offers 256 priority levels from 0 to 255.*

Listing 14.2 shows how you can set the priorities for `Thread` objects.

LISTING 14.2: USING THREAD PRIORITIES

```csharp
/*
  Example14_2.cs illustrates the use of thread priorities
*/

using System;
using System.Threading;

class Example14_2
{

    // the Countdown method counts down from 1000 to 1
    public static void Countdown()
    {
        for (int counter = 1000; counter > 0; counter--)
        {
            Console.Write(counter.ToString() + " ");
        }
    }
}
```

```
public static void Main()
{

    // create a second thread
    Thread t2 = new Thread(new ThreadStart(Countdown));

    // set the new thread to highest priority
    t2.Priority=ThreadPriority.Highest;

    // Locate the current thread and set it to the lowest priority
    Thread.CurrentThread.Priority=ThreadPriority.Lowest;

    // launch the second thread
    t2.Start();

    // and meanwhile call the Countdown method from the first thread
    Countdown();

}

}
```

TIP *Note the use of the* Thread.CurrentThread *property to return a* Thread *object representing the currently executing code. The* CurrentThread *property of any* Thread *object will return the executing* Thread.

Figure 14.5 shows the results of running this example.

FIGURE 14.5

Thread priorities in action

Inspecting this figure will show you that one thread finished its work before the other thread got control of the console. Comparing Figure 14.5 with Figure 14.4 shows that you can use thread priorities to reduce contention for shared resources.

WARNING *There is no guarantee that a higher-priority thread will finish executing before a lower-priority thread begins executing. First, not every operating system supports thread scheduling in that manner. Second, priority usually refers to the dedication of additional processing time, rather than an absolute pecking order. So, a long-running, high-priority thread may end up finishing after a shorter but lower-priority thread. Finally, modern operating systems contain code to resolve cases of priority inversion. Priority inversion occurs when a low-priority thread is holding a resource that a high-priority thread needs to continue its work. In this case, the scheduler may choose to boost the priority of the lower-priority thread so that the thread can release the shared resource.*

Retrieving Thread States

Thread objects go through a lifecycle characterized by a set of states. You can retrieve the state of any given `Thread` by reading its `ThreadState` property, which will return one of 10 values:

Unstarted   The `Thread` has not yet been started.

Running   The `Thread` is being executed.

Background   The `Thread` is being executed as a background thread.

WaitSleepJoin   The `Thread` is blocked as a result of a call to the `Wait`, `Sleep`, or `Join` methods.

SuspendRequested   The `Thread` object is in the process of being suspended.

Suspended   The `Thread` object has been suspended.

StopRequested   The `Thread` object is in the process of being stopped.

Stopped   The `Thread` object has stopped.

AbortRequested   The `Abort` method has been called, but the `Thread` object has not yet received the `ThreadAbortException`.

Aborted   The `Thread` object was aborted.

A `Thread` object initially starts in the `Unstarted` state when it's created. When you call the `Thread` `.Start` method, it enters the `Running` state. If you then set the `IsBackground` method to `true`, the `Thread` object will be in the `Background` state, and so on.

A `Thread` object can be in more than one state at a time. For example, a `Thread` object that's waiting for a resource might be in both the `WaitSleepJoin` and `AbortRequested` state if the `Abort` method has been called while it's waiting. For this reason, you must use Boolean logic to test thread states. Listing 14.3 shows this technique.

LISTING 14.3: ANALYZING THREAD STATES

```
/*
   Example14_3.cs illustrates the ThreadState property
*/

using System;
using System.Threading;
```

```csharp
class Example14_3
{

    // the Countdown method counts down from 10 to 1
    public static void Countdown()
    {
        for (int counter = 10; counter > 0; counter--)
        {
            Console.Write(counter.ToString() + " ");
        }
        Console.WriteLine();
    }


    // the DumpThreadState method displays the current Thread's state
    // Note that ThreadState is a bitmask, and multiple states for the
    // same thread are valid
    public static void DumpThreadState (
        Thread t
        )
    {
        Console.Write("Current state: ");
        if ((t.ThreadState & ThreadState.Aborted) == ThreadState.Aborted)
            Console.Write("Aborted ");
        if ((t.ThreadState & ThreadState.AbortRequested) ==
         ThreadState.AbortRequested)
            Console.Write("AbortRequested ");
        if ((t.ThreadState & ThreadState.Background) ==
         ThreadState.Background)
            Console.Write("Background ");
        if ((t.ThreadState &
         (ThreadState.Stopped | ThreadState.Unstarted |
          ThreadState.Aborted)) == 0)
            Console.Write("Running ");
        if ((t.ThreadState & ThreadState.Stopped) == ThreadState.Stopped)
            Console.Write("Stopped ");
        if ((t.ThreadState & ThreadState.StopRequested) ==
         ThreadState.StopRequested)
            Console.Write("StopRequested ");
        if ((t.ThreadState & ThreadState.Suspended) ==
         ThreadState.Suspended)
            Console.Write("Suspended ");
        if ((t.ThreadState & ThreadState.SuspendRequested) ==
         ThreadState.SuspendRequested)
            Console.Write("SuspendRequested ");
        if ((t.ThreadState & ThreadState.Unstarted) ==
         ThreadState.Unstarted)
            Console.Write("Unstarted ");
        if ((t.ThreadState & ThreadState.WaitSleepJoin) ==
```

```
        ThreadState.WaitSleepJoin)
            Console.Write("WaitSleepJoin ");
        Console.WriteLine();
    }

    public static void Main()
    {

        // create a second thread
        Thread t2 = new Thread(new ThreadStart(Countdown));
        DumpThreadState(t2);

        // launch the second thread
        t2.Start();
        DumpThreadState(t2);

        // and meanwhile call the Countdown method from the first thread
        Countdown();

        // shut down the second thread
        t2.Abort();
        DumpThreadState(t2);

    }

}
```

The output from this program might be as follows:

```
Current state: Unstarted
Current state: Unstarted
10 9 8 7 6 5 4 3 2 1
Current state: Aborted
```

You'll notice that we said *might be*. The output might also be as follows:

```
Current state: Unstarted
Current state: Unstarted
10 9 8 7 6 5 4 3 2 1
Current state: AbortRequested
```

Or it might be as follows:

```
Current state: Unstarted
Current state: Running
10 9 8 7 6 5 4 3 2 1
Current state: Running
```

You might even see output from Thread t2's call to the CountDown method in the output. It all depends on when the Abort request is processed compared to when the scheduler executes the second thread. Thinking about the actions that lead to the various possible outputs will help convince you of the unpredictable nature of threads.

TIP   In Listing 14.3, you'll see that testing for the Running *state is a special case. That's because the literal value of the* ThreadState.Running *constant is zero, so it can't be tested for by applying a bitmask. Instead, the code takes advantage of the knowledge that if a* Thread *object isn't unstarted, stopped, or aborted, it must be running.*

Using Data Slots

Sometimes it's convenient to store information on a per-thread basis, available only to that thread. This is called *thread-local storage*. That's the purpose of the various methods that manipulate LocalDataStore-Slot objects. Listing 14.4 shows some of these methods in action.

LISTING 14.4: USING THREAD-LOCAL STORAGE

```
/*
  Example14_4.cs illustrates the use of thread-local storage
*/

using System;
using System.Threading;

class Example14_4
{

    // the WriteError method writes error info from the current thread
    public static void WriteError()
    {
        Console.WriteLine("Error number = " +
         Thread.GetData(Thread.GetNamedDataSlot("ErrNo")));
        Console.WriteLine("Error source = " +
         Thread.GetData(Thread.GetNamedDataSlot("ErrSource")));
    }

    // the SetError method sets a random error number
    public static void SetError()
    {
        Random r = new Random();
        Thread.SetData(Thread.GetNamedDataSlot("ErrNo"), r.Next(100));
        Thread.SetData(Thread.GetNamedDataSlot("ErrSource") ,
         Thread.CurrentThread.Name);
        WriteError();
    }
```

```
public static void Main()
{
    // allocate some named data slots
    Thread.AllocateNamedDataSlot("ErrNo");
    Thread.AllocateNamedDataSlot("ErrSource");

    // create and start a second thread
    Thread t2 = new Thread(new ThreadStart(SetError));
    t2.Name = "t2";
    t2.Start();

    // create a third thread
    Thread t3 = new Thread(new ThreadStart(SetError));
    t3.Name = "t3";
    t3.Start();

    // clean up the data slots
    Thread.FreeNamedDataSlot("ErrNo");
    Thread.FreeNamedDataSlot("ErrSource");


}

}
```

This program starts by setting up two named data slots, ErrNo and ErrSource. (You can also use unnamed data slots by passing LocalDataStoreSlot objects around, but named data slots are usually more convenient.) It then spawns two threads, each of which executes at the SetError method when the Thread object is started. This method generates and stores some information in the data slots and then calls the WriteError method to print that information. The output from this program is as follows (though, of course, you'll see different random numbers if you run it):

```
Error number = 29
Error source = t2
Error number = 52
Error source = t3
```

Though both threads use the "same" data slot, they each get their own instance of the data slot to use. In fact, threads cannot see a data slot from another thread under any circumstances.

TIP *If you want threads to be able to share data, just declare and instantiate an object in a scope that's common to the two threads.*

Managing Threads

As you've seen so far in this chapter, thread execution is by nature nondeterministic. That is, you can't be sure when a particular thread will execute or what order threads will execute in. But there are ways to manage the behavior of threads to make them more deterministic. In this section, we'll investigate the Timer class, which allows you to run threads at periodic intervals; the Join method, which lets one thread wait for another thread to complete; and the Lock, Interlocked, Monitor, and Mutex classes, which enable you to coordinate the activities and resource usage of multiple threads.

Using the *Timer* Class

The Timer class provides you with the ability to add a "fire-and-forget" thread to your program. When you instantiate a Timer object, you specify four parameters:

callback   A TimerCallback delegate that supplies a method that the Timer will call.

state   An object that should be passed to the TimerCallback method. You can use this to keep persistent state available to the Timer. If you don't need any persistent state, this parameter can be null.

dueTime   The number of milliseconds until the Timer should fire the first time.

Period   The number of milliseconds between invocations of the Timer.

Listing 14.5 shows an example of the Timer class.

LISTING 14.5: USING A Timer OBJECT

```
/*
  Example14_5.cs illustrates the use of the Timer class
*/

using System;
using System.Threading;

class Example14_5
{

    // the CheckTime method is called by the Timer
    public static void CheckTime(Object state)
    {
        Console.WriteLine(DateTime.Now);
    }

    public static void Main()
    {

        // create the delegate that the Timer will call
        TimerCallback tc = new TimerCallback(CheckTime);

        // create a Timer that runs twice a second, starting in one second
        Timer t = new Timer(tc, null, 1000, 500);
```

```
      // Wait for user input
      Console.WriteLine("Press Enter to exit");
      int i = Console.Read();

      // clean up the resources
      t.Dispose();
      t = null;

   }

}
```

The output from this program is as follows:

```
Press Enter to exit
03/30/2002 4:02:06 PM
03/30/2002 4:02:06 PM
03/30/2002 4:02:07 PM
03/30/2002 4:02:07 PM
03/30/2002 4:02:08 PM
03/30/2002 4:02:08 PM
```

The method specified in the `Timer` executes in a separate thread allocated by the system, not in the thread that creates the `Timer` object. Note the call to the `Dispose` method of the `Timer` object. This is essential to make sure that the resources assigned to this separate thread are properly cleaned up when you no longer need them.

TIP   To alter the priority of the method invoked by a `Timer` object, you can set the value of `Thread.Current-Thread.Priority` within that method.

Using the *Join* Method

The `Thread.Join` method allows you to put one thread "on hold" until another thread completes its work. Listing 14.6 shows this method at work.

LISTING 14.6: USING THE `Thread.Join` METHOD

```
/*
   Example14_6.cs shows the Thread.Join method in action
*/

using System;
using System.Threading;

class Example14_6
{
```

```
// the Countdown method counts down from 1000 to 1
public static void Countdown()
{
    for (int counter = 1000; counter > 0; counter--)
    {
        Console.Write(counter.ToString() + " ");
    }
}

public static void Main()
{

    // create a second thread
    Thread t2 = new Thread(new ThreadStart(Countdown));

    // launch the second thread
    t2.Start();

    // block the first thread until the second is done
    t2.Join();

    // and  call the Countdown method from the first thread
    Countdown();

}

}
```

If you run this example and look at the results, you'll discover that the output from the two calls to the Countdown method are not interspersed, even though the main thread and the secondary thread are both executing at normal priority. That's because the call to t2.Join prevents the main thread from continuing until the secondary thread finishes executing the Countdown method.

There are also overloaded versions of the Join method that enable you to specify a maximum period to wait. For example, you can wait for another thread to complete for a maximum of five seconds with this syntax:

```
t2.Join(5000);
```

Using Locks

There are many potential problems with threaded code that you won't run into if you're not using threads. For example, what happens when two different threads are working with a shared variable? The results aren't always what you expect. Listing 14.7 shows some threaded code that has a problem.

```csharp
/*
  Example14_7.cs shows code with a problem
*/

using System;
using System.Threading;

class Example14_7
{
    // a shared counter
    private int Runs = 0;

    // the CountUp method increments the shared counter
    public  void CountUp()
    {
        while (Runs <= 10)
        {
            int Temp = Runs;
            Temp++;
            Console.WriteLine(Thread.CurrentThread.Name + " " + Temp);
            Thread.Sleep(1000);
            Runs = Temp;
        }
    }

    public static void Main()
    {
        // Make an instance of this class
        Example14_7 ex = new Example14_7();

        // And run the test outside of the static method
        ex.RunThreads();
    }

    public void RunThreads()
    {
        // create and launch two threads
        Thread t2 = new Thread(new ThreadStart(CountUp));
        t2.Name = "t2";
        Thread t3 = new Thread(new ThreadStart(CountUp));
        t3.Name = "t3";
        t2.Start();
        t3.Start();

    }

}
```

The output from this program is as follows:

```
t2 1
t3 1
t2 2
t3 2
t2 3
t3 3
t2 4
t3 4
t2 5
t3 5
t2 6
t3 6
t2 7
t3 7
t2 8
t3 8
t2 9
t3 9
t2 10
t3 10
```

If you were expecting a total of 10 executions of the CountUp method, you probably find this output rather surprising. The problem is that incrementing the Runs variable is not an atomic operation. That is, other things can happen in the middle of the process of retrieving the current value of this variable, incrementing it, and saving the new variable. The Thread.Sleep method tells a Thread object to give up its processing time for a number of milliseconds. In this case, here's what happens:

1. Thread t2 gets the value of the Runs variable into the Temp variable and increments it.

2. Thread t2 goes to sleep for a second.

3. The scheduler passes control to Thread t3.

4. Thread t3 gets the value of the Runs variable into the Temp variable and increments it. This is the same value that Thread t2 saw previously because t2 hasn't yet written the new value back.

5. Thread t3 goes to sleep for a second.

6. Thread t2 wakes up and writes the incremented value back to the Runs variable.

7. Thread t3 wakes up and writes the incremented value back to the Runs variable, overwriting the value that was written by Thread t2.

8. The cycle repeats.

NOTE   *The call to the Sleep method is in this code to make sure that the resource contention is obvious. In fact, you can see this same pattern even without the Sleep method because the scheduler can switch away from a Thread object in the middle of an increment operation, before the new value is stored.*

This is a classic resource contention problem, with two threads fighting over a single resource. Fortunately, the .NET Framework provides several ways to solve this type of issue. The simplest way to do so is to use a Lock object. Lock objects don't need to be explicitly created in your code; they're supported in C# by a special lock keyword. Listing 14.8 shows how you can patch this program to work properly by using a Lock object.

```csharp
/*
  Example14_8.cs illustrates the use of the lock object
*/

using System;
using System.Threading;

class Example14_8
{
    // a shared counter
    private int Runs = 0;

    // the CountUp method increments the shared counter
    public  void CountUp()
    {
        while (Runs < 10)
        {
            lock(this)
            {
                int Temp = Runs;
                Temp++;
                Console.WriteLine(Thread.CurrentThread.Name + " " + Temp);
                Thread.Sleep(1000);
                Runs = Temp;
            }
        }
    }

    public static void Main()
    {
        // Make an instance of this class
        Example14_8 ex = new Example14_8();

        // And run the test outside of the static method
        ex.RunThreads();
    }

    public void RunThreads()
    {
        // create and launch two threads
        Thread t2 = new Thread(new ThreadStart(CountUp));
        t2.Name = "t2";
```

```
            Thread t3 = new Thread(new ThreadStart(CountUp));
            t3.Name = "t3";
            t2.Start();
            t3.Start();

        }

    }
```

What the lock statement says is, "Don't let any other thread use this section of code while I'm using it."

TIP   You can lock any object. This example uses the this keyword with the lock to lock all of the code within the class.

In this case, the output looks like this:

```
t2 1
t3 2
t2 3
t3 4
t2 5
t3 6
t2 7
t3 8
t2 9
t3 10
t2 11
```

NOTE   The count goes to 11 because the t2 thread sees the counter value of 9 and starts a new loop; it then blocks while the other thread increments the value to 10. When t2 unblocks, it works with this newly incremented value.

Using the *Interlocked* Class

Safely incrementing a variable in a thread is so common that a special object exists to handle the task: the Interlocked class. This class has no properties. Table 14.5 shows the public Interlocked methods.

TABLE 14.5: Interlocked METHODS

METHOD	STATIC?	DESCRIPTION
CompareExchange()	Yes	Compares two values; if they are equal, returns a third value
Decrement()	Yes	Decrements a variable
Exchange()	Yes	Sets a variable equal to a value
Increment()	Yes	Increments a variable

Listing 14.9 shows the use of the Interlocked object.

LISTING 14.9: USING THE Interlocked OBJECT

```
/*
  Example14_9.cs illustrates the use of the Interlocked object
*/

using System;
using System.Threading;

class Example14_9
{
    // a shared counter
    private int Runs = 0;

    // the CountUp method increments the shared counter
    public  void CountUp()
    {
        while (Runs < 10)
        {
            Interlocked.Increment(ref Runs);
            Console.WriteLine(Thread.CurrentThread.Name + " " + Runs);
            Thread.Sleep(1000);
        }
    }

    public static void Main()
    {
        // Make an instance of this class
        Example14_9 ex = new Example14_9();

        // And run the test outside of the static method
        ex.RunThreads();
    }

    public void RunThreads()
    {
        // create and launch two threads
        Thread t2 = new Thread(new ThreadStart(CountUp));
        t2.Name = "t2";
        Thread t3 = new Thread(new ThreadStart(CountUp));
        t3.Name = "t3";
        t2.Start();
        t3.Start();

    }

}
```

The output from this program is as follows:

```
t2 1
t3 2
t2 3
t3 4
t2 5
t3 6
t2 7
t3 8
t2 9
t3 10
```

Using the *Monitor* Class

The lock keyword, which you saw earlier, is in fact a shorthand way of using the Monitor class. The Monitor class offers flexible options for synchronizing access to any object in your code. Listing 14.10 shows how you can rewrite the code to explicitly use the Monitor class.

LISTING 14.10: USING A Monitor OBJECT

```csharp
/*
   Example14_10.cs illustrates the use of the Monitor object
*/

using System;
using System.Threading;

class Example14_10
{
    // a shared counter
    private int Runs = 0;

    // the CountUp method increments the shared counter
    public  void CountUp()
    {
        while (Runs < 10)
        {
            Monitor.Enter(this);
            int Temp = Runs;
            Temp++;
            Console.WriteLine(Thread.CurrentThread.Name + " " + Temp);
            Thread.Sleep(1000);
            Runs = Temp;
            Monitor.Exit(this);
        }
    }
```

```
public static void Main()
{
    // Make an instance of this class
    Example14_10 ex = new Example14_10();

    // And run the test outside of the static method
    ex.RunThreads();
}

public void RunThreads()
{
    // create and launch two threads
    Thread t2 = new Thread(new ThreadStart(CountUp));
    t2.Name = "t2";
    Thread t3 = new Thread(new ThreadStart(CountUp));
    t3.Name = "t3";
    t2.Start();
    t3.Start();

}

}
```

The output from this code is as follows:

```
t2 1
t3 2
t2 3
t3 4
t2 5
t3 6
t2 7
t3 8
t2 9
t3 10
t2 11
```

The `Monitor.Enter` and `Monitor.Exit` methods together function exactly the same as the `lock` keyword. But the `Monitor` has capabilities beyond this sort of simple locking. Table 14.6 shows the public `Monitor` methods.

TABLE 14.6: MONITOR METHODS

METHOD	STATIC?	DESCRIPTION
Enter()	Yes	Obtains a lock on the object passed to the Monitor. If another Thread has already locked the object, this Thread will be blocked until that thread releases the object.
Exit()	Yes	Releases the lock held by the Monitor.
Pulse()	Yes	Signals the next waiting Thread that the Monitor is temporarily done with this object and that Thread can continue.
PulseAll()	Yes	Signals all waiting Thread objects that an object is about to be released.
TryEnter()	Yes	Attempts to obtain a lock on the object passed to the Monitor. If the lock can be obtained, returns true; otherwise returns false.
Wait()	Yes	Releases any lock held on the object and blocks this Thread until another Thread calls Pulse.

Using the *Mutex* Class

Finally, you can synchronize threads by using the Mutex object. Listing 14.11 shows the Mutex object for the same code you've been looking at in the last several examples.

LISTING 14.11: USING A Mutex OBJECT

```
/*
  Example14_11.cs illustrates the use of the Mutex object
*/

using System;
using System.Threading;

class Example14_11
{
    // a shared counter
    private static int Runs = 0;

    // a mutex
    static Mutex mtx;

    // the CountUp method increments the shared counter
    public static void CountUp()
    {
        while (Runs < 10)
        {
```

```
            // acquire the mutex
            mtx.WaitOne();
            int Temp = Runs;
            Temp++;
            Console.WriteLine(Thread.CurrentThread.Name + " " + Temp);
            Thread.Sleep(1000);
            Runs = Temp;
            // release the mutex
            mtx.ReleaseMutex();
        }
    }

    public static void Main()
    {

        // create the mutex
        mtx = new Mutex(false, "RunsMutex");

        // create and launch two threads
        Thread t2 = new Thread(new ThreadStart(CountUp));
        t2.Name = "t2";
        Thread t3 = new Thread(new ThreadStart(CountUp));
        t3.Name = "t3";
        t2.Start();
        t3.Start();

    }

}
```

A Mutex is an object that can be owned by a single Thread at one time. The constructor for the Mutex takes two parameters in this example (there are other overloaded versions of this constructor). The first Boolean parameter specifies whether the object should initially be owned by the Thread that creates it. The second parameter supplies a name for the Mutex.

A Thread can call the WaitOne method to acquire the Mutex. If no other Thread is holding the Mutex, the Thread that calls WaitOne will receive ownership of the Mutex; otherwise, it will block until the Mutex is available. When it's done with the Mutex, the thread can call ReleaseMutex to release the Mutex for the next waiting Thread.

NOTE *The* Mutex *also supports a* WaitAll *method to wait for all* Mutex *objects in a group to be free and a* WaitAny *method to wait for any* Mutex *object in a group to be free.*

The output from this code is as follows:

```
t2 1
t3 2
t2 3
```

```
t3  4
t2  5
t3  6
t2  7
t3  8
t2  9
t3  10
t2  11
```

When should you use a `Mutex` instead of another synchronization object such as a `Monitor`? You should use a `Mutex` when you need to synchronize threads across processes. That's because the `Mutex` is implemented as an object in the Windows kernel, rather than an object in a particular application. If two processes both call the `Mutex` constructor and supply identical names for the `Mutex`, then they will both get the same `Mutex` with which to work.

WARNING *Because it's implemented in the kernel, the* `Mutex` *is slower than the* `Monitor`. *You should not use a* `Mutex` *unless you require its cross-process communications capabilities.*

Dealing with Thread Problems

The nondeterministic nature of thread scheduling can lead to problems in your code even more serious than the resource-contention issues already discussed. Although modern operating systems contain some ways to automatically avoid these problems, you should still know about two potential classes of trouble for your threaded applications: deadlocks and race conditions.

Avoiding Deadlocks

A *deadlock* occurs when two threads are each waiting for an object locked by the other. Suppose that one thread in your application is executing these statements:

```
lock(employee)
{
    lock(payroll)
    {
        // processing here
    }
}
```

Meanwhile, a second thread in your application is executing these statements:

```
lock(payroll)
{
    lock(employee)
    {
        // processing here
    }
}
```

If you are unlucky (and in the long run, you will be very unlucky), the processor will switch from the first thread to the second thread just after the first thread has locked the `employee` object. In this case, the second thread will lock the `payroll` object and then wait for the `employee` object to be free. When the CPU gets back to the first thread, it will have to wait for the `payroll` object to be free. Neither thread can proceed in this situation.

To avoid deadlocks in your code, follow these guidelines:

- Lock objects in the same order in all threads.

- Lock all objects you need in calls located together in the code; similarly, release all objects in calls located close together.

- Lock as few objects as possible and for as short a time as possible.

- If you must lock multiple objects, make sure all the locks were successful and abort processing if they're not. You can use the `Monitor.TryEnter` method for this purpose, as in the following code:

```
if (Monitor.TryEnter(employee))
{
    if (Monitor.TryEnter(payroll))
    {
        // processing here
    }
    else
        // couldn't lock payroll
        Monitor.Exit(employee)
}
```

Avoiding Race Conditions

A *race condition* occurs when your code depends on one thread completing some work before another thread is called. Once again, in the long run you'll get unlucky and the second thread will execute before the first thread finishes its work. To avoid race conditions in your code, follow these guidelines:

- Keep work that must be completed sequentially in one thread, instead of spreading it across multiple threads.

- If one thread must be completed before another thread can continue, use `Thread.Join` to force the second thread to wait for the first thread.

- If one thread must complete work with a shared resource before a second thread can use that shared resource, use a synchronization object such as a `Monitor` or a `Mutex` to control access to the resource.

Thread Pooling

In some cases, you may want to use threads without creating them for yourself. That's the purpose of the `ThreadPool` class, which gives you access to a pool of threads managed by the operating system. These threads are shared between all processes that access the thread pool. The system can manage these threads more efficiently than threads represented by independent `Thread` objects.

Table 14.7 shows the public `ThreadPool` methods.

TABLE 14.7: ThreadPool METHODS

METHOD	STATIC?	DESCRIPTION
BindHandle()	Yes	Binds an operating system handle to the ThreadPool. This is only useful from unmanaged code; you won't use it in C#.
GetAvailableThreads()	Yes	Returns the number of work items that you can add to the ThreadPool.
GetMaxThreads()	Yes	Returns the maximum number of threads in the ThreadPool. If you request more work items than this, the extras will block until some work items are completed.
QueueUserWorkItem()	Yes	Adds a work item to the ThreadPool via a callback.
RegisterWaitFor-SingleObject()	Yes	Registers a delegate to wait for a WaitHandle via the ThreadPool.
UnsafeQueueUser-WorkItem()	Yes	A version of QueueUserWorkItem that does not copy the stack to the worker thread.
UnsafeRegisterWait-ForSingleObject	Yes	A version of RegisterWaitForSingleObject that does not copy the stack to the worker thread.

Listing 14.12 shows code that uses the operating system thread pool.

LISTING 14.12: USING THE ThreadPool OBJECT

```
/*
  Example14_12.cs illustrates the use of the system thread pool
*/

using System;
using System.Threading;

class Example14_12
{

    // the Countdown method counts down from 1000 to 1
    public static void Countdown(Object o)
    {
        for (int counter = 1000; counter > 0; counter--)
        {
            Console.Write(counter.ToString() + " ");
        }
    }
```

```
public static void Main()
{

    // ask the system to create and launch a second thread
    ThreadPool.QueueUserWorkItem(new WaitCallback(Countdown), null);

    // and meanwhile call the Countdown method from the first thread
    Countdown(null);

}

}
```

As you can see, the `QueueUserWorkItem` method takes two parameters. The first is a `WaitCallBack` object, which specifies the method that should be executed by the worker thread. The second is an object to be passed to the worker thread, which in turn will pass this object to the method that it executes. The object can be `null` if you don't need to pass any information, but the signature for the method must include an `Object` parameter.

WARNING   *If you run this example, you'll discover that some of the expected output may vanish. When the* Countdown *call from the main thread finishes executing, the system abandons the worker thread, even if the worker thread hasn't finished its work.*

The system limits the default thread pool to 25 threads per CPU. Worker threads from the thread pool always execute as background threads with normal priority.

Worker threads from the thread pool are not appropriate in all cases. Situations where you should create your own `Thread` objects include the following:

◆ You need a thread to execute in the foreground.

◆ You need a thread to execute at a priority other than normal.

◆ You have a task that may run for a long time. If you don't create your own `Thread` object for this process, it will block threads in other processes.

◆ You need many threads (more than the thread pool provides).

◆ You need to signal threads with the `Join` method.

Avoid creating your own threads when you don't really need them, though. It's much faster to use a thread from the thread pool than it is to instantiate your own thread.

Summary

The .NET Framework Class Library contains thousands of useful objects that you can use in your C# code. These objects are consolidated in about a hundred namespaces, which group them together on the basis of functionality. You can use the Object Browser, the .NET documentation, or the Windows Forms Class Viewer to explore the namespaces in the class library.

The System.Threading namespace contains objects that are useful for threaded operations. Threads provide the illusion of multiple operations executing at the same time.

You can create a thread by creating a new Thread object. Properties of the Thread object let you control its priority and state. You can associate data slots with a Thread to hold data in thread-local storage.

The Timer class enables you to create a thread that will execute on a periodic basis. Other management tools let you synchronize and coordinate threads. These tools include the Join method, the lock statement, and the Interlocked, Monitor, and Mutex objects.

When you're writing threaded code, you need to be aware of problems that can be caused by the nondeterministic nature of thread scheduling. These include deadlocks (where two threads are each waiting for a resource locked by the other) and race conditions (where you depend on one thread to execute code before another).

For background operations, the system provides a pool of worker threads that you can use. Access to these worker threads is via the ThreadPool object. In the next chapter, you'll learn about streams and input/output.

Chapter 15

Streams and Input/Output

IT'S HARD TO IMAGINE a computer program that doesn't perform input and output operations (usually called *I/O*). Even applications that don't interact with the user, such as Windows services, must still acquire data and return results. Considering the fundamental nature of I/O operations, it's not surprising that the .NET Framework Class Library provides a rich set of classes for handling these operations.

These classes include support for working directly with files and directories, but that's only part of the story. Much of the I/O support in the .NET Framework revolves around the twin concepts of *streams* and *backing stores*. A stream represents data being moved from one place to another; a backing store is a place where you can keep data for an extended period of time.

In this chapter we'll explore the ins and outs of working with data the .NET way. We'll start with basic file and directory operations. From there, you'll learn how to read and write data in a variety of ways, including ways to use the network as a data transport. Finally, we'll take a look at the concept of *serialization*, which lets you move entire objects to a backing store. The primary namespace that we'll explore in this chapter is System.IO, though we'll also use objects from other namespaces including System.Net and System.Runtime.Serialization.

Featured in this chapter:

- ◆ Dealing with Files and Directories
- ◆ Introducing Streams and Backing Stores
- ◆ Using Readers and Writers
- ◆ Implementing Asynchronous I/O
- ◆ Understanding Serialization

Dealing with Files and Directories

Although the .NET concept of I/O is much broader than that of simply reading and writing disk files, that's a convenient place to start. The class library includes classes to handle just about any file or directory operation that you can think of, from creating a new directory to monitoring a file for changes.

Browsing for Files

For many of our examples, we'll need to specify a file with which to work. Rather than hard-coding a filename into the source code, let's take a slight detour and introduce the OpenFileDialog class. This class is a part of the System.Windows.Forms namespace, and its job is to display the standard Windows Open dialog box. Listing 15.1 illustrates the simplest use of this class.

LISTING 15.1: BROWSING FOR A FILE

```
/*
  Example15_1.cs shows browsing for a file
*/

using System;
using System.Windows.Forms;

class Example15_1
{

  public static void Main()
  {

    // create and show an open file dialog
    OpenFileDialog dlgOpen = new OpenFileDialog();
    if (dlgOpen.ShowDialog() == DialogResult.OK)
      {
        Console.Write(dlgOpen.FileName);
      }

  }

}
```

When you run this example, it will display the Open dialog box, as shown in Figure 15.1. If you select a file and click Open, the Console.Write method will print the name of the selected file.

The OpenFileDialog class has an assortment of methods and properties. Table 15.1 shows the public OpenFileDialog properties. This table includes both properties of the OpenFileDialog class itself and properties inherited from the FileDialog class.

FIGURE 15.1

Browsing for a file

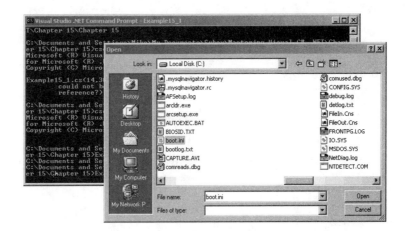

TABLE 15.1: OpenFileDialog PROPERTIES

PROPERTY	TYPE	DESCRIPTION
AddExtension	bool	Gets or sets a value indicating whether the dialog box should add an extension to the filename if the user omits one
CheckFileExists	bool	Gets or sets a value indicating whether the dialog box should display a warning if a file does not exist
CheckPathExists	bool	Gets or sets a value indicating whether the dialog box should display a warning if a specified path does not exist
DefaultExt	string	Gets or sets the default file extension
DereferenceLinks	bool	Gets or sets a value indicating whether the target of a link should be returned instead of the link
FileName	string	Gets or sets the filename displayed in the dialog box
FileNames	string[]	Gets or sets an array of all filenames selected in the dialog box
Filter	string	Gets or sets the filename filter
FilterIndex	int	Gets or sets the current filter
InitialDirectory	string	Gets or sets the initial directory displayed when the dialog box is shown
Multiselect	bool	Gets or sets a value indicating whether multiple files can be selected
ReadOnlyChecked	bool	Gets or sets a value indicating whether the Read Only checkbox on the dialog box is checked
RestoreDirectory	bool	Gets or sets a value indicating whether the original current directory should be restored when the dialog box is closed

Continued on next page

TABLE 15.1: OpenFileDialog PROPERTIES *(continued)*

PROPERTY	TYPE	DESCRIPTION
ShowHelp	bool	Gets or sets a value indicating whether the Help button should be shown in the dialog box
ShowReadOnly	bool	Gets or sets a value indicating whether the Read Only checkbox should be shown in the dialog box
Title	string	Gets or sets the title of the dialog box
ValidateNames	bool	Gets or sets a value indicating whether the dialog box will only accept valid filenames

Table 15.2 shows the public OpenFileDialog methods.

TABLE 15.2: OpenFileDialog METHODS

METHOD	STATIC?	DESCRIPTION
OpenFile()	No	Opens the file selected by the user with readonly permissions
Reset()	No	Resets all properties of the dialog box to their default values
ShowDialog()	No	Shows the dialog box and waits for the user to click Open or Cancel

Listing 15.2 illustrates several of the properties of the OpenFileDialog class. This example lets you select multiple files and then prints the names of all of the selected files.

LISTING 15.2: SELECTING MULTIPLE FILES

```
/*
  Example15_2.cs shows browsing for a set of files
*/

using System;
using System.Windows.Forms;

class Example15_2
{

    public static void Main()
    {

        // create an open file dialog
        OpenFileDialog dlgOpen = new OpenFileDialog();
```

```
        // set properties for the dialog
        dlgOpen.Title = "Select one or more files";
        dlgOpen.ShowReadOnly = true;
        dlgOpen.Multiselect = true;

        // display the dialog and return results
        if (dlgOpen.ShowDialog() == DialogResult.OK)
        {
            foreach (string s in dlgOpen.FileNames)
                Console.WriteLine(s);
        }

    }

}
```

Retrieving File Information

The class library provides two different classes for manipulating files: the `File` class and the `FileInfo` class. The `File` class is the simpler of the two and is implemented as a collection of static methods. This class is intended for manipulating entire files. For example, it's the easiest way to move, copy, create, or delete files. Being a collection of static methods, it's also low overhead. If you want more detailed access to the contents or attributes of a file, you should use the `FileInfo` class (discussed later in the chapter) instead.

Listing 15.3 shows the `File` class in action.

LISTING 15.3: RETRIEVING INFORMATION WITH THE `File` CLASS

```
/*
  Example15_3.cs illustrates the File class
*/

using System;
using System.Windows.Forms;
using System.IO;

class Example15_3
{

    public static void Main()
    {

        // create and show an open file dialog
        OpenFileDialog dlgOpen = new OpenFileDialog();
        if (dlgOpen.ShowDialog() == DialogResult.OK)
        {
```

```
                     // use the File class to return info about the file
                     string s = dlgOpen.FileName;
                     Console.WriteLine("Filename " + s);
                     Console.WriteLine(" Created at " + File.GetCreationTime(s));
                     Console.WriteLine(" Accessed at " +
                      File.GetLastAccessTime(s));
                 }

            }

        }
```

The output from this program might be as follows:

```
Filename C:\bootlog.txt
 Created at 10/30/2001 5:01:53 PM
 Accessed at 11/13/2001 5:33:20 AM
```

Of course, because the methods of the File class are static, you don't need to declare an instance of the class to use it. In this particular example, we used the File class to retrieve the creation and last access dates of the selected file, but the methods of this class implement a good deal more functionality than that. Table 15.3 shows the public File methods.

TABLE 15.3: File METHODS

METHOD	STATIC?	DESCRIPTION
AppendText()	Yes	Appends text to an existing file
Copy()	Yes	Copies a file
Create()	Yes	Creates a file
CreateText()	Yes	Creates a file and opens it to receive text
Delete()	Yes	Deletes a file
Exists()	Yes	Determines whether the file exists
GetAttributes()	Yes	Gets the file attributes for the file
GetCreationTime()	Yes	Gets the creation time for the file
GetLastAccessTime()	Yes	Gets the last access time for the file
GetLastWriteTime()	Yes	Gets the last time the file was written to
Move()	Yes	Moves a file
Open()	Yes	Opens a file
OpenRead()	Yes	Opens a file for reading

Continued on next page

TABLE 15.3: File METHODS *(continued)*

METHOD	STATIC?	DESCRIPTION
OpenText()	Yes	Opens a file for reading text
OpenWrite()	Yes	Opens a file for writing
SetAttributes()	Yes	Sets the file attributes for the file
SetCreationTime()	Yes	Sets the creation time for the file
SetLastAccessTime()	Yes	Sets the last access time for the file
SetLastWriteTime()	Yes	Sets the last written time for the file

NOTE   *You'll see the* Open *methods later in the chapter (starting with Listing 15.10) after you've looked at the* Stream *object.*

Listing 15.4 shows how you can use the File class to retrieve the attributes of any file.

LISTING 15.4: RETRIEVING FILE ATTRIBUTES

```
/*
  Example15_4.cs illustrates the FileAttributes enumeration
*/

using System;
using System.Windows.Forms;
using System.IO;

class Example15_4
{

    // the DecipherAttributes method turns file attributes
    // into something easier for people to read
    public static void DecipherAttributes(FileAttributes f)
    {
        if ((f & FileAttributes.Archive) == FileAttributes.Archive)
            Console.WriteLine("Archive");
        if ((f & FileAttributes.Compressed) == FileAttributes.Compressed)
            Console.WriteLine("Compressed");
        if ((f & FileAttributes.Device) == FileAttributes.Device)
            Console.WriteLine("Device");
        if ((f & FileAttributes.Directory)   == FileAttributes.Directory)
            Console.WriteLine("Directory");
        if ((f & FileAttributes.Encrypted)  == FileAttributes.Encrypted)
            Console.WriteLine("Encrypted");
        if ((f & FileAttributes.Hidden)  == FileAttributes.Hidden)
            Console.WriteLine("Hidden");
```

```
        if ((f & FileAttributes.NotContentIndexed) ==
         FileAttributes.NotContentIndexed)
            Console.WriteLine("NotContentIndexed");
        if ((f & FileAttributes.Offline) == FileAttributes.Offline)
            Console.WriteLine("Offline");
        if ((f & FileAttributes.ReadOnly) == FileAttributes.ReadOnly)
            Console.WriteLine("ReadOnly");
        if ((f & FileAttributes.ReparsePoint) ==
         FileAttributes.ReparsePoint)
            Console.WriteLine("ReparsePoint");
        if ((f & FileAttributes.SparseFile) == FileAttributes.SparseFile)
            Console.WriteLine("SparseFile");
        if ((f & FileAttributes.System) == FileAttributes.System)
            Console.WriteLine("System");
        if ((f & FileAttributes.Temporary) == FileAttributes.Temporary)
            Console.WriteLine("Temporary");
    }

    public static void Main()
    {

        // create and show an open file dialog
        OpenFileDialog dlgOpen = new OpenFileDialog();
        if (dlgOpen.ShowDialog() == DialogResult.OK)
        {
            // retrieve and show the file attributes
            FileAttributes f = File.GetAttributes(dlgOpen.FileName);
            Console.WriteLine("Filename " + dlgOpen.FileName +
                " has attributes:");
            DecipherAttributes(f);
        }

    }

}
```

As you can see, the FileAttributes value is a set of bit flags. You can extract the individual flags with Boolean logic when you want to know which bits are set. The output from this program might be as follows:

```
Filename C:\boot.ini has attributes:
Hidden
System
```

TIP   *Some of the bits in the* FileAttributes *enumeration don't apply to files. As you'll see shortly, you use this same enumeration for the attributes of directories.*

An important point is that some of the File methods (such as Create and Exists) can use a filename that refers to a file that doesn't yet exist. You can do the same with the FileInfo class, which you'll see next. The FileInfo class represents a single disk file. Unlike the File class, the FileInfo class needs to be instantiated to refer to a particular file. Listing 15.5 shows the FileInfo class in use.

LISTING 15.5: USING THE FileInfo CLASS

```
/*
  Example15_5.cs illustrates the FileInfo class
*/

using System;
using System.Windows.Forms;
using System.IO;

class Example15_5
{

    public static void Main()
    {

        // create and show an open file dialog
        OpenFileDialog dlgOpen = new OpenFileDialog();
        if (dlgOpen.ShowDialog() == DialogResult.OK)
        {
            // use the File class to return info about the file
            FileInfo fi = new FileInfo(dlgOpen.FileName);
            Console.WriteLine("Filename " + fi.FullName );
            Console.WriteLine(" Created at " + fi.CreationTime );
            Console.WriteLine(" Accessed at " + fi.LastAccessTime );
        }

    }

}
```

Table 15.4 shows the public FileInfo properties. This table includes properties of the FileInfo class itself and properties inherited from the FileSystemInfo class.

TABLE 15.4: FileInfo PROPERTIES

PROPERTY	TYPE	DESCRIPTION
Attributes	FileAttributes	Gets or sets the file attributes
CreationTime	DateTime	Gets or sets the creation time of the file
Directory	DirectoryInfo	Gets the directory that contains this file
DirectoryName	string	Gets the name of the directory that contains this file
Exists	bool	Gets a value indicating whether the file exists
Extenson	string	Gets the extension of the file
FullName	string	Gets the full path and filename of the file
LastAccessTime	DateTime	Gets or sets the last access time for the file
LastWriteTime	DateTime	Gets or sets the last write time for the file
Length	long	Gets the size of the file
Name	string	Gets the name of the file

Table 15.5 shows the public FileInfo methods.

TABLE 15.5: FileInfo METHODS

METHOD	STATIC?	DESCRIPTION
AppendText()	No	Appends text to the file
CopyTo()	No	Copies the file
Create()	No	Creates a file
CreateText()	No	Creates a text file
Delete()	No	Deletes the file
MoveTo()	No	Moves the file
Open()	No	Opens the file
OpenText()	No	Opens the file to read text
OpenWrite()	No	Opens the file for writing

When choosing between the File and FileInfo classes, there are several points to keep in mind. First, the File object is faster if you're only performing a single operation because it has less overhead. But for multiple operations on the same file, the FileInfo object will be faster because it only has to check the user's permissions when it's created rather than at every operation. Also, the File-Info class implements a few features that aren't present in the File class, such as the ability to extract the extension for the file. And, as you'll see in the "Walking the Hierarchy" section, the FileInfo class is ideally suited (together with the companion DirectoryInfo class) for operations that require you to navigate the disk hierarchy.

Retrieving Directory Information

Just as there are two classes to represent disk files, there are two classes that you can use to represent directories: the Directory class and the DirectoryInfo class. Like the File class, the Directory class is entirely composed of static methods. Listing 15.6 shows the Directory class in use.

LISTING 15.6: LISTING THE FILES IN A DIRECTORY

```
/*
  Example15_6.cs illustrates the Directory class
*/

using System;
using System.IO;

class Example15_6
{

    public static void Main()
    {

        // get the files from the root directory
        string[] aFiles = Directory.GetFiles("c:\\");

        // and display them
        foreach (string s in aFiles)
            Console.WriteLine(s);
    }

}
```

The output from this program might start as follows:

```
c:\.mysqlnavigator.history
c:\.mysqlnavigator.rc
c:\AFSetup.log
c:\arcldr.exe
c:\arcsetup.exe
c:\AUTOEXEC.BAT
c:\BIOSID.TXT
c:\boot.ini
c:\bootlog.txt
```

Table 15.6 shows the public Directory methods.

TABLE 15.6: Directory METHODS

METHOD	STATIC?	DESCRIPTION
CreateDirectory()	Yes	Creates a new directory
Delete()	Yes	Deletes a directory and its contents
Exists()	Yes	Determines whether a specified directory exists
GetCreationTime()	Yes	Gets the creation time of a directory
GetCurrentDirectory()	Yes	Gets the current working directory
GetDirectories()	Yes	Gets the names of all subdirectories of a directory
GetDirectoryRoot()	Yes	Gets the root directory for a directory
GetFiles()	Yes	Gets the names of all files in a directory
GetFileSystemEntries()	Yes	Gets the names of all files and subdirectories in a directory
GetLastAccessTime()	Yes	Gets the last time a directory was accessed
GetLastWriteTime()	Yes	Gets the last time a directory was written to
GetLogicalDrives()	Yes	Returns the names of all logical drives on the computer
GetParent()	Yes	Gets the parent directory of a directory
Move()	Yes	Move a directory
SetCreationTime	Yes	Sets the creation time of a directory
SetCurrentDirectory()	Yes	Sets the current working directory
SetLastAccessTime()	Yes	Sets the last access time of a directory
SetLastWriteTime()	Yes	Sets the last write time of a directory

For the most part, the difference between the Directory and DirectoryInfo classes resembles the difference between the File and FileInfo classes. Listing 15.7 shows the DirectoryInfo class being used to retrieve the attributes of a directory.

LISTING 15.7: USING THE DirectoryInfo CLASS

```
/*
   Example15_7.cs illustrates the Directory class
*/
```

```csharp
using System;
using System.IO;

class Example15_7
{

    // the DecipherAttributes method turns file attributes
    // into something easier for people to read
    public static void DecipherAttributes(FileAttributes f)
    {
        if ((f & FileAttributes.Archive) == FileAttributes.Archive)
            Console.WriteLine("Archive");
        if ((f & FileAttributes.Compressed) == FileAttributes.Compressed)
            Console.WriteLine("Compressed");
        if ((f & FileAttributes.Device) == FileAttributes.Device)
            Console.WriteLine("Device");
        if ((f & FileAttributes.Directory)  == FileAttributes.Directory)
            Console.WriteLine("Directory");
        if ((f & FileAttributes.Encrypted)  == FileAttributes.Encrypted)
            Console.WriteLine("Encrypted");
        if ((f & FileAttributes.Hidden)  == FileAttributes.Hidden)
            Console.WriteLine("Hidden");
        if ((f & FileAttributes.NotContentIndexed)  ==
         FileAttributes.NotContentIndexed)
            Console.WriteLine("NotContentIndexed");
        if ((f & FileAttributes.Offline)  == FileAttributes.Offline)
            Console.WriteLine("Offline");
        if ((f & FileAttributes.ReadOnly)  ==
         FileAttributes.ReadOnly)
            Console.WriteLine("ReadOnly");
        if ((f & FileAttributes.ReparsePoint)  == FileAttributes.ReparsePoint)
            Console.WriteLine("ReparsePoint");
        if ((f & FileAttributes.SparseFile)  == FileAttributes.SparseFile)
            Console.WriteLine("SparseFile");
        if ((f & FileAttributes.System)  == FileAttributes.System)
            Console.WriteLine("System");
        if ((f & FileAttributes.Temporary)  == FileAttributes.Temporary)
            Console.WriteLine("Temporary");
    }

    public static void Main()
    {

        // create a DirectoryInfo object
        DirectoryInfo di = new DirectoryInfo("c:\\");
```

```
        // retrieve and show the directory attributes
        FileAttributes f = di.Attributes;
        Console.WriteLine("Directory c:\\ has attributes:");
        DecipherAttributes(f);

    }

}
```

The output from this program might be as follows:

```
Directory c:\ has attributes:
Archive
Directory
Hidden
System
```

Table 15.7 shows the public DirectoryInfo properties. This table includes properties of the DirectoryInfo class itself and properties inherited from the FileSystemInfo class.

TABLE 15.7: DirectoryInfo PROPERTIES

PROPERTY	TYPE	DESCRIPTION
Attributes	FileAttributes	Gets or sets the file attributes
CreationTime	DateTime	Gets or sets the creation time of the directory
Exists	bool	Gets a value indicating whether the directory exists
Extenson	string	Gets the extension of the directory
FullName	string	Gets the full path and name of the directory
LastAccessTime	DateTime	Gets or sets the last access time for the directory
LastWriteTime	DateTime	Gets or sets the last write time for the directory
Length	long	Gets the size of the directory
Name	string	Gets the name of the directory
Parent	string	Gets the name of the parent directory of this directory
Root	string	Gets the name of the root directory of this directory

Table 15.8 shows the public DirectoryInfo methods.

TABLE 15.8: DirectoryInfo METHODS

METHOD	STATIC?	DESCRIPTION
Create()	No	Creates a directory
CreateSubdirectory()	No	Creates a subdirectory
Delete()	No	Deletes the directory
GetDirectories()	No	Returns the subdirectories of this directory
GetFiles()	No	Returns the files in this directory
MoveTo()	No	Moves the directory

Walking the Hierarchy

The GetDirectories and GetFiles methods of the DirectoryInfo class provide you with an easy way to navigate the structure of a hard drive. Listing 15.8 shows the use of the DirectoryInfo class to recursively list all of the directories on the C drive.

LISTING 15.8: RECURSIVELY LISTING DIRECTORIES

```csharp
/*
   Example15_8.cs illustrates recursive Directory use
*/

using System;
using System.IO;

class Example15_8
{

    // ShowDirectory prints the directory name
    // and retrieves its children
    public static void ShowDirectory(DirectoryInfo di, int intLevel)
    {
        try
        {
            // print out the directory name, after 2*intLevel spaces
            string strPad = new String(' ', 2*intLevel);
            Console.WriteLine(strPad + di.Name);

            // get its children and recursively call this routine
            // with one more level of indenting
            foreach (DirectoryInfo diChild in di.GetDirectories())
                ShowDirectory(diChild, intLevel+1);
        }
```

```
        catch {} // just keep going in case of any error
        finally{}
    }

    public static void Main()
    {

        // create a DirectoryInfo object
        DirectoryInfo di = new DirectoryInfo("c:\\");

        // And pass it to the recursive printing routine
        ShowDirectory(di, 0);

    }

}
```

TIP *Note the use of the* try/catch/finally *block to continue in case of any error. If you omit this code, you may discover that you don't have sufficient permissions to list all of the directories on your computer.*

Here's a small part of the output from running this program:

```
Program Files
  3M
    PSN2Lite
      Help
  AA
  abcDB
    Samples
      Local
      Remote
  Access2MySQL
    Help
  Accessories
    Imagevue
  Active Network Monitor
    Plugins
    Projects
```

WARNING *This program can produce a lot of output if you've got a large hard drive with many applications installed! On our test computer, the output was more than 300KB in size.*

Watching for Changes

Before we get to actually reading and writing data, we're going to look at one more file-related class: the `FileSystemWatcher` class. This class enables you to set up a callback from the operating system to notify your application when a file or directory is changed. Listing 15.9 shows a simple application of this class.

```
/*
  Example15_9.cs illustrates the FileSystemWatcher class
*/

using System;
using System.IO;

class Example15_9
{

    // event handler for file change
    public static void OnChanged(object source, FileSystemEventArgs e)
    {
        // dump info to the screen
        Console.WriteLine("Change to " + e.FullPath + ": " +
          e.ChangeType);
    }

    public static void Main()
    {

        // create a watcher for the c: drive
        FileSystemWatcher fsw = new FileSystemWatcher("c:\\");
        fsw.IncludeSubdirectories = true;

        // hook up the event handler
        fsw.Changed += new FileSystemEventHandler(OnChanged);

        // turn on file watching
        fsw.EnableRaisingEvents = true;

        // And wait for the user to quit
        Console.WriteLine("Press any key to exit");
        int i = Console.Read();

    }

}
```

WARNING   *The* FileSystemWatcher *only functions on Windows NT 4 or Windows 2000 (or later) operating systems. You won't be able to test this code on Windows 98 or Windows Me, even if you install the .NET redistributable.*

This program creates a FileSystemWatcher object and then tells it to watch the C drive, including the root and all subdirectories. It then adds an event handler that the FileSystemWatcher will call when it gets a notification from the operating system. Whenever a file is changed, the code in the event handler will execute. Here's what the output from this program might look like:

```
Change to c:\documents and settings\mike\local settings\
➥ history\history.ie5\mshist012002040620020407\index.dat: Changed
Change to c:\documents and settings\mike\recent\temp (10).lnk: Changed
Change to c:\documents and settings\mike\ntuser.dat.log: Changed
Change to c:\documents and settings\mike\ntuser.dat.log: Changed
Change to c:\documents and settings\mike\recent: Changed
Change to c:\temp\sfquery.txt: Changed
Change to c:\temp\sfquery.txt: Changed
```

Table 15.9 shows the public `FileSystemWatcher` properties.

TABLE 15.9: `FileSystemWatcher` PROPERTIES

PROPERTY	TYPE	DESCRIPTION
EnableRaisingEvents	bool	Controls whether the object will raise events in response to operating system notifications.
Filter	string	Controls which files to watch. The default is *.*.
IncludeSubdirectories	bool	Gets or sets a value indicating whether to monitor subdirectories for events.
InternalBufferSize	int	Gets or sets the size of the buffer that the operating system uses to set events. The default is 8KB.
NotifyFilter	NotifyFilters	Gets or sets a list of events to monitor.
Path	string	Gets or sets the path to monitor.
SynchronizingObject	ISynchronizeInvoke	Controls the thread that monitors changes.

Table 15.10 shows the public `FileSystemWatcher` events.

TABLE 15.10: `FileSystemWatcher` EVENTS

EVENT	DESCRIPTION
Changed	Raised when a file or directory is changed
Created	Raised when a file or directory is created
Deleted	Raised when a file or directory is deleted
Error	Raised if the internal buffer overflows
Renamed	Raised when a file or directory is renamed

Windows is a fairly "busy" operating system. Even if you're not doing anything with files, it's likely that the operating system will be writing log files, cleaning up temporary files, or otherwise modifying the file system. If you monitor for all possible file events (which is what the code in Listing 15.9 does), you may be overwhelmed with events. To avoid this, you should use one of these techniques to limit the notifications that you get:

◆ Use the `Path` property (or the `FileSystemWatcher` constructor) to specify the particular directory you want to monitor.

◆ Set the `IncludeSubdirectories` property to `false`.

◆ Use the `Filter` property to limit the files that you watch.

◆ Use the `NotifyFilter` property to limit the activities that you monitor.

The `NotifyFilter` property is a collection of flags from the `NotifyFilters` enumeration. Table 15.11 lists the values of this enumeration.

TABLE 15.11: `NotifyFilters` VALUES

VALUE	MEANING
`Attributes`	Monitor for changes in file attributes
`CreationTime`	Monitor for changes to file or folder creation time
`DirectoryName`	Monitor for changes to directory names
`FileName`	Monitor for changes to filenames
`LastAccess`	Monitor for changes to the last accessed time
`LastWrite`	Monitor for changes to the last written time
`Security`	Monitor for changes to security settings
`Size`	Monitor for changes to size

The default value for the `NotifyFilter` property is to monitor last written, filename, and directory name changes.

Exploring Streams and Backing Stores

In many programming languages, I/O has a monolithic feel: You open a file, do stuff with it, and then close the file. If that's what you're used to, you'll need to start thinking differently to make effective use of .NET I/O because .NET separates the thing you act on from the actions you perform.

Specifically, .NET I/O revolves around the twin notions of *streams* and *backing stores*. A stream represents a flow of raw data. A backing store represents some place you can put data. A backing store might be a file—but it might also be a network connection, an Internet address, or even a section of memory. In this section, we'll investigate the stream classes from the class library:

◆ `Stream`

◆ `FileStream`

◆ `NetworkStream`

- ◆ MemoryStream
- ◆ BufferedStream
- ◆ CryptoStream

Stream

The Stream class is the abstract class from which all other stream classes derive. Although you're unlikely to use the Stream class itself, understanding its interface is crucial to working with the more specific I/O classes. Table 15.12 shows the public Stream properties.

TABLE 15.12: Stream PROPERTIES

PROPERTY	TYPE	DESCRIPTION
CanRead	bool	Gets a value indicating whether you can read from the Stream object
CanSeek	bool	Gets a value indicating whether you can seek to a specific position within the Stream object
CanWrite	bool	Gets a value indicating whether you can write to the Stream object
Length	long	Gets the length of the Stream object in bytes
Position	long	Gets the current position within the Stream object

Table 15.13 shows the public Stream methods.

TABLE 15.13: Stream METHODS

METHOD	STATIC?	DESCRIPTION
BeginRead()	No	Starts an asynchronous read operation
BeginWrite()	No	Starts an asynchronous write operation
Close()	No	Closes the Stream and releases any associated resources
EndRead()	No	Waits for an asynchronous read to complete
EndWrite()	No	Ends an asynchronous write operation
Flush()	No	Writes any buffered data to the backing store
Read()	No	Reads a sequence of bytes
ReadByte()	No	Reads a single byte
Seek()	No	Sets the position within the Stream
SetLength()	No	Sets the length of the Stream
Write()	No	Writes a sequence of bytes
WriteByte()	No	Writes a single byte

The `Stream` class also implements a `Stream.Null` field, which returns a stream with no backing store. `Stream.Null` gives you a place to read or write data that doesn't consume any system resources. When you read from `Stream.Null`, you don't get any data back; when you write to `Stream.Null`, the data simply vanishes.

You won't be using the `Stream` class directly in your applications. Instead, you'll use one or more of the subclasses that derive from `Stream`: `FileStream`, `NetworkStream`, `MemoryStream`, `BufferedStream`, and `CryptoStream`. We'll cover these classes next.

FileStream

The `FileStream` class implements the `Stream` class for reading and writing from disk files (and other objects for which the operating system provides file handles, such as the standard input and standard output). Listing 15.10 shows how you can use the `FileStream` class to read and write files.

LISTING 15.10: READING AND WRITING FILES

```
/*
   Example15_10.cs illustrates use of FileStreams
*/

using System;
using System.Windows.Forms;
using System.IO;

class Example15_10
{

    public static void Main()
    {

        // use an open file dialog to get a filename
        OpenFileDialog dlgOpen = new OpenFileDialog();
        dlgOpen.Title="Select file to back up";

        if (dlgOpen.ShowDialog() == DialogResult.OK)
        {
            FileStream inStream = File.OpenRead(dlgOpen.FileName);
            FileStream outStream =
             File.OpenWrite(dlgOpen.FileName + ".bak");
            int b;

            // copy all data from in to out
            while ((b = inStream.ReadByte()) > -1)
                outStream.WriteByte( (byte) b);

            // clean up
            outStream.Flush();
```

```
            outStream.Close();
            inStream.Close();

        }

    }

}
```

WARNING *Be careful when testing this program. If the output file already exists, it will be overwritten without warning.*

Note the disparity between the `ReadByte` method, which returns an `int`, and the `WriteByte` method, which writes a `byte`. That's because the `ReadByte` method uses the special value –1 (which can't be stored in a `byte`) to indicate that it's reached the end of the data.

NOTE *This sample reads and writes the data synchronously. We'll look at asynchronous streams in the "Using Asynchronous I/O" section, after we've introduced the remainder of the stream classes.*

Table 15.14 shows the public `FileStream` properties.

TABLE 15.14: `FileStream` PROPERTIES

PROPERTY	TYPE	DESCRIPTION
CanRead	bool	Gets a value indicating whether you can read from the `FileStream` object
CanSeek	bool	Gets a value indicating whether you can seek to a specific position within the `FileStream` object
CanWrite	bool	Gets a value indicating whether you can write to the `FileStream` object
Handle	IntPtr	The operating system file handle for the open file
IsAsync	bool	Gets a value indicating whether the file was opened asynchronously
Length	long	Gets the length of the `FileStream` object in bytes
Name	string	Gets the name of the `FileStream` object
Position	long	Gets the current position within the `FileStream` object

Table 15.15 shows the public `FileStream` methods.

TABLE 15.15: FileStream METHODS

METHOD	STATIC?	DESCRIPTION
BeginRead()	No	Starts an asynchronous read operation
BeginWrite()	No	Starts an asynchronous write operation
Close()	No	Closes the FileStream object and releases any associated resources
EndRead()	No	Waits for an asynchronous read to complete
EndWrite()	No	Ends an asynchronous write operation
Flush()	No	Writes any buffered data to the backing store
Lock()	No	Prevents other processes from accessing the file
Read()	No	Reads a sequence of bytes
ReadByte()	No	Reads a single byte
Seek()	No	Sets the position within the FileStream object
SetLength()	No	Sets the length of the FileStream object
Unlock()	No	Unlocks a previously locked file
Write()	No	Writes a sequence of bytes
WriteByte()	No	Writes a single byte

Reading and writing files one byte at a time is inefficient. Listing 15.11 shows a second version of the program from Listing 15.10. The second version reads and writes the file via a buffer and the Read and Write methods.

LISTING 15.11: READING AND WRITING FILES WITH A BUFFER

```
/*
  Example15_11.cs illustrates use of FileStreams
*/

using System;
using System.Windows.Forms;
using System.IO;

class Example15_11
{

    public static void Main()
    {
```

```
// use an open file dialog to get a filename
OpenFileDialog dlgOpen = new OpenFileDialog();
dlgOpen.Title="Select file to back up";

if (dlgOpen.ShowDialog() == DialogResult.OK)
{
    FileStream inStream = File.OpenRead(dlgOpen.FileName);
    FileStream outStream =
        File.OpenWrite(dlgOpen.FileName + ".bak");
    byte[] buf = new byte[4096];
    int bytesRead;

    // copy all data from in to out
    while ((bytesRead = inStream.Read(buf, 0, 4096)) > 0)
        outStream.Write(buf, 0, bytesRead);

    // clean up
    outStream.Flush();
    outStream.Close();
    inStream.Close();

}

}

}
```

The Read method takes three parameters. The first is the buffer to place the bytes read into, the second is an offset in the buffer where the new data should be placed, and the third is the maximum number of bytes to read. The return value from the Read method is the number of bytes actually read. The Write method takes a buffer, an offset in the buffer where it should start getting bytes to write, and the number of bytes to write.

NetworkStream

The NetworkStream class provides a second implementation of the abstract Stream class. Network-Stream sends and receives bytes over a network to a process on the other end of a network connection, without caring whether that process is a file or another backing store.

NOTE   *The* NetworkStream *class is a member of the* System.Net.Sockets *namespace.*

Using a NetworkStream class requires some additional plumbing. Network connections are based on the concept of a *socket*. A socket in turn is identified by two pieces of information. First, there's a host address, which can be either a numeric TCP/IP address or a host name that can be converted into a numeric address by the host operating system. Second, there's a port number. Port numbers range from 0 to 65,536 and are divided into three groups:

◆ Ports from 0 to 1,023 are assigned to "well-known" services. For example, port 80 is normally used for HTTP traffic.

◆ Ports from 1,024 to 49,151 are *registered ports*, which are set aside for less well-known services.

◆ Ports from 49,152 to 65,536 are reserved for private applications or dynamic use.

TIP   *To avoid possible conflicts with other network services, you should use ports from the private application range in your own .NET programs.*

For two programs to communicate through a network connection, each one needs to create a socket that the other can address. The System.Net.Sockets namespace provides a Socket class that can be used for this purpose. In our code, we've used two other classes that derive from Socket but that provide more focused functionality. The TcpListener class opens a socket and waits for a client to connect to it. The TcpClient class opens a socket and connects it to another program.

With these additional classes, we're ready to demonstrate the NetworkStream class. Listing 15.12 shows a program to implement a server using the NetworkStream class. This server waits for a client to connect, and when a client does connect, it uses a NetworkStream to send a hard-coded buffer.

LISTING 15.12: IMPLEMENTING A SERVER WITH NetworkStream

```
/*
  Example15_12a.cs implements a NetworkStream server
*/

using System;
using System.IO;
using System.Net.Sockets ;

class Example15_12a
{

    // Listen waits for connections
    private void Listen()
    {
        // listen on port 50001
        TcpListener tcpl = new TcpListener(50001);
        tcpl.Start();

        // wait for clients
        for (;;)
        {

            // Block here waiting for client connections
            Socket newSocket = tcpl.AcceptSocket();
```

```
                        if (newSocket.Connected)
                        {

                            // create a NetworkStream on the socket
                            NetworkStream ns = new NetworkStream(newSocket);

                            // send some data
                            byte[] buf = {(byte)'H', (byte)'e', (byte)'l', (byte)'l',
                             (byte)'o', (byte)' ', (byte)'N', (byte)'e', (byte)'t'};
                            ns.Write(buf, 0, 9);

                            // cleanup
                            ns.Flush();
                            ns.Close();

                        }

                        // clean up and quit
                        newSocket.Close();
                        break;

                    }

                }

                public static void Main()
                {

                    // launch a listening thread
                    Example15_12a listener = new Example15_12a();
                    listener.Listen();

                }

            }
```

This code uses two methods of the `TcpListener` class. First, the `Start` method tells the class to start listening for new connections across the network, according to the port number that was supplied to the constructor. Second, the `AcceptSocket` method waits for a client to actually connect, and when it does, returns a `Socket` object that can be used to send data to that client.

If you look at the code that uses the `NetworkStream` object, you'll see that it's similar to the examples you already saw that used the `FileStream` object. The major difference is that the `NetworkStream` constructor accepts a `Socket` rather than a filename.

Listing 15.13 shows the corresponding client code.

```
/*
  Example15_12b.cs implements a NetworkStream client
*/

using System;
using System.IO;
using System.Net.Sockets ;

class Example15_12b
{

    public static void Main()
    {

        // create a client socket
        TcpClient newSocket = new TcpClient("localhost", 50001);

        // create a NetworkStream to read from the host
        NetworkStream ns = newSocket.GetStream();

        // fill a byte array from the stream
        byte[] buf = new byte[100];
        ns.Read(buf, 0, 100);

        // convert to a char array and print
        char[] buf2 = new char[100];
        for(int i=0;i<100;i++)
            buf2[i]=(char)buf[i];
        Console.WriteLine(buf2);

        // clean up
        ns.Close();
        newSocket.Close();

    }

}
```

The TcpClient class is even simpler to use than the TcpListener class. You supply it with an address and a port number in the constructor, and it tries to connect to a network socket at that address and port (in our code, we use the special localhost name that automatically refers to the local computer). When the TcpClient is connected, the code uses its GetStream method to return a NetworkStream. Then, as you probably expect by now, you can use the Read method of the NetworkStream to retrieve data from the socket.

NOTE   You'll see that this code has to jump through some hoops to format the returned buffer for display on the console. We'll introduce you to classes to make the job of working with streamed text easier later in this section.

To test these examples, run `Example15_12a` on your computer. It will launch and then wait, listening for a client to connect. Open another command window and run `Example 15_12b`. The client will connect to the server, and you'll see this output in the client window:

```
Hello Net
```

After the message has been transmitted, both client and server will shut down.

WARNING   If you launch the client before the server, the client will abort with a `SocketException` *because it won't find anything on port 50,001 with which to connect.*

Table 15.16 shows the public `NetworkStream` properties.

TABLE 15.16: NetworkStream PROPERTIES

PROPERTY	TYPE	DESCRIPTION
CanRead	bool	Gets a value indicating whether you can read from the NetworkStream object.
CanSeek	bool	Gets a value indicating whether you can seek to a specific position within the NetworkStream object.
CanWrite	bool	Gets a value indicating whether you can write to the NetworkStream object.
DataAvailable	bool	Gets a value indicating whether there is data on the NetworkStream object waiting to be read.
Length	long	Gets the length of the NetworkStream object in bytes. Accessing this property always throws a NotSupportedException.
Position	long	The current position within the NetworkStream object. Accessing this property always throws a NotSupportedException.

Table 15.17 shows the public `NetworkStream` methods.

TABLE 15.17: NetworkStream METHODS

METHOD	STATIC?	DESCRIPTION
BeginRead()	No	Starts an asynchronous read operation.
BeginWrite()	No	Starts an asynchronous write operation.
Close()	No	Closes the NetworkStream object and releases any associated resources.
EndRead()	No	Waits for an asynchronous read to complete.

Continued on next page

TABLE 15.17: NetworkStream METHODS *(continued)*

METHOD	STATIC?	DESCRIPTION
EndWrite()	No	Ends an asynchronous write operation.
Flush()	No	Writes any buffered data to the backing store.
Read()	No	Reads a sequence of bytes.
ReadByte()	No	Reads a single byte.
Seek()	No	Sets the position within the NetworkStream object. Calling this method always throws a NotSupportedException.
SetLength()	No	Sets the length of the FileStream object. Calling this method always throws a NotSupportedException.
Write()	No	Writes a sequence of bytes.
WriteByte()	No	Writes a single byte.

MemoryStream

In the Example15_11 class, we used a byte array as a buffer to hold data as it was being moved from one FileStream to another. The MemoryStream class provides an abstraction of that sort of buffer. You can think of a MemoryStream as a stream whose backing store is an area of memory. Listing 15.14 shows how you might use a MemoryStream to transfer data from one area of a program to another.

LISTING 15.14: COPYING DATA WITH A MemoryStream

```
/*
   Example15_13.cs illustrates use of MemoryStreams
*/

using System;
using System.Windows.Forms;
using System.IO;

class Example15_13
{

    // SaveMemoryStream saves the MemoryStream as a file
    public static void SaveMemoryStream(
        MemoryStream ms, string FileName)
    {
        FileStream outStream = File.OpenWrite(FileName);
        ms.WriteTo(outStream);
```

```
        outStream.Flush();
        outStream.Close();
    }


    public static void Main()
    {

        // use an open file dialog to get a filename
        OpenFileDialog dlgOpen = new OpenFileDialog();
        dlgOpen.Title="Select file to back up";

        if (dlgOpen.ShowDialog() == DialogResult.OK)
        {
            // Read the file into a MemoryStream
            FileStream inStream = File.OpenRead(dlgOpen.FileName);
            MemoryStream storeStream = new MemoryStream();

            // copy all data from in to store
            storeStream.SetLength(inStream.Length);
            inStream.Read(storeStream.GetBuffer(), 0,
             (int)inStream.Length);

            // clean up
            storeStream.Flush();
            inStream.Close();

            // pass the store to a method to write it out
            SaveMemoryStream(storeStream, dlgOpen.FileName + ".bak");
            storeStream.Close();

        }

    }

}
```

The default constructor for MemoryStream returns an expandable buffer whose initial capacity is zero. As you can see in Listing 15.14, you can extend this buffer by calling the SetLength method of the MemoryStream. You also have direct access to the buffer through the GetBuffer method. Table 15.18 shows the full range of constructor overloads for the MemoryStream.

TABLE 15.18: MemoryStream CONSTRUCTORS

CONSTRUCTOR	DETAILS
MemoryStream()	Creates a MemoryStream with an expandable buffer initialized to zero bytes.
MemoryStream(byte[])	Creates a MemoryStream that reads and writes the supplied byte array. The array cannot be resized or retrieved with GetBuffer.
MemoryStream(int)	Creates a MemoryStream with an expandable buffer initialized to the specified number of bytes.
MemoryStream(byte[], bool)	Creates a MemoryStream that reads and writes the supplied byte array. The Boolean value specifies the value of the CanWrite property. The array cannot be resized or retrieved with GetBuffer.
MemoryStream(byte[], int, int, bool)	Creates a MemoryStream that reads and writes the region of the supplied byte array between the first offset and the second. The Boolean value specifies the value of the CanWrite property. The array cannot be resized or retrieved with GetBuffer.
MemoryStream(byte[], int, int, bool, bool)	Creates a MemoryStream that reads and writes the region of the supplied byte array between the first offset and the second. The first Boolean value specifies the value of the CanWrite property. The array cannot be resized. The second Boolean value specifies whether the array can be retrieved with GetBuffer.

Table 15.19 shows the public MemoryStream properties.

TABLE 15.19: MemoryStream PROPERTIES

PROPERTY	TYPE	DESCRIPTION
CanRead	bool	Gets a value indicating whether you can read from the MemoryStream
CanSeek	bool	Gets a value indicating whether you can seek to a specific position within the MemoryStream
CanWrite	bool	Gets a value indicating whether you can write to the MemoryStream
Capacity	int	Gets or sets the number of bytes allocated for the MemoryStream
Length	long	Gets the length of the MemoryStream in bytes
Position	long	Gets the current position within the MemoryStream

Table 15.20 shows the public MemoryStream methods.

TABLE 15.20: MemoryStream METHODS

METHOD	STATIC?	DESCRIPTION
BeginRead()	No	Starts an asynchronous read operation
BeginWrite()	No	Starts an asynchronous write operation
Close()	No	Closes the MemoryStream and releases any associated resources
EndRead()	No	Waits for an asynchronous read to complete
EndWrite()	No	Ends an asynchronous write operation
Flush()	No	Writes any buffered data to the backing store
GetBuffer()	No	Returns the internal buffer used by the MemoryStream
Read()	No	Reads a sequence of bytes
ReadByte()	No	Reads a single byte
Seek()	No	Sets the position within the MemoryStream
SetLength()	No	Sets the length of the MemoryStream
Write()	No	Writes a sequence of bytes
WriteByte()	No	Writes a single byte
WriteTo()	No	Writes the contents of the MemoryStream directly to another stream

BufferedStream

Another way to abstract and improve stream operations is to use the BufferedStream class. Listing 15.15 shows a file-copying routine that makes use of this class.

LISTING 15.15: COPYING FILES VIA BufferedStream OBJECTS

```
/*
  Example15_14.cs illustrates use of BufferedStreams
*/

using System;
using System.Windows.Forms;
using System.IO;

class Example15_14
{

    public static void Main()
    {
```

```
        // use an open file dialog to get a filename
        OpenFileDialog dlgOpen = new OpenFileDialog();
        dlgOpen.Title="Select file to back up";

        if (dlgOpen.ShowDialog() == DialogResult.OK)
        {
            // create the raw streams
            FileStream inStream = File.OpenRead(dlgOpen.FileName);
            FileStream outStream =
                File.OpenWrite(dlgOpen.FileName + ".bak");

            // add a buffering layer
            BufferedStream bufInStream = new BufferedStream(inStream);
            BufferedStream bufOutStream = new BufferedStream(outStream);

            byte[] buf = new byte[4096];
            int bytesRead;

            // copy all data from in to out via the buffer layer
            while ((bytesRead = bufInStream.Read(buf, 0, 4096)) > 0)
                bufOutStream.Write(buf, 0, bytesRead);

            // clean up
            bufOutStream.Flush();
            bufOutStream.Close();
            bufInStream.Close();
            outStream.Close();
            inStream.Close();

        }

    }

}
```

The BufferedStream constructor takes an existing stream as a parameter and builds the new BufferedStream object on top of that existing stream. After that's done, you can use the methods of the BufferedStream class to read and write the ultimate data. But why would you add this layer on top of existing streams? Well, it can make your code more efficient. That's because there's seldom going to be a perfect match between the data that you want to read and write and the most efficient way for the operating system to supply that data.

For example, suppose you want to read five bytes from a file. It's possible that the operating system can grab 4KB, 8KB, or more of the file in a single operation. With a BufferedStream, the operating system will supply data in the most efficient chunks, and the BufferedStream class will take care of handing over only the chunks for which you asked. On the other side of the coin, the BufferedStream may store multiple writes in memory until enough writes accumulate to make writing the data to disk efficient.

WARNING   *Because of this internal buffering, it's critical to remember to call the* Flush *method when you want to be sure that the contents of a* BufferedStream *have actually been transferred to the underlying backing store.*

Table 15.21 shows the public BufferedStream properties.

TABLE 15.21: BufferedStream PROPERTIES

PROPERTY	TYPE	DESCRIPTION
CanRead	bool	Gets a value indicating whether you can read from the BufferedStream
CanSeek	bool	Gets a value indicating whether you can seek to a specific position within the BufferedStream
CanWrite	bool	Gets a value indicating whether you can write to the BufferedStream
Length	long	Gets the length of the BufferedStream in bytes
Position	long	Gets the current position within the BufferedStream

Table 15.22 shows the public BufferedStream methods.

TABLE 15.22: BufferedStream METHODS

METHOD	STATIC?	DESCRIPTION
BeginRead()	No	Starts an asynchronous read operation
BeginWrite()	No	Starts an asynchronous write operation
Close()	No	Closes the BufferedStream and releases any associated resources
EndRead()	No	Waits for an asynchronous read to complete
EndWrite()	No	Ends an asynchronous write operation
Flush()	No	Writes any buffered data to the backing store
Read()	No	Reads a sequence of bytes
ReadByte()	No	Reads a single byte
Seek()	No	Sets the position within the BufferedStream
SetLength()	No	Sets the length of the BufferedStream
Write()	No	Writes a sequence of bytes
WriteByte()	No	Writes a single byte

CryptoStream

There's one more class derived from Stream that you should know about: System.Security .Cryptography.CryptoStream. The CryptoStream class provides a streaming implementation of cryptography. Just as you can use a BufferedStream object to add a buffering layer to an existing stream implementation, so you can use a CryptoStream object to add an encryption layer.

NOTE *We'll discuss encryption in Chapter 19, "Security."*

Using Readers and Writers

So far, we've been working directly with the raw, typeless data delivered by the Stream class and its subclasses. That's convenient when you just want to move data from place to place, but it's less so if you actually need to work with the data. To provide a more structured view of data from streams, the System.IO namespace provides a number of *reader* and *writer* classes. In this section, we'll look at eight of these classes, which group conveniently into four pairs:

◆ BinaryReader and BinaryWriter

◆ TextReader and TextWriter

◆ StreamReader and StreamWriter

◆ StringReader and StringWriter

BinaryReader and BinaryWriter

The BinaryReader class can read data from a stream directly into typed variables. The corresponding BinaryWriter class can write data from typed variables to a stream. The process is lossless. That is, data written by the BinaryWriter can be retrieved exactly by the BinaryReader (assuming that you read the same data types that you wrote). Listing 15.16 shows these two classes in action.

LISTING 15.16: WORKING WITH BINARY DATA

```
/*
  Example15_15.cs illustrates reading and writing binary data
*/

using System;
using System.IO;

class Example15_15
{

    public static void Main()
    {

        // create a new file to work with
        FileStream outStream = File.Create("c:\\BinaryTest.dat");
```

```
// use a BinaryWriter to write formatted data to the file
BinaryWriter bw = new BinaryWriter(outStream);

// write various data to the file
bw.Write( (int) 32);
bw.Write( (decimal) 4.567);
string s = "Test String";
bw.Write(s);

// flush and close
bw.Flush();
bw.Close();

// now open the file for reading
FileStream inStream = File.OpenRead("c:\\BinaryTest.dat");

// use a BinaryReader to read formatted data and dump it to the screen
BinaryReader br = new BinaryReader(inStream);

int i = br.ReadInt32();
decimal d = br.ReadDecimal();
string s2 = br.ReadString();

Console.WriteLine(i);
Console.WriteLine(d);
Console.WriteLine(s2);

// clean up
br.Close();

    }

}
```

The output from this program is as follows:

```
32
4.567
Test String
```

One thing you need to remember is that the BinaryReader and BinaryWriter classes use a data representation format convenient for them, not for you. Figure 15.2 shows the BinaryTest.dat file generated by this program open in a hex editor.

FIGURE 15.2

File created by
`BinaryWriter` class

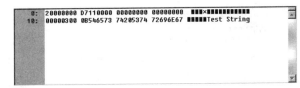

Without worrying about the details of the representation, you can see that the `BinaryWriter` class encoded the various data types as it wrote them to disk.

Table 15.23 shows the public `BinaryWriter` properties.

TABLE 15.23: `BinaryWriter` PROPERTIES

PROPERTY	TYPE	DESCRIPTION
BaseStream	Stream	Gets the underlying Stream that the BinaryWriter writes to

Table 15.24 shows the public `BinaryWriter` methods.

The `BinaryWriter` class doesn't have many methods, but its `Write` method is heavily overloaded to handle most of the common data types.

WARNING *The* `Close` *and* `Flush` *methods of the* `BinaryWriter` *also affect the underlying* `Stream`. *If you try to close the* `Stream` *after closing the* `BinaryWriter`, *you'll get an error.*

TABLE 15.24: `BinaryWriter` METHODS

METHOD	STATIC?	DESCRIPTION
Close()	No	Closes the BinaryWriter and the underlying Stream
Flush()	No	Flushes all data to the ultimate backing store of the underlying Stream
Seek()	No	Sets the position within the underlying Stream
Write()	No	Writes a value to the underlying Stream

Table 15.25 shows the public `BinaryReader` properties.

TABLE 15.25: `BinaryReader` PROPERTIES

PROPERTY	TYPE	DESCRIPTION
BaseStream	Stream	Gets the underlying Stream that the BinaryReader reads from

Table 15.26 shows the public `BinaryReader` methods.

TABLE 15.26: BinaryReader METHODS

METHOD	STATIC?	DESCRIPTION
Close()	No	Closes the BinaryReader and the underlying Stream
PeekChar()	No	Returns the next available character without advancing the Stream's position
Read()	No	Reads characters from the underlying Stream
ReadBoolean()	No	Reads a Boolean value from the underlying Stream
ReadByte()	No	Reads a byte from the underlying Stream
ReadBytes()	No	Reads a byte array from the underlying Stream
ReadChar()	No	Reads a character from the underlying Stream
ReadChars()	No	Reads a character array from the underlying Stream
ReadDecimal()	No	Reads a decimal value from the underlying Stream
ReadDouble()	No	Reads a double value from the underlying Stream
ReadInt16()	No	Reads a 2-byte signed integer from the underlying Stream
ReadInt32()	No	Reads a 4-byte signed integer from the underlying Stream
ReadInt64()	No	Reads an 8-byte signed integer from the underlying Stream
ReadSByte	No	Reads a signed byte from the underlying Stream
ReadSingle	No	Reads a single value from the underlying Stream
ReadString()	No	Reads a string from the underlying Stream
ReadUInt16()	No	Reads a 2-byte unsigned integer from the underlying Stream
ReadUInt32()	No	Reads a 4-byte unsigned integer from the underlying Stream
ReadUInt64()	No	Reads an 8-byte unsigned integer from the underlying Stream

TextReader and TextWriter

The BinaryReader and BinaryWriter classes are a good choice for dealing with arbitrary data such as a file of internal settings. But for human-readable data, you should look to the TextReader and TextWriter classes. These are abstract base classes with subclasses available for particular situations such as working with streams or working with strings. The TextReader and TextWriter classes aren't terribly useful by themselves because, although they understand text, they don't have any way to work with streams or backing stores.

StreamReader and StreamWriter

The StreamReader and StreamWriter classes provide implementations of TextReader and TextWriter that are designed to work with streams. As such, they can work with any of the types of streams you saw earlier in this chapter. Listing 15.17 shows how you might use these classes to work with data that uses a file as a backing store.

LISTING 15.17: USING StreamReader AND StreamWriter

```
/*
  Example15_16.cs illustrates reading and writing text data
*/

using System;
using System.IO;

class Example15_16
{

    public static void Main()
    {

        // create a new file to work with
        FileStream outStream = File.Create("c:\\TextTest.txt");

        // use a StreamWriter to write data to the file
        StreamWriter sw = new StreamWriter(outStream);

        // write some text to the file
        sw.WriteLine("This is a test of the StreamWriter class");

        // flush and close
        sw.Flush();
        sw.Close();

        // now open the file for reading
        StreamReader sr = new StreamReader("c:\\TextTest.txt");

        // read the first line of the file into a buffer and display it
        string FirstLine;

        FirstLine = sr.ReadLine();
        Console.WriteLine(FirstLine);

        // clean up
        sr.Close();

    }

}
```

This is the output of this program:

`This is a test of the StreamWriter class`

The StreamReader and StreamWriter classes have a variety of constructors. In this particular case, we've based the StreamWriter on a FileStream but opened the StreamReader directly from a filename. Other overloaded constructors let you specify the encodings and buffer sizes to use with these classes.

Table 15.27 shows the public StreamWriter properties.

TABLE 15.27: StreamWriter PROPERTIES

PROPERTY	TYPE	DESCRIPTION
AutoFlush	bool	Gets or sets a value that indicates whether the StreamWriter will flush its buffer after every call to Write or WriteLine
BaseStream	Stream	Gets the underlying Stream that the StreamWriter writes to
Encoding	Encoding	Gets the current text encoding
FormatProvider	IFormatProvider	Gets an object that controls culture-specific formatting
NewLine	string	Gets or sets the line terminator string used by this StreamWriter

TIP   For more information on cultures and formatting, see Chapter 21, "Other Classes in the Base Class Library."

Table 15.28 shows the public StreamWriter methods.

TABLE 15.28: StreamWriter METHODS

METHOD	STATIC?	DESCRIPTION
Close()	No	Closes the StreamWriter and the underlying Stream
Flush()	No	Flushes the StreamWriter and the underlying Stream
Write()	No	Writes to the underlying Stream
WriteLine()	No	Writes to the underlying Stream and appends the line terminator string

Table 15.29 shows the public StreamReader properties.

TABLE 15.29: StreamReader PROPERTIES

PROPERTY	TYPE	DESCRIPTION
BaseStream	Stream	Gets the underlying Stream that the StreamReader reads from
CurrentEncoding	Encoding	Gets the current text encoding

Table 15.30 shows the public `StreamReader` methods.

TABLE 15.30: StreamReader METHODS

METHOD	STATIC?	DESCRIPTION
Close()	No	Closes the StreamReader and the underlying Stream
DiscardBufferedData()	No	Discards any data in the StreamReader
Peek()	No	Returns the next available character without advancing the position of the underlying Stream
Read()	No	Reads characters from the underlying Stream
ReadBlock()	No	Reads a buffer from the underlying Stream
ReadLine()	No	Reads a line of characters from the underlying Stream
ReadToEnd()	No	Reads from the current position to the end of the Stream

StringReader and *StringWriter*

The `StringReader` and `StringWriter` classes also inherit from the `TextReader` and `TextWriter` classes. As you can probably guess, these classes use a string as the backing store. Listing 15.18 shows the use of the `StringReader` and `StringWriter` classes.

LISTING 15.18: USING StringReader AND StringWriter

```
/*
  Example15_17.cs illustrates reading and writing string data
*/

using System;
using System.IO;
using System.Text;

class Example15_17
{

    public static void Main()
    {

        // create a new string to work with
        StringBuilder sb = new StringBuilder();

        // use a StringWriter to write data to the string
        StringWriter sw = new StringWriter(sb);
```

```
// write some text to the string
sw.Write("This is a test of the StringWriter class");
sw.Close();

// now open the string for reading
StringReader sr = new StringReader(sb.ToString());

// read the entire string into a buffer and display it
string EntireString;

EntireString = sr.ReadToEnd();
Console.WriteLine(EntireString);

// clean up
sr.Close();

    }

}
```

This is the output from this program:

```
This is a test of the StringWriter class
```

Table 15.31 shows the public `StringWriter` properties.

TABLE 15.31: `StringWriter` PROPERTIES

PROPERTY	TYPE	DESCRIPTION
Encoding	Encoding	Gets the current text encoding
FormatProvider	IFormatProvider	Gets an object that controls culture-specific formatting
NewLine	string	Gets or sets the line terminator string used by this `StringWriter`

Table 15.32 shows the public `StringWriter` methods.

TABLE 15.32: `StringWriter` METHODS

METHOD	STATIC?	DESCRIPTION
Close()	No	Closes the `StringWriter`
Flush()	No	Flushes the `StringWriter`
GetStringBuilder()	No	Returns the underlying `StringBuilder`

Continued on next page

TABLE 15.32: StringWriter METHODS *(continued)*

METHOD	STATIC?	DESCRIPTION
ToString()	No	Returns a string containing the characters written to the StringWriter
Write()	No	Writes to the underlying Stream
WriteLine()	No	Writes to the underlying Stream and appends the line terminator string

The StringReader has no public properties. Table 15.33 shows the public StringReader methods.

TABLE 15.33: StringReader METHODS

METHOD	STATIC?	DESCRIPTION
Close()	No	Closes the StringReader
Peek()	No	Returns the next available character without advancing the position of the underlying string
Read()	No	Reads characters from the underlying string
ReadBlock()	No	Reads a buffer from the underlying string
ReadLine()	No	Reads a line of characters from the underlying string
ReadToEnd()	No	Reads from the current position to the end of the string

Using Asynchronous I/O

All of the examples you've seen so far in this chapter have used the default *synchronous* I/O methods. With synchronous I/O, execution of your program is blocked while I/O is being performed. For example, if you call the Read or Write methods of any of the objects you've seen, your program will wait right there for the input or output operation to conclude.

This may represent an unacceptable delay, particularly if your application deals with large files and there is other work that it can be doing. That's why the .NET Framework also supports *asynchronous* I/O operations. With asynchronous I/O, a separate thread is allocated to perform the input or output. When the operation is completed, your program gets notified via a callback to a delegate passed to the I/O call. Of course, you need to tell the .NET Framework what to do when you get the callback. At this point, the results of the operation will be available for you to work with.

Listing 15.19 demonstrates asynchronous file reading. You can apply the same principles to any of the objects you've seen in this chapter.

LISTING 15.19: READING A FILE ASYNCHRONOUSLY

```
/*
  Example15_18.cs illustrates asynchronous I/O
*/

using System;
using System.IO;
using System.Windows.Forms;

class Example15_18
{
    // stream to handle reading
    private static FileStream inStream;

    // delegated method to handle callback
    private static AsyncCallback acb;

    // allocate a big buffer for reading
    static byte[] buf = new byte[500000];

    // callback to use when read is complete
    static void OnComplete(IAsyncResult asyncResult)
    {
        int bytesRead = inStream.EndRead(asyncResult);
        Console.Write(bytesRead);
        Console.WriteLine(" bytes read!");
    }

    public static void Main()
    {
        // use an open file dialog to get a filename
        OpenFileDialog dlgOpen = new OpenFileDialog();
        dlgOpen.Title="Select file to read";

        if (dlgOpen.ShowDialog() == DialogResult.OK)
        {
            // open the file
            inStream = new FileStream(dlgOpen.FileName, FileMode.Open,
             FileAccess.Read, FileShare.None, 2048, true);

            // assign the callback delegate
            acb = new AsyncCallback(OnComplete);

            // read asynchronously
            inStream.BeginRead(buf, 0, 500000, acb, null);

            // do some work in the meantime
```

```
        for(int i=0; i<10; i++)
            Console.WriteLine(i);
        // And wait for the user to quit
        Console.WriteLine("Press Enter to exit");
        int resp = Console.Read();
    }

}

}
```

The output from this program might look like this:

```
0
1
2
3
4
5
6
7
8
9
Press Enter to exit
425337 bytes read!
```

When you run the program, it first prompts you for the name of a file to read. Then it creates a FileStream object to read the file. As you can see, it uses an overloaded version of the FileStream constructor that takes more parameters than the ones used earlier in the chapter. That's because this version of the constructor enables you to specify that the file should be opened asynchronously; the simpler versions open the file synchronously.

WARNING *If you open a file synchronously, even the asynchronous I/O methods will execute synchronously.*

The parameters to the constructor are as follows:

path   Full path and filename of the file to open

mode   A FileMode enumeration that specifies whether to open or create the file

access   A FileAccess enumeration that specifies how the file can be accessed

share   A FileShare enumeration that specifies whether the file will be opened shared or exclusively

buffersize   An integer that specifies the internal buffer size to use when reading

useAsync   A Boolean value that specifies whether to open the file asynchronously

NOTE *Operating systems are not required to respect the useAsync setting. If you're not sure whether your current platform supports asynchronous I/O, you can check the value of the IsAsync property after opening the FileStream.*

After the file is open, the program creates a new delegate to handle the callback when the read is complete. The delegate specifies that the Framework should call the `OnComplete` method when the operation is finished. This delegate is passed—along with the buffer to use, starting position, length of read, and an object (`null` in this case)—to the `BeginRead` method. `BeginRead` launches a separate thread to perform the read operation. When the operation is done, it calls the method specified by the callback. Within the callback method, you can use the `EndRead` method to determine the number of bytes that were read. The program concludes the asynchronous operation by writing the number of bytes read to the console.

Meanwhile, the code after the call to `BeginRead` continues executing. In this case, that code simply performs a loop, writing status information to the console to show that it's working.

If you look at the output from the program, you'll see that the code was able to continue executing while the background thread read the file. You can use this same method of asynchronous reading with any of the classes in this chapter. The `BeginWrite` and `EndWrite` methods function the same way to support asynchronous writing.

Introducing Serialization

To conclude this chapter, we'll take a short look at *serialization*. Serialization refers to the process of storing an object. As you might guess, the serialization support in the .NET Framework enables you to take an object and write it out to a backing store via a stream. Later, you can *deserialize* the object from the backing store via a stream to re-create the object.

Listing 15.20 shows the process of serializing a simple object.

LISTING 15.20: SERIALIZING AND DESERIALIZING

```
/*
   Example15_19.cs illustrates binary serialization
*/

using System;
using System.IO;
using System.Runtime.Serialization;
using System.Runtime.Serialization.Formatters.Binary;

// the Customer class gives us something to serialize
[Serializable]
class Customer
{
    // some private data members
    private int CustomerNumber;
    private string CustomerName;
    private string CustomerCountry;

    // the WriteCustomer method formats info to the screen
    public void WriteCustomer()
    {
        Console.WriteLine("Customer Number: " + this.CustomerNumber);
```

```
            Console.WriteLine("Customer Name: " + this.CustomerName);
            Console.WriteLine("Customer Country: " + this.CustomerCountry);
        }

        // the constructor accepts all the info to create a customer
        public Customer(
            int newCustomerNumber,
            string newCustomerName,
            string newCustomerCountry)
        {
            this.CustomerNumber = newCustomerNumber;
            this.CustomerName = newCustomerName;
            this.CustomerCountry = newCustomerCountry;
        }
    }

    class Example15_19
    {

        public static void Main()
        {

            // create a new customer and dump to screen
            Customer MyCustomer = new Customer(1, "X Corporation", "France");
            MyCustomer.WriteCustomer();

            // Create a FileStream to hold the serialized customer
            FileStream serializeStream = new FileStream("c:\\MyCustomer.dat",
             FileMode.Create);

            // use the CLR's binary formatting support
            BinaryFormatter bf = new BinaryFormatter();

            // serialize the object
            bf.Serialize(serializeStream, MyCustomer);
            serializeStream.Flush();
            serializeStream.Close();

            // retrieve the serialized version to a second object and dump that
            FileStream retrieveStream = new FileStream("c:\\MyCustomer.dat",
             FileMode.Open);
            Customer NewCustomer = (Customer) bf.Deserialize(retrieveStream);
            NewCustomer.WriteCustomer();
        }

    }
```

The output from this program is as follows:

```
Customer Number: 1
Customer Name: X Corporation
Customer Country: France
Customer Number: 1
Customer Name: X Corporation
Customer Country: France
```

By default, the Common Language Runtime (CLR) does not assume you will want to serialize your objects. The [Serializable] attribute for the Customer class in the previous example specifies that this object should be constructed in such a way that it can be serialized.

The actual code to serialize and then deserialize the object is straightforward. To serialize the object, follow these steps:

1. Create a stream that will convey the serialized object to whatever backing store you like.

2. Create a formatting object to manage the serialization.

3. Call the Serialize method of the formatting object to actually serialize the object.

To deserialize the object, follow these steps:

1. Open a stream that can access the serialized object.

2. Create a formatting object to manage the deserialization.

3. Call the Deserialize method of the formatting object, casting the result to the object that you're deserializing.

Figure 15.3 shows the MyCustomer.dat file from this example open in a hex editor. Once again, you can see that the CLR has stored the object in a format that it can interpret later.

FIGURE 15.3

Class serialized via a BinaryFormatter object

The BinaryFormatter is only one choice for serialization. This is a good choice for objects you'll only be using from within your own applications because it uses an efficient binary representation of the information. For objects you want to share with other applications, though, you may prefer a more easily deciphered format. You can get such a format by using the SoapFormatter class. This class serializes objects using Simple Object Access Protocol (SOAP). Listing 15.21 shows this example rewritten to use a SoapFormatter as the formatting object.

TIP   *To use the* SoapFormatter *class, you'll need to add a reference to the* System.Runtime.Serialization .Formatters.Soap *library.*

LISTING 15.21: SERIALIZING AS SOAP

```
/*
   Example15_19.cs illustrates SOAP serialization
*/

using System;
using System.IO;
using System.Runtime.Serialization;
using System.Runtime.Serialization.Formatters.Soap;

// the Customer class gives us something to serialize
[Serializable]
class Customer
{
    // some private data members
    private int CustomerNumber;
    private string CustomerName;
    private string CustomerCountry;

    // the WriteCustomer method formats info to the screen
    public void WriteCustomer()
    {
        Console.WriteLine("Customer Number: " + this.CustomerNumber);
        Console.WriteLine("Customer Name: " + this.CustomerName);
        Console.WriteLine("Customer Country: " + this.CustomerCountry);
    }

    // the constructor accepts all the info to create a customer
    public Customer(
        int newCustomerNumber,
        string newCustomerName,
        string newCustomerCountry)
    {
        this.CustomerNumber = newCustomerNumber;
        this.CustomerName = newCustomerName;
        this.CustomerCountry = newCustomerCountry;
    }
}

class Example15_20
{
```

```
public static void Main()
{

    // create a new customer and dump to screen
    Customer MyCustomer = new Customer(1, "X Corporation", "France");
    MyCustomer.WriteCustomer();

    // Create a FileStream to hold the serialized customer
    FileStream serializeStream = new FileStream("c:\\MyCustomer.xml",
        FileMode.Create);

    // use SOAP formatting
    SoapFormatter sf = new SoapFormatter();

    // serialize the object
    sf.Serialize(serializeStream, MyCustomer);
    serializeStream.Flush();
    serializeStream.Close();

    // retrieve the serialized version to a second object and dump that
    FileStream retrieveStream = new FileStream("c:\\MyCustomer.xml",
        FileMode.Open);
    Customer NewCustomer = (Customer) sf.Deserialize(retrieveStream);
    NewCustomer.WriteCustomer();
}

}
```

The output from this program is as follows:

```
Customer Number: 1
Customer Name: X Corporation
Customer Country: France
Customer Number: 1
Customer Name: X Corporation
Customer Country: France
```

If you open the `MyCustomer.xml` file, you'll discover it contains the object in SOAP format:

```
<SOAP-ENV:Envelope xmlns:xsi="http://www.w3.org/2001/
➥ XMLSchema-instance" xmlns:xsd="http://www.w3.org/2001/XMLSchema"
➥ xmlns:SOAP-ENC="http://schemas.xmlsoap.org/soap/encoding/"
➥ xmlns:SOAP-ENV="http://schemas.xmlsoap.org/soap/envelope/"
➥ xmlns:clr="http://schemas.microsoft.com/soap/encoding/clr/1.0"
➥ SOAP-ENV:encodingStyle="http://schemas.xmlsoap.org/soap/encoding/">
<SOAP-ENV:Body>
<a1:Customer id="ref-1"
➥ xmlns:a1="http://schemas.microsoft.com/clr/assem/Example15_20
```

➥ %2C%20Version%3D0.0.0.0%2C%20Culture%3Dneutral%2C%20
➥ PublicKeyToken%3Dnull">
<CustomerNumber>1</CustomerNumber>
<CustomerName id="ref-3">X Corporation</CustomerName>
<CustomerCountry id="ref-4">France</CustomerCountry>
</a1:Customer>
</SOAP-ENV:Body>
</SOAP-ENV:Envelope>

NOTE   *You'll learn more about SOAP in Chapter 26, "Web Services."*

Summary

In this chapter you learned about input/output. The `System.IO` namespace provides thorough support for input and output operations.

You can manipulate files and directories by using the `File` and `Directory` objects, which include an extensive list of static methods, or by using the `FileInfo` and `DirectoryInfo` objects, which can be instantiated to represent individual files and directories. Methods of the `DirectoryInfo` object let you easily navigate around a file hierarchy.

You can use the `FileSystemWatcher` class to monitor all or part of your file system for changes to files and directories.

The main I/O classes in .NET are based on the ideas of streams and backing stores. A stream represents a flow of raw data. A backing store represents some place that you can put data. A backing store might be a file—but it might also be a network connection, an Internet address, or even a section of memory.

Stream classes provide a view of data as a stream of bytes. The stream classes include `Stream`, `FileStream`, `NetworkStream`, `MemoryStream`, `BufferedStream`, and `CryptoStream`. You can combine these classes to achieve additional functionality, such as buffered, encrypted network communications.

For a more structured view of your data, the .NET Framework Class Library also provides a set of `Reader` and `Writer` classes. The `BinaryReader` and `BinaryWriter` can deal with the basic data types. The classes derived from `TextReader` and `TextWriter` are optimized to handle character data.

In addition to synchronous (blocking) I/O, the .NET Framework also allows asynchronous I/O. Asynchronous I/O is performed by a background thread and sends notifications to your code via a callback when it's completed.

The class library also includes support for serializing any object to a backing store via a stream and later deserializing the stored version back to an object. You can choose to format the serialized object in an efficient binary format or in industry-standard SOAP format. In the next chapter, you'll learn about assemblies.

Chapter 16

Assemblies

.NET GROUPS CODE INTO units called *assemblies*. Even though we haven't discussed assemblies explicitly in this book, each piece of sample code that you've compiled and run on your computer has been incorporated into a single .NET assembly. .NET uses assemblies for version tracking, security, deployment, and type identity—among other things.

In this chapter, we'll introduce you to assemblies. You'll learn how to create assemblies and how to include more than one file in the same assembly. We'll also discuss strong names and signing (which provide means for verifying the identity of an assembly) and versioning (which provides a way to specify which version of an assembly to use in any given circumstance).

You'll also learn about the distinction between private and shared assemblies and why you might want to use each type.

Featured in this chapter:

◆ Introducing and Building Assemblies

◆ Viewing Assembly Contents

◆ Using Strong Names and Signing

◆ Assembly Versioning

◆ Working with the Global Assembly Cache

◆ Finding an Assembly

Looking at the Big Picture

NET groups code into units called *assemblies*. Before drilling into the details of assemblies, let's look at the big picture. An assembly can consist of a single file or of components distributed across multiple files. In all cases, there is one file that contains the *assembly manifest*, a part of the metadata that lists the contents of the assembly. This can be a stand-alone file or part of another file in the assembly.

When you're writing .NET code, you can designate which files will go into an assembly and which other assemblies a particular assembly works with. The CLR uses assemblies as a fundamental unit of management in many respects:

- Permissions are requested and granted on an assembly as a whole.

- A type retains its identity within an assembly. That is, if you declare a type named `CustomType` within an assembly, that type will be identical in all files contained in the assembly. But different assemblies may contain two different types named `CustomType`.

- The assembly manifest specifies which of the types that are implemented within the assembly may be used by code outside the assembly.

- Version tracking is done on the assembly level. An assembly can specify the version of another assembly that it requires, but it cannot specify a version for an individual file within an assembly.

- Assemblies are deployed as a unit. When an application requires code contained in an assembly, it must install the entire assembly.

Why Use Assemblies?

To understand the motivation behind assemblies, you need to look back in Windows history. One of the key advances of Windows over MS-DOS was the inclusion of the dynamic link library (DLL file). A DLL can encapsulate common functionality used by more than one application. For example, the standard Windows treeview control is included in a DLL. Having more than one program share this file results in less disk space being taken by software and gives all of the programs access to similar functionality.

Although DLLs and other shared components (notably COM components, which are largely implemented in DLLs) have benefits in terms of disk space and functionality, over the long run they've led to a condition commonly known as *DLL hell*. This happens because the existing solutions for shared components do not allow robust versioning rules. Suppose you're already using an application, WhizBang 1, which installed the WunderBar Control 1 DLL. Then you install a new application, SurfFest 1, which in turn includes WunderBar 2. Because there can be only a single WunderBar control on the computer, version 2 replaces version 1. That means that WhizBang now uses version 2. If version 2 of the control is completely backward compatible with version 1, this isn't a problem. Unfortunately, complete backward compatibility is rare. In all too many cases, upgrading a shared component breaks older applications that depended on a previous version of that component.

That's DLL hell, and that's the main problem that .NET assemblies help solve with enhanced versioning and side-by-side execution. If you work at it, you can still end up with similar problems in .NET applications, but the .NET tools are designed to help you avoid these problems.

NOTE *As you'll see in the rest of the chapter, there's a lot more to assemblies than just solving DLL hell issues. But those issues were the motivation for the design of assemblies.*

Enhanced Versioning

In the world of COM, an application generally could not precisely specify the version of components on which it depends. If you used WunderBar 1 in building your application, it would load WunderBar 1 *or any later version* that it found on the computer at run-time.

.NET changes this by allowing assemblies to specify the *exact version* of components on which they depend. In fact, this enhanced versioning is the default behavior of applications built with .NET. If you build your .NET application with WunderBar 1, it will load precisely that version at run-time, no matter what other versions may exist on your computer. If it can't find that exact version, then the program won't run.

TIP *Later in the chapter you'll see how you can override this default behavior.*

Side-by-Side Execution

The flip side of enhanced versioning is *side-by-side execution*. What happens if you run two applications at the same time, and one of them wants WunderBar 1, while the other wants WunderBar 2? If the applications were written in .NET, the answer is that both versions of the library get loaded, and each application uses only the version that it needs.

Support for side-by-side execution is one of the many services provided by the Common Language Runtime (CLR). When you're designing assemblies, you need to keep the potential of side-by-side execution in mind. All of the files included in an assembly should continue to work together, no matter which version of the assembly is loaded; the CLR cannot reach into an assembly and extract a single file to couple with a later version of the same assembly.

What's in an Assembly?

An assembly can contain any of these items:

- Assembly manifest
- Type metadata
- Microsoft Intermediate Language (MSIL) code
- Resources

Only the assembly manifest is required, although an assembly containing only a manifest is pretty useless.

The Assembly Manifest

Every assembly contains a collection of metadata that describes the assembly and its components. This metadata is referred to as the *assembly manifest*. In a single-file assembly, the manifest is in the single file. In a multifile assembly, the manifest can be included in one of the executable files, or it can be present as a separate file.

The manifest contains the following pieces of information:

Assembly Name This is a text string that specifies the name of the assembly.

Assembly Version The version number consists of a major version, a minor version, a revision, and a build number.

Culture If an assembly is a satellite assembly designed to aid in globalization, it will contain information on the culture that it supports. You'll learn more about cultures in Chapter 21, "Other Classes in the Base Class Library."

Strong Name Information   This is the public key from the assembly publisher, if the assembly has been given a strong name. You'll learn about strong names later in this chapter, in the "Understanding Strong Names and Signing" section.

List of Files   The assembly manifest contains a list of all files in the assembly. Each file is identified by a hash value that's designed to make the assembly tamper resistant.

Type Reference Information   For types exported from the assembly, the manifest identifies the file within the assembly that contains the declaration and implementation of the type.

Information on Referenced Assemblies   For each assembly referenced by this assembly, the manifest contains identifying information (name, version, culture, and public key).

Type Metadata

Metadata, of course, is data about data. In the case of *type metadata*, this is data that describes the types in the assembly—or more precisely, the types that the assembly chooses to make externally available. This metadata includes information on class names, methods and their parameters, calling conventions, properties, fields, events, nested types, and anything else necessary for an external application to use the classes. This information is all stored in a common format understood by the CLR so that types written in one language can easily be called by code written in another language.

MSIL Code

Regardless of whether you write your original source code with C#, VB .NET, ActivePerl, or any of dozens of other .NET languages, it's always translated into MSIL and stored as MSIL. It's this MSIL that the CLR compiles and executes, not your own source code.

MSIL is an entire language with operations for loading, storing, and using objects, arithmetic and logical operations, looping and conditional code, and so on. We'll show you how to inspect MSIL code later in this chapter, in the "Viewing Assembly Contents" section.

Resources

An assembly can also contain resources. *Resources* is a catchall term for any other file you care to stuff into the assembly. Often this will be graphics such as BMP or JPG files. Resources can also include the text necessary to produce a localized version of an application.

Building Assemblies

Every time you create an executable (`.exe`) file using the `csc` command-line compiler, you're building a simple assembly. But there are many ways to customize this process. In this section, you'll explore some of the issues involved in building assemblies. First, you'll take a brief look at the concept of assembly attributes. Then you'll see the tools you can use to build either single-file or multifile assemblies.

Assembly Attributes

Assembly attributes are special values that function as properties of an assembly. Assembly attributes are grouped into four classes:

♦   Identity attributes determine the identity of an assembly.

◆ Informational attributes provide additional company or product information.

◆ Manifest attributes provide information for the manifest.

◆ Strong name attributes set the strong name for an assembly.

Table 16.1 lists the available assembly attributes.

TABLE 16.1: ASSEMBLY ATTRIBUTES

ATTRIBUTE	CLASS	DESCRIPTION
AssemblyCompanyAttribute	Informational	Name of the company that produced the assembly.
AssemblyConfigurationAttribute	Manifest	Configuration (such as Retail or Debug for the assembly).
AssemblyCopyrightAttribute	Informational	Copyright information for the assembly.
AssemblyCultureAttribute	Identity	Indicates the culture that the assembly supports. An assembly with a non-null AssemblyCultureAttribute is automatically treated as a satellite assembly.
AssemblyDefaultAliasAttribute	Manifest	An alternative name for the assembly. Useful when the full name is a GUID or other non-friendly name.
AssemblyDelaySignAttribute	Strong Name	A Boolean value that indicates whether delay signing is being used.
AssemblyDescriptionAttribute	Manifest	Short description of the assembly.
AssemblyFileVersionAttribute	Informational	Human-readable version string.
AssemblyFlagsAttribute	Identity	An enumerated attribute that indicates what type of side-by-side execution this assembly supports.
AssemblyInformationalVersion-Attribute	Informational	Extra version information that is not part of the version number.
AssemblyKeyFileAttribute	Strong Name	Name of the file containing cryptographic key information.
AssemblyKeyNameAttribute	Strong Name	Name of the key container containing cryptographic key information.
AssemblyProductAttribute	Informational	Product information for the assembly.
AssemblyTitleAttribute	Manifest	Human-friendly name for the assembly.
AssemblyTrademarkAttribute	Informational	Trademark information for the assembly.
AssemblyVersionAttribute	Identity	The version of the assembly.

NOTE *In addition to the standard attributes listed in Table 16.1, you can create your own custom attributes. You can also manipulate attributes programmatically. We'll cover these tasks in Chapter 17, "Attributes and Reflection."*

To set an attribute for an assembly in C#, you use this syntax:

```
[assembly:AttributeName("AttributeValue")]
```

Note that because this is a directive to the compiler, rather than a part of the language itself, this statement is not terminated with a semicolon.

TIP *You need to set a reference to the* System.Reflection *namespace to include assembly attributes.*

Listing 16.1 shows a simple class that includes two assembly attributes, a version number, and a title.

LISTING 16.1: SETTING ASSEMBLY ATTRIBUTES IN CODE

```
/*
  Example16_1.cs shows the use of assembly attributes
*/

using System;
using System.Reflection;

[assembly:AssemblyVersionAttribute("1.0.0.0")]
[assembly:AssemblyTitleAttribute("Example 16.1")]

class Example16_1
{
    string privateString;

    public string inString
    {
        get
        {
            return privateString;
        }
        set
        {
            privateString = inString;
        }
    }

    public void upper(out string upperString)
    {
        upperString = privateString.ToUpper();
    }
```

```
    public static void Main()
    {

    }

}
```

Later in this chapter, you'll see how to view the results of this code by inspecting the assembly's executable file directly.

Single-File Assemblies

You already know how to create a single-file assembly: Run a C# source file through the `csc` command-line compiler. But there are numerous ways to customize the process. Let's look at a few of those.

First, you can create an assembly from a single `.cs` file as a single `.exe` file by using the source file-name as the only parameter to the compiler call:

```
csc Example16_1.cs
```

The next step in customization is to specify the output filename. You can do this with the `/out` switch. For example, to compile `Example16_1.cs` into `NewExample.exe`, you could use this command line:

```
csc /out:NewExample.exe Example16_1.cs
```

So far, everything we've done has involved an entry point named `Main`. But there are times when you don't want an assembly to have an entry point. This happens when you want to use an assembly strictly to hold classes for other code to call. The term for this is *library assembly*. Listing 16.2 shows the code for a typical library assembly.

LISTING 16.2: A LIBRARY ASSEMBLY

```
/*
   Example16_2.cs creates a library assembly
*/

using System;
using System.Reflection;

[assembly:AssemblyVersionAttribute("1.0.0.0")]
[assembly:AssemblyTitleAttribute("Example 16.2")]

class Example16_2
{
    string privateString;

    public string inString
    {
        get
```

```
            {
                return privateString;
            }
            set
            {
                privateString = inString;
            }
        }

        public void upper(out string upperString)
        {
            upperString = privateString.ToUpper();
        }

    }
```

If you just try to compile this assembly without special switches, you'll get an error:

```
C>csc Example16_2.cs
Microsoft (R) Visual C# .NET Compiler version 7.00.9466
for Microsoft (R) .NET Framework version 1.0.3705
Copyright (C) Microsoft Corporation 2001. All rights reserved.

error CS5001: Program 'Example16_2.exe' does not have an entry point defined
```

To compile a library assembly, you should use the /out switch to specify an output file name with the extension .dll, and the /t:library switch to specify that you're creating a library (and thus, an entry point is not required). For example:

```
csc /out:Example16_2.dll /t:library Example16_2.cs
```

There are many other switches available for csc. To see them all, you can execute this command:

```
csc /?
```

Table 16.2 lists the command-line switches for the csc compiler.

TABLE 16.2: csc Compiler Switches

Switch	Description
/? or /help	Lists all compiler switches
/addmodule	Specifies modules to add to this assembly
/baseaddress	Specifies the preferred base address to use when loading a DLL into memory
/bugreport	Creates a text file with information useful for filing a compiler bug report
/checked	Overflows will cause a run-time exception

Continued on next page

TABLE 16.2: CSC COMPILER SWITCHES *(continued)*

SWITCH	DESCRIPTION
/codepage	Specifies the code page to be used for this assembly
/debug	Creates a debug file for the assembly
/define	Defines a preprocessor symbol
/doc	Converts documentation comments to an XML file
/filealign	Specifies the size of sections in the output file
/fullpaths	Includes full paths in any compiler errors or warnings
/incremental	Enables incremental compilation
/lib	Specifies the location for libraries referenced from this assembly
/linkresource	Creates a link to a managed resource
/main	Specifies the location of the main method
/noconfig	Does not include references that are in the csc.rsp file
/nologo	Tells the compiler not to display compiler version information
/nostdlib	Does not link in the standard library
/nowarn	Suppresses compiler warnings
/optimize	Enables or disables optimizations
/recurse	Searches subdirectories for files to compile
/reference	Imports metadata from another assembly
/resource	Embeds a resource file in the assembly
/target:exe or /t:exe	Creates an executable file
/target:library or /t:library	Creates a library file
/target:module or /t:module	Creates a module
/target:winexe or /t:winexe	Creates a Windows executable file
/unsafe	Enables you to compile code containing the unsafe keyword
/utf8output	Displays compiler output using the UTF-8 character set
/warn	Sets the warning level
/warnaserror	Treats all warnings as errors
/win32icon	Includes an icon file in the assembly
/win32res	Includes a Win32 resource file in the assembly

You can also create single-file assemblies by using the Visual Studio .NET Integrated Development Environment (IDE). When you select Build or Rebuild from the Visual Studio .NET Build menu, the product invokes the compiler to create an assembly file. In Visual Studio .NET projects, assembly attributes are specified (by default) in a separate file named `AssemblyInfo.cs`. Listing 16.3 shows a default `AssemblyInfo.cs` file.

LISTING 16.3: DEFAULT CONTENTS OF THE `AssemblyInfo.cs` FILE

```
using System.Reflection;
using System.Runtime.CompilerServices;

//
// General Information about an assembly is controlled through the
➡ following
// set of attributes. Change these attribute values to modify the
➡ information
// associated with an assembly.
//
[assembly: AssemblyTitle("")]
[assembly: AssemblyDescription("")]
[assembly: AssemblyConfiguration("")]
[assembly: AssemblyCompany("")]
[assembly: AssemblyProduct("")]
[assembly: AssemblyCopyright("")]
[assembly: AssemblyTrademark("")]
[assembly: AssemblyCulture("")]


//
// Version information for an assembly consists of the following four
➡ values:
//
//      Major Version
//      Minor Version
//      Build Number
//      Revision
//
// You can specify all the values or you can default the Revision and
➡ Build Numbers
// by using the '*' as shown below:

[assembly: AssemblyVersion("1.0.*")]


//
// In order to sign your assembly you must specify a key to use. Refer to
➡ the
// Microsoft .NET Framework documentation for more information on assembly
➡ signing.
```

```
//
// Use the attributes below to control which key is used for signing.
//
// Notes:
//   (*) If no key is specified, the assembly is not signed.
//   (*) KeyName refers to a key that has been installed in the Crypto
➥ Service
//       Provider (CSP) on your machine. KeyFile refers to a file which
➥ contains
//       a key.
//   (*) If the KeyFile and the KeyName values are both specified, the
//       following processing occurs:
//       (1) If the KeyName can be found in the CSP, that key is used.
//       (2) If the KeyName does not exist and the KeyFile does exist, the
➥ key
//           in the KeyFile is installed into the CSP and used.
//   (*) In order to create a KeyFile, you can use the sn.exe (Strong
➥ Name) utility.
//       When specifying the KeyFile, the location of the KeyFile should
➥ be
//       relative to the project output directory which is
//       %Project Directory%\obj\<configuration>. For example, if your
➥ KeyFile is
//       located in the project directory, you would specify the
➥ AssemblyKeyFile
//       attribute as [assembly: AssemblyKeyFile("..\\..\\mykey.snk")]
//   (*) Delay Signing is an advanced option - see the Microsoft .NET
➥ Framework
//       documentation for more information on this.
//
[assembly: AssemblyDelaySign(false)]
[assembly: AssemblyKeyFile("")]
[assembly: AssemblyKeyName("")]
```

You can also set compiler options from within the Visual Studio .NET IDE. To do so, right-click the project file in the Solution Explorer and select Properties. The Property Pages dialog box, shown in Figure 16.1, lets you set values for many of the command-line compiler switches. For example, selecting True in the Allow Unsafe Code Blocks section is the equivalent of supplying the /unsafe command-line switch.

FIGURE 16.1

Setting compiler options

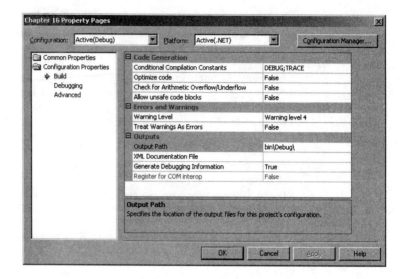

Multifile Assemblies

You must create multifile assemblies using the command-line tools; you cannot create a multifile assembly for a C# application within the Visual Studio .NET IDE.

NOTE   You can create multifile assemblies from the IDE if you're working with C++ rather than C# or Visual Basic .NET.

To create a multifile assembly, you can use a combination of the command-line compiler csc and the assembly linker al. To demonstrate the use of these programs together, we'll build an assembly that contains the compiled versions of three C# files plus a bitmap resource.

The first C# file, shown in Listing 16.4, contains a definition for a namespace that includes a single class.

LISTING 16.4: DEFINING A NAMESPACE WITH A SINGLE CLASS

```
/*
  Example16_3a.cs creates a namespace with a single class
*/

using System;

namespace StringSwitch
{
    class MySwitch
    {
        string privateString;
```

```
    public string inString
    {
        get
        {
            return privateString;
        }
        set
        {
            privateString = value;
        }
    }

    public void upper(out string upperString)
    {
        upperString = privateString.ToUpper();
    }

    }
}
```

Note that this source file does not contain an entry point. We could compile it as a library file, but that would defeat the purpose of including it into a multifile assembly. Instead, we'll compile this code into a module:

`csc /t:module Example16_3a.cs`

The result will be a file named `Example16_3a.netmodule`. This file contains executable code, but it does not contain an assembly manifest or an entry point.

The second source code file, shown in Listing 16.5, includes a reference to the `StringSwitch` namespace that was declared in the first code file. This file also includes an entry point.

LISTING 16.5: USING A CLASS FROM ANOTHER NAMESPACE

```
/*
  Example16_3b.cs uses a class from Example16_3a.cs
*/

using System;
using StringSwitch;

class Example16_3b
{

    public static void Main()
    {
        string localString;
        MySwitch s = new MySwitch();
```

```
            s.inString="abcdef";
            s.upper(out localString);
            Console.WriteLine(localString);
        }

    }
```

Again, we'll compile this source file into a module. However, this time we need to tell the compiler where to find the `StringSwitch` namespace. We can do that by using the `/addmodule` command-line switch:

```
csc /addmodule:Example16_3a.netmodule /t:module Example16_3b.cs
```

The third source file, shown in Listing 16.6, contains only information for the assembly manifest.

LISTING 16.6: MANIFEST INFORMATION IN A SOURCE FILE

```
/*
   Example16_3c.cs provides manifest information for Example 16_3
*/

using System.Reflection;

[assembly: AssemblyTitle("Example 16.3")]
[assembly: AssemblyVersion("1.0.0.0")]
```

This source file too can be compiled into a separate module:

```
csc /t:module Example16_3c.cs
```

Finally, Figure 16.2 shows the bitmap resource that we're going to include in this assembly.

Merging these files together into a single executable is the job of the assembly linker, `al.exe`. For this particular job, we can use this command line:

```
al Example16_3a.netmodule Example16_3b.netmodule Example16_3c.netmodule
➥ /embed:CSharp.bmp /main:Example16_3b.Main /out:Example16_3.exe /t:exe
```

This command line starts by listing the three modules that should be used to create the assembly. It then uses the `/embed` command-line switch to specify an embedded resource. The `/main` switch specifies the fully qualified (class and method) entry point for the assembly, and the `/out` switch specifies the name of the assembly to create.

Of course, there are many other command-line switches for `al`. Table 16.3 summarizes these switches.

NOTE   *Square brackets in Table 16.3 indicate optional parts of the switches.*

FIGURE 16.2

A bitmap resource

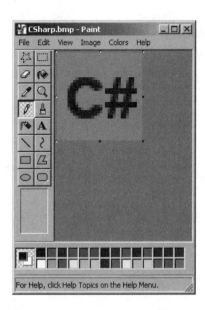

TABLE 16.3: al COMMAND-LINE SWITCHES

SWITCH	DESCRIPTION
/? or /help	Displays options for the linker.
/algid:id	Specifies the algorithm to compute hash values used in the assembly manifest. You can specify CALG_SHA1 or CALG_MD5 to use the SHA1 or MD5 algorithms respectively.
/base[address]:address	Specifies the base address where the assembly will load by default.
/bugreport:filename	Creates a file with bug report information.
/comp[any]:text	Specifies the company name to associate with the assembly.
/config[uration]:text	Specifies configuration information to associate with the assembly.
/copy[right]:text	Specifies a copyright string for the assembly.
/c[ulture]:text	Specifies the culture identifier for the assembly.
/delay[sign][+|-]	Used to allow delayed signing of strong-named assemblies.
/descry[iption]:text	Specifies a description string for the assembly.
/embed[resource]: file[,name[,private]]	Embeds the specified file as a resource in the assembly. You can specify an internal name for the resource if you like. If you mark the resource as private it is not available to other assemblies.

Continued on next page

TABLE 16.3: al COMMAND-LINE SWITCHES *(continued)*

SWITCH	DESCRIPTION
/e[vidence]:*file*	Embeds the specified file in the assembly with the resource name of Security.Evidence. Evidence is a special class that contains information for verifying code permissions.
/fileversion:*version*	Specifies a file version string for the assembly.
/flags:*flags*	Specifies side-by-side execution modes for the assembly.
/fullpaths	Causes the linker to use full paths in any error messages.
/keyf[ile]:*filename*	Specifies a key file for the assembly.
/keyn[ame]:*text*	Specifies a key container for the assembly.
/link[resource]: *file*[,*name*[,*target* [,*private*]]]	Links a resource to the assembly. You can specify an internal name and a target directory for the resource. If you mark the resource as private it is not available to other assemblies.
/main:*method*	Specifies the fully qualified name of the entry point for the assembly.
/nologo	Suppresses the banner displayed by the linker.
/out:*filename*	Specifies the output file name.
/prod[uct]:*text*	Specifies a product string for the assembly.
/productv[ersion]:*text*	Specifies a product version for the assembly.
/t[arget]:lib	Creates a library.
/t[arget]:exe	Creates a console executable.
/t[arget]:win	Creates a Windows executable.
/template:*filename*	Specifies another assembly from which to inherit all attributes except culture.
/title:text	Specifies a title string for the assembly.
/trade[mark]:*text*	Specifies a trademark string for the assembly.
/v[ersion]:*text*	Specifies a version string for the assembly.
/win32icon:*filename*	Specifies an icon for a Windows executable assembly.
/win32res:*filename*	Inserts the specified resource file into the assembly.

TIP   For complex assembly tasks, you'll find it's much easier to use the Visual Studio .NET IDE to compile your applications. The IDE will take care of constructing the appropriate command lines for both csc and al to include all of the files that are a part of your project in the final assembly.

As you can see, many of the switches for the assembly linker control the same information that you can set with assembly attributes. If you should specify the same information twice (for example, with an `AssemblyTitle` attribute setting and with the `/title` command-line switch), you'll get a linker error AL1021, and the information supplied in the command-line switch will take precedence over the information in the attribute.

Viewing Assembly Contents

We've now built several assemblies and told you what they contain. But wouldn't you like to see for yourself? Fortunately, the .NET Framework Software Development Kit (SDK) ships with an excellent tool for investigating the contents of assemblies. This tool is the MSIL Disassembler, `ildasm.exe` (usually referred to as ILDasm). It can show you all of the data contained within any .NET assembly.

ILDasm is launched from the command line but displays its results in a graphical user interface (GUI) window by default (it can also display results in a console window or send output to a file). The easiest way to learn what ILDasm can do for you is to simply start using it. For example, to disassemble the first assembly created in this chapter, you can use this command line:

```
ildasm Example16_1.exe
```

Alternatively, you can launch ILDasm and then browse for a file to disassemble. The results of the disassembly are displayed in a treeview control, as shown in Figure 16.3.

FIGURE 16.3

Using the MSIL Disassembler

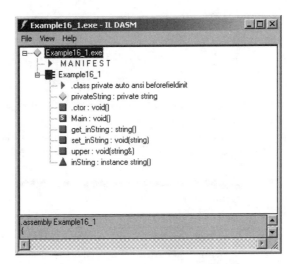

The different icons in the ILDasm display indicate different entities in the assembly. Table 16.4 shows these icons and their meanings.

TABLE 16.4: ILDASM ICONS

ICON	MEANING
▶	Manifest or class information
⬟	Namespace
▤	Class
▥	Interface
▤	Value class
▤	Enum
▪	Method
S	Static method
◇	Field
◈	Static field
▽	Event
▲	Property

If you compare Figure 16.3 to Listing 16.1, you should be able to identify the code construct that maps to each icon in the treeview.

Double-clicking any item in the ILDasm treeview will show you the MSIL code for that item. For example, Figure 16.4 shows the detailed disassembly view for the Manifest node from Figure 16.3.

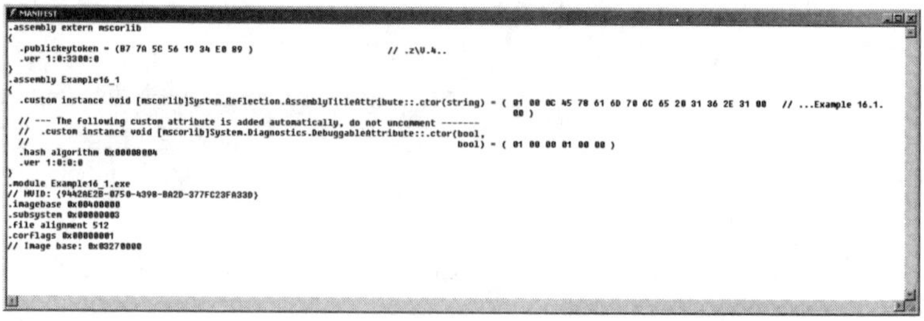

FIGURE 16.4

MSIL listing

We're not going to try to teach you the details of MSIL in this book. But just by looking at this MSIL listing, you can see how some parts of the original source file were translated. For example, consider the version attribute from the original source file:

```
[assembly:AssemblyVersionAttribute("1.0.0.0")]
```

This translates directly into a single line in the MSIL:

```
.ver 1:0:0:0
```

ILDasm can disassemble executables, libraries, and modules. Figure 16.5 shows the result of disassembling the Example16_3a.netmodule file.

FIGURE 16.5

Disassembling a module

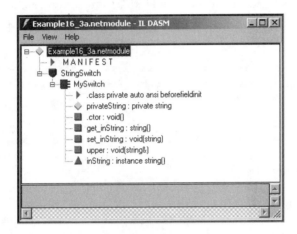

TIP *ILDasm can only disassemble .NET files. If you're not sure whether a particular EXE or DLL file is a .NET file, one quick way to check is to attempt to disassemble it with ILDasm.*

Understanding Strong Names and Signing

One of the most important tasks that the CLR performs is to verify the identity of assemblies at run-time. .NET is designed with strong protections to prevent malicious code from substituting for trusted code. In particular, *strong names* guarantee that the contents of an assembly have not been changed since the assembly was built, and *code signing* provides a level of trust for the assembly.

Strong Names

When you give an assembly a strong name, you're really applying public-key encryption to the assembly. Public-key cryptography depends on a *key pair*, consisting of a public key and a private key. The public key is shared with the world, but the private key is kept as a closely guarded secret.

You may be familiar with public-key cryptography from such applications as PGP. In those applications, a message is encrypted with a public key, and it can then be decrypted with the matching private key. But there's another way to use public-key cryptography. If a message is signed with a private key, it can be verified with the public key. That's how the .NET Framework uses key pairs in assigning strong names.

The CLR uses the keys in strong names to verify assembly identity at run-time. The process works like this:

1. When you develop a library, you assign a key pair to the assembly.

2. When you create the assembly (using the Visual Studio .NET IDE or the command-line tools), the hash for the assembly is signed with the private key from the key pair.

3. When you reference the library from another piece of code, the reference includes the public key for the assembly.

4. At run-time, the CLR uses the public key in the second file to verify that the hash in the first file was signed with the expected private key. The hash can then be used to verify the contents of the referenced assembly.

The net effect of these steps is that the CLR can know at run-time that the referenced assembly came from the expected developer (because otherwise the key would not have verified) and that the bits inside the assembly have not been tampered with (because otherwise the hash values would not have matched the files).

Now that you understand the concept, we can look at the mechanics of assigning a strong name to an assembly. The first step is to create a cryptographic key pair. To do this, you can use the Strong Name tool, `sn.exe`. This tool includes a variety of command-line switches that can manage key files, but for the purpose of assigning a strong name, all you need is the `-k` switch. That switch tells the tool to generate a new file containing a key pair. You call it with a filename to hold the key pair:

```
sn -k Example16_3.snk
```

The next step is to assign this particular key file to the assembly. You can do this in one of two ways:

◆ Use the `AssemblyKeyFileAttribute` attribute in the source code for the assembly.

◆ Use the `/keyfile` switch for the assembly linker.

For example, to relink `Example16_3.exe`, using the key pair in `Example16_3.snk` to assign a strong name, we could use this command line with `al.exe`:

```
al Example16_3a.netmodule Example16_3b.netmodule Example16_3c.netmodule
➥ /embed:CSharp.bmp /main:Example16_3b.Main /out:Example16_3.exe
➥ /t:exe /keyfile:Example16_3.snk
```

To reference this assembly from another assembly, you use the `/reference` switch when compiling the other assembly. This will cause the compiler to retrieve the public key for this assembly and store it with the assembly reference.

If you're using the Visual Studio .NET IDE, public keys for strong-named assemblies are automatically retrieved when you compile an application.

Code Signing

Although strong names let you verify that an assembly hasn't been tampered with by anyone since it was compiled, they don't give you any reason to trust the creator of the assembly. After all, it could be that the original developer was interested in doing something malicious and has shipped an assembly with a strong name that will wipe your hard drive. The .NET Framework includes a second code security mechanism that's designed to help you determine whether to trust a particular assembly. Code signing is a way to add an Authenticode digital signature to an assembly.

Authenticode is a method for verifying the identity of a software publisher. When working with an Authenticode-signed assembly, you can verify that the publisher is known by a certificate authority. You should expect commercial software publishers to have a digital certificate from a recognized authority such as VeriSign (`www.verisign.com`) or Thawte (`www.thawte.com`).

Getting a "real" certificate from a certificate authority generally requires you prove your identity and pay a fee. But the .NET Framework includes tools to let you work with code signing on a test basis:

- The Certificate Creation Tool
- The Software Publisher Certificate Test Tool
- The File Signing Tool

You can follow these steps to create a test certificate and then use it to sign an assembly:

1. Use the Certificate Creation Tool, `makecert.exe`, to create an X.509 digital certificate. This tool has many options, but the basic one you should know is the `-n` option, which enables you to specify the company name for the certificate. This name needs to be specified in X.500 format; you can accomplish this by putting the name in quotes and prepending `CN=` to it. You'll also need to use the `-sv` option to create a file containing the private key for the certificate:

   ```
   makecert -n "CN=Chapter 16 Test Company" -sv Chapter16.pvk Chapter16.cer
   ```

2. When you run `makecert`, it will prompt you to assign a password for the private key file. Be sure to pick a password you can remember.

3. The next step is to turn the X.509 certificate into a software publisher's certificate (SPC). You can do this with the Software Publisher Certificate Test Tool, `cert2spc.exe`:

   ```
   cert2spc Chapter16.cer Chapter16.spc
   ```

4. You can then use the File Signing Tool, `signcode.exe`, to sign an assembly with the software publisher's certificate. Signcode has many command-line switches, but the simplest way to use it is to run it with no options. This will launch the Digital Signature Wizard.

5. Read the introductory text for the wizard and click Next.

6. On the file selection panel, select the assembly file you want to sign. Click Next.

7. On the Signing Options panel, select Custom and click Next. Although the wizard will tell you that most users should select Typical, you can only specify a certificate file if you select custom.

8. On the signature certificate panel, click Select from File and select the `.spc` file. Click Next.

9. On the private key panel, browse to the private key file you created in step 1. Leave the rest of the options at their default, as shown in Figure 16.6. Click Next.

FIGURE 16.6

Setting the private key for code signing

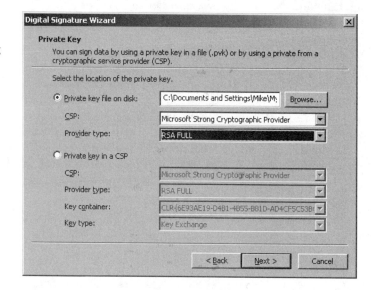

10. Enter the private key password you assigned in step 2 and click OK.

11. Select a hash algorithm and click Next.

12. On the Additional Certificates panel, leave the defaults selected and click Next.

13. On the Data Description panel, leave the description blank and click Next.

14. On the Timestamping panel, leave the default options and click Next.

15. Click Finish to sign the file. Enter your private key password when prompted and click OK.

Of course, code signing would not be worth much if you couldn't check the signature. Fortunately, there is yet another tool that you can use to check digital signatures. This is the Certificate Verification tool, `chktrust.exe`. To use the tool, you pass it the name of the file to check on the command line:

```
chktrust Example16_3.exe
```

If you check the trust on a file that you've signed with your own test certificate, you'll see a warning such as the one shown in Figure 16.7. That happens because the certificate wasn't issued by a recognized certificate authority.

FIGURE 16.7

Invalid certificate warning from `chktrust`

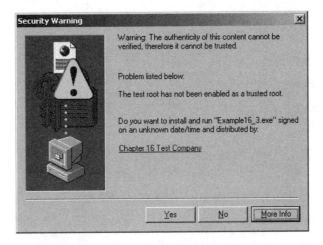

If you run `chktrust` on a program that was signed with a valid certificate, you'll see a dialog box such as the one in Figure 16.8.

FIGURE 16.8

Verifying certificate authenticity with `chktrust`

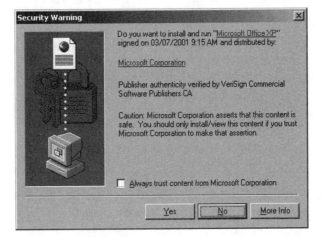

Assembly Versioning

When you create an assembly, you assign a version number to that assembly. The version number serves to identify the particular code in the assembly to other code that calls the assembly. In this section we'll discuss the format of version numbers and the way that the .NET Framework uses version information to make sure that it loads the exact assembly that the calling code expects.

Understanding Version Numbers

Version numbers in .NET have four parts:

- ◆ Major part
- ◆ Minor part
- ◆ Build part
- ◆ Revision

You can set all the parts of the version number explicitly by using the `AssemblyVersion` attribute, as you saw earlier in the chapter:

```
[assembly: AssemblyVersion("1.3.7.18914")]
```

You can also choose to set only part of the version number yourself:

```
[assembly: AssemblyVersion("1.0.*")]
```

Setting the `AssemblyVersion` attribute to `1.0.*` tells the .NET Framework to use 1 for the major part, 0 for the minor part, and to come up with build and private part numbers automatically. In this case, .NET will assign an arbitrary build part and an arbitrary private part, and it will change the private part each time you rebuild the assembly.

Version numbers are stored as a 128-bit number logically partitioned into four 32-bit numbers. Each of the four parts of the version number must be in the range of 0 to 65,536, although 32 bits should allow storing more than that.

Retrieving Version Numbers

To retrieve the version number of an application from Visual Basic .NET, you can use the `Assembly-Name` class from the `System.Reflection` namespace. This class has a `Version` property that returns an instance of the `Version` class. The `Version` class in turn implements a set of properties that you can use to retrieve version number information:

- ◆ `Major` returns an integer containing the major part.
- ◆ `Minor` returns an integer containing the minor part.
- ◆ `Build` returns an integer containing the build part.
- ◆ `Revision` returns an integer containing the revision part.

Listing 16.7 shows how you can use the classes in the `System.Reflection` namespace to retrieve version information.

LISTING 16.7: RETRIEVING VERSION INFORMATION

```
/*
  Example16_4.cs demonstrates retrieving version information
*/
```

```
using System;
using System.Reflection;

[assembly:AssemblyVersionAttribute("1.2.3.4")]
[assembly:AssemblyTitleAttribute("Example 16_4")]

class Example16_4
{
    public static void Main()
    {
        // get the version object for this assembly
        Version v = System.Reflection.Assembly.GetExecutingAssembly().
         GetName().Version;
        // write out the whole version number
        Console.WriteLine(v.ToString());
        // or do it in pieces
        Console.WriteLine(v.Major + "." + v.Minor + "." + v.Build +
         "." + v.Revision);

        // now get an external assembly
        AssemblyName anm = AssemblyName.GetAssemblyName(
         "c:\\winnt\\microsoft.net\\framework\\v1.0.3705\\mscorlib.dll");
        // and show its version
        Console.WriteLine(anm.Version.ToString());

    }

}
```

The output from this program is as follows:

```
1.2.3.4
1.2.4.3
1.0.3300.0
```

WARNING *If you get an error running this program, make sure that the* GetAssemblyName *call is pointing to the folder where you have the .NET run-time files installed.*

Version Compatibility and Policy Files

The main use of version information is to help applications and developers determine whether a particular version of a component is compatible with an application that makes use of the component. By default, .NET uses only the versions of components that were present when an assembly was compiled.

You're free to use whatever version numbering you'd like as you release new versions. However, it's useful to establish standards for choosing new version numbers. This is one common standard for assigning version numbers:

◆ A new major or minor part indicates that the new version is incompatible with the old one. For example, version 3.0.0.0 should be incompatible with version 2.4.8.1932. You should change major version numbers whenever you introduce an incompatibility into your code.

◆ A new build part indicates probable compatibility. Typically you should change minor version numbers when you introduce a service pack or a minor upgrade. For example, version 2.8.0.0 is probably compatible with version 2.7.0.1.

◆ A new revision part indicates a Quick Fix Engineering (QFE) release that is compatible with the previous version and that should be installed. For example, version 4.12.0.22 might be a mandatory bug-fix upgrade to version 4.12.0.23.

Sometimes you don't want the .NET Framework to enforce strict version-number compatibility. For example, you might want assemblies to use version 4.12.0.23 of your library, even though they were originally compiled to use version 4.12.0.22. You can use *policy files* to override the version information stored in the assembly.

Policy files are XML files that can specify the version of a component to use. The general structure of a policy file follows this template:

```
<configuration>
    <runtime>
        <assemblyBinding xmlns="urn:schemas-microsoft-com:asm.v1">
            <dependentAssembly>
                <assemblyIdentity name="ComponentName"
                    publicKeyToken="PublicKey" />
                <bindingRedirect oldVersion="version"
                                 newVersion="version"/>
            </dependentAssembly>
        </assemblyBinding>
    </runtime>
</configuration>
```

The version for the `oldVersion` attribute can be either a single version number such as `4.12.0.22` or a range of version numbers such as `4.12.0.1-4.12.0.22`. The version for the `newVersion` attribute is the version number of the component that should be loaded instead of the version specified in the calling assembly's manifest.

The CLR checks three policy files for version information:

◆ The application policy file has the same name as the application plus the extension `.config` and resides in the same directory as the application. For example, the application configuration file for `MyApp.exe` would be named `MyApp.exe.config`. In some cases the name of the application policy file is dictated by .NET. For example, the application policy file for an ASP.NET application is always named `web.config`.

◆ The publisher policy file is distributed by a component publisher together with a new version of a component. The publisher policy file must be installed in the Global Assembly Cache (GAC), even though the assembly itself need not be. In the majority of cases, though, finding a policy file in the GAC probably means you'll find the assembly in the GAC as well. You'll learn about the GAC in the next section, "Working with the Global Assembly Cache."

◆ The machine configuration file is named `machine.config` and is stored in the `CONFIG` directory beneath the directory where the .NET run-time is installed.

You don't have to edit policy files by hand. The .NET Framework includes a snap-in for the Microsoft Management Console (MMC) to handle this and other .NET Configuration tasks. To create a new policy file, follow these steps:

1. Select Start ➢ Programs ➢ Administrative Tools ➢ Microsoft .NET Framework Configuration.

2. Select the Configured Assemblies node in the left pane of the .NET Framework Configuration application.

3. Click the Configure an Assembly task in the right pane.

4. In the Configure an Assembly dialog box, click the Choose Assembly button.

5. In the Choose Assembly from Assembly Cache dialog box, highlight the assembly whose version information you want to override and click Select.

6. In the Configure an Assembly dialog box, click Finish. This will open the Properties dialog box for the selected assembly.

7. Select the Binding Policy tab of the Properties dialog box. Enter the old and new version numbers as shown in Figure 16.9. Click OK.

FIGURE 16.9

Overriding a binding policy

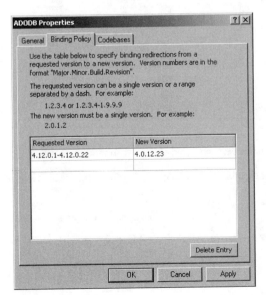

Working with the Global Assembly Cache

When you ship an assembly as part of an application, you generally install it in your own application's directory. That makes the assembly private to that application. But there are times when you'd like to share one assembly among multiple applications. That sharing is the job of the Global Assembly Cache (GAC).

The GAC is a collection of assemblies maintained by the CLR. Assemblies in the GAC are available to all applications on the computer. This is where you'll find the assemblies that are provided by the .NET Framework itself, which explains why every application can use code from assemblies such as `System.Data` or `System.Reflection`.

There are several ways to work with the GAC. One is to locate it in Windows Explorer. You'll find the GAC installed as a folder such as `c:\WINNT\assembly`. There's also a command-line tool, `gacutil .exe`, which can add assemblies to the GAC. However, it's probably easier to manage the GAC by using the .NET Framework Configuration tool. You can launch this tool by selecting Start ➤ Programs ➤ Administrative Tools ➤ Microsoft .NET Framework Configuration. Click the Assembly Cache node and then click the hyperlink to view the list of assemblies in the cache, as shown in Figure 16.10.

FIGURE 16.10

Viewing the contents of the GAC

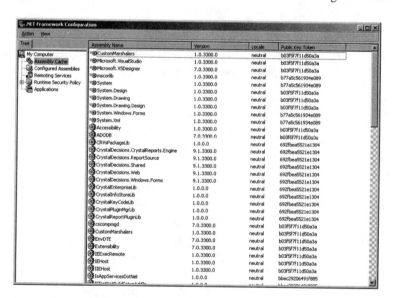

From here, you can perform the basic GAC-management functions:

◆ To add an assembly to the GAC, right-click the Assembly Cache node in the treeview and select Add.

◆ To delete an assembly from the GAC, right-click the assembly and select Delete.

◆ To view the properties of an assembly, right-click the assembly and select Properties.

TIP *To add an assembly to the GAC, you must first sign the assembly with a strong name.*

Finding an Assembly

When you run a .NET application that uses a component from an external assembly, the CLR checks four places to determine which version of the component to load:

1. The original version listed in the assembly manifest is the default version to load.

2. The CLR then checks for the presence of an application policy file that overrides the version information for this application only.

3. The CLR then checks for the presence of a publisher policy file that overrides the version information for this component in all applications.

4. The CLR then checks for the presence of an administrator policy file that overrides the version information for this component systemwide.

WARNING   *Version checking is only performed on files that have strong names.*

After it's determined which version of an assembly to use, the CLR has to find the assembly. It does so using these rules in order:

1. If the application has already used code from this assembly, the CLR uses the version of the assembly that's already loaded.

2. If the assembly is in the GAC, the CLR uses the assembly from the GAC.

3. The CLR next checks the policy files for the application to see whether a `<codeBase>` element exists for the assembly. If a `<codeBase>` element is found, the CLR uses the assembly that is specified by that element. The `<codebase>` element follows this template:

```
<configuration>
  <runtime>
    <assemblyBinding xmlns="urn:schemas-microsoft-com:asm.v1">
      <dependentAssembly>
        <assemblyIdentity name="ComponentName"
          publicKeyToken="PublicKey" />
        <codeBase version="version"
              href="url"/>
      </dependentAssembly>
    </assemblyBinding>
  </runtime>
</configuration>
```

You can use either file- or Internet-based URLs to specify the assembly location in this manner.

4. The CLR next checks the application's own directory for the assembly.

5. The CLR then probes subdirectories, based first on the assembly name and culture, and then looking at any other subdirectories of the application.

Summary

Assemblies are the fundamental unit of physical code grouping in .NET. They're also a fundamental unit of management for purposes such as permissions, type identity, public visibility, deployment, and version tracking. Assemblies are designed to solve DLL hell problems by enforcing enhanced versioning rules.

An assembly can contain an assembly manifest, type metadata, MSIL code, and other resources. Assembly metadata can be specified by using assembly attributes in a source-code file or by supplying command-line switches to the assembly linker.

You can build assemblies by using the Visual Studio .NET IDE or by using the command-line compiler and assembly linker. Assemblies can be single-file or multifile. You can only build multifile assemblies by using the command-line tools. To view the contents of an assembly, you can use the ILDasm tool.

Strong names and code signing can help guarantee that the contents of an assembly have not changed since the assembly was compiled and that the supplier of the assembly is a trusted source.

You can specify assembly version numbers with the `AssemblyVersion` attribute and retrieve them with classes from the `System.Reflection` namespace. Policy files allow you to override version information stored in an assembly manifest.

The CLR stores shared assemblies in the Global Assembly Cache (GAC). .NET provides an MMC-based tool to manage the GAC.

When you request code from an assembly, the CLR applies a series of rules to determine the version of the assembly to load and then to find that version of the assembly. In the next chapter, you'll learn about attributes and reflection, .NET features that allow you to view and manipulate code metadata from within the code itself.

Chapter 17

Attributes and Reflection

IN THE PREVIOUS CHAPTER you learned a bit about *metadata*—the data within .NET assemblies that describes the contents of those assemblies. In this chapter, you're going to dig more deeply into the metadata concept and its implementation in .NET. The key concept is that you can actually manipulate metadata directly from .NET code, rather than depending on external tools.

Metadata consists of attributes that describe types, members, modules, and assemblies. The .NET Framework supports both intrinsic attributes and custom attributes. The first part of this chapter will cover working with attributes, including the creation of your own custom attributes to extend the metadata stored in assemblies.

After that, you'll look at the two namespaces within the base class library that let you work with metadata. The `System.Reflection` namespace offers support for manipulating existing types through their metadata. The `System.Reflection.Emit` namespace supports creating entirely new types from within your code. You'll see that these two namespaces combine to offer you powerful tools for writing code about code.

Featured in this chapter:

◆ Introducing and Using Attributes

◆ Discovering Types at Run-Time

◆ Creating Types at Run-Time

Using Attributes

The metadata that describes types, members, modules, and assemblies is contained in *attributes*. An attribute is a single piece of metadata about some component within your .NET application. You already saw some attributes in Chapter 16, "Assemblies." For example, the `AssemblyDescription-Attribute` attribute enables you to attach a description to an assembly. This description is not formally part of the assembly. Rather, it is a piece of information about the assembly.

You can broadly divide attributes into two classes, *intrinsic attributes* and *custom attributes*. The .NET Framework defines intrinsic attributes. Custom attributes are attributes you define programmatically in your own applications.

In the following sections, you'll learn about the syntax and uses of both intrinsic and custom attributes.

Using Intrinsic Attributes

Metadata plays a crucial world in the .NET Framework, telling the Common Language Runtime (CLR) how it should handle various pieces of code and carrying information for other pieces of the .NET development environment. This metadata is expressed in attributes, which are classes derived from System.Attribute.

As an example of attribute use by Visual Studio .NET, consider the issues involved in designing your own custom control for use on Windows forms. You can write controls for .NET in any .NET language. One of the tasks you'll need to perform as part of the design process is providing a bitmap to be used in the Visual Studio .NET Toolbox. The way you do this is by specifying a value for the ToolboxBitmapAttribute attribute:

```
[ToolboxBitmap(typeof(Button))]
public class ACustomControl : UserControl
```

When you're designing a form and you've added this control to the project, Visual Studio .NET will read the attributes of the class (using the System.Reflection namespace, discussed later in this chapter) and, in this case, use the bitmap assigned to the Button control to represent the custom control.

This code snippet demonstrates two other points that apply to both intrinsic attributes and custom attributes. First, an attribute can have parameters. Second, you can omit the Attribute portion of the attribute name when using the attribute in code. The .NET Framework will handle the attribute correctly either way.

The .NET Framework includes hundreds of intrinsic attributes. Most of them are specialized, so we won't try to provide a full list here. Instead, you'll look at the System.Attribute class and then see a couple of the most commonly used intrinsic attributes.

UNDERSTANDING THE *SYSTEM.ATTRIBUTE* CLASS

All attributes (both intrinsic and custom) inherit either directly or indirectly from the System.Attribute class. This class is an abstract class that defines the minimum interface that the CLR expects from an attribute. Table 17.1 shows the public Attribute property.

TABLE 17.1: Attribute PROPERTY

PROPERTY	TYPE	DESCRIPTION
TypeId	Object	When implemented in a derived class, returns a unique identifier for the Attribute

Table 17.2 shows the public Attribute methods.

TABLE 17.2: Attribute METHODS

METHOD	STATIC?	DESCRIPTION
GetCustomAttribute()	Yes	Returns a particular custom attribute of a specified type from a specified class
GetCustomAttributes()	Yes	Returns an array of custom attributes of a specified class
IsDefaultAttribute()	No	Indicates whether the value of this instance is the default value for the derived class
IsDefined()	Yes	Determines whether a particular custom attribute has been applied to a specified class
Match()	No	Determines whether one attribute equals another

As you can see, there isn't much to the `Attribute` class itself. This class merely provides a template into which you can add your own functionality. You'll see how to do that a bit later in the chapter in the "Using Custom Attributes" section.

USING THE *OBSOLETE* ATTRIBUTE

Some attributes are so useful that they're defined as part of the C# language itself. One of these is the `Obsolete` attribute. The `Obsolete` keyword in C# is an alias for the `System.ObsoleteAttribute` attribute. The purpose of this attribute is to help you identify obsolete bits of code and their preferred replacements. Listing 17.1 shows how you might use the `Obsolete` attribute in code.

LISTING 17.1: USING THE `Obsolete` ATTRIBUTE

```
/*
    Example17_1.cs illustrates use of the Obsolete attribute
*/

using System;

class Example17_1
{

    // warn the user that Method1 is obsolete
    [Obsolete("Method1 has been replaced by NewMethod1", false)]
    public static int Method1()
    {
        return 1;
    }

    // throw an error if the user tries to use Method2
    [Obsolete("Method2 has been replaced by NewMethod2", true)]
```

```
public static int Method2()
{
    return 2;
}

public static void Main()
{

    Console.WriteLine(Method1());
    Console.WriteLine(Method2());

}

}
```

The Obsolete attribute takes two parameters. The first is a string value that the attribute should return at run-time. The second is a Boolean value that is true to treat the use of this item as an error or false to treat it as a warning. If you try to compile this example, you'll receive this output:

```
Microsoft (R) Visual C# .NET Compiler version 7.00.9466
for Microsoft (R) .NET Framework version 1.0.3705
Copyright (C) Microsoft Corporation 2001. All rights reserved.

Example17_1.cs(29,21): warning CS0618: 'Example15_10.Method1()' is obsolete:
    'Method1 has been replaced by NewMethod1'
Example17_1.cs(30,21): error CS0619: 'Example15_10.Method2()' is obsolete:
    'Method2 has been replaced by NewMethod2'
```

The Obsolete attribute will be of great use to you if you're building shared libraries. No matter how much thought you put into the interface of your classes, you will probably decide that some things can be improved the next time you revise the code. By using the Obsolete attribute, you can let users of your library know automatically when they can use your library in a new way. The presence of the human-readable string as a parameter to the attribute gives you an easy way to provide additional guidance to the user. The Obsolete attribute thus enables you to infuse new functionality into a library without the DLL hell pitfalls of introducing incompatibilities with previous versions.

USING THE *CONDITIONAL* ATTRIBUTE

Another attribute that's useful enough to have become a part of the C# language is the Conditional attribute (which is an alias for the System.Diagnostics.ConditionalAttribute attribute). The Conditional keyword gives you an attribute-oriented way to perform conditional compilation. You can use this attribute with any method contained in a class or struct declaration that has a return type of void. Listing 17.2 shows an example of using the Conditional attribute.

LISTING 17.2: USING THE `Conditional` ATTRIBUTE

```
/*
  Example17_2.cs illustrates use of the Conditional attribute
*/

#define USE_METHOD_1

using System;
using System.Diagnostics;

class Example17_2
{

    // use conditional compilation with Method1
    [Conditional("USE_METHOD_1")]
    public static void Method1()
    {
        Console.WriteLine("In Method 1");
    }

    public static void Main()
    {

        Console.WriteLine("In Main");
        Method1();

    }

}
```

The output from this program is as follows:

```
In Main
In Method 1
```

If you remove the definition of the USE_METHOD_1 symbol and recompile the program, the output is as follows:

```
In Main
```

The Conditional attribute doesn't add anything to the compilation process that can't be handled with the #if…#endif preprocessor directive. But it does add important flexibility that the preprocessor directive lacks: You can use reflection from other code to determine the value of the Conditional attribute. This makes it easier to write tools that are aware of conditional compilation.

Using Custom Attributes

Intrinsic attributes are useful, but for the most part they have specific uses. One of the nice things about the .NET Framework is that when you need an attribute for some purpose that the .NET designers didn't contemplate, you can create your own. In this section, you'll see how to create custom attributes and (just as importantly) how to interrogate your own code at run-time to find the value of such attributes.

UNDERSTANDING ATTRIBUTE SYNTAX

Before working with custom attributes, you should understand a bit more about the syntax involved in actually using attributes. The simplest possible use of an attribute is to specify the attribute name in square brackets before the entity to which it applies. For instance, you can use the `DebuggerStepThrough-Attribute` to indicate a class where the debugger should not stop:

```
[DebuggerStepThroughAttribute]
class DontStopHereClass
```

Most attributes have one or more parameters. Attribute parameters can be either positional or named. The parameters of the `ObsoleteAttribute` attribute, for instance, are positional. You must specify a string value to display and a Boolean value that indicated whether to throw an error or a warning, in precisely that order. On the other hand, the `DllImportAttribute` attribute, which declares a Win32 API call from within the .NET Framework, uses a single positional parameter (the name of the file containing the API) and numerous named parameters. You can specify the named parameters in any order. One valid use of `DllImportAttribute` would be this:

```
[DllImport("user32.dll", EntryPoint="MessageBox")]
```

You can apply more than one attribute to a single entity. In that case, you can place both attributes within a single set of brackets or use two sets of brackets. The two forms are equivalent to the compiler. For example, this is a valid use of attributes:

```
[Obsolete("Method1 has been replaced by NewMethod1", false)]
[Conditional("USE_METHOD_1")]
public static void Method1()
```

And this form is equally valid:

```
[Obsolete("Method1 has been replaced by NewMethod1", false),
 Conditional("USE_METHOD_1")]
public static void Method1()
```

Finally, you can apply some attributes more than once to a single entity. The `Conditional` attribute is such a multiuse attribute:

```
[Conditional("USE_METHOD_1"),
 Conditional("DEBUG")]
public static void Method1()
```

CREATING CUSTOM ATTRIBUTES

To create a custom attribute, you define a class that derives from System.Attribute. Listing 17.3 shows an example of creating a custom attribute.

TIP   *Any parameters to the constructor of a custom attribute class will become the mandatory positional parameters of the attribute. Public fields and public writeable properties of the class will become the optional named parameters of the attribute.*

LISTING 17.3: CREATING A CUSTOM ATTRIBUTE

```
/*
  Example17_3.cs shows how to create a custom attribute
*/

using System;

// declare an attribute named UnitTest
// UnitTest.Written is either true or false
public class UnitTest : Attribute
{
    bool bWritten;

    public bool Written()
    {
        return bWritten;
    }

    public UnitTest(bool Written)
    {
        bWritten = Written;
    }
}

// apply the UnitTest attribute to two classes
[UnitTest(true)]
public class Class1
{
}

[UnitTest(false)]
public class Class2
{
}

class Example17_3
{
```

```
    public static void Main()
    {

        UnitTest u;

        // retrieve and display the UnitTest attributes of the classes
        Console.Write("Class1 UnitTest attribute: ");
        u = (UnitTest) Attribute.GetCustomAttribute(
            typeof(Class1), typeof(UnitTest));
        Console.WriteLine(u.Written());
        Console.Write("Class2 UnitTest attribute: ");
        u = (UnitTest) Attribute.GetCustomAttribute(
            typeof(Class2), typeof(UnitTest));
        Console.WriteLine(u.Written());

    }

}
```

The output from this program is as follows:

```
Class1 UnitTest attribute:True
Class2 UnitTest attribute:False
```

If you've never worked with a language that included run-time code-inspection facilities, you may find this confusing. It's worth thinking about this code step-by-step:

1. The UnitTest class is declared as being derived from the Attribute class. This makes UnitTest eligible to be used as an attribute on other entities in the code. The UnitTest constructor requires a single Boolean value. The UnitTest class has a Written method that simply returns the value of its internal bWritten variable.

2. Because UnitTest derives from Attribute, it can be applied as an attribute to the Class1 and Class2 classes. The Boolean values in the lines using UnitTest get passed to the UnitTest constructor.

3. At run-time, the code uses the static Attribute.GetCustomAttribute method to retrieve the information in these attributes. The GetCustomAttribute method takes two types as parameters. The first is the type to inspect, and the second is the type of attribute for which to look. No matter what type of attribute you're looking for, though, the GetCustomAttribute method returns an Attribute object. The code immediately casts this back to a UnitTest object.

4. Given a UnitTest object, you can use Console.WriteLine to write the value of its Written property to the console.

The values of attributes within a program are stored in the Microsoft Intermediate Language (MSIL) for that program. Figure 17.1 shows a portion of the Example17_3.exe program open in ILDasm. You can clearly see the name and value of the UnitTest attribute.

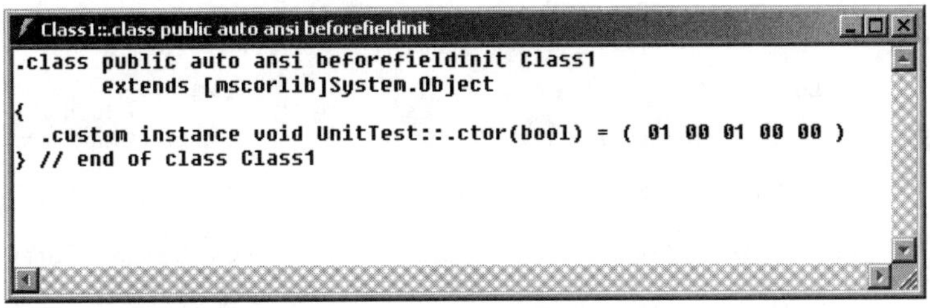

FIGURE 17.1

Viewing a custom
attribute with
ILDasm

```
Class1::.class public auto ansi beforefieldinit               _ □ x

.class public auto ansi beforefieldinit Class1
        extends [mscorlib]System.Object
{
    .custom instance void UnitTest::.ctor(bool) = ( 01 00 01 00 00 )
} // end of class Class1
```

TIP *Because the attribute values are in the MSIL, they're available to any application that can read the MSIL structure. You can do this with the* System.Reflection *classes. This makes it easy to build tools that operate on attributes. For example, it would be fairly easy to build an application that could scan .NET programs and determine which, if any, had classes with the* UnitTest *attribute's* Written *property set to* false.

LIMITING ATTRIBUTE USAGE

By default, you can apply a custom attribute to any entity in your code. For example, the UnitTest attribute (as defined in Listing 17.3) can be applied to a class, a method, a return value, and so on. You may want to limit your custom attributes to appearing only on certain types of entities. You can use the AttributeUsage attribute to control to which entities a particular custom attribute can be applied. The AttributeUsage attribute takes up to three parameters:

♦ A positional parameter that specifies the valid targets for this attribute. This parameter can be any combination of the values listed in Table 17.3. The default value of this parameter is ApplicationTargets.All.

♦ A bool parameter named allowmultiple. If this parameter is set to true, then the attribute is multiuse. The default value of this parameter is false.

♦ A bool parameter named inherited. If this parameter is set to true, then the value of the attribute is inherited by derived classes. The default value of this parameter is false.

TABLE 17.3: AttributeTargets VALUES

VALUE	TARGET
AttributeTargets.All	Can be applied to any entity in the application
AttributeTargets.Assembly	Can be applied to an assembly
AttributeTargets.Class	Can be applied to a class
AttributeTargets.Constructor	Can be applied to a constructor
AttributeTargets.Delegate	Can be applied to a delegate
AttributeTargets.Enum	Can be applied to an enumeration

Continued on next page

TABLE 17.3: AttributeTargets VALUES *(continued)*

VALUE	TARGET
AttributeTargets.Event	Can be applied to an event
AttributeTargets.Field	Can be applied to a field
AttributeTargets.Interface	Can be applied to an interface
AttributeTargets.Method	Can be applied to a method
AttributeTargets.Module	Can be applied to a module within an assembly
AttributeTargets.Parameter	Can be applied to a parameter
AttributeTargets.Property	Can be applied to a property
AttributeTargets.ReturnValue	Can be applied to a return value
AttributeTargets.Struct	Can be applied to a structure

You can combine as many constants as you like from this enumeration. For example, you could define the UnitTest attribute to apply only to classes and structures this way:

```
// declare an attribute named UnitTest
// UnitTest.Written is either true or false
[AttributeUsage(AttributeTargets.Class |
 AttributeTargets.Struct)]
public class UnitTest : Attribute
{
    bool bWritten;

    public bool Written()
    {
        return bWritten;
    }

    public UnitTest(bool Written)
    {
        bWritten = Written;
    }
}
```

Any attempt to apply this attribute to anything other than a class or a struct will raise a run-time error.

RETRIEVING ATTRIBUTE VALUES AT RUN-TIME

There are two ways for your code to retrieve attribute values at run-time. First, you can call the Get-CustomAttribute static method of the Attribute class. This method takes as its parameters the type to inspect and the attribute type to return. It returns an `Attribute` object, which you can then cast back to the type you want. You saw this method used in Listing 17.3:

```
u = (UnitTest) Attribute.GetCustomAttribute(
    typeof(Class1), typeof(UnitTest));
```

WARNING   *Remember that you specify a type, not an object, when you want to retrieve an attribute. Attributes are applied at design-time to types. It doesn't make any sense to talk about the attributes of an object, which is a run-time instance of a type.*

The second method of retrieving attributes is to use the `GetCustomAttributes` static method of the `Attribute` class. Listing 17.4 shows this technique in action.

LISTING 17.4: RETRIEVING ATTRIBUTES WITH `GetCustomAttribute`

```
/*
  Example17_4.cs illustrates the GetCustomAttributes method
*/

using System;

// declare an attribute named UnitTest
// UnitTest.Written is either true or false
public class UnitTest : Attribute
{
    bool bWritten;

    public bool Written()
    {
        return bWritten;
    }

    public UnitTest(bool Written)
    {
        bWritten = Written;
    }
}


// declare another attribute named LifeCycle
// LifeCycle.Stage returns a string
public class LifeCycle : Attribute
{
    string sStage;

    public string Stage()
    {
        return sStage;
    }
}
```

```
        public LifeCycle(string Stage)
        {
            sStage = Stage;
        }
    }

// apply the attributes to a class
[UnitTest(true)]
[LifeCycle("Coding")]
public class Class1
{
}

class Example17_4
{

    public static void Main()
    {

        // retrieve all attributes of Class1
        Console.WriteLine("Class1 attributes: ");
        object[] aAttributes = Attribute.GetCustomAttributes(
            typeof(Class1));
        foreach (object attr in aAttributes)
        {
            Console.WriteLine(attr);
        }

    }

}
```

The output from this program is as follows:

```
Class1 attributes:
UnitTest
LifeCycle
```

The GetCustomAttributes method returns an array containing all of the attributes of the specified type. If you're not sure which attributes apply to a particular type, you can iterate through this array. Then you can use GetCustomAttribute to return the details of any particular attribute that you want.

Discovering Types at Run-Time

Attributes are a particular example of a more general area of .NET programming: *reflection*. Reflection is the means by which you can discover information about an assembly and the types that it contains at run-time. Reflection encompasses more than just returning attribute values. You can easily discover the implementation details of a constructor, the data type of any property, or the return type of any method, at run-time. Reflection is most useful if you want to write tools that work with .NET assemblies, but it can also be used to enable extremely late binding, where the type you're working with isn't known when you're writing the code.

In the following sections you'll see some of the power of the System.Reflection namespace, which contains the classes that enable reflection.

Building a Run-Time Library

One way to learn about reflection is simply to use it to inspect existing code. You can, for example, use reflection to list all of the classes implemented in the .NET Framework libraries. Being able to exhaustively explore code is useful to people who are writing object browsers and other developer tools, but less so for those writing application programs. Instead, you'll see how you can use reflection to add run-time flexibility to your code. With the right coding, you can actually change the behavior of your code after it has been shipped by installing new libraries.

Suppose, for example, that you're shipping an application that depends on random numbers for part of its operation. You've decided to ship a relatively low-quality randomizer in the first version of the application so that you can get it to market quickly. But you'd like to be able to use a higher-quality randomizer later. How can you arrange your code so that the randomizer is a pluggable component, without having fully designed its interface?

In this section, you'll build three library assemblies with code to reflect over. One of these libraries contains custom attributes named RandomSupplier and RandomMethod. The other two libraries contain classes marked with these attributes. Listing 17.5 shows the definition for the RandomSupplier attribute and the RandomMethod attribute.

LISTING 17.5: DEFINING A PAIR OF CUSTOM ATTRIBUTES

```
/*
   Example17_5a compiles into a library defining the RamdomSupplier attribute
   and the RandomMethod attribute
*/

using System;

// declare an attribute named RandomSupplier
[AttributeUsage(AttributeTargets.Class)]
public class RandomSupplier : Attribute
{
    public RandomSupplier()
    {
        // doesn't have to do anything
        // we just use this attribute to mark selected methods
    }
}
```

```
// declare an attribute named RandomMethod
[AttributeUsage(AttributeTargets.Method )]
public class RandomMethod : Attribute
{
    public RandomMethod()
    {
        // doesn't have to do anything
        // we just use this attribute to mark selected methods
    }
}
```

The RandomSupplier attribute is simple. It has no properties, either positional or named. Its purpose is just to supply a marker that you can use to indicate classes that supply random numbers. Similarly, the RandomMethod attribute is there to mark the methods within those classes that supply the random numbers. To compile this code into a library assembly, use this command line:

```
csc /out:Example17_5a.dll /t:library Example17_5a.cs
```

NOTE   *For more information on the options for compiling assemblies, refer to Chapter 16, "Assemblies."*

The next step is to build two different library assemblies, each of which contains a class marked with the RandomSupplier attribute, which in turn contains a method marked with the RandomMethod attribute. Listing 17.6 shows the source code for the first of these libraries.

LISTING 17.6: DEFINING A CLASS WITH THE RandomSupplier AND RandomMethod ATTRIBUTES

```
/*
  Example17_5b implements one class to supply random numbers
*/

// flag the class as a random supplier
[RandomSupplier]
public class OriginalRandom
{
    [RandomMethod]
    public int GetRandom()
    {
        return 5;
    }
}
```

To compile this code into a library assembly, use this command line:

```
csc /out:Example17_5b.dll /t:library /r:Example17_5a.dll Example17_5b.cs
```

Remember, the /r switch tells the compiler which library to use as a reference to resolve external symbols. If you accidentally omit that switch, then the RandomSupplier and RandomMethod attributes won't be defined.

NOTE *You might think you could omit marking the method. After all, if the class just contains a single method, can't you just assume that any method you can find is the method that returns random numbers? But in fact the class does not contain just a single method. Like all other classes, this one ultimately derives from* System.Object, *meaning that it will contain an* Equals *method, a* GetHashCode *method, and all of the other methods inherited from* System.Object.

Finally, Listing 17.7 shows a second source code file that also defines a class marked with the RandomSupplier attribute and a method marked with the RandomMethod attribute.

LISTING 17.7: DEFINING A SECOND CLASS WITH THE RandomSupplier ATTRIBUTE

```
/*
  Example17_5c implements one class to supply random numbers
*/

using System;

// flag the class as a random supplier
[RandomSupplier]
public class NewRandom
{
    [RandomMethod]
    public int ImprovedRandom()
    {
        Random r = new Random();
        return r.Next(1, 100);
    }
}

// this class has nothing to do with random numbers
public class AnotherClass
{
    public int NotRandom()
    {
        return 1;
    }
}
```

Again, to compile this file into a library assembly you need to use the /r switch:

```
csc /out:Example17_5c.dll /t:library /r:Example17_5a.dll Example17_5c.cs
```

Note that the Example17_5c assembly also contains a second class (named AnotherClass) that is *not* flagged with the RandomSupplier attribute.

Discovering Type Information

Now that you've created some assemblies to examine, you can finally see how reflection works. Listing 17.8 shows code to find classes marked with the RandomSupplier attribute.

LISTING 17.8: USING REFLECTION TO FIND CLASSES MARKED WITH THE RandomSupplier ATTRIBUTE

```
/*
  Example17_5d illustrates runtime type discovery
*/

using System;
using System.Reflection;

class Example17_5d
{

    public static void Main(string[] args)
    {

        RandomSupplier rs;
        RandomMethod rm;

        // iterate over all command-line arguments
        foreach(string s in args)
        {
            Assembly a = Assembly.LoadFrom(s);

            // Look through all the types in the assembly
            foreach(Type t in a.GetTypes())
            {
                rs = (RandomSupplier) Attribute.GetCustomAttribute(
                 t, typeof(RandomSupplier));
                if(rs != null)
                {
                    Console.WriteLine("Found RandomSupplier class {0} in {1}",
                     t, s);
                    foreach(MethodInfo m in t.GetMethods())
                    {
                        rm = (RandomMethod) Attribute.GetCustomAttribute(
                         m, typeof(RandomMethod));
                        if(rm != null)
                        {
                            Console.WriteLine("Found RandomMethod method {0}"
                             , m.Name );
                        }
                    }
                }
            }
        }
```

```
            }
        }
    }
}
```

To compile this code, you need to remember to link in the definition of the `RandomSupplier` attribute:

```
csc /r:Example17_5a.dll Example17_5d.cs
```

To use this program, you enter a command line that specifies assemblies to examine, such as:

```
Example17_5d Example17_5b.dll Example17_5c.dll
```

The output from this program is as follows:

```
Found RandomSupplier class OriginalRandom in Example17_5b.dll
Found RandomMethod method GetRandom
Found RandomSupplier class NewRandom in Example17_5c.dll
Found RandomMethod method ImprovedRandom
```

As you can see, it properly found the two classes marked with the `RandomSupplier` attribute. Just as important, it rejected the third class that is lacking that attribute.

How does this code work? It uses three classes to look into the library assemblies. The first of these classes, `Assembly`, is a member of the `System.Reflection` namespace. It represents a single assembly and can be loaded from a disk file (as it was in this example). The second class, `Type`, is a member of the `System` namespace. As you'll see shortly, it has members to describe all the types that you'll find in a .NET program. The third class in this code is the `MethodInfo` class, which is another member of the `System.Reflection` namespace. As you can probably guess, this class supplies information about reflected methods. Let's look at the `Assembly` class first. Table 17.3 shows the public `Assembly` properties.

TABLE 17.3: ASSEMBLY PROPERTIES

PROPERTY	TYPE	DESCRIPTION
CodeBase	String	The original location of the `Assembly`
EntryPoint	MedthoInfo	The entry point of the `Assembly`
EscapedCodeBase	String	URI, including any escaped characters, for the location of the `Assembly`
Evidence	Evidence	The evidence (information for security policies) of this `Assembly`
FullName	String	The display name of the `Assembly`
GlobalAssemblyCache	Boolean	Indicates whether the `Assembly` was loaded from the GAC
Location	String	The loaded location of this `Assembly`

Table 17.4 shows the public Assembly methods.

TABLE 17.4: ASSEMBLY METHODS

METHOD	STATIC?	DESCRIPTION
CreateInstance()	No	Creates an instance of a type from this Assembly
CreateQualifiedName()	Yes	Creates the name of a type from this Assembly qualified by the Assembly name
GetAssembly()	Yes	Gets an Assembly containing a specified class
GetCallingAssembly()	Yes	Gets the Assembly that contains the method that invoked the current method
GetCustomAttributes()	No	Gets an array of custom attributes for this Assembly
GetEntryAssembly()	Yes	Gets the executable file that launched this code
GetExecutingAssembly()	Yes	Gets the Assembly containing the currently executing code
GetExportedTypes()	No	Gets all types exported from this Assembly
GetFile()	No	Gets a FileStream for a file included in the manifest of this Assembly
GetFiles()	No	Gets the files in the manifest of this Assembly
GetLoadedModules()	No	Gets all loaded modules that are a part of this Assembly
GetManifestResourceInfo()	No	Gets information about a specified resource
GetManifestResourceNames()	No	Gets the names of all resources in the Assembly
GetManifestResourceStream()	No	Loads the specified resource from the Assembly
GetModule()	No	Gets a specified module
GetModules()	No	Gets all modules that are a part of this Assembly
GetName()	No	Gets the AssemblyName for this Assembly
GetObjectData()	No	Gets serialization information for this Assembly
GetReferencedAssemblies()	No	Gets the names of Assembly objects referenced by this Assembly
GetSatelliteAssembly()	No	Gets a satellite (localized) Assembly
GetType()	No	Gets a specified type from the Assembly
GetTypes()	No	Gets all types defined in the Assembly
IsDefined()	No	Indicates whether a particular custom attribute is defined
Load()	Yes	Loads an Assembly by name
LoadFrom()	Yes	Loads an Assembly by filename
LoadModule()	No	Loads a module from this Assembly
LoadWithPartialName()	Yes	Loads an Assembly from the GAC using a partial name

The code in Listing 17.8 uses the assembly name passed in on the program's command line, together with the LoadFrom method of the Assembly class, to create an Assembly object that refers to the specified Assembly. This makes the contents of the Assembly available for reflection. The next step is to call the GetTypes method of the loaded Assembly. This returns an array of Type objects, one for every type defined in the Assembly.

To go further with this analysis, you'll need to take a look at the Type class. Although it's one of the key classes for reflection, the Type class is actually a member of the System namespace—perhaps because it's central to the operation of the entire .NET Framework. Table 17.5 shows the public Type fields.

TABLE 17.5: TYPE FIELDS

FIELD	TYPE	DESCRIPTION
Delimiter	Char	Separator for names in the namespace of the Type
EmptyTypes	Type	Returns an empty array of Type objects
FilterAttribute	MemberFilter	Filter applied to attributes to locate this Type
FilterName	MemberFilter	Filter applied to names to locate this Type
FilterNameIgnoreCase	MemberFilter	Case-insensitive filter applied to names to locate this Type
Missing	Object	A missing value in the Type information

Table 17.6 shows the public Type properties.

TABLE 17.6: TYPE PROPERTIES

PROPERTY	TYPE	DESCRIPTION
Assembly	Assembly	The Assembly containing this Type
AssemblyQualifiedName	String	Fully qualified name of the Type
Attributes	TypeAttributes	Attributes associated with the Type
BaseType	Type	Gets the Type from which the current Type directly inherits
DeclaringType	Type	Gets the class that declares this member
DefaultBinder	Binder	The default binder used by the system
FullName	String	The name of the Type qualified with the name of the containing namespace
GUID	Guid	The GUID associated with the Type
HasElementType	Boolean	Returns true if the Type is an array, a pointer, or is passed by reference

Continued on next page

Table 17.6: Type Properties *(continued)*

Property	Type	Description
IsAbstract	Boolean	Indicates whether the Type is abstract and must be overridden
IsAnsiClass	Boolean	Indicates whether the attribute AnsiClass is selected for the Type
IsArray	Boolean	Indicates whether the Type is an array
IsAutoClass	Boolean	Indicates whether the attribute AutoClass is selected for the Type
IsAutoLayout	Boolean	Indicates whether the attribute AutoLayout is selected for the Type
IsByRef	Boolean	Indicates whether the Type is passed by reference
IsClass	Boolean	Indicates whether the Type is a class
IsCOMObject	Boolean	Indicates whether the Type is a COM object
IsContextful	Boolean	Indicates whether the Type can be hosted in a context
IsEnum	Boolean	Indicates whether the Type is an enumeration
IsExplicitLayout	Boolean	Indicates whether the attribute ExplicitLayout is selected for the Type
IsImport	Boolean	Indicates whether the Type was imported from another class
IsInterface	Boolean	Indicates whether the Type is an interface
IsLayoutSequential	Boolean	Indicates whether the attribute SequentialLayout is selected for the Type
IsMarshalByRef	Boolean	Indicates whether the Type is marshaled by reference
IsNestedAssembly	Boolean	Indicates whether the Type is nested and only visible to classes that belong to its own assembly
IsNestedFamANDAssem	Boolean	Indicates whether the Type is nested and only visible to classes that belong to both its own family and its own assembly
IsNestedFamily	Boolean	Indicates whether the Type is nested and only visible to classes that belong to its own family
IsNestedFamORAssembly	Boolean	Indicates whether the Type is nested and only visible to classes that belong to either its own family or its own assembly
IsNestedPrivate	Boolean	Indicates whether the Type is nested and declared Private

Continued on next page

TABLE 17.6: TYPE PROPERTIES *(continued)*

PROPERTY	TYPE	DESCRIPTION
IsNestedPublic	Boolean	Indicates whether the Type is nested and declared Public
IsNotPublic	Boolean	Indicates whether the top-level Type containing this Type is declared Public
IsPointer	Boolean	Indicates whether the Type is a pointer
IsPrimitive	Boolean	Indicates whether the Type is one of the primitive types
IsPublic	Boolean	Indicates whether the Type is public
IsSealed	Boolean	Indicates whether the Type is sealed
IsSerializable	Boolean	Indicates whether the Type is serializable
IsSpecialName	Boolean	Indicates whether the name of the Type requires special handling
IsUnicodeClass	Boolean	Indicates whether the attribute UnicodeClass is selected for the Type
IsValueType	Boolean	Indicates whether the Type is a value type
MemberType	MemberTypes	Gets a bitmask indicating the member type
Module	Module	Gets the module in which the Type is defined
Name	String	Gets the name of the Type
Namespace	String	Gets the namespace of the Type
ReflectedType	Type	Gets the class object that was used to obtain this Type
TypeHandle	RuntimeTypeHandle	Gets the handle for the Type
TypeInitializer	ConstructorInfo	Gets the initializer for the Type
UnderlyingSystemType	Type	Returns the CLR type used for this Type

Table 17.7 shows the public Type methods.

TABLE 17.7: TYPE METHODS

METHOD	STATIC?	DESCRIPTION
Equals()	No	Determines whether two Types are the same
FindInterfaces()	No	Returns an array of Type objects representing the interfaces of the current Type

Continued on next page

TABLE 17.7: TYPE METHODS *(continued)*

METHOD	STATIC?	DESCRIPTION
FindMembers()	No	Returns an array of MemberInfo objects representing the members of the current Type
GetArrayRank()	No	Gets the number of dimensions in an array
GetConstructor()	No	Gets a constructor for the current Type
GetConstructors()	No	Gets all of the constructors for the current Type
GetCustomAttributes()	No	Gets the custom attributes defined on this Type
GetDefaultMembers()	No	Gets the default members for this Type
GetElementType()	No	Gets a Type representing elements in an array or other containing Type
GetEvent()	No	Gets a specific event for the current Type
GetEvents()	No	Gets all of the events for the current Type
GetField()	No	Gets a specific field of the current Type
GetFields()	No	Gets all of the fields of the current Type
GetHashCode()	No	Returns the hash code for this Type
GetInterface()	No	Gets a specific interface for the current Type
GetInterfaceMap()	No	Gets an interface mapping for the specified interface
GetInterfaces()	No	Gets all of the interfaces for the current Type
GetMember()	No	Gets a specified member of the current Type
GetMembers()	No	Gets all of the members of the current Type
GetMethod()	No	Gets a specific method of the current Type
GetMethods()	No	Gets all of the methods of the current Type
GetNestedType()	No	Gets a specific nested Type within the current Type
GetNestedTypes()	No	Gets all of the nested Types within the current Type
GetProperties()	No	Gets all of the properties of the current Type
GetProperty()	No	Gets a specific property of the current Type
GetType()	Yes	Gets a Type with a specified name
GetTypeArray()	Yes	Gets the Types of the objects in the specified array
GetTypeCode()	Yes	Gets the underlying type code of the specified Type
GetTypeFromCLSID()	Yes	Gets the Type associated with a specified class identifier

Continued on next page

TABLE 17.7: TYPE METHODS *(continued)*

METHOD	STATIC?	DESCRIPTION
GetTypeFromHandle()	Yes	Gets the Type associated with a specified type handle
GetTypeFromProgID()	Yes	Gets the Type associated with a specified program identifier
GetTypeHandle()	Yes	Gets the handle for the Type of a specified object
InvokeMember()	No	Invokes a specific member of the current Type
IsAssignableFrom()	No	Determines whether an instance of the current Type can be assigned from an instance of the specified Type
IsDefined()	No	Indicated whether a particular attribute is defined on this Type
IsInstanceOfType()	No	Indicates whether a specified object is an instance of this Type
IsSubclassOf()	No	Indicates whether this Type is a subclass of the specified Type
ToString()	No	Returns a string with the name of the current Type

It should be obvious that the code you've seen so far makes little use of the power of the Type class. If you refer to Listing 17.8, you'll see that you get Type objects back from the GetTypes method of the Assembly class. For each of these Type objects, the code attempts to retrieve the RandomSupplier attribute. If it's able to retrieve the attribute, then the code has found a class tagged with that attribute, and it outputs its name and the name of the containing library to the screen.

The next task is to find the method marked with the RandomMethod attribute. This makes use of the MethodInfo class. The GetMethods method of the Type class returns an array of MethodInfo objects. Table 17.8 shows the public MethodInfo properties.

NOTE *Many of these members are inherited from the* MemberInfo *class, which encompasses all members of a class, or the* MethodBase *class, which applies to both methods and constructors.*

TABLE 17.8: MethodInfo PROPERTIES

PROPERTY	TYPE	DESCRIPTION
Attributes	MethodAttributes	Gets the attributes associated with this method
CallingConvention	CallingConvention	Gets the calling convention for this method
DeclaringType	Type	Gets the class that declared this method
IsAbstract	Boolean	Indicates whether the method is abstract

Continued on next page

TABLE 17.8: MethodInfo PROPERTIES *(continued)*

PROPERTY	TYPE	DESCRIPTION
IsAssembly	Boolean	Indicates whether the method can be called by other classes in the same assembly
IsConstructor	Boolean	Indicates whether the method is a constructor
IsFamily	Boolean	Indicates whether this method can only be called by its own class and derived classes of that class
IsFamilyaAndAssembly	Boolean	Indicates whether the method can be called by family classes in the same assembly
IsFamilyOrAssembly	Boolean	Indicates whether the method can be called by family classes and by classes in the same assembly
IsFinal	Boolean	Indicates whether this method is final
IsHideBySig	Boolean	Indicates whether members with exactly the same signature are hidden in any derived class
IsPrivate	Boolean	Indicates whether the method is declared Private
IsPublic	Boolean	Indicates whether the method is declared Public
IsSpecialName	Boolean	Indicates whether the method has a special name
IsStatic	Boolean	Indicates whether the method is static
IsVirtual	Boolean	Indicates whether the method is virtual
MemberType	MemberTypes	Indicates that this member is a method
MethodHandle	RuntimeMethodHandle	Handle to the internal metadata for the method
Name	String	Name of the method
ReflectedType	Type	Gets the Type that was used to obtain this instance of MethodInfo
ReturnType		Gets the return type of the method
ReturnTypeCustomAttributes	ICustomAttributeProvider	Gets the custom attributes of the return type

Table 17.9 shows the public `MethodInfo` methods.

TABLE 17.9: MethodInfo METHODS

METHOD	STATIC?	DESCRIPTION
GetBaseDefinition()	No	Returns the MethodInfo object for the method from which this method derives
GetCustomAttributes()	No	Returns the custom attributes of the method
GetMethodImplementationFlags()	No	Returns a set of flags with information about the method
GetParameters()	No	Gets all of the parameters of the method
GetType()	No	Gets the type of the method
Invoke()	No	Invokes the method
IsDefined()	No	Indicates whether a specified attribute is defined on this method

With the `MethodInfo` object, the code can finally find the methods of interest. The `GetMethods` method of the `Type` object returns an array of `MethodInfo` objects, one for each method defined on the class that the `Type` object represents. The code then iterates through these methods, looking for one that has the `RandomMethod` custom attribute applied. When it finds one, it outputs the name to the console.

Late Binding via Reflection

Finding methods at run-time is interesting enough, but what about actually using them? After all, the point of this exercise was to plug in new methods for generating random numbers to an existing application. Using methods via reflection is the job of the `MethodInfo.Invoke` method (see Listing 17.9).

LISTING 17.9: USING MethodInfo.Invoke

```
/*
  Example17_6 illustrates runtime type invocation
*/

using System;
using System.Reflection;

class Example17_6
{

    public static void Main(string[] args)
    {
```

```csharp
RandomSupplier rs;
RandomMethod rm;

// iterate over all command-line arguments
foreach(string s in args)
{
    Assembly a = Assembly.LoadFrom(s);

    // Look through all the types in the assembly
    foreach(Type t in a.GetTypes())
    {
        rs = (RandomSupplier) Attribute.GetCustomAttribute(
            t, typeof(RandomSupplier));
        if(rs != null)
        {
            // find the method in this class. assume that
            // the class only contains a single method.
            // can't use GetMethod() because we don't know
            // what the method is named
            foreach(MethodInfo m in t.GetMethods())
            {
                rm = (RandomMethod) Attribute.GetCustomAttribute(
                 m, typeof(RandomMethod));
                if(rm != null)
                {
                    // create an instance of the class
                    Object o = Activator.CreateInstance(t);
                    // create an empty arguments array
                    Object[] aa = new Object[0];
                    // invoke the method
                    int i = (int) m.Invoke(o, aa);
                    Console.WriteLine("Class {0} in {1} returned {2}",
                        t, s, i);
                }
            }
        }
    }
}
```

Most of this code is identical to the code you saw in Listing 17.8. That makes sense; before you can execute a method via reflection, you need to find it. The remaining code creates an instance of the class that was located and then calls the appropriate method from that class. Creating the instance is the job of the `Activator` class, which is a member of the `System` namespace. The `Activator` has no properties and four methods, all of which are static (see Table 17.10).

TABLE 17.10: ACTIVATOR METHODS

METHOD	STATIC?	DESCRIPTION
`CreateComInstanceFrom()`	Yes	Creates an instance of a COM type by filename
`CreateInstance()`	Yes	Creates an instance of a specified type
`CreateInstanceFrom()`	Yes	Creates an instance of a specified type using a specified file
`GetObject()`	Yes	Creates a proxy for a currently running remote object, server-activated well-known object, or Web service

You need two things to invoke a method via reflection. The first is an instance of the class that contains the method; that's supplied by the call to `Activator.CreateInstance`. The second is an array of objects, each of which represents one of the parameters of the method. In this particular case, there are no parameters, but the array is still required. The code handles this by constructing an array of objects that contains zero members:

```
Object[] aa = new Object[0];
```

That may look odd, but it's legal C# code. The final step of the process is to call the `Invoke` method of the `MethodInfo` object that represents the method that you want to invoke, passing in the instance of the class and the array of arguments. The return value from the `Invoke` method will be the return value of the invoked method.

Here's the output of calling this code several times:

```
C:\>Example17_6 Example17_5b.dll
Class OriginalRandom in Example17_5b.dll returned 5

C:\>Example17_6 Example17_5c.dll
Class NewRandom in Example17_5c.dll returned 98
```

As you can see, this code has satisfied our original goal: to be able to call a method of an arbitrary class from a library, without knowing at the time you compiled the code anything more about the method than the name of a custom attribute that marks it.

What You Can Find with Reflection

The `System.Reflection` namespace contains a great many classes. That makes sense because it must be able to represent anything you can create in .NET code. These classes are broadly similar to the `Assembly` and `MethodInfo` classes you saw earlier in the chapter. Each contains properties to describe instances of the class and methods to return arrays and single instances of associated types. Rather than exhaustively list the members of these classes (you'll find them in the .NET Framework Class Library reference, of course), Table 17.11 lists the major classes and their purposes.

TABLE 17.11: IMPORTANT CLASSES FROM System.Reflection

CLASS	DESCRIPTION
Assembly	Represents a single assembly
ConstructorInfo	Represents a constructor for a class
EventInfo	Represents an event of a class
FieldInfo	Represents a field of a class
MemberInfo	Represents a single member (event, field, property, method, or type) within a class
MethodBase	Represents a method or a constructor
MethodInfo	Represents a method of a class
Module	Represents a single module of code
ParameterInfo	Represents a parameter of a member
PropertyInfo	Represents a property of a class

Creating Types at Run-Time

There's one use of reflection that we haven't covered yet. You can actually create new types at run-time. That's right: If the code you want doesn't exist yet, your program can write it. This is an extremely advanced use of the .NET Framework, and one that many developers will never need. It's worth knowing that it exists, though, if only because it's such an interesting technique. In this section you'll see an example of run-time type creation and learn how it works.

The classes in the System.Reflection.Emit namespace handle run-time type creation. Table 17.12 lists some of the classes from this namespace.

TABLE 17.12: IMPORTANT CLASSES FROM System.Reflection.Emit

CLASS	DESCRIPTION
AssemblyBuilder	Defines a new assembly
ConstructorBuilder	Defines a new constructor
EnumBuilder	Defines a new enumeration
EventBuilder	Defines a new event
FieldBuilder	Defines a new field
ILGenerator	Generates MSIL instructions
LocalBuilder	Defines a new local variable
MethodBuilder	Defines a new method
MethodRental	Provides a new body for an existing method

Continued on next page

TABLE 17.12: IMPORTANT CLASSES FROM `System.Reflection.Emit` *(continued)*

CLASS	DESCRIPTION
ModuleBuilder	Defines a new module
OpCodes	Provides field representations of MSIL instructions
ParameterBuilder	Defines a new parameter
PropertyBuilder	Defines a new property
TypeBuilder	Defines a new type

If you compare Table 17.12 with Table 17.11, you'll see there are many correspondences between the `System.Reflection` and `System.Reflection.Emit` namespaces. In general, `System.Reflection.Emit` can build anything that `System.Reflection` can discover. Listing 17.10 shows an example.

LISTING 17.10: USING `System.Reflection.Emit`

```
/*
  Example17_7 illustrates runtime type creation
*/

using System;
using System.Reflection;
using System.Reflection.Emit;

class Example17_7
{

    public static void Main()
    {
        // get the current appdomain
        AppDomain ad = AppDomain.CurrentDomain;

        // create a new dynamic assembly
        AssemblyName an = new AssemblyName();
        an.Name = "DynamicRandomAssembly";
        AssemblyBuilder ab = ad.DefineDynamicAssembly(
          an, AssemblyBuilderAccess.Run);

        // create a new module to hold code in the assembly
        ModuleBuilder mb = ab.DefineDynamicModule("RandomModule");

        // create a type in the module
        TypeBuilder tb = mb.DefineType(
          "DynamicRandomClass",TypeAttributes.Public);
```

```
// create a method of the type
Type returntype = typeof(int);
Type[] paramstype = new Type[0];
MethodBuilder methb=tb.DefineMethod("DynamicRandomMethod",
 MethodAttributes.Public, returntype, paramstype);

// generate the MSIL
ILGenerator gen = methb.GetILGenerator();
gen.Emit(OpCodes.Ldc_I4, 1);
gen.Emit(OpCodes.Ret);

// finish creating the type and make it available
Type t = tb.CreateType();

// create an instance of the new type
Object o = Activator.CreateInstance(t);
// create an empty arguments array
Object[] aa = new Object[0];
// get the method and invoke it
MethodInfo m = t.GetMethod("DynamicRandomMethod");
int i = (int) m.Invoke(o, aa);
Console.WriteLine("Method {0} in Class {1} returned {2}",
    m, t, i);

    }
}
```

The output of this program is as follows:

```
Method Int32 DynamicRandomMethod() in Class DynamicRandomClass returned 1
```

This is not all that impressive an output until you realize it came from code that didn't exist until you ran the program.

The code starts by retrieving the current *application domain*. An application domain is the unit of code isolation for the CLR. All assemblies execute within an application domain. As you can see, you can retrieve the current application domain by calling the static CurrentDomain method of the AppDomain object.

The next step is to create a new assembly. The AppDomain object supplies a DefineDynamicAssembly method to create dynamic assemblies. This method takes as parameters an AssemblyName object (which, not surprisingly, defines the name of the assembly) and a constant defining access modes for the assembly (in this case, that it will be run but not saved). This method returns an AssemblyBuilder object.

The code then calls the DefineDynamicModule method of the AssemblyBuilder to create a module, represented by a ModuleBuilder object. There's a pattern here, of course: The code starts with an AppDomain and then creates increasingly specific objects.

The next step is to use the `DefineType` method of the `ModuleBuilder` to create a new type, represented by a `TypeBuilder` object. The parameters of this method are the name of the new class and a set of flags indicating its attributes.

The `DefineMethod` method of the `TypeBuilder` object takes four parameters:

- The name of the new method

- The attributes of the new method

- A `Type` object that defines the return type of the new method

- An array of `Type` objects that define the parameter types of the new method

`DefineMethod` returns a `MethodBuilder` object. Now there's only one step left: writing the actual code. This requires you to supply MSIL instructions. How do you get those instructions? The easiest way is to compile the code you'd like to create and then use `ILDasm` to look at the resulting assembly. In this case, we wrote a very small C# program:

```csharp
using System;

public class DynamicRandomClass
{
    public int DynamicRandomMethod()
    {
        return 1;
    }
}
```

Then we compiled the program to a library, and used ILDasm to load the library. Figure 17.2 shows the results.

FIGURE 17.2

Inspecting MSIL instructions

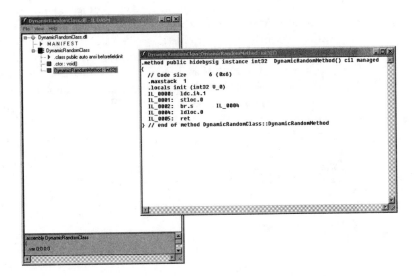

The MSIL that we're interested in is the section in the middle of the disassembly (the actual instructions, not the directives and signature information surrounding them). Here's the MSIL code that the C# compiler created for the DynamicRandomMethod method:

```
IL_0000:    ldc.i4.1
IL_0001:    stloc.0
IL_0002:    br.s        IL_0004
IL_0004:    ldloc.0
IL_0005:    ret
```

A step-by-step translation of this MSIL might be as follows:

1. Place a 4-byte integer with the value of 1 on top of the stack.

2. Store the value from the top of the stack into the first local variable.

3. Jump to instruction 4.

4. Load the value of the first local variable to the top of the stack.

5. Return the top of the stack to the calling program.

If you think about it, you can see that this code is doing too much work. The net result is to put the value of 1 on the top of the stack and then return it. So, in Listing 17.10, we've only generated the MSIL for those two steps:

```
// generate the MSIL
ILGenerator gen = methb.GetILGenerator();
gen.Emit(OpCodes.Ldc_I4, 1);
gen.Emit(OpCodes.Ret);
```

The ILGenerator object knows how to write MSIL instructions to a method. Getting an ILGenerator object from the GetILGenerator method of a MethodBuilder object gives you an ILGenerator to build the body of the method to which the MethodBuilder refers. Then it's just a matter of calling the Emit method of the ILGenerator object once for each instruction that you want to put into the body of the method. The OpCodes object has fields representing every possible MSIL instruction.

After all of the instructions have been written, the code calls the TypeBuilder.CreateType method. This method actually creates the type, together with the method that it contains (and any other members, if the code had built other members). With the type in hand, the code to instantiate it and call its method is the same as it would be for a type permanently stored in a library assembly.

If you find this code confusing, you're not alone. As mentioned earlier, creating types at run-time is an advanced use of the .NET Framework. If you just remember that the capability is there, you can look up the details when and if you need them.

Summary

The .NET Framework includes powerful capabilities for working with metadata—the data within .NET assemblies that describes the contents of those assemblies.

One important part of this metadata is the set of attributes that describe types, members, modules, and assemblies. The .NET Framework supplies a number of intrinsic attributes. You can also create your own custom attributes and retrieve their values at run-time from code.

Retrieving attribute values at run-time is one example of the more general technique of reflection. Reflection lets your .NET code find out almost anything about other .NET code. The classes in the `System.Reflection` namespace let you discover information about existing types and their members in detail. You can use these classes to enable late binding of code, even when you don't know the type names when you write the calling code.

The `System.Reflection.Emit` namespace rounds out the reflection picture. This namespace lets you create entirely new types at run-time and to specify the exact MSIL instructions that will be executed when you invoke their methods.

Chapter 18

Remoting

THE .NET FRAMEWORK IS designed to function in a world of distributed componentized software. You already know that classes defined in one file can be used by code in another file, but the distributed architecture of .NET goes much deeper than that. In this chapter, you'll learn about *remoting*, the generalized means by which objects in one application can communicate with objects in another application. Remoting can function between applications running on a single computer, between applications running on different computers on the same LAN, or even across the Internet.

We'll start by discussing application domains, which form a logical boundary for applications within .NET. Then you'll look at the concepts and code involved in marshaling an object through a proxy, which forms the basis for .NET remoting. *Contexts* provide a means for isolating objects from one another even within a single domain, and *channels* are the means for communication between applications. Finally, we'll put all of the pieces together to show how you can invoke methods on remote objects.

Featured in this chapter:

◆ Introducing Application Domains

◆ Understanding Marshaling with Proxies

◆ Understanding Contexts and Channels

◆ Using Remoting

Understanding Application Domains

Every application runs in a *process*. A process is the operating system's way of keeping applications separate. For example, if you're running Word and Excel on your computer, they're running in two separate processes. As you saw in Chapter 14, "Threads," a process can contain more than one thread of execution, each represented by a `Thread` object in the .NET Framework.

An *application domain* is an intermediate level of aggregation between the process and the thread, which is created and maintained by the Common Language Runtime (CLR). A process must contain at least one application domain, but it can contain more. An application domain must contain at least one thread, but it can contain more.

NOTE *Threads do not cross application domain boundaries. Each thread is associated with a particular application domain. The GetDomain method of the Thread object returns a reference to the application domain in which the thread is executing.*

By default the CLR creates a single application domain within the operating system process when you launch an application. All of your code executes within this single application domain. But if you like, you can create additional application domains within a single process. In this section, you'll see how to create an application domain and how to use an object in one application domain from another application domain, both within the same process.

Creating an Application Domain

The CLR creates a default application domain when you run an application. If you want to use additional application domains within that application, you'll need to create them yourself. Listing 18.1 shows how you can create an application domain.

LISTING 18.1: CREATING AN APPLICATION DOMAIN

```
/*
   Example18_1.cs illustrates creation of an application domain
*/

using System;

class Example18_1
{

    public static void Main()
    {

        AppDomain d = AppDomain.CreateDomain("NewDomain");
        Console.WriteLine(AppDomain.CurrentDomain.FriendlyName);
        Console.WriteLine(d.FriendlyName);

    }

}
```

The output from this application is as follows:

```
Example18_1.exe
NewDomain
```

As you can see, creating a new application domain is the job of the static CreateDomain method of the AppDomain object (which is a member of the System namespace). You can use this object to manage application domains in general. Table 18.1 shows the public AppDomain properties.

TABLE 18.1: AppDomain PROPERTIES

PROPERTY	TYPE	DESCRIPTION
BaseDirectory	String	Gets the base directory used to locate assemblies for this AppDomain
CurrentDomain	AppDomain	Static property that returns the AppDomain for the current Thread
DynamicDirectory	String	Gets the directory used to locate dynamic assemblies for this Appdomain
Evidence	Evidence	Gets the Evidence used for security policy for this AppDomain
FriendlyName	String	Gets the name of the AppDomain
RelativeSearchPath	String	Gets the path from the BaseDirectory to a directory to hold private assemblies
SetupInformation	AppDomainSetup	A class that contains configuration information for this AppDomain
ShadowCopyFiles	Boolean	Indicates whether assemblies loaded into this domain should be shadow copied

Table 18.2 shows the public AppDomain methods.

TABLE 18.2: AppDomain METHODS

METHOD	STATIC?	DESCRIPTION
AppendPrivatePath()	No	Adds a new directory to the private search path
ClearPrivatePath()	No	Resets the private search path to the empty string
ClearShadowCopyPath()	No	Resets the list of directories containing shadow-copied assemblies to the empty string
CreateComInstanceFrom()	No	Creates an instance of a COM type in the AppDomain
CreateDomain()	Yes	Creates a new AppDomain
CreateInstance()	No	Create an instance of a class in the AppDomain
CreateInstanceAndUnwrap()	No	Creates an instance of a class in the AppDomain and prepares it for remote marshaling
CreateInstanceFrom()	No	Creates an instance of a class from an assembly file in the AppDomain
CreateInstanceFromAndUnwrap()	No	Creates an instance of a class from an assembly file in the AppDomain and prepare it for remote marshaling

Continued on next page

TABLE 18.2: AppDomain METHODS *(continued)*

METHOD	STATIC?	DESCRIPTION
CreateObjRef()	No	Creates an object that can be used as a proxy
DefineDynamicAssembly()	No	Creates a new dynamic assembly in the AppDomain
DoCallback()	No	Executes code identified by a specific delegate object
ExecuteAssembly()	No	Executes an assembly in the AppDomain
GetAssemblies()	No	Gets the Assembly objects from this AppDomain
GetCurrentThreadID()	Yes	Gets the current Thread identifier
GetData()	No	Gets a data item stored in this AppDomain
GetLifetimeService()	No	Gets an object that controls the lifetime policy for this AppDomain
GetType()	No	Gets the type of the current instance
InitializeLifetimeService()	No	Gives the AppDomain an infinite lifetime
IsFinalizingForUnload()	No	Indicates whether this AppDomain is in the process of being unloaded
Load()	No	Loads an Assembly into the AppDomain
SetAppDomainPolicy()	No	Sets the security policy for this AppDomain
SetCachePath()	No	Sets a path for caching shadow copied assemblies
SetData()	No	Stores a data item in this AppDomain
SetDynamicBase()	No	Sets the base directory for dynamic assemblies
SetPrincipalPolicy()	No	Sets default authentication properties for threads in the AppDomain
SetShadowCopyFiles()	No	Turns on shadow copying
SetShadowCopyPath()	No	Specifies the folder for shadow copying
SetThreadPrincipal()	No	Sets a default Principal object that threads will bind to in this AppDomain
ToString()	No	Obtains a String representing the AppDomain
Unload()	No	Unloads the AppDomain

Using an Object in an Application Domain

By itself, a fresh application domain isn't very useful. To do anything with it, you'll need to load some code. As you saw in Table 18.2, there are a variety of methods to load things into an AppDomain object.

The one that you'll probably find most useful is `CreateInstance`, which can load an assembly and instantiate an object from that assembly in a single operation. Of course, before you can create an object, you need a class to instantiate. Listing 18.2 shows a simple class that we'll use for this purpose.

LISTING 18.2: CREATING A SIMPLE OBJECT

```
/*
   Example18_2.cs defines a simple object to create
*/

using System;

[Serializable]
public class SimpleObject
{

    public String ToUpper(String inString)
    {
        return(inString.ToUpper());
    }

}
```

NOTE *You'll see the reason that we've marked this class with the* `Serializable` *attribute in the section "Understanding Marshaling with Proxies" later in the chapter.*

To compile this example into a library assembly, use this command line:

```
csc /t:library /out:Example18_2.dll Example18_2.cs
```

Now that you have an object to use, you can see the mechanics of using it in another application domain (see Listing 18.3).

LISTING 18.3: USING AN OBJECT IN AN APPLICATION DOMAIN

```
/*
   Example18_3.cs uses an object in another application domain
*/

using System;
using System.Runtime.Remoting;
using System.Reflection;

class Example18_3
{
```

```
public static void Main()
{

    // create a new appdomain
    AppDomain d = AppDomain.CreateDomain("NewDomain");

    // load an instance of the System.Rand object
    ObjectHandle hobj = d.CreateInstance("Example18_2",
    "SimpleObject");
    // use a local variable to access the object
    SimpleObject so = (SimpleObject) hobj.Unwrap();
    Console.WriteLine(so.ToUpper("make this uppercase"));
}

}
```

After you've created an application domain, you can create an object in that application domain by calling the CreateInstance method. This method has several overloaded forms. The simplest form (which is the one we're using here) takes an assembly name and an object name and creates an instance of that object from that assembly. The CreateInstance method returns an *object handle* (a pointer through which you can access the object), which is itself an instance of the ObjectHandle class. You can *unwrap* an object handle by calling its Unwrap method to get back the original object.

Because this code uses the SimpleObject class, you need to compile it with a reference to the library that contains that class:

```
csc /r:Example18_2.dll Example18_3.cs
```

The output of this program is as follows:

```
MAKE THIS UPPERCASE
```

As you can see, after unwrapping the object handle you can use any of the native methods of the object that's in the other application domain.

Unloading an Application Domain

When you're done working with an application domain, you can unload it, destroying all of the objects it contains (see Listing 18.4).

LISTING 18.4: UNLOADING AN APPLICATION DOMAIN

```
/*
  Example18_4.cs illustrates unloading an application domain
*/

using System;
using System.Runtime.Remoting;
using System.Reflection;
```

```
class Example18_4
{

    public static void Main()
    {

        // create a new appdomain
        AppDomain d = AppDomain.CreateDomain("NewDomain");

        // load an instance of the SimpleObject class
        ObjectHandle hobj = d.CreateInstance("Example18_2", "SimpleObject");
        // use a local variable to access the object
        SimpleObject so = (SimpleObject) hobj.Unwrap();
        Console.WriteLine(so.ToUpper("make this uppercase"));

        // unload the application domain
        AppDomain.Unload(d);
        Console.WriteLine(so.ToUpper("make this uppercase"));

    }

}
```

Because this code uses the `SimpleObject` class, you need to compile it with a reference to the library that contains that class:

```
csc /r:Example18_2.dll Example18_4.cs
```

The output of this program is as follows:

```
MAKE THIS UPPERCASE
MAKE THIS UPPERCASE
```

If you've been following the discussion to this point, you may be surprised by that output. It seems that the instance of the `SimpleObject` object was able to execute its `ToUpper` method even after the application domain in which it was created was destroyed!

To understand how this can be, you need to understand the difference between marshaling an object by value and marshaling it by reference. That's the subject of the next section of the chapter.

Understanding Marshaling with Proxies

Marshaling is the process of preparing an object to cross the boundary between two application domains. There's a great deal of "plumbing" involved in this process, but fortunately the .NET Framework hides most of this complexity from you. However, it's imperative that you understand the difference between marshaling by value and marshaling by reference.

Marshaling by Value

When you marshal an object by value, you're making an exact copy of the object. The .NET Framework records all the type information about the object in its original application domain and sends that information to the calling application domain. There the information is used to reconstitute an exact copy of the original object.

The simplest way to cause an object to be marshaled by value is to mark the class with the `Serializable` attribute. As you'll recall from Chapter 15, "Streams and Input/Output," serialization refers to the process of writing the information about an object to a backing store. In this case, the .NET Framework seamlessly handles the process of serializing the object, passing the store to the calling domain and deserializing the store into a new object when it's delivered.

You can also cause an object to be marshaled by value by implementing the `ISerializable` interface so that the object performs its own serialization.

Now you can understand the results of the code from Listing 18.4. This code uses the `SimpleObject` object from `Example18_2.cs`. If you refer back to Listing 18.2, you'll see this class is marked as serializable. So when you call the `CreateInstance` method to make an instance of the object and then unwrap the object handle, what you get is a copy of the object that was marshaled by value across the application domain boundary. When the code in Listing 18.4 unloads the second application domain, the `SimpleObject` object that it contains is destroyed, but the copy continues to exist and its methods can still be invoked.

Marshaling by Reference

By contrast, when you marshal an object by reference, you tell the .NET Framework to create a *proxy* object. The proxy object has the same interfaces as the original, but it doesn't do any actual work. Instead, it uses the communications infrastructure built into .NET to communicate with the original object. When you set a property on the proxy object, the change is made on the original object in its original application domain. When you call a method on the proxy object, it invokes the same method on the original object and returns the results back from the proxy to the calling code.

The simplest way to force a class to marshal by reference is to derive it from the `MarshalObjByRef` class. Listing 18.5 shows a sample class that will be marshaled by reference.

LISTING 18.5: DEFINING A CLASS TO MARSHAL BY REFERENCE

```
/*
  Example18_5.cs defines a simple object to create
*/

using System;

public class SimpleObject : MarshalByRefObject
{

    public String ToUpper(String inString)
    {
```

```
        return(inString.ToUpper());
    }

}
```

To compile this code into a library, use this command line:

```
csc /out:Example18_5.dll /t:library Example18_5.cs
```

Listing 18.6 shows how you might call this object from one application domain to another.

LISTING 18.6: MARSHALING AN OBJECT BY REFERENCE

```
/*
   Example18_6.cs illustrates unloading an application domain
*/

using System;
using System.Runtime.Remoting;
using System.Reflection;

class Example18_6
{

    public static void Main()
    {

        // create a new appdomain
        AppDomain d = AppDomain.CreateDomain("NewDomain");

        // load an instance of the SimpleObject class
        ObjectHandle hobj = d.CreateInstance("Example18_5", "SimpleObject");
        // use a local variable to access the object
        SimpleObject so = (SimpleObject) hobj.Unwrap();
        Console.WriteLine(so.ToUpper("make this uppercase"));

        // unload the application domain
        AppDomain.Unload(d);
        Console.WriteLine(so.ToUpper("make this uppercase"));

    }

}
```

To compile this code, you need to tell it where to find the `SimpleObject` class:

```
csc /r:Example18_5.dll Example18_6.cs
```

The output from this program is as follows:

```
MAKE THIS UPPERCASE

Unhandled Exception: System.AppDomainUnloadedException:
➡ The target application domain has been unloaded.

Server stack trace:
   at System.Threading.Thread.EnterContextInternal(Context ctx,
➡ Int32 id, Int32 appDomainID, ContextTransitionFrame& frame)
   at System.Runtime.Remoting.Channels.CrossAppDomainSink.
➡ DoTransitionDispatch(Byte[] reqStmBuff, SmuggledMethodCallMessage
➡ smuggledMcm, SmuggledMethodReturnMessage& smuggledMrm)
   at System.Runtime.Remoting.Channels.CrossAppDomainSink.
➡ SyncProcessMessage(IMessage reqMsg)

Exception rethrown at [0]:
   at System.Runtime.Remoting.Proxies.RealProxy.HandleReturnMessage(
➡ IMessage reqMsg, IMessage retMsg)
   at System.Runtime.Remoting.Proxies.RealProxy.PrivateInvoke(
➡ MessageData& msgData, Int32 type)
   at SimpleObject.ToUpper(String inString)
   at Example18_6.Main()
```

As you can see, the first call to the `SimpleObject.ToUpper` method succeeded, but the second call to the same method failed because the object was destroyed when its application domain was unloaded.

Understanding Contexts

Another issue complicates remoting: objects have a *context* in which they execute. You can think of a context as being a set of rules within an application domain. Every application domain has a default context, and for the most part every object executes within that default context. An application domain, however, can have more than one context.

For example, suppose that some objects in your application perform database transactions. When you call the `BeginTransaction` method of the `System.Data.SqlClient` object, for example, you're creating a new context within the application domain. Objects that enlist in the transaction execute in the new context.

Another case in which contexts are used is synchronization. When you apply the `Synchronization` attribute to an object so that multiple threads accessing the object take turns, this creates a new set of rules that in turn leads to a new context.

In the case of remoting, there are two contexts involved: the context of the calling code and the context of the object being called. Objects are either context-bound or context-agile. A context-bound object will only function within its own context; a context-agile object operates within the context of the calling code. You can create a context-bound object by deriving it from the `ContextBoundObject` class.

The following rules control marshaling and agility across application domains and contexts. These rules apply to objects that are entirely contained within a single application:

◆ By default, objects are not marshaled. They are context-agile within application domains, and do not cross application domains.

◆ Objects marked with the `Serializable` attribute are marshaled by value across application domains and are context-agile.

◆ Objects derived from `MarshalByRefObject` are marshaled by reference across application domains and are context-agile.

◆ Objects derived from `ContextBoundObject` are marshaled by reference across application domains and are context-bound.

Understanding Channels

So far, the examples in this chapter have crossed application domains, but they're not true remoting. *Remoting* refers specifically to calling an object from another process (either on the same machine or on a different machine). There's one more concept you need to understand before looking at full-blown remoting code: *channels*. A channel is a transport mechanism that moves messages between applications across remoting boundaries. Although the .NET Framework will take care of much of this "plumbing" for you, it's a process you can also customize and modify if you want.

In the .NET Framework, a channel is an object that implements the `IChannel` interface. This interface has two public properties:

◆ `ChannelName` is an arbitrary string that is the name of the channel.

◆ `ChannelPriority` is an integer indicating the priority of the channel when compared to other channels working with the same object. Higher numbers indicate a higher priority.

The .NET Framework supplies several classes that implement `IChannel`. The two that you're most likely to use for remoting are `HttpChannel` and `TcpChannel`.

The `HttpChannel` class transports messages between objects by formatting the messages using the Simple Object Access Protocol (SOAP) and transporting them with the Hypertext Transfer Protocol (HTTP). This provides you with a general-purpose remoting channel that requires a minimum amount of setup. One potential problem with the `HttpChannel` class is that it's not compatible with the Internet Explorer automatic configuration of proxy server settings. If you're using `HttpChannel` and your computer uses a proxy server, you must explicitly set the proxy information in Internet Explorer.

For more flexible remoting, you can use the `TcpChannel` class. The `TcpChannel` class transports messages by formatting the messages as a binary stream and transporting them using the TCP protocol.

TIP If you attempt to mismatch channel types (for example, by using a `TcpChannel` on the server and an `HttpChannel` on the client), you'll receive this error message: "The underlying connection was closed: An unexpected error occurred on a receive."

Channels work in conjunction with *sinks*. A sink is an object that can perform an operation on the message being transported. Sinks are organized into sink chains because one channel can contain multiple sinks. Each sink processes the message and then passes it on to the next sink. For example, a channel always contains a formatting sink that's responsible for translating from the original message format to the transport format or vice versa. You can also use sinks for functions such as logging, encryption, or filtering.

Using Remoting

Now it's time to see remoting in action. In this section, you'll see how to build a server that listens for client connections on an HTTP channel, and then you'll see how to call an object on that server remotely from a client. Server objects come in three variations:

◆ Server-activated singleton objects are directly controlled by the server, and only one instance of the object can exist at one time. All client requests are handled by this one instance.

◆ Server-activated SingleCall objects are directly controlled by the server, which creates a new instance to handle each call from the client.

◆ Client-activated objects are objects whose lifetime is controlled by the client (this is exactly how local client objects are controlled). With client-activated objects (as opposed to server-activated objects), the client maintains a permanent connection to the object for the life of the object.

Server-activated objects are sometimes called *well-known objects*.

For the remainder of the chapter, you'll work through the steps involved in creating a well-known singleton object on the server and then calling it from the client:

◆ Defining an interface

◆ Building the server

◆ Building the client

Defining an Interface

Rather than implement the server as a simple object (as earlier in the chapter with the SimpleObject class), for this example we'll define an interface first and then implement this interface in an object. The benefit of this approach is that the client object need only consume the interface, and so it will not need to be recompiled if the server implementation changes (so long as the server interface remains constant). If the client used the server object directly, then the definition of that object's class would need to be compiled into the client (otherwise the client couldn't declare a remote instance of the server object).

Listing 18.7 shows the definition of the interface for this example.

LISTING 18.7: DEFINING AN INTERFACE FOR A WELL-KNOWN SERVER OBJECT

```
/*
  Example18_7.cs defines an interface for a simple object
*/

using System;
```

```
public interface ISimpleObject
{

    String ToUpper(String inString);

}
```

This code defines an interface that exposes a single method. To compile this into a library that can be used by both the server and the client, use this command line:

```
csc /t:library Example18_7.cs
```

Building the Server

Listing 18.8 shows the code for a server that will provide an implementation of the ISimpleObject interface that can be invoked remotely.

LISTING 18.8: A SERVER FOR ISimpleObject

```
/*
  Example18_8.cs provides a server for a well-known singleton object
*/

using System;
using System.Runtime.Remoting;
using System.Runtime.Remoting.Channels;
using System.Runtime.Remoting.Channels.Http;

    // implementation of ISimpleObject
    public class SimpleObject : MarshalByRefObject, ISimpleObject
    {
        public String ToUpper(String inString)
        {
            return(inString.ToUpper());
        }
    }

class Example18_8
{

    public static void Main()
    {

        // create and register a channel
        HttpChannel hchan = new HttpChannel(54321);
        ChannelServices.RegisterChannel(hchan);
```

```
        // get the type that we're managing
        Type SimpleObjectType = Type.GetType("SimpleObject");

        // register this type and set up an endpoint
     RemotingConfiguration.RegisterWellKnownServiceType(SimpleObjectType,
           "SOEndPoint", WellKnownObjectMode.Singleton);

        // wait for user input to terminate the server
        Console.WriteLine("Press Enter to halt server");
        Console.ReadLine();
     }

   }
```

To compile this server, you need to link in the library that defines the interface:

```
csc /r:Example18_7.dll Example18_8.cs
```

The server code starts by defining a class, SimpleObject, which implements the ISimpleObject interface. It's this class that will be invoked by the client.

When you run the server, of course, execution starts with the Main procedure. The first thing that Main does is declare a new HttpChannel object. The constructor for HttpChannel takes as its parameter a port number on which this channel will listen. Generally, you should select a port number in the private port range from 49152 to 65536 to avoid any chance of conflict with other applications.

The next step is to register the channel, using the static RegisterChannel method of the Channel-Services class. The ChannelServices class is responsible for managing all transport channels on the computer. Its RegisterChannel method tells the remoting infrastructure to start accepting messages on that channel and to direct the messages to this server.

The last step of setting up the server is to call the RegisterWellKnownServiceType static method of the RemotingConfiguration class. This method tells the remoting infrastructure that this server can create objects of the specified type, and that this will be a singleton server. It also supplies a name for the endpoint that will process results for this object. On the server side, multiple applications can share a single channel. The endpoint name allows the remoting infrastructure to determine which server-side application will service a particular request.

The remainder of the code in the server application causes this application to remain in memory (and thus capable of creating objects) until you press a key.

TIP You will probably choose to implement a production server as a Windows Service so that you can manage it from the Services application and so that it can be started without a user logging on to the server computer.

Building the Client

Listing 18.9 shows the code for a client that can invoke the remote server object.

LISTING 18.9: INVOKING AN OBJECT VIA REMOTING

```csharp
/*
  Example18_9.cs uses an object via remoting
*/

using System;
using System.Runtime.Remoting;
using System.Runtime.Remoting.Channels;
using System.Runtime.Remoting.Channels.Http;

class Example18_3
{

    public static void Main()
    {

        // create and register an HttpChannel
        HttpChannel hchan = new HttpChannel(0);
        ChannelServices.RegisterChannel(hchan);

        // Get an object from the other end of the channel
        Object remoteObject =
          RemotingServices.Connect(typeof(ISimpleObject),
          "http://localhost:54321/SOEndPoint");

        // Cast it back to the shared interface
        ISimpleObject so = remoteObject as ISimpleObject;

        // and use the object
        Console.WriteLine(so.ToUpper("make this uppercase"));
    }

}
```

Once again, this code needs to be compiled with a reference to the library that contains the
ISimpleObject interface:

```
csc /r:Example18_7.dll Example18_9.cs
```

Just like the server, the client starts by declaring a channel for communications. Because the client
won't be listening on the channel, though, it doesn't need to register a port number.

The next step is the one that actually creates and returns the server object. The call to the Connect
static method of the RemotingServices class takes two parameters. The first is the type of the object
to get from the server. The second is the URL to use to get the object. The URL is made up of the
server name (the special name localhost means that the HTTP server and the client will be running
on the same computer), the port number where the HttpChannel object is listening, and the name of
the endpoint.

The `Connect` method returns a generic `Object` instance. The code then proceeds to cast this to the expected `ISimpleObject` interface. Once that's been done, as far as the local code is concerned the object functions just as if it had been created locally. And that, after all, is the entire point of remoting.

Testing the Code

The final step is to find out whether everything works. To do so, you can open two command prompts. In the first one, run the server application, `Example18_8`. You'll get this output:

```
Press Enter to halt server
```

That shows that the server has successfully initialized and is listening for client object requests. In the second command prompt, run the client application, `Example18_9`. You'll see this output:

```
MAKE THIS UPPERCASE
```

Although it doesn't look like much on screen, this is actually fairly amazing. It means that the client code sent a message encapsulated as SOAP over HTTP to the server. This message told the server to instantiate an object and return a proxy to the client. The client then called a method on the server object and transparently received the result, which it printed to the client's output. In most previous programming environments, this would have taken hundreds, perhaps thousands, of lines of code. With the .NET Framework providing the infrastructure, we were able to write the entire application in fewer than 100 lines of code, including blank lines.

Summary

In this chapter, you learned the basics of remoting. First, you saw application domains, which provide a boundary between different parts of the same application. You learned how to create and unload application domains, and you saw how to use code in one application domain to call an object located in another application domain.

You then learned the two methods available for marshaling: marshaling by value, which makes an exact copy of an object, and marshaling by reference, which returns a proxy that acts for the original object.

Contexts provide another subdivision of applications. A context is a set of rules within an application domain. Some objects are bound to their original context, and others are agile and move between contexts.

Channels provide the means of communication between objects across processes or even across machines. The .NET Framework implements the `IChannel` interface in the `HttpChannel` and `TcpChannel` objects.

Finally, you saw how to use .NET remoting to call an object in a server process from code in a client process.

Chapter 19

Security

THE .NET FRAMEWORK OFFERS extensive security features. Indeed, it sometimes seems as if Microsoft tried to build in every possible security feature, which can make it difficult to understand the .NET approach to security. Broadly speaking, there are two main security areas in .NET: code-access security and role-based security.

Code-access security focuses on the .NET source code. You can tell the .NET Framework about the permissions that your code needs to execute properly, and the .NET Framework will check for these permissions on the machine at run-time. Code-access security is very flexible, including the ability to define your own sets of necessary permissions. Also, administrators can use code-access security to make sure that undesired code never gets the chance to run on a system.

Role-based security, in contrast, focuses on the user rather than the code. Using role-based security allows you to provide (or deny) access to resources based on an identity provided by the user who is running the code.

The .NET Framework also provides support for securing data through encryption. You can use the `CryptoStream` class to plug encryption into the stream and backing store model that .NET uses for all input/output (I/O) operations.

Featured in this chapter:

- ◆ Understanding Code-Access security
- ◆ Understanding Role-Based Security
- ◆ Implementing Encryption

Using Code-Access Security

Code-access security controls the access that code itself has to resources. Code-access security revolves around the notion of permissions that can be granted or denied. In the following sections, you'll learn about permissions and the factors that determine whether they're granted. Code-access security is independent of the identity of the user who is running the code.

NOTE   In general, the .NET security system functions completely only for type-safe code. Type-safe code is code that can only access memory that it's supposed to access. You can run non-type-safe code in .NET, but only if you grant it permission to skip the verification step that would otherwise take place. All C# code is type-safe by design, so we won't explore the details of skipping verification.

Understanding Permissions

For example, the ability to read or write files requires the `FileIOPermission` on the part of your code. In general, your code can request that it be granted a particular permission or demand that its callers have a particular permission. The Common Language Runtime (CLR) decides, based on a variety of factors (including the origin of the code and the local security policy), whether a particular permission will be granted. If a piece of code is unable to obtain all of the permissions that it requires, then that piece of code won't execute. The security settings of the computer determine the maximum permissions that code can be granted, but code is allowed to request (and receive) fewer permissions than that maximum. Of course, the developer can use a `try/catch` block to decide whether code should still attempt to run if it can't get all of the permissions that it requests.

There are three distinct types of permissions in the .NET Framework:

Code-Access Permissions   Code-access permissions represent access to a protected resource or the ability to perform a protected operation.

Identity Permissions   Identity permissions represent access based on credentials that are a part of the code itself, such as the identity of the code's publisher.

Role-Based Permissions   Role-based permissions represent access based on the user who is running the code.

For the most part, code-access security depends on code-access permissions, but we'll discuss all three types to give you an idea of the spectrum of available permissions.

All of the code-access permissions are classes that derive from the `System.Security.CodeAccess-Permission` class. Individual code-access permission classes are not contained within the `System.Security` namespace. Rather, they're in the same namespaces as the objects to which they're related. For example, the `OleDbPermission` class is a member of the `System.Data.OleDb` class. Table 19.1 lists the available code-access permission classes.

TABLE 19.1: CODE-ACCESS PERMISSION CLASSES

CLASS	CONTROLS ACCESS TO...
DirectoryServicesPermission	The System.DirectoryServices namespace
DnsPermission	Domain Name System (DNS)
EnvironmentPermission	Environment variables
EventLogPermission	The Windows event log
FileDialogPermission	Files selected from the Open dialog box

Continued on next page

TABLE 19.1: CODE-ACCESS PERMISSION CLASSES *(continued)*

CLASS	CONTROLS ACCESS TO...
FileIoPermission	Reading and writing files and directories
IsolatedStorageFilePermission	Private virtual file systems
IsolatedStoragePermission	Isolated storage
MessageQueuePermission	Message queuing via Microsoft Message Queue (MSMQ)
OleDbPermission	Data via the System.Data.OleDb namespace
PerformanceCounterPermission	Performance counters
PrintingPermission	Printers
ReflectionPermission	The reflection features of .NET
RegistryPermission	The Windows Registry
SecurityPermission	Unmanaged code
ServiceControllerPermission	Starting and stopping services
SocketPermission	Windows sockets
SqlClientPermission	Data via the System.Data.SqlClient namespace
UiPermission	The user interface
WebPermission	Making web connections

Identity permissions are also derived from the System.Security.CodeAccessPermissions class, but unlike code-access permissions, identity permissions are granted based on facts about the code. Although an application must request code-access permissions, identity permissions are automatically granted by the CLR based on a set of factors that are referred to as the *evidence* of the code. Table 19.2 lists the available identity permission classes.

TABLE 19.2: IDENTITY PERMISSION CLASSES

CLASS	REPRESENTS
PublisherIdentityPermission	The identity of the publisher, as determined by the code's digital signature.
SiteIdentityPermission	The website from which the code was downloaded.
StrongNameIdentityPermission	The strong name of the assembly.
URLIdentityPermission	The exact Uniform Resource Locator (URL) where the code originated.
ZoneIdentityPermission	The security zone where the code originated. You can view security zones on the Security tab of the Internet Explorer Options dialog box.

Finally, there is a single role-based permission class, `PrincipalPermission`. The class can determine whether a particular set of credentials for a user and a role match those required by a particular piece of code.

NOTE *If the permissions supplied by the .NET Framework aren't quite right for your application, you can design your own permission class by implementing the `IPermission` and `IUnrestrictedPermission` interfaces. Custom permissions are used in code just like built-in permissions.*

Requesting Minimum Permissions

To begin participating in the .NET security structure, your code can request the minimum permissions that it requires to run successfully (see Listing 19.1).

LISTING 19.1: REQUESTING MINIMUM PERMISSIONS

```
/*
   Example19_1.cs illustrates requesting minimum permissions
*/

using System;
using System.IO;
using System.Security.Permissions;

[assembly:FileIOPermissionAttribute(SecurityAction.RequestMinimum,
 All=@"c:\\temp")]

class Example19_1
{

    public static void Main()
    {

        // Create a new file to work with
        FileStream fsOut = File.Create(@"c:\\temp\\test.txt");
        // Create a StreamWriter to handle writing
        StreamWriter sw = new StreamWriter(fsOut);
        // And write some data
        sw.WriteLine("'Twas brillig, and the slithy toves");
        sw.WriteLine("Did gyre and gimble in the wabe.");
        sw.Flush();
        sw.Close();

    }

}
```

To request a permission, you apply an attribute to a class or an assembly. Each possible code-access permission has its own attribute with a set of properties. Specifying the `SecurityAction.Request-Minimum` action tells the CLR that your application needs this particular permission to function at all. The `All` property in the case of the `FileIOPermissionAttribute` requests all access to files in the specified directory.

> **NOTE** *The technique used in this example (and in the rest of the examples in this section) of handling permissions through attributes is called declarative security. There is also a second security syntax (using instances of the* `Permission` *objects) called imperative security. Imperative security is only necessary if you want to assign permissions based on information known only at run-time (for example, the name of a file to be opened). For more information, refer to the "Security Syntax" section of the .NET Framework help file.*

If you compile and run this application, you won't see any output, but it will create the specified file in your `c:\Temp` directory. That's because by default you have full permissions to run any code that originates on your own computer. To see code-access security in action, you'll have to learn how to manage the permissions granted to code on your computer. Before you can manage permissions, you need to understand the concepts of *code groups* and *permission sets*.

Code Groups

A *code group* is a logical grouping of code. As part of the process of determining the permissions that apply to a particular piece of code, the CLR determines which code groups have the code in question as a member. Permissions are assigned to code groups, rather than to individual pieces of code. This is analogous to assigning operating system permissions to groups rather than users and has the same major benefit: It makes things easier to understand.

You define code groups by specifying the membership condition for the group; each code group has precisely one membership condition. Table 19.3 shows the membership conditions you can use to define code groups.

TABLE 19.3: CODE GROUP MEMBERSHIP CONDITIONS

CONDITION	GROUP INCLUDES...
All code	All code.
Application directory	All code in the installation directory of the running application.
Cryptographic hash	All code matching a particular cryptographic hash.
Software publisher	All code from a particular publisher, as validated by an Authenticode signature.
Site membership	All code from a particular Internet site (includes HTTP, HTTPS, and FTP URLs).
Strong name	All code with a particular strong name.
URL	All code that originates from a particular URL.
Zone	All code that originates from a particular security zone. The available zones include Internet, Local Intranet, Trusted Sites, My Computer, and Untrusted Sites.

TIP   To define a code group that includes a single application, you can use a strong name membership condition if the application has been signed with a strong name or a cryptographic hash membership condition.

Permission Sets

Permissions are granted in *permission sets*. A permission set is a set of one or more code-access permissions that can be granted as a unit. The .NET Framework supplies six built-in permission sets (see Table 19.4). You can also create your own permission sets, as you'll see later in this chapter.

TABLE 19.4: BUILT-IN PERMISSION SETS

PERMISSION SET NAME	DESCRIPTION
Nothing	No permissions
Execution	Permission to run but not to access protected resources
Internet	Limited permissions designed for code of unknown origin
LocalIntranet	High permissions designed for code within an enterprise
Everything	All permissions except the permission to skip verification
FullTrust	Full access to all resources

Granting Permissions

The .NET Framework supplies two tools for managing permissions:

◆ The Code Access Security Policy tool (`caspol.exe`) is a command-line tool.

◆ The .NET Framework Configuration tool is a tool that works within the Microsoft Management Console (MMC).

Although the Code Access Security Policy tool has benefits in some situations (for example, you can call it from a batch file), it's generally easier to work with the .NET Framework Configuration tool, especially when you're first learning about .NET security.

To demonstrate the effect of setting a more restrictive security policy on the `Example19_1` application, follow these steps:

1. Select Start ➢ Program Files ➢ Administrative Tools ➢ Microsoft .NET Framework Configuration Tool.

2. Expand the Runtime Security Policy node, and then the User node, to see the security settings that apply to the current user on the computer, as shown in Figure 19.1. As you can see, there are also security settings for the machine and the enterprise. The "Computing Permissions" section later in the chapter discusses those settings.

FIGURE 19.1

Security settings in the .NET Framework Configuration tool

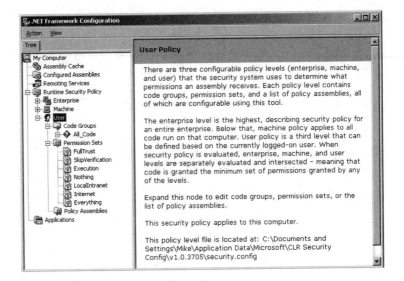

3. Right-click the Everything permission set and select Duplicate to create an exact copy of the permission set. The tool will name this permission set Copy of Everything.

4. Select the Copy of Everything permission set and click the Rename Permission Set link in the right panel of the tool. Change the permission set name to No File IO and then click OK.

5. Click the Change Permissions link. Select the File IO permission in the list of assigned permissions and click Remove to remove File IO permission from this permission set. Click Finish to save your changes.

6. Click the All Code code group.

7. Click the Add a Child Code Group link. Select the option button for Create a New Code Group. Name the new code group **Example19_1** and supply a description. Click Next.

8. Choose the Hash Condition for Membership in this code group. Select the SHA1 hash algorithm. Click the Import button and browse to `Example19_1.exe`. This will compute the hash for this file and insert the results into the Hash textbox. Click Next.

9. Select the No File IO permission set as the permission set for this code group. Click Next.

10. Click Finish to create the new code group. It will be created as a child of the `Example19_1` code group.

11. Right-click the new code group and select Properties. Check the box to assign only permissions from this code group on this policy level. Click OK.

Now run `Example19_1.exe` again. The Just-In-Time debugging dialog box will open. Click No to dismiss the dialog box. The output will be as follows:

```
Unhandled Exception: System.Security.Policy.PolicyException:
Required permissions cannot be acquired.
```

Computing Permissions

Computing the actual permissions applied to any given piece of code is a complex process. To begin the process, think about permissions at the Enterprise level only. The CLR starts by examining the *evidence* that a particular piece of code presents to determine its membership in code groups at that level. Evidence is just an overall term for the various factors (publisher, strong name, hash, and so on) that can go into code group membership.

As you saw in the previous section, code groups are organized into a hierarchy. In general, the CLR will examine all of the code groups in the hierarchy to determine membership. However, any code group in the hierarchy may be marked as `Exclusive` (that's the effect of the check box you selected when creating the code group for `Example19_1`). When code is found to be a member of an `Exclusive` code group, then the CLR stops checking for group membership.

The next step is to determine the permission set for each relevant code group. If the code is a member of an `Exclusive` code group, then only the permission set of that code group is taken into account. If the code is a member of more than one code group, and none of them is an `Exclusive` code group, then all of the permission sets of those code groups are taken into account. The permission set for the code is the *union* of the permission sets of all relevant code groups. That is, if code is a member of Code Group A and Code Group B, and Code Group A grants Registry permission but Code Group B does not, then the code *will* have Registry permission.

That accounts for the permissions at one level (the Enterprise level). But there are actually four levels of permissions:

◆ Enterprise

◆ Machine

◆ User

◆ Application Domain

Only the first three of these levels can be managed within the .NET Framework Configuration tool, but if you need specific security checking within an application domain you can do this in code. An application domain can reduce the permissions granted to code within that application domain, but it cannot expand them.

The CLR determines which of the four levels are relevant by starting at the top (the Enterprise level) and working down. Any given code group can have the `LevelFinal` property, in which case the examination stops there. For example, if code is a member of a code group on the Machine level that has the `LevelFinal` property, then only the Enterprise and Machine levels are relevant. The CLR computes the permissions for each level separately, and then assigns the code the *intersection* of the permissions of all relevant levels. That is, if code is granted Registry permission on the Enterprise level, but is not granted Registry permission on the Machine level, then the code will *not* have Registry permission.

At this point, the CLR knows what permissions should be granted to the code in question, considered in isolation. But code does not run in isolation; it runs as part of an application. The final step of evaluating code-access permissions is to perform a *stack walk*. In a stack walk, the CLR examines all code in the calling chain from the original application to the code being evaluated. The final permission set for the code is the *intersection* of the permission sets of all code in the calling chain. That is, if code is granted Registry permission but the code that called it was not granted Registry permission, then the code will *not* be granted Registry permission.

The .NET Framework Configuration tool includes a wizard that will help you determine the permission set for any given piece of code. To use this tool, click the Runtime Security Policy node within the Configuration tool and then click the Evaluate Assembly link. Browse to the file you'd like to evaluate and then select whether to evaluate code group membership or permissions. Decide whether to evaluate all levels or only a selected level and click Next. The wizard will show you the results. For example, Figure 19.2 shows the code groups to which the Example19_1.exe assembly belongs.

FIGURE 19.2

Checking code group membership

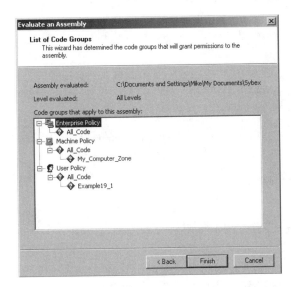

When you install the .NET Framework, it includes a default set of code groups and permission sets. On the Enterprise and User level, there is a single code group that uses the All Code membership condition. This code group is assigned the Full Trust permission set. The net effect of this is that the Enterprise and User levels grant all code rights to do anything. Because of the intersection rules, this means that the code groups on the Machine level control everything by default. Table 19.5 shows the default code groups at the Machine level.

TABLE 19.5: DEFAULT .NET SECURITY SETTINGS AT THE MACHINE LEVEL

CODE GROUP	MEMBERSHIP CONDITION	PERMISSION SET
My Computer Zone Code Group	Zone=My Computer	Full Trust
Microsoft Strong Name Code Group	Strong name uses Microsoft's public key	Full Trust
ECMA Strong Name Code Group	Strong name uses ECMA public key	Full Trust
Local Intranet Code Group	Zone=Local Intranet	Local Intranet
Internet Code Group	Zone=Internet	Internet
Trusted Zone Code Group	Zone=Trusted Sites	Internet
All Code Group	All Code	Nothing
Restricted Zone Code Group	Zone=Untrusted Sites	Nothing

Requesting Optional Permissions

In addition to requesting the minimum permissions that it must have to run, a block of code can request optional permissions that it would like to have but doesn't necessarily need. Listing 19.2 shows an example.

LISTING 19.2: REQUESTING OPTIONAL PERMISSIONS

```
/*
   Example19_2.cs illustrates requesting optional permissions
*/

using System;
using System.IO;
using System.Security.Permissions;

[assembly:FileIOPermissionAttribute(SecurityAction.RequestOptional,
All=@"c:\\temp")]

class Example19_2
{

    public static void Main()
    {

        // Create a new file to work with
        FileStream fsOut = File.Create(@"c:\\temp\\test.txt");
        // Create a StreamWriter to handle writing
        StreamWriter sw = new StreamWriter(fsOut);
        // And write some data
        sw.WriteLine("'Twas brillig, and the slithy toves");
        sw.WriteLine("Did gyre and gimble in the wabe.");
        sw.Flush();
        sw.Close();

    }

}
```

If you compile this example and set up a code group to assign it the No File IO permission set, you'll find that it still throws a security exception when it requests the permission, even though the permission is marked as optional. The difference between minimum and optional permissions is that with an optional permission your code can catch the exception and continue execution; the CLR won't force the application to exit just because an optional permission cannot be granted.

Requesting Permission Sets

Instead of requesting individual permissions, your code can request one of the built-in permission sets. This is done using the PermissionSetAttribute attribute (see Listing 19.3).

LISTING 19.3: REQUESTING A PERMISSION SET

```
/*
  Example19_3.cs illustrates requesting a permission set
*/

using System;
using System.IO;
using System.Security.Permissions;

[assembly:PermissionSetAttribute(SecurityAction.RequestMinimum,
 Name="FullTrust")]

class Example19_3
{

    public static void Main()
    {

        // Create a new file to work with
        FileStream fsOut = File.Create(@"c:\\temp\\test.txt");
        // Create a StreamWriter to handle writing
        StreamWriter sw = new StreamWriter(fsOut);
        // And write some data
        sw.WriteLine("'Twas brillig, and the slithy toves");
        sw.WriteLine("Did gyre and gimble in the wabe.");
        sw.Flush();
        sw.Close();

    }

}
```

You can't use this syntax to request a custom permission set because the permissions contained in a custom permission set can vary.

Refusing Permissions

Your code can also tell the CLR what permissions it does *not* want to have. Listing 19.4 shows code that refuses a particular permission.

LISTING 19.4: REFUSING PERMISSIONS

```
/*
   Example19_4.cs illustrates refusing permissions
*/

using System;
using System.IO;
using System.Security.Permissions;

[assembly:FileIOPermissionAttribute(SecurityAction.RequestRefuse,
Unrestricted=true)]

class Example19_4
{

    public static void Main()
    {

        // Create a new file to work with
        FileStream fsOut = File.Create(@"c:\\temp\\test.txt");
        // Create a StreamWriter to handle writing
        StreamWriter sw = new StreamWriter(fsOut);
        // And write some data
        sw.WriteLine("'Twas brillig, and the slithy toves");
        sw.WriteLine("Did gyre and gimble in the wabe.");
        sw.Flush();
        sw.Close();

    }

}
```

This code tells the CLR that it does not want to run if it's granted unrestricted file I/O permissions. You might use permission refusal to limit the amount of damage that your code can do if an attacker were able to exploit a bug in the code.

Demanding Permissions

Finally, you can use code within .NET to demand permissions. Demanding permissions establishes the permissions that calling code must have to use your code. Listing 19.5 shows a class that demands permissions.

LISTING 19.5: DEMANDING PERMISSIONS

```
/*
  Example19_5.cs illustrates demanding permissions
*/

using System;
using System.IO;
using System.Security.Permissions;

[FileIOPermissionAttribute(SecurityAction.Demand,
All=@"c:\\temp")]
class Example19_5
{

    public static void MakeFile()
    {

        // Create a new file to work with
        FileStream fsOut = File.Create(@"c:\\temp\\test.txt");
        // Create a StreamWriter to handle writing
        StreamWriter sw = new StreamWriter(fsOut);
        // And write some data
        sw.WriteLine("'Twas brillig, and the slithy toves");
        sw.WriteLine("Did gyre and gimble in the wabe.");
        sw.Flush();
        sw.Close();

    }

}
```

Note that the demand is made on the level of the class in this case; you can't demand permissions on the assembly level. You can also place a security demand at the method level in your code.

You should only need to demand permissions if you're using custom permissions. The .NET Framework classes already demand the permissions that they need to properly function. For example, the StreamWriter class demands file I/O permissions, so there's no need to demand the same permissions in your code that calls the StreamWriter class.

Using Role-Based Security

So far, all of the security features you've seen depend on the code itself. The code requests, refuses, or demands features regardless of who is running the application. But there's a second security system built into the .NET Framework. This role-based security lets you assign privileges based not on the code but on the user who is running the code.

In the following sections, you'll learn the terminology that applies to role-based security and see how you can use role-based security to assign permissions to code.

NOTE We'll use security based on Windows user accounts in this section. The .NET Framework also supports custom role-based security in which you define all of the applicable permissions of the security objects, allowing you to develop your own logon system that's independent of the Windows logon system. This is an advanced use of the security objects that we won't cover in this book.

Identity and Principal Objects

Role-based security is based largely on two interfaces: IIdentity and IPrincipal. For applications that use Windows accounts in role-based security these interfaces are implemented in the Windows-Identity and WindowsPrincipal objects, respectively.

The simpler of these two objects is the WindowsIdentity object, which represents the user running the current block of code. Properties of this object allow you to retrieve the username and authentication method that they used, among other things.

The WindowsPrincipal object builds on the WindowsIdentity object. This object represents the entire security context of the user who is running the current code, including their identity and any roles to which they belong. The WindowsPrincipal object is the object that the CLR inspects when deciding which role-based permissions to assign to your code.

Listing 19.6 shows some of the properties you can retrieve from these two objects.

LISTING 19.6: WindowsIdentity **AND** WindowsPrincipal **OBJECTS**

```csharp
/*
  Example19_6.cs demonstrates principal & identity objects
*/

using System;
using System.Security.Principal;


class Example19_6
{

    public static void Main()
    {

        // get the current identity
        WindowsIdentity wi = WindowsIdentity.GetCurrent();

        Console.WriteLine("Identity information:");
        Console.WriteLine("  Authentication Type: {0}",wi.AuthenticationType);
        Console.WriteLine("  Is Anonymous: {0}", wi.IsAnonymous);
        Console.WriteLine("  Is Authenticated: {0}", wi.IsAuthenticated);
        Console.WriteLine("  Is Guest: {0}", wi.IsGuest);
        Console.WriteLine("  Is System: {0}", wi.IsSystem);
```

```
        Console.WriteLine("  Name: {0}", wi.Name);
        Console.WriteLine("  Token: {0}", wi.Token);

        // get the associated principal
        WindowsPrincipal prin = new WindowsPrincipal(wi);

        Console.WriteLine("Principal information:");
        Console.WriteLine("  Authentication Type: {0}",
         prin.Identity.AuthenticationType);
        Console.WriteLine("  Is authenticated: {0}",
         prin.Identity.IsAuthenticated);
        Console.WriteLine("  Name: {0}", prin.Identity.Name);


    }


}
```

The output from this program might be as follows:

```
Identity information:
  Authentication Type: NTLM
  Is Anonymous: False
  Is Authenticated: True
  Is Guest: False
  Is System: False
  Name: LARKGROUP\Mike
  Token: 532
Principal information:
  Authentication Type: NTLM
  Is authenticated: True
  Name: LARKGROUP\Mike
```

Table 19.6 shows the public `WindowsIdentity` properties.

TABLE 19.6: `WindowsIdentity` PROPERTIES

PROPERTY	TYPE	DESCRIPTION
AuthenticationType	String	Type of authentication used to identify the user
IsAnonymous	Boolean	Indicates whether this is an anonymous user
IsAuthenticated	Boolean	Indicates whether this is an authenticated user
IsGuest	Boolean	Indicates whether this is a guest user
IsSystem	Boolean	Indicates whether this is a system account
Name	String	User's Windows login name
Token	IntPtr	The Windows account token for the user

Table 19.7 shows the public `WindowsIdentity` methods.

TABLE 19.7: `WindowsIdentity` METHODS

METHOD	STATIC?	DESCRIPTION
GetAnonymous()	Yes	Returns a `WindowsIdentity` object representing an anonymous user
GetCurrent()	Yes	Returns a `WindowsIdentity` object representing the current user
Impersonate()	No	Allows code to impersonate a different Windows user

Table 19.8 shows the public `WindowsPrincipal` property.

TABLE 19.8: `WindowsPrincipal` PROPERTY

PROPERTY	TYPE	DESCRIPTION
Identity	WindowsIdentity	Gets the `WindowsIdentity` object representing the user for this `Principal`

Table 19.9 shows the public `WindowsPrincipal` method.

TABLE 19.9: `WindowsPrincipal` METHOD

METHOD	STATIC?	DESCRIPTION
IsInRole()	No	Determines whether the current `Principal` belongs to a specified Windows group

Verifying Role Membership

The simplest use of role-based security is to determine whether the current user is a member of a particular Windows group. Listing 19.7 shows an example.

LISTING 19.7: DETERMINING GROUP MEMBERSHIP

```
/*
   Example19_7.cs demonstrates determining group identity
*/

using System;
using System.Security.Principal;
```

```
class Example19_6
{

    public static void Main()
    {

        // get the current identity
        WindowsIdentity wi = WindowsIdentity.GetCurrent();
        // get the associated principal
        WindowsPrincipal prin = new WindowsPrincipal(wi);

        if (prin.IsInRole(WindowsBuiltInRole.PowerUser))
        {
            Console.WriteLine("You are a member of the Power User group");
        }
        else
        {
            Console.WriteLine("You are not a member of the Power User group");
        }

    }

}
```

There are three available overloaded forms of the `IsInRole` method. The first, shown in Listing 19.7, uses one of the `WindowsBuiltInRole` constants to check for membership in the standard Windows groups. The second accepts a string parameter, which can be the name of any group, whether built-in or custom. The third accepts a string parameter, which can be the role identifier (RID) of any group. RIDs are assigned by the operating system and provide a language-independent way to identify groups.

Using the *PrincipalPermission* Class

You can also perform security checking with role-based security by using the `PrincipalPermission` class or the `PrincipalPermissionAttribute` attribute. Listing 19.8 shows an example of this technique with declarative security checking.

LISTING 19.8: DECLARATIVE ROLE-BASED SECURITY

```
/*
   Example19_8.cs illustrates declarative role-based security
*/

using System;
using System.IO;
using System.Security.Permissions;
```

```
[PrincipalPermissionAttribute(SecurityAction.Demand, Role="Administrators")]
class Example19_8
{
    public static void Main()
    {

        // Create a new file to work with
        FileStream fsOut = File.Create(@"c:\\temp\\test.txt");
        // Create a StreamWriter to handle writing
        StreamWriter sw = new StreamWriter(fsOut);
        // And write some data
        sw.WriteLine("'Twas brillig, and the slithy toves");
        sw.WriteLine("Did gyre and gimble in the wabe.");
        sw.Flush();
        sw.Close();

    }

}
```

Checking permissions with role-based security is similar to checking permissions with code-access security. The difference lies in what you are checking. Listing 19.8 checks to see whether the user running the code is in the local Administrators group. If so, the code will run; if not, a security exception will be thrown. You can also use the `Name` property of the `PrincipalPermissionAttribute` class to check whether a user has a particular logon name.

Using Encryption

Besides code-access and role-based permissions, the .NET Framework offers one more important security feature: encryption. Classes in the .NET Framework support both symmetric and asymmetric cryptography. In this section, you'll see how to use the built-in support for both types of cryptography.

NOTE   *The .NET cryptography model also includes classes to handle digital signatures (which let you verify the origin of messages) and hash values (which let you verify that a message has not been altered illicitly). For more details on these classes, refer to the "Cryptographic Services" section of the .NET Framework documentation.*

Symmetric and Asymmetric Cryptography

To effectively use encryption, you need to understand the difference between *symmetric* cryptography (sometimes called *private-key* cryptography) and *asymmetric* cryptography (sometimes called *public-key* cryptography).

In symmetric cryptography, the same key encrypts and decrypts data. Anyone who has the encrypted data as well as the key can decrypt the data and read it. The .NET Framework uses a slightly more complicated form of symmetric encryption called *cipher-block chaining*, in which you must know both the key and the initialization vector (IV) to decrypt the encrypted message. Over the years, cryptographers have developed many different algorithms to perform symmetric cryptography. These algorithms are designed to be difficult to break by brute-force attacks (such as trying to decrypt a message using every possible key). The .NET Framework includes implementations of four of these algorithms:

◆ DES

◆ RC2

◆ Rijndael

◆ Triple DES

Asymmetric cryptography uses two keys: a public key and a private key. Data encrypted with the public key can only be decrypted with the matching private key. If you distribute your public key widely, anyone can encrypt a message that only you can decrypt (as long as you keep your private key a secret). The .NET Framework includes implementations of two asymmetric algorithms:

◆ DSA

◆ RSA

In practice, asymmetric encryption is much harder to break without the private key than symmetric encryption. But asymmetric encryption also requires much more computational effort to encrypt a message. To communicate securely with another person, you can use a combination of asymmetric and symmetric encryption to balance security against computation:

1. Your friend generates a key pair (consisting of a public key and a private key) for asymmetric cryptography. She publicizes her public key.

2. To initiate a conversation, you generate a key and an IV for a symmetric algorithm. Encrypt this information with your friend's public key and send it to her.

3. Your friend can now decrypt the symmetric key and IV by using her own private key, and the remainder of the conversation can consist of messages encrypted with the symmetric key.

This technique uses asymmetric cryptography to transmit the symmetric key and then allows the participants to continue the conversation using the faster symmetric cryptography.

Encrypting a File

The .NET Framework uses a stream-based approach to encryption. Encryption is managed through the `CryptoStream` object. You'll recall from Chapter 15, "Streams and Input/Output," that you can use the output of one stream as the input to the next stream, so the `CryptoStream` object is a natural way to plug into file or network operations (see Listing 19.9).

LISTING 19.9: CREATING AN ENCRYPTED FILE

```
/*
  Example19_9.cs illustrates encrypting a file
*/
```

```csharp
using System;
using System.IO;
using System.Security.Cryptography;

class Example19_9
{
    public static void Main()
    {

        // Create a new file to work with
        FileStream fsOut = File.Create(@"c:\temp\encrypted.txt");

        // Create a new crypto provider
        TripleDESCryptoServiceProvider tdes =
            new TripleDESCryptoServiceProvider();

        // Create a cryptostream to encrypt to the filestream
        CryptoStream cs = new CryptoStream(fsOut, tdes.CreateEncryptor(),
            CryptoStreamMode.Write);

        // Create a StreamWriter to format the output
        StreamWriter sw = new StreamWriter(cs);

        // And write some data
        sw.WriteLine("'Twas brillig, and the slithy toves");
        sw.WriteLine("Did gyre and gimble in the wabe.");
        sw.Flush();
        sw.Close();

        // save the key and IV for future use
        FileStream fsKeyOut = File.Create(@"c:\temp\encrypted.key");

        // use a BinaryWriter to write formatted data to the file
        BinaryWriter bw = new BinaryWriter(fsKeyOut);

        // write data to the file
        bw.Write( tdes.Key );
        bw.Write( tdes.IV );

        // flush and close
        bw.Flush();
        bw.Close();

    }

}
```

The `System.Security.Cryptography` framework contains the cryptographic classes. This framework includes a hierarchy of objects at three levels:

◆ Algorithm type classes, such as `SymmetricAlgorithm`, are abstract classes that represent particular types of cryptography.

◆ Algorithm classes, such as `TripleDES`, inherit from the algorithm type classes. Algorithm classes are abstract classes that describe a particular algorithm.

◆ Implementation classes, such as `TripleDESCryptoServiceProvider`, inherit from algorithm classes and provide an implementation of the inherited algorithm.

This code starts by creating an instance of the `TripleDESCryptoServiceProvider` class to supply the actual encryption service. When you instantiate an implementation class, the constructor automatically creates a new, random key for the class to use. The `TripleDESCryptoServiceProvider` is representative of all the implementation classes. Table 19.10 shows the public properties of this class.

TABLE 19.10: `TripleDESCryptoServiceProvider` PROPERTIES

PROPERTY	TYPE	DESCRIPTION
BlockSize	int	The number of bits encrypted or decrypted in a single operation.
FeedbackSize	int	The amount of data from each block that is used in encrypting the next block.
IV	Byte[]	The initialization vector used by this algorithm.
Key	Byte[]	The key used by the algorithm.
KeySize	int	The number of bits in the key.
LegalBlockSizes	KeySizes[]	Block sizes supported by this algorithm.
LegalKeySizes	KeySizes[]	Key sizes supported by this algorithm.
Mode	CipherMode	Indicates details of the encryption algorithm. The .NET Framework automatically initializes this to the most secure value.
Padding	PaddingMode	Determines the bytes to be added if the last block in the message is not long enough for the algorithm.

Table 19.11 shows the public `TripleDESCryptoServiceProvider` methods.

TABLE 19.11: `TripleDESCryptoServiceProvider` METHODS

METHOD	STATIC?	DESCRIPTION
Clear()	No	Releases all resources used by the algorithm
CreateDecryptor()	No	Creates an object that can be used to perform decryption operations

Continued on next page

TABLE 19.11: `TripleDESCryptoServiceProvider` METHODS *(continued)*

METHOD	STATIC?	DESCRIPTION
`CreateEncryptor()`	No	Creates an object that can be used to perform encryption operations
`GenerateIV()`	No	Generates a new random initialization vector
`GenerateKey()`	No	Generates a new random key
`ValidKeySize()`	No	Determines whether the current key size is valid

With the algorithm implementation available, the code can create a `CryptoStream` object to handle the actual encryption. In this case, the `CryptoStream` takes in bytes from the `StreamWriter` object, encrypts them, and writes the encrypted bytes out to the `FileStream` object. The `CryptoStream` constructor takes three parameters:

♦ A stream object to use for input or output

♦ An transform, which can be supplied by the `CreateEncryptor` or `CreateDecryptor` method of one of the algorithm implementation classes

♦ A mode, which specifies whether this `CryptoStream` should read or write encrypted data

In this case, the `CryptoStream` is initialized to write data, using the transform supplied by the `tdes.CreateEncryptor` method.

The code then creates a `StreamWriter` to write to the `CryptoStream`, and writes some data out. The data goes from the `StreamWriter` to the `CryptoStream`, which encrypts it, and then to the `FileStream`, which writes it to a disk file.

This program concludes its operations by using a `BinaryWriter` object to write the key and IV that were used for the encryption operations to a disk file.

TIP   The "pluggable" nature of the `CryptoStream` *means you can use it in contexts other than disk files. For example, you can use a* `CryptoStream` *in conjunction with a* `NetworkStream` *to encrypt data being sent over the network.*

Figure 19.3 shows the encrypted file in a hex editor. As you can see, it bears no resemblance to the original data.

FIGURE 19.3

Contents of an encrypted file

Decrypting a File

Decrypting a file uses many of the same objects as encrypting a file. Listing 19.10 shows an example.

LISTING 19.10: DECRYPTING AN ENCRYPTED FILE

```csharp
/*
  Example19_10.cs illustrates decrypting a file
*/

using System;
using System.IO;
using System.Security.Cryptography;

class Example19_10
{
    public static void Main()
    {

        // Create a new crypto provider
        TripleDESCryptoServiceProvider tdes =
            new TripleDESCryptoServiceProvider();

        // open the file containing the key and IV
        FileStream fsKeyIn = File.OpenRead(@"c:\temp\encrypted.key");

        // use a BinaryReader to read formatted data from the file
        BinaryReader br = new BinaryReader(fsKeyIn);

        // read data from the file and close it
        tdes.Key = br.ReadBytes(24);
        tdes.IV = br.ReadBytes(8);

        // Open the encrypted file
        FileStream fsIn = File.OpenRead(@"c:\temp\encrypted.txt");

        // Create a cryptostream to decrypt from the filestream
        CryptoStream cs = new CryptoStream(fsIn, tdes.CreateDecryptor(),
            CryptoStreamMode.Read);

        // Create a StreamReader to format the input
        StreamReader sr = new StreamReader(cs);

        // And decrypt the data
        Console.WriteLine(sr.ReadToEnd());
        sr.Close();

    }

}
```

The output from this program is as follows:

```
'Twas brillig, and the slithy toves
Did gyre and gimble in the wabe.
```

As you can see, reading an encrypted file is similar to writing it in the first place. The code constructs a `TripleDESCryptoServiceProvider` object, but it then overwrites the random `Key` and `IV` properties with the values saved in the `encrypted.key` file. Having created an implementation object with the same properties used to encrypt the file, the code then creates a `CryptoStream` object using the `CreateDecryptor()` method of this object. The data is read from the disk file by a `FileStream` object, decrypted by the `CryptoStream` object, and then passed by the `StreamReader` object to the `Console` object, which displays the result.

Using Asymmetric Cryptography

The code for using asymmetric cryptography is somewhat simpler than that for symmetric cryptography because asymmetric cryptography is intended to handle small amounts of data rather than data streams. As a result, you can call methods of the implementation class directly to perform encryption and decryption (see Listing 19.11).

LISTING 19.11: USING ASYMMETRIC CRYPTOGRAPHY

```
/*
   Example19_11.cs illustrates asymmetric cryptography
*/

using System;
using System.IO;
using System.Security.Cryptography;

class Example19_11
{
    public static void Main()
    {

        // Create a new crypto provider
        RSACryptoServiceProvider rsa =
            new RSACryptoServiceProvider();

        // Data to encrypt
        Byte[] testData = {1, 2, 3, 4, 5, 6, 7, 8, 9, 10};

        // Encrypt the data
        Byte[] encryptedData = rsa.Encrypt(testData, false);
        Console.WriteLine("Encrypted data:");
        for(int i=0; i<encryptedData.GetLength(0); i++)
        {
```

```
            Console.Write("{0} ", encryptedData[i]);
        }
        Console.WriteLine();

        // Decrypt the data
        Byte[] decryptedData = rsa.Decrypt(encryptedData, false);
        Console.WriteLine("Decrypted Data:");
        for(int i=0; i<decryptedData.GetLength(0); i++)
        {
            Console.Write("{0} ", decryptedData[i]);
        }
        Console.WriteLine();
    }

}
```

The output from this program is as follows:

```
Encrypted data:
104 188 153 19 34 115 49 163 115 33 93 49 170 233 92 101 110 39 91 219 245 95 19
9 113 138 69 177 143 96 174 133 250 191 141 28 65 21 192 234 13 9 54 112 121 232
 250 149 253 224 181 94 178 51 229 111 18 238 254 244 86 238 243 45 81 91 21 44
175 189 64 57 149 163 72 46 125 54 192 36 241 218 131 177 33 144 96 185 196 206
193 7 160 129 51 196 218 29 70 20 164 221 70 128 253 245 230 152 24 147 183 178
1 128 95 219 62 139 251 175 202 203 211 192 81 105 140 231 137
Decrypted Data:
1 2 3 4 5 6 7 8 9 10
```

As you can see, the encryption process pads out the data to the full block size that the RSA cipher uses. The decryption process recovers the original byte array exactly.

Summary

The .NET Framework includes an extensive security system. You've only seen the basics in this chapter, but that should be enough for most applications.

You can use code-access security to specify exactly which operations an application is allowed to perform. Code-access security allows you to select individual permissions to apply to code based on the code's membership in code groups. A code group can be based on the publisher of the code, the identity of the code, the location from which the code was obtained, or other factors.

You can also use role-based security to limit execution of an application to members of a particular group, or even to individual users.

Either code-access security or role-based security can be applied to assemblies, classes, or members.

The .NET Framework also includes classes to support both symmetric (private key) and asymmetric (public key) cryptography.

Chapter 20

XML

BY NOW YOU'VE ALMOST certainly run across the Extensible Markup Language (XML). XML is a pervasive Internet standard that's also omnipresent within the .NET Framework. .NET uses XML for many things, from storing configuration files to serializing objects for transmission to a remote application.

In addition to this infrastructure, the .NET Framework also includes the System.Xml namespace, which contains classes for working explicitly with XML. You can read and write XML files, analyze their structure, transform XML files into new formats, or use them to work with data.

In this chapter, we'll start by reviewing the basics of XML. Then we'll show you how you can work with XML files from your C# applications in a variety of ways.

Featured in this chapter:

◆ Understanding, Reading, and Writing XML

◆ Using the Document Object Model

◆ Transforming XML

Understanding XML

Although XML is sometimes thought of as simply an enhanced version of Hypertext Markup Language (HTML), the truth is a bit more complicated. XML as it's commonly used in the development world refers to an overlapping set of dozens of standards for data persistence, interchange, transformation, and display. Fortunately, you can use XML for many things without knowing every single one of these standards. In this section, you'll learn the basics of the standards that are most used in the .NET Framework:

◆ XML

◆ Extensible Stylesheet Language Transformation (XSLT)

◆ XML Schema Standard (XSD)

Introducing XML

If you've been avoiding XML, you may find the number of acronyms surrounding the subject a bit daunting. Or you may have been put off by descriptions such as that in the official World Wide Web Consortium (W3C) Recommendation, which starts off like this: "The Extensible Markup Language (XML) is a subset of SGML..." (SGML being the Standardized General Markup Language, another complex language from which both HTML and XML are derived). Fortunately, there is a simple way to think about XML: XML is just human-readable data combined with human-readable metadata.

Yes, there is a lot of complexity beyond that simple definition, but most of the complexity lies in defining the syntax of XML. Just as you need to learn keywords and their legitimate uses to write C# code, you need to learn the syntax of XML to read or write XML documents. But the basic concept is simple.

Listing 20.1 shows a file named Cust.xml.

LISTING 20.1: Cust.xml

```
<?xml version="1.0" encoding="UTF-8"?>
<NewDataSet>
    <Customers>
        <CustomerID>ALFKI</CustomerID>
        <CompanyName>Alfreds Futterkiste</CompanyName>
        <ContactName>Maria Anders</ContactName>
        <ContactTitle>Sales Representative</ContactTitle>
        <Address>Obere Str. 57</Address>
        <City>Berlin</City>
        <PostalCode>12209</PostalCode>
        <Country>Germany</Country>
        <Phone>030-0074321</Phone>
        <Fax>030-0076545</Fax>
    </Customers>
    <Customers>
        <CustomerID>BONAP</CustomerID>
        <CompanyName><![CDATA[Bon app']]></CompanyName>
        <ContactName>Laurence Lebihan</ContactName>
        <ContactTitle>Owner</ContactTitle>
        <Address>12, rue des Bouchers</Address>
        <City>Marseille</City>
        <PostalCode>13008</PostalCode>
        <Country>France</Country>
        <Phone>91.24.45.40</Phone>
        <Fax>91.24.45.41</Fax>
    </Customers>
</NewDataSet>
```

One of the nice things about XML is that, like C#, it allows you to use whitespace to enhance readability or to rearrange the XML to your liking. Listing 20.2 shows another representation of the same XML document, which is exactly the same as far as an XML parser is concerned.

LISTING 20.2: Cust.xml, **REFORMATTED**

```xml
<?xml version="1.0" encoding="UTF-8"?>
<NewDataSet>
    <Customers>
        <CustomerID>
            ALFKI
        </CustomerID>
        <CompanyName>
            Alfreds Futterkiste
        </CompanyName>
        <ContactName>
            Maria Anders
        </ContactName>
        <ContactTitle>
            Sales Representative
        </ContactTitle>
        <Address>
            Obere Str. 57
        </Address>
        <City>
            Berlin
        </City>
        <PostalCode>
            12209
        </PostalCode>
        <Country>
            Germany
        </Country>
        <Phone>
            030-0074321
        </Phone>
        <Fax>
            030-0076545
        </Fax>
    </Customers>
    <Customers>
        <CustomerID>
            BONAP
        </CustomerID>
        <CompanyName>
            <![CDATA[Bon app']]>
        </CompanyName>
        <ContactName>
            Laurence Lebihan
        </ContactName>
        <ContactTitle>
            Owner
```

```
            </ContactTitle>
            <Address>
                12, rue des Bouchers
            </Address>
            <City>
                Marseille
            </City>
            <PostalCode>
                13008
            </PostalCode>
            <Country>
                France
            </Country>
            <Phone>
                91.24.45.40
            </Phone>
            <Fax>
                91.24.45.41
            </Fax>
        </Customers>
    </NewDataSet>
```

Even without knowing anything about the syntax of XML, you can probably learn some things from this rearrangement of the data. In particular, XML consists of *tags* (which are set off inside of angle brackets, <>) and data. Tags are always arranged in pairs, with the closing tag being the same as the opening tag but prefixed with a forward slash.

NOTE   There's a shorthand form you can use for tags that have no content. This form combines both the opening and closing tags in a single tag that ends with a slash. For example, <p></p> can be replaced by the shorthand form <p/>.

THE XML DECLARATION

The first line of the sample XML file is the *XML declaration*:

```
<?xml version="1.0" encoding="UTF-8"?>
```

This line specifies several things about the document:

- It is an XML document.

- It conforms to the XML version 1.0 specification.

- It uses the UTF-8 character set.

You'll find an XML declaration at the start of any XML file that conforms to the XML standard, though it won't necessarily have the version or encoding attributes.

TAGS AND ELEMENTS

Most of the XML file consists of pairs of tags. There are three types of tags:

◆ Start tags start with < and end with >.

◆ End tags start with </ and end with >.

◆ Empty tags start with < and end with /> (the sample document does not contain any empty tags).

Within a tag you'll find the name of an element. If you know HTML, you know that there are certain elements whose names are dictated by the language; for example, <H1> for a first-level heading. XML takes a different approach here. You can make up any name you like for an element, subject to some simple rules of naming:

◆ Names can contain any alphanumeric character (English or otherwise).

◆ Names can contain the special characters such as the underscore (_), hyphen (-), and period (.).

◆ Names may not contain any whitespace.

◆ Names must start with a letter or the underscore character.

A start tag plus an end tag (or a single empty tag) defines an *element*. For example, this is a single element from the sample file:

```
<City>
    Berlin
</City>
```

The name of this element is `City`, and the value of this element is `Berlin`.

Elements can be nested, but they cannot overlap. That is, the following is a legal XML structure, with an element named `Customers` containing three child elements:

```
<Customers>
    <CustomerID>
        ALFKI
    </CustomerID>
    <CompanyName>
        Alfreds Futterkiste
    </CompanyName>
    <ContactName>
        Maria Anders
    </ContactName>
</Customers>
```

But the following structure is not legal because the `CompanyName` and `ContactName` elements overlap:

```
<Customers>
    <CustomerID>
        ALFKI
    </CustomerID>
    <CompanyName>
        Alfreds Futterkiste
```

```
    <ContactName>
    </CompanyName>
        Maria Anders
    </ContactName>
</Customers>
```

Every XML document contains a single *root element*. In the case of sample document in Listing 20.1, the root element has the name `NewDataSet`. The net effect of these rules (a single root element, no overlapping tags, nested elements) is that any XML file can be represented as a tree, where each element has precisely one parent and zero or more children. One way to see the structure of an XML document is to open it in a recent version of Internet Explorer. Figure 20.1 shows the `Cust.xml` document in Internet Explorer 6.0.

FIGURE 20.1

XML document displayed by Internet Explorer

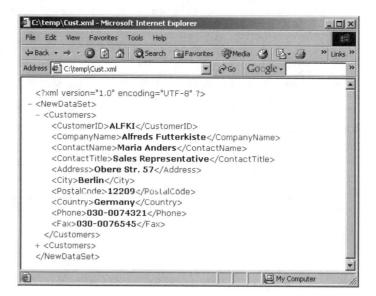

When you use Internet Explorer to view an XML document, you can use the minus (−) signs to collapse the view of child elements—at which point they turn to plus (+) signs to expand the child elements again.

XML NAMESPACES

Listing 20.3 shows another XML document.

LISTING 20.3: AN XML DOCUMENT CONTAINING SEVERAL NAMESPACES

```
<?xml version="1.0" encoding="utf-8" ?>
<xs:schema id="Dataset1" targetNamespace="http://tempuri.org/Dataset1.xsd"
  elementFormDefault="qualified" attributeFormDefault="qualified"
  xmlns="http://tempuri.org/Dataset1.xsd"
```

```
xmlns:mstns="http://tempuri.org/Dataset1.xsd"
xmlns:xs="http://www.w3.org/2001/XMLSchema"
xmlns:msdata="urn:schemas-microsoft-com:xml-msdata">
  <xs:element name="Dataset1" msdata:IsDataSet="true">
   <xs:complexType>
    <xs:choice maxOccurs="unbounded">
     <xs:element name="Customers">
      <xs:complexType>
       <xs:sequence>
        <xs:element name="CustomerID" type="xs:string" />
        <xs:element name="CompanyName" type="xs:string" />
        <xs:element name="ContactName" type="xs:string" minOccurs="0" />
        <xs:element name="ContactTitle" type="xs:string" minOccurs="0" />
        <xs:element name="Address" type="xs:string" minOccurs="0" />
        <xs:element name="City" type="xs:string" minOccurs="0" />
        <xs:element name="Region" type="xs:string" minOccurs="0" />
        <xs:element name="PostalCode" type="xs:string" minOccurs="0" />
        <xs:element name="Country" type="xs:string" minOccurs="0" />
        <xs:element name="Phone" type="xs:string" minOccurs="0" />
        <xs:element name="Fax" type="xs:string" minOccurs="0" />
       </xs:sequence>
      </xs:complexType>
     </xs:element>
    </xs:choice>
   </xs:complexType>
   <xs:unique name="Dataset1Key1" msdata:PrimaryKey="true">
    <xs:selector xpath=".//mstns:Customers" />
    <xs:field xpath="mstns:CustomerID" />
   </xs:unique>
  </xs:element>
</xs:schema>
```

This particular document is an XSD file; you'll learn more about XSD later in the "XSD" section. For now, just focus on the starting tag for the schema element. This tag contains a set of *XML namespace declarations*:

```
xmlns="http://tempuri.org/Dataset1.xsd"
xmlns:mstns="http://tempuri.org/Dataset1.xsd"
xmlns:xs="http://www.w3.org/2001/XMLSchema"
xmlns:msdata="urn:schemas-microsoft-com:xml-msdata"
```

An XML namespace declaration has three parts. First, xmlns tells the XML parser that there's an XML namespace declaration coming. Next, there's an optional prefix assigned to this namespace (in this case, mstns, xs, and msdata are the namespace prefixes). Finally, there is a resource indicator for the namespace. The resource indicator uniquely identifies the namespace and sets it apart from all other XML namespaces.

The use of an XML namespace is to allow tags in an XML document to be qualified with their namespace. This avoids the possibility of the same tag being used in a single document to mean two different things. For example, many different namespaces might have a tag named element, and you could risk using that tag for two different things in the same document. The elements in this particular document come from the xs namespace:

```
<xs:element name="Address" type="xs:string" minOccurs="0" />
```

TIP   Although the resource indicator may be the same format as a URL, it doesn't actually have to point to a web page. It simply has to be unique. Just knowing there is a namespace does not help you determine which tags might exist in that namespace.

ATTRIBUTES

So far, we've represented the individual fields in the data by using one element for each field. XML allows an alternate representation of information by using attributes. Listing 20.4 shows a more attribute-oriented view of the data with which we've been working.

LISTING 20.4: Cust2.xml

```
<?xml version="1.0" encoding="UTF-8"?>
<NewDataSet>
    <Customers CustomerID="ALFKI" ContactName="Maria Anders"
     CompanyName="Alfreds Futterkiste" ContactTitle="Sales Representative"
     Address="Obere Str. 57" City="Berlin" PostalCode="12209"
     Country="Germany" Phone="030-0074321" Fax="030-0076545"
    </Customers>
    <Customers CustomerID="BONAP" ContactName="Laurence Lebihan"
     CompanyName="Bon app&apos;" ContactTitle="Owner"
     Address="12, rue des Bouchers" City="Marseille" PostalCode="13008"
     Country="France" Phone="91.24.45.40" Fax="91.24.45.41"
    </Customers>
</NewDataSet>
```

An XML element may contain zero or more attributes. Each attribute has a name and a value, with the name coming first, then an equals (=) sign, and then the value in double quotes (""). For example, the attributes of the first Customers element include:

◆ A CustomerID attribute with the value ALFKI

◆ A ContactName attribute with the value Maria Anders

◆ A CompanyName attribute with the value Alfreds Futterkiste

In many cases, you can represent the same information using either elements (as in Listing 20.1) or attributes (as in Listing 20.2). Sometimes attributes are said to be for metadata about the element, and elements are for data. But it can be difficult to tell metadata from data. In contrast, some databases will use attributes for primary keys and elements for other data.

SPECIAL CHARACTERS

XML offers two ways to handle special characters. You've seen both of them in the examples in this chapter. First, for individual characters you can use what are called *entity references*. There are five entity references defined by XML:

- < translates to an opening angle bracket (<).
- > translates to a closing angle bracket (>).
- & translates to an ampersand (&).
- ' translates to an apostrophe (').
- " translates to a quotation mark (").

Thus, in this XML element:

```
<Customers CustomerID="BONAP" ContactName="Laurence Lebihan"
  CompanyName="Bon app&apos;" ContactTitle="Owner"
  Address="12, rue des Bouchers" City="Marseille" PostalCode="13008"
  Country="France" Phone="91.24.45.40" Fax="91.24.45.41"
</Customers>
```

The value of the `CompanyName` attribute is `Bon App'`, with the entity reference replaced by the apostrophe.

You can also use a *CDATA section* to represent any arbitrary amount of literal data. A CDATA section has the following general format:

```
<![CDATA[literal data]]>
```

Thus, in Listing 20.1 one of the elements has the following value:

```
<![CDATA[Bon app']]>
```

This entire string is also translated to the value `Bon App'` when the XML parser processes the document.

COMMENTS AND PROCESSING INSTRUCTIONS

There are two other important parts of XML you haven't seen yet. First, XML allows *comments*. You set off comments with the opening string <!-- and the closing string -->. For example, this would be a valid comment in an XML file:

```
<!-- New version December 4, 2002 -->
```

Comments may appear almost anywhere in an XML document. But they may not appear inside of a tag (like an attribute), and comments may not be nested.

Comments are intended for human beings to read. The equivalent for programs to read is the *processing instruction*. You set off a processing instruction with the opening string <? and the closing string ?>. For example, this processing instruction would associate the style sheet named `customers.css` with the current document:

```
<?xml-stylesheet href="customers.css" type="text/css"?>
```

Introducing XSLT

XML is all about representing information. Think about the examples you've seen so far in this chapter: They describe customers, along with pertinent data for each customer. But that's all that XML files contain. In particular, there is nothing in an XML file that dictates a presentation format for the information that the file contains.

Of course, sooner or later this poses a problem when you want to see the information. To solve this problem, you can use the Extensible Stylesheet Language Transformation (XSLT). XSLT files (which usually have the extension .xsl) are combined with XML files by an XSLT processor, producing an output file. That output file might be HTML, pure text, a Word document, or just about anything else.

TIP   When you open an XML file in Internet Explorer, you're actually using a default XSLT file that is built into Internet Explorer. This XSLT file transforms the XML into the color-coded treeview that IE then displays.

LOOKING AT AN XSLT EXAMPLE

To see XSL in action, consider the XML file shown in Listing 20.5, Cust3.xml.

LISTING 20.5: Cust3.xml

```
<?xml version="1.0" encoding="UTF-8"?>
<?xml-stylesheet type="text/xsl" href="Cust.xsl"?>
<NewDataSet>
    <Customers>
        <CustomerID>ALFKI</CustomerID>
        <CompanyName>Alfreds Futterkiste</CompanyName>
        <ContactName>Maria Anders</ContactName>
        <ContactTitle>Sales Representative</ContactTitle>
        <Address>Obere Str. 57</Address>
        <City>Berlin</City>
        <PostalCode>12209</PostalCode>
        <Country>Germany</Country>
        <Phone>030-0074321</Phone>
        <Fax>030-0076545</Fax>
    </Customers>
    <Customers>
        <CustomerID>BONAP</CustomerID>
        <CompanyName><![CDATA[Bon app']]></CompanyName>
        <ContactName>Laurence Lebihan</ContactName>
        <ContactTitle>Owner</ContactTitle>
        <Address>12, rue des Bouchers</Address>
        <City>Marseille</City>
        <PostalCode>13008</PostalCode>
        <Country>France</Country>
        <Phone>91.24.45.40</Phone>
        <Fax>91.24.45.41</Fax>
    </Customers>
</NewDataSet>
```

The only difference between this XML file and Listing 20.1 is that this one has a processing directive that specifies a style sheet:

```
<?xml-stylesheet type="text/xsl" href="Cust.xsl"?>
```

Any XSLT processor that is handed this XML file will read this processing directive. It specifies a style sheet of XSLT commands Cust.xsl, in the same folder as Cust3.xml (you could also use an absolute rather than a relative URL).

Listing 20.6 shows the contents of Cust.xsl, the XSL file referred to by Cust3.xml.

LISTING 20.6: Cust.xsl

```
<?xml version="1.0" encoding="UTF-8"?>
<html xsl:version="1.0" xmlns:xsl="http://www.w3.org/1999/XSL/Transform">
<body>
    <xsl:for-each select="/NewDataSet/Customers">
        <p><h2>Customer</h2>
         <br><b><xsl:value-of select="CustomerID"/></b></br>
          <br><xsl:value-of select="CompanyName"/></br>
          <br><xsl:value-of select="ContactName"/></br></p>
    </xsl:for-each>
</body>
</html>
```

As you can see, this particular XSLT file is sort of a cross between HTML and XML. Technically, this is known as an XHTML file, which is a form of XML that contains HTML tags. When this pair of files is run through an XSLT processor, the result in fact will be an HTML file. For example, if you open Cust3.xml with Internet Explorer (which contains a built-in XSLT processor), the result will be as shown in Figure 20.2.

FIGURE 20.2

XML file displayed with XSLT style sheet

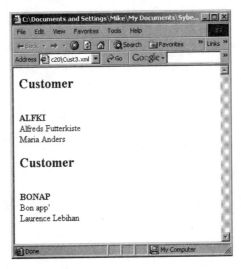

UNDERSTANDING THE EXAMPLE

The simplest way to understand the output of this process is to start with the XSLT file. Anything in this file that's not tagged with the `xsl:` namespace prefix is simply copied verbatim to the output file. So in this case, the output (which is what Internet Explorer displays) starts with the following:

```
<html xsl:version="1.0" xmlns:xsl="http://www.w3.org/1999/XSL/Transform">
<body>
```

NOTE   Note that the namespace information for XSLT is packed into the HTML tag. The XSLT processor can still find it there, and it has no effect on the output file's presentation as HTML.

The next thing in the XSLT file is the starting tag of a `for-each` element in the XSL namespace:

```
<xsl:for-each select="/NewDataSet/Customers">
```

The `/NewDataSet/Customers` attribute in this element matches any `Customers` element that is a child of the `NewDataSet` element in the XML document. If you refer back to the XML document in Listing 20.5, you'll see that there is one such tag for each customer.

All of the code within the `for-each` element (which, of course, ends with the `</xsl:for-each>` tag) is executed once for each instance of the `Customers` element in the XML file. This code starts by simply outputting some more literal text (which happens to be HTML, though of course the XSLT processor has no knowledge of how its output will be used):

```
<p><h2>Customer</h2>
        <br><b>
```

Next comes an XSLT `value-of` element:

```
<xsl:value-of select="CustomerID"/>
```

The `value-of` element returns the value of the element to which it refers. The value of an XML element is just the text within that element, with all tags stripped away. For example, the value of the following:

```
<CustomerID>ALFKI</CustomerID>
```

is this:

```
ALFKI
```

For each customer, then, this XSLT file inserts the value of the `CustomerID`, `CompanyName`, and `ContactName` elements, with HTML break tags used to place them on separate lines when the HTML is displayed.

TIP   Note that the `<br>` tags are terminated explicitly with `</br>` tags. Although HTML doesn't require the closing tag here, XML does, and XSLT files must be well-formed by the rules of XML. Alternatively, you can use the empty `<br />` tag, which is legal for both XML and HTML.

Finally, the XSLT file ends its output with two more literal HTML tags:

```
</body>
</html>
```

Putting the pieces together, Listing 20.7 shows the generated HTML file that results from this process.

TIP   If you're using Internet Explorer to view this example, the only way to see the generated HTML is to work it out for yourself. If you choose View ➤ Source in Internet Explorer, you'll see the XML file, not the generated HTML.

LISTING 20.7: OUTPUT OF APPLYING Cust.xsl TO Cust3.xml

```
<html xsl:version="1.0" xmlns:xsl="http://www.w3.org/1999/XSL/Transform">
<body>
<p><h2>Customer</h2><br><b>ALFKI</b><br>Alfreds Futterkiste<br>Maria Anders</p>
<p><h2>Customer</h2><br><b>BONAP</b><br>Bon app'<br>Laurence Lebihan</p>
</body>
</html>
```

Introducing XSD

The third important XML standard to know about when working with the .NET Framework is the XML Schema Definition standard (XSD). XSD provides a way of describing the data contained in an XML file in terms of its underlying data types. This means that XSD files are good for carrying database schema information to go along with XML files.

For example, Listing 20.8 shows an XSD file generated by Visual Studio .NET to represent the schema of the Customers table from the Northwind SQL Server sample database.

LISTING 20.8: Customers.xsd

```
<?xml version="1.0" encoding="utf-8" ?>
<xs:schema id="Dataset1" targetNamespace="http://tempuri.org/Dataset1.xsd"
 elementFormDefault="qualified" attributeFormDefault="qualified"
xmlns="http://tempuri.org/Dataset1.xsd"
xmlns:mstns="http://tempuri.org/Dataset1.xsd"
xmlns:xs="http://www.w3.org/2001/XMLSchema"
xmlns:msdata="urn:schemas-microsoft-com:xml-msdata">
  <xs:element name="Dataset1" msdata:IsDataSet="true">
   <xs:complexType>
    <xs:choice maxOccurs="unbounded">
      <xs:element name="Customers">
       <xs:complexType>
        <xs:sequence>
         <xs:element name="CustomerID" type="xs:string" />
         <xs:element name="CompanyName" type="xs:string" />
         <xs:element name="ContactName" type="xs:string" minOccurs="0" />
         <xs:element name="ContactTitle" type="xs:string" minOccurs="0" />
         <xs:element name="Address" type="xs:string" minOccurs="0" />
```

```
        <xs:element name="City" type="xs:string" minOccurs="0" />
        <xs:element name="Region" type="xs:string" minOccurs="0" />
        <xs:element name="PostalCode" type="xs:string" minOccurs="0" />
        <xs:element name="Country" type="xs:string" minOccurs="0" />
        <xs:element name="Phone" type="xs:string" minOccurs="0" />
        <xs:element name="Fax" type="xs:string" minOccurs="0" />
      </xs:sequence>
     </xs:complexType>
    </xs:element>
   </xs:choice>
  </xs:complexType>
  <xs:unique name="Dataset1Key1" msdata:PrimaryKey="true">
   <xs:selector xpath=".//mstns:Customers" />
   <xs:field xpath="mstns:CustomerID" />
  </xs:unique>
 </xs:element>
</xs:schema>
```

Starting at the top, you can see that this XSD file references several namespaces. This includes the xs namespace, which is the proposed XSD standard at the W3C's website, and the mstns and msdata namespaces developed by Microsoft. This file provides a good example of how you can intermingle tags from two namespaces by using prefixes.

The first thing that the XSD file defines is the contents of an element named DataSet1, which is marked (through an attribute from the msdata namespace) as representing a DataSet:

```
<xs:element name="Dataset1" msdata:IsDataSet="true">
 <xs:complexType>
  <xs:choice maxOccurs="unbounded">
   <xs:element name="Customers">
```

The DataSet1 element is identified as a complex type—that is, one that contains more than one piece of data. The xs:choice tag with the maxOccurs attribute set to "unbounded" says that the contents of the DataSet1 element can occur an unlimited number of times in the file that this XSD schema describes. The xsd:element tag shows that the Customers element is the element that can reoccur within the DataSet1 element.

The Customers element is defined next. The start of this definition is as follows:

```
<xs:element name="Customers">
 <xs:complexType>
  <xs:sequence>
```

The xs:element tag supplies the name of the element. The XSD file then states that the Customers data type is a complex type consisting of a sequence of other types. A sequence in this context is a set of tags that must occur in a particular order.

The other types contained within Customers are then defined in sequence. For example, this is the definition for CustomerName, the first of the contained types:

```
<xs:element name="CustomerID" type="xs:string" />
```

The `CustomerID` type is defined as a simple data type based on the XSD string data type.

The definitions of the other elements within the `Customers` type are similar. When all of the elements in the `Customers` type have been defined, the file includes a section to define the unique key for the table:

```
<xs:unique name="Dataset1Key1" msdata:PrimaryKey="true">
  <xs:selector xpath=".//mstns:Customers" />
  <xs:field xpath="mstns:CustomerID" />
</xs:unique>
```

Finally, the file is closed with tags to correspond to all of the opening tags.

NOTE   *For the complete details on how the .NET Framework structures XSD files, refer to the "XSD Schema Reference" section in the .NET Framework General Reference (part of the online help for the .NET Framework).*

Reading and Writing XML

After that whirlwind introduction to XML, you're probably ready to find out what you can do with XML from the .NET Framework. We'll start with the basics: reading and writing XML files. Reading and writing XML files are integrated into the streams and stores model of I/O that you saw in Chapter 15, "Streams and Input/Output."

Writing XML Files

Listing 20.9 shows how you can use an `XmlTextWriter` object to create an XML file.

LISTING 20.9: WRITING XML WITH AN `XmlTextWriter`

```
/*
  Example20_1.cs illustrates the XmlTextWriter class
*/

using System;
using System.Xml;

class Example20_1
{

    public static void Main()
    {

        // use the XmlTextWriter to open a new XML file
        XmlTextWriter xw = new XmlTextWriter(@"c:\temp\Cust4.xml",
            System.Text.Encoding.UTF8);

        // write the document declaration
        xw.WriteStartDocument();
```

```
        // write the first element
        xw.WriteStartElement("NewDataSet");

        // write the first customer
        xw.WriteStartElement("Customers");
        xw.WriteElementString("CustomerID", "ALFKI");
        xw.WriteElementString("CompanyName", "Alfreds Futterkiste");
        xw.WriteElementString("ContactName", "Maria Anders");
        xw.WriteElementString("ContactTitle", "Sales Representative");
        xw.WriteElementString("Address", "Obere Str. 57");
        xw.WriteElementString("City", "Berlin");
        xw.WriteElementString("PostalCode", "12209");
        xw.WriteElementString("Country", "Germany");
        xw.WriteElementString("Phone", "030-0074321");
        xw.WriteElementString("Fax", "030-0076545");
        xw.WriteEndElement();

        // write the second customer
        xw.WriteStartElement("Customers");
        xw.WriteElementString("CustomerID", "BONAPP");
        xw.WriteElementString("CompanyName", "Bon App'");
        xw.WriteElementString("ContactName", "Laurence Lebihan");
        xw.WriteElementString("ContactTitle", "Owner");
        xw.WriteElementString("Address", "12, rue des Bouchers");
        xw.WriteElementString("City", "Marseille");
        xw.WriteElementString("PostalCode", "13008");
        xw.WriteElementString("Country", "France");
        xw.WriteElementString("Phone", "91.24.45.40");
        xw.WriteElementString("Fax", "91.24.45.41");
        xw.WriteEndElement();

        // end the NewDataSet element
        xw.WriteEndElement();

        // end the document
        xw.WriteEndDocument();

        // flush and close
        xw.Flush();
        xw.Close();
    }

}
```

The output of this code will be a file, Cust4.xml, in the c:\temp folder. This file will contain the same information as the Cust.xml file that you saw earlier in this chapter. Note that you don't need to worry about proper tag syntax or even the XML declaration when using the XmlTextWriter class.

Just as the BinaryWriter class takes care of binary formatting for you, the XmlTextWriter class takes care of XML formatting.

TIP *The file created by this application will be a single long string of text with no whitespace. You can use the* Indentation *property and the* WriteWhitespace *method of the* XmlTextWriter *to add whitespace to an XML file.*

Table 20.1 shows the public XmlTextWriter properties.

TABLE 20.1: XmlTextWriter PROPERTIES

PROPERTY	TYPE	DESCRIPTION
BaseStream	Stream	Gets the underlying Stream that the XmlTextWriter writes to
Formatting	Formatting	Controls how the output file is formatted.
Indentation	int	Sets the number of IndentChar characters to write for each level of indentation
IndentChar	char	Gets or sets the character used for indenting the XML
Namespaces	bool	Indicates whether this XmlTextWriter supports namespaces
QuoteChar	char	Represents the character used to quote attribute values
WriteState	WriteState	Indicates the progress of the write operation
XmlLang	string	Indicates the current language being used in the file
XmlSpace	XmlSpace	Indicates the current state of the XmlTextWriter

Table 20.2 shows the public XmlTextWriter methods.

TABLE 20.2: XmlTextWriter METHODS

METHOD	STATIC?	DESCRIPTION
Close()	No	Closes the XmlTextWriter and the underlying Stream
Flush()	No	Flushes any remaining data in the buffer to the underlying Stream
LookupPrefix()	No	Returns the prefix, if any, for a given namespace
WriteAttributes()	No	Writes out a set of attributes
WriteAttributeString()	No	Writes out a single attribute as a string
WriteBase64()	No	Writes out Base64-encoded information
WriteBinHex()	No	Writes out BinHex-encoded information
WriteCData()	No	Writes out a CDATA section

Continued on next page

TABLE 20.2: XmlTextWriter METHODS *(continued)*

METHOD	STATIC?	DESCRIPTION
WriteCharEntity()	No	Writes out a character entity
WriteChars()	No	Writes out a text buffer
WriteComment()	No	Writes out an XML comment
WriteDocType()	No	Writes out a DOCTYPE declaration
WriteElementString()	No	Writes out a single element as a string
WriteEndAttribute()	No	Writes out a closing tag for an attribute
WriteEndDocument()	No	Writes out a closing tag for a document
WriteEndElement()	No	Writes out a closing tag for an element
WriteEntityRef()	No	Writes out an entity reference
WriteFullEndElement()	No	Writes out a closing tag for an element and stops using a namespace
WriteName()	No	Writes out a name
WriteNmToken()	No	Writes out a name using the NmToken format
WriteNode()	No	Writes out an XML node
WriteProcessingInstruction()	No	Writes out a processing instruction
WriteQualfiedName()	No	Writes out a namespace-qualified name
WriteRaw()	No	Writes out raw markup
WriteStartAttribute()	No	Writes out the start of an attribute
WriteStartDocument()	No	Writes out the start of an XML document
WriteStartElement()	No	Writes out the start of an element
WriteString()	No	Writes out a string of text
WriteSurrogateCharEntity()	No	Writes out a surrogate character entity
WriteWhitespace()	No	Writes out whitespace

NOTE *The* XmlTextWriter *class is an implementation of the abstract* XmlWriter *class.*

Reading XML Files

Just as you can write XML files using the .NET Framework, you can also read them. Reading XML files is handled by the XmlReader abstract base class, which is implemented in the XmlTextReader, XmlValidatingReader, and XmlNodeReader classes.

To understand how the XmlReader class works, though, we'll need to take a slight detour. That's because the XmlReader returns information about XML files through the Document Object Model (DOM). So, before you can understand code using the XmlReader, you'll need to be familiar with the DOM, which is the subject of the next section of this chapter.

Using the Document Object Model

The key .NET Framework class for synchronizing a DataSet with an XML representation of the same data is the XmlDataDocument. Before you can understand this class, though, you should have a grasp of the XmlDocument class; XmlDataDocument inherits from and extends XmlDocument. The XmlDocument class, in turn, is an implementation of the DOM. So, to start working with DataSet objects and XML, the first thing to explore is the DOM.

Understanding the Document Object Model

The DOM is an Internet standard for representing the information contained in an HTML or XML document as a tree of nodes. Like many other Internet standards, the DOM is an official standard of the W3C. According to the W3C, the DOM specification "defines the Document Object Model, a platform- and language-neutral interface that will allow programs and scripts to dynamically access and update the content, structure, and style of documents. The Document Object Model provides a standard set of objects for representing HTML and XML documents, a standard model of how these objects can be combined, and a standard interface for accessing and manipulating them."

NOTE *To be precise, there are several Document Object Models. The one we'll be using in this chapter is the XML DOM. There is also a DHTML DOM, a standard for representing Dynamic HTML documents.*

You can't count on any vendor to implement the entire DOM standard. The .NET Framework includes support for the DOM Level 1 Core and DOM Level 2 Core specifications, but it also extends the DOM by adding additional objects, methods, and properties to the specification. This is typical of Internet vendors. Although a grasp of the applicable standard will get you started understanding a technology such as the DOM, you'll need to look at a particular vendor's tools to determine exactly how that vendor implements its technology.

TIP *For the official DOM specifications, see* **www.w3.org/DOM**. *The XML Cover Pages website also has a nice set of DOM-related links at* **www.oasis-open.org/cover/dom.html**.

Within the .NET Framework, the DOM is implemented in two classes, XmlNode and XmlDocument. An XmlNode object represents a single atomic portion of the XML file. An XmlDocument object represents the entire file as a collection of XmlNode objects.

Introducing the *XmlNode* Class

As you've seen, an XML document is a series of nested items, including elements and attributes. Any nested structure can be transformed to an equivalent tree structure, by making the outermost nested item the root of the tree, the next-in items the children of the root, and so on.

In converting an XML document to a tree, many different items may become nodes. For example, both elements and attributes are represented as nodes within the DOM. The DOM assigns a node type to each node to identify its source in the XML. The .NET Framework includes an XmlNodeType enumeration that distinguishes the possible node types in Microsoft's DOM implementation. Table 20.3 lists the members of the XmlNodeType enumeration.

TABLE 20.3: XmlNodeType ENUMERATION

MEMBER	REPRESENTS
Attribute	An XML attribute
CDATA	An XML CDATA section
Comment	An XML comment
Document	The outermost element of the XML document (that is, the root of the tree representation of the XML)
DocumentFragment	The outermost element of a subsection of an XML document
DocumentType	A Document Type Description (DTD) reference
Element	An XML element
EndElement	The closing tag of an XML element
EndEntity	The end of an included entity
Entity	An XML entity declaration
EntityReference	A reference to an entity
None	Indication of an XmlReader that has not been initialized
Notation	An XML notation
ProcessingInstruction	An XML processing instruction
SignificantWhitespace	Whitespace that must be preserved to re-create the original XML document
Text	The text content of an attribute, element, or other node
Whitespace	Space between actual XML markup items
XmlDeclaration	The XML declaration

NOTE *Technically, attributes are not part of the DOM tree. Rather, they're considered properties of their parent element. Later in the chapter, in the section "Reading an XML Document with the XmlTextReader Class," you'll see how to retrieve a collection containing all the attributes belonging to a particular element.*

Individual nodes in the DOM representation of an XML document are represented in the .NET Framework by XmlNode objects. After instantiating an XmlNode object that represents a particular portion of an XML file, you can alter the properties of the XmlNode object and then write the changes back to the XML file. The DOM provides two-way access to the underlying XML and is thus a convenient means for manipulating XML files.

NOTE *The* System.Xml *namespace also contains a set of classes that represent particular types of nodes:* XmlAttribute, XmlComment, XmlElement, *and so on. These classes all inherit from the* XmlNode *class.*

Table 20.4 shows the public XmlNode properties.

TABLE 20.4: XmlNode PROPERTIES

PROPERTY	TYPE	DESCRIPTION
Attributes	XmlAttributeCollection	Gets the attributes of this XmlNode
BaseURI	string	Gets the base URI of this XmlNode
ChildNodes	XmlNodeList	Gets the child nodes of this XmlNode
FirstChild	XmlNode	Gets the first child of this XmlNode
HasChildNodes	bool	Indicates whether this XmlNode has child nodes
InnerText	string	Gets the value of this XmlNode and all of its children
InnerXml	string	Gets the markup representing the children of this XmlNode
IsReadOnly	bool	Indicates whether the XmlNode is read-only
Item	XmlElement	Gets the specified child element of this XmlNode
LastChild	XmlNode	Gets the last child of this XmlNode
LocalName	string	Gets the local name of this XmlNode
Name	string	Gets the qualified name of this XmlNode
NamespaceURI	string	Gets the namespace URI for this XmlNode
NextSibling	XmlNode	Gets the next XmlNode in the tree
NodeType	XmlNodeType	Gets the type of this XmlNode
OuterXml	string	Gets the markup representing this XmlNode and all of its children
OwnerDocument	XmlDocument	Gets the document that contains this XmlNode
ParentNode	XmlNode	Gets the parent of this XmlNode
Prefix	string	Gets the namespace prefix of this XmlNode
PreviousSibling	XmlNode	Gets the previous XmlNode in the tree
Value	string	Gets the value of this XmlNode

Table 20.5 shows the public XmlNode methods.

TABLE 20.5 XmlNode METHODS

METHOD	STATIC?	DESCRIPTION
AppendChild()	No	Adds a new XmlNode to the end of the list of children of this XmlNode
Clone()	No	Creates a duplicate of this XmlNode
CloneNode()	No	Creates a duplicate of this XmlNode
CreateNavigator()	No	Creates an XPathNavigator object
GetEnumerator()	No	Supports iteration over the children of this XmlNode
GetNamespaceOfPrefix()	No	Looks up the namespace for a given prefix
GetPrefixOfNamespace()	No	Looks up the prefix for a given namespace
InsertAfter()	No	Inserts an Xml node immediately after this XmlNode
InsertBefore()	No	Inserts an XmlNode immediately before this XmlNode
Normalize()	No	Reformats an XmlNode and its children to a standard format
PrependChild()	No	Adds a new XmlNode to the beginning of the list of children of this XmlNode
RemoveAll()	No	Removes all children of this XmlNode
RemoveChild()	No	Removes a specified child of this XmlNode
ReplaceChild()	No	Replaces a specified child of this XmlNode
SelectNodes()	No	Selects a list of nodes matching an XPath expression
SelectSingleNode()	No	Selects a single node matching an XPath expression
Supports()	No	Tests for implementation behavior of the DOM
WriteContentTo()	No	Saves the children of this XmlNode to an XmlWriter
WriteTo()	No	Saves this XmlNode to an XmlWriter

As you can see, the XmlNode object has a comparatively rich interface. But note that although every node has a property to navigate directly to its parent node, the parent node does not have a property for every child node.

Introducing the *XmlDocument* Class

The XmlNode class represents one particular piece of an XML document. To represent the document as a whole, you need another class. Not surprisingly, this is the XmlDocument class. An instance of the XmlDocument class can be instantiated from an XML document, and it then provides access to the individual XmlNode objects that describe the document. The XmlDocument class has a rich interface, with many properties, methods, and events. Table 20.6 shows the public XmlDocument properties.

NOTE The XmlDocument *class inherits from the* XmlNode *class. In addition to the methods and properties shown in Tables 20.6 and 20.7, the* XmlDocument *class has all of the methods and properties shown in Tables 20.4 and 20.5.*

TABLE 20.6: XmlDocument PROPERTIES

PROPERTY	TYPE	DESCRIPTION
DocumentElement	XmlElement	Gets the root XML element of the document
DocumentType	XmlDocumentType	Gets the node containing the DOCTYPE declaration, if any
Implementation	XmlImplementation	Returns an object that defines the context for this XML file
NameTable	XmlNameTable	Returns an internal data structure used in parsing the XML file
PreserveWhitespace	bool	Indicates whether whitespace should be preserved when working with this XmlDocument
XmlResolver	XmlResoolver	The XmlResolver is used to resolve external resources.

Table 20.7 shows the public XmlDocument methods.

TABLE 20.7 XmlDocument METHODS

METHOD	STATIC?	DESCRIPTION
CreateAttribute()	No	Creates a new attribute
CreateCDataSection()	No	Creates a new CDATA section
CreateComment()	No	Creates a new comment
CreateDocumentFragment()	No	Creates a new document fragment
CreateDocumentType()	No	Creates a new document type
CreateElement()	No	Creates a new element
CreateEntityReference()	No	Creates a new entity reference
CreateNavigator()	No	Creates a new XPathNavigator object
CreateNode()	No	Creates a new XmlNode
CreateProcessingInstruction()	No	Creates a new processing instruction
CreateSignificantWhitespace()	No	Creates new whitespace
CreateTextNode()	No	Creates a new node representing text
CreateWhitespace()	No	Creates new whitespace
CreateXmlDeclaration()	No	Creates a node representing the XML declaration

Continued on next page

TABLE 20.7 XmlDocument METHODS *(continued)*

METHOD	STATIC?	DESCRIPTION
GetElementById()	No	Gets an XML element corresponding to a particular ID
GetElementsByTagName()	No	Gets a list of elements with a particular tag name
ImportNode()	No	Imports an XmlNode from another document
Load()	No	Loads the XML document
LoadXml()	No	Loads the XML document from the specified string
ReadNode()	No	Reads the next node in the XML file

Reading an XML Document with the *XmlTextReader* Class

Listing 20.10 shows how you can use an XmlTextReader to read an XML file into an XmlDocument.

LISTING 20.10: READING AN XML FILE

```
/*
   Example20_2.cs illustrates the XmlTextReader class
*/

using System;
using System.Xml;

class Example20_2
{
    // Display a node and its children
    private static void AddChildren(XmlNode xnod, int level)
    {
        XmlNode xnodWorking;
        String pad = new String(' ', level * 2);

        Console.WriteLine(pad + xnod.Name + "(" + xnod.NodeType.ToString()
         + ": " + xnod.Value + ")");

        // if this is an element, extract any attributes
        if (xnod.NodeType == XmlNodeType.Element)
        {
            XmlNamedNodeMap mapAttributes = xnod.Attributes;
            for(int i=0; i<mapAttributes.Count; i+=1)
            {
                Console.WriteLine(pad + " " + mapAttributes.Item(i).Name
                    + " = " +  mapAttributes.Item(i).Value);
            }
        }
    }
```

```
        // call recursively on all children of the current node
        if (xnod.HasChildNodes)
        {
            xnodWorking = xnod.FirstChild;
            while (xnodWorking != null)
            {
                AddChildren(xnodWorking, level+1);
                xnodWorking = xnodWorking.NextSibling;
            }
        }


    }

    public static void Main()
    {

        // use an XmlTextReader to open an XML document
        XmlTextReader xtr = new XmlTextReader(@"c:\temp\Cust4.xml");
        xtr.WhitespaceHandling = WhitespaceHandling.None;

        // load the file into an XmlDocuent
        XmlDocument xd = new XmlDocument();
        xd.Load(xtr);

        // get the document root node
        XmlNode xnodDE = xd.DocumentElement;

        // recursively walk the node tree
        AddChildren(xnodDE, 0);

        // close the reader
        xtr.Close();
    }

}
```

After reading the XML file into the XmlDocument, this program does some work with the resulting structure. It moves recursively through all of the nodes in the DOM, outputting the name and type of each node along with its contents. The output from this program is as follows:

```
NewDataSet(Element: )
  Customers(Element: )
    CustomerID(Element: )
      #text(Text: ALFKI)
```

```
        CompanyName(Element: )
          #text(Text: Alfreds Futterkiste)
        ContactName(Element: )
          #text(Text: Maria Anders)
        ContactTitle(Element: )
          #text(Text: Sales Representative)
        Address(Element: )
          #text(Text: Obere Str. 57)
        City(Element: )
          #text(Text: Berlin)
        PostalCode(Element: )
          #text(Text: 12209)
        Country(Element: )
          #text(Text: Germany)
        Phone(Element: )
          #text(Text: 030-0074321)
        Fax(Element: )
          #text(Text: 030-0076545)
    Customers(Element: )
      CustomerID(Element: )
        #text(Text: BONAPP)
      CompanyName(Element: )
        #text(Text: Bon App&apos;)
      ContactName(Element: )
        #text(Text: Laurence Lebihan)
      ContactTitle(Element: )
        #text(Text: Owner)
      Address(Element: )
        #text(Text: 12, rue des Bouchers)
      City(Element: )
        #text(Text: Marseille)
      PostalCode(Element: )
        #text(Text: 13008)
      Country(Element: )
        #text(Text: France)
      Phone(Element: )
        #text(Text: 91.24.45.40)
      Fax(Element: )
        #text(Text: 91.24.45.41)
```

In this particular case, we've used the XmlTextReader as a pipe to fill the XmlDocument. But you can also work with an XmlTextReader directly through its rich set of members. Table 20.8 shows the public XmlTextReader properties.

TABLE 20.8: XmlTextReader PROPERTIES

PROPERTY	TYPE	DESCRIPTION
AttributeCount	int	Gets the number of attributes on the current node
BaseURI	string	Gets the base URI of the current node
CanResolveEntity	bool	Indicates whether this XmlTextReader can resolve entity references
Depth	int	Returns the depth of the current node in the document
Encoding	Encoding	Gets the encoding of the document
EOF	bool	Indicates whether the XmlTextReader is at the end of the stream
HasAttributes	bool	Indicates whether the current node has any attributes
HasValue	bool	Indicates whether the current node can have a value
IsDefault	bool	Indicates whether the current node was generated from a default value defined in a DTD or schema
IsEmptyElement	bool	Indicates whether the current node is an empty element
Item	string	Returns an indexer for the XmlTextReader
LineNumber	int	Gets the current line number in the original file
LinePosition	int	Gets the current line position in the original file
LocalName	string	Gets the local name of the current node
Name	string	Gets the qualified name of the current node
Namespaces	bool	Indicates whether the XmlTextReader supports namespaces
NamespaceURI	string	Gets the namespace URI for the current node
NameTable	XmlNameTable	Gets the name table for this XmlTextReader
NodeType	XmlNodeType	Gets the type of the current node
Normalization	bool	Indicates whether to normalize whitespace
Prefix	string	Gets the Namespace prefix for the current node
QuoteChar	char	Gets the character used to quote attributes
ReadState	ReadState	Gets the state of the XmlTextReader
Value	string	Value of the current node
WhitespaceHandling	WhitespaceHandling	Indicates how whitespace is handled
XmlLang	string	Gets the current language
XmlResolver	XmlResolver	Gets the object used to resolve external references
XmlSpace	XmlSpace	Indicates the state of the XmlTextReader

Table 20.9 shows the public XmlTextReader methods.

TABLE 20.9 XmlTextReader METHODS

METHOD	STATIC?	DESCRIPTION
Close()	No	Closes the XmlTextReader
GetAttribute()	No	Gets the value of an attribute
GetRemainder()	No	Gets the rest of the buffered XML
IsStartElement()	No	Tests whether the current node is a start tag for an element
LookupNamespace()	No	Resolves a namespace reference
MoveToAttribute()	No	Moves to the specified attribute
MoveToContent()	No	Moves to the next node with content
MoveToElement()	No	Moves to the element node that contains the current attribute
MoveToFirstAttribute()	No	Moves to the first attribute
MoveToNextAttribute()	No	Moves to the next attribute
Read()	No	Reads the next node
ReadAttributeValue()	No	Reads the value of an attribute
ReadBase64()	No	Decodes and returns a Base64 value
ReadBinHex()	No	Decodes and returns a BinHex value
ReadChars()	No	Reads the text of an element
ReadElementString()	No	Reads an element into a string
ReadEndElement()	No	Processes an end tag
ReadInnerXml()	No	Reads all content and markup of a node
ReadOuterXml()	No	Reads all content and markup of a node and its children
ReadStartElement()	No	Processes a start tag
ReadString()	No	Reads the current node contents
ResetState()	No	Resets the XmlTextReader
ResolveEntity()	No	Resolves an entity reference
Skip()	No	Skips the children of the current node

Transforming XML

The .NET Framework also includes support for transforming XML via XSLT. This support is provided through objects in the System.Xml.Xsl namespace. Listing 20.11 demonstrates the use of the XslTransform class to apply a transform.

LISTING 20.11: USING THE XslTransform CLASS

```
/*
  Example20_3.cs illustrates the XslTransform class
*/

using System;
using System.Xml;
using System.Xml.Xsl;
using System.IO;

class Example20_3
{

    public static void Main()
    {

        // use an XmlTextReader to open an XML document
        XmlTextReader xtr = new XmlTextReader("Cust3.xml");
        xtr.WhitespaceHandling = WhitespaceHandling.None;

        // load the file into an XmlDocuent
        XmlDocument xd = new XmlDocument();
        xd.Load(xtr);

        // load an XSLT file
        XslTransform xslt = new XslTransform();
        xslt.Load("Cust.xsl");

        // perform the transformation in memory
        MemoryStream stm = new MemoryStream();
        xslt.Transform(xd, null, stm);

        // and dump the results
        stm.Position = 1;
        StreamReader sr = new StreamReader(stm);
        Console.Write(sr.ReadToEnd());

        // close the reader
        xtr.Close();
    }

}
```

The output from this program is as follows:

```
<html>
  <body>
    <p>
      <h2>Customer</h2>
      <br>
        <b>ALFKI</b>
      <br>Alfreds Futterkiste
      <br>Maria Anders
    </p>
    <p>
      <h2>Customer</h2>
      <br>
        <b>BONAP</b>
      <br>Bon app'
      <br>Laurence Lebihan
    </p>
  </body>
</html>
```

The XslTransform class is one of those simple classes that exists to perform a single task. Table 20.10 shows the public XslTransform property.

TABLE 20.10: XslTransform PROPERTY

PROPERTY	TYPE	DESCRIPTION
XmlResolver	XmlResolver	The object used to resolve any external references in the XML file

Table 20.11 shows the public XslTransform methods.

TABLE 20.11: XslTransform METHODS

METHOD	STATIC?	DESCRIPTION
Load()	No	Loads an XSL style sheet into the XslTransform
Transform()	No	Transforms the specified XML data with the loaded style sheet

There are several overloaded versions of the Transform method. These allow you to use a variety of objects including files and XPathNavigator objects for input and to output the results to a file, stream, XmlReader, or TextWriter object. In this particular case, we used the version that reads the XML from a class that implements IXPathNavigable and outputs the results to a stream. This version has three parameters. The first is the name of the XmlDocument object that contains the XML. The second is an instance of the XsltArgumentList class, which lets you pass arguments to the style sheet. This particular style sheet doesn't take any arguments so we passed a null parameter in the second position. The third parameter is the stream to be used for the output. Note that in this case we used a `MemoryStream` object to avoid the overhead of writing the transformed file to disk. If you send the results of the transform to another `Stream` class, such as a `NetworkStream` or a `StringWriter`, you can send the transformed data across the network or to a file.

Summary

In this chapter we introduced you to the basics of XML and some of the classes that the .NET Framework provides for working with XML.

The major XML standards supported by the .NET Framework include XML, XSLT, and XSD.

The `XmlTextWriter` class provides a high-level interface for writing XML files that encapsulates knowledge of the XML file structure. The `XmlTextReader` class provides a corresponding way to read an XML file with knowledge of the file's structure.

The `XmlNode` and `XmlDocument` classes let you investigate the structure of an XML file.

The `XslTransform` class allows you to apply an XSLT transform to an XML file.

There is much more to XML in the .NET Framework than we can cover in a short chapter. For example, the .NET Framework also supports XPath, a standard for executing queries on XML data. If you're working seriously with XML, you'll want to dig into these additional classes on your own.

Chapter 21

Other Classes in the Base Class Library

AS MENTIONED IN CHAPTER 14, "Threads," the .NET Framework Base Class Library contains hundreds of classes. In a book this size, we can't even attempt to cover all of the available classes. Now that you've seen some of the major chunks of functionality that the class library provides, we'll take a quick survey of some other portions. The classes covered in this chapter do not exhaust the class library by any means; if you're after something else, refer to the .NET Framework documentation where you may well find a class to fill your needs.

The class library contains a full set of graphics classes that work with GDI+, the latest round of graphical application programming interfaces (APIs) for the Windows operating system. We'll start this chapter with a look at some of the graphics classes.

In today's world, globalization is becoming an increasingly important topic. Globalization refers to the process of preparing your software to be used in other locales and other languages. The class library provides a well-designed set of classes designed to support globalization.

Diagnostics and debugging are also built into the class library. We'll look at the `Debug` and `Trace` classes, which let you see debugging information either at design-time or run-time.

Finally, we'll check out some of the advanced feature support of the class library. These include classes that support the features of the .NET run-time itself, of the operating system, and of advanced component services.

Featured in this chapter:

- ◆ Looking at the Graphics Classes
- ◆ Understanding Globalization
- ◆ Diagnostics and Debugging
- ◆ Getting into Advanced Facilities

Understanding the Graphics Classes

The .NET Framework graphics classes are designed to work with GDI+, the latest version of the Windows Graphics Device Interface libraries. Graphics classes in the .NET Framework allow you to draw lines and shapes, as well as to work with image files and typographic fonts. In this section, we'll discuss some of the basics of GDI+ and then show you a few samples so you can get an idea of what GDI+ and the .NET Framework can do together.

Introducing the GDI+

GDI+ is the latest revision to the core graphics library used by Windows, designed especially for use by managed-code applications. GDI+ is installed with the operating system as a part of Windows XP and Windows .NET server. For older operating systems (Windows 98, Windows Me, Windows NT 4.0, and Windows 2000), you can download and install the GDI+ library from www.microsoft.com/downloads/release.asp?releaseid=32738. The .NET Framework also installs GDI+.

Like previous Windows graphics libraries, the purpose of GDI+ is to insulate developers from the details of different display devices. Your code can call a uniform set of classes from GDI+, and the library will worry about the details of using the hardware in your computer to display the results of those calls.

Broadly speaking, the GDI+ classes handle three functions:

- Displaying vector graphics, such as points, lines, and shapes
- Displaying image files, such as files in the JPG or PNG formats
- Displaying fonts

We'll look at sample code from the first two of these areas in the following sections.

Using Pens, Lines, and Rectangles

To get a feel for the use of GDI+, we'll draw some simple shapes: lines and rectangles. This requires using both the Graphics class and the Pen class. Listing 21.1 shows how to draw a single line.

LISTING 21.1: DRAWING A LINE

```
/*
  Example21_1.cs illustrates the use of Pens and Lines
*/

using System;
using System.Drawing;
using System.Collections;
using System.ComponentModel;
using System.Windows.Forms;
using System.Data;
```

```
public class Example21_1 : System.Windows.Forms.Form
{
    private System.ComponentModel.Container components = null;

    public Example21_1()
    {
        InitializeComponent();
    }

    protected override void Dispose( bool disposing )
    {
        if( disposing )
        {
            if (components != null)
            {
                components.Dispose();
            }
        }
        base.Dispose( disposing );
    }

    private void InitializeComponent()
    {
        this.BackColor = System.Drawing.Color.White;
        this.ClientSize = new System.Drawing.Size(400, 400);
        this.Name = "Example21_1";
        this.Text = "Example21_1";
        this.Paint += new System.Windows.Forms.
         PaintEventHandler(this.Example21_1_Paint);
    }


    static void Main()
    {
        Application.Run(new Example21_1());
    }

    private void Example21_1_Paint(object sender,
     System.Windows.Forms.PaintEventArgs e)
    {
        Graphics g = e.Graphics;
        Pen p = new Pen(Color.Black, 10);
        g.DrawLine(p, 25, 25, 375, 375);
    }
}
```

NOTE   *Unlike most of the samples that you've seen in this book, this example (and the other graphics examples in this chapter) works as a Windows application rather than as a command-prompt application. You can still launch it from the command line if you like. Alternatively, you can compile it with the /t:winexe switch and launch it directly from Windows Explorer by double-clicking the executable.*

You'll see that this example has much more scaffolding code than most of the examples so far in this book. That's because you can't use the graphics classes with a console application. Instead, we're using these classes to draw on a Windows form. You'll learn about Windows forms in Chapter 24, "Introduction to Windows Applications." For now, you can just treat forms as a canvas to draw on, and instead concentrate on the code that does the actual drawing, which is contained entirely within the `Paint` event handler. Figure 21.1 shows the result of running this application.

TIP   *This application uses the `Paint` event of the form to retrieve a `Graphics` object, which represents the client area of the form.*

FIGURE 21.1

A single line on a form

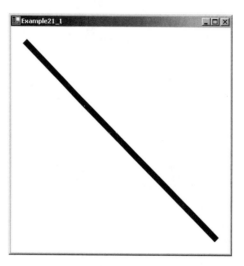

As you can see in the source code, it takes two objects (at least) to manage graphics operations. The `Graphics` object represents the overall GDI+ drawing environment. You can think of it as a blank page that you can use to hold graphical elements. The `Pen` object represents the properties of a line used to draw such elements.

Table 21.1 shows the public `Pen` properties.

TABLE 21.1: Pen PROPERTIES

PROPERTY	TYPE	DESCRIPTION
Alignment	PenAlignment	Gets the alignment of the Pen object
Brush	Brush	Gets the Brush object used by this Pen object
Color	Color	Gets the color of the Pen object
CompoundArray	float[]	Allows you to create a Pen that draws multiple parallel lines
CustomEndCap	CustomLineCap	Sets the style to use in drawing the end of the line
CustomStartCap	CustomLineCap	Sets the style to use in drawing the start of the line
DashCap	DashCap	Sets the style to use at the end of any dashes in the line
DashOffset	float	Sets the distance from the start of the line to a dashed pattern
DashPattern	float[]	An array of dashes and spaces
DashStyle	DashStyle	Sets the style of dashes drawn with this pen
EndCap	LineCap	Sets the style to use in drawing the end of the line
LineJoin	LineJoin	Sets the style of join between multiple lines drawn with this pen
MiterLimit	float	Sets the thickness of mitered corners when joining multiple lines
PenType	PenType	The style of lines to draw with this pen
StartCap	LineCap	The style used in drawing the start of the line
Transform	Matrix	Specifies a geometric transformation
Width	float	The width (in pixels) of lines drawn with this pen

Table 21.2 shows the public Pen methods.

TABLE 21.2: Pen METHODS

METHOD	STATIC?	DESCRIPTION
Clone()	No	Creates a copy of this Pen object
MultiplyTransform()	No	Applies matrix math to a transform
ResetTransform()	No	Returns a transform to its original state
RotateTransform()	No	Rotates a transform
ScaleTransform()	No	Scales a transform
SetLineCap()	No	Sets the values of the StartCap and EndCap properties
TranslateTransform()	No	Moves a transform

All graphics operations are measured in pixels, with the origin of the measurement being the upper-left corner of the Graphics object. In this sample, this line of code draws the following line:

```
g.DrawLine(p, 25, 25, 375, 375);
```

That starts the line 25 pixels down from the top of the form and 25 pixels in from the left of the form. The line is continued to a point 375 pixels down and 375 pixels in.

Drawing the line takes three steps:

1. Obtain a Graphics object that represents the form. In this code, the Graphics object is obtained from the PaintEventArgs object that's passed into the Paint event.

2. Create a new Pen object that has properties matching the line you'd like to draw. In this case, that's a black line 10-pixels wide.

3. Use the DrawLine method of the Graphics object, together with the Pen object, to draw a line between two specified points.

You can use a single pen repeatedly or use multiple pens in a single application. Listing 21.2 illustrates these points.

LISTING 21.2: USING MULTIPLE PENS

```
/*
  Example21_2.cs illustrates the use of multiple Pens
*/

using System;
using System.Drawing;
using System.Drawing.Drawing2D;
using System.Collections;
using System.ComponentModel;
using System.Windows.Forms;
using System.Data;

public class Example21_2 : System.Windows.Forms.Form
{
    private System.ComponentModel.Container components = null;

    public Example21_2()
    {
        InitializeComponent();
    }

    protected override void Dispose( bool disposing )
    {
        if( disposing )
        {
            if (components != null)
```

```
            {
                components.Dispose();
            }
        }
        base.Dispose( disposing );
    }

    private void InitializeComponent()
    {
        this.BackColor = System.Drawing.Color.White;
        this.ClientSize = new System.Drawing.Size(400, 400);
        this.Name = "Example21_2";
        this.Text = "Example21_2";
        this.Paint += new System.Windows.Forms.
         PaintEventHandler(this.Example21_2_Paint);
    }


    static void Main()
    {
        Application.Run(new Example21_2());
    }

    private void Example21_2_Paint(
     object sender, System.Windows.Forms.PaintEventArgs e)
    {
        Graphics g = e.Graphics;
        // draw two lines with one pen
        Pen p = new Pen(Color.Black, 10);
        g.DrawLine(p, 25, 25, 375, 375);
        g.DrawLine(p, 25, 375, 375, 25);
        // draw four lines with another pen
        Pen p2 = new Pen(Color.Gray, 7);
        p2.EndCap = LineCap.Round;
        p2.StartCap = LineCap.ArrowAnchor;
        g.DrawLine(p2, 25, 35, 25, 365);
        g.DrawLine(p2, 35, 375, 365, 375);
        g.DrawLine(p2, 375, 365, 375, 35);
        g.DrawLine(p2, 365, 25, 35, 25);
    }
}
```

This code creates a Pen object named p and uses it to draw two lines. It then creates a second Pen object named p2, sets its properties to have custom start and end points, and uses it to draw four lines. Figure 21.2 shows the results of running this application.

FIGURE 21.2

Drawing multiple lines

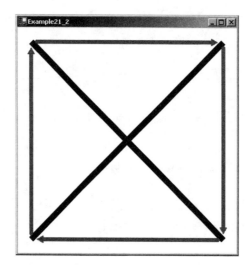

The other essential class for drawing this sort of simple graphics is the `Graphics` class. Table 21.3 shows the public `Graphics` properties.

TABLE 21.3: `Graphics` PROPERTIES

PROPERTY	TYPE	DESCRIPTION
Clip	Region	Sets the region available on which to draw
ClipBounds	Rectangle	Gets a RectangleF object representing the clipping region
CompositingMode	CompositingMode	Specifies how composited images are drawn
CompositingQuality	CompositingQuality	Specifies the quality of composited images
DpiX	float	Sets the horizontal resolution of the Graphics object
DpiY	float	Sets the vertical resolution of the Graphics object
InterpolatingMode	InterpolatingMode	Determines how values between two endpoints are calculated
IsClipEmpty	bool	Indicates whether the clipping region is empty
PageScale	float	Sets a scaling factor for the Graphics object
PageUnit	GraphicsUnit	Identifies the unit of measurement to use
PixelOffsetMode	PixelOffsetMode	Determines how pixels are offset during rendering
RenderingOrigin	Point	Sets the origin for hatches and brushes
SmoothingMode	SmoothingMode	Controls the smoothness used to draw on this object

Continued on next page

TABLE 21.3: Graphics PROPERTIES *(continued)*

PROPERTY	TYPE	DESCRIPTION
TextContrast	int	Sets a contrast value for text
TextRenderingHint	TextRenderingHint	Sets a hinting value for text
Transform	Matrix	Specifies a geometric transformation
VisibleClipbounds	Rectanlge	Gets the visible clipping region of the Graphics object

Table 21.4 shows the public Graphics methods.

TABLE 21.4: Graphics METHODS

METHOD	STATIC?	DESCRIPTION
AddMetafileComment()	No	Adds a comment to a Metafile object
BeginContainer()	No	Opens a new graphics container
Clear()	No	Clears the drawing surface
DrawArc()	No	Draws an arc
DrawBezier()	No	Draws a Bezier spline
DrawBeziers()	No	Draws a series of Bezier splines
DrawClosedCurve()	No	Draws a closed cardinal spline
Drawcurve()	No	Draws a cardinal spline
DrawEllipse()	No	Draws an ellipse
DrawIcon()	No	Displays an icon
DrawIconUnstretched()	No	Displays an icon with no scaling
DrawImage()	No	Displays an image
DrawImageUnscaled()	No	Displays an image with no scaling
DrawLine()	No	Draws a line
DrawLines()	No	Draws a series of lines
DrawPath()	No	Draws a GraphicsPath object
DrawPie()	No	Draws a "pie piece" shape
DrawPolygon()	No	Draws a polygon
DrawRectangle()	No	Draws a rectangle
DrawRectangles()	No	Draws a series of rectangles

Continued on next page

TABLE 21.4: Graphics METHODS *(continued)*

METHOD	STATIC?	DESCRIPTION
DrawString()	No	Draws a string of text
EndContainer()	No	Closes a graphics container
EnumerateMetafile()	No	Renders the contents of a metafile
ExcludeClip()	No	Adds a rectangle to the clipping region
FillClosedCurve()	No	Fills a closed curve
FillEllipse()	No	Fills an ellipse
FillPath()	No	Fills the interior of a GraphicsPath object
FillPie()	No	Fills the interior of a pie shape
FillPolygon()	No	Fills the interior of a polygon
FillRectangle()	No	Fills the interior of a rectangle
FillRectangles()	No	Fills the interior of a series of rectangles
FillRegion()	No	Fills the interior of a Region object
Flush()	No	Forces execution of all pending operations
FromHdc()	Yes	Creates a Graphics object from a device context handle
FromHwnd()	Yes	Creates a Graphics object from a Window handle
FromImage()	Yes	Creates a Graphics object from an Image object
GetHalftonePalette()	Yes	Gets a handle to the current Windows halftone palette
GetHdc()	No	Gets the device context handle for this Graphics object
GetNearestColor()	No	Gets a near match for a color
IntersectClip()	No	Updates the clipping region by intersecting it with a Rectangle
IsVisible()	No	Indicates whether a point is visible
MeasureCharacterRanges()	No	Gets size information for a text string
MeasureString()	No	Gets the size of a string in a specified font
MultipleTransform()	No	Changes the transform for this Graphics object
ReleaseHdc()	No	Releases a device context
ResetClip()	No	Resets the clipping region
ResetTransform()	No	Resets the transform for this Graphics object
Restore()	No	Restores state stored in a GraphicsState object

Continued on next page

TABLE 21.4: Graphics METHODS *(continued)*

METHOD	STATIC?	DESCRIPTION
RotateTransform()	No	Rotates the transform for this Graphics object
Save()	No	Saves state into a GraphicsState object
ScaleTransform()	No	Changes the scale of the transform for this Graphics object
SetClip()	No	Sets the clipping region
TransformPoints()	No	Transforms an array of points from one coordinate space to another
TranslateClip()	No	Moves the clipping region
TranslateTransform()	No	Applies a translation to the transform for this Graphics region

The Graphics object doesn't have a public constructor, but there are several ways to obtain a Graphics object when you need it:

◆ Retrieving it from the arguments to a Paint event. This is the method I've used in the examples in this chapter.

◆ Calling the CreateGraphics method of a Control or Form

◆ Retrieving it from a Window handle or a device context

◆ Retrieving it from an image

As you can tell from the methods in Table 21.4, the Graphics class is not limited to drawing simple lines. Listing 21.3 demonstrates some of the other drawing capabilities of the Graphics object.

LISTING 21.3: DRAWING SHAPES

```
/*
  Example21_3.cs illustrates drawing shapes
*/

using System;
using System.Drawing;
using System.Drawing.Drawing2D;
using System.Collections;
using System.ComponentModel;
using System.Windows.Forms;
using System.Data;

public class Example21_3 : System.Windows.Forms.Form
{
    private System.ComponentModel.Container components = null;
```

```
public Example21_3()
{
    InitializeComponent();
}

protected override void Dispose( bool disposing )
{
    if( disposing )
    {
        if (components != null)
        {
            components.Dispose();
        }
    }
    base.Dispose( disposing );
}

private void InitializeComponent()
{
    this.BackColor = System.Drawing.Color.White;
    this.ClientSize = new System.Drawing.Size(400, 400);
    this.Name = "Example21_3";
    this.Text = "Example21_3";
    this.Paint += new System.Windows.Forms.
        PaintEventHandler(this.Example21_3_Paint);
}


static void Main()
{
    Application.Run(new Example21_3());
}

private void Example21_3_Paint(
    object sender, System.Windows.Forms.PaintEventArgs e)
{
    Graphics g = e.Graphics;
    // draw a rectangle
    Pen p = new Pen(Color.Black, 5);
    g.DrawRectangle(p, 10, 10, 200, 200);
    // draw an ellipse
    Pen p2 = new Pen(Color.Gray, 7);
    g.DrawEllipse(p2, 200, 200, 150, 190);
}
}
```

If you refer to Table 21.2, you'll see that the `Graphics` object supplies a wide variety of `DrawX` methods to draw various objects. This example uses two of these: the `DrawRectangle` method to draw a rectangle and the `DrawEllipse` method to draw an ellipse. Each of these methods (and the other methods of the `Graphics` object) takes a `Pen` to draw with and a set of numeric values that specify the coordinates of the new object that it draws. You'll need to refer to the .NET Framework help documentation to determine the correct numeric parameters for each of these methods.

Figure 21.3 shows the result of running this program.

FIGURE 21.3

Using the `DrawRectangle` and `DrawEllipse` methods

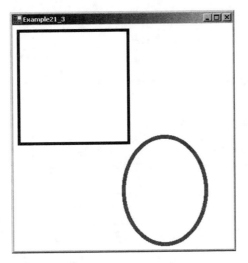

Filling Shapes with a Brush

Another useful graphics class is the `Brush`, which lets you apply fancy patterns to objects. Listing 21.4 shows the `Brush` class in action.

LISTING 21.4: CREATING FILLED SHAPES

```
/*
  Example21_4.cs illustrates filling shapes with a brush
*/

using System;
using System.Drawing;
using System.Drawing.Drawing2D;
using System.Collections;
using System.ComponentModel;
using System.Windows.Forms;
using System.Data;

public class Example21_4 : System.Windows.Forms.Form
{
    private System.ComponentModel.Container components = null;
```

```csharp
public Example21_4()
{
    InitializeComponent();
}

protected override void Dispose( bool disposing )
{
    if( disposing )
    {
        if (components != null)
        {
            components.Dispose();
        }
    }
    base.Dispose( disposing );
}

private void InitializeComponent()
{
    this.BackColor = System.Drawing.Color.White;
    this.ClientSize = new System.Drawing.Size(400, 400);
    this.Name = "Example21_4";
    this.Text = "Example21_4";
    this.Paint += new System.Windows.Forms.
        PaintEventHandler(this.Example21_4_Paint);
}


static void Main()
{
    Application.Run(new Example21_4());
}

private void Example21_4_Paint(
    object sender, System.Windows.Forms.PaintEventArgs e)
{
    Graphics g = e.Graphics;
    // build some brushes
    Brush brSolid = new SolidBrush(Color.Blue);
    Brush brHatch = new HatchBrush(HatchStyle.HorizontalBrick,
        Color.Red, Color.Yellow);
    Brush brGradient = new LinearGradientBrush(
        new Rectangle(0, 0, 200, 200),
        Color.Black, Color.LightGray, 45, false);
    // and draw some filled shapes
    g.FillRectangle(brGradient, 10, 10, 200, 200);
    g.FillEllipse(brHatch, 200, 200, 150, 190);
    g.FillPie(brSolid, 0, 0, 300, 300, 285, 75);
}
}
```

Figure 21.4 shows the result of running this application.

FIGURE 21.4

Drawing filled shapes with GDI+

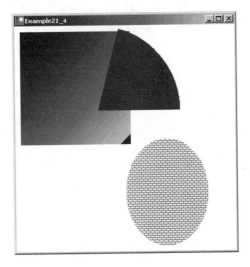

Creating a filled shape is a two-step process. First, you need to create a `Brush` object that will provide the fill. Second, you call one of the `Fill` methods of the `Graphics` object, passing it the `Brush` to use. The various methods take parameters to indicate the size and orientation of the objects that they draw.

In this particular example, I've created three different types of `Brush` object. The `brSolid` object is filled with a solid blue color. The `brHatch` object is filled with horizontal brick shapes in red and yellow. The `brGradient` object is filled with a gradient (a smooth blend) between black and light gray. Each brush is then used to draw a single filled shape on the `Graphics` object.

The `Brush` class itself is an abstract base class that cannot be instantiated. Instead, you can use one of the `Brush` subclasses listed in Table 21.5.

TABLE 21.5: Brush SUBCLASSES

SUBCLASS	USE
`HatchBrush`	Used to fill a drawing object with one of a set of standard hatching patterns
`LinearGradientBrush`	Used to fill a drawing object with a smooth blend between two colors along a straight line.
`PathGradientBrush`	Used to fill a drawing object with a smooth blend between two colors along an arbitrary path.
`SolidBrush`	Used to fill a drawing object with a solid color
`TextureBrush`	Used to fill a drawing object with an image file

Working with Images

The .NET Framework also has the ability to display images in the BMP, GIF, JPG, PNG, or TIF file formats (see Listing 21.5).

LISTING 21.5: DISPLAYING AN IMAGE FILE

```
/*
  Example21_5.cs illustrates using a graphics file
*/

using System;
using System.Drawing;
using System.Drawing.Drawing2D;
using System.Collections;
using System.ComponentModel;
using System.Windows.Forms;
using System.Data;

public class Example21_5 : System.Windows.Forms.Form
{
    private System.ComponentModel.Container components = null;

    public Example21_5()
    {
        InitializeComponent();
    }

    protected override void Dispose( bool disposing )
    {
        if( disposing )
        {
            if (components != null)
            {
                components.Dispose();
            }
        }
        base.Dispose( disposing );
    }

    private void InitializeComponent()
    {
        this.BackColor = System.Drawing.Color.White;
        this.ClientSize = new System.Drawing.Size(400, 400);
        this.Name = "Example21_5";
        this.Text = "Example21_5";
        this.Paint += new System.Windows.Forms.
            PaintEventHandler(this.Example21_5_Paint);
    }
```

```
static void Main()
{
    Application.Run(new Example21_5());
}

private void Example21_5_Paint(
    object sender, System.Windows.Forms.PaintEventArgs e)
{
    Graphics g = e.Graphics;
    // Load the image
    Bitmap b = new Bitmap("CSharp.tif");
    // and display it
    g.DrawImage(b, 10, 10, 350, 300);
}
}
```

TIP   Despite the name, the Bitmap class can be used with many types of image files.

Figure 21.5 shows the result of running this application.

FIGURE 21.5

Drawing an image
with the Bitmap
class

Displaying images in .NET is simple: Create the Bitmap object, and then use the DrawImage method of the Graphics object to display it on the screen. The parameters of the DrawImage method provide a bounding box for the displayed image; GDI+ will automatically resize the image to fit the supplied box. Table 21.6 shows the public Bitmap properties.

TABLE 21.6: Bitmap PROPERTIES

PROPERTY	TYPE	DESCRIPTION
Flags	int	A set of attribute flags
FrameDimensionsList	Guid[]	An array that specifies the dimensions of frames within the image
Height	int	Unscaled height of the image
HorizontalResolution	float	Horizontal resolution in pixels per inch
Palette	ColorPalette	The color palette of the image
PhysicalDimension	SizeF	Width and height of the image
PixelFormat	PixelFormat	Pixel format for the image
PropertyIDList	int[]	Array of IDs of properties stored in this image
PropertyItems	PropertyItem[]	Array of PropertyItem objects that describe this image
RawFormat	ImageFormat	Format of the image
Size	Size	Width and height of the image
VerticalResolution	float	Vertical resolution in pixels per inch
Width	int	Unscaled width of the image

Table 21.7 shows the public Bitmap methods.

TABLE 21.7: Bitmap METHODS

METHOD	STATIC?	DESCRIPTION
Clone()	No	Creates a copy of this bitmap
FromHicon()	Yes	Creates a bitmap from a Windows icon handle
FromResource()	Yes	Creates a bitmap from a Windows resource
GetBounds()	No	Gets a bounding rectangle for the bitmap
GetEncoderParameterList()	No	Returns information about the parameters used to save the image
GetFrameCount()	No	Returns the number of frames in the image
GetHbitmap()	No	Gets a Windows bitmap handle for the bitmap
GetHicon()	No	Gets a Windows icon handle for the bitmap
GetPixel()	No	Gets the color of a specified pixel in the bitmap
GetPropertyItem()	No	Gets a specified PropertyItem

Continued on next page

TABLE 21.7: Bitmap METHODS *(continued)*

METHOD	STATIC?	DESCRIPTION
GetThumbnailImage()	No	Gets a thumbnail version of the Bitmap
LockBits()	No	Locks the bitmap into memory
MakeTransparent()	No	Makes portions of the bitmap transparent
RemovePropertyItem()	No	Removes a PropertyItem from the bitmap
RotateFlip()	No	Rotates and/or flips the bitmap
Save()	No	Saves the bitmap to a Stream
SaveAdd()	No	Combines two bitmaps
SelectActiveFrame()	No	Selects one frame from a multiframe bitmap
SetPixel()	No	Sets the color of a specified pixel in the bitmap
SetPropertyItem()	No	Sets the value of a PropertyItem in the bitmap
SetResolution()	No	Sets the resolution for the bitmap
UnlockBits()	No	Unlocks the bitmap from memory

Supporting Globalization

As the Internet makes it easier for software to cross international boundaries, globalization has taken on additional importance. The .NET Framework includes extensive support for globalization. The basic goal of the classes in the System.Globalization namespace is to enable you to quickly customize a common code base for new languages, currency symbols, numeric display conventions, and so on. In the following sections, you'll learn about some of the classes that support this customization.

Overview of Localization and Globalization

The process of preparing an application for shipment in a new language is called *localization*. Microsoft divides the process of preparing a "world-ready application" into three phases:

Globalization   *Globalization* is the process of preparing an application to be localized. This step involves identifying all the localizable resources in an application and separating them from executable code so that they can be modified easily.

Localizability   In the *localizability* phase of the process, you check to make sure that translating the application won't require code changes.

Localization   Finally, in the *localization* phase of the process, you customize your application for new *cultures*. You'll learn about cultures in the next section of this chapter.

Understanding Cultures

The .NET Framework identifies the target audience for localized content by specifying a *culture*. A culture is a more precise concept than a language. For example, U.S. English and U.K. English are two different cultures in the .NET Framework. To completely localize an application, you must depend on cultures rather than on languages. This should be obvious if you think about the things that may need to be localized. For example, the formatting of currency and date values differs between the United States and the United Kingdom, even though these countries share (for the most part) a single language.

CULTURE CODES

The .NET Framework identifies cultures by a set of abbreviations. Each abbreviation consists of a culture code followed by one or more subculture codes. By convention, culture codes are written in lowercase, and subculture codes are written in uppercase. Here are some examples:

◆ **es** identifies the Spanish culture. This is a *neutral culture*—that is, one that doesn't specify a subculture code. Generally, you won't use neutral cultures in your applications because they're not specific enough to tell you how some things (such as currency or date values) should be displayed.

◆ **nl-BE** identifies the Dutch (Belgium) culture. This *specific culture* includes enough information to localize an application for use by Dutch speakers who live in Belgium.

◆ **sr-SP-Latn** is an example of a specific culture with multiple subculture codes. It identifies Serbian in Serbia written in Latin characters.

At this point, you may be wondering which cultures the .NET Framework supports. To answer that question, you'll need to know something about the `System.Globalization` namespace.

THE *SYSTEM.GLOBALIZATION* NAMESPACE

The `System.Globalization` namespace in the .NET Framework contains classes that handle culture-specific information. Table 21.8 lists some of the classes in this namespace. As you can see, they cover many of the things that need to change when you move your software from one culture to another.

TABLE 21.8: `System.Globalization` CLASSES

CLASS	DESCRIPTION
Calendar	An abstract class that represents the general notion of a culture-specific calendar. Subclasses such as `GregorianCalendar` and `HebrewCalendar` represent calendars for particular cultures.
CompareInfo	A collection of methods for culture-specific string comparisons.
CultureInfo	Contains information about all aspects of a particular culture.
DateTimeFormatInfo	Contains information about formatting dates and times.
DaylightTime	Contains information about daylight savings time.
NumberFormatInfo	Contains information about formatting numbers and currency values.

Continued on next page

TABLE 21.8: System.Globalization CLASSES *(continued)*

CLASS	DESCRIPTION
RegionInfo	Contains information about a particular region or country.
SortKey	Contains information for sorting strings.
StringInfo	Provides methods to split a string into elements and iterate over those elements.
TextInfo	Contains information about formatting text.

You can use the CultureInfo class in conjunction with other classes from the System.Globalization namespace to retrieve information on any culture that the .NET Framework supports. Listing 21.6 shows how you can use the CultureInfo and associated classes.

LISTING 21.6: RETRIEVING CULTURE INFORMATION

```
/*
  Example21_6.cs illustrates the CultureInfo class
*/

using System;
using System.Globalization;

class Example21_6
{

    public static void Main()
    {
        // create a CultureInfo object for the nl-BE culture
        CultureInfo ci = new CultureInfo("nl-BE");

        // show some basic information
        Console.WriteLine("Native Name: " + ci.NativeName);
        Console.WriteLine("English Name: " + ci.EnglishName);

        // get datetime formatting info
        DateTimeFormatInfo dtfi = ci.DateTimeFormat;
        Console.WriteLine("Long date pattern: " + dtfi.LongDatePattern);

        // get numeric formatting info
        NumberFormatInfo nfi = ci.NumberFormat;
        Console.WriteLine("Currency symbol: " + nfi.CurrencySymbol);
        Console.WriteLine("Decimal seperator: " + nfi.NumberDecimalSeparator);

    }

}
```

This program first creates a `CultureInfo` object that represents the culture for Dutch as it is spoken in Belgium. It then retrieves various properties of this `CultureInfo` object, including its name, long date format, currency, and decimal separators. The output from this program is as follows:

```
Native Name: Nederlands (België)
English Name: Dutch (Belgium)
Long date pattern: dddd d MMMM yyyy
Currency symbol: ?
Decimal seperator: ,
```

If you think that currency separator looks wrong, you're right. The problem is that the Windows console is incapable of displaying Unicode characters properly. Unicode is a standard way of representing characters from many languages that's used extensively by .NET.

Fortunately, there's an easy way to see the proper Unicode results because Windows Notepad is Unicode-enabled. Listing 21.7 shows a revised version of the code that writes to a file instead of to the console window.

LISTING 21.7: RETRIEVING CULTURE INFORMATION TO A FILE

```csharp
/*
  Example21_7.cs illustrates the CultureInfo class
*/

using System;
using System.Globalization;
using System.IO;

class Example21_7
{

    public static void Main()
    {
        // create a CultureInfo object for the nl-BE culture
        CultureInfo ci = new CultureInfo("nl-BE");

        // create a file to hold the results
        FileStream outStream = File.Create("CultureInfo.txt");

        // use a StreamWriter to write data to the file
        StreamWriter sw = new StreamWriter(outStream);

        // show some basic information
        sw.WriteLine("Native Name: " + ci.NativeName);
        sw.WriteLine("English Name: " + ci.EnglishName);

        // get datetime formatting info
        DateTimeFormatInfo dtfi = ci.DateTimeFormat;
        sw.WriteLine("Long date pattern: " + dtfi.LongDatePattern);
```

```
// get numeric formatting info
NumberFormatInfo nfi = ci.NumberFormat;
sw.WriteLine("Currency symbol: " + nfi.CurrencySymbol);
sw.WriteLine("Decimal seperator: " + nfi.NumberDecimalSeparator);

// flush and close the file
sw.Flush();
sw.Close();

    }

}
```

Figure 21.6 shows the output file from this program open in Notepad. Here you can see the Euro symbol for currency properly displayed.

NOTE *For more information on the* FileStream *and* StreamWriter *classes, refer to Chapter 15, "Streams and Input/Output."*

FIGURE 21.6

Culture information in Notepad

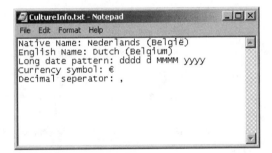

The key class in working with cultures is the CultureInfo class. Table 21.9 shows the public CultureInfo properties.

TABLE 21.9: CultureInfo PROPERTIES

PROPERTY	TYPE	DESCRIPTION
Calendar	Calendar	Gets the default calendar for the culture
CompareInfo	CompareInfo	Gets the string comparison information for the culture
CurrentCulture	CultureInfo	Static property that returns the current culture for this thread
CurrentUICulture	CultureInfo	Static property that returns the current culture for the user interface

Continued on next page

TABLE 21.9: `CultureInfo` PROPERTIES *(continued)*

PROPERTY	TYPE	DESCRIPTION
DateTimeFormat	DateTimeFormatInfo	Gets the date and time formatting information for the culture
DisplayName	string	Gets the display name of the culture
EnglishName	string	Gets the English name of the culture
InstalledUICulture	CultureInfo	Static property that returns the culture installed with the operating system
InvariantCulture	CultureInfo	Static property that returns the invariant culture
IsNeutralCulture	bool	Indicates whether this CultureInfo represents a neutral culture
IsReadOnly	bool	Indicates whether this CultureInfo is readonly
LCID	string	Gets the culture identifier for this CultureInfo
Name	string	Gets the name of the culture
NativeName	string	Gets the name of the culture in its own language
NumberFormat	NumberFormatInfo	Gets the numeric formatting information for the culture
OptionalCalendars	Calendar[]	Gets a list of alternate calendars for the culture
Parent	CultureInfo	Gets the parent of the current culture
TextInfo	TextInfo	Gets the text formatting information for the culture
ThreeLetterISOLanguageName	string	Gets the ISO code for the language of this culture
TwoLetterISOLanguageName	string	Gets the two-letter ISO code for the language of this culture
UseUserOverride	bool	Indicates whether this CultureInfo is using user-selected settings

Table 21.10 shows the public `CultureInfo` methods.

TABLE 21.10: `CultureInfo` METHODS

METHOD	STATIC?	DESCRIPTION
ClearCachedData()	No	Refreshes any cached information about the culture
CreateSpecificCulture()	Yes	Creates a CultureInfo object from a culture name
GetCultures()	Yes	Gets a list of available cultures
ReadOnly()	Yes	Returns a readonly version of this CultureInfo

THE *CURRENTCULTURE* AND *CURRENTUICULTURE* PROPERTIES

The .NET Common Language Runtime (CLR) keeps track of two different cultures on a per-thread basis. The CurrentCulture property is used for data formatting, and the CurrentUICulture is used for language formatting. Listing 21.8 shows the use of the CurrentCulture and CurrentUICulture properties of the Thread and CultureInfo classes.

LISTING 21.8: WORKING WITH CURRENT CULTURES

```
/*
  Example21_8.cs illustrates the current cultures
*/

using System;
using System.Globalization;
using System.Threading;

class Example21_8
{

    public static void Main()
    {
        // set the current culture for the executing thread
        Thread.CurrentThread.CurrentCulture=new CultureInfo("de-DE");
        // and display it
        Console.WriteLine(Thread.CurrentThread.CurrentCulture.Name);
        // create another new culture
        CultureInfo ci = new CultureInfo("en-US");
        // prove that this doesn't change the current culture
        Console.WriteLine(CultureInfo.CurrentCulture.Name);

        // set the current UI culture for the executing thread
        Thread.CurrentThread.CurrentUICulture=new CultureInfo("fr-FR");
        // and display it
        Console.WriteLine(Thread.CurrentThread.CurrentUICulture.Name);
        // create another new culture
        CultureInfo ci2 = new CultureInfo("en-US");
        // prove that this doesn't change the current culture
        Console.WriteLine(CultureInfo.CurrentUICulture.Name);

    }

}
```

The output from this program is as follows:

```
de-DE
de-DE
fr-FR
fr-FR
```

The code in this listing sets the current thread's culture to German (Germany) by creating a new `CultureInfo` object and then assigning it to the `Thread.CurrentThread.CurrentCulture` property. As you'd expect, the first `WriteLine` statement returns de-DE as the name of the `CultureInfo` retrieved from the thread at that point. The code then goes on to create an independent `CultureInfo` object representing the English (United States) culture. What you might not expect is that the second `WriteLine` statement also returns de-DE. Just creating a new `CultureInfo` object doesn't change the culture of the current thread. To change the culture of the current thread, you need to explicitly assign a new `CultureInfo` object to it.

The remaining code repeats these steps using the `CurrentUICulture` property and the French (France) culture.

The difference between `CurrentCulture` and `CurrentUICulture` is in their use by the .NET Framework. The `CurrentUICulture` property is used to retrieve culture-specific resources (most importantly, text for the user interface) from an appropriate file. The `CurrentCulture` property sets the format for dates, times, currency, and numbers, as well as other culture-specific functionality, including sorting order, string comparison rules, and casing rules.

ENUMERATING CULTURES

The `GetCultures` method of the `CultureInfo` object takes a `CultureTypes` parameter that specifies a set of cultures to be returned. Table 21.11 shows the possible values for the `CultureTypes` parameter.

TABLE 21.11: VALUES FOR THE `CultureTypes` PARAMETER

VALUE	MEANING
AllCultures	All cultures understood by the .NET Framework
InstalledWin32Cultures	All cultures installed on the operating system
NeutralCultures	All neutral cultures
SpecificCultures	All specific cultures

The `GetCultures` method returns an array of `CultureInfo` objects. So, to see all the cultures that the .NET Framework supports, you can retrieve an array using `GetCultures(AllCultures)` and iterate through its contents. Listing 21.9 shows code to accomplish this task. This program displays the English names and abbreviations of all of the cultures that the .NET Framework supports.

LISTING 21.9: ENUMERATING CULTURES

```
/*
  Example21_9.cs enumerates all available cultures
*/

using System;
using System.Globalization;

class Example21_9
{

    public static void Main()
    {
        foreach (CultureInfo ci in
            CultureInfo.GetCultures(CultureTypes.AllCultures))
        {
            Console.WriteLine("{0} | {1}", ci.EnglishName, ci.Name);
        }
    }

}
```

The output from this program starts as follows:

```
Arabic | ar
Arabic (Saudi Arabia) | ar-SA
Arabic (Iraq) | ar-IQ
Arabic (Egypt) | ar-EG
Arabic (Libya) | ar-LY
Arabic (Algeria) | ar-DZ
Arabic (Morocco) | ar-MA
Arabic (Tunisia) | ar-TN
Arabic (Oman) | ar-OM
Arabic (Yemen) | ar-YE
Arabic (Syria) | ar-SY
Arabic (Jordan) | ar-JO
Arabic (Lebanon) | ar-LB
Arabic (Kuwait) | ar-KW
Arabic (U.A.E.) | ar-AE
Arabic (Bahrain) | ar-BH
Arabic (Qatar) | ar-QA
Bulgarian | bg
Bulgarian (Bulgaria) | bg-BG
```

If you run this program and view the entire output, you'll see that the .NET Framework supports a wide variety of cultures—more than 200 of them.

THE INVARIANT CULTURE

The last culture you'll find in the list of all cultures is Invariant Language (Invariant Country) This culture has two purposes:

♦ Interacting with other software, such as system services, where no user is involved

♦ Storing data in a culture-independent format that won't be displayed directly to end users

You can create a CultureInfo object for the invariant culture in one of two ways. These two lines of code produce exactly the same result:

```
CultureInfo ciInv = new CultureInfo("")
CultureInfo ciInv = CultureInfo.InvariantCulture
```

Displaying Localized Information

Listing 21.10 shows how you can use a CultureInfo object to format information for particular cultures (in this case, the United States English and Great Britain English cultures).

LISTING 21.10: USING THE CultureInfo OBJECT

```csharp
/*
  Example21_10.cs demonstrates culture formatting
*/

using System;
using System.Globalization;

class Example21_10
{

    public static void Main()
    {

        // create a date and a currency value
        DateTime dtNow = DateTime.Now;
        Double curOriginal = 12345.67;

        // and format the variables for a specific culture
        CultureInfo ci = new CultureInfo("en-US");
        string sLocalizedDate = dtNow.ToString("d", ci);
        string sLocalizedCur = curOriginal.ToString("c", ci);

        // print them out
        Console.WriteLine(sLocalizedDate);
        Console.WriteLine(sLocalizedCur);

        // and format them for a second culture
        CultureInfo ci2 = new CultureInfo("en-GB");
```

```
        string sLocalizedDate2 = dtNow.ToString("d", ci2);
        string sLocalizedCur2 = curOriginal.ToString("c", ci2);

        // print them out again
        Console.WriteLine(sLocalizedDate2);
        Console.WriteLine(sLocalizedCur2);

    }

}
```

The output from this program is as follows:

```
05/28/2002
$12,345.67
28/06/2002
£12,345.67
```

The code uses an overloaded form of the `ToString` method of the variables in question to format them for the specified culture.

NOTE   *In addition to the `CultureInfo`-based formatting of variables, the .NET Framework also supports localizing user interface text by using the `ResourceManager` class and satellite DLLs. A satellite DLL is a .NET file that contains the text (and possibly other localized resources) for a particular culture. This user-interface technique is beyond the scope of this book, but you can refer to the "Developing World-Ready Applications" topic in the .NET Framework help file for more information.*

Diagnostics and Debugging

The .NET Framework was designed from the start to be able to monitor itself. You've already seen one facet of that monitoring in the discussion of the `System.Reflection` classes in Chapter 17, "Attributes and Reflection." In the following sections you'll see some of the classes from the `System.Diagnostics` namespace, which provides classes for many diagnostic-related tasks:

◆ Reading and writing event log entries

◆ Monitoring, stopping, starting, and investigating processes

◆ Creating and reading performance counters

◆ Tracing and debugging code

In the next section, you'll see a small portion of the `System.Diagnostics` namespace that handles tracing and debugging functions.

The *Trace* and *Debug* Classes

The .NET Framework includes two classes with identical interfaces: Trace and Debug. Either class can provide diagnostic information and messages from a running program. The difference between the two is in their intent. The Debug class must be explicitly turned on with a #define DEBUG directive. If that directive (or the equivalent command-line switch) isn't present in the source code, then Debug statements generate no output in the program's Microsoft Intermediate Language (MSIL) and hence have no effect at run-time.

The Trace class, on the other hand, always includes statements in the MSIL. At run-time, though, you can control whether a Trace class is active by configuring the application.

You should use the Debug class when you're testing and debugging a program before deployment. The Trace class should be saved for situations when you might need diagnostic information back from a copy of the program that's been deployed to end users. It's also worth keeping in mind that shipping debug code can open security holes by giving a potential attacker extra information on the structure of your program.

Table 21.12 shows the public Debug and Trace properties.

TABLE 21.12: Debug AND Trace PROPERTIES

PROPERTY	TYPE	DESCRIPTION
AutoFlush	bool	Indicates whether every write should be flushed
IndentLevel	int	The current indent level for output
IndentSize	int	The number of spaces in each indent level
Listeners	TraceListenerCollection	The listeners to this class

Table 21.13 shows the public Debug and Trace methods.

TABLE 21.13: Debug AND Trace METHODS

METHOD	STATIC?	DESCRIPTION
Assert()	Yes	Outputs a message if a condition evaluates to false
Close()	Yes	Flushes the output buffer and stops tracing
Fail()	Yes	Outputs an error message
Flush()	Yes	Flushes all content in the output buffer
Indent()	Yes	Increases the indent level by one
Unindent()	Yes	Decreases the indent level by one
Write()	Yes	Writes output
WriteIf()	Yes	Writes output if a condition evaluates to true
WriteLine()	Yes	Writes output followed by a newline
WriteLineIf()	Yes	Writes output if a condition evaluates to true, followed by a newline

Listing 21.11 shows the Debug class in action

```csharp
#define DEBUG

/*
  Example21_11.cs demonstrates debug output
*/

using System;
using System.Globalization;
using System.Diagnostics;

class Example21_11
{

    public static void Main()
    {
        TextWriterTraceListener tl = new TextWriterTraceListener(Console.Out);
        Debug.Listeners.Add(tl);

        Debug.WriteLine("Starting Main()");
        // create a date and a currency value
        DateTime dtNow = DateTime.Now;
        Double curOriginal = 12345.67;

        // and format the variables for a specific culture
        CultureInfo ci = new CultureInfo("en-US");
        string sLocalizedDate = dtNow.ToString("d", ci);
        string sLocalizedCur = curOriginal.ToString("c", ci);
        Debug.Assert(sLocalizedDate != null, "Localized date has no content");

        // print them out
        Console.WriteLine(sLocalizedDate);
        Console.WriteLine(sLocalizedCur);

        Debug.WriteLine("Exiting Main()");
    }

}
```

The output from this program is as follows:

```
Starting Main()
05/28/2002
$12,345.67
Exiting Main()
```

Each `Debug.WriteLine` statement in the code is reflected in the output. The `Debug.Assert` statement does not produce any output because the condition it asserts is true.

If you remove the `#define DEBUG` statement and recompile the code, you can verify that the `Debug` class no longer produces any output. You can also reenable debugging by adding the `/d:DEBUG` switch to the compiler options when you compile the program.

Using *Trace* Listeners

One problem with the code in Listing 21.11 is that it intermingles the debug output with the program's regular output. Another is that you need to recompile the program each time you want to switch from debugging to not debugging. Listing 21.12 shows how you might solve this problem.

LISTING 21.12: USING Trace LISTENERS

```
#define DEBUG

/*
  Example21_12.cs demonstrates the use of TraceListener objects
*/

using System;
using System.Globalization;
using System.Diagnostics;

class Example21_12
{

    public static void Main()
    {
        // Set up a TraceListener to a file
        TextWriterTraceListener t1 =
         new TextWriterTraceListener("Example21_12.txt");
        Debug.Listeners.Add(t1);
        // And a second TraceListener to the event log
        EventLogTraceListener t2 =
         new EventLogTraceListener("Application");
        Debug.Listeners.Add(t2);

        Debug.WriteLine("Starting Main()");
        // create a date and a currency value
        DateTime dtNow = DateTime.Now;
        Double curOriginal = 12345.67;

        // and format the variables for a specific culture
        CultureInfo ci = new CultureInfo("en-US");
        string sLocalizedDate = dtNow.ToString("d", ci);
```

```
        string sLocalizedCur = curOriginal.ToString("c", ci);
        Debug.Assert(sLocalizedDate != null, "Localized date has no content");

        // print them out
        Console.WriteLine(sLocalizedDate);
        Console.WriteLine(sLocalizedCur);

        Debug.WriteLine("Exiting Main()");
        Debug.Flush();
        Debug.Close();
    }

}
```

The output of this program is as follows:

```
05/29/2002
$12,345.67
```

If you run the program, you'll find that it also creates a file named `Example21_12.txt`. That file contains the debug output:

```
Starting Main()
Exiting Main()
```

If you use Windows Event Viewer to inspect the Application event log, you'll also find the debug output there, in the form of individual events. Of course, you can choose to include as much or as little detail as you like in a trace file by adding more `Debug.WriteLine` statements.

The `Debug` and `Trace` classes share a `TraceListeners` collection, consisting of individual instances of subclasses of the `TraceListener` class. Every `TraceListener` class gets sent a copy of all of the debug output and can decide what to do with it. Table 21.14 lists the types of `TraceListener` that you can use.

TABLE 21.14: `TraceListener` SUBCLASSES

CLASS	FUNCTION
`DefaultTraceListener`	Sends output to any attached debugger or to the Visual Studio .NET Output window if your code is running in the IDE
`EventLogTraceListener`	Sends output to a specified Windows event log
`TextWriterTraceListener`	Sends output to a `TextWriter` or a `Stream`

The .NET Framework automatically adds a `DefaultTraceListener` object to the `TraceListeners` collection. You can add additional `TraceListener` instances by calling the `Listeners.Add` method.

Using Trace Output After Deployment

There are times when you'd like to ship your application with the ability to provide debugging information, but only turn that ability on when it's needed (see Listing 21.13).

LISTING 21.13: ENABLING TRACE OUTPUT AFTER DEPLOYMENT

```
#define TRACE

/*
  Example21_13.cs demonstrates post-deployment tracing
*/

using System;
using System.Globalization;
using System.Diagnostics;

class Example21_13
{

    public static void Main()
    {
        // Set up a switch to turn tracing on
        BooleanSwitch bsEnableTrace = new BooleanSwitch("TraceOutput",
            "Turn on tracing");

        // Set up a TraceListener to a file
        TextWriterTraceListener tl =
         new TextWriterTraceListener("Example21_13.txt");
        Trace.Listeners.Add(tl);
        // And a second TraceListener to the event log
        EventLogTraceListener t2 = new EventLogTraceListener("Application");
        Trace.Listeners.Add(t2);

        Trace.WriteLineIf(bsEnableTrace.Enabled,"Starting Main()");
        // create a date and a currency value
        DateTime dtNow = DateTime.Now;
        Double curOriginal = 12345.67;

        // and format the variables for a specific culture
        CultureInfo ci = new CultureInfo("en-US");
        string sLocalizedDate = dtNow.ToString("d", ci);
        string sLocalizedCur = curOriginal.ToString("c", ci);
        if (bsEnableTrace.Enabled)
        {
            Trace.Assert(sLocalizedDate != null, "Localized date has no content");
        }
```

```
        // print them out
        Console.WriteLine(sLocalizedDate);
        Console.WriteLine(sLocalizedCur);

        Trace.WriteLineIf(bsEnableTrace.Enabled, "Exiting Main()");
        Trace.Flush();
        Trace.Close();
    }

}
```

The output of this program is as follows:

```
05/29/2002
$12,345.67
```

You might expect to find an `Example21_13.txt` file after running the program, but you won't. That's because the `Enabled` property of the `BooleanSwitch` class defaults to `false`. So even though the `Trace` class is compiled into the application, it won't do anything because that property is never set to `true`, and it's used in the `WriteLineIf` statements to control whether there should be any trace output.

TIP *There is no `AssertIf` method. This example shows how you can use the `BooleanSwitch` object to control the execution of an `Assert` method.*

The nice thing about the `BooleanSwitch` object is that you can set its `Enabled` property at run-time by supplying a configuration file. The configuration file must have the same name as the executable file plus the extension `config`—in this case, `Example21_13.exe.config`. Here are the contents of a configuration file to turn on tracing:

```
<configuration>
    <system.diagnostics>
        <switches>
            <add name="TraceOutput" value="1" />
        </switches>
    </system.diagnostics>
</configuration>
```

If you create this file in the directory that holds `Example21_13.exe` and run the program again, it will create the debug output in the `Example21_13.txt` file and in the Application event log, even though you didn't change or recompile the program.

Using Advanced Facilities

The .NET Framework also includes a number of classes that are tightly integrated with .NET or the Windows operating system. These include classes that support the features of the .NET run-time itself, of the operating system and of advanced component services such as COM+, MSMQ, and Active Directory. In the following sections you'll see some examples of these classes.

Controlling the Garbage Collector

You already know that the CLR includes a component called the *garbage collector*, whose job it is to remove unused objects from memory and to invoke their destructors. Normally, the CLR decides when to run the garbage collector. However, you can also attempt to run the garbage collector whenever you think it's a good idea, as shown in Listing 21.14.

LISTING 21.14: INVOKING GARBAGE COLLECTION

```csharp
/*
   Example21_14.cs demonstrates forced garbage collection
*/

using System;

class Junk
{
    public Junk()
    {
        Console.WriteLine("Created Junk");
    }

    ~Junk()
    {
        Console.WriteLine("Destroyed Junk");
    }

}

class Example21_14
{

    public static void Main()
    {

        Console.WriteLine("Starting Main");
        // create a Junk object
        Junk j = new Junk();

        // and destroy it
        j = null;

        // force a garbage collection
        GC.Collect();

        Console.WriteLine("Exiting Main");
    }

}
```

The output from the program is as follows:

```
Starting Main
Created Junk
Exiting Main
Destroyed Junk
```

WARNING *Even though you can force garbage collection to start, you still can't predict when any particular object will be garbage collected. In this case, the* Junk *object isn't destroyed until the main class exits, because garbage collection isn't instantaneous.*

The System namespace provides the GC object to manage the garbage collection process. Table 21.15 shows the public GC property.

TABLE 21.15: GC PROPERTY

PROPERTY	TYPE	DESCRIPTION
MaxGenerations	int	Maximum number of generations (different age classes for objects) that the system supports

Table 21.16 shows the public GC methods.

TABLE 21.16: GC METHODS

METHOD	STATIC?	DESCRIPTION
Collect()	Yes	Forces a garbage collection
GetGeneration()	Yes	Returns the current generation of an object
GetTotalMemory()	Yes	Returns the number of bytes currently allocated
KeepAlive()	Yes	Prevents an object from being garbage collected
ReRegisterForFinalize()	Yes	Reverses a call to SuppressFinalize()
SuppressFinalize()	Yes	Suppresses the Finalize method for an object
WaitForCurrentFinalizers()	Yes	Suspends the current thread until finalization is finished

Starting and Stopping Services

The System.ServiceProcess namespace includes classes to let you control existing Windows services, as well as to implement your own system services. Listing 21.15 shows an example of service control using this namespace.

LISTING 21.15: WORKING WITH A SERVICE

```
/*
  Example21_15.cs demonstrates service control
*/

using System;
using System.ServiceProcess;

class Example21_15
{

    public static void Main()
    {

        // connect to the Alerter service
        ServiceController scAlerter = new ServiceController("Alerter");

        Console.WriteLine(scAlerter.DisplayName);
        Console.WriteLine(scAlerter.CanStop);

        scAlerter.Stop();
        Console.WriteLine("Service stopped");
        scAlerter.Start();
        Console.WriteLine("Service started");
    }

}
```

The output from this program is as follows:

```
Alerter
True
Service stopped
Service started
```

The ServiceController object represents a running service, either on the local computer (as in this sample) or on a remote computer (an overloaded constructor for the class accepts a machine name as a second parameter). This sample shows how you can connect to a running service, stop it, and then start it again. Table 21.17 shows the public ServiceController properties.

TABLE 21.17: ServiceController PROPERTIES

PROPERTY	TYPE	DESCRIPTION
CanPauseAndContinue	bool	Indicates whether the service can be paused
CanShutdown	bool	Indicates whether the service should be notified of system shutdowns
CanStop	bool	Indicates whether the service can be stopped
DependentServices	ServiceController[]	Gets the set of services that depend on this service
DisplayName	string	Gets the friendly name for the service
MachineName	string	Gets the name of the computer on which the service is running
ServiceName	string	Gets the name of the service
ServicesDependedOn	ServiceController[]	Gets the set of services on which this service depends
ServiceType	ServiceType	Gets the type of this service
Status	ServiceControllerStatus	Gets the current status of \the service

Table 21.18 shows the public ServiceController methods.

TABLE 21.18: ServiceController METHODS

METHOD	STATIC?	DESCRIPTION
Close()	No	Disconnects from the service
Continue()	No	Continues a service after it has been paused
ExecuteCommand()	No	Executes a custom command on the service
GetDevices()	Yes	Retrieves the device driver services on a computer
GetServices()	Yes	Retrieves the non-device driver services on a computer
Pause()	No	Suspends a service
Refresh()	No	Refreshes property values of a service
Start()	No	Starts a service
Stop()	No	Stops a service
WaitForStatus()	No	Waits for a service to enter a specified status

Working with Active Directory

The System.DirectoryServices namespace contains classes for working with Active Directory. These classes use Active Directory Services Interface (ADSI) to communicate directly with Active Directory servers. Listing 21.16 shows one of these classes. Active Directory is a complex topic in its own right, and this sample shows just a small corner of Active Directory operations. If you work with Active Directory on a regular basis, you'll find that the System.DirectoryServices namespace includes comprehensive Active Directory support.

LISTING 21.16: ENUMERATING ACTIVE DIRECTORY ENTRIES

```
/*
  Example21_16.cs retrieves Active Directory information
*/

using System;
using System.DirectoryServices;

class Example21_16
{

    public static void Main()
    {

        // connect to AD
        DirectoryEntry de = new DirectoryEntry(
            "WinNT://DomanName/MachineName", "Administrator", "Password");

        foreach(DirectoryEntry child in de.Children)
        {
            Console.WriteLine(child.SchemaClassName + ": " + child.Name);
        }
    }

}
```

NOTE   *To use this code, you'll need to supply valid parameters to the constructor for the* DirectoryEntry *object. This includes your domain name, machine name, and a username and password with access to Active Directory.*

The output of this program will start something like this:

```
User: __vmware_user__
User: ACTUser
User: Administrator
User: ASPNET
User: Guest
```

You'll see all the users, groups, and services in Active Directory enumerated in the output. Table 21.19 shows the public `DirectoryEntry` properties.

TABLE 21.19: `DirectoryEntry` PROPERTIES

PROPERTY	TYPE	DESCRIPTION
AuthenticationType	AuthenticationTypes	Gets or sets the type of authentication to use
Children	DiretoryEntries	Gets a collection containing the child nodes of this Active Directory node
Guid	guid	Gets the GUID of this Active Directory node
Name	string	Gets the name of the object represented by this AD node
NativeGuid	guid	Gets the GUID as returned by the Active Directory provider
NativeObject		The underlying ADSI object
Parent	DirectoryEntry	Gets the parent of this Active Directory node
Password	string	Sets the password to use for authentication
Path	string	Gets the path to this `DirectoryEntry`
Properties	PropertyCollection	Gets the properties set on this object
SchemaClassName	string	Gets the name of the schema class to which this AD node belongs
SchemaEntry	DirectoryEntry	Gets the Active Directory entry containing the schema information for this Active Directory node
UsePropertyCache	bool	Indicates whether properties should be cached or immediately committed
UserName	string	Sets the username to use for authentication

Table 21.20 shows the public `DirectoryEntry` methods.

TABLE 21.20: `DirectoryEntry` METHODS

METHOD	STATIC?	DESCRIPTION
Close()	No	Disconnects from the Active Directory node
CommitChanges()	No	Saves any changes
CopyTo()	No	Creates a copy of this Active Directory node
DeleteTree()	No	Deletes the entry and its children from Active Directory

Continued on next page

TABLE 21.20: DirectoryEntry METHODS *(continued)*

METHOD	STATIC?	DESCRIPTION
Exists()	Yes	Determines whether a specified Active Directory entry exists
Invoke()	No	Calls a method on the object
MoveTo()	No	Moves this Active Directory node to a new place in the tree
RefreshCache()	No	Reloads properties for the Active Directory object
Rename()	No	Changes the name of the Active Directory object

Summary

By now you've probably realized that the .NET Framework Base Class Library contains classes to handle nearly any common task that you might like to perform in an application. This chapter touched on a few areas that we haven't explored in depth, but it's certainly not exhaustive. Before you do any coding, you should explore the class library to see whether the job has already been done for you.

The graphics capabilities of the class library include drawing lines and shapes, displaying images, and displaying text.

The globalization capabilities of the class library let you easily modify the user interface and output of an application to match a new culture.

The Trace and Debug classes let you manage diagnostic information both before and after deployment of your application.

More advanced functions supported by the class library include on-demand garbage collection, starting and stopping Windows services, and retrieving information from Active Directory.

Part 3

.NET Programming with C#

In this section you will find:

Chapter 22

Introduction to Databases

IN THIS CHAPTER, YOU'LL learn the basics of databases and see how to use the Structured Query Language (SQL) to access a database. You'll need to understand these subjects prior to reading the following three chapters, where you'll see how to access a database using ADO.NET. This chapter shows the use of a SQL Server database named Northwind. This database contains the information for the fictitious Northwind Company, which sells food products. This database is one of the example databases typically installed with SQL Server. There is also a version of the Northwind database that comes with Microsoft Access.

Featured in this chapter:

◆ Introducing Databases

◆ Exploring the Northwind Database

◆ Using the Structured Query Language (SQL)

◆ Introducing Stored Procedures

◆ Accessing a Database Using Visual Studio .NET

Introducing Databases

A database is an organized collection of information. A *relational database* is a collection of related information that has been organized into structures known as *tables*. Each table contains *rows* that are further organized into *columns*. You should already be familiar with information being represented in the form of a table with columns. For example, Table 22.1 shows the details of some products sold by the Northwind Company. Table 22.1 lists the product ID, name, quantity per unit, and unit price for the first 10 products; this information comes from the Products table of the Northwind database.

TABLE 22.1: Products TABLE

ID	NAME	QUANTITY PER UNIT	UNIT PRICE
1	Chai	10 boxes by 20 bags	$18
2	Chang	24–12oz bottles	$19
3	Aniseed Syrup	12–550ml bottles	$10
4	Chef Anton's Cajun Seasoning	48–6oz jars	$22
5	Chef Anton's Gumbo Mix	36 boxes	$21.35
6	Grandma's Boysenberry Spread	12–8oz jars	$25
7	Uncle Bob's Organic Dried Pears	12–1lb packages	$30
8	Northwoods Cranberry Sauce	12–12oz jars	$40
9	Mishi Kobe Niku	18–500g packages	$97
10	Ikura	12–200ml jars	$31

You can store the information in a database on pieces of paper in a filing cabinet or in electronic format stored in the memory and file system of a computer. The system used to manage the information in the database is known as the *database management system*. In the case of an electronic database in a computer, the database management system is the software that manages the information in the computer's memory and files. One example of such software is SQL Server (this is the relational database management system, or RDBMS, used in this book). Other examples include Oracle and DB2.

NOTE   A database schema is a representation of the structure of data, and includes the definition of the tables and columns that make up the database.

In the following section, you'll learn what is meant by the term *relational* in the context of a relational database, and you'll explore some of the tables in the Northwind database.

Exploring the Northwind Database

A database may have many tables, some of which are related to each other. For example, the Northwind database contains many tables, four of which are named Customers, Orders, Order Details, and Products. Figure 22.1 shows a diagram that illustrates how these tables are related; this diagram was created using SQL Server's Enterprise Manager tool.

FIGURE 22.1

Relationships
between the
Customers,
Orders, Order
Details, and
Products tables

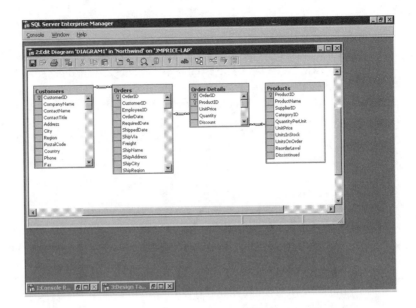

The columns for each table are shown within each box. For example, the Customers table contains 11 columns: CustomerID, CompanyName, ContactName, ContactTitle, Address, City, Region, PostalCode, Country, Phone, and Fax.

In the next few sections, you'll learn some database theory, and then you'll learn how each of the previous columns is defined in the Customers table.

Primary Keys

Typically, each table in a database has one or more columns that uniquely identify each row in the table. This column (or columns) is known as the *primary key* for the table.

NOTE   *The value for the primary key in each row of a table must be unique.*

In the case of the Customers table, the primary key is the CustomerID column. The key icon shown to the left of the CustomerID column in Figure 22.1 indicates that this column is the primary key for the Customers table.

Foreign Keys

The lines that connect the tables show relationships between the tables. The infinity sign at the end of each line indicates a one-to-many relationship between two tables—meaning that a row in one table can be related to multiple rows in the other table.

For example, the Customers table has a one-to-many relationship with the Orders table. You read the relationships as follows: Each customer can place many orders. Each order is made up of many order details (you can think of an order detail as a line in a purchase order list, and each line in the list refers to a specific product that is ordered). Each product can appear in many order details.

These relationships are modeled using *foreign keys*. For example, the Orders table has a column named CustomerID. This column is related to the CustomerID column in the Customers table through a foreign key. This means that every row in the Orders table must have a corresponding row in the Customers table.

Similarly, the Order Details table has a column named OrderID that is related to the OrderID column of the Orders table. The Order Details table also has a column named ProductID that is related to the ProductID column of the Products table.

NOTE *The relational term comes from the fact that tables in a relational database can be related to each other through foreign keys.*

Null Values

Databases must also provide the ability to handle values that are unknown. Unknown values are called *null values*, and a column is defined as allowing or disallowing null values. When a column allows null values, that column is defined as null; otherwise it is defined as not null. A not null column always has value stored in it. If you tried to add a row but didn't supply a value to a not null column, then the database would throw an exception and wouldn't add your new row.

You'll see the column definitions for the Customers, Orders, Order Details, and Products tables in the following sections.

The *Customers* Table

The Customers table contains rows that store the details of a company that may place orders with the Northwind Company. Figure 22.2 shows some of the rows and columns stored in the Customers table.

FIGURE 22.2

Rows from the Customers table

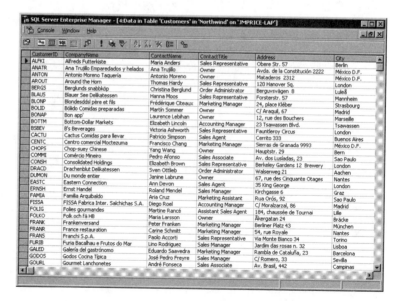

As you can see, the first row displayed is for a customer with the name Alfreds Futterkiste—this name is stored in the CompanyName column of the Customers table.

The CustomerID for the first row is ALFKI, and as you can see, the CustomerID is unique for each row. As mentioned earlier, the primary key for the Customers table is the CustomerID column. If you tried to add a row with a primary key already used by a row, then the database would refuse to add your new row. For example, if you tried to add a row to the Customers table with a CompanyID of ALFKI, then that row would be rejected because ALFKI is already used by a row in the table.

COLUMN TYPES

Each column in a table has a specific database type. This type is similar to the class of an object in C#, except that a database type applies to the kind of value you can store in a column of a table. Table 22.2 lists some of the SQL Server database types.

TABLE 22.2: SQL SERVER DATABASE TYPES

TYPE	DESCRIPTION
bigint	Integer value from -2^{63} ($-9,223,372,036,854,775,808$) to $2^{63} - 1$ ($9,223,372,036,854,775,807$)
int	Integer value from -2^{31} ($-2,147,483,648$) to $2^{31} - 1$ ($2,147,483,647$)
smallint	Integer value from 2^{15} ($-32,768$) to $2^{15} - 1$ ($32,767$)
tinyint	Integer value from 0 to 255
bit	Integer value with either a 1 or 0 value
decimal	Fixed precision and scale numeric value from $-10^{38} + 1$ to $10^{38} - 1$
numeric	Same as decimal
money	Monetary data value from -2^{63} ($-922,337,203,685,477.5808$) to $2^{63} - 1$ ($922,337,203,685,477.5807$), with an accuracy to one ten-thousandth of a monetary unit
smallmoney	Monetary data value from $-214,748.3648$ to $214,748.3647$, with an accuracy to one ten-thousandth of a monetary unit
float	Floating-point value from $-1.79E + 308$ to $1.79E + 308$
real	Floating-point value from $-3.40E + 38$ to $3.40E + 38$
datetime	Date and time value from January 1, 1753, to December 31, 9999, with an accuracy of three-hundredths of a second (3.33 milliseconds)
smalldatetime	Date and time value from January 1, 1900, to June 6, 2079, with an accuracy of one minute
char	Fixed-length non-Unicode characters with a maximum length of 8,000 characters
varchar	Variable-length non-Unicode characters with a maximum of 8,000 characters
text	Variable-length non-Unicode characters with a maximum length of $2^{31} - 1$ ($2,147,483,647$) characters

Continued on next page

TABLE 22.2: SQL SERVER DATABASE TYPES *(continued)*

TYPE	DESCRIPTION
nchar	Fixed-length Unicode characters with a maximum length of 4,000 characters
nvarchar	Variable-length Unicode characters with a maximum length of 4,000 characters
ntext	Variable-length Unicode characters with a maximum length of $2^{30} - 1$ (1,073,741,823) characters
binary	Fixed-length binary data with a maximum length of 8,000 bytes
varbinary	Variable-length binary data with a maximum length of 8,000 bytes
image	Variable-length binary data with a maximum length of $2^{31} - 1$ (2,147,483,647) bytes

DEFINITION OF THE *CUSTOMERS* TABLE

Table 22.3 shows the definition for the columns of the Customers table. This table shows the column name, database type, length, and whether the column allows null values.

TABLE 22.3: DEFINITION FOR THE COLUMNS OF THE Customers TABLE

COLUMN NAME	DATABASE TYPE	LENGTH	ALLOWS NULL VALUES?
CustomerID	nchar	5	No
CompanyName	nvarchar	40	No
ContactName	nvarchar	30	Yes
ContactTitle	nvarchar	30	Yes
Address	nvarchar	60	Yes
City	nvarchar	15	Yes
Region	nvarchar	15	Yes
PostalCode	nvarchar	10	Yes
Country	nvarchar	15	Yes
Phone	nvarchar	24	Yes
Fax	nvarchar	24	Yes

The *Orders* Table

The Orders table contains rows that store the orders placed by customer.

The primary key for the Orders table is the OrderID column—meaning that the value for this column must be unique for each row.

In Figure 22.3, we've restricted the rows retrieved from the Orders table to those where the CustomerID column is equal to ALFKI (this is the same as the CustomerID column for the first row in the Customers table shown earlier in Figure 22.2). As you'll see in the "Using the *WHERE* Clause to Restrict Retrieved Rows" section, you restrict the rows retrieved from a table using a WHERE clause.

FIGURE 22.3

Restricted rows from the Orders table

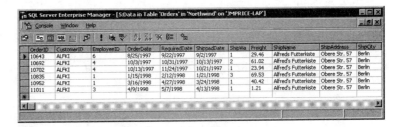

You can now see how foreign keys relate information. The CustomerID column of the Orders table is a foreign key that references the CustomerID column of the Customers table. The table containing the foreign key is known as the *detail table*, and the table whose column is referenced by the foreign key is known as the *master table*. In this example, the Orders table is the detail table, and the Customers table is the master table. Foreign key relationships are for this reason known as *master-detail relationships*. Sometimes the master and detail tables are also known as *parent* and *child* tables, and foreign key relationships are also known as *parent-child relationships*.

Table 22.4 shows the definition for the columns of the Orders table.

TABLE 22.4: DEFINITION FOR THE COLUMNS OF THE Orders TABLE

COLUMN NAME	DATABASE TYPE	LENGTH	ALLOWS NULL VALUES?
OrderID	int	4	No
CustomerID	nchar	5	Yes
EmployeeID	int	4	Yes
OrderDate	datetime	8	Yes
RequiredDate	datetime	8	Yes
ShippedDate	datetime	8	Yes
ShipVia	int	4	Yes
Freight	money	8	Yes
ShipName	nvarchar	40	Yes
ShipAddress	nvarchar	60	Yes
ShipCity	nvarchar	15	Yes
ShipRegion	nvarchar	15	Yes
ShipPostalCode	nvarchar	10	Yes
ShipCountry	nvarchar	15	Yes

The *Order Details* Table

The Order Details table contains rows that store the details of each order.

The primary key for the Order Details table is the combination of the OrderID and CustomerID columns—meaning that the combination of the values in these two columns must be unique for each row. Also, the OrderID column of the Order Details table is a foreign key that references the OrderID column of the Orders table. The ProductID column of the Order Details table is a foreign key that references the ProductID column of the Products table. You'll learn about the Products table shortly.

In Figure 22.4, we've restricted the rows retrieved from the Order Details table to those where the OrderID column is equal to 10643 (this is the same as the OrderID column for the first row in the Orders table shown earlier in Figure 22.3).

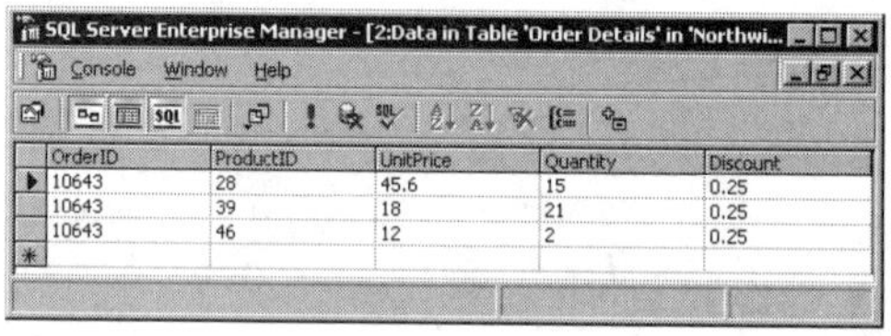

FIGURE 22.4

Restricted rows from the Order Details table

Table 22.5 shows the definition for the columns of the Order Details table.

TABLE 22.5: DEFINITION FOR THE COLUMNS OF THE Order Details TABLE

COLUMN NAME	DATABASE TYPE	LENGTH	ALLOWS NULL VALUES?
OrderID	int	4	Yes
ProductID	int	4	Yes
UnitPrice	money	8	Yes
Quantity	smallint	2	Yes
Discount	real	4	Yes

The *Products* Table

The Products table contains rows that store the details of each product sold by the Northwind Company.

The primary key for the Products table is the ProductID column. The CategoryID column of the Products table is a foreign key that references the CategoryID column of the Categories table. The Categories table contains the various categories of products.

The SupplierID column of the Products table is a foreign key that references the SupplierID column of the Suppliers table. The Suppliers table contains the suppliers of products to the Northwind Company.

In Figure 22.5, we've restricted the rows retrieved from the Products table to those where the ProductID column is equal to 22, 39, and 46 (these are the same as the values for the ProductID column for the rows in the Order Details table shown earlier in Figure 22.4).

FIGURE 22.5

Restricted rows from the Products table

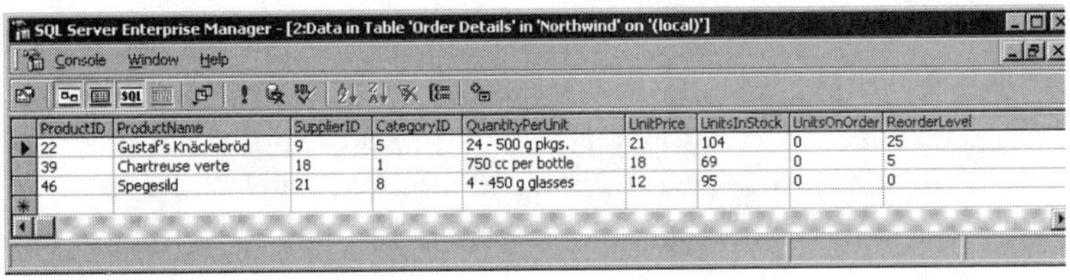

Table 22.6 shows the definition for the columns of the Products table.

TABLE 22.6: DEFINITION FOR THE COLUMNS OF THE Products TABLE

COLUMN NAME	DATABASE TYPE	LENGTH	ALLOWS NULL VALUES?
ProductID	int	4	No
ProductName	nvarchar	40	No
SupplierID	int	4	Yes
CategoryID	int	4	Yes
QuantityPerUnit	nvarchar	20	Yes
UnitPrice	money	8	Yes
UnitsInStock	smallint	2	Yes
UnitsOnOrder	smallint	2	Yes
ReorderLevel	smallint	2	Yes
Discontinued	bit	1	Yes

Using the Structured Query Language (SQL)

The Structured Query Language, or SQL (pronounced *sequel*), is the standard language for accessing relational databases. As you'll see in this section, SQL is easy to learn and use. With SQL, you tell the database what data you want to access, and the database software figures out exactly how to get that data.

There are many types of SQL statements, but the most commonly used types of SQL statements are these:

- Data Manipulation Language (DML) statements
- Data Definition Language (DDL) statements

DML statements allow you to retrieve, add, modify, and delete rows stored in database tables. DDL statements allow you to create database structures such as tables. DDL statements are of interest to people who manage the database and are beyond the scope of this book.

NOTE   *For further details of writing DDL statements for SQL Server, you may consult the book Mastering SQL Server 2000 by Mike Gunderloy and Joseph L. Jorden (Sybex, 2000).*

Before you learn the basics of DML statements, you need to know how you can enter and run SQL statements. You can enter and run SQL statements against a SQL Server database using the Query Analyzer, and you'll learn about this tool in the following section.

TIP   *You can also use the Query Builder through Visual Studio .NET to create SQL statements. The Query Builder is a graphical tool that allows you to create SQL statements visually, rather than typing them.*

Using the Query Analyzer

You can use the Query Analyzer to enter and run SQL statements. You start the Query Analyzer by selecting Start ➢ Microsoft SQL Server ➢ Query Analyzer.

CONNECTING TO A SQL SERVER INSTANCE

When you start the Query Analyzer, the first thing it displays is the Connect to SQL Server dialog box. In the SQL Server field, you enter the name of the SQL Server instance to which you want to connect. You can click the drop-down list box and select an instance of SQL Server, or you can click the ellipsis button to the right of the drop-down list box to display a list of SQL Server instances running on your network.

If you select the Windows authentication radio button, then SQL Server will use the Windows 2000/NT user information to validate your request to connect to SQL Server. If you select the SQL Server authentication radio button, then you will need to enter a login name and password in the Login Name and Password fields, respectively.

For example, to connect to our database, we enter **localhost** in the SQL Server field; this corresponds to the instance of SQL Server installed on the local computer. We also select the SQL Server authentication radio button, and enter **sa** in the Login Name field and **sa** in the Password field (this password was set when we installed SQL Server). These details are then used to connect to SQL Server. If you have an instance of SQL Server running on your local computer or on your network, enter the relevant details and click the OK button to connect to SQL Server.

ENTERING AND RUNNING A SQL STATEMENT

Once you've connected to SQL Server using the Query Analyzer, you can use the Object Browser to view the parts of a database, and you enter and run SQL statements using a Query window. Figure 22.6 shows the Object Browser and an example Query window, along with the results of retrieving the `CustomerID` and `CompanyName` columns from the `Customers` table.

FIGURE 22.6

Viewing database items using the Object Browser and executing a **SELECT** statement using the Query window

As you can see from Figure 22.6, you enter SQL statements into the top part of the Query window, and the results retrieved from the database are displayed in the bottom part. You specify the database to access with the USE statement, and you retrieve rows from the database using the SELECT statement.

If you want to follow along with this example, go ahead and enter the following USE statement into your Query window:

```
USE Northwind
```

This USE statement indicates that you want to use the Northwind database. Next, on a separate line, enter the following SELECT statement:

```
SELECT CustomerID, CompanyName FROM Customers;
```

This SELECT statement indicates that you want to retrieve the CustomerID and CompanyName columns from the Customers table.

NOTE *SELECT and FROM are SQL keywords. Although SQL isn't case sensitive, we use uppercase when specifying SQL keywords and mixed case when specifying column and table names. You may terminate a SQL statement using a semicolon (;)—although this isn't mandatory.*

You can run the SQL statement entered in the Query window in four ways:

- Selecting Execute from the Query menu

- Clicking the Execute Query button on the toolbar (the button with the green triangle)

- Pressing the F5 button on the keyboard

- Pressing Ctrl+E on the keyboard

Once you run the SQL statement, your statement is sent to the database for execution. The database runs your statement and sends results back. These results are then displayed in the bottom of your Query window.

SAVING AND LOADING A SQL STATEMENT

You can save a SQL statement entered into the Query Analyzer into a text file. You can then load and run the SQL statement in that file later. You can save a SQL statement by:

◆ Selecting Save or Save As from the File menu

◆ Pressing the Save Query/Result button on the toolbar (the button with the disk)

◆ Pressing Ctrl+S on the keyboard

When you do any of these actions, the Query Analyzer opens the Save Query dialog box. Let's say you save the file as CustomerSelect.sql.
Once you've saved the file, you can open it by:

◆ Selecting Open from the File menu

◆ Pressing the Load SQL Script button on the toolbar (the button with the open folder)

◆ Pressing Ctrl+Shift+P on the keyboard

When you do any of these actions, the Query Analyzer opens the Open Query File dialog box. Let's say you open CustomerSelect.sql. Once you've opened a query file, you can run it using one the techniques described earlier.

Understanding Data Manipulation Language (DML) Statements

As mentioned earlier, Data Manipulation Language (DML) statements allow you to retrieve, add, modify, and delete rows stored in database tables. There are four types of DML statements:

SELECT Statements   You use a SELECT statement to retrieve rows from one or more tables.

INSERT Statements   You use an INSERT statement to add one or more new rows to a table.

UPDATE Statements   You use an UPDATE statement to modify one or more rows in a table.

DELETE Statements   You use a DELETE statement to remove one or more rows from a table.

You'll learn how to use these four statements in the following sections. You'll start off learning how to use a SELECT statement to retrieve rows from a single table.

USING A *SELECT* STATEMENT TO RETRIEVE ROWS FROM A SINGLE TABLE

You use the SELECT statement to retrieve rows from tables. The SELECT statement has many forms, and the simplest version allows you to specify a list of columns and the table name. For example, the following SELECT statement retrieves the CustomerID, CompanyName, ContactName, and Address columns from the Customers table:

```
SELECT CustomerID, CompanyName, ContactName, Address
FROM Customers;
```

The columns to retrieve are specified after the SELECT keyword, and the table is specified after the FROM keyword.

You can retrieve all columns from a table by specifying the asterisk character (*) immediately after the SELECT keyword.

*TIP   You should avoid using * in your SELECT statements because you might be retrieving more information than you need. You should list only the columns you actually want.*

For example, the following SELECT statement retrieves all the columns from the Customers table using *:

```
SELECT *
FROM Customers;
```

This example also retrieves all the rows from the Customers table.

USING THE *WHERE* CLAUSE TO RESTRICT RETRIEVED ROWS

You can use the WHERE clause to restrict the rows retrieved by a SELECT statement. For example, the following SELECT statement uses a WHERE clause to restrict the rows retrieved from the Customers table to those where the Country column is equal to 'UK':

```
SELECT CustomerID, CompanyName, City
FROM Customers
WHERE Country = 'UK';
```

Figure 22.7 shows the results of this SELECT statement.

FIGURE 22.7

Customers where Country is equal to 'UK'

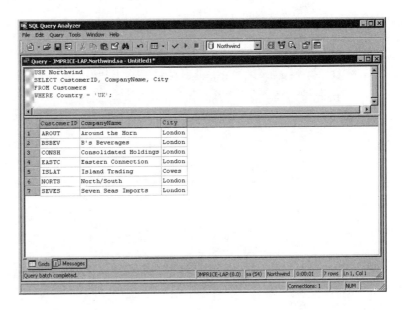

The next SELECT statement uses a WHERE clause to restrict the row retrieved from the Products table to the one where ProductID is equal to 10:

```
SELECT ProductID, ProductName, QuantityPerUnit, UnitPrice
FROM Products
WHERE ProductID = 10;
```

The equal operator (=) is not the only operator you can use in a WHERE clause. Table 22.7 shows other mathematical operators you can use.

TABLE 22.7: SQL MATHEMATICAL OPERATORS

OPERATOR	DESCRIPTION
=	Equal
<> or !=	Not equal
<	Less than
>	Greater than
<=	Less than or equal
>=	Greater than or equal

The following SELECT statement uses the less than or equal operator (<=) to retrieve the rows from the Products table where the ProductID column is less than or equal to 10:

```
SELECT ProductID, ProductName, QuantityPerUnit, UnitPrice
FROM Products
WHERE ProductID <= 10;
```

The next SELECT statement uses the not equal operator (!=) to retrieve the rows from the Products table where the ProductID column is not equal to 10:

```
SELECT ProductID, ProductName, QuantityPerUnit, UnitPrice
FROM Products
WHERE ProductID != 10;
```

USING THE *LIKE* OPERATOR TO PERFORM PATTERN MATCHING

You can use the LIKE operator in a WHERE clause to perform pattern matching. You specify one or more *wildcard* characters to use in your pattern matching string. Table 22.8 lists the wildcard characters.

TABLE 22.8: WILDCARD CHARACTERS

CHARACTERS	DESCRIPTION
_	Matches any one character. For example, J_y matches Joy and Jay.
%	Matches any number of characters. For example, %wind matches Northwind and Southwind; %fire% matches starfire, firestarter, and fireman.
[ ]	Matches any one character in the brackets. For example, [sm]ay matches say and may.
[^]	Matches any one character not in the brackets. For example, [^a] matches any character except a.
[-]	Matches a range of characters. For example, [a-c]bc matches abc, bbc, and cbc.
#	Matches any one number. For example, A# matches A1 through A9.

Let's take a look at some examples that use some of the wildcard characters shown in Table 22.7. The following SELECT statement uses the LIKE operator to retrieve products where the ProductName column is like 'Cha_':

```
SELECT ProductID, ProductName
FROM Products
WHERE ProductName LIKE 'Cha_';
```

The next SELECT statement uses the LIKE operator to retrieve products where the ProductName column is like 'Cha%':

```
SELECT ProductID, ProductName
FROM Products
WHERE ProductName LIKE 'Cha%';
```

The next SELECT statement uses the LIKE operator to retrieve products where the ProductName column is like '[ABC]%':

```
SELECT ProductID, ProductName
FROM Products
WHERE ProductName LIKE '[ABC]%';
```

The next SELECT statement uses the LIKE operator to retrieve products where the ProductName column is like '[^ABC]%':

```
SELECT ProductID, ProductName
FROM Products
WHERE ProductName LIKE '[^ABC]%';
```

The next SELECT statement uses the LIKE operator to retrieve products where the ProductName column is like '[A-E]%':

```
SELECT ProductID, ProductName
FROM Products
WHERE ProductName LIKE '[A-E]%';
```

USING THE *IN* OPERATOR TO SPECIFY A LIST OF VALUES

You can use the IN operator in a WHERE clause to retrieve rows whose columns contain values in a specified list. For example, the following SELECT statement uses the IN operator to retrieve products whose ProductID is 1, 2, 5, 15, 20, 22, 25, 35, 37, 40, 42, 45, or 50:

```
SELECT ProductID, ProductName, QuantityPerUnit, UnitPrice
FROM Products
WHERE ProductID IN (1, 2, 5, 15, 20, 22, 25, 35, 37, 40, 42, 45, 50);
```

Here's another example that displays the OrderID column from the Orders table for the rows where the CustomerID column is in the list retrieved by a subquery; the subquery retrieves the CustomerID column from the Customers table where the CompanyName is like 'Fu%':

```
SELECT OrderID
FROM Orders
WHERE CustomerID IN (
  SELECT CustomerID
  FROM Customers
  WHERE CompanyName like 'Fu%'
);
```

The results of the subquery are used in the outer query.

USING THE *BETWEEN* OPERATOR TO SPECIFY A RANGE OF VALUES

You can use the BETWEEN operator in a WHERE clause to retrieve rows whose columns contain values in a specified range. For example, the following SELECT statement uses the BETWEEN operator to retrieve products whose ProductID is between 1 and 12:

```
SELECT ProductID, ProductName, QuantityPerUnit, UnitPrice
FROM Products
WHERE ProductID BETWEEN 1 AND 12;
```

This is another example that displays the OrderID column for the rows from the Orders table where the OrderDate is between '1996-07-04' and '1996-07-08':

```
SELECT OrderID
FROM Orders
WHERE OrderDate BETWEEN '1996-07-04' AND '1996-07-08';
```

USING THE *NOT* KEYWORD TO REVERSE THE MEANING OF AN OPERATOR

You can use the NOT keyword with an operator in a WHERE clause to reverse the meaning of that operator. For example, the following SELECT statement uses the NOT keyword to reverse the meaning of the BETWEEN operator shown in the previous example:

```
SELECT ProductID, ProductName, QuantityPerUnit, UnitPrice
FROM Products
WHERE ProductID NOT BETWEEN 1 AND 12;
```

NOTE   *You can use the NOT keyword to reverse other operators: NOT LIKE, NOT IN—for example.*

USING THE *IS NULL* OPERATOR TO RETRIEVE ROWS WHOSE COLUMNS ARE SET TO NULL

Earlier, we mentioned that columns can contain null values. A null value is different from a blank string or zero: A null value represents a value that hasn't been set, or is unknown. You can use the IS NULL operator in a WHERE clause to determine if a column contains a null value. For example, the following SELECT statement uses the IS NULL operator to retrieve customers where the Fax column contains a null value:

```
SELECT CustomerID, CompanyName, Fax
FROM Customers
WHERE Fax IS NULL;
```

Figure 22.8 shows the results of this SELECT statement.

FIGURE 22.8

Customers where Fax contains a null value

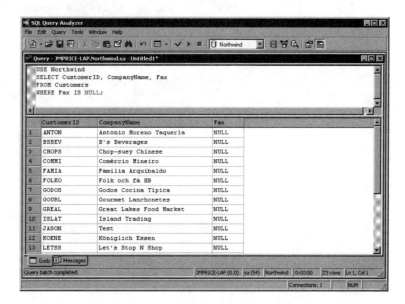

NOTE   *As you can see, null values are displayed as* NULL *in the Query Analyzer.*

USING LOGICAL OPERATORS TO SPECIFY MULTIPLE CONDITIONS

You can use the logical operators shown in Table 22.9 to specify multiple conditions in a WHERE clause.

TABLE 22.9: LOGICAL OPERATORS

OPERATOR	DESCRIPTION
a AND b	Evaluates to true when a and b are both true
a OR b	Evaluates to true when either a or b are true
NOT a	Evaluates to true if a is false, and false if a is true

For example, the following SELECT statement uses the AND operator to retrieve products where the UnitsInStock column is less than 10 and the ReorderLevel column is less than or equal to 20:

```
SELECT ProductID, ProductName, UnitsInStock, ReorderLevel
FROM Products
WHERE UnitsInStock < 10
AND ReorderLevel <= 20;
```

Figure 22.9 shows the results of this SELECT statement.

FIGURE 22.9

Products where UnitsInStock is less than 10 and ReorderLevel is less than or equal to 20

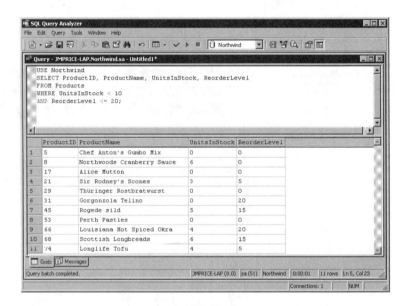

In the next example, the SELECT statement uses the OR operator to retrieve products where either the UnitsInStock column is less than 10 or the ReorderLevel column is less than or equal to 20:

```
SELECT ProductID, ProductName, UnitsInStock, ReorderLevel
FROM Products
WHERE UnitsInStock < 10
OR ReorderLevel <= 20;
```

The next SELECT statement uses the NOT operator to retrieve products where the UnitsInStock column is not less than 10:

```
SELECT ProductID, ProductName, UnitsInStock, ReorderLevel
FROM Products
WHERE NOT (UnitsInStock < 10);
```

USING THE *ORDER BY* CLAUSE TO SORT ROWS

You can use the ORDER BY clause to sort rows retrieved from the database. You specify the column (or columns) to sort in the ORDER BY clause. By default, rows are sorted in ascending order. For example, the following SELECT statement orders the rows using the ProductName column:

```
SELECT ProductID, ProductName, UnitsInStock, ReorderLevel
FROM Products
ORDER BY ProductName;
```

Figure 22.10 shows the results of this SELECT statement. As you can see, the rows are ordered in ascending order using the ProductName column.

FIGURE 22.10

Products ordered by ascending ProductName

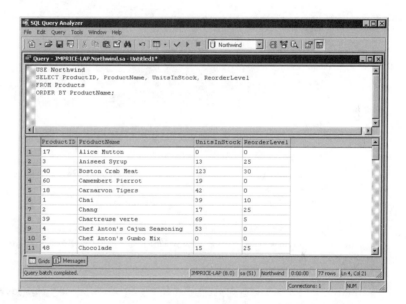

You can explicitly state the order for a column using the ASC or DESC keyword. ASC orders the columns in ascending order (the default, which is smallest item first), and DESC orders the columns in descending order (largest item first). For example, the following SELECT statement orders the products in descending order using the ProductName column:

```
SELECT ProductID, ProductName, UnitsInStock, ReorderLevel
FROM Products
ORDER BY ProductName DESC;
```

Figure 22.11 shows the results of this SELECT statement. As you can see, the rows are ordered in descending order using the ProductName column.

FIGURE 22.11

Products ordered
by descending
`ProductName`

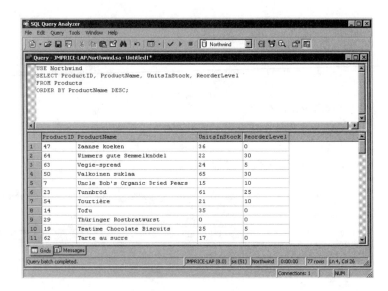

You can specify multiple columns in an `ORDER BY` clause. For example, the following `SELECT` statement orders the rows using both the `UnitsInStock` and `ReorderLevel` columns:

```
SELECT ProductID, ProductName, UnitsInStock, ReorderLevel
FROM Products
ORDER BY UnitsInStock DESC, ReorderLevel ASC;
```

Figure 22.12 shows the results of this `SELECT` statement. As you can see, the rows are ordered by the `UnitsInStock` column first (in descending order), and then by the `ReorderLevel` column (in ascending order).

FIGURE 22.12

Products ordered by
`UnitsInStock` and
`ReorderLevel`

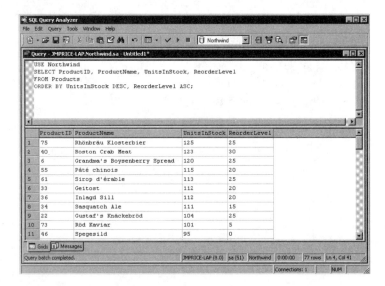

USING A *SELECT* STATEMENT TO RETRIEVE ROWS FROM MULTIPLE TABLES

So far, you've only seen SELECT statements that retrieve rows from one table at a time. You'll often need to retrieve rows from multiple tables using the same SELECT statement.

For example, you might want to see all the orders placed by a customer. To do this, you must specify both the Customers and the Orders tables after the FROM keyword in the SELECT statement and use a *table join* in the WHERE clause. You must also specify the name of the table when referencing columns of the same name in both tables. The following SELECT statement shows this and retrieves the orders placed by the customer with a CustomerID of ALFKI:

```
SELECT Customers.CustomerID, CompanyName, Address, OrderID, ShipAddress
FROM Customers, Orders
WHERE Customers.CustomerID = Orders.CustomerID
AND Customers.CustomerID = 'ALFKI';
```

Notice that the Customers and Orders tables are specified after the FROM keyword, and because both tables contain a column named CustomerID, the table name is placed before each reference to the respective column in each table. The table join is done on the CustomerID column of each table (Customers.CustomerID = Orders.CustomerID).

Figure 22.13 shows the results of this SELECT statement.

FIGURE 22.13

Orders placed by a specific customer

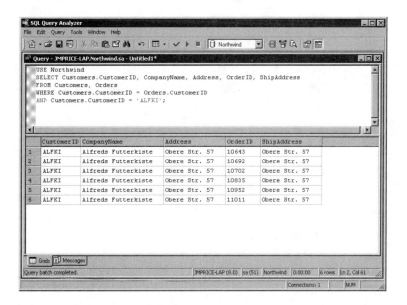

The previous SELECT statement used the SQL standard format for joining tables. With SQL Server, you can also use the JOIN keyword for joining tables. The advantage of the JOIN keyword is you can use it to perform outer joins, which you'll learn about shortly. The following example rewrites the previous SELECT statement using the JOIN keyword:

```
SELECT Customers.CustomerID, CompanyName, Address, OrderID, ShipAddress
FROM Customers
```

```
JOIN Orders
ON Customers.CustomerID = Orders.CustomerID
AND Customers.CustomerID = 'ALFKI';
```

This SELECT statement returns the same results as the previous example.

The disadvantage of the previous two SELECT statements is that they only return rows where the join columns both contain a value—in other words, neither column contains a null. This can be a problem if you have rows that have a null value in either of the columns used in the join—and you need to actually retrieve those rows. Outer joins solve this problem. There are three types of outer joins:

LEFT OUTER JOIN   The LEFT OUTER JOIN (usually shortened to LEFT JOIN) returns all the rows from the table on the left of the join—including those whose column contains a null.

RIGHT OUTER JOIN   The RIGHT OUTER JOIN (usually shortened to RIGHT JOIN) returns all the rows from the table on the right of the join—including those whose column contains a null.

FULL OUTER JOIN   The FULL OUTER JOIN (usually shortened to FULL JOIN) returns all the rows from the tables on the left and right of the join—including those whose column contains a null.

Let's take a look at a couple of examples. First, go ahead and perform the following INSERT to add a row to the Products table:

```
INSERT INTO Products (ProductName, SupplierID)
VALUES ('DVD Player', NULL);
```

You don't need to specify the ProductID column because SQL Server will automatically supply a value. You'll notice that the SupplierID column is null. If you now perform the following SELECT statement, you won't see the new row because the SupplierID column of the new row is null and the JOIN won't return that row:

```
SELECT ProductID
FROM Products
JOIN Suppliers
ON Products.SupplierID = Suppliers.SupplierID;
```

To see the new row, you use LEFT JOIN in the SELECT statement to retrieve all rows from the table on the left of the join (in this case, the table on the left is the Products table):

```
SELECT ProductID
FROM Products
LEFT JOIN Suppliers
ON Products.SupplierID = Suppliers.SupplierID;
```

You can also use LEFT JOIN with IS NULL in the same SELECT statement to retrieve just the new row:

```
SELECT ProductID
FROM Products
LEFT JOIN Suppliers
ON Products.SupplierID = Suppliers.SupplierID
WHERE Products.SupplierID IS NULL;
```

USING THE *AS* KEYWORD TO SPECIFY THE DISPLAY NAME FOR A COLUMN OR ALIAS A TABLE

You can use the AS keyword to specify the name of a column when it is displayed in the output from a SELECT statement. You might want to do this when you need to display more friendly names or descriptive names for columns. For example, the following SELECT statement uses the AS keyword to set the display name of the ProductName column to Product, and the UnitPrice column to Price for each unit:

```sql
SELECT ProductName AS Product, UnitPrice AS 'Price for each unit'
FROM products;
```

Figure 22.14 shows the results of this SELECT statement.

FIGURE 22.14

Using the AS keyword to specify the display name for columns

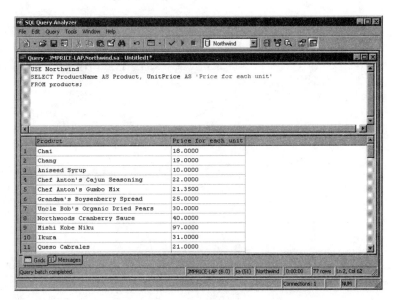

You can also use the AS keyword to alias a table. You might want to do this if your table names are long. The following example uses the AS keyword to alias the Customers and Orders tables as Cust and Ord, respectively:

```sql
SELECT Cust.CustomerID, CompanyName, Address, OrderID, ShipAddress
FROM Customers AS Cust, Orders AS Ord
WHERE Cust.CustomerID = Ord.CustomerID
AND Cust.CustomerID = 'ALFKI';
```

USING AN *INSERT* STATEMENT TO ADD A NEW ROW TO A TABLE

You use the INSERT statement to add a new row to a table. When adding a new row, you specify the name of the table, the optional column names, and the values for those columns. For example, the following INSERT statement adds a new row to the Customers table:

```sql
INSERT INTO Customers (
  CustomerID, CompanyName, ContactName, ContactTitle, Address,
```

```
   City, Region, PostalCode, Country, Phone, Fax
) VALUES (
   'JPCOM', 'Jason Price Company', 'Jason Price', 'Owner', '1 Main Street',
   'New York', NULL, '12345', 'USA', '(800)-555-1212', NULL
);
```

The CustomerID column is the primary key of the Customers table, and therefore the new row must contain a unique value for this column. You'll notice that the INSERT statement specifies a null value for the Region and Fax columns (this is specified using the NULL keyword).

You can use the Query Analyzer to enter INSERT statements, and Figure 22.15 shows the previous INSERT, along with a SELECT statement that retrieves the new row.

FIGURE 22.15

Using an INSERT statement to add a new row to the Customers table

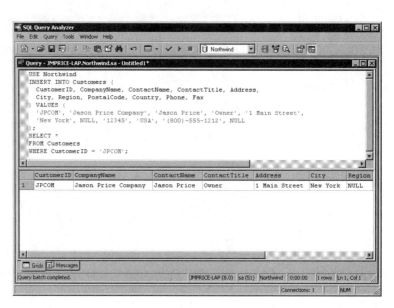

NOTE   *You must supply values for all columns that are defined as* not null *in a table. Also, the number of columns in the* INSERT *and* VALUES *lists much match, and the data type of each column in the* INSERT *and* VALUES *lists must also match.*

When supplying values to all columns in a row, you may omit the column names and just supply the values for each column. For example:

```
INSERT INTO Customers VALUES (
   'CRCOM', 'Cynthia Red Company', 'Cynthia Red', 'Owner', '2 South Street',
   'New York', NULL, '12345', 'USA', '(800)-555-1212', NULL
);
```

USING AN *UPDATE* STATEMENT TO MODIFY ROWS IN A TABLE

You use the UPDATE statement to update rows in a table. When updating a row, you specify the name of the table, the columns to update, and the new values for the columns.

WARNING   *Typically, you should also use a* **WHERE** *clause to restrict the rows being updated. If you don't supply a* **WHERE** *clause, then all the rows in the specified table will be updated. In many cases, you'll specify the value for the primary key in your* **WHERE** *clause.*

The following UPDATE statement modifies the Address column for the row in the Customers table with a CustomerID of JPCOM:

```
UPDATE Customers
SET Address = '3 North Street'
WHERE CustomerID = 'JPCOM';
```

Figure 22.16 shows this UPDATE statement, along with a SELECT statement that retrieves the modified row.

FIGURE 22.16

Using an UPDATE statement to modify the Address column of a row in the Customers table

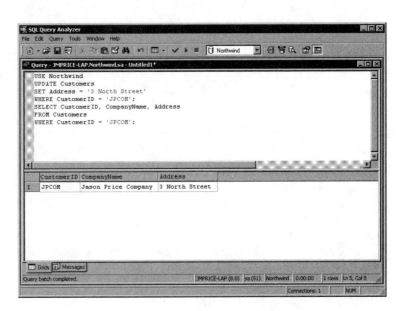

You can use an UPDATE statement to modify multiple columns. For example, the following UPDATE statement modifies the Address and ContactTitle columns:

```
UPDATE Customers
SET Address = '5 Liberty Street', ContactTitle = 'CEO'
WHERE CustomerID = 'JPCOM';
```

Figure 22.17 shows this UPDATE statement, along with a SELECT statement that retrieves the modified row.

FIGURE 22.17

Modifying the
`Address` and
`ContactTitle`
columns of a row in
the `Customers` table

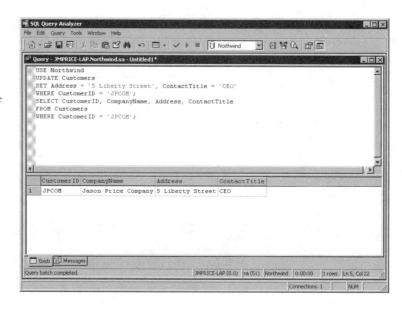

USING A *DELETE* STATEMENT TO REMOVE ROWS FROM A TABLE

You use the DELETE statement to remove rows from a table. When removing a row, you specify the name of the table and the rows to delete using a WHERE clause.

WARNING   *If you omit the WHERE clause in a DELETE statement, all rows from the table will be deleted. Make sure you provide a WHERE clause if you don't want to remove all the rows from the table. Typically, you'll specify the value for the primary key in your WHERE clause.*

The following DELETE statement removes the row from the Customers table where the CustomerID is CRCOM:

```
DELETE FROM Customers
WHERE CustomerID = 'CRCOM';
```

Figure 22.18 shows this DELETE statement, along with a SELECT statement that demonstrates that the row has been removed.

MAINTAINING DATABASE INTEGRITY

The database software ensures that the information stored in the tables is consistent. In technical terms, it maintains the integrity of the information. Two examples of this are the following:

◆   The primary key of a row is always contains a unique value.

◆   The foreign key of a row always references a value that exists in the master table.

WARNING   *In the real world, people who don't know how to design databases often end up actually creating the database. Because of this, they don't always add primary or foreign keys to their tables—and therefore the database cannot enforce consistency in the data.*

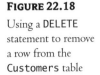

FIGURE 22.18

Using a DELETE statement to remove a row from the **Customers** table

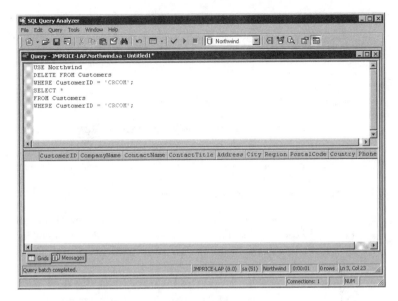

Let's take a look at what happens when you try to insert a row into a table with a primary key that already exists. The following INSERT statement attempts to add a row to the Customers table with a CustomerID of ALFKI (a row with this primary key already exists in the Customers table):

```
INSERT INTO Customers (
    CustomerID, CompanyName, ContactName, ContactTitle, Address,
    City, Region, PostalCode, Country, Phone, Fax
) VALUES (
    'ALFKI', 'Jason Price Company', 'Jason Price', 'Owner', '1 Main Street',
    'New York', NULL, '12345', 'USA', '(800)-555-1212', NULL
);
```

If you attempt to run this INSERT statement, you'll get the following error message from the database:

```
Violation of PRIMARY KEY constraint 'PK_Customers'.
Cannot insert duplicate key in object 'Customers'.
The statement has been terminated.
```

This INSERT statement fails because an existing row in Customers table already contains the primary key value ALFKI. The message tells you that the primary key specified in the INSERT statement already exists in the Customers table. The constraint name PK_Customers is the name of the table constraint assigned to the primary key when the Customers table was originally created. At the end, the message indicates that the statement has been terminated—meaning that the INSERT statement has not been performed.

Let's take a look at what happens when you try to modify a primary key in a master table whose value is referenced in a foreign key in a detail table. The following UPDATE statement attempts to modify the CustomerID from ALFKI to ALFKZ (this row is referenced by rows in the Orders table):

```
UPDATE Customers
SET CustomerID = 'ALFKZ'
WHERE CustomerID = 'ALFKI';
```

If you attempt to run this UPDATE statement, you'll get the following error message:

```
UPDATE statement conflicted with COLUMN REFERENCE constraint
'FK_Orders_Customers'. The conflict occurred in database
'Northwind', table 'Orders', column 'CustomerID'.
The statement has been terminated.
```

This UPDATE statement fails because the row containing the primary key value ALFKI is referenced by rows in the Orders table. The message tells you that the new value for the CustomerID column violates the foreign key constraint on the CustomerID column of the Orders table. This constraint is named FK_Orders_Customers.

Also, you can't remove a row from a master table that is referenced by a row in a detail table. For example, the following DELETE statement attempts to remove the row from the Customers table where the CustomerID column equals ALFKI (this row is referenced by rows in the Orders table):

```
DELETE FROM Customers
WHERE CustomerID = 'ALFKI';
```

If you attempt to run this DELETE statement, you'll get the same error message that was shown for the previous UPDATE statement. This DELETE statement fails because the Orders table contains rows that reference the row in the Customers table, and removing this row would make the database inconsistent because the rows in the Orders table wouldn't reference a valid row.

USING DATABASE TRANSACTIONS

By default, when you run an INSERT, UPDATE, or DELETE statement, SQL Server permanently records the results of the statement in the database. This may not always be your desired result. For example, in the case of a banking transaction, you might want to withdraw money from one account and deposit it into another account. If you had two separate UPDATE statements that performed the withdraw and deposit, then you would only want to make the results of each UPDATE statement permanent as one unit. If either UPDATE failed for some reason, then you would want to undo the results of both UPDATE statements.

NOTE *Permanently recording the results of SQL statements is known as a commit, or committing the SQL statements. Undoing the results of SQL statements is known as a rollback, or rolling back the SQL statements.*

You can group SQL statements together into a *transaction*. You can then commit or roll back the SQL statements in that transaction as one unit. For example, the two UPDATE statements in the banking example could be placed into a transaction, and then you could commit or roll back that transaction as one unit, depending on whether both of the UPDATE statements succeeded.

You start a transaction using the BEGIN TRANSACTION statement, or the shorthand version BEGIN TRANS. You then perform your SQL statements that make up the transaction. To commit the transaction, you perform a COMMIT TRANSACTION statement, or the shorthand version COMMIT TRANS or COMMIT. To roll back the transaction, you perform a ROLLBACK TRANSACTION statement, or the shorthand version ROLLBACK TRANS or ROLLBACK.

Let's take a look at an example. The following transaction consists of two INSERT statements: the first adds a row to the Customers table and the second adds a row to the Orders table. At the end, the transaction is committed using a COMMIT statement:

```
BEGIN TRANSACTION;
INSERT INTO Customers (
  CustomerID, CompanyName
) VALUES (
  'SOCOM', 'Steve Orange Company'
);
INSERT INTO Orders (
  CustomerID
) VALUES (
  'SOCOM'
);
COMMIT;
```

Figure 22.19 shows this transaction, along with two SELECT statements that show the two new rows.

FIGURE 22.19

Committing a transaction

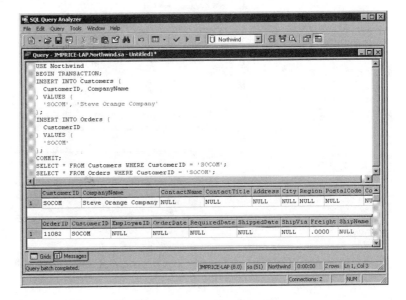

The next transaction consists of similar INSERT statements, except this time the transaction is rolled back using a ROLLBACK statement.

```
BEGIN TRANSACTION;
INSERT INTO Customers (
  CustomerID, CompanyName
) VALUES (
  'SYCOM', 'Steve Yellow Company'
);
INSERT INTO Orders (
  CustomerID
) VALUES (
  'SYCOM'
);
ROLLBACK;
```

Because the transaction is rolled back, the two rows added by the INSERT statements are undone. Figure 22.20 shows this transaction along with two SELECT statements that show the two new rows were not added.

FIGURE 22.20

Rolling back a transaction

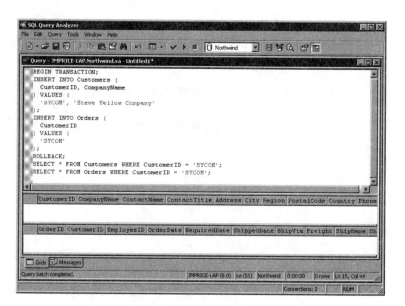

You should check for errors in a transaction before deciding to perform a COMMIT or ROLLBACK because errors do not always stop the next line from processing. To do this in SQL Server, you use the @@ERROR variable. This variable contains zero whenever a statement is executed and doesn't cause an error; if @@ERROR contains a non-zero value, you know an error occurred. Therefore, you perform a COMMIT if @@ERROR equals 0; otherwise you perform a ROLLBACK.

You can also assign a name to your transaction in the BEGIN TRANSACTION statement. This is useful as it shows which transaction you are working on.

The following example shows the naming of a transaction, along with the use of the @@ERROR variable to determine whether to perform a COMMIT or ROLLBACK:

```
BEGIN TRANSACTION MyTransaction;
INSERT INTO Customers (
  CustomerID, CompanyName
) VALUES (
  'SYCOM', 'Steve Yellow Company'
);
INSERT INTO Orders (
  CustomerID
) VALUES (
  'SYCOM'
);
IF @@Error = 0
  COMMIT TRANSACTION MyTransaction;
ELSE
  ROLLBACK TRANSACTION MyTransaction;
```

Notice that the name of the transaction is MyTransaction, and that this name is used in the COMMIT and ROLLBACK statements.

Introducing Stored Procedures

Many databases allow you to store procedures in the database. These are known as *stored procedures*. You can later run these procedures from within the database or call them from a C# program. SQL Server and Oracle are two examples of databases that allow you to use stored procedures.

Stored procedures are written in vendor-specific languages. For example, stored procedures in SQL Server are written in a language known as *Transact-SQL*; in Oracle, stored procedures are written in a language known as *PL/SQL*.

In this section, you'll see a simple stored procedure that already exists in the SQL Server Northwind database. You'll also see how to run this procedure using the Query Analyzer tool. In Chapter 23, "Active Data Objects: ADO.NET," you'll learn how to run the procedure from a C# program.

Looking at an Example SQL Server Stored Procedure

The following stored procedure, named Ten Most Expensive Products is defined in the SQL Server Northwind database:

```
CREATE PROCEDURE "Ten Most Expensive Products" AS
SET ROWCOUNT 10
SELECT Products.ProductName AS TenMostExpensiveProducts, Products.UnitPrice
FROM Products
ORDER BY Products.UnitPrice DESC
GO
```

As you can see, you create procedures in SQL Server using the CREATE PROCEDURE statement. The SET ROWCOUNT statement sets the maximum number of rows retrieved by the SELECT statement; in this case, 10 rows are retrieved. In a nutshell, this procedure returns the ProductName and Unitprice for the top 10 rows in the Products table, ordered by the UnitPrice column.

Running a SQL Server Stored Procedure

You can run a procedure in the Query Analyzer tool using the EXEC statement. For example, the following statement runs the Ten Most Expensive Products procedure:

```
EXEC "Ten Most Expensive Products";
```

Figure 22.21 shows the result of running this procedure.

FIGURE 22.21

Running the Ten Most Expensive Products stored procedure

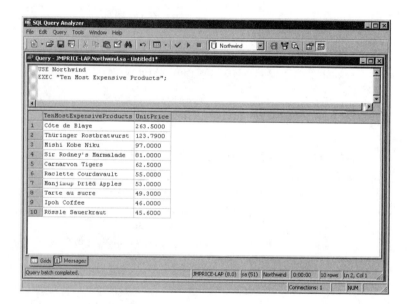

In the next section, you'll see how to access a database using Visual Studio .NET.

Accessing a Database Using Visual Studio .NET

Visual Studio .NET (VS .NET) contains functions that allow you to connect to a database and explore elements such as tables. These functions are contained in the Server Explorer. In this section, you'll be introduced to Server Explorer and some of its functions.

First, you need to connect to a database. To do this, you select Connect to Database from the Tools menu. This displays the Data Link Properties dialog box. Figure 22.22 shows this dialog box with appropriate entries to connect to the Northwind database running on the computer JMPRICE-LAP.

FIGURE 22.22

Entering database details using the Data Link Properties dialog box

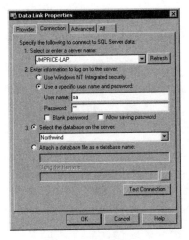

Second, once you've entered you database details, click the Test Connection button to verify the database connection details. Click the OK button once your test succeeds.

Finally, once you've connected to the database, you can view things like the tables. You can also retrieve and modify rows in the tables. You can drill down to the tables in the database by clicking the Add icon in the tree in Server Explorer, and you can retrieve the rows from a table by clicking the right mouse button on the table in the tree and selecting Retrieve Data from Table in the pop-up window. Figure 22.23 shows the rows from the Customers table.

FIGURE 22.23

Viewing the rows in the Customers table using the Server Explorer

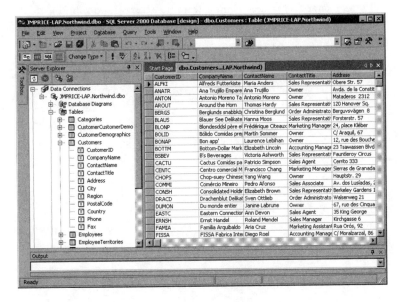

You can enter SQL statements by clicking the Show SQL Pane button in the toolbar, as shown in Figure 22.24.

FIGURE 22.24

Entering a SQL statement

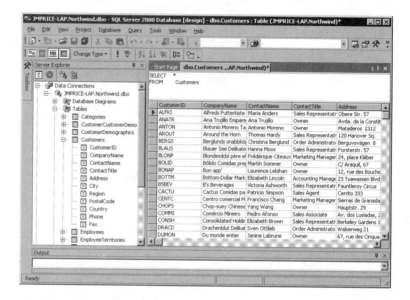

You can build SQL statements visually using the by clicking the Show Diagram button in the toolbar and selecting columns from the table, as shown in Figure 22.25. As you can see, we've selected the ContactName, CompanyName, and CustomerID columns from the Customers table.

FIGURE 22.25

Building a SQL statement visually

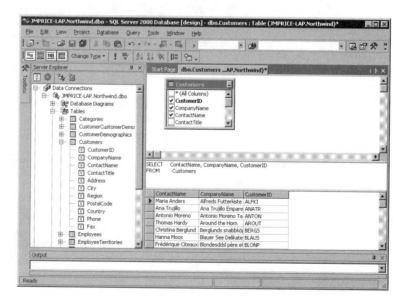

You can view the properties of a column in a table by clicking the right mouse button over the column and selecting Properties from the pop-up window. Figure 22.26 shows the properties of the CustomerID column of the Customers table.

FIGURE 22.26

Properties of the CustomerID columns

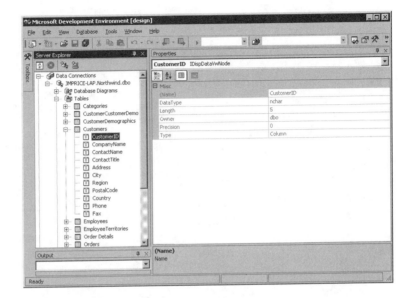

We've only scratched the surface of the Server Explorer in this section. If you have VS .NET, you should feel free to experiment with the Server Explorer—that's the best way to learn.

Summary

In this chapter, you learned the basics of databases and saw how to use SQL (pronounced *sequel*) to access a database.

A database is an organized collection of information. A *relational database* is a collection of related information that has been organized into structures known as *tables*. Each table contains *rows* that are further organized into *columns*.

SQL is the standard language for accessing relational databases. With SQL, you tell the database what data you want to access, and the database software figures out exactly how to get that data.

Many databases allow you to store small programs in the database. These programs are known as *stored procedures*. You can run these programs from with the database. SQL Server and Oracle are two examples of databases that allow you to use stored procedures.

Visual Studio .NET (VS .NET) contains functions that allow you to connect to a database and explore elements such as tables. This functionality is contained in the Server Explorer tool.

In the next chapter, you'll learn how to access a database in a C# program using ADO.NET.

Chapter 23

Active Data Objects: ADO.NET

IN THIS CHAPTER, YOU'LL learn how to access a database from a C# program using Active Data Objects for the .NET Framework (ADO.NET). The example programs in this chapter use the SQL Server Northwind database. You were introduced to the Northwind database in the previous chapter. This database contains the information for a fictitious company that sells food products.

Featured in this chapter:

◆ Introducing ADO.NET and the ADO.NET Classes

◆ Performing a SQL SELECT Statement Using ADO.NET

◆ Connecting to Microsoft Access and Oracle Databases

◆ Performing SQL INSERT, UPDATE, and DELETE Statements Using ADO.NET

◆ Modifying a DataTable Object and Synchronizing the Changes with the Database

◆ Using a Transaction in ADO.NET

◆ Using a DataView Object to Filter and Sort Rows

◆ Running a SQL Server Stored Procedure Using ADO.NET

◆ Defining and Using a Relationship Between Two DataTable Objects

◆ Writing and Reading XML Files Using ADO.NET

Overview of ADO.NET

When accessing a database using ADO.NET, you connect to the database, retrieve the information you're interested in, and store that information in the memory of the computer on which the C# program is running. Once you have that information in the memory, you can then read and manipulate that information. For example, you can display the columns for the rows, add new rows, modify rows, and delete rows in one or more tables. Periodically, you'll reconnect to the database to synchronize your changes you've made locally with the database.

> **NOTE** *ADO.NET provides a disconnected model for database access. You store the information you're interested in locally on the computer on which your C# program is running.*

Typically, the database will be running on a different computer from the one on which your program runs. Depending on the demands of your organization, the database will run on a powerful computer that will service the demands of many programs and users running many SQL statements at the same time.

In the next section, you'll get an overview of the ADO.NET classes, and then you'll see a simple program that uses ADO.NET to retrieve rows from the Customers table of the Northwind database. Later, you'll see the details of the ADO.NET classes, followed by some programs that illustrate the most common tasks you'll perform with ADO.NET.

Overview of the ADO.NET Classes

To provide disconnected database access, ADO.NET defines two sets of classes:

- Generic data classes

- Managed provider classes

You use objects of the generic data classes to store a local copy of information retrieved from the database. This local copy of the information is stored in the memory of the computer where the C# program is running. The main generic data class is the System.Data.DataSet class.

You use objects of the managed provider classes to connect to the database and to read and write information to and from your DataSet object. Managed provider objects provide directly access to the database and allow you to synchronize your locally stored data with the database.

You'll get an overview of the generic data classes and managed provider classes in this section.

Generic Data Classes and Objects

The generic data objects enable you to store a local copy of the information stored in the database. The following are some of the generic data classes:

DataSet Class You use an object of the DataSet class to represent a local copy of the information stored in the database. It has the capability of representing database structures such as tables, rows, and columns, among others. You can also use a DataSet object to represent XML data.

DataTable Class You use an object of the DataTable class to represent a table. You can store multiple DataTable objects in a DataSet.

DataRow Class You use an object of the DataRow class to represent a row. You can store multiple DataRow objects in a DataTable.

DataColumn Class You use an object of the DataColumn class to represent a column. You can store multiple DataColumn objects in a DataRow.

DataRelation Class You use an object of the DataRelation class to represent a relationship between two DataTable objects. You can use a DataRelation object to model parent-child relationships between two database tables. You can store multiple DataRelation objects in a DataSet.

Constraint Class   You use an object of the Constraint class to represent a database constraint—such as unique values for a column or that a particular column is a foreign key into another table. You can store multiple Constraint objects in a DataTable.

DataView Class   You use an object of the DataView class to view only specific rows in a DataTable object using a filter. You can store multiple DataView objects in a DataSet.

NOTE   The DataSet, DataTable, DataRow, DataColumn, DataRelation, Constraint, and DataView classes are all declared in the System.Data namespace. This namespace contains other classes that you can use in your programs. You can view the full set of classes declared in the System.Data namespace using the .NET documentation. Chapter 1, "Introduction to Visual C# and the .NET Framework," explained how you access this documentation.

Managed Provider Classes and Objects

The managed provider objects allow you to directly access a database. You use the managed provider objects to connect to the database and to read and write information to and from the database. The following are some of the managed provider classes:

SqlConnection, OleDbConnection, OdbcConnection Classes   You use an object of the Sql-Connection class to connect to a SQL Server database. You use an object of the OleDbConnection class to connect to any database that supports OLEDB (Object Linking and Embedding for Databases), such as Access or Oracle. You use an object of the OdbcConnection class to connect to any database that supports ODBC (Open Database Connectivity). All the major databases support ODBC, but ODBC is typically slower than the other two options when working with .NET.

SqlCommand, OleDbCommand, OdbcCommand Classes   You use an object of the SqlCommand, OleDb-Command, or OdbcCommand class to represent a SQL statement or stored procedure call that you then execute using one of the appropriate connection classes.

SqlDataReader, OleDbDataReader, OdbcDataReader Classes   You use an object of the Sql-DataReader, OleDbDataReader, or OdbcDataReader class to read rows retrieved from a SQL Server, OLEDB-compliant, or ODBC-compliant database, respectively. You use these objects to read rows in a forward direction only and to act as an alternative to a DataSet. Reading data using these objects is typically faster than using a DataSet.

SqlDataAdapter, OleDbDataAdapter, OdbcDataAdapter Classes   You use an object of the Sql-DataAdapter, OleDbDataAdapter, or OdbcDataAdapter class to move rows between a DataSet object and a SQL Server, OLEDB-compliant, or ODBC-compliant database, respectively. You use one of these data adapters to synchronize your locally stored information with the database.

SqlTransaction, OleDbTransaction, OdbcTransaction Classes   You use an object of the Sql-Transaction, OleDbTransaction, or OdbcTransaction class to represent a database transaction in a SQL Server, OLEDB-compliant, or ODBC-compliant database, respectively.

The managed provider classes for SQL Server (SqlConnection and so on) are declared in the System.Data.SqlClient namespace. The classes for OLEDB-compliant databases (SqlDbConnection and so on) are declared in the System.Data.OleDb namespace. The classes for ODBC-compliant databases (OdbcConnection and so on) are declared in the System.Data.Odbc namespace.

NOTE *At time of writing, you have to download the ODBC managed provider classes from Microsoft's website at* http://msdn.microsoft.com/downloads. *This download is separate from the .NET SDK.*

Before you see the details of the ADO.NET classes, we'll show you a simple example that illustrates how to issue a SQL SELECT statement. This SELECT statement will retrieve rows from the Customers table and display them. This program will give you a basic understanding on how to use the ADO.NET classes.

Performing a SQL *SELECT* Statement Using ADO.NET

In the example featured in this section, you'll see how to connect to the SQL Server Northwind database and perform a SQL SELECT statement to retrieve the CustomerID, CompanyName, ContactName, and Address columns for the first 10 rows from the Customers table. You can use the following steps to do this:

1. Formulate a string containing the details of the database connection.

2. Create a SqlConnection object to connect to the database, passing the connection string to the constructor.

3. Formulate a string containing a SELECT statement to retrieve the columns for the rows from the Customers table.

4. Create a SqlCommand object to hold the SELECT statement.

5. Set the CommandText property of the SqlCommand object to the SELECT string.

6. Create a SqlDataAdapter object.

7. Set the SelectCommand property of the SqlAdapter object to the SqlCommand object.

8. Create a DataSet object to store the results of the SELECT statement.

9. Open the database connection using the Open() method of the SqlConnection object.

10. Call the Fill() method of the SqlDataAdapter object to retrieve the rows from the table, storing the rows locally in a DataTable of the DataSet object.

11. Get the DataTable object from the DataSet object.

12. Display the columns for each row in the DataTable, using a DataRow object to access each row in the DataTable.

13. Close the database connection, using the Close() method of the SqlConnection object created in step 2.

In the following sections, you'll learn the details of these steps and see example code.

Step 1: Formulate a String Containing the Details of the Database Connection

The first step is to formulate a string containing the details of the database connection. When connecting to a SQL Server database, your string must specify the following:

◆ The name of the computer on which SQL Server is running. You set this in the `server` part of the string. If SQL Server is running on your local computer, you can use `localhost` as the server name. For example: `server=localhost`.

◆ The name of the database. You set this in the `database` part of the string. For example: `database=Northwind`.

◆ The name of the user to connect to the database as. You set this in the `uid` part of the string. For example: `uid=sa`.

◆ The password for the database user. You set this in the `pwd` part of the string. For example: `pwd=sa`.

NOTE   *Typically, your organization's Database Administrator (DBA) will provide you with the appropriate values for the connection string. The DBA is responsible for administering the database.*

The following example creates a string named `connectionString` and sets it to an appropriate string to connect to the Northwind database running on the local computer, using the `sa` user (with a password of `sa`) to connect to that database:

```
string connectionString =
  "server=localhost;database=Northwind;uid=sa;pwd=sa";
```

Step 2: Create a *SqlConnection* Object to Connect to the Database

The second step is to create a `SqlConnection` object to connect to the database, passing the connection string created in the previous step to the constructor. You use an object of the `SqlConnection` class to connect to a SQL Server database.

The following example creates a `SqlConnection` object named `mySqlConnection`, passing `connection-String` (created in the previous step) to the constructor:

```
SqlConnection mySqlConnection =
  new SqlConnection(connectionString);
```

Step 3: Formulate a String Containing the *SELECT* Statement

The third step is to formulate a string containing the `SELECT` statement to retrieve the `CustomerID`, `CompanyName`, `ContactName`, and `Address` columns for the first 10 rows from the `Customers` table. For example:

```
string selectString =
  "SELECT CustomerID, CompanyName, ContactName, Address " +
  "FROM Customers " +
  "WHERE CustomerID < 'BSBEV'";
```

NOTE *With the initial set of rows in the* Customers *table, the* WHERE *clause used in this* SELECT *statement returns the first 10 rows* (CustomerID < 'BSBEV').

Step 4: Create a *SqlCommand* Object to Hold the *SELECT* Statement

The fourth step is to create a SqlCommand object to hold your SELECT statement. You can call the CreateCommand() method of mySqlConnection to create a new SqlCommand object for that connection. The CreateCommand() method returns a new SqlCommand object for the SqlConnection object.

In the following example, a new SqlCommand object named mySqlCommand is set to the SqlCommand object returned by calling the CreateCommand() method of mySqlConnection:

```
SqlCommand mySqlCommand = mySqlConnection.CreateCommand();
```

You can then use mySqlCommand to run SQL statements or stored procedures.

Step 5: Set the *CommandText* Property of the *SqlCommand* Object to the *SELECT* String

The fifth step is to set the CommandText property of your SqlCommand object to the SELECT string created in step 4. The CommandText property contains the SQL statement (or the stored procedure call) you want to perform.

In the following example, the CommandText property of mySqlCommand is set to selectString:

```
mySqlCommand.CommandText = selectString;
```

Step 6: Create a *SqlDataAdapter* Object

The sixth step is to create a SqlDataAdapter object. You use a SqlDataAdapter object to move information between your DataSet object and the database. You'll see how to create a DataSet object later in step 8.

The following example creates a SqlDataAdapter object named mySqlDataAdapter:

```
SqlDataAdapter mySqlDataAdapter = new SqlDataAdapter();
```

Step 7: Set the *SelectCommand* Property of the *SqlAdapter* Object to the *SqlCommand* Object

The seventh step is to set the SelectCommand property of your SqlAdapter object to your SqlCommand object. In the following example, the SelectCommand property of mySqlDataAdapter is set to mySqlCommand:

```
mySqlDataAdapter.SelectCommand = mySqlCommand;
```

This enables you to perform the SELECT statement defined in mySqlCommand. Step 10 actually performs the SELECT statement.

Step 8: Create a *DataSet* Object to Store the Results of the *SELECT* Statement

The eighth step is to create a DataSet object to store the results of the SELECT statement. You use a DataSet object to store a local copy of information retrieved from the database.

The following example creates a DataSet object named myDataSet:

```
DataSet myDataSet = new DataSet();
```

Step 9: Open the Database Connection Using the *Open()* Method of the *SqlConnection* Object

The ninth step is to open the database connection using the Open() method of your SqlConnection object. The following example calls the Open() method for mySqlConnection:

```
mySqlConnection.Open();
```

Once you've opened the database connection, you can access the database.

Step 10: Call the *Fill()* Method of the *SqlDataAdapter* Object to Retrieve the Rows from the Table

The tenth step is to call the Fill() method of the SqlDataAdapter object to retrieve the rows from the table, storing the rows locally in a DataTable of the DataSet object.

The Fill() method is overloaded, and the version you'll see in the example accepts two parameters: the first is a DataSet object and the second is a string containing the name of the DataTable object to create. The Fill() method then creates a DataTable in the DataSet with the specified name and runs the SELECT statement. The DataTable created in your DataSet is then populated with the rows retrieved by the SELECT statement.

The following example creates a string named dataTableName and sets it to "Customers" and then calls the Fill() method of mySqlDataAdapter, passing myDataSet and dataTableName to the method:

```
string dataTableName = "Customers";
mySqlDataAdapter.Fill(myDataSet, dataTableName);
```

The Fill() method creates a DataTable object named Customers in myDataSet and populates it with the rows retrieved by the SELECT statement.

Step 11: Get the *DataTable* Object from the *DataSet* Object

The eleventh step is to get the DataTable object created in the previous step from the DataSet object. You get a DataTable from your DataSet using the Tables property, passing the name of the DataTable in brackets (Customers, for example). The Tables property will then return your requested DataTable, which you can store in a new DataTable object that you declare.

In the following example, myDataSet.Tables[dataTableName] returns the Customers DataTable created in myDataSet in the previous step, and stores the returned DataTable in myDataTable:

```
DataTable myDataTable = myDataSet.Tables[dataTableName];
```

Remember that the dataTableName string is set to "Customers".

NOTE *You can also specify the* DataTable *you want to get by passing a numeric value to the* Tables *property. For example,* myDataSet.Tables[0] *also returns the* Customers *DataTable.*

Step 12: Display the Columns for Each Row in the *DataTable*

The twelfth step is to display the columns for each row in the DataTable, using a DataRow object to access each row in the DataTable. The DataTable class defines a property named Rows that gets the collection of DataRow objects stored in a DataTable. You can use the Rows property in a foreach loop to iterate over the DataRow objects. For example:

```
foreach (DataRow myDataRow in myDataTable.Rows)
{
  // ... access the myDataRow object
}
```

Each DataRow object stores DataColumn objects that contain the values retrieved from the columns of the database table. You can access these column values by passing the name of the column in brackets to the DataRow object. For example, myDataRow["CustomerID"] returns the value of the CustomerID column.

In the following example, a foreach loop iterates over the DataRow objects in myDataTable, and the column values are displayed for each row:

```
foreach (DataRow myDataRow in myDataTable.Rows)
{
  Console.WriteLine("CustomerID = " + myDataRow["CustomerID"]);
  Console.WriteLine("CompanyName = " + myDataRow["CompanyName"]);
  Console.WriteLine("ContactName = " + myDataRow["ContactName"]);
  Console.WriteLine("Address = " + myDataRow["Address"]);
}
```

As you can see, the name of each column is passed in brackets to each DataRow object, which then returns the column value.

NOTE *You can also specify the column you want to get by passing a numeric value in brackets. For example,* myDataRow[0] *also returns the* CustomerID *column value.*

Step 13: Close the Database Connection

The thirteenth and final step is to close the database connection using the Close() method of the SqlConnection object created in the second step. For example:

```
mySqlConnection.Close();
```

Listing 23.1 shows a complete program that uses these steps.

LISTING 23.1: PERFOMING A SQL SELECT STATEMENT USING ADO.NET

```
/*
  Example23_1.cs illustrates how to perform a SELECT statement
  using ADO.NET
*/
```

```
using System;
using System.Data;
using System.Data.SqlClient;

class Example23_1
{

  public static void Main()
  {

    // step 1: formulate a string containing the details of the
    // database connection
    string connectionString =
      "server=localhost;database=Northwind;uid=sa;pwd=sa";

    // step 2: create a SqlConnection object to connect to the
    // database, passing the connection string to the constructor
    SqlConnection mySqlConnection =
      new SqlConnection(connectionString);

    // step 3: formulate a SELECT statement to retrieve the
    // CustomerID, CompanyName, ContactName, and Address
    // columns for the first ten rows from the Customers table
    string selectString =
      "SELECT CustomerID, CompanyName, ContactName, Address " +
      "FROM Customers " +
      "WHERE CustomerID < 'BSBEV'";

    // step 4: create a SqlCommand object to hold the SELECT statement
    SqlCommand mySqlCommand = mySqlConnection.CreateCommand();

    // step 5: set the CommandText property of the SqlCommand object to
    // the SELECT string
    mySqlCommand.CommandText = selectString;

    // step 6: create a SqlDataAdapter object
    SqlDataAdapter mySqlDataAdapter = new SqlDataAdapter();

    // step 7: set the SelectCommand property of the SqlAdapter object
    // to the SqlCommand object
    mySqlDataAdapter.SelectCommand = mySqlCommand;

    // step 8: create a DataSet object to store the results of
    // the SELECT statement
    DataSet myDataSet = new DataSet();
```

```
// step 9: open the database connection using the
// Open() method of the SqlConnection object
mySqlConnection.Open();

// step 10: use the Fill() method of the SqlDataAdapter object to
// retrieve the rows from the table, storing the rows locally
// in a DataTable of the DataSet object
Console.WriteLine("Retrieving rows from the Customers table");
string dataTableName = "Customers";
mySqlDataAdapter.Fill(myDataSet, dataTableName);

// step 11: get the DataTable object from the DataSet object
DataTable myDataTable = myDataSet.Tables[dataTableName];

// step 12: display the columns for each row in the DataTable,
// using a DataRow object to access each row in the DataTable
foreach (DataRow myDataRow in myDataTable.Rows)
{
  Console.WriteLine("CustomerID = " + myDataRow["CustomerID"]);
  Console.WriteLine("CompanyName = " + myDataRow["CompanyName"]);
  Console.WriteLine("ContactName = " + myDataRow["ContactName"]);
  Console.WriteLine("Address = " + myDataRow["Address"]);
}

// step 13: close the database connection using the Close() method
// of the SqlConnection object created in Step 2
mySqlConnection.Close();

  }

}
```

The output from this program is as follows:

```
Retrieving rows from the Customers table
CustomerID = ALFKI
CompanyName = Alfreds Futterkiste
ContactName = Maria Anders
Address = Obere Str. 57
CustomerID = ANATR
CompanyName = Ana Trujillo Emparedados y helados
ContactName = Ana Trujillo
Address = Avda. de la Constitución 2222
CustomerID = ANTON
CompanyName = Antonio Moreno Taquería
ContactName = Antonio Moreno
Address = Mataderos  2312
```

```
CustomerID = AROUT
CompanyName = Around the Horn
ContactName = Thomas Hardy
Address = 120 Hanover Sq.
CustomerID = BERGS
CompanyName = Berglunds snabbköp
ContactName = Christina Berglund
Address = Berguvsvägen  8
CustomerID = BLAUS
CompanyName = Blauer See Delikatessen
ContactName = Hanna Moos
Address = Forsterstr. 57
CustomerID = BLONP
CompanyName = Blondesddsl père et fils
ContactName = Frédérique Citeaux
Address = 24, place Kléber
CustomerID = BOLID
CompanyName = Bólido Comidas preparadas
ContactName = Martín Sommer
Address = C/ Araquil, 67
CustomerID = BONAP
CompanyName = Bon app'
ContactName = Laurence Lebihan
Address = 12, rue des Bouchers
CustomerID = BOTTM
CompanyName = Bottom-Dollar Markets
ContactName = Elizabeth Lincoln
Address = 23 Tsawassen Blvd.
```

Connecting to a Microsoft Access Database

If you want to connect to a Microsoft Access database, you use a connection string with the following format:

```
provider=Microsoft.Jet.OLEDB.4.0;data source=databaseFile
```

where *databaseFile* is the directory and filename of the Microsoft Access database. Notice that you specify the provider in the connection string. You can also specify a database username and password with Access.

The following example creates a string with this format:

```
string connectionString =
   "provider=Microsoft.Jet.OLEDB.4.0;data source=C:\\Northwind.mdb";
```

NOTE   *Notice the use of two backslash characters in the filename* C:\\Northwind.mdb.

You'll need to use OleDbConnection and OleDbDataAdapter objects when accessing a Microsoft Access database.

Connecting to an Oracle Database

If you want to connect to an Oracle database, you use a connection string with the following syntax:

```
provider=MSDAORA; data source=OracleNetServiceName; user id=username;
  password=password
```

where *OracleNetServiceName* is the Oracle Net service name for the database, *username* is the name of the database user, and *password* is the password for that user.

The following example creates a string with this format:

```
string connectionString =
  "provider=MSDAORA; data source=ORCL; user id=SCOTT; password=TIGER";
```

NOTE *The user ID of* SCOTT *with a password of* TIGER *is the default for accessing one of the example schemas that come with the Oracle database. This schema contains a different set of tables to those previously described for the SQL Server Northwind database.*

You'll need to use an OleDbConnection and OleDbDataAdapter object when accessing an Oracle database.

In the next section, you'll learn the details of the ADO.NET classes.

Exploring the Details of the ADO.NET Classes

In this section, you'll see some of the properties and methods for the SqlConnection, SqlCommand, SqlDataReader, SqlDataAdapter, SqlTransaction, DataSet, DataTable, DataRow, DataColumn, DataRelation, Constraint, and DataView classes. You can use the tables shown in the following sections as quick references to the various ADO.NET classes.

SqlConnection Class

You use an object of the SqlConnection class to connect to a SQL Server database.

NOTE *Although this class is specific to SQL Server, many of the properties and methods in this class are the same as those for the* OleDbConnection *and* OdbcConnection *classes. If a property or method is specific to* SqlConnection, *it says so in the Description column of the tables shown in this section. This applies to the other SQL Server–specific classes described in the later sections.*

Table 23.1 shows some of the SqlConnection properties.

TABLE 23.1: SqlConnection PROPERTIES

PROPERTY	TYPE	DESCRIPTION
ConnectionString	string	Gets or sets the string used to open a database.
ConnectionTimeout	int	Gets the number of seconds to wait while trying to establish a connection to a database.

Continued on next page

TABLE 23.1: SqlConnection PROPERTIES *(continued)*

PROPERTY	TYPE	DESCRIPTION
Database	string	Gets the name of the current database (or the database to be used once the connection to the database is made).
DataSource	string	Gets the name of the database server.
PacketSize	int	Gets the size (in bytes) of network packets used to communicate with SQL Server. This property only applies to the SqlConnection class.
ServerVersion	string	Gets a string containing the version of SQL Server.
State	ConnectionState	Gets the current state of the connection.
WorkstationId	string	Gets a string that identifies the client computer that is connected to SQL Server. This property only applies to the SqlConnection class.

Table 23.2 shows some of the SqlConnection methods.

TABLE 23.2: SqlConnection METHODS

METHOD	RETURN TYPE	DESCRIPTION
BeginTransaction()	SqlTransaction	Overloaded. Begins a database transaction.
ChangeDatabase()	void	Changes the current database for an open connection.
Close()	void	Closes the connection to the database.
CreateCommand()	SqlCommand	Creates and returns a command object.
Open()	void	Opens a database connection with the property settings specified by the ConnectionString property.

SqlCommand Class

You use an object of the SqlCommand class to represent a SQL statement or stored procedure call that you then execute. Table 23.3 shows some of the SqlCommand properties.

TABLE 23.3: SqlCommand PROPERTIES

PROPERTY	TYPE	DESCRIPTION
CommandText	string	Gets or sets the SQL statement or stored procedure to execute.
CommandTimeout	int	Gets or sets the number of seconds to wait before ending an attempt to execute the command.

Continued on next page

TABLE 23.3: SqlCommand PROPERTIES *(continued)*

PROPERTY	TYPE	DESCRIPTION
CommandType	CommandType	Gets or sets a value that indicates how the CommandText property is to be interpreted. Typically, the only time you'll need to set this property is when calling a stored procedure, in which case you set it to CommandType.StoredProcedure.
Connection	string	Gets the name of the database connection.
Parameters	SqlParameter-Collection	Gets the parameters (if any) to supply to the command. When using a SqlConnection, the parameters are stored in a SqlParameter-Collection object.
Transaction	SqlTransaction	Gets or sets the database transaction for the command.

Table 23.4 shows some of the SqlCommand methods.

TABLE 23.4: SqlCommand METHODS

METHOD	RETURN TYPE	DESCRIPTION
Cancel()	void	Cancels the execution of the command.
CreateParameter()	SqlParameter	Creates a new parameter for the command.
ExecuteNonQuery()	int	Used to execute SQL INSERT, UPDATE, and DELETE statements or stored procedures. The int value returned is the number of database rows affected by the command.
ExecuteReader()	SqlDataReader	Also used to execute SQL SELECT statements or stored procedures. Returns the results of the command in a data reader.
ExecuteScalar()	object	Also used to execute SQL SELECT statements or stored procedures that return a single value. Returns the result of the command as an object.
ExecuteXmlReader()	XmlReader	Executes a command and returns results in an XmlReader object. This method only applies to the SqlCommand class.
Prepare()	void	Creates a prepared version of the command. This sometimes results in faster execution of the command.
ResetCommandTimeout()	void	Resets the CommandTimeout property to its default value.

SqlDataReader *Class*

You use an object of the SqlDataReader class to read rows retrieved from a SQL Server database.

TIP   Data reader objects only allow you to access rows one after another from beginning to end. For this reason, these objects aren't the most flexible when accessing rows, but they do offer the fastest access to the rows stored in them. If you don't need flexible access to rows, you might want to consider using a data reader object.

Table 23.5 shows some of the `SqlDataReader` properties.

TABLE 23.5: `SqlDataReader` PROPERTIES

PROPERTY	TYPE	DESCRIPTION
Depth	int	Gets a value indicating the depth of nesting for the current row.
FieldCount	int	Gets the number of columns in the current row.
IsClosed	bool	Gets a bool value indicating whether the data reader is closed.
RecordsAffected	int	Gets the number of rows added, modified, or removed by execution of the SQL statement.

Table 23.6 shows some of the public `SqlDataReader` methods.

TABLE 23.6: `SqlDataReader` METHODS

METHOD	RETURN TYPE	DESCRIPTION
GetBoolean()	bool	Returns the value of the specified column as a bool.
GetByte()	byte	Returns the value of the specified column as a byte.
GetBytes()	long	Reads a stream of byte values from the specified column into a byte array. The long value returned is the number of byte values read from the column.
GetChar()	char	Returns the value of the specified column as a char.
GetChars()	long	Reads a stream of char values from the specified column into a char array. The long value returned is the number of char values read from the column.
GetDataTypeName()	string	Returns the name of the source data type for the specified column.
GetDateTime()	DateTime	Returns the value of the specified column as a DateTime.
GetDecimal()	decimal	Returns the value of the specified column as a decimal.
GetDouble()	double	Returns the value of the specified column as a double.
GetFieldType()	Type	Returns the Type of the specified column.
GetFloat()	float	Returns the value of the specified column as a float.
GetGuid()	Guid	Returns the value of the specified column as a globally unique identifier (GUID).

Continued on next page

TABLE 23.6: SqlDataReader METHODS *(continued)*

METHOD	RETURN TYPE	DESCRIPTION
GetInt16()	short	Returns the value of the specified column as a short.
GetInt32()	int	Returns the value of the specified column as an int.
GetInt64()	long	Returns the value of the specified column as a long.
GetName()	string	Returns the name of the specified column.
GetOrdinal()	int	Returns the numeric position, or *ordinal*, of the specified column (first column has an ordinal of 0).
GetSchemaTable()	DataTable	Returns a DataTable that contains details of the columns stored in the data reader.*
GetSqlBinary()	SqlBinary	Returns the value of the specified column as a SqlBinary object. The SqlBinary class is declared in the System.Data.SqlTypes namespace.**
GetSqlBoolean()	SqlBoolean	Returns the value of the specified column as a SqlBoolean object.
GetSqlByte()	SqlByte	Returns the value of the specified column as a SqlByte object.
GetSqlDateTime()	SqlDateTime	Returns the value of the specified column as a SqlDateTime object.
GetSqlDecimal()	SqlDecimal	Returns the value of the specified column as a SqlDecimal object.
GetSqlDouble()	SqlDouble	Returns the value of the specified column as a SqlDouble object.
GetSqlGuid()	SqlGuid	Returns the value of the specified column as a SqlGuid object.
GetSqlInt16()	SqlInt16	Returns the value of the specified column as a SqlInt16 object.
GetSqlInt32()	SqlInt32	Returns the value of the specified column as a SqlInt32 object.
GetSqlInt64()	SqlInt64	Returns the value of the specified column as a SqlInt64 object.
GetSqlMoney()	SqlMoney	Returns the value of the specified column as a SqlMoney object.
GetSqlSingle()	SqlSingle	Returns the value of the specified column as a SqlSingle object.
GetSqlString()	SqlString	Returns the value of the specified column as a SqlString object.
GetSqlValue()	object	Returns the value of the specified column as an object.
GetSqlValues()	int	Copies the value of all the columns in the current row into a specified object array. The int returned by this method is the number of elements in the array.
GetString()	string	Returns the value of the specified column as a string.
GetValue()	object	Returns the value of the specified column in its native format.
GetValues()	int	Copies the value of all the columns in the current row into a specified object array. The int returned by this method is the number of elements in the array.

Continued on next page

TABLE 23.6: SqlDataReader METHODS *(continued)*

METHOD	RETURN TYPE	DESCRIPTION
IsDBNull()	bool	Returns a bool that indicates whether the specified column contains a null value.
NextResult()	bool	Moves the data reader to the next row in the result set. The bool returned by this method indicates whether there are more rows in the result set.
Read()	bool	Moves the data reader to the next row in the result set and reads the row. The bool returned by this method indicates whether there are more rows in the result set.

* The DataTable column details include the name (stored in the ColumnName column of the returned DataTable), ordinal (stored in ColumnOrdinal), maximum length of the value that may be stored in the column (stored in Column-Size), precision and scale of a numeric column (stored in NumericPrecision and NumericScale), among others.

** The System.Data.SqlTypes namespace provides classes for native data types used within SQL Server. These classes provide a safer and faster alternative to other data types returned by the other Get* methods. Using the classes in this namespace helps prevent type conversion errors caused in situations where loss of precision could occur. Because other data types are converted to and from SqlTypes behind the scenes, explicitly creating and using objects within this namespace results in faster code as well.

SqlDataAdapter Class

You use an object of the SqlDataAdapter class to move rows between a DataSet object and a SQL Server database. A SqlDataAdapter object allows you to synchronize your locally stored information with the database. Table 23.7 shows some of the SqlDataAdapter properties.

TABLE 23.7: SqlDataAdapter PROPERTIES

PROPERTY	TYPE	DESCRIPTION
AcceptChangesDuringFill (inherited from DbDataAdapter)	bool	Gets or sets a value indicating whether the AcceptChanges() method is called after a DataRow object has been added, modified, or removed in a DataTable object. The default is true.
DeleteCommand	SqlCommand	Gets or sets a command containing a SQL DELETE statement to remove rows from the database.
InsertCommand	SqlCommand	Gets or sets a command containing a SQL INSERT statement to add rows to the database.
SelectCommand	SqlCommand	Gets or sets a command containing a SQL SELECT statement to retrieve rows from the database.
UpdateCommand	SqlCommand	Gets or sets a command containing a SQL UPDATE statement to modify rows in the database.

Table 23.8 shows some of the `SqlDataAdapter` methods.

TABLE 23.8: `SqlDataAdapter` METHODS

METHOD	RETURN TYPE	DESCRIPTION
`Fill()` (inherited from DbDataAdapter)	`int`	Overloaded. Synchronizes the rows in the `DataSet` object to match those in the data source. The `int` returned by this method is the number of rows synchronized in the `DataSet` with the database.
`FillSchema()` (inherited from DbDataAdapter)	`DataTable` `DataTable[]`	Overloaded. Adds a `DataTable` to a `DataSet` object.
`GetFillParameters()` (inherited from DbDataAdapter)	`IDataParameter[]`	Returns an array of any parameters set for the SQL SELECT statement.
`Update()` (inherited from DbDataAdapter)	`int`	Overloaded. Calls the respective SQL INSERT, UPDATE, or DELETE statements (stored in the `InsertCommand`, `UpdateCommand`, and `DeleteCommand` properties, respectively) for each row that has been added, modified, or removed from a `DataTable` object. The `int` returned by this method is the number of rows updated.

SqlTransaction Class

You use an object of the `SqlTransaction` class to represent a database transaction in a SQL Server database. Table 23.9 shows some of the `SqlTransaction` properties.

TABLE 23.9: `SqlTransaction` PROPERTIES

PROPERTY	TYPE	DESCRIPTION
`Connection`	`SqlConnection`	Gets the connection for the transaction.
`IsolationLevel`	`IsolationLevel`	Gets the isolation level for the transaction.

Table 23.10 shows some of the `SqlTransaction` methods.

TABLE 23.10: `SqlTransaction` METHODS

METHOD	RETURN TYPE	DESCRIPTION
`Commit()`	`void`	Performs a commit to permanently record the SQL statements in the transaction.
`Rollback()`	`void`	Overloaded. Performs a rollback to undo the SQL statements in the transaction.

Continued on next page

TABLE 23.10: SqlTransaction METHODS *(continued)*

METHOD	RETURN TYPE	DESCRIPTION
Save()	void	Creates a save point in the transaction that can be used to undo a portion of that transaction. The string passed to this method specifies the save point name. You can then roll back the transaction to that save point.

Now that you've seen the managed provider classes, you'll learn about the generic data classes—starting with the DataSet class.

DataSet Class

You use an object of the DataSet class to represent a local copy of the information stored in a database. You can also use a DataSet object to represent XML data. Table 23.11 shows some of the DataSet properties.

TABLE 23.11: DataSet PROPERTIES

PROPERTY	TYPE	DESCRIPTION
CaseSensitive	bool	Gets or sets a bool value that indicates whether string comparisons within DataTable objects are case sensitive.
DataSetName	string	Gets or sets the name of the current DataSet object.
EnforceConstraints	bool	Gets or sets a bool value that indicates whether constraint rules are followed when updating information in the DataSet object.
HasErrors	bool	Gets a bool value that indicates whether there are errors in any of the rows in the tables of the DataSet object.
Relations	DataRelationCollection	Gets the collection of relations (DataRelationCollection) that allows navigation from a parent table to a child table. A DataRelationCollection consists of DataRelation objects.
Tables	DataTableCollection	Gets the collection of tables (DataTableCollection) that contains the DataTable objects stored in the DataSet.

Table 23.12 shows some of the DataSet methods.

TABLE 23.12: DataSet METHODS

METHOD	RETURN TYPE	DESCRIPTION
AcceptChanges()	void	Commits all the changes made to the DataSet object since it was loaded or since the last time the AcceptChanges() method was called.
Clear()	void	Removes all rows from all tables in the DataSet object.
Clone()	DataSet	Clones the structure of the DataSet object and returns that clone. The clone contains all the schemas, relations, and constraints.
GetChanges()	DataSet	Overloaded. Gets a copy of all the changes made to the DataSet object since it was last loaded or since the last time the AcceptChanges() method was called.
GetXml()	string	Returns the XML representation of the data stored in the DataSet object.
GetXmlSchema()	string	Returns the XML representation of the schema for the DataSet object.
HasChanges()	bool	Overloaded. Returns a bool value that indicates whether the DataSet object has changes that haven't been committed.
Merge()	void	Overloaded. Merges this DataSet with another specified DataSet object.
ReadXml()	XmlReadMode	Overloaded. Loads the data from an XML file into the DataSet object.
ReadXmlSchema()	void	Overloaded. Loads a schema from an XML file into the DataSet object.
RejectChanges()	void	Undoes all the changes made to the DataSet object since it was created or since the last time the AcceptChanges() method was called.
Reset()	void	Resets the DataSet object to its original state.
WriteXml()	void	Overloaded. Writes the data from the DataSet object out to an XML file.
WriteXmlSchema()	void	Overloaded. Writes the schema of the DataSet object out to an XML file.

DataTable Class

You use an object of the DataTable class to represent a table. You can store multiple DataTable objects in a DataSet. Table 23.13 shows some of the DataTable properties.

TABLE 23.13: DataTable PROPERTIES

PROPERTY	TYPE	DESCRIPTION
CaseSensitive	bool	Gets or sets a bool value that indicates whether string comparisons within DataTable objects are case sensitive.
ChildRelations	DataRelationCollection	Gets the collection of relations (DataRelationCollection) that allows navigation from a parent table to a child table. A DataRelationCollection consists of DataRelation objects.
Columns	DataColumnCollection	Gets the collection of columns (DataColumnCollection) that contains DataColumn objects that represent the columns in the DataTable object.
Constraints	ConstraintCollection	Gets the collection of constraints (ConstraintCollection) that contains Constraint objects that represent primary key (UniqueConstraint) or foreign key constraints (ForeignKeyConstraint) in the DataTable object.
DataSet	DataSet	Gets the DataSet to which the DataTable belongs.
HasErrors	bool	Returns a bool value that indicates whether any of the rows in the DataTable has errors.
PrimaryKey	DataColumn[]	Gets or sets an array of DataColumn objects that are the primary keys for the DataTable.
Rows	DataRowCollection	Gets the collection of rows (DataRowCollection) that contains the DataRow objects stored in the DataTable.
TableName	string	Gets the name of the DataTable object.

Table 23.14 shows some of the DataTable methods.

TABLE 23.14: DataTable METHODS

METHOD	RETURN TYPE	DESCRIPTION
AcceptChanges()	void	Commits all the changes made to the DataTable object since it was loaded or since the last time the AcceptChanges() method was called.
Clear()	void	Removes all rows from the DataTable object.
Clone()	DataTable	Clones the structure of the DataTable object and returns that clone.
Compute()	object	Computes the given expression on the current rows that pass the filter criteria.

Continued on next page

TABLE 23.14: DataTable METHODS *(continued)*

METHOD	RETURN TYPE	DESCRIPTION
GetChanges()	DataTable	Overloaded. Returns a copy of the DataTable object since it was last loaded or since the last time the AcceptChanges() method was called.
GetErrors()	DataRow[]	Overloaded. Gets a copy of all the DataRow objects that have errors.
LoadDataRow()	DataRow	Finds and updates a specified DataRow object. If no matching DataRow object is found, a new row is created using the specified values.
NewRow()	DataRow	Creates a new DataRow object in the DataTable.
RejectChanges()	void	Undoes all the changes made to the DataTable object since it was created or since the last time the AcceptChanges() method was called.
Select()	DataRow[]	Overloaded. Returns the array of DataRow objects stored in the DataTable that match the specified criteria.

DataRow Class

You use an object of the DataRow class to represent a row. You can store multiple DataRow objects in a DataTable. Table 23.15 shows some of the DataRow properties.

TABLE 23.15: DataRow PROPERTIES

PROPERTY	TYPE	DESCRIPTION
HasErrors	bool	Returns a bool value that indicates whether any of the DataColumn objects in the DataRow have errors.
ItemArray	object[]	Gets or sets all the DataColumn objects in the DataRow.
RowState	DataRowState	Gets the current state of the DataRow. The state can be Added, Deleted, Detached (the row has been created but isn't part of a DataRowCollection object; a DataRow is in this state immediately after it has been created and before it is added to a collection, or if it has been removed from a collection), Modified, or Unchanged. The state depends in the operation performed on the DataRow and whether the AcceptChanges() method has been called to commit the changes.
Table	DataTable	Gets the DataTable object to which the DataRow belongs.

Table 23.16 shows some of the DataRow methods.

TABLE 23.16: DataRow METHODS

METHOD	RETURN TYPE	DESCRIPTION
AcceptChanges()	void	Commits all the changes made to the DataRow object since it was loaded or since the last time the AcceptChanges() method was called.
BeginEdit()	void	Starts an edit for the DataRow object.
CancelEdit()	void	Cancels an edit for the DataRow object.
ClearErrors()	void	Clears any errors for the DataRow object.
Delete()	void	Deletes the DataRow object.
EndEdit()	void	Stops an edit for the DataRow object.
GetChildRows()	DataRow[]	Overloaded. Returns an array of DataRow objects that contain the child rows using the specified DataRelation object.
GetColumnError()	string	Overloaded. Returns the description of the error for the specified DataColumn object.
GetColumnsInError()	DataColumn[]	Returns an array of DataColumn objects that have errors.
GetParentRow()	DataRow	Overloaded. Returns a DataRow object that contains the parent row using the specified DataRelation object.
GetParentRows()	DataRow[]	Overloaded. Returns an array of DataRow objects that contain the parent rows using the specified DataRelation object.
IsNull()	bool	Overloaded. Returns a bool value that indicates whether the specified DataColumn object contains a null value.
RejectChanges()	void	Undoes all changes made to the DataRow object since the AcceptChanges() method was called.
SetNull()	void	Sets the specified DataColumn object to a null value.
SetParentRow()	void	Overloaded. Sets the parent row to the specified DataRow object.

DataColumn Class

You use an object of the DataColumn class to represent a column. You can store multiple DataColumn objects in a DataRow. Table 23.17 shows some of the DataColumn properties.

TABLE 23.17: DataColumn PROPERTIES

PROPERTY	TYPE	DESCRIPTION
AllowDBNull	bool	Gets or sets a bool value that indicates whether null values are allowed in this DataColumn object.
AutoIncrement	bool	Gets or sets a bool value that indicates whether the DataColumn object automatically increments the value of the column for new rows.
AutoIncrementSeed	long	Gets or sets the starting value for the DataColumn object. Only applies when the AutoIncrement property is set to true.
AutoIncrementStep	long	Gets or sets the increment used. Only applies when the AutoIncrement property is set to true.
Caption	string	Gets or sets the caption for the column. The caption for the column is shown in Windows forms.
ColumnName	string	Gets or sets the name of the column.
DataType	Type	Gets or sets the type of data stored in the DataColumn object. This can be Boolean, Byte, Char, DateTime, Decimal, Double, Int16, Int32, Int64, SByte, Single, String, TimeSpan, UInt16, or UInt64.
DefaultValue	object	Gets or sets the default value for the DataColumn when new rows are created.
MaxLength	int	Gets or sets the maximum length of text that may be stored in a DataColumn object.
Ordinal	int	Gets the numeric position of the DataColumn object (0 is the first object).
ReadOnly	bool	Gets or sets a bool value that indicates whether the DataColumn object can be changed once it has been added to a DataRow.
Table	DataTable	Gets the DataTable to which the DataColumn object belongs.
Unique	bool	Gets or sets a bool value that indicates whether the DataColumn values in each DataRow object must be unique.

DataRelation Class

You use an object of the DataRelation class to represent a relationship between two DataTable objects. You can use a DataRelation object to model parent-child relationships between two database tables. You can store multiple DataRelation objects in a DataSet. Table 23.18 shows some of the DataRelation properties.

TABLE 23.18: DataRelation PROPERTIES

PROPERTY	TYPE	DESCRIPTION
ChildColumns	DataColumn[]	Gets the array of DataColumn objects that represent the child columns for the DataRelation.
ChildKeyConstraint	ForeignKeyConstraint	Gets the ForeignKeyConstraint object for the DataRelation.
ChildTable	DataTable	Gets the child DataTable object for the DataRelation.
DataSet	DataSet	Gets the DataSet to which the DataRelation belongs.
Nested	bool	Gets or sets a bool value that indicates whether the DataRelation objects are nested. This is useful when defining hierarchical relationships in XML.
ParentColumns	DataColumn[]	Gets the array of DataColumn objects that represent the parent columns for the DataRelation.
ParentKeyConstraint	UniqueConstraint	Gets the UniqueConstraint object that ensures values in the parent column of the DataRelation are unique.
ParentTable	string	Gets the parent DataTable object for the DataRelation.
RelationName	string	Gets the name of the DataRelation object.

Constraint Class

You use an object of the Constraint class to represent a database constraint—such as unique values for a column or that a particular column is a foreign key into another table. You can store multiple Constraint objects in a DataTable. Table 23.19 shows some of the Constraint properties.

TABLE 23.19: Constraint PROPERTIES

PROPERTY	TYPE	DESCRIPTION
ConstraintName	string	Gets or sets the name of the Constraint object.
Table	DataTable	Gets the DataTable to which the Constraint object belongs.

DataView Class

You use an object of the DataView class to view only specific rows in a DataTable object using a filter. You can store multiple DataView objects in a DataSet. Table 23.20 shows some of the DataView properties.

TABLE 23.20: DataView PROPERTIES

PROPERTY	TYPE	DESCRIPTION
AllowDelete	bool	Gets or sets a bool value that indicates whether deletion of rows from the DataView object is permitted.
AllowEdit	bool	Gets or sets a bool value that indicates whether editing of rows in the DataView object is permitted.
AllowNew	bool	Gets or sets a bool value that indicates whether adding of new rows to the DataView object is permitted.
ApplyDefaultSort	bool	Gets or sets a bool value that indicates whether to use the default sorting algorithm to sort rows in the DataView object.
Count	int	Gets the number of rows in the DataView object after the rows have been filtered using a RowFilter or RowStateFilter object.
RowFilter	string	Gets or sets the expression used to filter rows in the DataView object.
RowStateFilter	DataViewRowSet	Gets or sets the expression used to filter rows based on the row state.
Sort	string	Gets or sets the sort column or columns, and sort order for the table. The string contains the column names followed by "ASC" (for ascending sort) or "DESC" (for descending sort). Columns are sorted ascending by default. Multiple columns are be separated by commas in the string.
Table	DataTable	Gets or sets the DataTable object.

Table 23.21 shows some of the DataView methods.

TABLE 23.21: DataView METHODS

METHOD	RETURN TYPE	DESCRIPTION
AddNew()	DataViewRow	Adds a new row to the DataView object.
Delete()	void	Deletes a row at the specified index of the DataView object.
Find()	int	Overloaded. Finds and returns the index of a row with the specified primary key in the DataView object. The int returned by this method is the index of row if the row was found; otherwise null is returned.
GetEnumerator()	IEnumerator	Returns an enumerator for the DataView object.
Delete()	void	Deletes the row at the specified index of the DataView object.

In the following sections, you'll see some example programs that use the ADO.NET classes.

Performing SQL *INSERT*, *UPDATE*, and *DELETE* Statements Using ADO.NET

In this section, you'll see the steps required to perform SQL INSERT, UPDATE, and DELETE statements to add, modify, and remove rows from a database table. The steps for issuing each of these types of SQL statement are similar, and you'll see code that adds a row to the Customers table of the Northwind database using an INSERT statement.

NOTE *The code for performing UPDATE and DELETE statements is similar to issuing an INSERT statement. Therefore, the code examples in the text will only show how to perform an INSERT statement. However, in Listing 23.2, you'll see a complete program that performs INSERT, UPDATE, and DELETE statements.*

You can use the following steps to perform a SQL INSERT, UPDATE, or DELETE statement using ADO.NET:

1. Formulate a string containing the SQL statement. Your string may specify special substrings that represent parameters (if any) for the column values.

2. Create a SqlCommand object to hold your SQL statement.

3. Set the CommandText property of your SqlCommand object to your string containing the SQL statement.

4. Use the Add() method through the Parameters property of your SqlCommand object to add the parameters to that object.

5. Set the parameters to specified values. These values are then used in your SQL statement.

6. Use the ExecuteNonQuery() method to run your SQL statement.

In the following sections, you'll learn the details of these steps and see example code that issues an INSERT statement that adds a row to the Customers table.

Step 1: Formulate a String Containing the SQL Statement

The first step is to formulate a string containing your SQL statement. For example, the following string contains an INSERT statement that adds a row to the Customers table:

```
string insertString =
  "INSERT INTO Customers (" +
  " CustomerID, CompanyName, ContactName, Address" +
  ") VALUES (" +
  " @CustomerID, @CompanyName, @ContactName, @Address" +
  ")";
```

This string contains substrings that have an at character (@) at the start. These substrings represent placeholders for the parameter types and their values. The actual parameter types and values will be provided later—you'll see that in steps 4 and 5.

You could, of course, just use literal values in the SQL string. For example, you could use the following string to add a new row:

```
string insertString =
  "INSERT INTO Customers (" +
  "  CustomerID, CompanyName, ContactName, Address" +
  ") VALUES (" +
  "  'T1COM', 'T1 Company', 'Jason Price', '1 Main Street' " +
  ")";
```

This limitation of this second string is that you can't change the column values at run-time. With the first string, you can use the placeholders to define variables for the column values, and you can specify these column values at run-time.

Step 2: Create a *SqlCommand* Object to Hold the SQL Statement

The second step is to create a SqlCommand object to hold your SQL statement. For example:

```
SqlCommand mySqlCommand = mySqlConnection.CreateCommand();
```

Step 3: Set the *CommandText* Property of the *SqlCommand* Object to the SQL String

The third step is to set the CommandText property of your SqlCommand object to your SQL string. For example:

```
mySqlCommand.CommandText = insertString;
```

Step 4: Use the *Add()* Method to Add the Parameters

The fourth step is to use the Add() method through the Parameters property of your SqlCommand object. The Add() method adds the parameters to your SqlCommand object. The Add() method is overloaded, and the version used in this example accepts three parameters:

◆ The placeholder string for the parameter in your SQL statement. For example, "@CustomerID" is the first placeholder in the insertString created in step 1.

◆ The type for the column in the database. For SQL server, these types are defined in the SqlDbType enumeration. Table 23.22 shows these database types.

◆ The maximum length of the parameter value (optional).

TABLE 23.22: SqlDbType ENUMERATION MEMBERS

MEMBER	DESCRIPTION
BigInt	A 64-bit signed integer between -2^{63} ($-9,223,372,036,854,775,808$) and $2^{63} - 1$ ($9,223,372,036,854,775,807$).
Binary	An array of bytes with a maximum length of 8,000.

Continued on next page

TABLE 23.22: SqlDbType ENUMERATION MEMBERS *(continued)*

MEMBER	DESCRIPTION
Bit	An unsigned numeric value that can be 0, 1, or a null reference.
Char	A string of non-Unicode characters with a maximum length of 8,000.
DateTime	A date and time between January 1, 1753 to December 31, 9999. This is accurate to 3.33 milliseconds.
Decimal	A fixed precision and scale numeric value between $-10^{38} - 1$ ($-79,228,162,514,264,337,593,543,950,335$) and $10^{38} - 1$ ($79,228,162,514,264,337,593,543,950,335$).
Float	A floating point number between $-1.79E + 308$ and $1.79E + 308$.
Image	An array of bytes with a maximum length of $2^{31} -1$ ($2,147,483,647$).
Int	A 32-bit signed integer between -2^{31} ($-2,147,483,648$) and $2^{31} - 1$ ($2,147,483,647$).
Money	A currency value between $-922,337,203,685,477.5808$ and $922,337,203,685,477.5807$. This is accurate to 1/10,000th of a currency unit.
NChar	A string of Unicode characters with a maximum length of 4,000.
NText	A string of Unicode characters with a maximum length of $2^{30} - 1$ ($1,073,741,823$).
NVarChar	A string of Unicode characters with a maximum length of 4,000.
Real	A floating point number between $-3.40E + 38$ and $3.40E + 38$.
SmallDateTime	A date and time between January 1, 1900 and June 6, 2079. This is accurate to 1 minute.
SmallInt	A 16-bit signed integer.
SmallMoney	A currency value between $-214,748.3648$ and $214,748.3647$. Accurate to 1/10,000th of a currency unit.
Text	A string of non-Unicode characters with a maximum length of $2^{31} - 1$ ($2,147,483,647$).
Timestamp	A date and time in the format yyyymmddhhmmss.
TinyInt	An 8-bit unsigned integer between 0 and $2^8 - 1$ (255).
UniqueIdentifier	A globally unique identifier (GUID).
VarBinary	An array of bytes with a maximum length of 8,000.
VarChar	A string of non-Unicode characters with a maximum length of 4,000.
Variant	A data type that can contain numbers, strings, bytes, or dates.

Earlier in step 1, `insertString` was set to an `INSERT` statement that contains placeholders for four parameters. The following statements use the `Add()` method to add four parameters to `mySqlCommand`:

```
mySqlCommand.Parameters.Add("@CustomerID", SqlDbType.NChar, 5);
mySqlCommand.Parameters.Add("@CompanyName", SqlDbType.NVarChar, 40);
mySqlCommand.Parameters.Add("@ContactName", SqlDbType.NVarChar, 30);
mySqlCommand.Parameters.Add("@Address", SqlDbType.NVarChar, 60);
```

As you can see, the parameter for the `"@CustomerID"` placeholder is defined as an `NChar`—a string of Unicode characters with a maximum length of 4,000. A value of 5 is passed as the third parameter to the `Add()` method for `"@CustomerID"`, meaning that a maximum of five characters may be supplied as the parameter value. You'll see the setting of the parameter values in the next step.

Step 5: Set the Parameters to Specified Values Using the Value Property

The fifth step is to set the parameters defined in the previous step to specified values. You do this using the `Value` property of each parameter. These values are then used in the `INSERT` statement when the new row is added to the `Customers` table. For example:

```
mySqlCommand.Parameters["@CustomerID"].Value = "T1COM";
mySqlCommand.Parameters["@CompanyName"].Value = "T1 Company";
mySqlCommand.Parameters["@ContactName"].Value = "Jason Price";
mySqlCommand.Parameters["@Address"].Value = "1 Main Street";
```

In this example, `"@CustomerID"` is set to `"T1COM"`. Therefore, the `INSERT` statement will set the `CustomerID` column for the new row to T1COM. The entire `INSERT` statement is as follows:

```
INSERT INTO Customers (
  CustomerID, CompanyName, ContactName, Address
) VALUES (
  'T1COM', 'T1 Company', 'Jason Price', '1 Main Street'
);
```

As you can see, the column values are the same as those specified in the `Value` property for each parameter. This `INSERT` statement is run in the next step.

Step 6: Use the *ExecuteNonQuery()* Method to Run the SQL Statement

The final step is to use the `ExecuteNonQuery()` method to run your SQL statement. For example:

```
mySqlCommand.ExecuteNonQuery();
```

This runs the `INSERT` statement and adds the new row to the `Customers` table. The reason why we're using the `ExecuteNonQuery()` method is that we don't need anything to be returned by the database. This is because an `INSERT` statement is being performed.

Example Program

Listing 23.2 shows a program that performs an INSERT, UPDATE, and DELETE statement to add, modify, and remove a row from the Customers table. This program contains five methods:

DisplayDataTable()   The DisplayDataTable() method displays the CustomerID, CompanyName, ContactName, and Address columns for the rows contained in a DataTable object. This DataTable object is passed as a parameter to the DisplayDataTable() method.

AddRow()   The AddRow() method performs an INSERT statement that adds a new row to the Customers table.

ModifyRow()   The ModifyRow() method performs an UPDATE statement that modifies the new row in the Customers table.

RemoveRow()   The RemoveRow() method performs a DELETE statement that removes the new row from the Customers table.

Main()   The Main() method retrieves rows from the Customers table into a DataSet object and then calls the AddRow(), ModifyRow(), and RemoveRow() methods to add, modify, and remove the row from the Customers table. After each of these methods is called, Main() calls the Display-DataTable() method to display the changes made to the Customers table.

LISTING 23.2: PERFORMING SQL INSERT, UPDATE, AND DELETE STATEMENTS USING ADO.NET

```
/*
  Example23_2.cs illustrates how to perform INSERT, UPDATE,
  and DELETE statements using ADO.NET
*/

using System;
using System.Data;
using System.Data.SqlClient;

class Example23_2
{

  public static void DisplayDataTable(
    SqlDataAdapter mySqlDataAdapter,
    DataSet myDataSet,
    DataTable myDataTable
  )
  {

    // use the Clear() method of the DataSet object
    // to remove all the rows in the DataSet
    myDataSet.Clear();
```

```
// use the Fill() method of the SqlDataAdapter object
// to synchronize any changes made to the database
// with the DataSet object
mySqlDataAdapter.Fill(myDataSet, "Customers");

// display the columns for each row in the DataTable,
// using a DataRow object to access each row in the DataTable
foreach (DataRow myDataRow in myDataTable.Rows)
{
  Console.WriteLine("CustomerID = " + myDataRow["CustomerID"]);
  Console.WriteLine("CompanyName = " + myDataRow["CompanyName"]);
  Console.WriteLine("ContactName = " + myDataRow["ContactName"]);
  Console.WriteLine("Address = " + myDataRow["Address"]);
}

}

public static void AddRow(
  SqlConnection mySqlConnection,
  SqlDataAdapter mySqlDataAdapter,
  DataSet myDataSet
)
{

  Console.WriteLine("\nAdding a new row with CustomerID of 'T1COM'");

  // step 1: formulate a string containing the SQL statement
  string insertString =
    "INSERT INTO Customers (" +
    "  CustomerID, CompanyName, ContactName, Address" +
    ") VALUES (" +
    "  @CustomerID, @CompanyName, @ContactName, @Address" +
    ")";

  // step 2: create a SqlCommand object to hold the SQL statement
  SqlCommand mySqlCommand = mySqlConnection.CreateCommand();

  // step 3: set the CommandText property of the SqlCommand object to
  // the SQL string
  mySqlCommand.CommandText = insertString;

  // step 4: use the Add() method through the Parameters property
  // of the SqlCommand object to add the parameters to the SqlCommand
  // object
  mySqlCommand.Parameters.Add("@CustomerID", SqlDbType.NChar, 5);
  mySqlCommand.Parameters.Add("@CompanyName", SqlDbType.NVarChar, 40);
  mySqlCommand.Parameters.Add("@ContactName", SqlDbType.NVarChar, 30);
  mySqlCommand.Parameters.Add("@Address", SqlDbType.NVarChar, 60);
```

```
    // step 5: set the parameters to specified values using the
    // Value property
    mySqlCommand.Parameters["@CustomerID"].Value = "T1COM";
    mySqlCommand.Parameters["@CompanyName"].Value = "T1 Company";
    mySqlCommand.Parameters["@ContactName"].Value = "Jason Price";
    mySqlCommand.Parameters["@Address"].Value = "1 Main Street";

    // step 6: use the ExecuteNonQuery() method to run the
    // SQL statement
    mySqlCommand.ExecuteNonQuery();

}

public static void ModifyRow(
  SqlConnection mySqlConnection,
  SqlDataAdapter mySqlDataAdapter,
  DataSet myDataSet
)
{

    Console.WriteLine("\nModifying the new row");

    // step 1: formulate the SQL statement
    string updateString =
      "UPDATE Customers " +
      "SET " +
      "  CompanyName = @CompanyName, " +
      "  ContactName = @ContactName, " +
      "  Address = @Address " +
      "WHERE CustomerID = @CustomerID";

    // step 2: create a SqlCommand object to hold the SQL statement
    SqlCommand mySqlCommand = mySqlConnection.CreateCommand();

    // step 3: set the CommandText property of the SqlCommand object to
    // the SQL string
    mySqlCommand.CommandText = updateString;

    // step 4: use the Add() method through the Parameters property
    // to add the parameters
    mySqlCommand.Parameters.Add("@CustomerID", SqlDbType.NChar, 5);
    mySqlCommand.Parameters.Add("@CompanyName", SqlDbType.NVarChar, 40);
    mySqlCommand.Parameters.Add("@ContactName", SqlDbType.NVarChar, 30);
    mySqlCommand.Parameters.Add("@Address", SqlDbType.NVarChar, 60);

    // step 5: set the parameters to values using the Value property
    mySqlCommand.Parameters["@CustomerID"].Value = "T1COM";
    mySqlCommand.Parameters["@CompanyName"].Value = "Widgets Inc.";
```

```
    mySqlCommand.Parameters["@ContactName"].Value = "John Smith";
    mySqlCommand.Parameters["@Address"].Value = "1 Any Street";

    // step 6: use the ExecuteNonQuery() method to run the
    // SQL statement
    mySqlCommand.ExecuteNonQuery();

  }

  public static void RemoveRow(
    SqlConnection mySqlConnection,
    SqlDataAdapter mySqlDataAdapter,
    DataSet myDataSet
  )
  {

    Console.WriteLine("\nRemoving the new row");

    // step 1: formulate the SQL statement
    string deleteString =
      "DELETE FROM Customers " +
      "WHERE CustomerID = @CustomerID";

    // step 2: create a SqlCommand object to hold the SQL statement
    SqlCommand mySqlCommand = mySqlConnection.CreateCommand();

    // step 3: set the CommandText property of the SqlCommand object to
    // the SQL string
    mySqlCommand.CommandText = deleteString;

    // step 4: use the Add() method through the Parameters property
    // to add the parameter
    mySqlCommand.Parameters.Add("@CustomerID", SqlDbType.NChar, 5);

    // step 5: set the parameters to values using the Value property
    mySqlCommand.Parameters["@CustomerID"].Value = "T1COM";

    // step 6: use the ExecuteNonQuery() method to run the
    // SQL statement
    mySqlCommand.ExecuteNonQuery();

  }

  public static void Main()
  {

    // formulate a string containing the details of the
    // database connection
```

```
string connectionString =
  "server=localhost;database=Northwind;uid=sa;pwd=sa";

// create a SqlConnection object to connect to the
// database, passing the connection string to the constructor
SqlConnection mySqlConnection =
  new SqlConnection(connectionString);

// formulate a SELECT statement to retrieve the
// CustomerID, CompanyName, ContactName, and Address
// columns for rows from the Customers table
string selectString =
  "SELECT CustomerID, CompanyName, ContactName, Address " +
  "FROM Customers " +
  "WHERE CustomerID IN ('ALFKI', 'T1COM')";

// create a SqlCommand object to hold the SELECT statement
SqlCommand mySqlCommand = mySqlConnection.CreateCommand();

// set the CommandText property of the SqlCommand object to
// the SELECT string
mySqlCommand.CommandText = selectString;

// create a SqlDataAdapter object
SqlDataAdapter mySqlDataAdapter = new SqlDataAdapter();

// set the SelectCommand property of the SqlAdapter object
// to the SqlCommand object
mySqlDataAdapter.SelectCommand = mySqlCommand;

// create a DataSet object to store the results of
// the SELECT statement
DataSet myDataSet = new DataSet();

// open the database connection using the
// Open() method of the SqlConnection object
mySqlConnection.Open();

// use the Fill() method of the SqlDataAdapter object to
// retrieve the rows from the table, storing the rows locally
// in a DataTable of the DataSet object
string dataTableName = "Customers";
Console.WriteLine("Retrieving a row from the Customers table");
mySqlDataAdapter.Fill(myDataSet, dataTableName);

// get the DataTable object from the DataSet object
DataTable myDataTable = myDataSet.Tables[dataTableName];
```

```
        // display the rows in the DataTable object
        DisplayDataTable(mySqlDataAdapter, myDataSet, myDataTable);

        // add a new row
        AddRow(mySqlConnection, mySqlDataAdapter, myDataSet);
        DisplayDataTable(mySqlDataAdapter, myDataSet, myDataTable);

        // modify the new row
        ModifyRow(mySqlConnection, mySqlDataAdapter, myDataSet);
        DisplayDataTable(mySqlDataAdapter, myDataSet, myDataTable);

        // remove the new row
        RemoveRow(mySqlConnection, mySqlDataAdapter, myDataSet);
        DisplayDataTable(mySqlDataAdapter, myDataSet, myDataTable);

        // close the database connection using the Close() method
        // of the SqlConnection object
        mySqlConnection.Close();

    }

}
```

The output from this program is as follows:

```
Retrieving a row from the Customers table
CustomerID = ALFKI
CompanyName = Alfreds Futterkiste
ContactName = Maria Anders
Address = Obere Str. 57

Adding a new row with CustomerID of 'T1COM'
CustomerID = ALFKI
CompanyName = Alfreds Futterkiste
ContactName = Maria Anders
Address = Obere Str. 57
CustomerID = T1COM
CompanyName = T1 Company
ContactName = Jason Price
Address = 1 Main Street

Modifying the new row
CustomerID = ALFKI
CompanyName = Alfreds Futterkiste
ContactName = Maria Anders
Address = Obere Str. 57
CustomerID = T1COM
```

```
CompanyName = Widgets Inc.
ContactName = John Smith
Address = 1 Any Street

Removing the new row
CustomerID = ALFKI
CompanyName = Alfreds Futterkiste
ContactName = Maria Anders
Address = Obere Str. 57
```

Modifying a *DataTable* Object and Synchronizing the Changes with the Database

In this section, you'll see the steps required to add, modify, and remove rows from a DataTable object and then synchronize those changes with the database.

When you make changes to the rows in a DataTable, it frees you from writing SQL INSERT, UPDATE, and DELETE statements. Your changes are made to the local copy of the rows on your local computer. When you're ready to synchronize your changes with the database, you simply call the Fill() method of your data adapter to permanently record your changes in the database.

Adding a New Row to a *DataTable* Object

To add a new row to a DataTable object, you can use the following steps:

1. Use the NewRow() method of the DataRow object to create a new row in your DataTable.

2. Set the values for the columns of the new row.

3. Use the Add() method through the Rows property of your DataTable object to add the new DataRow to the DataTable.

4. Use the AcceptChanges() method of your DataTable to commit the changes.

NOTE *To permanently record the new row in the database, you must call the Fill() method of your data adapter. This rule also applies when modifying or deleting a row. The Fill() method synchronizes the changes made to your DataSet with the database.*

The following method, named AddRow(), illustrates these four steps to add a new row to a DataTable object (the DataTable object is assumed to have already been created and populated with the CustomerID, CompanyName, ContactName, and Address columns from the Customers table):

```
public static void AddRow(
  DataTable myDataTable
)
{

    Console.WriteLine("\nAdding a new row with CustomerID of 'T1COM'");
```

```
    // step 1: use the NewRow() method of the DataRow object to create
    // a new row in the DataTable
    DataRow myNewDataRow = myDataTable.NewRow();

    // step 2: set the values for the columns of the new row
    myNewDataRow["CustomerID"] = "T1COM";
    myNewDataRow["CompanyName"] = "T1 Company";
    myNewDataRow["ContactName"] = "Jason Price";
    myNewDataRow["Address"] = "1 Main Street";

    // step 3: use the Add() method through the Rows property to add
    // the new DataRow to the DataTable
    myDataTable.Rows.Add(myNewDataRow);

    // step 4: use the AcceptChanges() method of the DataTable to commit
    // the changes
    myDataTable.AcceptChanges();

}
```

At the end, you need to call the Fill() method of your SqlDataAdapter object to synchronize the changes made to your DataSet with the database. For example:

```
mySqlDataAdapter.Fill(myDataSet, "Customers");
```

This causes the new row to be added to the Customers table.

Modifying a Row in a *DataTable* Object

To modify a row in a DataTable object, you can use the following steps:

1. Set the PrimaryKey property for the DataTable. You need to set this to find the DataRow in the next step.

2. Use the Find() method to locate the DataRow that you want to modify in your DataTable. You locate the DataRow using the value for its primary key column.

3. Change the column values for your DataRow.

4. Use the AcceptChanges() method of your DataTable to commit the changes.

The following method, named ModifyRow(), illustrates these four steps to modify the row that was previously added by the AddRow() method:

```
public static void ModifyRow(
  DataTable myDataTable
)
{

    Console.WriteLine("\nModifying the new row");
```

```
// step 1: set the PrimaryKey property for the DataTable object
DataColumn[] myPrimaryKey = new DataColumn[1];
myPrimaryKey[0] = myDataTable.Columns["CustomerID"];
myDataTable.PrimaryKey = myPrimaryKey;

// step 2: use the Find() method to locate the DataRow
// in the DataTable using the primary key value
DataRow myEditDataRow = myDataTable.Rows.Find("T1COM");

// step 3: change the column values
myEditDataRow["CompanyName"] = "Widgets Inc.";
myEditDataRow["ContactName"] = "John Smith";
myEditDataRow["Address"] = "1 Any Street";

// step 4: use the AcceptChanges() method of the DataTable to commit
// the changes
myDataTable.AcceptChanges();
Console.WriteLine("myEditDataRow.RowState = " + myEditDataRow.RowState);

}
```

Remember: You need to call the `Fill()` method of your `SqlDataAdapter` object to synchronize the changes made to your `DataSet` with the database.

Removing a Row from a *DataTable* Object

To remove a row from a `DataTable` object, you can use the following steps:

1. Set the `PrimaryKey` property for your `DataTable` object.

2. Use the `Find()` method to locate your `DataRow`.

3. Use the `Delete()` method to remove your `DataRow`.

4. Use the `AcceptChanges()` method of your `DataTable` to commit the changes.

The following method, named `DeleteRow()`, illustrates these four steps to delete the row that was previously added by the `AddRow()` method:

```
public static void RemoveRow(
  DataTable myDataTable
)
{

  Console.WriteLine("\nRemoving the new row");

  // step 1: set the PrimaryKey property for the DataTable object
  DataColumn[] myPrimaryKey = new DataColumn[1];
  myPrimaryKey[0] = myDataTable.Columns["CustomerID"];
  myDataTable.PrimaryKey = myPrimaryKey;
```

```
  // step 2: use the Find() method to locate the DataRow
  DataRow myRemoveDataRow = myDataTable.Rows.Find("T1COM");

  // step 3: use the Delete() method to remove the DataRow
  myRemoveDataRow.Delete();

  // step 4: use the AcceptChanges() method of the DataTable to commit
  // the changes
  myDataTable.AcceptChanges();

}
```

Remember: You need to call the Fill() method of your SqlDataAdapter object to synchronize the changes made to your DataSet with the database.

Examining an Example Program

Listing 23.3 shows a program that uses the AddRow(), ModifyRow(), and RemoveRow() methods to add, modify, and remove a row from the Customers table.

LISTING 23.3: ADDING, MODIFYING, AND DELETING ROWS FROM A DataTable OBJECT

```
/*
   Example23_3.cs illustrates the use of adding, modifying, and deleting
   a row in a DataTable object and synchronizing those changes with the
   database
*/

using System;
using System.Data;
using System.Data.SqlClient;

class Example23_3
{

  public static void DisplayDataTable(DataTable myDataTable)
  {

    // display the columns for each row in the DataTable,
    // using a DataRow object to access each row in the DataTable
    foreach (DataRow myDataRow in myDataTable.Rows)
    {
      Console.WriteLine("CustomerID = " + myDataRow["CustomerID"]);
      Console.WriteLine("CompanyName = " + myDataRow["CompanyName"]);
      Console.WriteLine("ContactName = " + myDataRow["ContactName"]);
      Console.WriteLine("Address = " + myDataRow["Address"]);
    }
```

```
}

public static void AddRow(
  DataTable myDataTable
)
{

  Console.WriteLine("\nAdding a new row with CustomerID of 'T1COM'");

  // step 1: use the NewRow() method of the DataRow object to create
  // a new row in the DataTable
  DataRow myNewDataRow = myDataTable.NewRow();

  // step 2: set the values for the columns of the new row
  myNewDataRow["CustomerID"] = "T1COM";
  myNewDataRow["CompanyName"] = "T1 Company";
  myNewDataRow["ContactName"] = "Jason Price";
  myNewDataRow["Address"] = "1 Main Street";

  // step 3: use the Add() method through the Rows property to add
  // the new DataRow to the DataTable
  myDataTable.Rows.Add(myNewDataRow);

  // step 4: use the AcceptChanges() method of the DataTable to commit
  // the changes
  myDataTable.AcceptChanges();

}

public static void ModifyRow(
  DataTable myDataTable
)
{

  Console.WriteLine("\nModifying the new row");

  // step 1: set the PrimaryKey property for the DataTable object
  DataColumn[] myPrimaryKey = new DataColumn[1];
  myPrimaryKey[0] = myDataTable.Columns["CustomerID"];
  myDataTable.PrimaryKey = myPrimaryKey;

  // step 2: use the Find() method to locate the DataRow
  // in the DataTable using the primary key value
  DataRow myEditDataRow = myDataTable.Rows.Find("T1COM");

  // step 3: change the column values
  myEditDataRow["CompanyName"] = "Widgets Inc.";
```

```
    myEditDataRow["ContactName"] = "John Smith";
    myEditDataRow["Address"] = "1 Any Street";

    // step 4: use the AcceptChanges() method of the DataTable to commit
    // the changes
    myDataTable.AcceptChanges();
    Console.WriteLine("myEditDataRow.RowState = " + myEditDataRow.RowState);

}

public static void RemoveRow(
  DataTable myDataTable
)
{

  Console.WriteLine("\nRemoving the new row");

  // step 1: set the PrimaryKey property for the DataTable object
  DataColumn[] myPrimaryKey = new DataColumn[1];
  myPrimaryKey[0] = myDataTable.Columns["CustomerID"];
  myDataTable.PrimaryKey = myPrimaryKey;

  // step 2: use the Find() method to locate the DataRow
  DataRow myRemoveDataRow = myDataTable.Rows.Find("T1COM");

  // step 3: use the Delete() method to remove the DataRow
  myRemoveDataRow.Delete();

  // step 4: use the AcceptChanges() method of the DataTable to commit
  // the changes
  myDataTable.AcceptChanges();

}

public static void Main()
{

  // formulate a string containing the details of the
  // database connection
  string connectionString =
    "server=localhost;database=Northwind;uid=sa;pwd=sa";

  // create a SqlConnection object to connect to the
  // database, passing the connection string to the constructor
  SqlConnection mySqlConnection =
    new SqlConnection(connectionString);
```

```
// formulate a SELECT statement to retrieve the
// CustomerID, CompanyName, ContactName, and Address
// columns for the first row from the Customers table
string selectString =
  "SELECT CustomerID, CompanyName, ContactName, Address " +
  "FROM Customers " +
  "WHERE CustomerID = 'ALFKI'";

// create a SqlCommand object to hold the SELECT statement
SqlCommand mySqlCommand = mySqlConnection.CreateCommand();

// set the CommandText property of the SqlCommand object to
// the SELECT string
mySqlCommand.CommandText = selectString;

// create a SqlDataAdapter object
SqlDataAdapter mySqlDataAdapter = new SqlDataAdapter();

// set the SelectCommand property of the SqlAdapter object
// to the SqlCommand object
mySqlDataAdapter.SelectCommand = mySqlCommand;

// create a DataSet object to store the results of
// the SELECT statement
DataSet myDataSet = new DataSet();

// open the database connection using the
// Open() method of the SqlConnection object
mySqlConnection.Open();

// use the Fill() method of the SqlDataAdapter object to
// retrieve the rows from the table, storing the rows locally
// in a DataTable of the DataSet object
Console.WriteLine("Retrieving a row from the Customers table");
mySqlDataAdapter.Fill(myDataSet, "Customers");

// get the DataTable object from the DataSet object
DataTable myDataTable = myDataSet.Tables["Customers"];

// display the rows in the DataTable object
DisplayDataTable(myDataTable);

// add a new row
AddRow(myDataTable);
DisplayDataTable(myDataTable);
```

```
                        // modify a row
                        ModifyRow(myDataTable);
                        DisplayDataTable(myDataTable);

                        // remove a row
                        RemoveRow(myDataTable);
                        DisplayDataTable(myDataTable);

                        // use the Fill() method of the SqlDataAdapter object
                        // to synchronize the changes with the database
                        mySqlDataAdapter.Fill(myDataSet, "Customers");

                        // close the database connection using the Close() method
                        // of the SqlConnection object
                        mySqlConnection.Close();

                    }

                }
```

The output from this program is as follows:

```
Retrieving a row from the Customers table
CustomerID = ALFKI
CompanyName = Alfreds Futterkiste
ContactName = Maria Anders
Address = Obere Str. 57

Adding a new row with CustomerID of 'T1COM'
CustomerID = ALFKI
CompanyName = Alfreds Futterkiste
ContactName = Maria Anders
Address = Obere Str. 57
CustomerID = T1COM
CompanyName = T1 Company
ContactName = Jason Price
Address = 1 Main Street

Modifying the new row
myEditDataRow.RowState = Unchanged
CustomerID = ALFKI
CompanyName = Alfreds Futterkiste
ContactName = Maria Anders
Address = Obere Str. 57
CustomerID = T1COM
CompanyName = Widgets Inc.
```

```
ContactName = John Smith
Address = 1 Any Street

Removing the new row
CustomerID = ALFKI
CompanyName = Alfreds Futterkiste
ContactName = Maria Anders
Address = Obere Str. 57
```

Using a Transaction in ADO.NET

In the previous chapter, you saw how you can group SQL statements together into transactions. The transaction is then committed or rolled back as one unit. You can use a `SqlTransaction` object to represent a transaction in ADO.NET with a SQL Server database.

1. When using a transaction to run two `INSERT` statements, you can use the following steps:

2. Create a `SqlTransaction` object and start the transaction by calling the `BeginTransaction()` method of your `SqlConnection` object.

3. Create a `SqlCommand` object to hold your SQL statement.

4. Set the `Transaction` property for your `SqlCommand` object.

5. Formulate a string containing your first `INSERT` statement.

6. Set the `CommandText` property of your `SqlCommand` object to the first `INSERT` string.

7. Run the first `INSERT` statement using the `ExecuteNonQuery()` method of your `SqlCommand` object.

8. Formulate a string contain your second `INSERT` statement.

9. Set the `CommandText` property of your `SqlCommand` object to the second `INSERT` string.

10. Run the second `INSERT` statement using the `ExecuteNonQuery()` method of your `SqlCommand` object.

11. Commit the transaction using the `Commit()` method of your `SqlTransaction` object. This makes the two new rows added by the `INSERT` statements permanent in the database. You can use the `Rollback()` method to undo the `INSERT` statements.

Listing 23.4 shows a program that illustrates these steps. Two `INSERT` statements are performed in the transaction. Each `INSERT` statement adds a row to the `Customers` table. At the end of the program, the transaction is committed.

NOTE   *If you want to run the program more than once, you'll need to remove the two rows added to the* `Customers` *table using the following* `DELETE` *statement (you can do this using the Query Analyzer tool):* `DELETE FROM Customers WHERE CustomerID IN ('T1COM', 'T2COM');`.

LISTING 23.4: USING A TRANSACTION IN ADO.NET

```
/*
  Example23_4.cs illustrates the use of transactions
*/

using System;
using System.Data;
using System.Data.SqlClient;

class Example23_4
{

  public static void Main()
  {

    // formulate a string containing the details of the
    // database connection
    string connectionString =
      "server=localhost;database=Northwind;uid=sa;pwd=sa";

    // create a SqlConnection object to connect to the
    // database, passing the connection string to the constructor
    SqlConnection mySqlConnection =
      new SqlConnection(connectionString);

    // open the database connection using the
    // Open() method of the SqlConnection object
    mySqlConnection.Open();

    // step 1: create a SqlTransaction object and start the transaction
    // by calling the BeginTransaction() method of the SqlConnection
    // object
    SqlTransaction mySqlTransaction =
      mySqlConnection.BeginTransaction();

    // step 2: create a SqlCommand object to hold a SQL statement
    SqlCommand mySqlCommand = mySqlConnection.CreateCommand();

    // step 3: set the Transaction property for the SqlCommand object
    mySqlCommand.Transaction = mySqlTransaction;

    // step 4: formulate a string containing the first INSERT statement
    string insertString =
      "INSERT INTO Customers (" +
      "  CustomerID, CompanyName, ContactName, Address" +
      ") VALUES (" +
```

```
          "  'T2COM', 'T2 Company', 'Jason Price', '1 Main Street'" +
          ")";

        // step 5: set the CommandText property of the SqlCommand object to
        // the INSERT string
        mySqlCommand.CommandText = insertString;

        // step 6: run the first INSERT statement
        Console.WriteLine("Running first INSERT statement");
        mySqlCommand.ExecuteNonQuery();

        // step 7: formulate a second INSERT statement
        insertString =
          "INSERT INTO Orders (" +
          "  CustomerID" +
          ") VALUES (" +
          "  'T2COM'" +
          ")";

        // step 8: set the CommandText property of the SqlCommand object to
        // the second INSERT string
        mySqlCommand.CommandText = insertString;

        // step 9: run the second INSERT statement
        Console.WriteLine("Running second INSERT statement");
        mySqlCommand.ExecuteNonQuery();

        // step 10: commit the transaction using the Commit() method
        // of the SqlTransaction object
        Console.WriteLine("Committing transaction");
        mySqlTransaction.Commit();

        // close the database connection using the Close() method
        // of the SqlConnection object
        mySqlConnection.Close();

  }

}
```

The output from this program is as follows:

```
Running first INSERT statement
Running second INSERT statement
Committing transaction
```

Using a *DataView* Object to Filter and Sort Rows

You can use a DataView object to filter rows previously retrieved into a DataTable. You set the row filter for a DataView object using the RowFilter property. You can also sort the rows in the DataView—you specify the columns to sort using the Sort property.

TIP *You can also use the* Select() *method of a* DataTable *object to filter and sort rows.*

For example, say you had a DataSet object named myDataSet that has already been populated with a DataTable object that contains the CustomerID, CompanyName, City, and Country columns for the rows from the Customers table. Let's say you want to filter those rows to view customers in the UK, and you want to sort those rows by the CustomerID column. You can create a DataView object and use it to get the rows in that DataTable using the following statement:

```
DataView myDataView =
    new DataView(myDataSet.Tables["Customers"]);
```

You can then filter the rows to those where the Country column is equal to 'UK' by setting the RowFilter property of myDataView to "Country = 'UK'":

```
myDataView.RowFilter = "Country = 'UK'";
```

You can then sort those rows by the CustomerID column in ascending order by setting the Sort property of myDataView to "CustomerID ASC":

```
myDataView.Sort = "CustomerID ASC";
```

NOTE *You can sort in descending order by using* DESC *rather than* ASC *in the* Sort *property string.*

Listing 23.5 shows a program that uses a DataView object to filter the rows retrieved from the Customers table to those where the Country column is equal to 'UK'; these rows are then sorted by the CustomerID column in ascending order. The contents of the DataView object are then displayed.

LISTING 23.5: USING A DataView OBJECT TO FILTER AND SORT ROWS

```
/*
  Example23_5.cs illustrates the use of a DataView object to
  filter and sort rows
*/

using System;
using System.Data;
using System.Data.SqlClient;

class Example23_5
{

  public static void Main()
  {
```

```csharp
// formulate a string containing the details of the
// database connection
string connectionString =
  "server=localhost;database=Northwind;uid=sa;pwd=sa";

// create a SqlConnection object to connect to the
// database, passing the connection string to the constructor
SqlConnection mySqlConnection =
  new SqlConnection(connectionString);

// formulate a string containing a SELECT statement
string selectString =
  "SELECT CustomerID, CompanyName, City, Country " +
  "FROM Customers";

// create a SqlCommand object to hold the SELECT statement
SqlCommand mySqlCommand = mySqlConnection.CreateCommand();

// set the CommandText property of the SqlCommand object to
// the SELECT string
mySqlCommand.CommandText = selectString;

// create a SqlDataAdapter object
SqlDataAdapter mySqlDataAdapter = new SqlDataAdapter();

// set the SelectCommand property of the SqlAdapter object
// to the SqlCommand object
mySqlDataAdapter.SelectCommand = mySqlCommand;

// create a DataSet object to store the results of
// the SELECT statement
DataSet myDataSet = new DataSet();

// open the database connection using the
// Open() method of the SqlConnection object
mySqlConnection.Open();

// use the Fill() method of the SqlDataAdapter object to
// retrieve the rows from the table, storing the rows locally
// in a DataTable of the DataSet object
Console.WriteLine("Retrieving rows from the Customers table");
mySqlDataAdapter.Fill(myDataSet, "Customers");

// create a DataView object
DataView myDataView =
  new DataView(myDataSet.Tables["Customers"]);
```

```
            // set the RowFilter property of the DataView object
            myDataView.RowFilter = "Country = 'UK'";

            // set the Sort property of the DataView object
            myDataView.Sort = "CustomerID ASC";

            // display the rows in the DataView object
            foreach (DataRowView myDataRowView in myDataView)
            {
              for (int count = 0; count < myDataView.Table.Columns.Count; count++)
              {
                Console.WriteLine(myDataRowView[count]);
              }
            }

            // close the database connection using the Close() method
            // of the SqlConnection object
            mySqlConnection.Close();

        }

    }
```

The output from this program is as follows:

```
Retrieving rows from the Customers table
AROUT
Around the Horn
London
UK
BSBEV
B's Beverages
London
UK
CONSH
Consolidated Holdings
London
UK
EASTC
Eastern Connection
London
UK
ISLAT
Island Trading
Cowes
UK
NORTS
```

North/South
London
UK
SEVES
Seven Seas Imports
London
UK

Defining and Using a Relationship between Two *DataTable* Objects

You can define a relationship between two DataTable objects in a DataSet object. By doing this, you can model the parent-child relationship that exists between two database tables.

For example, the Customers table and Orders table have a parent-child relationship. The CustomerID column of the Orders table is a foreign key that links to the CustomerID column of the Customers table. You can model this parent-child relationship in your program. By doing this, you can use the GetChildRows() method for your parent DataTable object to obtain the rows of your child DataTable object.

For example, let's say you already have a DataSet object named myDataSet that contains two DataTable objects named "Customers" and "Orders". Assume that the "Customers" DataTable was populated with the row retrieved by the following SELECT statement:

```
SELECT CustomerID, CompanyName
FROM Customers
WHERE CustomerID = 'ALFKI';
```

Also assume that the "Orders" DataTable was populated with the rows retrieved by the following SELECT statement:

```
SELECT OrderID, CustomerID
FROM Orders
WHERE CustomerID = 'ALFKI';
```

As you can see, the "Orders" DataTable contains the orders placed by the customer with the CustomerID of ALFKI.

Now, as mentioned, there is a parent-child relationship between the Customers and Orders tables. You can model this in your DataSet object by defining a relationship between the "Customers" and "Orders" DataTable objects. You access the relationships in a DataSet object through the Relationships property—and you define a new relationship by calling the Add() method through the Relationships property.

NOTE *The* Relationships *property of a* DataSet *returns an object of the* DataRelationCollection *class. Like the name suggests, this object is collection, and a* DataRelationCollection *object is a collection of* DataRelation *objects. The* Add() *method is defined in the* DataRelationCollection *class and allows you to add a* DataRelation *object to the* DataRelationCollection *object in the* DataSet.

The following statement uses the Add() method to add a relationship to myDataSet; this relationship is between the "Customers" and the "Orders" DataSet objects:

```
myDataSet.Relations.Add(
  "Orders",
  myDataSet.Tables["Customers"].Columns["CustomerID"],
  myDataSet.Tables["Orders"].Columns["CustomerID"]
);
```

The first parameter to the Add() method is a string containing the name you want to assign to the relationship. The second and third parameters of the relationship are the DataColumn objects of the DataTable objects. The first DataColumn object is the primary key column of the parent table; the second DataColumn is the foreign key of the child table.

As you can see from the previous example, the name of the relationship is set to "Orders". The primary key DataColumn object is the CustomerID column from the Customers DataTable. The foreign key DataColumn object is the CustomerID column from the Orders DataTable.

You can then use the following code to display the rows in the Customers DataTable and the Orders DataTable; notice the use of the GetChildRows() method to read the orders placed by the customer:

```
DataTable customers = myDataSet.Tables["Customers"];
foreach (DataRow customer in customers.Rows)
{
  Console.WriteLine("CustomerID = " + customer["CustomerID"]);
  Console.WriteLine("CompanyName = " + customer["CompanyName"]);

  DataRow[] orders = customer.GetChildRows("Orders");
  Console.WriteLine("This customer placed the following orders:");
  foreach (DataRow order in orders)
  {
    Console.WriteLine("  OrderID = " + order["OrderID"]);
  }

}
```

Listing 23.6 illustrates how to define and use a relationship.

LISTING 23.6: DEFINING AND USING A RELATIONSHIP BETWEEN TWO DataTable OBJECTS

```
/*
  Example23_6.cs illustrates how to specify and use a
  relationship between two DataTable objects
*/

using System;
using System.Data;
using System.Data.SqlClient;
```

```csharp
class Example23_6
{

  public static void Main()
  {

    // formulate a string containing the details of the
    // database connection
    string connectionString =
      "server=localhost;database=Northwind;uid=sa;pwd=sa";

    // create a SqlConnection object to connect to the
    // database, passing the connection string to the constructor
    SqlConnection mySqlConnection =
      new SqlConnection(connectionString);

    // formulate a string containing a SELECT statement to
    // retrieve a row from the Customers table
    string selectString =
      "SELECT CustomerID, CompanyName " +
      "FROM Customers " +
      "WHERE CustomerID = 'ALFKI'";

    // create a SqlCommand object to hold the SELECT statement
    SqlCommand mySqlCommand = mySqlConnection.CreateCommand();

    // set the CommandText property of the SqlCommand object to
    // the SELECT string
    mySqlCommand.CommandText = selectString;

    // create a SqlDataAdapter object
    SqlDataAdapter mySqlDataAdapter = new SqlDataAdapter();

    // set the SelectCommand property of the SqlAdapter object
    // to the SqlCommand object
    mySqlDataAdapter.SelectCommand = mySqlCommand;

    // create a DataSet object to store the results of
    // the SELECT statement
    DataSet myDataSet = new DataSet();

    // open the database connection using the
    // Open() method of the SqlConnection object
    mySqlConnection.Open();

    // use the Fill() method of the SqlDataAdapter object to
    // retrieve the rows from the database, storing the rows
```

```csharp
// in a DataTable named "Customers"
mySqlDataAdapter.Fill(myDataSet, "Customers");

// formulate a string containing a SELECT statement to
// retrieve the rows from the Orders table where the CustomerID
// column is equal to ALFKI
selectString =
  "SELECT OrderID, CustomerID " +
  "FROM Orders " +
  "WHERE CustomerID = 'ALFKI'";

// set the CommandText property of the SqlCommand object to
// the SELECT string
mySqlCommand.CommandText = selectString;

// use the Fill() method of the SqlDataAdapter object to
// retrieve the rows from the database, storing the rows
// in a DataTable named "Orders"
mySqlDataAdapter.Fill(myDataSet, "Orders");

// use the Add() method through the Relations property
// to define a relationship between the Customers and
// Orders DataTable objects
myDataSet.Relations.Add(
  "Orders",
  myDataSet.Tables["Customers"].Columns["CustomerID"],
  myDataSet.Tables["Orders"].Columns["CustomerID"]
);

// display the rows in the Customers and Orders DataTable objects,
// using the GetChildRows() method to get the orders for the
// customer
DataTable customers = myDataSet.Tables["Customers"];
foreach (DataRow customer in customers.Rows)
{
  Console.WriteLine("CustomerID = " + customer["CustomerID"]);
  Console.WriteLine("CompanyName = " + customer["CompanyName"]);

  DataRow[] orders = customer.GetChildRows("Orders");
  Console.WriteLine("This customer placed the following orders:");
  foreach (DataRow order in orders)
  {
    Console.WriteLine("  OrderID = " + order["OrderID"]);
  }

}
```

```
    // close the database connection using the Close() method
    // of the SqlConnection object
    mySqlConnection.Close();

  }

}
```

The output from this program is as follows:

```
CustomerID = ALFKI
CompanyName = Alfreds Futterkiste
This customer placed the following orders:
  OrderID = 10643
  OrderID = 10692
  OrderID = 10702
  OrderID = 10835
  OrderID = 10952
  OrderID = 11011
```

Running a SQL Server Stored Procedure Using ADO.NET

In the previous chapter, you saw how to run a SQL Server stored procedure using the Query Analyzer tool. Specifically, you saw how to run the Ten Most Expensive Products stored procedure. You can also run stored procedure using ADO.NET.

Running a stored procedure using ADO.NET is similar to running any other type of SQL statement. You formulate a string containing the name of the procedure, add any parameters along with their values for the procedure call, and then use the ExecuteNonQuery() method to run the stored procedure.

One difference is that you must set the CommandType property of the SqlCommand object to CommandType.StoredProcedure. This tells ADO.NET that the SqlCommand is intended to run a stored procedure. For example:

```
mySqlCommand.CommandType = CommandType.StoredProcedure;
```

Listing 23.7 illustrates how to call the Ten Most Expensive Products stored procedure and display the returns results.

LISTING 23.7: RUNNING A SQL SERVER STORED PROCEDURE USING ADO.NET

```
/*
  Example23_7.cs illustrates how to call a SQL Server
  stored procedure
*/
```

```csharp
using System;
using System.Data;
using System.Data.SqlClient;

class Example23_7
{

  public static void Main()
  {

    // formulate a string containing the details of the
    // database connection
    string connectionString =
      "server=localhost;database=Northwind;uid=sa;pwd=sa";

    // create a SqlConnection object to connect to the
    // database, passing the connection string to the constructor
    SqlConnection mySqlConnection =
      new SqlConnection(connectionString);

    // formulate a string containing the name of the
    // stored procedure
    string procedureString =
      "Ten Most Expensive Products";

    // create a SqlCommand object to hold the SQL statement
    SqlCommand mySqlCommand = mySqlConnection.CreateCommand();

    // set the CommandText property of the SqlCommand object to
    // procedureString
    mySqlCommand.CommandText = procedureString;

    // set the CommandType property of the SqlCommand object
    // to CommandType.StoredProcedure
    mySqlCommand.CommandType = CommandType.StoredProcedure;

    // open the database connection using the
    // Open() method of the SqlConnection object
    mySqlConnection.Open();

    // run the stored procedure
    mySqlCommand.ExecuteNonQuery();

    // create a SqlDataAdapter object
    SqlDataAdapter mySqlDataAdapter = new SqlDataAdapter();
```

```
// set the SelectCommand property of the SqlAdapter object
// to the SqlCommand object
mySqlDataAdapter.SelectCommand = mySqlCommand;

// create a DataSet object to store the results of
// the stored procedure call
DataSet myDataSet = new DataSet();

// use the Fill() method of the SqlDataAdapter object to
// retrieve the rows from the stored procedure call,
// storing the rows in a DataTable named Products
mySqlDataAdapter.Fill(myDataSet, "Products");

// display the rows in the Products DataTable
Console.WriteLine("The ten most expensive products are:");
DataTable products = myDataSet.Tables["Products"];
foreach (DataRow product in products.Rows)
{
  Console.WriteLine("Product name = " +
    product["TenMostExpensiveProducts"]);
  Console.WriteLine("Unit price = " +
    product["UnitPrice"]);

}

// close the database connection using the Close() method
// of the SqlConnection object
mySqlConnection.Close();

}

}
```

The output from this program is as follows:

```
Product name = Côte de Blaye
Unit price = 263.5
Product name = Thüringer Rostbratwurst
Unit price = 123.79
Product name = Mishi Kobe Niku
Unit price = 97
Product name = Sir Rodney's Marmalade
Unit price = 81
Product name = Carnarvon Tigers
Unit price = 62.5
Product name = Raclette Courdavault
Unit price = 55
```

```
Product name = Manjimup Dried Apples
Unit price = 53
Product name = Tarte au sucre
Unit price = 49.3
Product name = Ipoh Coffee
Unit price = 46
Product name = Rössle Sauerkraut
Unit price = 45.6
```

Writing and Reading XML Files Using ADO.NET

You can write the contents of the DataTable objects contained in a DataSet out to an XML file using the WriteXml() method. The XML file written by this method contains the DataTable name, the column names, and the column values.

You can write the schema of a DataSet object out to an XML file using the WriteXmlSchema() method. The XML file written by this method contains the structure of the DataTable objects contained in the DataSet.

Similarly, you can read the contents of the DataTable objects in an XML file into a DataSet object using the ReadXml() method. You can also read the schema contained in an XML file using the ReadXmlSchema() method.

Using the *WriteXml()* Method

Let's say you have a DataSet object named myDataSet. Assume that myDataSet has a DataTable that contains the CustomerID, CompanyName, ContactName, and Address columns for the first two rows from the Customers table. You can write the contents of myDataSet out to an XML file using the WriteXml() method. For example:

```
myDataSet.WriteXml("myXmlFile.xml");
```

This writes an XML file named myXmlFile.xml that contains the following lines:

```xml
<?xml version="1.0" standalone="yes"?>
<NewDataSet>
  <Customers>
    <CustomerID>ALFKI</CustomerID>
    <CompanyName>Alfreds Futterkiste</CompanyName>
    <ContactName>Maria Anders</ContactName>
    <Address>Obere Str. 57</Address>
  </Customers>
  <Customers>
    <CustomerID>ANATR</CustomerID>
    <CompanyName>Ana Trujillo Emparedados y helados</CompanyName>
    <ContactName>Ana Trujillo</ContactName>
    <Address>Avda. de la Constitución 2222</Address>
  </Customers>
</NewDataSet>
```

As you can see, this file contains the columns for the rows retrieved from the Customers table.

Using the *WriteXmlSchema()* Method

You can write the schema of myDataSet out to an XML file using the WriteXmlSchema() method. For example:

```
myDataSet.WriteXmlSchema("myXmlSchemaFile.xml");
```

This writes an XML file named myXmlSchemaFile.xml that contains the following lines:

```xml
<?xml version="1.0" standalone="yes"?>
<xsd:schema id="NewDataSet" targetNamespace="" xmlns=""
 xmlns:xsd="http://www.w3.org/2001/XMLSchema"
 xmlns:msdata="urn:schemas-microsoft-com:xml-msdata">
  <xsd:element name="NewDataSet" msdata:IsDataSet="true">
    <xsd:complexType>
      <xsd:choice maxOccurs="unbounded">
        <xsd:element name="Customers">
          <xsd:complexType>
            <xsd:sequence>
              <xsd:element name="CustomerID" type="xsd:string" minOccurs="0" />
              <xsd:element name="CompanyName" type="xsd:string" minOccurs="0" />
              <xsd:element name="ContactName" type="xsd:string" minOccurs="0" />
              <xsd:element name="Address" type="xsd:string" minOccurs="0" />
            </xsd:sequence>
          </xsd:complexType>
        </xsd:element>
      </xsd:choice>
    </xsd:complexType>
  </xsd:element>
</xsd:schema>
```

This file contains the structure of the DataSet object.

Using the *ReadXml()* Method

You can read the contents of an XML file into a DataSet object using the ReadXml() method. This method reads the rows and columns from the XML file into DataTable objects of the DataSet. For example, the following statement uses the ReadXml() method to read the XML file myXmlFile.xml previously written by the WriteXml() method:

```
myDataSet.ReadXml("myXmlFile.xml");
```

Listing 23.8 illustrates how to write and read XML files using ADO.NET.

LISTING 23.8: WRITING AND READING XML FILES USING ADO.NET

```
/*
  Example23_8.cs illustrates how to write and read XML files
*/
```

```csharp
using System;
using System.Data;
using System.Data.SqlClient;

class Example23_8
{

  public static void Main()
  {

    // formulate a string containing the details of the
    // database connection
    string connectionString =
      "server=localhost;database=Northwind;uid=sa;pwd=sa";

    // create a SqlConnection object to connect to the
    // database, passing the connection string to the constructor
    SqlConnection mySqlConnection =
      new SqlConnection(connectionString);

    // formulate a SELECT statement to retrieve the
    // CustomerID, CompanyName, ContactName, and Address
    // columns for the first two rows from the Customers table
    string selectString =
      "SELECT CustomerID, CompanyName, ContactName, Address " +
      "FROM Customers " +
      "WHERE CustomerID IN ('ALFKI', 'ANATR')";

    // create a SqlCommand object to hold the SELECT statement
    SqlCommand mySqlCommand = mySqlConnection.CreateCommand();

    // set the CommandText property of the SqlCommand object to
    // the SELECT string
    mySqlCommand.CommandText = selectString;

    // create a SqlDataAdapter object
    SqlDataAdapter mySqlDataAdapter = new SqlDataAdapter();

    // set the SelectCommand property of the SqlAdapter object
    // to the SqlCommand object
    mySqlDataAdapter.SelectCommand = mySqlCommand;

    // create a DataSet object to store the results of
    // the SELECT statement
    DataSet myDataSet = new DataSet();

    // open the database connection using the
    // Open() method of the SqlConnection object
    mySqlConnection.Open();
```

```
// use the Fill() method of the SqlDataAdapter object to
// retrieve the rows from the table, storing the rows locally
// in a DataTable of the DataSet object
Console.WriteLine("Retrieving rows from the Customers table");
mySqlDataAdapter.Fill(myDataSet, "Customers");

// get the DataTable object from the DataSet object
DataTable myDataTable = myDataSet.Tables["Customers"];

// use the WriteXml() method to write the DataSet out to an
// XML file
Console.WriteLine("Writing rows out to an XML file named " +
  "myXmlFile.xml");
myDataSet.WriteXml("myXmlFile.xml");

// use the WriteXmlSchema() method to write the schema of the
// DataSet out to an XML file
Console.WriteLine("Writing schema out to an XML file named " +
  "myXmlSchemaFile.xml");
myDataSet.WriteXmlSchema("myXmlSchemaFile.xml");

// use the Clear() method to clear the current rows in the DataSet
myDataSet.Clear();

// use the ReadXml() method to read the contents of the XML file
// into the DataSet
myDataSet.ReadXml("myXmlFile.xml");

// display the columns for each row in the DataTable,
// using a DataRow object to access each row in the DataTable
foreach (DataRow myDataRow in myDataTable.Rows)
{
  Console.WriteLine("CustomerID = " + myDataRow["CustomerID"]);
  Console.WriteLine("CompanyName = " + myDataRow["CompanyName"]);
  Console.WriteLine("ContactName = " + myDataRow["ContactName"]);
  Console.WriteLine("Address = " + myDataRow["Address"]);
}

// close the database connection using the Close() method
// of the SqlConnection object
mySqlConnection.Close();

  }

}
```

The output from this program is as follows:

```
Retrieving rows from the Customers table
Writing rows out to an XML file named myXmlFile.xml
Writing schema out to an XML file named myXmlSchemaFile.xml
CustomerID = ALFKI
CompanyName = Alfreds Futterkiste
ContactName = Maria Anders
Address = Obere Str. 57
CustomerID = ANATR
CompanyName = Ana Trujillo Emparedados y helados
ContactName = Ana Trujillo
Address = Avda. de la Constitución 2222
```

Summary

In this chapter, you learned how to access a database from a C# program using ADO.NET.

When accessing a database using ADO.NET, you connect to the database, retrieve the information you're interested in, and store that information in the memory of the computer on which the C# program is running. Once you have that information in memory, you can then read and manipulate that information. Periodically, you reconnect to the database to synchronize your changes you've made locally with the database.

You use an object of the DataSet class to store a local copy of information retrieved from the database, and you can store various objects in a DataSet that represents database or XML information. For example, you use an object of the DataTable class to represent a database table.

You use objects of the managed provider classes to connect to the database and to read and write information to and from your DataSet object. Managed provider objects provide direct access to the database and allow you to synchronize your locally stored data with the database.

Some of the managed provider classes include SqlConnection, SqlCommand, SqlDataReader, Sql-DataAdapter, and SqlTransaction. You use an object of the SqlConnection class to connect to a SQL Server database. You use an object of the SqlCommand class to represent a SQL statement or stored procedure call that you then execute. You use an object of the SqlDataReader class to read rows retrieved from a SQL Server database. You use an object of the SqlDataAdapter class to move rows between a DataSet object and a SQL Server database. You use an object of the SqlTransaction class to represent a database transaction in a SQL Server database.

You use an object of the DataSet class to represent a local copy of the information stored in a database. You can also use a DataSet object to represent XML data. Within a DataSet object, you can store objects of the following classes: DataTable, DataRow, DataColumn, DataRelation, and DataView.

Specifically, you use an object of the DataTable class to represent a table. You use an object of the DataRow class to represent a row. You use an object of the DataColumn class to represent a column. You use an object of the DataRelation class to represent a relationship between two DataTable objects. You use a DataRelation object to model parent-child relationships between two database tables. You use an object of the DataView class to view only specific rows in a DataTable object using a filter.

In the next chapter, you'll learn how to create Windows programs.

Chapter 24

Introduction to Windows Applications

IN THE PREVIOUS CHAPTERS, you ran programs using the Windows Command Prompt tool. In this chapter, you'll be introduced to Windows applications. A Windows application takes advantage of displaying and using the mouse, as well as the keyboard, for input. Windows provides graphical items such as menus, text boxes, and radio buttons so you can build a visual interface that will be easy to use.

As you know, Windows applications are simple to learn and use because human beings are used to interacting with machines in a visual manner. Some widely successful Windows applications include Microsoft Word and Excel.

The idea of using graphical user interfaces (GUIs) and a mouse to interact with a computer is not unique to Windows. In fact, these concepts were originally developed back in the early 1970s by engineers at Xerox Corporation's Palo Alto Research Center (PARC) in California, and one of the first computers to use a GUI and a mouse was the Alto. Unfortunately, the Alto was expensive, and it wasn't until Apple Computer launched the Macintosh in 1984 that the GUI became popular. Later, Microsoft developed the Windows operating system that built on the ideas made popular by Apple.

NOTE *You'll see the use of Visual Studio .NET (VS .NET) to build some Windows applications in this chapter. You could develop Windows applications without the use of VS .NET by hand-coding them using Notepad—but that's typically not the way most real Windows applications are built.*

Featured in this chapter:

◆ Developing a Simple Windows Application

◆ Using Windows Controls

◆ Accessing a Database with a *DataGrid* Control

◆ Creating a Windows Form with the Data Form Wizard

Developing a Simple Windows Application

In this section, you'll see how to create a simple Windows application using Visual Studio .NET (VS .NET). This application will consist of a single form that contains a label and a button. When you click the button, the text for the label will change to a quote from Shakespeare's play, *Macbeth*. You'll also see how to compile and run the example application.

Creating the Windows Application

Start VS .NET by selecting Start ➤ Programs ➤ Microsoft Visual Studio .NET ➤ Microsoft Visual Studio .NET. To create a new Windows application, click the New Project button on the Start page or select File ➤ New ➤ Project.

TIP *You can also create a new project by pressing Ctrl+Shift+N on your keyboard.*

You'll see the New Project dialog box, which you use to select the type of project that you want to create. Because you're going to create a Windows application, select Windows Application from the Templates area of the New Project dialog box. VS .NET will assign a default name to your project; this default name will be `WindowsApplication1` or something similar. You can specify your own name for your project by changing the text in the Name field; enter **MyWindowsApplication** in the Name field, as shown in Figure 24.1.

FIGURE 24.1

Creating a Windows application in Visual Studio .NET

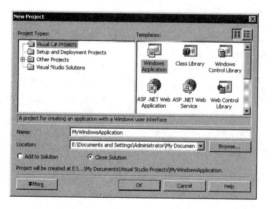

NOTE *The Location field specifies the directory where the files for your new project are stored. VS .NET will set a default directory, but you can change this by entering your own directory. This default directory is the* `Documents and Settings/YourLogon/My Documents/Visual Studio Projects` *directory on your hard drive.*

Click the OK button to continue. VS .NET will create a new subdirectory named `MyWindows-Application` in the directory specified in the Location field. Once VS .NET creates the directory, along with some initial files for your project, VS .NET will display a blank form, as shown in Figure 24.2. You can think of the form as the canvas on which you can place standard Windows controls, such as labels, text boxes, and buttons. You'll be adding controls to your form shortly.

FIGURE 24.2

A blank form

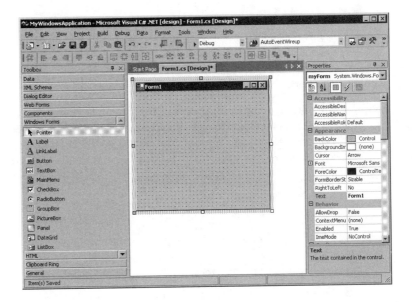

In the next section, you'll learn about the Toolbox, which you use to add controls to your form.

WORKING WITH THE TOOLBOX

You add controls to your form by selecting the control from the Toolbox and dragging the control to your form. You can also click and draw, or you can double-click the control to have a new one of that type of control dropped onto your form. As you can see in Figure 24.2 shown earlier, the Toolbox is to the left of the blank form.

NOTE *If you don't see the Toolbox, you can display it by selecting View ➤ Toolbox or by pressing Ctrl+Alt+X on your keyboard.*

You can see that the available items in the Toolbox are categorized into groups with names such as Data and XML Schema. The Toolbox will only show categories that are relevant to the type of application you are developing. The following list describes the contents of some of these categories:

Data   The Data category contains classes that allow you to access and store information from a database. The Data category includes the following classes: `SqlConnection`, `SqlCommand`, `DataSet`, and `DataView`, among others. You learned about these classes in Chapter 23, "Active Data Objects: ADO.NET."

XML Schema   The XML Schema category contains classes that allow you to access XML data. The XML Schema category doesn't show up when you're developing a Windows application.

Dialog Editor   The Dialog Editor category contains controls that you can place on Windows dialog boxes. The Dialog Editor category doesn't show up when you're developing a Windows application.

Web Forms   The Web Forms category contains controls that are for web forms. You can design web forms using VS .NET and deploy them to Microsoft's Internet Information Server (IIS). These web forms may then be run over the Internet. You'll learn about web forms in Chapter 25, "Active Server Pages: ASP.NET." The Web Forms category doesn't show up when you're developing a Windows application.

Components   The Components category contains classes such as `FileSystemWatcher`, which allows you to monitor changes in a computer's file system. Other classes include `EventLog`, `DirectoryEntry`, `DirectorySearcher`, `MessageQueue`, `PerformanceCounter`, `Process`, `Service-Controller`, and `Timer`. These allow you to perform various system operations.

Windows Forms   The Windows Forms category contains controls that you can add to a Windows form. These include labels, buttons, and text boxes, among others. You'll use some of these controls in this chapter.

HTML   The HTML category contains controls that you can add to a web form. These include labels, buttons, tables, and images, among others. The HTML category doesn't show up when you're developing a Windows application.

In the next section, you'll learn about the Properties window.

WORKING WITH THE PROPERTIES WINDOW

The Properties window contains aspects of a control that you can set. For example, you can set the background color of your form using the `BackColor` property. Some other properties of the form control include `ForeColor` (the foreground color) and `BackgroundImage` (an image displayed in the background). Different types of controls have different types of properties.

As you can see from Figure 24.2 shown earlier, the Properties window is to the right of the blank form.

NOTE   *If you don't see the Properties window, you can display it by selecting View* ➤ *Properties Window or by pressing F4 on your keyboard.*

You set the property by clicking the area to the right of the property name. Click to the right of the `BackColor` property to view some of the colors to which you can set this property.

In the next section, you'll learn how to add a label and button control to your form. You'll also set a couple of the properties for those controls.

ADDING A LABEL AND A BUTTON CONTROL

Add a label and button control to your form. You do this by selecting the appropriate control from the Toolbox and dragging it to your form. For example, to add a label to your form, you select the label control from the Toolbox. Once you've dragged a label to your form, you can resize it by using the mouse or by setting the `Size` property in the Properties window. You can also click the label in the Toolbox and draw it on your form, which is more efficient as this is a single operation.

Make your label big enough so that that it stretches across the length of your form. Next, add a button control below your label, as shown in Figure 24.3.

FIGURE 24.3

The form with a label and button control

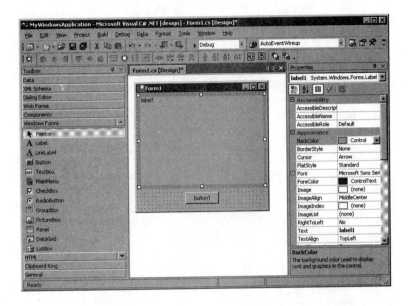

Next, you'll change some of the properties for your label and button. You do this using the Properties window. Set the Name property of your label to myLabel. Set the Name and Text properties for your button to myButton and Press Me!, respectively. Also, set the Name and Text properties for your form to myForm and My Form, respectively.

NOTE *You use the* Name *property when referencing a Windows control in C# code.*

Next, you'll add a line of code to the myButton_Click() method. This method is executed when myButton is clicked in your running form. The statement you'll add to myButton_Click() will set the Text property of myLabel to a string. This string will contain a line from Shakespeare's play, *Macbeth*. To add the code, double-click myButton and enter the following code in the myButton_Click() method:

```
myLabel.Text =
  "Is this a dagger which I see before me,\n" +
  "The handle toward my hand? Come, let me clutch thee.\n" +
  "I have thee not, and yet I see thee still.\n" +
  "Art thou not, fatal vision, sensible\n" +
  "To feeling as to sight? or art thou but\n" +
  "A dagger of the mind, a false creation,\n" +
  "Proceeding from the heat-oppressed brain?";
```

NOTE *If you're a Shakespeare fan, you'll recognize this line from the scene before Macbeth kills King Duncan.*

You've now finished your form. Build your project by selecting Build ➤ Build Solution or by pressing Ctrl+Shift+B on your keyboard.

To run your form, select Debug ➤ Start without Debugging, or press Ctrl+F5 on your keyboard.

TIP *You can take a shortcut when building and running your form: If you simply start your form without first building it, VS .NET will check to see if you made any changes to your form since you last ran it. If you did make a change, VS .NET will first rebuild your project and then run it.*

Figure 24.4 shows the running form after the button is clicked.

FIGURE 24.4

The running form

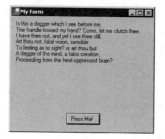

Now that you've created and run the form, let's take a look at the code generated by VS .NET for your form. The C# code for your form is contained in the file Form1.cs file. You'll examine this code in the next section.

Examining the *Form1.cs* File

The Form1.cs file contains the code for your form. This code is often referred to as the *code behind* your form because you can think of it as being behind the visual design for your form. You can view the code for your form by selecting View ➤ Code or by pressing the F7 key on your keyboard.

Listing 24.1 shows the contents of the Form1.cs file.

LISTING 24.1: Form1.cs

```
using System;
using System.Drawing;
using System.Collections;
using System.ComponentModel;
using System.Windows.Forms;
using System.Data;

namespace MyWindowsApplication
{
  /// <summary>
  /// Summary description for Form1.
  /// </summary>
  public class Form1 : System.Windows.Forms.Form
  {
    private System.Windows.Forms.Label myLabel;
    private System.Windows.Forms.Button myButton;
    /// <summary>
    /// Required designer variable.
```

```csharp
/// </summary>
private System.ComponentModel.Container components = null;

public Form1()
{
  //
  // Required for Windows Form Designer support
  //
  InitializeComponent();

  //
  // TODO: Add any constructor code after InitializeComponent call
  //
}

/// <summary>
/// Clean up any resources being used.
/// </summary>
protected override void Dispose( bool disposing )
{
  if( disposing )
  {
    if (components != null)
    {
      components.Dispose();
    }
  }
  base.Dispose( disposing );
}

#region Windows Form Designer generated code
/// <summary>
/// Required method for Designer support - do not modify
/// the contents of this method with the code editor.
/// </summary>
private void InitializeComponent()
{
  this.myLabel = new System.Windows.Forms.Label();
  this.myButton = new System.Windows.Forms.Button();
  this.SuspendLayout();
  //
  // myLabel
  //
  this.myLabel.Location = new System.Drawing.Point(8, 8);
  this.myLabel.Name = "myLabel";
  this.myLabel.Size = new System.Drawing.Size(288, 184);
  this.myLabel.TabIndex = 0;
  this.myLabel.Text = "label1";
```

```
//
// myButton
//
this.myButton.Location = new System.Drawing.Point(120, 200);
this.myButton.Name = "myButton";
this.myButton.Size = new System.Drawing.Size(72, 24);
this.myButton.TabIndex = 1;
this.myButton.Text = "Press Me!";
this.myButton.Click += new System.EventHandler(this.myButton_Click);
//
// Form1
//
this.AutoScaleBaseSize = new System.Drawing.Size(5, 13);
this.ClientSize = new System.Drawing.Size(304, 237);
this.Controls.AddRange(new System.Windows.Forms.Control[] {
  this.myButton,
  this.myLabel});
this.Name = "Form1";
this.Text = "My Form";
this.ResumeLayout(false);

}
#endregion

/// <summary>
/// The main entry point for the application.
/// </summary>
[STAThread]
static void Main()
{
  Application.Run(new Form1());
}

private void myButton_Click(object sender, System.EventArgs e)
{
  myLabel.Text =
    "Is this a dagger which I see before me,\n" +
    "The handle toward my hand? Come, let me clutch thee.\n" +
    "I have thee not, and yet I see thee still.\n" +
    "Art thou not, fatal vision, sensible\n" +
    "To feeling as to sight? or art thou but\n" +
    "A dagger of the mind, a false creation,\n" +
    "Proceeding from the heat-oppressed brain?";

  }
 }
}
```

As you can see, the `Form1` class is derived from the `System.Windows.Forms.Form` class. The `Form` class represents a Windows form.

NOTE   The `System.Windows.Forms` namespace contains the various classes for creating Windows applications. Most of the classes in this namespace are derived from the `System.Windows.Forms.Control` class; this class provides the basic functionality for the controls you can place on a form.

The `Form1` class declares two private objects named `myLabel` and `myButton`, which are the label and button controls you added to your form earlier. Private is an access modifier that was covered in Chapter 5, "Object-Oriented Programming." Because the `myLabel` and `myButton` objects are private, this means they are only accessible in the `Form1` class.

The `Form1` class constructor calls the `InitializeComponent()` method. This method adds `myLabel` and `myButton` to the form and sets the properties for those objects. These properties include the `Location` (the position in the form), `Name`, `Size`, `TabIndex` (the order in which the control is accessed using the tab key), and `Text`. For example, the following code sets the properties of `myLabel`:

```
this.myLabel.Location = new System.Drawing.Point(8, 8);
this.myLabel.Name = "myLabel";
this.myLabel.Size = new System.Drawing.Size(288, 184);
this.myLabel.TabIndex = 0;
this.myLabel.Text = "label1";
```

You'll notice that the `InitializeComponent()` method is within `#region` and `#endregion` preprocessor directives. These directives enclose an area of code that may be hidden in VS .NET's code editor, leaving only the text that immediately follows `#region` visible. Figure 24.5 shows how the hidden code appears in VS .NET.

FIGURE 24.5

Hiding code in VS .NET using the `#region` directive

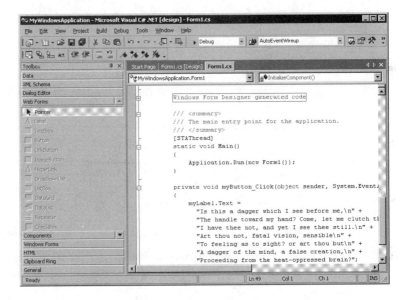

To view hidden code, all you have to do is to click the plus icon to the left of the code. Figure 24.6 shows the code within the #region and #endregion directives.

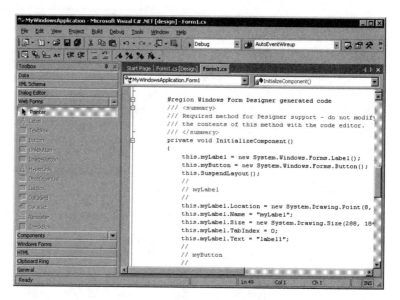

FIGURE 24.6

Viewing hidden code in VS .NET

The Main() method runs the form by calling the Application.Run() method. The Application class is static and provides a number of methods you can use in your Windows programs. Because this class is static, you don't create an instance of this class and its members are always available within your form. When the Run() method is called, your form waits for events from the mouse and keyboard. One example of an event is the clicking of the button in your form.

The myButton_Click() method is the method you modified earlier that sets the Text property of myLabel to a string containing the quote from *Macbeth*. When myButton is clicked, the myButton_Click() method is called and the text in myLabel is changed—you saw this when you ran your form earlier.

In the next section, you'll learn about the VS .NET Solution Explorer.

Working with the Solution Explorer

You can use the VS .NET Solution Explorer to view the items in your project—such as the namespace for your project. Of course, a project may contain more than one namespace. To view the Solution Explorer, you select View ➤ Solution Explorer.

TIP   You can also view the Solution Explorer by pressing Ctrl+Alt+L on your keyboard.

You can use Solution Explorer to view the following items in a project's namespace:

References   References include other namespaces and classes to which your form's code refers. You can use the using statement to reference other namespaces and classes.

Icon File   An icon file has the extension .ico. You use an icon file to set the image displayed in Windows Explorer for your application.

Assembly File   An assembly file contains the metadata for your application's assembly.

Code Files   A code file is a program source file, such as the code for a form. You saw an example of this in the earlier "The *Form1.cs* File" section.

Figure 24.7 shows the Solution Explorer for this example.

FIGURE 24.7

The Solution
Explorer

As you can see from Figure 24.7, you can expand the items shown in the Solution Explorer by clicking an icon containing the plus sign. Similarly, you can collapse an item by clicking an icon containing the minus sign. You can also display the properties for an item in Solution Explorer: When you have the Properties window displayed, selecting an item in Solution Explorer will also display the properties for that item. For example, in Figure 24.7, the properties for the MyWindowsApplication project are displayed; you can see that the project file is MyWindowsApplication.csproj.

In the next section, you'll learn about the VS .NET Class View.

Working with the Class View

You use the VS .NET Class View to examine the classes, methods, and objects in your project. To see the Class View, you select View ➤ Class View.

TIP   *You can also see the Class View by pressing Ctrl+Shift+C on your keyboard.*

Figure 24.8 shows the Class View for the example.

FIGURE 24.8

The Class View

As you can see from Figure 24.8, you can see the classes, methods, and objects for the example. You can also view the properties for a selected item in the Properties window. For example, Figure 24.8 also shows the properties for the Form1 class.

Next, you'll be introduced to the other types of Windows controls.

Using Windows Controls

Table 24.1 lists the commonly used Windows form controls that you can pick from the Windows Forms section of the Toolbox. You can place any of these controls on your Windows form.

TABLE 24.1: COMMONLY USED WINDOWS FORM CONTROLS

CONTROL	DESCRIPTION
Label	Displays text. You set the text that you want to display using the Text property.
LinkLabel	Similar to a label, except it displays hyperlinks. You set the hyperlink that you want to display using the Text property. You set the navigation via the LinkClicked event.
Button	A clickable button. The Text property determines the text shown on the button.
TextBox	A box containing text that the user of your form may edit at run-time. The Text property contains the text contained in the TextBox.
MainMenu	A menu you can add to a form.
CheckBox	A check box contains a Boolean true/false value that is set to true by the user if they check the box. The Checked property indicates the Boolean value.
RadioButton	A radio button contains a Boolean true/false value that is set to true by the user if they click the button. The Checked property indicates the Boolean value.
GroupBox	A group box allows you to group related controls together. For example, you can group related radio buttons together. Most importantly, it allows you to treat multiple controls as a group. This differentiates between a panel, which allows you to move controls as a group in VS .NET.
PictureBox	A picture box displays an image that you set using the Image property.
Panel	A container for other controls such as radio buttons or group boxes.
DataGrid	A grid containing data retrieved from a data source, such as a database. You set the data source using the DataSource property. You'll learn about databases in Chapter 25.
ListBox	A list of options. You set the list of options using the Add() method of the Items collection property.
CheckedListBox	Similar to a list box except that a check mark is placed to the left of each item in the list. The check mark allows the user to select the items via a check box, as opposed to multiselecting with the Shift and/or Control keys.
ComboBox	Combines an editable field with a list box.

In the next section, you'll learn how to use a DataGrid control to access the rows in a database table.

Using a *DataGrid* Control to Access a Database

In this section, you'll learn how to use a `DataGrid` control to access the rows in a database table. A `DataGrid` allows you to access rows in a database table. You can create a `DataGrid` using VS .NET.

First, select File ➤ New Project. In the New Project dialog box, select Windows Application and enter **DataGridWindowsApplication** in the Name field. Second, click OK to continue. Your new project will contain a blank form.

Next, you'll add a `DataGrid` control to the form. To do this, select View ➤ Toolbox and then select `DataGrid`. Move the mouse pointer over the form to add a `DataGrid` to the form, as shown in Figure 24.9. Go ahead and make the `DataGrid` bigger.

FIGURE 24.9

Form with a
`DataGrid`

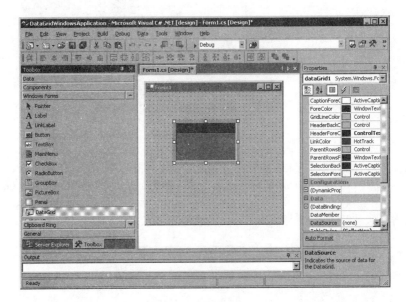

Next, you'll add a `SqlConnection` object and a `SqlDataAdapter` object to your form.

NOTE   *In Chapter 23, you learned that you use a `SqlConnection` object to connect to a SQL Server database, and you use a `SqlDataAdapter` object to move rows between SQL Server and a `DataSet` object.*

In certain versions of VS .NET, such as Enterprise Architect (the version used in this book), you can drag a table from a SQL Server database onto your form and have the `SqlConnection` and `SqlDataAdapter` objects created in one step. You use the Server Explorer for this. In other versions of VS .NET, or with databases that do not show up in the Server Explorer, your choices are limited. You can use the controls in Data category of the Toolbox to drag each item to your form and then set properties for each data object with the Properties window. We'll assume you are using the Enterprise Architect version of VS .NET.

To add a `SqlConnection` and `SqlDataAdapter` object to your form, select the `Customers` table in the Server Explorer and drag it to your form. This creates a `SqlConnection` object named `sqlConnection1` and a `SqlDataAdapter` object named `sqlDataAdapter1`, as shown in Figure 24.10.

FIGURE 24.10

Form with
`SqlConnection` and
`SqlDataAdapter`
objects

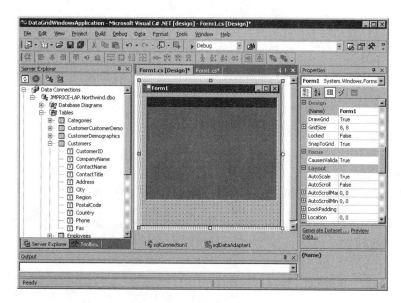

Click your `sqlConnection1` object to display the properties for this object in the Properties window. To enable `sqlConnection1` to access the database, you need to set the password for the connection. To do this, you need to add a substring containing `pwd` to the `ConnectionString` property of `sqlConnection1`. Add `pwd=sa` (or use the password suggested by your database administrator) to the `ConnectionString` property, as shown in Figure 24.13.

FIGURE 24.11

Setting the
`ConnectionString`
property for the
`sqlConnection1`
object

NOTE   *You may need to get the password for the* sa *user from your database administrator.*

Next, you'll modify the SQL SELECT statement used to retrieve the rows from the Customers table. Click your `sqlDataAdapter1` object to display the properties for this object. Then click the addition icon to the left of the `SelectCommand` property to display the dynamic properties; one of the dynamic properties is the `CommandText` property, which contains the `SELECT` statement (see Figure 24.12).

FIGURE 24.12

`SelectCommand`
property for the
`sqlDataAdapter1`
object

Click `CommandText` and then click the button with the ellipsis to display the Query Builder, as shown in Figure 24.13.

FIGURE 24.13

The Query Builder

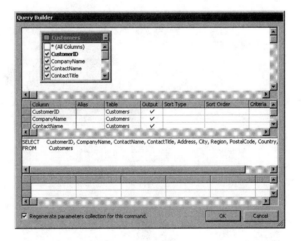

You use the Query Builder to define SQL statements. You can type in the SQL statement, or you can build it up visually. Uncheck all the columns except `CustomerID` and `CompanyName` from the `Customers` table using the `Customers` box at the top left of Query Builder. This results in the SQL `SELECT` statement being set to the following (see Figure 24.16):

```
SELECT CustomerID, CompanyName
FROM Customers
```

FIGURE 24.14

The modified
SELECT statement

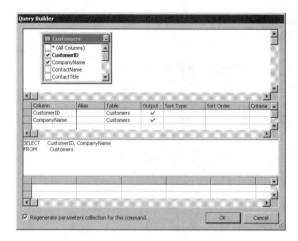

Click OK to continue. To check the rows returned by this SELECT statement, you click the Preview Data link near the bottom of the Properties window. This displays the Data Adapter Preview dialog box. Click this link and then click the Fill Dataset button in the Data Adapter Preview dialog box to run the SELECT statement, as shown in Figure 24.15.

FIGURE 24.15

Previewing the rows
retrieved by the
SELECT statement

Click the Close button to close the Data Adapter Preview dialog box. Next, you need to create a DataSet object.

NOTE *You use a* DataSet *object to a store local copy of the information stored in the database. A* DataSet *object has the capability of representing database structures such as tables, rows, and columns, among others. In this example, you'll use a* DataSet *object to store the rows from the* Customers *table.*

Click an area of your form outside of the DataGrid. Next, click the Generate Dataset link near the bottom of the Properties window. This displays the Generate Dataset dialog box. Select the New radio button and make sure the field to the right of this radio button contains DataSet1, as shown in Figure 24.18.

FIGURE 24.16

Entering the DataSet details in the Generate Dataset dialog box

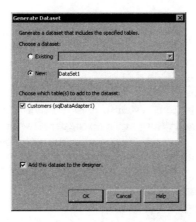

Click the OK button to continue. This adds a new DataSet object named dataSet1 to your form.

Next, you'll need to set the DataSource property of your DataGrid to your DataSet object. This sets the source of the data for your DataGrid—this allows the rows from your DataSet to be displayed in your DataGrid. To set the DataSource property, click your DataGrid object and set the DataSource property to dataSet1.Customers.

Next, you'll add a button that will fill sqlDataAdapter1 with the rows retrieved by your SELECT statement. Select Button from the Toolbox and drag it onto your form to a position just below your DataGrid. This creates a new button. Set the Text property for your button to Run SELECT in the Properties window.

To populate sqlDataAdapter1 with the rows retrieved by the SELECT statement, you'll need to call the Fill() method for this object. You'll call this method when the button is clicked. To add the required code, double-click the button you added earlier. This opens the code window and positions the cursor in the button1_Click() method. Enter the following code in this method:

```
dataSet11.Clear();
sqlDataAdapter1.Fill(dataSet11, "Customers");
```

NOTE *You could also call the* Fill() *method in the* Form1_Load *event. This event occurs when the form is initially loaded.*

Next, you'll add another button that will allow you to save any changes you make to the rows in the DataGrid. Add another button and set the Text property of this button to Update. Double-click this button and add the following statement to the button2_Click() method:

```
sqlDataAdapter1.Update(dataSet11, "Customers");
```

This statement calls the `Update()` method for the `sqlDataAdpater1` object. This method commits any changes you make to the rows in your `DataGrid` to the database.

One last thing you need to do is to set the `CommandText` property of the `sqlUpdateCommand1` object. Set this property to the following `UPDATE` statement:

```
UPDATE Customers
SET CustomerID = @CustomerID, CompanyName = @CompanyName
WHERE (CustomerID = @Original_CustomerID)
```

This `UPDATE` statement updates a row with the new column values you enter in your `DataGrid`. You've now finished your form. Build the project by selecting Build ➤ Build Solution.

Finally, you're ready to run your form! Select Debug ➤ Start without Debugging to start your form. Click the Run SELECT button on your form to run your `SELECT` statement. This retrieves the rows from the `Customers` table and displays them in the `DataGrid` of your form. Next, modify the `CompanyName` column of the first row to `Alfreds Futterkiste Shoppe` and click the Update button—this commits the change you made to the row in the `Customers` table (see Figure 24.17).

FIGURE 24.17

The running form

In the next section, you learn how to use the VS .NET Data Form Wizard to create a more advanced Windows application that accesses the Northwind database.

Using the Data Form Wizard to Create a Windows Form

In this section, you'll use the VS .NET Data Form Wizard to create a Windows application that accesses both the `Customers` and `Orders` tables. The `Orders` table contains rows that represent orders placed by the customers.

The rows in the `Orders` table are related to the rows in the `Customers` table through a foreign key: The `Orders` table contains a column named `CustomerID` that is a foreign key to the `CustomerID` column of the `Customers` table. The use of the foreign key defines a parent-child relationship between the `Customers` and `Orders` tables.

The form you'll learn how to create in this section will display a row from the `Customers` table, along with any related rows from the `Orders` table. To give you a clear idea of the final goal of this section, Figure 24.18 shows the completed form up and running. Notice that the top part of the form shows the details for the row from the `Customers` table where the `CustomerID` is `ALFKI`; the bottom part of the form contains a `DataGrid` control that displays the rows from the `Orders` table for that customer. When you move to the next row in the Customers table, the rows from the Orders table for that customer are automatically displayed in the DataGrid.

FIGURE 24.18

The running form

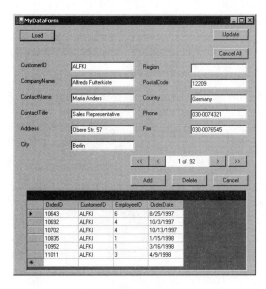

To get started building the form, select File ➤ New Project. In the New Project dialog box, select Empty Project and enter **DataFormWindowsApplication** in the Name field. Because you'll be adding a new form to your new application shortly, there's no need to have VS .NET generate the usual blank form for you—that's why you're creating an empty project.

Click OK to continue. VS .NET will create a new, empty project for you.

Next, you'll use the Data Form Wizard to create a form that accesses the Customers and Orders tables in the Northwind database. Select Project ➤ Add New Item. Then select Data Form Wizard from the Templates section on the right and click Open (see Figure 24.19).

FIGURE 24.19

Adding a data form using the Data Form Wizard

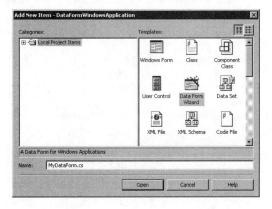

You'll then see the welcome page for the Data Form Wizard. Click the Next button to proceed.

Your next step is to enter the `DataSet` object you want to use in your form. You can pick an existing `DataSet`, or you can create a new one. Because this is a new project, you'll be creating a new `DataSet`. Enter **myDataSet** as the name for your `DataSet`, as shown in Figure 24.20.

FIGURE 24.20

Entering the name of the new `DataSet`

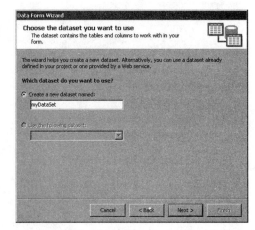

Click the Next button to go to the next step.

You must now choose a data connection to access the database. You can pick an existing connection, or you can create a new one. You already created a connection earlier when you created the example application named `DataGridWindowsApplication` in the previous section. That earlier application used a `DataGrid` control that connected to the Northwind database. Select the connection you created earlier. Figure 24.21 shows selecting the connection for our computer; of course, your connection name will differ from ours. If you don't have a connection, refer back to the previous section to see how to create one.

FIGURE 24.21

Choosing the data connection

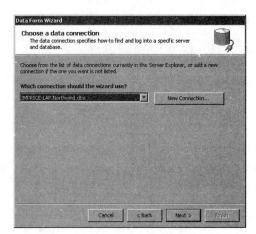

Click the Next button to continue.

Your next step is to log in to the database. You do this by specifying the password for the database user. You used the **sa** user when creating the database connection earlier, and you therefore need to reenter the password for that user, as shown in Figure 24.22.

FIGURE 24.22

Logging into the
SQL Server database

Click the OK button to proceed.

You now select the database tables or views you want to use in your form. The area on the bottom left of the dialog box shows the tables and views you can access using your form. The area on the bottom right shows the tables and views you've added. You add a table or view to your form by selecting it from the area on the left and clicking the button with the right arrow. You can also double-click the table or view and they will be added to your form. When you do this, the table or view moves to the right, indicating that you've selected them for use in your form. If you change your mind and decide you don't want to use a table or view, you can unselect them using the button with the left arrow. You can also double-click the table or view and they will be unselected. Select the **Customers** and **Orders** tables, as shown in Figure 24.23.

FIGURE 24.23

Selecting the
Customers and
Orders tables for
use in the form

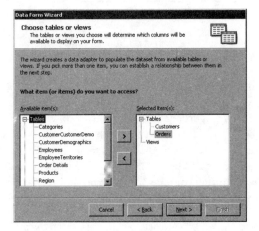

Click the Next button to proceed.

Because you selected two tables—the **Customers** and **Orders** tables—your next step is to define a relationship between those tables. This relationship is used in your form to synchronize navigation between the rows in the **Customers** table with the rows in the **Orders** table: When you move to a new row in the Customers table, the rows from the Orders table will be displayed in your form. Set the following in the dialog box (as shown in Figure 24.24):

◆ Enter **myRelationship** in the Name field.

◆ Select Customers as the parent table.

◆ Select Orders as the child table.

◆ Select CustomerID as the key for each table.

FIGURE 24.24

Creating a
relationship between
two tables

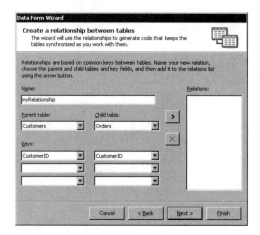

WARNING   *To add the relationship to your form, click the button with the right arrow. If you don't do this, your relationship won't be added to your form.*

Click the Next button to continue.

In the next step, you select the columns from the tables you want to display in your form. Because you added the Customers and Orders tables to your form, you'll be selecting the columns to display from these two tables. By default, all the columns from the tables are selected. You won't be displaying all the columns from the Customers or the Orders table. Unselect the City column for the Customers table —later, you'll see how to add this column to your form manually.

Next, deselect the following columns for the Orders table: RequiredDate, ShippedDate, ShipVia, Freight, ShipName, ShipAddress, ShipCity, ShipRegion, ShipPostalCode, and ShipCountry.

NOTE   *Remember: You're unselecting these columns, so you uncheck the columns for the Orders table.*

Figure 24.25 shows the completed dialog box with the selected columns to display from each table. Click the Next button to proceed.

Next, you select the display style for the rows (also known as *records*) in the parent table that are displayed in your form.

NOTE   *In this example, the parent table is the Customers table, and the child table is the Orders table. The rows for the child table are displayed in a DataGrid control.*

FIGURE 24.25

Selecting the
columns to display
from each table

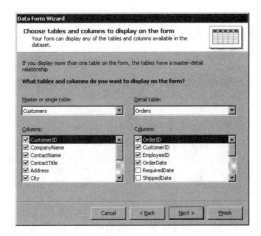

You can display the rows in a grid, or you can display each column using a separate control. You'll use a separate control for the columns, so select the Single Record in Individual Controls radio button. The other check boxes in the dialog box allow you pick the controls you want to add to your form. These controls affect the rows in the master table, and you can add the following controls to your form:

Cancel All   The Cancel All button allows you to undo any changes you've made to the current row.

Add   The Add button allows you to add a new row.

Delete   The Delete button allows you to delete the current row.

Cancel   The Cancel button allows you to cancel a change made to the current row.

Navigation Controls   The Navigation controls allow you to move to a different row. The Navigation controls consist of four buttons that allow you to move to first row, the previous row, the next row, and the last row. An indicator is also displayed to show the current row.
Figure 24.26 shows the completed dialog box.

FIGURE 24.26

Choosing the
display style

You've now completed all the steps in the Data Form Wizard. Click the Finish button to create your form.

VS .NET will now display the new form, as shown in Figure 24.27.

FIGURE 24.27

The completed form

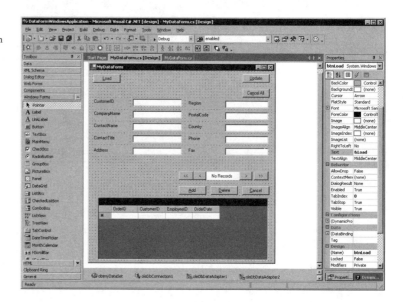

The managed provider objects in the form use the OLEDB classes contained in the `System .Data.OleDb` namespace—even though a SQL Server database is used. These objects work with any OLEDB-compliant database. The code would be more efficient if the managed provider classes in the `System.Data.SqlClient` namespace were used instead—these classes are specifically for use with a SQL Server database. This is the price of using the VS .NET wizard generate the code for you.

In the next section, you'll learn how the text box controls in your form access the columns in the `Customers` table.

Data Binding

Each text box control in the upper part of your form is bound to a column in the `Customers` table using a process known as *data binding*. When a control is bound to a column in a `DataSet` object, the value for that column is displayed in the control through the `Text` property in the `DataBindings` group. The `Text` property in the `DataBindings` group sets the text displayed in a control. To examine or set the data binding for a control, you select the control in the form designer and expand the `DataBindings` properties in the Properties window. You'll see these properties in the Data area of the Properties window.

Next, you'll see how the text box for the Customer ID is set. Select the text box to the right of the `CustomerID` label in your form—this text box is named `editCustomerID`. Make sure the `DataBindings` properties are expanded in the Properties window. Finally, click the drop-down list for the `Text` property to view the current column to which the text box is bound. As you can see from Figure 24.28, editCustomerID is bound to the CustomerID column of the Customers table. This means that when you run the form and load data from the database, the CustomerID column value will be displayed in the editCustomerID text box.

FIGURE 24.28

The edit-
CustomerID text
box is bound to the
CustomerID
column.

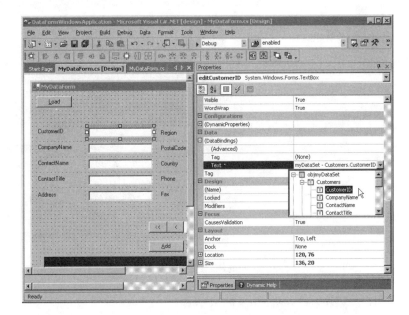

In the next section, you'll add a label and a text box control to display the City column in your form.

Adding Controls to the Form

When you ran the Data Form Wizard earlier to create your form, you'll recall that we told you to unselect the City column of the Customers table so that it didn't appear on your form. We asked you to do this so that you can now see how to manually add a control and bind it to the City column. That way, you can see how begin building your own forms that access the database.

You'll add a label and a text box to your form. Add a label below the Address label in your form. Set the Name property for your new label to lblCity. Set the Text property for your label to City. Next, add a text box below the editAddress text box. Set the Name property for your new text box to editCity. Remove the current text from the Text property so that no default text is shown in the control.

Next, you need to bind editCity to the City column of the Customers table. To do this, you open the DataBindings properties and select City from the Customers table, as shown in Figure 24.29.

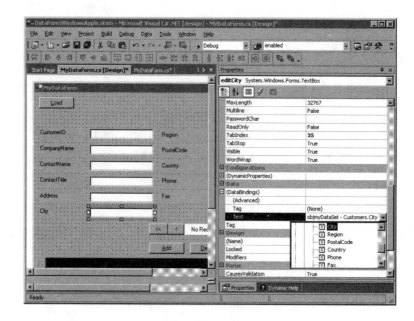

FIGURE 24.29

The new label and text box

In the next section, you'll add a Main() method to the code of your form.

Adding the *Main()* Method

As you know, all programs must have a Main() method. The Main() method is executed when you run your program. In this section, you'll add a Main() method to your form. To do this, select View ➤ Code and add the following Main() method inside your MyDataForm class (a good place to add Main() would be at the start of your MyDataForm class after the open curly bracket {):

```
public static void Main()
{
  Application.Run(new MyDataForm());
}
```

This code creates a new object of the MyDataForm class, causing your form to be displayed on the screen.

Setting the *pwd* Property

Before you can run your form, you need to set the password for the database user in the Connection-String property of the data connection object. This object was automatically created by VS .NET when you ran the Data Form Wizard, and the object has the default name oleDbConnection1.

To modify the ConnectionString property for oleDbConnection1, select oleDbConnection1 from the drop-down list in the Properties window. Add the text pwd=sa in the ConnectionString property, as shown in Figure 24.30.

FIGURE 24.30

Setting the
ConnectionString
property

You're now ready to run your form.

Running the Form

To run your form, select Debug ➤ Start without Debugging. Figure 24.31 shows the running form. You click the Load button to display the rows from the Customers and Orders tables in your form.

FIGURE 24.31

The running form

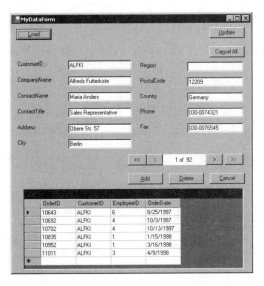

Notice that the top part of the form shows the details for the row from the Customers table where the CustomerID is ALFKI; the bottom part of the form contains a DataGrid control that displays the rows from the Orders table for that customer. When you move to the next row in the Customers table, the rows from the Orders table for that customer are automatically displayed in the DataGrid.

Feel free to try out the other buttons on your form to add, modify, and delete rows in the `Customers` table. You can also use the `DataGrid` control to add, modify, and delete rows from the `Orders` table for the current customer.

Summary

In this chapter, you leaned how to create Windows programs using Visual Studio .NET. Windows provides graphical items such as menus, text boxes, radio buttons, and text boxes that allow you to build a visual interface that users of your programs will find easy to use. In the next chapter, you'll learn about Active Server Pages for the .NET platform (ASP.NET).

Chapter 25

Active Server Pages: ASP.NET

WITH THE ADVENT OF the Internet, you can view information that companies and individuals have posted on web servers. These servers can be located anywhere in the world, and you can view that information using a web browser such as Internet Explorer. In addition, many companies allow you to order items such as books and music CDs and have them shipped right to your door.

No doubt you're already familiar with Hypertext Markup Language (HTML), which is used to display web pages in your web browser. You create a file containing information that is marked up with HTML tags to specify how the information is to be presented, or *rendered*, in your web browser. For example, the <B> and </B> tags indicate that any text placed within these tags is to be rendered as bold text.

HTML is fine for static information that doesn't change. However, if you want the information to be dynamic, then you can use Active Server Pages for .NET (ASP.NET). ASP.NET allows you to create web pages with content that can change at run-time, and it allows you to develop applications that are accessed using a web browser. For example, you could develop an application that allows users to order products over the Web or a stock trading application that allows users to place trades for shares in companies.

In this chapter, you'll learn the basics of ASP.NET, and you'll see how to use Visual Studio .NET (VS .NET) to create ASP.NET applications. Featured in this chapter:

- ◆ Creating ASP.NET Web Applications
- ◆ Using Web Form Controls
- ◆ Using DataGrid and DataList Controls to Access a Database

Creating a Simple ASP.NET Web Application

In the following sections, you'll see how to create a simple ASP.NET web application that contains a text box and a button. When you press the button, a string of text will appear in your text box. You'll learn how to deploy this application to Microsoft's Internet Information Server (IIS). You'll also see how to run the example web application from Internet Explorer.

NOTE   IIS is a piece of software that allows you to run ASP.NET web applications as well as display HTML pages. To deploy the ASP.NET applications shown in this chapter, you'll need access to a computer that runs IIS, along with the FrontPage Server Extensions. These extensions allow you to deploy an ASP.NET web application from Visual Studio .NET.

Start Visual Studio .NET (VS .NET) and select File ➤ New Project. Select Visual C# Projects from the Project Types area on the left of the New project dialog box, and select ASP .NET Web Application from the Templates area on the right. Enter **http://localhost/MyWebApplication** in the Location field, as shown in Figure 25.1.

FIGURE 25.1

Creating an ASP.NET web application in Visual Studio .NET

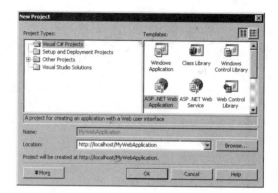

NOTE   The name localhost *represents your local computer on which you are developing your web application. If you're using IIS that is running on a computer other than your local computer, you should replace* localhost *with the name of the remote computer.*

Click the OK button to continue. VS .NET will create a new directory named MyWebApplication in the wwwroot directory; this is the directory where IIS stores published web pages and applications. After you click the OK button, you'll see the new application being sent to IIS.

Once your application has been deployed to IIS, VS .NET will display a blank web form. You can think of the web form as the canvas on which you can place controls, such as text boxes and buttons. When you later run your form, you'll see that the page displayed by the web browser is laid out in a similar manner to your form.

Go ahead and add a TextBox control to your form. The default value for the ID property of your TextBox control is TextBox1.

NOTE   You use the ID *property when referencing a web control in C# code. You'll see an example of code that does this shortly.*

Set the TextMode property for TextBox1 to MultiLine—this allows the text to be displayed on more than one line. Next, add a Button control to your form. The default ID for your Button control is Button1. Set the Text property for Button1 to Press Me!

Figure 25.2 shows the form with the TextBox and Button controls.

FIGURE 25.2

Adding a TextBox
and Button control
to the form

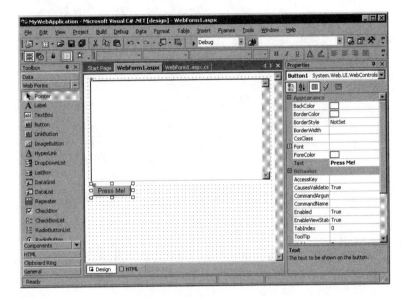

Next, you'll add a line of code to the Button1_Click() method. This method is executed when Button1 is pressed in your running form. The statement you'll add to Button1_Click() will set the Text property of TextBox1 to a string. This string will contain a line from Shakespeare's play, *Romeo and Juliet*. To add the code, double-click Button1 and enter the following code in the Button1_Click() method:

```
TextBox1.Text =
  "But, soft! what light through yonder window breaks?\n" +
  "It is the east, and Juliet is the sun.\n" +
  "Arise, fair sun, and kill the envious moon,\n" +
  "Who is already sick and pale with grief,\n" +
  "That thou her maid art far more fair than she";
```

NOTE *If you're a Shakespeare fan, you'll recognize this line from the magnificent balcony scene where from Romeo professes his true love for Juliet.*

You're now ready to run your form. Select Debug ➤ Start without Debugging, or press Ctrl+F5 on the keyboard to run your form (see Figure 25.3).

FIGURE 25.3

The running form

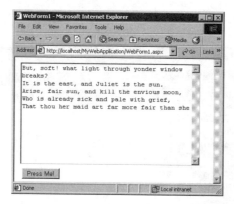

Now that you've created and run the form, let's examine the code generated by VS .NET. There are two main parts to the code:

◆ The WebForm1.aspx file, which contains HTML and ASP.NET code.

◆ The WebForm1.aspx.cs file, which contains C# code that supports the web form. You can think of this C# code as *running behind* the form, and for this reason the WebForm1.aspx.cs file is known as the *code-behind file*.

You'll examine the details of the WebForm1.aspx and WebForm1.aspx.cs files in the following sections.

The *WebForm1.aspx* File

You can view the HTML containing the ASP.NET tags for your form by clicking the HTML link at the bottom of the form designer. Click the HTML link to view the code for your form. Listing 25.1 shows the contents of the WebForm1.aspx file.

NOTE   *The exact values for the positions and sizes of the controls in your own code may differ slightly from those shown in Listing 25.1.*

LISTING 25.1: WebForm1.aspx

```
<%@ Page language="c#" Codebehind="WebForm1.aspx.cs"
AutoEventWireup="false"
Inherits="MyWebApplication.WebForm1" %>
<!DOCTYPE HTML PUBLIC "-//W3C//DTD HTML 4.0 Transitional//EN" >
<HTML>
  <HEAD>
    <title>WebForm1</title>
    <meta content="Microsoft Visual Studio 7.0" name="GENERATOR">
    <meta content="C#" name="CODE_LANGUAGE">
    <meta content="JavaScript" name="vs_defaultClientScript">
    <meta content="http://schemas.microsoft.com/intellisense/ie5"
```

```
      name="vs_targetSchema">
  </HEAD>
  <body MS_POSITIONING="GridLayout">
    <form id="Form1" method="post" runat="server">
      <asp:TextBox id="TextBox1" style="Z-INDEX: 101; LEFT: 13px;
        POSITION: absolute; TOP: 11px" runat="server"
          Width="386px" Height="212px"
        TextMode="MultiLine"></asp:TextBox>
      <asp:Button id="Button1" style="Z-INDEX: 102; LEFT: 17px;
        POSITION: absolute; TOP: 231px" runat="server" Width="82px" Height="22px"
        Text="Press Me!"></asp:Button>
    </form>
  </body>
</HTML>
```

Let's examine the lines in this file. The first lines are:

```
<%@ Page language="c#" Codebehind="WebForm1.aspx.cs"
 AutoEventWireup="false"
 Inherits="MyWebApplication.WebForm1" %>
```

The `language` attribute indicates that the file uses the C# language. The `Codebehind` attribute specifies the code-behind file that supports the form, and in this case the code-behind file is `WebForm1.aspx.cs`. The `AutoEventWireUp` attribute indicates whether the ASP.NET framework automatically calls the `Page_Init()` and `Page_Load()` event handler methods. These methods are defined in the `WebForm1.aspx.cs`; you'll learn more about these event handler methods shortly. The `Inherits` attribute specifies the name of the class in the `WebForm1.aspx.cs` file from which the form inherits.

The next few lines are standard HTML that specify the header and some meta information describing the file:

```
<!DOCTYPE HTML PUBLIC "-//W3C//DTD HTML 4.0 Transitional//EN" >
<HTML>
  <HEAD>
    <title>WebForm1</title>
    <meta content="Microsoft Visual Studio 7.0" name="GENERATOR">
    <meta content="C#" name="CODE_LANGUAGE">
    <meta content="JavaScript" name="vs_defaultClientScript">
    <meta content="http://schemas.microsoft.com/intellisense/ie5"
      name="vs_targetSchema">
  </HEAD>
```

The next line starts the body of the file:

```
<body MS_POSITIONING="GridLayout">
```

The `MS_POSITIONING` attribute indicates that the form controls are laid out in a grid. The alternative to `GridLayout` is `LinearLayout`, which specifies that the form controls are to be laid out one after another in the browser, rather than in a grid.

The next line starts a form:

```
<form id="Form1" method="post" runat="server">
```

The `id` attribute specifies the name of the form is `Form1`. The `method` attribute indicates that the form uses an HTTP post request to send information to the server. The `runat` attribute specifies that the form is executed on the server.

The next lines contain the details of the `TextBox` control that you added to your form:

```
<asp:TextBox id="TextBox1" style="Z-INDEX: 101; LEFT: 13px;
 POSITION: absolute; TOP: 11px" runat="server"
 Width="386px" Height="212px"
 TextMode="MultiLine"></asp:TextBox>
```

The next lines contain the details of the `Button` control that you added to your form:

```
<asp:Button id="Button1" style="Z-INDEX: 102; LEFT: 17px;
 POSITION: absolute; TOP: 231px" runat="server"
 Width="82px" Height="22px" Text="Press Me!"></asp:Button>
```

The remaining lines in the `WebForm1.aspx` file end the form, the body, and the file:

```
    </form>
  </body>
</HTML>
```

The *WebForm1.aspx.cs* File

The `WebForm1.aspx.cs` file contains the code behind your form. You can view this code by selecting View ➤ Code, or you can press F7 on your keyboard.

Listing 25.2 shows the contents of the `WebForm1.aspx.cs` file.

LISTING 25.2: `WebForm1.aspx.cs`

```
using System;
using System.Collections;
using System.ComponentModel;
using System.Data;
using System.Drawing;
using System.Web;
using System.Web.SessionState;
using System.Web.UI;
using System.Web.UI.WebControls;
using System.Web.UI.HtmlControls;

namespace MyWebApplication
{
  /// <summary>
  /// Summary description for WebForm1.
```

```
/// </summary>
public class WebForm1 : System.Web.UI.Page
{
  protected System.Web.UI.WebControls.TextBox TextBox1;

  protected System.Web.UI.WebControls.Button Button1;

  private void Page_Load(object sender, System.EventArgs e)
  {
    // Put user code to initialize the page here
  }

  #region Web Form Designer generated code
  override protected void OnInit(EventArgs e)
  {
    //
    // CODEGEN: This call is required by the ASP.NET Web Form Designer.
    //
    InitializeComponent();
    base.OnInit(e);
  }

  /// <summary>
  /// Required method for Designer support - do not modify
  /// the contents of this method with the code editor.
  /// </summary>
  private void InitializeComponent()
  {
    this.Button1.Click += new System.EventHandler(this.Button1_Click);
    this.Load += new System.EventHandler(this.Page_Load);

  }
  #endregion

  private void Button1_Click(object sender, System.EventArgs e)
  {
    TextBox1.Text =
      "But, soft! what light through yonder window breaks?\n" +
      "It is the east, and Juliet is the sun.\n" +
      "Arise, fair sun, and kill the envious moon,\n" +
      "Who is already sick and pale with grief,\n" +
      "That thou her maid art far more fair than she";
  }
}
}
```

As you can see, the WebForm1 class is derived from the System.Web.UI.Page class. The WebForm1 class declares two protected objects named TextBox1 and Button1, which represent the TextBox and Button controls you added to your form.

The Page_Load() event handler method is called when the Page_Load event is raised. The Page_Load event is raised whenever the web form is loaded by a browser. Typically, you'll place any initialization code in the Page_Load() method. For example, if you wanted to access a database, you would open the database connection in the Page_Load() method.

The OnInit() and InitializeComponent() methods are placed within #region and #endregion preprocessor directives. These directives enclose an area of code that may then be collapsed in VS .NET's code editor, leaving only the text that immediately follows #region visible. You saw how to expand and collapse code in Chapter 24, "Introduction to Windows Programming."

The OnInit() method is called when the form is initialized when it is started up. This method calls the InitializeComponent() method and adds the button Click and the form Load events to the System.EventHandler object. This informs the system that these two events are to be handled by the Button1_Click() and Page_Load() methods, respectively.

The Button1_Click() method is the method you modified earlier with code that sets the Text property of your TextBox1 control to a string containing the quote from *Romeo and Juliet*.

In the next section, you'll be introduced to some of the other controls you can add to a web form.

Using Web Form Controls

Table 25.1 lists some of the various web form controls that you can pick from the Toolbox's Web Forms section.

TABLE 25.1: WEB FORM CONTROLS

CONTROL	DESCRIPTION
Label	Displays text. You set the text that you want to display using the Text property.
TextBox	A box containing text that the user of your form may edit at run-time. The TextMode property may be set to SingleLine (text appears on one line), MultiLine (text appears over multiple lines), and Password (text appears as asterisk characters). The Text property contains the text contained in the TextBox.
Button	A clickable button. The Text property determines the text shown on the button.
LinkButton	Similar to a Button, except that a LinkButton appears as a hypertext link. You set the link using the Text property.
ImageButton	Similar to a Button, except that an ImageButton shows an image. You set the image using the ImageUrl property.
HyperLink	A hyperlink. You set the hyperlink using the NavigateUrl property.

Continued on next page

1: WEB FORM CONTROLS *(continued)*

DESCRIPTION

nList

A list of options that drops down when clicked. You set the list of options using the Items property. The user can only select one option from the DropDownList when the form is run.

ox

A list of options. You set the list of options using the Items property. The user can select multiple options from the ListBox if the SelectionMode property is set to Multiple. The other value is Single, in which case the user can only select one option.

Grid

A grid containing data retrieved from a data source, such as a database. You set the data source using the DataSource property.

DataList

A list containing data retrieved from a data source. You set the data source using the DataSource property.

Repeater

A list containing data retrieved from a data source that you set using the DataSource property. Each item in the list may be displayed using a template. A template defines the content and layout of the items in the list.

CheckBox

A check box contains a Boolean true/false value that is set to true by the user if they check the box. The Checked property indicates the Boolean value currently set in the check box.

CheckBoxList

A multiple selection check box. You set the list of check boxes using the Items property.

RadioButton

A radio button contains a Boolean true/false value that is set to true by the user if they press the button. The Checked property indicates the Boolean value currently set in the radio button.

RadioButtonList

A group of radio buttons. You set the list of radio buttons using the Items property.

Image

Displays an image that you set using the ImageUrl property.

Panel

A container for other controls.

PlaceHolder

A container for controls that you can create at run-time—these are known as *dynamic controls*.

Calendar

Displays a calendar for a month and allows a user to select a date. The user can also navigate to the previous and next month. You use the SelectedDate property to get or set the selected date, and you use the VisibleDate property to get or set the month currently displayed.

AdRotator

Displays banner advertisements. Details on the advertisements, such as the image, URL when clicked, and frequency of display, are set in an XML file that you set using the AdvertisementFile property.

Table

Displays a table of rows, which you set using the Rows property.

Continued on next page

TABLE 25.1: WEB FORM CONTROLS *(continued)*

CONTROL	DESCRIPTION
RequiredFieldValidator	Used to ensure that the user has specified some input for a control. You set the control to validate using the ControlToValidate property. You'll see an example that uses a validation control shortly.
CompareValidator	Used to compare an entry made by a user in one control with another control or a constant value. You set the control to validate using the ControlToValidate property (this control contains the value entered by the user). You set the control to compare against using the ControlTo-Compare property, or you can set a value to compare against using the ValueToCompare property. You set the operator for the comparison using the Operator property.
RangeValidator	Used to ensure that the user has entered a value within a specified range in a control. You set the control to validate using the ControlToValidate property, and the range of values using the MinimumValue and MaximumValue properties.
RegularExpressionValidator	Used to ensure that the user has entered a value that satisfies a specified regular expression. You set the control to validate using the ControlTo-Validate property, and the regular expression using the Validation-Expression property.
CustomValidator	Used to perform your own custom validation for the value entered by a user. You set the control to validate using the ControlToValidate property, and your function to use in the validation using the ClientValidationFunction property.
ValidationSummary	Used to display a summary of all validation errors on the web form and/or a message box. You set whether you want to show the errors on your web form using the ShowSummary property. You set whether you want to show the errors in a message box using the ShowMessageBox property.
XML	Displays the contents of an XML file. You set the XML file to display using the DocumentSource property.
Literal	Displays static text. You set the text to display using the Text property.

You'll see the use of some of these controls in the rest of this chapter.

Building a More Complex Application

In this section, you'll see a more complex web form that uses Label, TextBox, RadioButtonList, DropDownList, and RequiredFieldValidator controls. The form will prompt the user for their name (a required field), favorite season (spring, summer, fall, or winter), and sex (male or female). The form will also feature a Button control, which when pressed will set the Text property of one of the Label controls to a string containing the user's name, sex, and favorite season. Figure 25.4 shows how your final form will appear.

FIGURE 25.4

The appearance of the final form

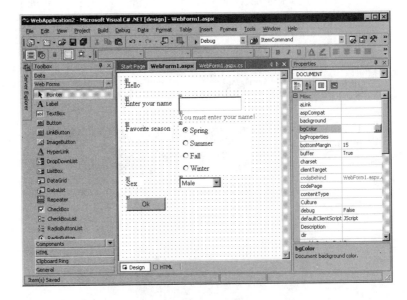

To create the new project, select File ➤ New Project in VS .NET. Select Visual C# Projects from the Project Types area on the left of the New project dialog box, and select ASP .NET Web Application from the Templates area on the right. Enter **http://localhost/MyWebApplication2** in the Location field. VS .NET will eventually display a blank form to which you can add controls.

Now, add the four `Label` controls listed in Table 25.2 to your blank form. This table shows the `ID` and `Text` property you should set for each of your `Label` controls.

TABLE 25.2: Label CONTROLS

ID PROPERTY	TEXT PROPERTY
HelloLabel	Hello
NameLabel	Enter your name
SeasonLabel	Favorite season
SexLabel	Sex

Next, add a `TextBox` control to the right of `HelloLabel`. Set the `ID` property for your `TextBox` control to `NameTextBox`. The user will enter their name in `NameTextBox` when the form is run.

We want the user to have to enter their name—if they don't, we want to display a message prompting them to do so. To achieve this, you use a `RequiredFieldValidator` control. Add a `RequiredField-Validator` control below `NameTextBox`. Set the `ID` property for your `RequiredFieldValidator` control to `NameRequiredFieldValidator`. Set the `Text` property to `You must enter your name!` Finally, set the `ControlToValidate` property to `NameTextBox`.

Next, add a `RadioButtonList` control to the right of `SeasonLabel`. The user will select their favorite season from this control. Set the `ID` property for your `RadioButtonList` control to `SeasonRadioButton-List`. To add radio buttons to `SeasonRadioButtonList`, click the ellipsis button in the `Items` property. This displays the `ListItem` Collection Editor, which you use to add, modify, or remove items in the `Items` collection for the control. When the form is run, any items you add to the collection are displayed as radio buttons. Figure 25.5 shows the `ListItem` Collection Editor with the required entries for your form.

FIGURE 25.5

The `ListItem`
Collection Editor

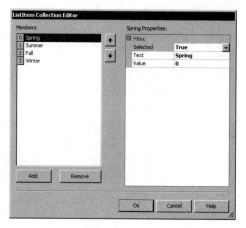

The `Selected` property indicates whether the item is initially selected in the running form. The `Text` property contains the text displayed with the item. The `Value` property is the returned value when the item is selected.

Now click the Add button to add the first item to your `RadioButtonList` control. Set the `Selected` property for the item to `True`—this causes the radio button to be initially selected. Set the `Text` property for the item to `Spring`—this is the text displayed in the radio button. Set the `Value` property to 0—this is the actual value selected. Table 25.3 shows the `Selected`, `Text`, and `Value` properties for this radio button, along with the three other radio buttons you should add to your `RadioButtonList` control.

TABLE 25.3: `RadioButtonList` ITEMS

`Selected` PROPERTY	`Text` PROPERTY	`Value` PROPERTY
`True`	`Spring`	0
`False`	`Summer`	1
`False`	`Fall`	2
`False`	`Winter`	3

Next, add a `DropDownList` control to your form. This control will allow a user to select their gender (male or female). Set the `ID` property for your `DropDownList` control to `SexDropDownList`. You add items to a `DropDownList` control using the `ListItem` Collection Editor, which you access using the ellipsis button through the `Items` property. Go ahead and open the `ListItem` Collection Editor and add the items shown in Table 25.4.

TABLE 25.4: `DropDownList` ITEMS

Selected **PROPERTY**	Text **PROPERTY**	Value **PROPERTY**
True	Male	0
False	Female	1

Finally, add a `Button` control to your form. Set the `ID` property for your `Button` control to `OkButton`. Double-click `OkButton` to edit the code for the `OkButton_Click()` method. add the following lines of code to this method:

```
HelloLabel.Text =
   "Hello " + NameTextBox.Text +
   ", you are " + SexDropDownList.SelectedItem.Text +
   " and your favorite season is " +
SeasonRadioButtonList.SelectedItem.Text;
```

As you can see, this line sets the `Text` property for the `HelloLabel` control to a string containing the user's entry in the `NameTextBox`, `SexDropDownList`, and `SeasonRadioButton` controls.

Run your completed form by pressing Ctrl+F5. Try pressing the OK button without entering a name, and you'll see the message `"You must enter your name!"`–as shown in Figure 25.6. This message comes from the `NameRequiredFieldValidator` control.

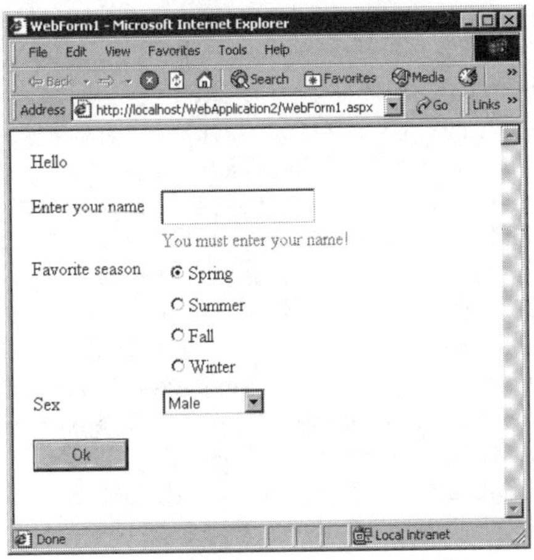

FIGURE 25.6

Message from the `NameRequired-FieldValidator` control

When you've finished running your form, close it and return to the VS .NET form designer. You can view the HTML containing the ASP.NET tags for your form by clicking the HTML link at the bottom of the form designer. Click the HTML link to view the code for your form. Listing 25.3 shows the WebForm1.aspx file for the form. You'll notice that this file contains the various controls that were added to the form.

LISTING 25.3: THE WebForm1.aspx FILE

```
<%@ Page language="c#" Codebehind="WebForm1.aspx.cs"
 AutoEventWireup="false"
 Inherits="WebApplication2.WebForm1" %>
<!DOCTYPE HTML PUBLIC "-//W3C//DTD HTML 4.0 Transitional//EN" >
<HTML>
  <HEAD>
    <title>WebForm1</title>
    <meta name="GENERATOR" Content="Microsoft Visual Studio 7.0">
    <meta name="CODE_LANGUAGE" Content="C#">
    <meta name="vs_defaultClientScript" content="JavaScript">
    <meta name="vs_targetSchema"
     content="http://schemas.microsoft.com/intellisense/ie5">
  </HEAD>
  <body MS_POSITIONING="GridLayout">
    <form id="Form1" method="post" runat="server">
      <asp:Label id="HelloLabel" style="Z-INDEX: 101; LEFT: 17px;
       POSITION: absolute; TOP: 16px" runat="server"
       Width="322px" Height="23px">Hello</asp:Label>
      <asp:Label id="NameLabel" style="Z-INDEX: 102; LEFT: 17px;
       POSITION: absolute; TOP: 54px" runat="server"
       Width="114px" Height="22px">Enter your name</asp:Label>
      <asp:Label id="SeasonLabel" style="Z-INDEX: 103; LEFT: 17px;
       POSITION: absolute; TOP: 107px" runat="server"
       Width="101px" Height="32px">Favorite season</asp:Label>
      <asp:Label id="SexLabel" style="Z-INDEX: 104; LEFT: 17px;
       POSITION: absolute; TOP: 221px" runat="server"
       Width="33px" Height="15px">Sex</asp:Label>
      <asp:TextBox id="NameTextBox" style="Z-INDEX: 105; LEFT: 130px;
       POSITION: absolute; TOP: 51px" runat="server"
       Width="135px" Height="30px"></asp:TextBox>
      <asp:RequiredFieldValidator id="NameRequiredFieldValidator"
       style="Z-INDEX: 106; LEFT: 130px; POSITION: absolute;
       TOP: 84px" runat="server" ErrorMessage="RequiredFieldValidator"
       ControlToValidate="NameTextBox">You must enter your name!
      </asp:RequiredFieldValidator>
      <asp:RadioButtonList id="SeasonRadioButtonList"
       style="Z-INDEX: 107; LEFT: 130px; POSITION: absolute;
       TOP: 107px" runat="server" Width="152px" Height="107px">
        <asp:ListItem Value="0" Selected="True">Spring</asp:ListItem>
```

```
            <asp:ListItem Value="1">Summer</asp:ListItem>
            <asp:ListItem Value="2">Fall</asp:ListItem>
            <asp:ListItem Value="3">Winter</asp:ListItem>
        </asp:RadioButtonList>
        <asp:DropDownList id="SexDropDownList" style="Z-INDEX: 108;
          LEFT: 130px; POSITION: absolute; TOP: 220px" runat="server"
         Width="90px" Height="27px">
            <asp:ListItem Value="0" Selected="True">Male</asp:ListItem>
            <asp:ListItem Value="1">Female</asp:ListItem>
        </asp:DropDownList>
        <asp:Button id="OkButton" style="Z-INDEX: 109; LEFT: 17px;
          POSITION: absolute; TOP: 261px" runat="server"
          Width="83px" Height="27px" Text="Ok"></asp:Button>
      </form>
    </body>
  </HTML>
```

Using a *DataGrid* Control to Access a Database

A `DataGrid` allows you to access rows in a database table. In the following sections, you'll learn how to create an ASP.NET web application that uses a `DataGrid` control to access the rows in a database table. The `DataGrid` you'll create will display the rows from the `Products` table of the Northwind database. You were introduced to the Northwind database in Chapter 22, "Introduction to Databases."

Creating the Web Application

To create the new project, select File ➢ New Project in VS .NET. Select Visual C# Projects from the Project Types area on the left of the New project dialog box, and select ASP.NET Web Application from the Templates area on the right. Enter **http://localhost/DataGridWebApplication** in the Location field. Click OK to continue. Your new project will contain a blank form.

Next, you'll add a `DataGrid` control to your form. To do this, select the `DataGrid` from the Toolbox and drag it to your form. Figure 25.7 shows the form with the `DataGrid`.

Next, you'll add a `SqlConnection` object and a `SqlDataAdapter` object to your form. To add these objects, select the `Products` table in Server Explorer and drag it to your form.

NOTE   *To display Server Explorer, select View ➢ Server Explorer, or press Ctrl+Alt+S on your keyboard.*

After you drag the `Products` table to your form, VS .NET creates a `SqlConnection` object named `sqlConnection1` and a `SqlDataAdapter` object named `sqlDataAdapter1`. Click your `sqlConnection1` object to display the properties for this object in the Properties window. To enable `sqlConnection1` to access the database, you need to set the password for the connection. To do this, you need to add a substring containing `pwd` to the `ConnectionString` property of `sqlConnection1`. Go ahead and add `pwd=sa;` to the `ConnectionString` property.

NOTE   *If you don't have the password for the sa user, you'll need to get it from your database administrator.*

FIGURE 25.7

Form with a
`DataGrid`

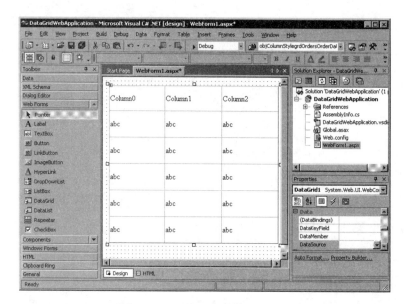

Next, you'll modify the SQL SELECT statement used to retrieve the rows from the Products table. Click the `sqlDataAdapter1` object to display the properties for this object. Click the addition icon to the left of the `SelectCommand` property to display the dynamic properties. One of the dynamic properties is the `CommandText` property, which contains the SELECT statement.

Click `CommandText` and then click the ellipsis button to display the Query Builder. You use Query Builder to define SQL statements. You can type in the SQL statement, or you can build it up visually. Uncheck all the columns except the following: `ProductID`, `ProductName`, `QuantityPerUnit`, and `UnitPrice`.

This results in the SQL SELECT statement being set to the following:

```
SELECT ProductID, ProductName, QuantityPerUnit, UnitPrice
FROM Products
```

Next, you need to create a `DataSet` object.

NOTE You use a `DataSet` object to a store local copy of the information stored in the database. A `DataSet` object has the capability of representing database structures such as tables, rows, and columns, among others. In the example in this section, you'll use a `DataSet` object to store the rows from the `Products` table.

Click an area of your form outside the `DataGrid`. Next, click the Generate Dataset link near the bottom of the Properties window. This displays the Generate Dataset dialog box. Select the New radio button and make sure the text field to the right of this radio button contains `DataSet1`. Click the OK button to continue. This adds a new `DataSet` object named `dataSet11` to your form.

Next, you'll need to set the `DataSource` property of your `DataGrid` to your `DataSet` object. This sets the source of the data for your `DataGrid` and allows the rows from your `DataSet` to be displayed in your `DataGrid`. To set the `DataSource` property, click your `DataGrid` object and set the `DataSource` property to dataSet11. Also, set the DataMember property to Products—this is table whose rows are to be displayed by your DataGrid.

Next, you'll need to add code to populate sqlDataAdapter1 with the rows retrieved by your SELECT statement. Typically, the best place to place this code is in the Page_Load() method of your form. The Page_Load() method is called when the web page containing your form is initially loaded or refreshed. The IsPostBack property of a page is false the first time the page is loaded and true when the submit button of a form is pressed. For performance, you'll generally only want to retrieve rows when the IsPostBack property is false—otherwise you might be needlessly reloading the rows from the database. To view the code for your form, open the code for your form by selecting View ➤ Code or by pressing F7 on your keyboard. Set your Page_Load() method to the following:

```
private void Page_Load(object sender, System.EventArgs e)
{
  // Put user code to initialize the page here
  if (!this.IsPostBack)
  {
    sqlDataAdapter1.Fill(dataSet11, "Products");
    this.DataBind();
  }
}
```

The Fill() method retrieves the rows from the Products table and populates dataSet11 with those rows. The DataBind() method then fills the Products DataTable in dataSet11 with the rows retrieved from the Products table. This causes the rows to be displayed in the DataGrid of your form.

To run your form, select Debug ➤ Start without Debugging, or press Ctl+F5 on your keyboard (see Figure 25.8).

FIGURE 25.8

The running form

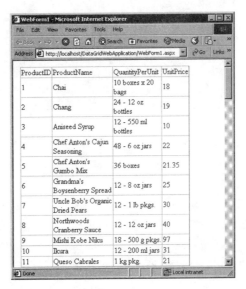

As you can see, a vertical scroll bar is displayed because of the number of rows retrieved from the Products table. In the next section, you'll learn how to customize your DataGrid. You'll see how you can control the number of rows displayed in your DataGrid so that no scroll bar appears, as well as control other aspects of your DataGrid.

Customizing the *DataGrid*

You customize your DataGrid by first selecting the DataGrid control and then clicking the Property Builder link at the bottom of the Properties window. This displays the Properties dialog box for your DataGrid. The Properties dialog is divided into five areas: General, Columns, Paging, Format, and Borders.

GENERAL PROPERTIES

The first set of properties displayed are the General properties. You use the General properties to set the data source for your DataGrid and whether you want a header and footer to displayed, among other properties. Set your General properties as shown in Figure 25.9.

FIGURE 25.9

The General properties

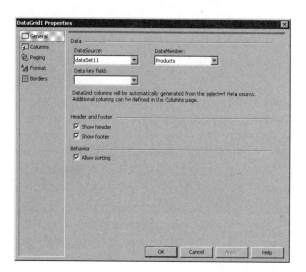

The General properties are as follows:

DataSource   The DataSource is the source of the data for your DataGrid. In this example, the DataSource is dataSet11.

DataMember   The DataMember is the name of the table to which your DataGrid is bound. In this example, the DataMember is Products.

Data Key Field   The Data Key Field is the name of a column or expression that is associated with each row in your DataGrid but isn't actually shown. You typically use it to specify the primary key.

Header and Footer   The header displays the name of the columns at the top of the DataGrid. The footer displays the name of the columns at the top of the DataGrid. Make sure you select Show Header and Show Footer.

Behavior   You can sort on columns in the header of your DataGrid. Make sure you select Allow Sorting so that your columns can be sorted.

COLUMNS PROPERTIES

Next, click the Columns link of the Properties dialog box to display the Columns properties. You use the Columns properties to select the columns to be displayed in your DataGrid and the header and footer text to be displayed for each column, among other properties. Set your Columns properties as shown in Figure 25.10.

FIGURE 25.10

The Columns properties

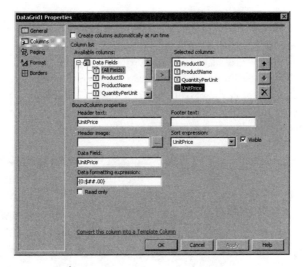

The Columns properties are as follows:

Create Columns Automatically at Run Time   The Create Columns Automatically at Run Time check box specifies whether to automatically include all the columns for the DataSet in your Data-Grid. When this check box is unselected, you can then set the other properties for each column individually. Make sure you unselect this check box.

Column List   The Column List allows you to select columns from your DataSet for display in your DataGrid. You select columns from the Available Columns area on the left and add them to Selected Columns area on the right using the button containing the right-arrow. Make sure you select (All Fields) from Available Columns and add them to the Selected Columns.

BoundColumn Properties   The BoundColumn properties allow you to set the properties for each column. You select the column you want to set in the Selected Columns area and then you set the properties for that column. The fields you can set for each column are as follows:

Header Text   The Header Text is the text you want to display in the header for a column.

Footer Text   The Footer Text is the text you want to display in the footer for a column.

Header Image   The Header Image is the image you want to display in the header for a column.

Sort Expression The Sort Expression is the column or expression you want to use to sort the column by. Make sure you select UnitPrice as the Sort expression.

Data Field The Data Field is the name of column.

Data Formatting Expression The Data Formatting Expression allows you to format a column value. You can use a formatting expression to format dates and numbers, among others. For example, {0:$##.00} formats a number and adds a dollar sign at the front and displays two digits after the decimal point; thus, 19 is formatted as $19.00. Make sure you set the formatting expression for the UnitPrice column to {0:$##.00}.

PAGING PROPERTIES

Next, click on the Paging link of the Properties dialog box. Normally, all the rows retrieved by a SELECT statement are displayed on a single page for the DataGrid. You can use the Paging properties to split up all the rows into separate pages with a fixed number of rows on each page in your Data-Grid. You can then select the buttons to navigate between those pages of rows. You'll be setting your page size to five rows with next and previous buttons to navigate between the pages of rows. Set your Paging properties as shown in Figure 25.11.

FIGURE 25.11

The Paging properties

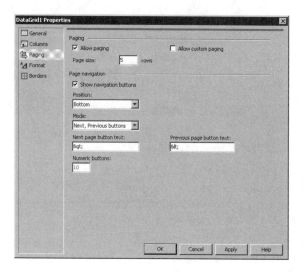

The Paging properties are as follows:

Allow Paging The Allow Paging check box controls whether paging is enabled. Make sure you check the Allow Paging box.

Page Size The Page Size field controls the number of rows displayed on each page. Make sure you set your Page Size to 5.

Show Navigation Buttons   The Show Navigation Buttons check box controls whether navigation buttons are displayed. These buttons allow you to navigate between pages of rows. Make sure you check the Show Navigation Buttons box.

Position   The Position field allows you to set the position of the navigation buttons. Make sure you set the Position to Bottom.

Mode   The Mode field controls the type of navigation buttons displayed. You can use next and previous buttons or page numbers to navigate between pages. Make sure you set the Mode to Next, Previous Buttons.

Next Page Button Text   The Next Page Button Text field sets the text displayed on the Next page button. Leave this as `&gt;` so that a greater than character (>) is displayed on the button.

Previous Page Button Text   The Previous Page Button Text field sets the text displayed on the Previous page button. Leave this as `&lt;` so that a less than character (<) is displayed on the button.

Numeric Buttons   The Numeric Buttons option controls whether numbers are displayed for each page when you set the Mode to Page Numbers. For example, 1 navigates to the first page, 2 to the second page, and so on.

In addition to enabling paging, you'll also need to add some code to your `DataGrid` to make navigation work and you'll do this shortly.

FORMAT PROPERTIES

Next, click the Format link of the Properties dialog box. You use the Format properties to control how each element on your `DataGrid` appears. You can set features such as the color of your `DataGrid`, as well as the font. You can also set the display properties of each column. You'll be setting the foreground and background color to black and white, respectively. You'll also be setting the font of the text displayed in your `DataGrid` to Arial. Set your Format properties as shown in Figure 25.12.

FIGURE 25.12

The Format properties

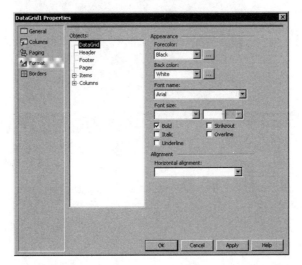

The Format properties are as follows:

Forecolor   The Forecolor option specifies the text color. Make sure you set the Forecolor to Black.

Back Color   The Back Color option specifies the color behind the text. Make sure you set the Back Color to White.

Font Name   The Font Name option specifies the font used to display the text. Make sure you set the Font Name to Arial.

Font Size   The Font Size option controls the size of the font used to display the text.

Bold, Italic, Underline, Strikeout, Overline   The Bold, Italic, Underline, Strikeout, and Overline options control the character formatting for the text.

Horizontal Alignment   The Horizontal Alignment option specifies the position of the text in the cell.

BORDERS PROPERTIES

Next, click on the Borders link of the Properties dialog box. You use the Borders properties to control the padding, spacing, and appearance of the grid lines in your `DataGrid`. You'll be setting the border color of the grid lines in your `DataGrid` to blue. Set your Borders properties as shown in Figure 25.13.

FIGURE 25.13

The Borders properties

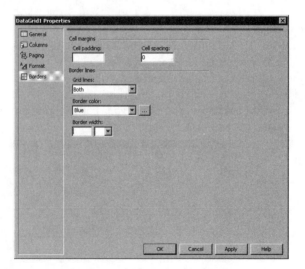

The Borders properties are as follows:

Cell Padding   The Cell Padding option controls the amount of space (in pixels) between the edge of a cell and the cell contents in your `DataGrid`.

Cell Spacing   The Cell Spacing option controls the amount of space (in pixels) between each element in your `DataGrid`.

Grid Lines   The Grid Lines option specifies the direction of the grid lines in your DataGrid.

Border Color   The Border Color option specifies the color of the grid lines in your DataGrid. Make sure you set this to blue.

Border Width   The Border Width option controls the width and units of the grid lines in your DataGrid.

Once you've set your properties, click the OK button to continue. Next, you'll be coding the PageIndexChanged() event handler to allow navigation of the rows in your DataGrid.

CODING THE *PAGEINDEXCHANGED()* EVENT HANDLER

As mentioned earlier, in addition to enabling paging in the Paging properties window, you'll also need to add some code to your DataGrid. Specifically, you'll need to add code to the PageIndexChanged() event handler method. This method is called whenever you change the page in the DataGrid on your running web page. Before you add the required code, you first select your DataGrid, and then you click the Events button to display the events for your DataGrid, as shown in Figure 25.14.

FIGURE 25.14

Displaying the DataGrid events

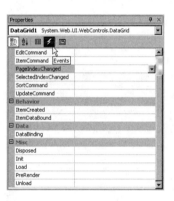

Double-click the PageIndexChanged event and set your DataGrid1_PageIndexChanged() method as follows:

```
private void DataGrid1_PageIndexChanged(
  object source,
  System.Web.UI.WebControls.DataGridPageChangedEventArgs e)
{
  DataGrid1.CurrentPageIndex = e.NewPageIndex;
  sqlDataAdapter1.Fill(dataSet11, "Products");
  DataGrid1.DataBind();
}
```

The first statement inside the method body is as follows:

```
DataGrid1.CurrentPageIndex = e.NewPageIndex;
```

This statement sets the current page displayed in `DataGrid1` to the new page that is selected using the navigation buttons in the running form. You set the current page for `DataGrid1` using the `CurrentPageIndex` property, and you get the new page from the `NewPageIndex` property of the `DataGridPageChangedEventArgs` object. By setting `DataGrid1.CurrentPageIndex` equal to `e.NewPageIndex`, the navigation to the new page of rows is performed.

The second statement is as follows:

```
sqlDataAdapter1.Fill(dataSet11, "Products");
```

This statement calls the `Fill()` method of `sqlDataAdapter1` to populate `dataSet11` with the next set of rows from the `Products` table:

The third statement is as follows:

```
DataGrid1.DataBind();
```

This statement calls the `DataBind()` method of `DataGrid1`, causing the new set of rows to displayed.

NOTE *With VS. NET, you can also go to the Code View and use the top drop-down lists to create the signature for events. This applies to any events you add. Of course, double-clicking events to get the "default" event is easier, but there are other events for each control.*

Run your form by pressing Ctrl+F5 on your keyboard. Figure 25.15 shows the running form.

FIGURE 25.15

The running form

Use the navigation buttons to move between pages of rows. Once you've finished running your form, close it and return to the VS .NET form designer. Click the HTML link to view the code for your form. Listing 25.4 shows the `WebForm1.aspx` file for the form. You'll notice that this file contains a `DataGrid` control with the appropriate columns.

LISTING 25.4: THE WebForm1.aspx FILE

```
<%@ Page language="c#" Codebehind="WebForm1.aspx.cs"
 AutoEventWireup="false"
 Inherits="DataGridWebApplication.WebForm1" %>
<!DOCTYPE HTML PUBLIC "-//W3C//DTD HTML 4.0 Transitional//EN" >
<HTML>
  <HEAD>
    <title>WebForm1</title>
    <meta content="Microsoft Visual Studio 7.0" name="GENERATOR">
    <meta content="C#" name="CODE_LANGUAGE">
    <meta content="JavaScript" name="vs_defaultClientScript">
    <meta content="http://schemas.microsoft.com/intellisense/ie5"
     name="vs_targetSchema">
  </HEAD>
  <body MS_POSITIONING="GridLayout">
    <form id="Form1" method="post" runat="server">
      <asp:datagrid id=DataGrid1 style="Z-INDEX: 101; LEFT: 16px;
       POSITION: absolute; TOP: 11px" runat="server"
       AutoGenerateColumns="False" BorderColor="Blue" Font-Bold="True"
       Font-Names="Arial" ForeColor="Black" BackColor="White"
       AllowPaging="True" PageSize="5" ShowFooter="True"
       DataMember="Products" AllowSorting="True"
       DataSource="<%# dataSet11 %>" Height="333px" Width="352px">
        <Columns>
          <asp:BoundColumn
           DataField="ProductID" HeaderText="ProductID">
          </asp:BoundColumn>
          <asp:BoundColumn DataField="ProductName"
           HeaderText="ProductName">
          </asp:BoundColumn>
          <asp:BoundColumn DataField="QuantityPerUnit"
           HeaderText="QuantityPerUnit">
          </asp:BoundColumn>
          <asp:BoundColumn DataField="UnitPrice"
           SortExpression="UnitPrice" HeaderText="UnitPrice"
           DataFormatString="{0:$##.00}">
          </asp:BoundColumn>
        </Columns>
      </asp:datagrid></form>
  </body>
</HTML>
```

In the next section, you'll learn how to use a DataList control to access a database.

Using a *DataList* Control to Access a Database

In this section, you'll learn how to use a `DataList` control to access the rows in the `Products` table.

TIP   A `DataList` offers you a lot more flexibility in the presentation of column values than that offered by a `DataGrid`.

To create the new project, select File ➤ New Project in VS .NET. Select Visual C# Projects from the Project Types area on the left of the New project dialog box, and select ASP .NET Web Application from the Templates area on the right. Enter **http://localhost/DataListWebApplication** in the Location field. Click OK to continue. Your new project will contain a blank form.

Next, you'll add a `SqlConnection` object and a `SqlDataAdapter` object to your form. Select the `Products` table in Server Explorer and drag it to your form.

NOTE   To display Server Explorer, select View ➤ Server Explorer, or press Ctrl+Alt+S on your keyboard.

After you drag the `Products` table to your form, VS .NET creates a `SqlConnection` object named `sqlConnection1` and a `SqlDataAdapter` object named `sqlDataAdapter1`.

Click your `sqlConnection1` object to display the properties for this object in the Properties window. To enable `sqlConnection1` to access the database, you need to set the password for the connection. Add `pwd=sa;` to the `ConnectionString` property.

Next, you'll modify the SQL `SELECT` statement used to retrieve the rows from the `Products` table. Click your `sqlDataAdapter1` object to display the properties for this object. Click the addition icon to the left of the `SelectCommand` property to display the dynamic properties; one of the dynamic properties is the `CommandText` property, which contains the `SELECT` statement. Next, click `Command-Text` and then click the ellipsis button to display the Query Builder. You can type in the SQL statement, or you can build it up visually. Go ahead and uncheck all the columns except `ProductID`, `ProductName`, `QuantityPerUnit`, and `UnitPrice`.

This results in the SQL `SELECT` statement being set to the following:

```
SELECT ProductID, ProductName, QuantityPerUnit, UnitPrice
FROM Products
```

Click OK to continue.

Next, you need to create a `DataSet` object. Click an area of your form outside of the `DataGrid`. Next, click the Generate Dataset link near the bottom of the Properties window. This displays the Generate Dataset dialog box. Select the New radio button and make sure the field to the right of this radio button contains `DataSet1`. Click the OK button to continue. This adds a new `DataSet` object named `dataSet11` to your form.

Next, you'll add a `DataList` control to your form. To do this, select the `DataList` from the Toolbox and drag it to your form. Figure 25.16 shows the form with the new `DataList`.

FIGURE 25.16

Form with a
`DataList`

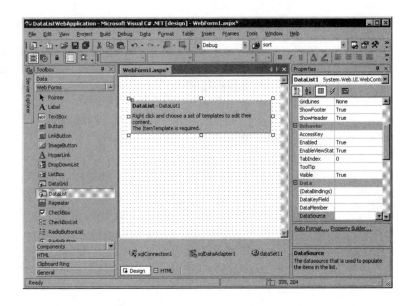

Next, you'll need to set the `DataSource` property of your `DataList` to your `DataSet` object created earlier. This sets the source of the data for your `DataList` and allows the rows from your `DataSet` to be displayed in your `DataList`. To set the `DataSource` property, click your `DataList` object and set its `DataSource` property to `dataSet11`. Also, set the `DataMember` property of your `DataList` to `Products`—this is the table whose rows are displayed by the `DataList`.

A `DataList` uses templates that define how its contents are laid out, and your next task is to set up those templates.

TIP   *It is the `DataList` templates that give you the flexibility for laying out controls that display column values.*

You'll be editing the template that defines the header and footer for the `DataList`, along with the template that defines the actual items displayed within your `DataList`. To edit the header and footer template, right-click your `DataList` and select Edit Template ➢ Header and Footer Templates.

You can add controls to the areas within the `HeaderTemplate` and `FooterTemplate` areas. Any controls you add will be displayed at the start and end of the `DataList`, respectively. Add a label in `Header-Template`; you do this by dragging a `Label` control from the Toolbox to the empty area below `HeaderTemplate`. Set the `Text` property for this `Label` to `Products`. Also, add a `Label` in the `Footer-Template` area and set its `Text` property to `End of list`. Figure 25.17 shows the modified header and footer templates with the `Label` controls.

FIGURE 25.17

The modified header and footer templates with Label controls

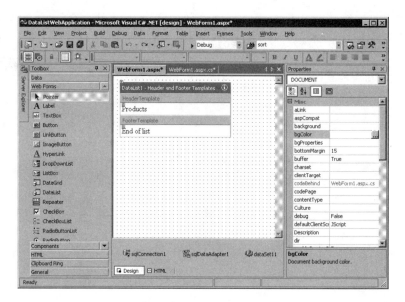

NOTE   You can end editing a template at any time by right-clicking your DataList and selecting End Template Editing.

Next, you'll be editing the item template and adding Label controls to display the ProductID, ProductName, QuantityPerUnit, and UnitPrice columns. Right-click your DataList and select Edit Template ➤ Item Templates. Figure 25.18 shows the Item Templates editor.

FIGURE 25.18

The Item Templates editor

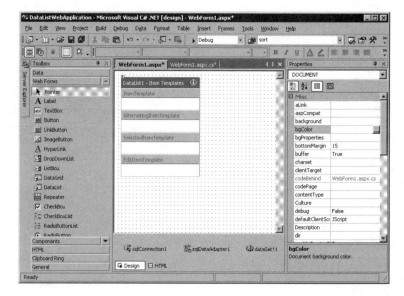

As you can see from Figure 25.18, the item templates editor is divided up into the following four areas:

ItemTemplate   The ItemTemplate area contains controls that you typically use to display column values.

AlternatingItemTemplate   The AlternatingItemTemplate area contains controls that are shown after the controls in the ItemTemplate.

SelectedItemTemplate   The SelectedItemTemplate area contains controls that are shown when you select an item.

EditItemTemplate   The EditItemTemplate area contains controls that are shown when you edit an item.

You'll be adding a table to the ItemTemplate area, and then you'll be adding four Label controls in the cells of your table. The four Label controls will display the values for the ProductID, Product-Name, QuantityPerUnit, and UnitPrice columns. To add a table, click anywhere in the ItemTemplate area and select Table ➢ Insert Table. Set the properties for the table as shown in Figure 25.19.

FIGURE 25.19

Setting the
properties of
the table

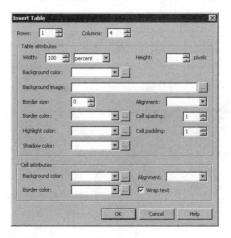

Next, drag a Label to the first cell in the table. You'll use this first Label to display the ProductID column. Set the ID property of your Label to ProductID, as shown in Figure 25.20.

FIGURE 25.20

Adding the Label

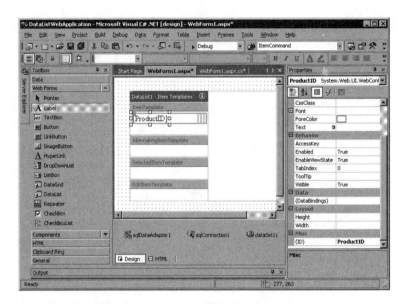

To get the Label to display the ProductID column, you'll need to bind it to that column. To do this, click the ellipsis button in the DataBindings property. You'll then see the DataBindings dialog box. Open the Container node by clicking the addition icon and then open the DataItem node; finally, select the ProductID column as shown in Figure 25.21.

FIGURE 25.21

Binding the Label to the ProductID column

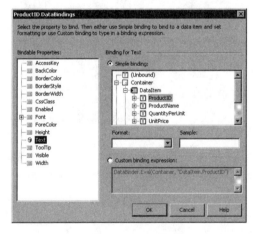

Next, add three more Label controls in the remaining cells of your table. Set the ID property for your three Label controls to ProductName, QuantityPerUnit, and UnitPrice, respectively. Also, bind each of your Label controls to the ProductName, QuantityPerUnit, and UnitPrice columns, respectively.

Next, you'll modify the HTML for your form to make the table a little easier to read. You'll be changing the width and border attributes of the TABLE tag and setting the width attribute of the TD tags.

NOTE *The* **TABLE** *tag defines a table, and the* **TD** *tag defines an element in a row in the table.*

To view the HTML code for your form, click the HTML link under the form designer to view the code for your form. Set the **width** and **border** attributes of your **TABLE** tag to 320 and 1, respectively, and set the **width** attributes of the four **TD** tags to 20, 100, 100, and 100, respectively. The following HTML shows these changes:

```
<TABLE id="Table5" cellSpacing="1" cellPadding="1" width="320" border="1">
  <TR>
    <TD width="20">
      <asp:Label id=ProductID runat="server" Text='
      <%# DataBinder.Eval(Container, "DataItem.ProductID") %>'>
      </asp:Label></TD>
    <TD width="100">
      <asp:Label id=ProductName runat="server" Text='
      <%# DataBinder.Eval(Container, "DataItem.ProductName") %>'>
      </asp:Label></TD>
    <TD width="100">
      <asp:Label id=QuantityPerUnit runat="server" Text='
      <%# DataBinder.Eval(Container, "DataItem.QuantityPerUnit") %>'>
      </asp:Label></TD>
    <TD width="100">
      <asp:Label id=UnitPrice runat="server" Text='
      <%# DataBinder.Eval(Container, "DataItem.UnitPrice") %>'>
      </asp:Label></TD>
  </TR>
</TABLE>
```

NOTE *The* **id** *attribute of your* **TABLE** *tag may differ from that shown in the previous code. Don't worry about changing the* **id** *attribute for your* **TABLE** *tag.*

Next, you'll need to add code to populate **sqlDataAdapter1** with the rows retrieved by your SELECT statement. Typically, the best place to place this code is in the **Page_Load()** method of your form. The **Page_Load()** method is called when the web page containing your form is initially loaded or refreshed. Open the code for your form by selecting View ➤ Code, or press F7 on your keyboard. Set your **Page_Load()** method to the following:

```
private void Page_Load(object sender, System.EventArgs e)
{
  // Put user code to initialize the page here
  if (!this.IsPostBack)
  {
    sqlDataAdapter1.Fill(dataSet11, "Products");
    this.DataBind();
  }
}
```

The Fill() method retrieves the rows from the Products table and populates the dataSet11 object with those rows. The DataBind() method then causes the rows to be displayed in the DataList of your form.

To run your form, select Debug ➤ Start without Debugging, or press Ctrl+F5 on your keyboard. Figure 25.22 shows the running form.

FIGURE 25.22

The running form

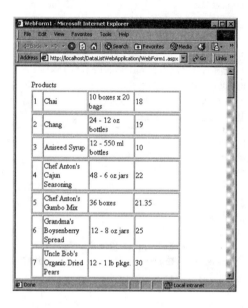

Once you've finished running your form, close it and return to the form designer. Click the HTML link to view the code for your form. Listing 25.5 shows the WebForm1.aspx file for the form. You'll notice that this file contains a DataGrid control with the appropriate columns.

LISTING 25.5: THE WebForm1.aspx FILE

```
<%@ Page language="c#" Codebehind="WebForm1.aspx.cs"
 AutoEventWireup="false"
 Inherits="DataListWebApplication.WebForm1" %>
<!DOCTYPE HTML PUBLIC "-//W3C//DTD HTML 4.0 Transitional//EN" >
<HTML>
  <HEAD>
    <title>WebForm1</title>
    <meta content="Microsoft Visual Studio 7.0" name="GENERATOR">
    <meta content="C#" name="CODE_LANGUAGE">
    <meta content="JavaScript" name="vs_defaultClientScript">
    <meta content="http://schemas.microsoft.com/intellisense/ie5"
      name="vs_targetSchema">
  </HEAD>
  <body MS_POSITIONING="GridLayout">
    <form id="Form1" method="post" runat="server">
```

```
<asp:datalist id=DataList1 style="Z-INDEX: 101; LEFT: 33px;
 POSITION: absolute; TOP: 28px" runat="server"
 DataMember="Products" Height="140" Width="297" DataSource="
<%# dataSet11 %>">
  <HeaderTemplate>
    <asp:Label id="Label1" runat="server">Products</asp:Label>
  </HeaderTemplate>
  <FooterTemplate>
    <asp:Label id="Label2" runat="server">End of list</asp:Label>
  </FooterTemplate>
  <ItemTemplate>
    <TABLE id="Table5" cellSpacing="1" cellPadding="1" width="320"
      border="1">
      <TR>
        <TD width="20">
          <asp:Label id=ProductID runat="server" Text='
          \<%# DataBinder.Eval(Container, "DataItem.ProductID") %>'>
          </asp:Label></TD>
        <TD width="100">
          <asp:Label id=ProductName runat="server" Text='
          <%# DataBinder.Eval(Container, "DataItem.ProductName") %>'>
          </asp:Label></TD>
        <TD width="100">
          <asp:Label id=QuantityPerUnit runat="server" Text='
          <%# DataBinder.Eval(Container,
            "DataItem.QuantityPerUnit") %>'>
          </asp:Label></TD>
        <TD width="100">
          <asp:Label id=UnitPrice runat="server" Text='
          <%# DataBinder.Eval(Container, "DataItem.UnitPrice") %>'>
          </asp:Label></TD>
      </TR>
    </TABLE>
  </ItemTemplate>
</asp:datalist></form>
</body>
</HTML>
```

Summary

HTML creates static web pages whose content doesn't change. However, if you want the information to be dynamic, then you can use ASP.NET. ASP.NET allows you to create web pages whose content may change at run-time, and it allows you to develop applications that are accessed using a web browser. In this chapter, you saw how to use Visual Studio .NET (VS .NET) to create some simple ASP.NET web applications. This chapter gave you a brief introduction to the large subject of ASP.NET.

In the next chapter, you'll learn about web services.

Chapter 26

Web Services

YOU'VE UNDOUBTEDLY HEARD OF *web services* by now. Indeed, Microsoft has made it clear that developing web services is one of the central goals of the .NET Framework and Visual Studio .NET. But despite the hype (or perhaps because of it), it's easy to be confused as to just what makes up a web service and how all of the pieces fit together.

Web services—sometimes called *XML web services*—enable the exchange of data and the remote invocation of methods by sending Extensible Markup Language (XML) messages from one application to another. Web services use a variety of standards to make these messages decipherable by a wide variety of applications. For instance, the messages themselves are formatted according to the SOAP standard, a particular XML application. There is no need for the web services server and client to share a platform, component model, or operating system.

In this chapter, we'll explore the standards that enable web services and show how you can use C# to build client and server programs that communicate via the web services model.

Featured in this chapter:

◆ Exploring the Architecture of Web Services

◆ Building Simple and Complex Web Services

◆ Monitoring the Conversation between Client and Server

◆ Looking Inside the Web Services Proxy

◆ Building a Client

◆ Understanding Web Services Registries

Exploring the Architecture of Web Services

Microsoft describes the .NET Framework as "an XML Web services platform that will enable developers to create programs that transcend device boundaries and fully harness the connectivity of the Internet." But just what is a web service? The easiest way to think of a web service is as a way of interacting with objects and their methods via Internet protocols.

You've already seen one method for interacting with objects via Internet protocols in Chapter 18, "Remoting." The difference between remoting and web services is in the degree of coupling required by the two methods of communicating. Two applications are said to be *tightly coupled* if they depend on knowledge of each other's internal structure or *loosely coupled* if they do not. Remoting is a tightly coupled solution: It only works from one .NET application to another, and the calling application requires an intimate knowledge of the called application. In contrast, web services provide a loosely coupled solution for using objects over Internet protocols. The two applications need only agree on a messaging format (which is based, as you'll see, in common Internet protocols). The internal implementations of the applications do not need to have any knowledge of each other. A web services client written in Java and running on Macintosh OSX can easily call a web services server written in .NET and running on Windows 2000. All of the web services protocols are implemented as XML messages, which are generally transported over Hypertext Transfer Protocol (HTTP).

NOTE *Web services are not absolutely required to interact over HTTP. The XML messages could be sent by another means such as Simple Mail Transport Protocol (SMTP) and they would still work. As a practical matter, though, web services built with Visual Studio .NET use HTTP as their default protocol. All of our examples in this chapter will do likewise.*

It's convenient to break up the interaction between a web services client and the web service that it calls into four aspects, each of which has an associated protocol:

Directory A web services *directory* works something like a telephone directory: You can search the directory to learn how to contact a particular web service. Web services clients communicate with a directory via the Universal Description, Discovery, and Integration (UDDI) protocol. There are several public UDDI registries available on the Internet, and any organization is free to set up its own UDDI registry internally or externally.

Discovery After you've located a particular web service, the next step is to engage in *discovery*. The purpose of discovery is to locate documents that describe the web service. Discovery is conducted by reading a discovery file from the web service. Normally the discovery file will contain the location of one or more description files for the web service.

Description A web services client can retrieve a *description* document from a server as a result of the discovery process. Description documents are written in Web Services Description Language (WSDL). A description document provides the information necessary for a client to construct a message that will actually call the web service. This includes details on service names, available methods, parameter data types, and so on.

Wire Format Finally, a client uses messages constructed according to a particular *wire format* to communicate with the server. With web services, the wire format is most often Simple Object Access Protocol (SOAP). SOAP messages can encapsulate method calls, return values, and parameter information passed between a client and server. This is the only aspect of communication that is absolutely required for a web service interaction.

We'll discuss each of these aspects of web services in more detail in the following pages. Depending on the client and the server, you might not require all four of these aspects in a particular application. For example, if you already know the address of the server, there's no need to consult a web services directory or to engage in a discovery process.

WARNING *Although web services are discovered by standards, those standards are still developing and are implemented in different ways by different vendors. In this chapter, we'll be describing the Microsoft approach to web services. The broad outlines will be the same for any vendor, but details may differ.*

Building a Simple Web Service

The easiest way to see how most of these protocols are used is to actually build a simple web service. Although you could construct all of the necessary documents by hand using only a text editor, it's much easier to let Visual Studio .NET do most of the work. Follow these steps to build a simple web service:

1. Launch Visual Studio .NET.

2. Click the New Project button on the Start page.

3. In the New Project dialog box, select Visual C# Projects as the project type and ASP.NET Web Service as the template. You'll need to supply a location that includes a server and a service name. Enter **http://localhost/Info** in the Location box to name the project Info and locate it on the computer where you're running Visual Studio .NET. Of course, you'll need to have Internet Information Services (IIS) installed on this computer. Alternatively, you can supply the name of any other server on which you have adequate rights and on which the .NET Framework in installed. For example, you could use http://SKYROCKET/Info to name the project Info and to locate it on a computer named SKYROCKET.

4. Visual Studio .NET will create your project and open a file named `Service1.asmx.cs`. Delete this file from Solution Explorer. Select Project ➢ Add Component and add a new web service named `InfoService.asmx` to the project.

TIP *Although you can rename a web service in Solution Explorer, this will only rename the file and not the underlying class. The mismatch in names can be confusing as you try to maintain the project.*

5. Switch to the code view of the web service. You'll find that it contains some sample code for creating a method: ·

```
// WEB SERVICE EXAMPLE
// The HelloWorld() example service returns the string Hello World
// To build, uncomment the following lines then save
and build the project
// To test this web service, press F5

//      [WebMethod]
//      public string HelloWorld()
//      {
//          return "Hello World";
//      }
```

Replace this sample code with your own custom code:

```
[WebMethod]
public DateTime LongDate()
{
    return DateTime.Now.ToLocalTime();
}

[WebMethod]
public string FormattedDate()
{
    return DateTime.Now.ToShortDateString();
}
```

6. Modify the class declaration by adding a WebService attribute:

```
[WebService(Namespace="http://MasteringCSharp/Info")]
public class InfoService : System.Web.Services.WebService
```

7. Select Build ➤ Build Solution to create the web service.

If you inspect the code within Visual Studio .NET, you'll see that the InfoService class is declared as a subclass of the System.Web.Services.WebService class:

```
public class InfoServices : System.Web.Services.WebService
```

Inheriting from System.Web.Services.WebService is what identifies this class as a web service. The WebMethod attribute marks methods that should be made available as methods of the web service.

TIP   *The Namespace property of the WebService attribute specifies an XML namespace that will be used to distinguish this web service from any other. By default, if you do not assign a Namespace property, the compiler will use http://tempuri.org as your web service's namespace. Although this will work fine in testing, you should always change it before you deploy a web service publicly.*

Understanding Discovery

Now that you've created a web service, you can see how discovery works with it. To do this, you can use the Web Services Discovery tool, disco.exe, which ships with the .NET Framework. Follow these steps to use this tool:

1. Select Start ➤ Programs ➤ Microsoft Visual Studio .NET ➤ Visual Studio .NET Tools ➤ Visual Studio .NET Command Prompt. This will open a command prompt window and set the environment up so that you can use any of the command-line tools from the .NET Framework SDK.

2. Execute this command line to invoke the Web Services Discovery tool:

```
disco http://localhost/Info/InfoService.asmx
```

The output from the Web Services Discovery tool is as follows:

```
Microsoft (R) Web Services Discovery Utility
[Microsoft (R) .NET Framework, Version 1.0.3705.0]
Copyright (C) Microsoft Corporation 1998-2001. All rights reserved.


Disco found documents at the following URLs:
http://localhost/Info/InfoService.asmx?wsdl
http://localhost/Info/InfoService.asmx?disco


The following files hold the content found at the corresponding URLs:
  .\InfoService.wsdl <- http://localhost/Info/InfoService.asmx?wsdl
  .\InfoService.disco <- http://localhost/Info/InfoService.asmx?disco
The file .\results.discomap holds links to each of these files.
```

As you can see, the Web Services Discovery tool creates three files on your local hard drive. The results.discomap file is simply an XML file that points to the other two files. The InfoService.wsdl file is a WSDL file for the InfoService web service. You'll see this file in the next section. Listing 26.1 shows the contents of the remaining file, InfoService.disco (slightly reformatted to fit on the page).

LISTING 26.1: InfoService.disco

```xml
<?xml version="1.0" encoding="utf-8"?>
<discovery xmlns:xsd="http://www.w3.org/2001/XMLSchema"
 xmlns:xsi="http://www.w3.org/2001/XMLSchema-instance"
 xmlns="http://schemas.xmlsoap.org/disco/">
  <contractRef ref="http://localhost/Info/InfoService.asmx?wsdl"
  docRef="http://localhost/Info/InfoService.asmx"
  xmlns="http://schemas.xmlsoap.org/disco/scl/" />
  <soap address="http://localhost/Info/InfoService.asmx"
    xmlns:q1="http://MasteringCSharp/Info"
    binding="q1:InfoServiceSoap"
    xmlns="http://schemas.xmlsoap.org/disco/soap/" />
</discovery>
```

In general, you won't need to be concerned with the details of disco files because they'll be processed by your tools. But it's worth taking a look at the overall structure:

◆ The discovery tag specifies the namespaces used by the Disco protocol.

◆ The contractRef tag points to other resources for this web service. In particular, the ref tag specifies where you can find the description of the service, and the docRef tag specifies where you can find the documentation for the service.

◆ The soap tag has the address to which SOAP requests can be sent, as well as the XML namespace that you specified for the web service.

NOTE *At this time, it's not clear whether Disco will end up being an especially important standard. If you believe it's likely that people will publish web services for others to use without notifying the other party, then the discovery process will be critical to using them. But if the majority of web services are used by partners who've negotiated things directly, discovery protocols will never be used.*

Understanding Description

As mentioned previously, discovery is a process that reveals the details of communicating with a web service. The Web Services Discovery tool returns a WSDL file from the server. Listing 26.2 shows this file for the example web service that we're using. Once again, the file has been reformatted to fit on the printed page.

LISTING 26.2: InfoService.wsdl

```xml
<?xml version="1.0" encoding="utf-8"?>
<definitions xmlns:http="http://schemas.xmlsoap.org/wsdl/http/"
 xmlns:soap="http://schemas.xmlsoap.org/wsdl/soap/"
 xmlns:s="http://www.w3.org/2001/XMLSchema"
 xmlns:s0="http://MasteringCSharp/Info"
 xmlns:soapenc="http://schemas.xmlsoap.org/soap/encoding/"
 xmlns:tm="http://microsoft.com/wsdl/mime/textMatching/"
 xmlns:mime="http://schemas.xmlsoap.org/wsdl/mime/"
 targetNamespace="http://MasteringCSharp/Info"
 xmlns="http://schemas.xmlsoap.org/wsdl/">
  <types>
    <s:schema elementFormDefault="qualified"
     targetNamespace="http://MasteringCSharp/Info">
      <s:element name="LongDate">
        <s:complexType />
      </s:element>
      <s:element name="LongDateResponse">
        <s:complexType>
          <s:sequence>
            <s:element minOccurs="1" maxOccurs="1" name="LongDateResult"
             type="s:dateTime" />
          </s:sequence>
        </s:complexType>
      </s:element>
      <s:element name="FormattedDate">
        <s:complexType />
      </s:element>
      <s:element name="FormattedDateResponse">
        <s:complexType>
          <s:sequence>
            <s:element minOccurs="0" maxOccurs="1"
             name="FormattedDateResult" type="s:string" />
          </s:sequence>
```

```
      </s:complexType>
    </s:element>
    <s:element name="dateTime" type="s:dateTime" />
    <s:element name="string" nillable="true" type="s:string" />
  </s:schema>
</types>
<message name="LongDateSoapIn">
  <part name="parameters" element="s0:LongDate" />
</message>
<message name="LongDateSoapOut">
  <part name="parameters" element="s0:LongDateResponse" />
</message>
<message name="FormattedDateSoapIn">
  <part name="parameters" element="s0:FormattedDate" />
</message>
<message name="FormattedDateSoapOut">
  <part name="parameters" element="s0:FormattedDateResponse" />
</message>
<message name="LongDateHttpGetIn" />
<message name="LongDateHttpGetOut">
  <part name="Body" element="s0:dateTime" />
</message>
<message name="FormattedDateHttpGetIn" />
<message name="FormattedDateHttpGetOut">
  <part name="Body" element="s0:string" />
</message>
<message name="LongDateHttpPostIn" />
<message name="LongDateHttpPostOut">
  <part name="Body" element="s0:dateTime" />
</message>
<message name="FormattedDateHttpPostIn" />
<message name="FormattedDateHttpPostOut">
  <part name="Body" element="s0:string" />
</message>
<portType name="InfoServiceSoap">
  <operation name="LongDate">
    <input message="s0:LongDateSoapIn" />
    <output message="s0:LongDateSoapOut" />
  </operation>
  <operation name="FormattedDate">
    <input message="s0:FormattedDateSoapIn" />
    <output message="s0:FormattedDateSoapOut" />
  </operation>
</portType>
<portType name="InfoServiceHttpGet">
  <operation name="LongDate">
    <input message="s0:LongDateHttpGetIn" />
    <output message="s0:LongDateHttpGetOut" />
```

```xml
      </operation>
      <operation name="FormattedDate">
        <input message="s0:FormattedDateHttpGetIn" />
        <output message="s0:FormattedDateHttpGetOut" />
      </operation>
    </portType>
    <portType name="InfoServiceHttpPost">
      <operation name="LongDate">
        <input message="s0:LongDateHttpPostIn" />
        <output message="s0:LongDateHttpPostOut" />
      </operation>
      <operation name="FormattedDate">
        <input message="s0:FormattedDateHttpPostIn" />
        <output message="s0:FormattedDateHttpPostOut" />
      </operation>
    </portType>
    <binding name="InfoServiceSoap" type="s0:InfoServiceSoap">
      <soap:binding transport="http://schemas.xmlsoap.org/soap/http"
       style="document" />
      <operation name="LongDate">
        <soap:operation soapAction="http://MasteringCSharp/Info/LongDate"
         style="document" />
        <input>
          <soap:body use="literal" />
        </input>
        <output>
          <soap:body use="literal" />
        </output>
      </operation>
      <operation name="FormattedDate">
        <soap:operation
         soapAction="http://MasteringCSharp/Info/FormattedDate"
         style="document" />
        <input>
          <soap:body use="literal" />
        </input>
        <output>
          <soap:body use="literal" />
        </output>
      </operation>
    </binding>
    <binding name="InfoServiceHttpGet" type="s0:InfoServiceHttpGet">
      <http:binding verb="GET" />
      <operation name="LongDate">
        <http:operation location="/LongDate" />
        <input>
          <http:urlEncoded />
        </input>
```

```
      <output>
        <mime:mimeXml part="Body" />
      </output>
    </operation>
    <operation name="FormattedDate">
      <http:operation location="/FormattedDate" />
      <input>
        <http:urlEncoded />
      </input>
      <output>
        <mime:mimeXml part="Body" />
      </output>
    </operation>
  </binding>
  <binding name="InfoServiceHttpPost" type="s0:InfoServiceHttpPost">
    <http:binding verb="POST" />
    <operation name="LongDate">
      <http:operation location="/LongDate" />
      <input>
        <mime:content type="application/x-www-form-urlencoded" />
      </input>
      <output>
        <mime:mimeXml part="Body" />
      </output>
    </operation>
    <operation name="FormattedDate">
      <http:operation location="/FormattedDate" />
      <input>
        <mime:content type="application/x-www-form-urlencoded" />
      </input>
      <output>
        <mime:mimeXml part="Body" />
      </output>
    </operation>
  </binding>
  <service name="InfoService">
    <port name="InfoServiceSoap" binding="s0:InfoServiceSoap">
      <soap:address location="http://localhost/Info/InfoService.asmx" />
    </port>
    <port name="InfoServiceHttpGet" binding="s0:InfoServiceHttpGet">
      <http:address location="http://localhost/Info/InfoService.asmx" />
    </port>
    <port name="InfoServiceHttpPost" binding="s0:InfoServiceHttpPost">
      <http:address location="http://localhost/Info/InfoService.asmx" />
    </port>
  </service>
</definitions>
```

As with the `disco` file, you shouldn't need to read the WSDL file yourself. But you should be able to see that it contains information identifying the public web methods of the web service, the data types that they take, the type of calls that you can make to them, and so on.

In fact, the WSDL file contains all of the information that you need to write an application that invokes the web service. The easiest way to build a client application for a web service is to create a proxy class that provides a local class with the same interfaces as the web service. Within the proxy class you include code to construct the actual messages to the web service. You can then include this proxy class in a client application to call the web service.

The .NET Framework includes another tool, the Web Services Description Language tool, which builds such proxy classes for you automatically. To use this tool, first retrieve the WSDL document from the server (either with the Web Services Discovery tool, or simply by knowing the location of the document on the server, and then enter this command line at a Visual Studio .NET command prompt:

```
wsdl /language:CS InfoService.wsdl
```

The result of this command line will be a file named **InfoService.cs** (see Listing 26.3).

LISTING 26.3: A WEB SERVICE PROXY CLASS

```
ï»¿//-------------------------------------------------------------------
---
// <autogenerated>
//     This code was generated by a tool.
//     Runtime Version: 1.0.3705.209
//
//     Changes to this file may cause incorrect behavior and will be lost if
//     the code is regenerated.
// </autogenerated>
//-------------------------------------------------------------------


//
// This source code was auto-generated by wsdl, Version=1.0.3705.209.
//
using System.Diagnostics;
using System.Xml.Serialization;
using System;
using System.Web.Services.Protocols;
using System.ComponentModel;
using System.Web.Services;


/// <remarks/>
[System.Diagnostics.DebuggerStepThroughAttribute()]
[System.ComponentModel.DesignerCategoryAttribute("code")]
[System.Web.Services.WebServiceBindingAttribute(Name="InfoServiceSoap",
```

```csharp
 Namespace="http://MasteringCSharp/Info")]
public class InfoService :
 System.Web.Services.Protocols.SoapHttpClientProtocol {

    /// <remarks/>
    public InfoService() {
        this.Url = "http://localhost/Info/InfoService.asmx";
    }

    /// <remarks/>
    [System.Web.Services.Protocols.SoapDocumentMethodAttribute(
     "http://MasteringCSharp/Info/LongDate",
     RequestNamespace="http://MasteringCSharp/Info",
     ResponseNamespace="http://MasteringCSharp/Info",
     Use=System.Web.Services.Description.SoapBindingUse.Literal,
     ParameterStyle=System.Web.Services.Protocols.
     SoapParameterStyle.Wrapped)]
    public System.DateTime LongDate() {
        object[] results = this.Invoke("LongDate", new object[0]);
        return ((System.DateTime)(results[0]));
    }

    /// <remarks/>
    public System.IAsyncResult BeginLongDate(System.AsyncCallback callback,
     object asyncState) {
        return this.BeginInvoke("LongDate", new object[0], callback,
         asyncState);
    }

    /// <remarks/>
    public System.DateTime EndLongDate(System.IAsyncResult asyncResult) {
        object[] results = this.EndInvoke(asyncResult);
        return ((System.DateTime)(results[0]));
    }

    /// <remarks/>
    [System.Web.Services.Protocols.SoapDocumentMethodAttribute(
     "http://MasteringCSharp/Info/FormattedDate",
     RequestNamespace="http://MasteringCSharp/Info",
     ResponseNamespace="http://MasteringCSharp/Info",
     Use=System.Web.Services.Description.SoapBindingUse.Literal,
     ParameterStyle=System.Web.Services.Protocols.
     SoapParameterStyle.Wrapped)]
    public string FormattedDate() {
        object[] results = this.Invoke("FormattedDate", new object[0]);
        return ((string)(results[0]));
    }
```

```csharp
        /// <remarks/>
        public System.IAsyncResult BeginFormattedDate(System.AsyncCallback
         callback, object asyncState) {
            return this.BeginInvoke("FormattedDate", new object[0], callback,
             asyncState);
        }

        /// <remarks/>
        public string EndFormattedDate(System.IAsyncResult asyncResult) {
            object[] results = this.EndInvoke(asyncResult);
            return ((string)(results[0]));
        }
    }
}
```

We'll examine this file in more detail in the section "Inside the Web Services Proxy." But first, we can use it to actually invoke the web service.

Using the Web Service

Listing 26.4 shows how you can use the InfoServices.cs proxy file to invoke the web service.

LISTING 26.4: INVOKING A WEB SERVICE THROUGH A PROXY CLASS

```csharp
/*
   Example26_1.cs invokes a web service via a proxy class
*/

using System;

class Example26_1
{

    public static void Main()
    {
        InfoService infsvc = new InfoService();
        DateTime dt = infsvc.LongDate();
        Console.WriteLine(dt.ToLongDateString());
        Console.WriteLine(infsvc.FormattedDate());
    }
}
```

To compile this program, you'll need to first compile the InfoServices.cs class to a module and then add the module to the program:

```
csc /t:module InfoService.cs
csc /addmodule:InfoService.netmodule Example26_1.cs
```

The output of running this program is as follows:

```
Tuesday, June 11, 2002
6/11/2002
```

Not too impressive—until you think about what's going on here. As far as the `Main` procedure is concerned, `InfoService` is a class like any other. It has two methods, one of which returns a `DateTime` value and the other of which returns a `string` value. This code would look exactly the same if the `InfoService` class were implemented in a local module.

The `InfoService.cs` proxy (and the .NET Framework) handles all the hard work. It converts all calls to the `InfoService` class into XML messages, sends them to the appropriate place on the server, retrieves the results, and formats them properly. There's a lot of "plumbing" behind this simple example. This nice thing about web services is that it all just works.

NOTE   *Chapter 16, "Assemblies," includes more information on linking multiple source files into a single executable.*

Before you get too excited about the prospect of web services, there's one thing to keep in mind: All of this plumbing adds a lot of overhead to the process. Translating parameters and results to and from XML takes time and increases the size of your code. Suppose you wanted to call the `FormattedDate` method from within the same project where the `InfoService` class is declared? In that case, you should call it just like any other method of a local class. Reserve the web services interface for times when you actually need to communicate via HTTP messages.

Watching the Conversation

Because web services use human-readable XML messages on standard ports, it's relatively easy to monitor the conversation between a web services client and the corresponding server. There are several tools available that can help you do this, either by acting as a proxy to an existing conversation or by using the discovery and description process to create an ad-hoc client. Tools in this class include NetTool, .NET Webservice Studio, and XML Spy:

♦ NetTool is a free Web services proxy tool from CapeClear. You can get a copy from `http://capescience.capeclear.com/articles/using_nettool/`.

♦ .NET Webservice Studio comes from Microsoft. You can download a free copy from `www.gotdotnet.com/team/tools/web_svc/default.aspx`.

♦ XML Spy includes a SOAP debugger that can be used to test Web services. You can download a trial copy of this XML editor and toolkit from `www.xmlspy.com/default.asp`.

Figure 26.1 shows .NET Webservice Studio in action.

FIGURE 26.1

Using .NET
Webservice Studio
to invoke a web
service

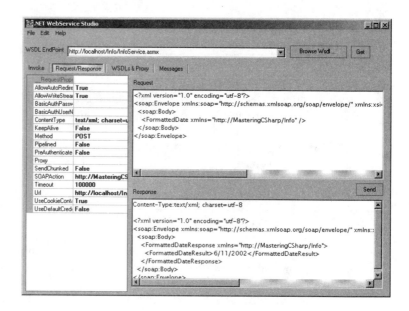

To use the .NET Webservice Studio to work with a web service, follow these steps:

1. Download and install the tool from www.gotdotnet.com/team/tools/web_svc/default.aspx.

2. Install and run the tool.

3. Enter the URL for the WSDL end point in the appropriate text box and click Get. The tool
   will download and parse the WSDL. If you're working with a web service created with Visual
   Studio .NET, you can use the name of the .asmx file for the WSDL end point. For other web
   services, you may need to specify the location of a WSDL file.

4. The tool will retrieve the WSDL file, parse it, and generate a proxy class to call the web service.
   Click the WSDLs & Proxy tab if you'd like to review any of the generated code.

5. Click the Invoke tab to view the objects that the web service makes available and their
   methods. Click a method to see the parameters (if any) that you must supply to the method.
   Click each parameter and assign a value. Then click the Invoke button.

6. You can see the results of the invocation in the lower half of the Invoke tab. To see the actual
   details of the conversation, click the Request/Response tab.

In the specific case of the `InfoService` object, here's the SOAP message from the client to the server:

```
<?xml version="1.0" encoding="utf-8"?>
<soap:Envelope xmlns:soap="http://schemas.xmlsoap.org/soap/envelope/"
 xmlns:xsi="http://www.w3.org/2001/XMLSchema-instance"
 xmlns:xsd="http://www.w3.org/2001/XMLSchema">
  <soap:Body>
    <FormattedDate xmlns="http://MasteringCSharp/Info" />
```

```
  </soap:Body>
</soap:Envelope>
```

Here's the matching response from the server to the client:

```
<?xml version="1.0" encoding="utf-8"?>
<soap:Envelope xmlns:soap="http://schemas.xmlsoap.org/soap/envelope/"
 xmlns:xsi="http://www.w3.org/2001/XMLSchema-instance"
 xmlns:xsd="http://www.w3.org/2001/XMLSchema">
  <soap:Body>
    <FormattedDateResponse xmlns="http://MasteringCSharp/Info">
      <FormattedDateResult>6/11/2002</FormattedDateResult>
    </FormattedDateResponse>
  </soap:Body>
</soap:Envelope>
```

You can see that each of these messages uses tags from the soap namespace and consists of a SOAP envelope containing a SOAP body. The SOAP body of the request contains the name of the method to be called on the web service. The SOAP body of the response contains the resulting data from the web service.

Looking Inside the Web Services Proxy

A closer look at the proxy class that you saw in Listing 26.3 will give you a better understanding of how the .NET Framework keeps track of all of the information necessary to instantiate and invoke objects from a web service. Much of the information is stored in attributes that the compiler can use as a source of metadata.

NOTE *For more information on attributes, see Chapter 17, "Attributes and Reflection."*

The InfoService class is declared this way:

```
[System.Diagnostics.DebuggerStepThroughAttribute()]
[System.ComponentModel.DesignerCategoryAttribute("code")]
[System.Web.Services.WebServiceBindingAttribute(Name="InfoServiceSoap",
 Namespace="http://MasteringCSharp/Info")]
public class InfoService :
 System.Web.Services.Protocols.SoapHttpClientProtocol {
```

The DebuggerStepThrough and DesignerCategory attributes provide information that tells the Visual Studio .NET IDE how to treat this code. The WebServiceBinding attribute indicates the binding within the WSDL file that this class will be a proxy for and specifies the XML namespace for the web service. A *binding* in WSDL is similar to an interface in .NET; web methods are operations that are contained within a particular binding.

The InfoService class derives from the System.Web.Services.Protocols.SoapHttpClientProtocol class. This class implements the basic operations to connect to a web service using SOAP messages with HTTP as the transport.

The constructor for the `InfoService` class hooks the class up to a particular server:

```
public InfoService() {
    this.Url = "http://localhost/Info/InfoService.asmx";
}
```

The `Url` property of the class specifies the base URL for the web service.

Each web method is represented in several ways in the proxy class. First, there's a declaration for the method itself:

```
[System.Web.Services.Protocols.SoapDocumentMethodAttribute(
 "http://MasteringCSharp/Info/LongDate",
 RequestNamespace="http://MasteringCSharp/Info",
 ResponseNamespace="http://MasteringCSharp/Info",
 Use=System.Web.Services.Description.SoapBindingUse.Literal,
 ParameterStyle=System.Web.Services.Protocols.
 SoapParameterStyle.Wrapped)]
public System.DateTime LongDate() {
    object[] results = this.Invoke("LongDate", new object[0]);
    return ((System.DateTime)(results[0]));
}
```

The `SoapDocumentMethod` attribute specifies the format of the SOAP messages that this method will send and receive, including the applicable namespaces. If you look back at the WSDL file for this service in Listing 26.2, you'll see that all of this information comes directly from the WSDL file. The body of the method uses the protected `Invoke` method to send the request to the web service and to return the result, cast to the appropriate data type.

The proxy class also contains methods to call the web methods asynchronously. For example, you can begin an asynchronous call to the `LongDate` method of the web service by calling the `BeginLong-Date` method:

```
public System.IAsyncResult BeginLongDate(System.AsyncCallback callback,
 object asyncState) {
    return this.BeginInvoke("LongDate", new object[0], callback,
     asyncState);
}
```

When you call the `BeginLongDate` method, you must supply a callback delegate that it can use to notify your code when the method is complete. When the callback is invoked, you should call the corresponding `EndLongDate` method to retrieve the result of the web method call:

```
public System.DateTime EndLongDate(System.IAsyncResult asyncResult) {
    object[] results = this.EndInvoke(asyncResult);
    return ((System.DateTime)(results[0]));
}
```

Building a More Complex Web Service

As you might have guessed by now, web methods can have input parameters as well as outputs. For this example, we'll build a more complex web service. This web service will return a `DataSet` containing all of the customers from a specified country, using the Northwind sample database.

NOTE *For this example to work, you'll need to have either the SQL Server or the MSDE version of Northwind, IIS, and Visual Studio .NET all installed on the same computer. You can split these services between multiple computers by adjusting connection and host names accordingly.*

Follow these steps to build the web service:

1. Launch Visual Studio .NET.

2. Click the New Project button on the Start page.

3. In the New Project dialog box, select Visual C# Projects as the project type and ASP.NET Web Service as the template. You'll need to supply a location that includes a server and a service name. Enter **http://localhost/NorthwindServer** to name the project `NorthwindServer` and locate it on the computer where you're running Visual Studio .NET.

4. Visual Studio .NET will create your project and open a file named `Service1.asmx.cs`. Delete this file from the Solution Explorer. Select Project ➤ Add Component and add a new web service named `CustomerService.asmx` to the project.

5. Switch to the code view of the web service. Add one line to the top of the code:

   ```
   using System.Data.SqlClient;
   ```

6. Add code for a web method:

   ```
   [WebMethod]
   public DataSet GetCustomers(string Country)
   {
       SqlConnection cnn = new SqlConnection(
         "data source=(local);initial catalog=Northwind;" +
         "integrated security=SSPI");
       SqlCommand cmd = cnn.CreateCommand();
       cmd.CommandText="SELECT * FROM Customers " +
         "WHERE Country = '" + Country + "'";
       DataSet ds = new DataSet();
       SqlDataAdapter da = new SqlDataAdapter();
       da.SelectCommand=cmd;
       da.Fill(ds, "Customers");
       return ds;
   }
   ```

7. Modify the class declaration by adding a `WebService` attribute:

   ```
   [WebService(Namespace="http://MasteringCSharp/Northwind")]
   public class CustomerService : System.Web.Services.WebService
   ```

8. Select Build ➤ Build Solution to create the web service.

At this point, you've created a web service that returns an entire `DataSet` via an XML message.

Building a Client the Easy Way

You could use the Web Services Discovery tool and the Web Services Description Language tool to construct a proxy class for the new web service. But there's an even easier way to handle all of the necessary connections: Use the tools built into Visual Studio. To do so, follow these steps:

1. Launch Visual Studio and create a new C# Windows application.

2. Add a text box named `txtCountry`, a button named `btnGetCustomers`, and a `DataGrid` named `dgCustomers` to the form.

3. Right-click the References node in the Solution Explorer and select Add Web Reference.

4. Enter **http://localhost/NorthwindServer/CustomerService.asmx** in the Address text box of the Add Web Reference dialog box and click Enter. Visual Studio .NET will retrieve the discovery and description information about the web service and display it as shown in Figure 26.2.

FIGURE 26.2

Adding a web reference

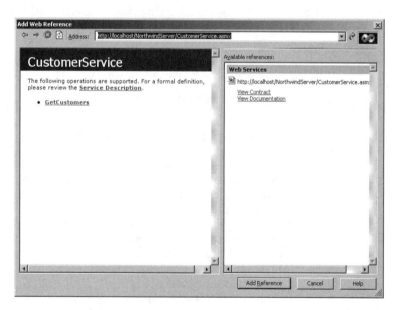

5. If you like, you can test the web service from this dialog box. Click the Get Customers link in the left pane. This will open a test page where you can enter a country name, as shown in Figure 26.3. Enter a country and click Invoke to test the web service. Visual Studio .NET will display the XML for the SOAP response in a new browser window.

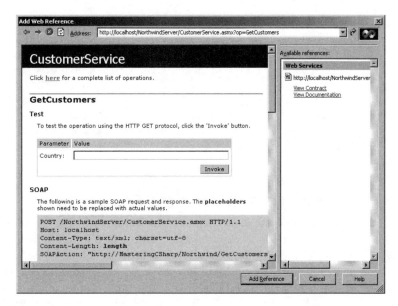

6. Click Add Reference to add a reference to the web service to the client solution.

7. Add code to the form's module to handle the button's click event:

```
private void btnGetCustomers_Click(object sender, System.EventArgs e)
{
    localhost.CustomerService cs = new localhost.CustomerService();
    dgCustomers.DataSource = cs.GetCustomers(txtCountry.Text);
    dgCustomers.DataMember = "Customers";
}
```

8. Run the project. Enter the name of a country and click the button. The form will contact the web service, retrieve the customers from that country, and display them on the DataGrid control, as shown in Figure 26.4.

FIGURE 26.4

Customers retrieved from a web service

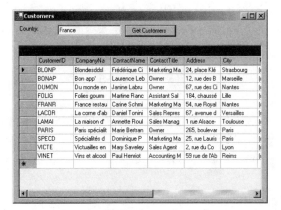

Once again, invoking a web method that accepts an input parameter and returns a complex object (such as a `DataSet`) is no different syntactically from invoking a local method with the same signature. You'll get the same results whether you construct the proxy class with the command-line tools or use Visual Studio .NET to build the connections with the web server through the graphical tools.

TIP There is a potentially major benefit to using a web reference (as compared to constructing proxy classes with the command-line tools). If the signature of the web service changes, it's easier to update the proxy classes if you've used a web reference to connect to the server. All that you need to do in that case is right-click the Web Reference node in the Solution Explorer and select Update Web Reference.

Exploring Web Services Registries

To close the chapter, we'll take a short look at UDDI and UDDI registries. Although you won't need UDDI if you're deploying web services on a small intranet, it can become essential if you need to locate a web service on an enterprise intranet or on the Internet.

UDDI is a method for finding services by referring to a central directory. *Services* in this context are not just web services. UDDI can help locate URLs for information, home pages, or the location of any other online service. UDDI registries are sites that contain information available via UDDI; you can search such a registry to find information about Web services.

UDDI registries come in two forms: public and private. A public UDDI registry is available to all comers via the Internet and serves as a central repository of information about Web and other services for businesses. A private UDDI registry follows the same specifications as a public UDDI registry but is located on an intranet for the use of workers at one particular enterprise.

The UDDI specification is being developed jointly by several industry partners including Microsoft and IBM. For more information and public UDDI registries, visit `www.uddi.org` or `http://uddi .microsoft.com/`.

Visual Studio .NET includes a wizard that helps you register your own web services with the Microsoft UDDI registry. You can register a web service in either a test or a production environment. To register the CustomerService web service, follow these steps:

1. Open Visual Studio .NET. On the Start page, click XML Web Services in the Contents column.

2. Click the Register a Service tab.

3. Click the hyperlink labeled Register Your XML Web Service today.

4. Select the UDDI Test Environment and click Submit.

5. Sign in to the UDDI registry with your Microsoft Passport.

6. Fill in your registration information and click Save to create a UDDI publisher account. Note that you will not be able to finish the process unless you supply a real e-mail address for an account to which you have access.

7. Read the terms of use and click Accept.

8. Wait for the validation e-mail to arrive and follow the instructions that it contains to verify your email address. Then click Continue.

9. Enter your business name and description and click Save.

10. Click Submit to specify the business that you just registered.

11. Fill in the information about your web service and click Submit. Note that you must supply a well-formed URL, but the URL does not have to be accessible from the public Internet.

That's all there is to registering a web service with the Microsoft UDDI Test Environment registry. After you've registered the service, you can add a reference to it by searching the registry. To do so, follow these steps:

1. Open Visual Studio .NET and create a new Windows application.

2. Right-click the References node in Solution Explorer and select Add Web Reference.

3. In the Add Web Reference dialog box, click the Test Microsoft UDDI Directory hyperlink.

4. Enter the name that you registered your business under and click the Search button. You can enter a partial name if you like.

5. The UDDI registry will return links to all of the matching web services. Select the one you like and click Add Reference to add the reference to your project.

With a web service that's listed in a public UDDI registry and Visual Studio .NET, you never have to see any of the XML involved in discovering, describing, and invoking the web service.

Summary

In this chapter, you learned the basics of creating and using web services with C# and Visual Studio .NET. You saw how web services allow you to instantiate and invoke objects over the Internet in a loosely coupled fashion.

Web services function by sending XML messages over common protocols such as HTTP. Several standards control the formatting of these XML messages. These include UDDI and Disco for web services discovery, WSDL for web services description, and SOAP for web services invocation. Although the connections may seem complex, if you keep in mind that a web service is just another way to invoke the members of a class, then you'll be able to see where this technique fits into your development.

Tools available with the .NET Framework and with Visual Studio .NET make it simple to create and invoke web services.

Appendix A

C# Keywords

In this appendix, you'll see a summary of the C# keywords.

abstract   You use the abstract modifier in a class declaration, method, or property. When you use abstract with a class, you indicate that the class is only used to derive other classes. You cannot create an object of an abstract class. When you use the abstract keyword in a method or property declaration, you indicate that the method or property doesn't contain an implementation. You provide the implementation in a derived class.

as   You use the as operator to convert a variable or object of one type to another compatible type. If the two types are not compatible, then the as operator returns null.

base   You use the base keyword to access the members of a base class from a derived class.

bool   You use the bool keyword to denote a Boolean true or false type.

break   You use the break statement to cause program control to exit a loop or a switch statement.

byte   You use the byte keyword to denote an unsigned 8-bit integer type.

case   You use the case statement in conjunction with a switch statement. The case statement denotes one possible branch of a switch statement that is executed when the value evaluated in the switch statement matches the value in the case statement.

catch   You use the catch statement in conjunction with a try statement. When an exception occurs in your try statement, program control searches for an appropriate catch statement to handle the exception. You can supply multiple catch statements after a try statement.

char   You use the char keyword to denote a 16-bit Unicode character type.

checked   You use the checked keyword to check that arithmetic expressions don't produce a value beyond the range that may be stored in your return type.

class   You use the class keyword to declare a class. You can think of a class as a template from which objects are created, although you can also create abstract classes that cannot be used to create objects.

const   You use the const modifier to indicate that value stored in variable or field is constant. Once set, you cannot change the initial value stored in the variable or field.

continue   You use the continue statement to cause program control to move to the next iteration of a loop, skipping over any remaining statements in the current iteration.

decimal   You use the decimal keyword to denote a signed 12-byte (or 96 bits) decimal number type.

default   You use a default statement in conjunction with a switch statement. The default statement is a branch in the switch statement that is executed when no matching catch statement is found.

delegate   You use the delegate keyword to declare a type that can be used to store a method signature. A delegate acts like a pointer to a function, and you can use them to call different functions that you specify at run-time.

do   You use the do statement to repeatedly execute one or more statements in a loop. The loop executes while a specified expression evaluates to true. This expression is evaluated at the end of each iteration of the loop, and therefore the statements in the loop are executed at least once.

double   You use the double keyword to denote a signed 64-bit floating-point number type.

else   You use the else statement in conjunction with an if statement. The else statement is a branch in the if statement that is executed when the expression in the if statement evaluates to false.

enum   You use the enum keyword to declare an enumeration. An enumeration is a list of numeric constants.

event   You use the event keyword to declare an event. Events are a special kind of delegate. You can use events to send notifications that something has occurred to a particular object.

explicit   You use the explicit keyword to declare an explicit type conversion operator.

extern   You use the extern modifier when you declare a method. The extern modifier indicates that your method is implemented outside of your C# code. For example, your method might be implemented in C++.

false   You use the false keyword to represent the negative Boolean value.

finally   You use a finally statement in conjunction with a try and catch statement. The code in your finally statement is always executed at the end of your try or catch statement regardless of whether an exception actually occurred.

fixed   You use the fixed keyword to prevent the garbage collector from relocating a variable or object. A pointer stores the memory location of the variable or object in the computer's memory. You only use the fixed keyword with a pointer in unsafe code.

float   You use the float keyword to denote a signed 32-bit floating-point number type.

for   You use the for statement to repeatedly execute one or more statements in a loop. The loop executes while a specified expression evaluates to true. This expression is evaluated at the end of each iteration of the loop. You can also supply expressions in the for statement that initialize a variable before the start of the loop and increment or decrement that variable at the end of each iteration.

foreach   You use the foreach statement to repeatedly execute one or more statements, iterating over the elements stored in an array or collection. One iteration is performed for each element in the array or collection.

goto   You use a goto statement to jump directly to a statement with a specified label. Typically, you shouldn't use a goto statement because they are considered a poor programming practice. Instead, you should restructure your code so that you don't use goto.

if   You use an if statement to execute a branch of code when a supplied expression evaluates to true.

implicit   You use the implicit keyword to declare an implicit type conversion operator.

in   You use the in keyword in conjunction with the foreach statement. The in keyword specifies the array or collection used in the foreach statement.

int   You use the int keyword to denote a signed 32-bit integer type.

interface   You use the interface keyword to declare an interface. An interface declares methods that must be defined by a class that implements the interface.

internal   You use the internal access modifier to specify that a type or member is only accessible within that type or a type in the same program or assembly.

is   You use the is operator to check if a variable or object of one type is compatible with another type.

lock   You use the lock keyword to ensure that one thread doesn't enter a section of code that is already being executed by another thread. You establish a lock on a specified object.

long   You use the long keyword to denote a signed 64-bit integer type.

namespace   You use the namespace keyword to declare a namespace. You use namespaces to group items such as class declarations into a named unit.

new   You use the new keyword as an operator or a modifier. When you use new as an operator, it creates an object. When you use new as a modifier, it hides a base class member in a derived class.

null   You use the null keyword to indicate that an object reference doesn't refer to an actual object.

object   You use the object type to denote an object of the System.Object class. The System.Object class is the base class from which all other types are derived.

operator   You use the operator keyword to overload an operator in a class or struct.

out   You use the out keyword to indicate that a parameter is to be passed by reference to a method. When you pass a parameter by reference, any changes you make to the parameter are retained when the method exits. When you use the out keyword, you don't have to initialize the parameter before calling your method, but you must set the value of the parameter in your method.

overrride   You use the override modifier with a method or property in a derived class. You then provide new code for the method or property in your derived class, which is run instead of the code in the base class whose method or property you have overridden.

params   You use the params keyword to indicate that a parameter to a method is actually made up of one or more values. These values are all of the same type. You can only use one params keyword in a method declaration.

private   You use the private access modifier to specify that a type or member is only accessible within that type.

protected   You use the protected access modifier to specify that a type or member is accessible within that type or a derived type.

public   You use the public access modifier to specify that a type or member is accessible without restriction.

readonly   You use the readonly modifier to indicate that a field can only be assigned a value once.

ref   You use the ref keyword to indicate that a parameter is to be passed by reference to a method. When you pass a parameter by reference, any changes you make to the parameter are retained when the method exits. When you use the ref keyword, you must initialize the parameter before calling your method, and you can change the value of the parameter in your method.

return   You use the return statement to exit a method. You can return a value from your method in a return statement. If your method returns void, you can omit the return statement.

sbyte   You use the sbyte keyword to denote a signed 8-bit integer type.

sealed   You use the sealed modifier to indicate that you can't derive anything from the class.

short   You use the short keyword to denote a signed 16-bit integer type.

sizeof   You use the sizeof operator to get the number of bytes used to store a value type.

stackalloc   You use the stackalloc keyword to allocate memory on the stack. You can only use stackalloc in unsafe code.

static   You use the static modifier to declare a static member. A static member belongs to the type, rather than an object or instance.

string   You use the string keyword to denote a sequence of Unicode characters.

struct   You use the struct keyword when declaring a struct. You can think of a struct as a lightweight alternative to a class.

switch   You use the `switch` statement to execute a branch of code that matches a particular value. Each branch is identified using a `case` statement. If a branch contains a matching value to the value in the `switch`, the code in that branch is executed. You can use the `default` statement to provide default code when no matching `case` is found.

this   You use the `this` keyword to access the current instance.

throw   You use the `throw` statement to raise an exception. An exception is an error or abnormal program condition.

true   You use the `true` keyword to represent the positive Boolean value.

try   You use the `try` statement in conjunction with a `catch` statement. When an exception occurs in your `try` statement, program control searches for an appropriate `catch` statement to handle the exception. You can supply multiple `catch` statements after a `try` statement.

typeof   You use the `typeof` operator to get the type of an object. The type is returned as an object of the `System.Type` class.

uint   You use the `uint` keyword to denote an unsigned 32-bit integer type.

ulong   You use the `uint` keyword to denote an unsigned 64-bit integer type.

unchecked   You use the `unchecked` keyword to truncate values beyond the range that may be stored in your return type.

unsafe   You use the `unsafe` keyword to mark code as unsafe. If you want to use pointers, then you must use the `unsafe` keyword to mark that code.

ushort   You use the `ushort` keyword to denote an unsigned 16-bit integer type.

using   You use the `using` keyword to create an alias for a namespace or define the scope for an object.

virtual   You use the `virtual` modifier to indicate that a method or property in a base class may be overridden in a derived class.

volatile   You use the `volatile` keyword to indicate that a field can be modified by an item such as the operating system or a concurrent thread. When your program accesses a volatile field it always reads the latest value from the field before using it.

void   You use the `void` keyword to indicate that a method doesn't return a value or to set an object reference to no object.

while   You use the `while` statement to repeatedly execute one or more statements in a loop. The loop executes while a specified expression evaluates to `true`.

Appendix B

C# Compiler Options

When you run the compiler, it takes your program source files and produces an executable output file. You can also pass one or more options to the compiler. For example, you can use the /out option to specify the name of the output file generated by the compiler. In this appendix, you'll see a summary of the C# compiler options.

You can also set some of the C# compiler options using Visual Studio .NET (VS .NET), and in this appendix you'll see references to the Property Pages dialog box of VS .NET. You use the Property Pages to set the compiler options. You access the Property Pages dialog box by following these steps:

1. Open your project.

2. Display the Solution Explorer by selecting View ➢ Solution Explorer.

3. Select the namespace of your project in Solution Explorer.

4. Select View ➢ Property Pages.

The following list summarizes the C# compiler options:

@file　You use the @ option to specify a response file. You specify the name of your response file using the *file* parameter that immediately follows @. Your response file may contain a list of compiler options and program source files; these options and source files are processed in the same way as if you were to type them on the command line. Using a response file therefore saves you from having to keep entering the same information on the command line every time you want to compile your program.

The following command uses the @ option:

```
csc @myRespFile.rsp
```

The @ option is not available in VS .NET.

/?　You use the /? option to view the list of compiler options. This list contains the options along with a description. The /? and /help options are identical.

The following command uses the /? option:

```
csc /?
```

The /? option is not available in VS .NET.

/addmodule:file_list   You use the /addmodule option to add one or more modules to an assembly. You specify the modules using the *file_list* parameter, which is a list of metadata files. Each file in *file_list* must be separated by a comma (,) or semicolon (;).

The following command uses the /addmodule option:

```
csc /addmodule:myMetaDataFile.netmodule mySourceFile.cs
```

The /addmodule option is not available in VS .NET.

/baseaddress:address   You use the /baseaddress option to specify the address to load a Dynamic Link Library (DLL). You specify this address using the *address* parameter, which is a decimal, hexadecimal, or octal number.

The following command uses the /baseaddress option:

```
csc /baseaddress:0x11110000 mySourceFile.cs
```

To set the /baseaddress option using VS .NET, you follow these steps:

1. Open the Property Pages dialog box. (For a description on how to open this dialog box, see the instructions at the start of this appendix.)

2. Click Configuration Properties.

3. Click Advanced.

4. Set the Base Address property.

/bugreport:file   You use the /bugreport option to write out to a file any bugs detected by the compiler. You specify the file using the *file* parameter. You can then send this file to Microsoft for resolution of the bug. The file written out contains the following items:

◆ A copy of all your source files

◆ The options you supplied to the compiler

◆ The version of your compiler, run-time, and operating system

◆ Any output from the compiler

◆ A description of the problem that you enter (if any)

◆ A description of how you think the problem could be fixed that you enter (if any)

The following command uses the /bugreport option:

```
csc /bugreport:myBugReportFile.txt mySourceFile.cs
```

The /bugreport option is not available in VS .NET.

/checked[+|-] You use the /checked option to specify whether you want the compiler to check the integer arithmetic expressions in your code.

If you use /checked+, then any integer expressions that produce a value beyond the supported range for the return type will cause a run-time exception.

If you use /checked- (the default), then any integer expressions that produce a value beyond the supported range for the return type won't cause a run-time exception—but the returned value will not be correct. You can see why the returned value is not correct in Chapter 2, "Basic C# Programming."

If you use the checked or unchecked keywords in your code, then the /checked option has no effect on the code placed in the scope of those keywords. The checked and unchecked keywords are described in Appendix A, "C# Keywords."

The following command uses the /checked option:

```
csc /checked+ mySourceFile.cs
```

To set the /checked option using VS .NET, you follow these steps:

1. Open the Property Pages dialog box. (For a description on how to open this dialog box, see the instructions at the start of this appendix.)

2. Click Configuration Properties.

3. Click Build.

4. Set the Check for Arithmetic Overflow/Underflow property.

/codepage:id You use the /codepage option to specify the code page (character set) for your source files during compilation. You specify the code page using the *id* parameter. You use the /codepage option when your source files are written using a code page different from the code page for your computer or if your files are not written in Unicode or UTF-8. This happens when you use an editor set to a different codepage or you explicitly save as another codepage. It is also fine with source files saved using ASCII, as it is a subset of UTF-8. In general, a different codepage only comes into play in countries other than the United States.

The following command uses the /codepage option:

```
csc /codepage:1 mySourceFile.cs
```

The /codepage option is not available in VS .NET.

/debug[+|-] and **/debug:[full|pbonly]**   You use the /debug option to specify whether you want the compiler to produce debugging information. You can also specify the type of debugging information produced.

If you use /debug or /debug+, the compiler produces debugging information and writes it out to a program database .pdb file.

If you use /debug- (the default), the compiler doesn't produce any debugging information.

If you use /debug:full (the default), this enables the attachment of a debugger to your program.

If you use /debug:pbonly, this enables source code debugging when your program is started in the debugger but only displays the assembler when your running program is attached to the debugger.

The following command uses the /debug option:

```
csc /debug+ /debug:full mySourceFile.cs
```

To set the /debug option using VS .NET, you follow these steps:

1. Open the Property Pages dialog box. (For a description on how to open this dialog box, see the instructions at the start of this appendix.)

2. Click Configuration Properties.

3. Click Build.

4. Set the Generate Debugging Information property.

/define:symbol_list   You use the /define option to set one or more symbols in your program. The preprocessor reads these symbols. You specify the symbols using the *symbol_list* parameter. Each symbol in *symbol_list* must be separated by a comma (,) or semicolon (;). You can also set symbols in your source files using the #define preprocessor directive.

The following command uses the /define option:

```
csc /define:DEBUG mySourceFile.cs
```

To set the /define option using VS .NET, you follow these steps:

1. Open the Property Pages dialog box. (For a description on how to open this dialog box, see the instructions at the start of this appendix.)

2. Click Configuration Properties.

3. Click Build.

4. Set the Conditional Compilation Constants property.

/doc:file   You use the /doc option to get the compiler to read the XML comments (marked using three forward slash characters: ///) in your source files and write them out to the file specified by the *file* parameter.

The following command uses the /doc option:

```
csc /doc:myDocFile.xml mySourceFile.cs
```

To set the /doc option using VS .NET, you follow these steps:

1. Open the Property Pages dialog box. (For a description on how to open this dialog box, see the instructions at the start of this appendix.)

2. Click Configuration Properties.

3. Click Build.

4. Set the XML Documentation File property.

/filealign:section_size You use the /filealign option to specify the size of the sections in the output file produced by the compiler. This size is specified using the *section_size* parameter and is the size in bytes of each section. Valid values for *section_size* are: 512, 1024, 2048, 4096, 8192, and 16384. The /filealign option is useful when you're developing programs that run on small devices such as handheld computers.

The following command uses the /filealign option:

```
csc /filealign:1024 mySourceFile.cs
```

To set the /filealign option using VS .NET, you follow these steps:

1. Open the Property Pages dialog box. (For a description on how to open this dialog box, see the instructions at the start of this appendix.)

2. Click Configuration Properties.

3. Click Build.

4. Set the File Alignment property.

/fullpaths You use the /fullpaths option to get the compiler to display the full path to each file that have compilation errors and warnings. By default, the compiler only displays the name of the file.

The following command uses the /fullpaths option:

```
csc /fullpaths mySourceFile.cs
```

The /fullpaths option is not available in VS .NET.

/help You use the /help option to view the list of compiler options. This list contains the options along with a description. The /help and /? options are identical.

The following command uses the /help option:

```
csc /help
```

The /help option is not available in VS .NET.

/incremental[+|-]   You use the /incremental option to enable or disable the incremental compiler. The incremental compiler only compiles the methods that have changed since the last compilation of your program. When you use the /incremental option, you must also use the /out option to name the output file produced by the compiler.

The information about the last compilation is placed in a file with the extension .incr. The .incr file contains the status of the compilation. If you also use the /debug option, a file with the extension .dbg will also be created. The .dbg file contains the status of the debugging information. Every time you recompile your files with the /incremental option, the .incr file is updated. If you also use the /debug option, then the .dbg file is also updated.

If you use /incremental or /incremental+, the incremental compiler is enabled.

If you use /incremental- (the default), the incremental compiler is disabled.

The following command uses the /incremental option:

```
csc /incremental+ /out:myOutputFile.exe mySourceFile.cs
```

To set the /incremental option using VS .NET, you follow these steps:

1. Open the Property Pages dialog box. (For a description on how to open this dialog box, see the instructions at the start of this appendix.)

2. Click Configuration Properties.

3. Click Advanced.

4. Set the Incremental Build property.

/lib:directory_list   You use the /lib option to specify one or more directories to look for a referenced assembly when the assembly wasn't found in the current directory or the Common Language Runtime (CLR) system directory. You specify the directories using the *directory_list* parameter. Each directory in *directory_list* must be separated by a comma (,) or semicolon (;).

The following command uses the /lib option:

```
csc /lib:myDirectory mySourceFile.cs
```

The /lib option is not available in VS .NET, although you can create a config file to do the same thing.

/linkresource:file[,identifier]   You use the /linkresource option to create a link to a .NET Framework resource file in the output file produced by the compiler. You specify the resource file that you want to link using the *file* parameter. You can also specify an optional logical name for the resource file using the *identifier* parameter.

The following command uses the /linkresource option:

```
csc /linkresource:myResourceFile.resource,myResourceName mySourceFile.cs
```

The /linkresource option is not available in VS .NET. Instead, you have to include the resource in your project to have it compiled in VS .NET.

/main:class   You use the /main option to specify the class that contains the Main() method you want to use in the output file. You specify the class that contains your required Main() method using the *class* parameter. The /main option is useful when you have more than one class than contains a Main() method.

The following command uses the /main option:

```
csc /main:myClass myClass.cs myClass2.cs
```

To set the /main option using VS .NET, you follow these steps:

1. Open the Property Pages dialog box. (For a description on how to open this dialog box, see the instructions at the start of this appendix.)

2. Click Common Properties.

3. Click General.

4. Set the Startup Object property.

/noconfig   You use the /noconfig option to tell the compiler not use the global or local versions of the csc.rsp file during compilation. The csc.rsp file contains compiler options.

The following command uses the /noconfig option:

```
csc /noconfig mySourceFile.cs
```

The /noconfig option is not available in VS .NET.

/nologo   You use the /nologo option to stop the compiler from displaying the copyright message at the start.

The following command uses the /nologo option:

```
csc /nologo mySourceFile.cs
```

The /nologo option is not available in VS .NET.

/nostdlib[+|-]   You use the /nostdlib option to enable or disable the compiler from importing the mscorlib.dll file. This file contains the System namespace. You use the /nostdlib option when you want to define your own System namespace.

If you use /nostdlib or /nostdlib+, the mscorlib.dll file is not imported.

If you use /nostdllib- (the default), the mscorlib.dll file is imported.

The following command uses the /nostdlib option:

```
csc /nostdlib+ mySourceFile.cs
```

The /nostdlib option is not available in VS .NET.

/nowarn:warn_list   You use the /nowarn option to stop the compiler from displaying one or more warnings. You specify the warnings you want to stop using the *warn_list* parameter. Each warning is the numeric part of the warning identifier with any leading zeros removed. For example, to stop warning CS0010 from being displayed, you use /nowarn:10. Each number in *warn_list* must be separated by a comma (,) or semicolon (;).

The following command shows an example that uses the /nowarn option:

```
csc /nowarn:10 mySourceFile.cs
```

The /nowarn option is not available in VS .NET.

/optimize[+|-]   You use the /optimize option to enable or disable the compiler from optimizing the output file. Optimizing the output file makes it smaller, faster to run, and more efficient.

If you use /optimize or /optimize+ (the default), optimization is enabled and your output file will be optimized by the compiler.

If you use /optimize-, optimization is disabled and your output file won't be optimized by the compiler.

The following command uses the /optimize option:

```
csc /optimize+ mySourceFile.cs
```

To set the /optimize option using VS .NET, you follow these steps:

1. Open the Property Pages dialog box. (For a description on how to open this dialog box, see the instructions at the start of this appendix.)

2. Click Configuration Properties.

3. Click Build.

4. Set the Optimize Code property.

/out:file   You use the /out option to specify the name of the output file produced by the compiler. You specify the name of the output file using the *file* parameter. If you don't use the /out option, the name of the output file produced by the compiler is the same as your source file that contains your Main() method (without the file extension). If you're compiling a .dll or .netmodule file, the name of the file will be the same as your first source file.

The following command uses the /out option:

```
csc /out:myOutputFile.exe mySourceFile.cs
```

To set the /out option using VS .NET, you follow these steps:

1. Open the Property Pages dialog box. (For a description on how to open this dialog box, see the instructions at the start of this appendix.)

2. Click Common Properties.

3. Click General.

4. Set the Assembly Name property.

/recurse:[directory\]file   You use the /recurse option to search for and compile source files in all subdirectories of a specified directory or the current directory. You specify the directory using the optional *directory* parameter. If you omit *directory*, the current directory is used. You specify the file to search for using the *file* parameter, which may contain wildcard characters to match multiple files.

The following command uses the /recurse option:

```
csc /recurse:myDirectory\*.cs mySourceFile.cs
```

The /recurse option is not available in VS .NET.

/reference:file_list   You use the /reference option to import metadata from one or more files that contain an assembly manifest. You specify the files to import using the *file_list* parameter. Each file in *file_list* must be separated by a comma (,) or semicolon (;).

The following command uses the /reference option:

```
csc /reference:myMetaDataFile1.dll;myMetaDataFile2.dll mySourceFile.cs
```

To import metadata from assembly manifest files using VS .NET, you select Project ➢ Add Reference and then add your files.

/resource:file[,identifier]   You use the /resource option to link a .NET Framework resource file to the output file produced by the compiler. Only a link is added to the output file—not the resource file itself. You specify the name of the file using the *file* parameter. You can also specify an optional logical name for your resource file using the *identifier* parameter.

The following command uses the /resource option:

```
csc /resource:myResourceFile.resource,myResourceFile mySourceFile.cs
```

To set the /resource option using VS .NET, you follow these steps:

1. Add the resource file to your project.

2. Select that file in Solution Explorer.

3. Set the Build Action property to Embedded Resource in the Properties window.

/target:format   You use the /target option to specify the format of the output file produced by the compiler. You specify the format using the *format* parameter, which may be set to one of the following values:

exe   You use the exe format to create an executable file. By default, this file has an extension of .exe. The exe format is the default.

library   You use the `library` format to create a code library. By default, this file has an extension of `.dll`.

module   You use the `module` format to create a module. By default, this file has an extension of `.netmodule`. The module format doesn't contain an assembly manifest and cannot be loaded by the CLR. However, you can use the `/addmodule` option to incorporate the file into the manifest of an assembly.

winexe   You use the `winexe` format to create a Windows program. By default, this file has an extension of `.exe`.

The following command uses the `/target` option:

```
csc /target:winexe mySourceFile.cs
```

To set the `/target` option using VS .NET, you follow these steps:

1. Open the Property Pages dialog box. (For a description on how to open this dialog box, see the instructions at the start of this appendix.)

2. Click Common Properties.

3. Click General.

4. Set the Output Type property.

/unsafe   You use the `/unsafe` option to enable compilation of code that contains the **unsafe** keyword. Unsafe code uses pointers, and you can learn about the **unsafe** keyword in Appendix A.

The following command uses the `/unsafe` option:

```
csc /unsafe mySourceFile.cs
```

To set the `/unsafe` option using VS .NET, you follow these steps:

1. Open the Property Pages dialog box. (For a description on how to open this dialog box, see the instructions at the start of this appendix.)

2. Click Configuration Properties.

3. Click Build.

4. Set the Allow Unsafe Code Blocks property.

/utf8output   You use the `/utf8output` option to get the compiler to display output in the UTF-8 character set. This is the output from the compiler and not from the compiled executable.

The following command uses the `/utf8output` option:

```
csc /utf8output mySourceFile.cs
```

The `/utf8output` option is not available in VS .NET.

/warn:warning_level   You use the /warn option to set the minimum warning level reported by the compiler. You specify the level using the *warning_level* parameter, which may be set to one of the following values:

0   The compiler displays no warnings.

1   The compiler displays severe warnings.

2   The compiler displays level 1 warnings plus medium severity warnings. Medium severity warnings include hiding class members.

3   The compiler displays level 2 warnings plus low severity warnings. Low severity warnings include expressions that always evaluate to true or false.

4   The compiler displays level 3 warnings plus informational warnings. This is the default level.

The following command uses the /warn option:

```
csc /warn:3 mySourceFile.cs
```

To set the /warn option using VS .NET, you follow these steps:

1. Open the Property Pages dialog box. (For a description on how to open this dialog box, see the instructions at the start of this appendix.)

2. Click Configuration Properties.

3. Click Build.

4. Set the Warning Level property.

/warnaserror[+|-]   You use the /warnaserror option to enable or disable the compiler from treating warnings as errors.

If you use /warnaserror or /warnaserror+, the compiler treats warnings as errors. When the compiler reports a warning, the build process terminates and no output file is produced. Typically, you should always treat warnings as errors and correct them in your code. That way, your code will be higher quality.

If you use /warnaserror- (the default), the compiler doesn't treat warnings as errors.

The following command uses the /warnaserror option:

```
csc /warnaserror:+ mySourceFile.cs
```

To set the /warnaserror option using VS .NET, you follow these steps:

1. Open the Property Pages dialog box. (For a description on how to open this dialog box, see the instructions at the start of this appendix.)

2. Click Configuration Properties.

3. Click Build.

4. Set the Treat Warnings As Errors property.

/win32icon:file   You use the /win32icon option to add a Win32 .ico file to the output file. A Win32 .ico file contains an icon displayed in Windows Explorer. You specify the .ico file using the *file* parameter.

The following command uses the /win32icon option:

```
csc /win32icon:myIconFile.ico mySourceFile.cs
```

To set the /win32icon option using VS .NET, you follow these steps:

1. Open the Property Pages dialog box. (For a description on how to open this dialog box, see the instructions at the start of this appendix.)

2. Click Common Properties.

3. Click General.

4. Set the Application Icon property.

/win32res:file   You use the /win32res option to add a Win32 .res file to the output file. A Win32 .res file is a resource file containing a version or bitmap (icon) that helps identify your program in Windows Explorer. You specify the .res file using the *file* parameter.

The following command uses the /win32res option:

```
csc /win32res:myResourceFile.res mySourceFile.cs
```

The /win32res option is not available in VS .NET.

Appendix C

Regular Expressions

In Chapter 9, "Strings, Dates, Times, and Time Spans," you examined the details of strings. In this appendix, you'll learn about *regular expressions*, which extend the search capabilities for strings and allow you to search for a specified set of characters or pattern of characters. Regular expressions are useful when you need to search and extract a web address or an area code and phone number from a string. You can even use regular expressions to modify a string. For example, you could a regular expression to modify the format of a date in a string.

Regular expressions actually originate from the Unix operating system and were fully developed in the Perl scripting language. In fact, the regular expressions available in C# are based on the Perl 5 standard. This appendix will give you a brief introduction to the subject of regular expressions.

Concepts

A regular expression is a pattern you use to match against a string. For example, let's say you have a string that contains the following quote from Shakespeare's *Romeo and Juliet*:

```
But, soft! what light through yonder window breaks?
It is the east, and Juliet is the sun.
Arise, fair sun, and kill the envious moon,
Who is already sick and pale with grief,
That thou her maid art far more fair than she.
```

Let's say you want to get all the words that start with the letter *s*. You can do this by applying the following regular expression to the string:

```
\bs\S*
```

The regular expression contains a number of *metacharacters*. In this example, \b, \S and * are the metacharacters. \b matches a word *boundary*, which is the position between a word and a space, and \bs matches the first character in a word that starts with the letter *s*. \S matches any non-whitespace character. * matches the preceding character (in this case, any non-whitespace character) zero or more times. When \S and * are combined, they match any non-whitespace character that is repeated zero or more times. When \bs and \S* are put together, they match words that start with *s*. Therefore, when the regular expression \bs\S* is applied to the string, the matches are as follows:

```
soft!
sun.
sun,
sick
she
```

As you can see, these are all the words in the string that start with the letter *s*.

Metacharacters

Table C.1 lists the metacharacters you can use in a regular expression, along with their meaning and a simple example or their use. You'll see some more advanced examples of regular expressions shortly.

TABLE C.1: REGULAR EXPRESSION METACHARACTERS

METACHARACTERS	MEANING	EXAMPLES
\	Indicates that the match character is a special character, a literal, a backreference, or an octal escape character. (A *backreference* repeats the previous match.)	\n matches the newline character, \\ matches \, \(matches (, and \) matches).
^	Matches the position at the start of the string.	^A matches A if A is the first character in the string.
$	Matches the position at the end of the string.	$B matches B if B is the last character in the string.
*	Matches the preceding character zero or more times.	ba*rk matches brk, bark, baark, and so on.
+	Matches the preceding character one or more times.	ba+rk matches bark, baark, and so on, but not brk.
?	Matches the preceding character zero or one time.	ba?rk matches brk and bark only.
{*n*}	Matches a character exactly *n* times, where *n* is an integer.	hob{2}it matches hobbit.
{*n*,}	Matches a character at least *n* times.	hob{2,}it matches hobbit, hobbbit, and so on, but not hobit.
{*n*,*m*}	Matches a character at least *n* times and at most *m* times, where *n* and *m* are both integers.	hob{2,3}it matches hobbit and hobbbit only.

Continued on next page

TABLE C.1: REGULAR EXPRESSION METACHARACTERS *(continued)*

METACHARACTERS	MEANING	EXAMPLES
.	Matches any single character except \n. If you need to match any character including \n, you use a pattern such as [\s\S].	hob.it matches hobait, hobbit, and so on.
(*pattern*)	A subexpression that matches the specified *pattern*. You use sub expressions to build up complex regular expressions. You can access the individual matches, known as *captures*, from this type of subexpression.	anatom(y|ies) matches anatomy and anatomies.
(?:*pattern*)	A subexpression that matches the specified *pattern* but doesn't store the captures.	anatom(?:y|ies) matches anatomy and anatomies.
(?=*pattern*)	A subexpression that performs a positive lookahead search. This matches a string at the point where a string that matches *pattern* starts.	Ford (?=Probe|Mustang) matches Ford in Ford Probe and Ford Mustang.
(?!*pattern*)	A sub-expression that performs a negative lookahead search. This matches a string at the point where a string that doesn't match *pattern* starts.	Ford (?!Probe|Mustang) matches Ford in Ford Escort and Ford Explorer, but not Ford in Ford Probe or Ford Mustang.
x|*y*	Matches *x* or *y*, where *x* and *y* are one or more characters.	war|peace matches war or peace.
[*abc*]	Matches any of the enclosed characters.	[ab]bc matches abc and bbc.
[^*abc*]	Matches any characters not equal to the enclosed characters.	[^ab]bc matches cbc, dbc, and so on, but not abc or bbc.
[*a-z*]	Matches any character in the specified range.	[a-c]bc matches abc, bbc, and cbc.
[^*a-z*]	Matches any character not in the specified range.	[^a-c]bc matches dbc, ebc, and fbc, but not abc, bbc, or cbc.
\b	Matches a word boundary, which is the position between a word and a space.	You can use this to match items at the start or end of words by placing the \b after or before the characters to be matched. For example, ed\b matches the ed in edward, and \bed matches the ed in drugged.
\B	Matches a non-word boundary. You can use this to match items in the middle of words.	ed\B matches the ed in predator but not the ed in bed.

Continued on next page

TABLE C.1: REGULAR EXPRESSION METACHARACTERS *(continued)*

METACHARACTERS	MEANING	EXAMPLES
\cx	Matches a control character x.	\cM matches a Ctrl-M or a carriage return character.
\d	Matches any numeric character (0 to 9).	\d matches 0 to 9.
\D	Matches any non-numeric character.	\D matches any character except 0 to 9.
\t	Matches a tab character.	\ta matches \ta.
\v	Matches a vertical tab character.	\va matches \va.
\f	Matches a form-feed character.	\fa matches \fa.
\r	Matches a carriage return character.	\ra matches \ra.
\n	Matches a newline character.	\na matches \na.
\s	Matches any whitespace character (space, tab \t, vertical tab \v, form-feed \f, carriage return \r, and new-line \n).	\sa matches <space>a, \ta, \fa, and so on. Note: <space> represents a space character.
\S	Matches any non-whitespace character.	\Sa matches aa, ba, ca, and so on, but not <space>a, \ta, \fa, and so on.
\w	Matches any alphabetical (A to Z and a to z), digit (0 to 9), or underscore (_) character.	\wa matches Aa, Ba, and so on.
\W	Matches any non-alphabetical, non-digit, or non-underscore character.	\Wa matches *a, +a, and so on.
\xn	Matches n, where n is a hexadecimal escape value. Hexadecimal escape values must be exactly two digits long. This allows you to use ASCII codes in your regular expressions.	\x43 matches C.
\num	This is a backreference to an earlier capture, where num is a positive integer.	(.)\1 matches two consecutive identical characters. The (.) captures any single character except \n, and the \1 repeats the capture, matching the same character again, therefore matching two consecutive identical characters.
\n	This is either an octal escape value or a backreference. If \n is preceded by at least n captures, n is a backreference. Otherwise, n is an octal escape value, where n is an octal digit (0 to 7).	\6

Continued on next page

TABLE C.1: REGULAR EXPRESSION METACHARACTERS *(continued)*

METACHARACTERS	MEANING	EXAMPLES
nm	This is either an octal escape value or a backreference. If *nm* is preceded by at least *nm* captures, *nm* is a backreference. If *nm* is preceded by at least *n* captures, *n* is a backreference followed by literal *m*. If neither of these, then *nm* matches the octal escape value *nm* when *n* and *m* are both octal digits (0 to 7).	\\34
nml	Matches an octal escape value *nml*, where *n* is a number from 0 to 3, and *m* and *l* are octal digits (0 to 7).	\\234
\\u*n*	Matches *n*, where *n* is a Unicode character expressed as four hexadecimal digits.	\\u0044 matches the D character.

The Regular Expression Classes

The System.Text.RegularExpressions namespace contains classes that allow you to use regular expressions your C# programs. This namespace contains the classes listed in Table C.2.

TABLE C.2: CLASSES IN THE System.Text.RegularExpressions NAMESPACE

CLASS	DESCRIPTION
Capture	The Capture class represents the results of a subexpression capture.
CaptureCollection	The CaptureCollection class represents a set of subexpression captures. This is a collection of Capture objects.
Group	The Group class represents a capturing group.
GroupCollection	The GroupCollection class represents a set of capturing groups. This is a collection of Group objects.
Match	The Match class represents a matched result from a regular expression.
MatchCollection	The MatchCollection class represents a set of matched results from a regular expression. This is a collection of Match objects.
Regex	The Regex class represents a regular expression.
RegexCompilationInfo	The RegexCompilationInfo class represents information that is used by the compiler to create a stand-alone assembly from a regular expression.

You'll see example programs that use objects of some of these classes shortly.

Regular Expression Examples

Let's take a look at some more complex examples that use regular expressions to match words in the earlier quote from *Romeo and Juliet*. The first example matches words that start with *s* and end with *e*:

```
\bs\S*e\b
```

The `\bs\S*` part of the expression matches words that start with *s*, and the `e\b` part matches words that end with *e*.

Next, the following regular expression matches words that contain two consecutive identical characters:

```
\S*(.)\1\S*
```

The `\S*` pairs at the beginning and end match any non-whitespace characters in a word and `(.)\1` matches two consecutive identical characters.

This example matches words that contain *u*:

```
\S*u+\S*
```

The `u+` matches *u* one or more times.

The next example matches words that contain the pattern *ai*:

```
\S*(ai)\S*
```

This example matched words that contain the pattern *ai* or *ie*:

```
\S*(ai|ie)\S*
```

The next example matches words that contain *k* or *f*:

```
\S*[kf]\S*
```

This final example matches words that contain any letters in the range *b* through *d*:

```
\S*[b-d]\S*
```

Let's examine some code you can use in a C# program to obtain the words that match one of these example regular expressions. Let's assume that the quote from *Romeo and Juliet* is stored in a string named `text`. To store the words that match a regular expression, you can use a `MatchCollection` object; this object is a collection of `Match` objects, each of which stores a match from a regular expression.

The following example creates a `MatchCollection` object named `myMatchCollection` and calls the static `Regex.Matches()` method. This method accepts two parameters: a string containing the text you want to find matches in and another string containing your regular expression:

```
MatchCollection myMatchCollection =
  Regex.Matches(text, @"\S*[b-d]\S*");
```

The `Regex.Matches()` method applies the regular expression to the `text` string and returns the matches in a `MatchCollection` object. You'll notice that the regular expression is the literal string `@"\S*[b-d]\S*"`. The at character (@) indicates that this is a literal string so that the backslash character (\) is not interpreted as an escape character.

You can then use the following foreach loop to iterate over the Match objects in myMatchCollection:

```
foreach (Match myMatch in myMatchCollection)
{
  Console.WriteLine(myMatch);
}
```

This loop displays all the matches that were found in the text string.
Listing C.1 illustrates the use of this code and the regular expressions shown earlier.

LISTING C.1: USING REGULAR EXPRESSIONS

```
/*
  ExampleC_1.cs illustrates the use of regular expressions
*/

using System;
using System.Text.RegularExpressions;

class ExampleC_1
{

  private static void DisplayMatches(
    string text,
    string regularExpressionString
  )
  {

    Console.WriteLine("using the following regular expression: " +
      regularExpressionString);

    // create a MatchCollection object to store the words that
    // match the regular expression
    MatchCollection myMatchCollection =
      Regex.Matches(text, regularExpressionString);

    // use a foreach loop to iterate over the Match objects in
    // the MatchCollection object
    foreach (Match myMatch in myMatchCollection)
    {
      Console.WriteLine(myMatch);
    }

  }

  public static void Main()
  {
```

```
            string text =
              "But, soft! what light through yonder window breaks?\n" +
              "It is the east, and Juliet is the sun.\n" +
              "Arise, fair sun, and kill the envious moon,\n" +
              "Who is already sick and pale with grief,\n" +
              "That thou her maid art far more fair than she";

            // match words that start with 's'
            Console.WriteLine("Matching words that start with 's'");
            DisplayMatches(text, @"\bs\S*");

            // match words that start with 's' and end with 'e'
            Console.WriteLine("Matching words that start with 's' and end with 'e'");
            DisplayMatches(text, @"\bs\S*e\b");

            // match words that contain two consecutive identical characters
            Console.WriteLine("Matching words that that contain two " +
              "consecutive identical characters");
            DisplayMatches(text, @"\S*(.)\1\S*");

            // match words that contain 'u'
            Console.WriteLine("Matching words that contain 'u'");
            DisplayMatches(text, @"\S*u+\S*");

            // match words that contain the pattern 'ai'
            Console.WriteLine("Matching words that contain the pattern 'ai'");
            DisplayMatches(text, @"\S*(ai)\S*");

            // match words that contain the pattern 'ai' or 'ie'
            Console.WriteLine("Matching words that contain the pattern 'ai' or 'ie'");
            DisplayMatches(text, @"\S*(ai|ie)\S*");

            // match words that contain 'k' or 'f'
            Console.WriteLine("Matching words that contain 'k' or 'f'");
            DisplayMatches(text, @"\S*[kf]\S*");

            // match words that contain any letters in the range 'b' through 'd'
            Console.WriteLine("Matching words that contain any " +
              "letters in the range 'b' through 'd'");
            DisplayMatches(text, @"\S*[b-d]\S*");

        }

    }
```

The output from this program is as follows:

```
Matching words that start with 's'
using the following regular expression: \bs\S*
soft!
sun.
sun,
sick
she
Matching words that start with 's' and end with 'e'
using the following regular expression: \bs\S*e\b
she
Matching words that that contain two consecutive identical characters
using the following regular expression: \S*(.)\1\S*
kill
moon,
Matching words that contain a 'u'
using the following regular expression: \S*u+\S*
But,
through
Juliet
sun.
sun,
envious
thou
Matching words that contain the pattern 'ai'
using the following regular expression: \S*(ai)\S*
fair
maid
fair
Matching words that contain the pattern 'ai' or 'ie'
using the following regular expression: \S*(ai|ie)\S*
Juliet
fair
grief,
maid
fair
Matching words that contain 'k' or 'f'
using the following regular expression: \S*[kf]\S*
soft!
breaks?
fair
kill
sick
grief,
far
fair
Matching words that contain any letters in the range 'b' through 'd'
```

```
using the following regular expression: \S*[b-d]\S*
yonder
window
breaks?
and
and
already
sick
and
maid
```

Groups and Captures

Let's take a look at an example that uses groups and captures. To show this, you'll see an example that matches the area code and phone numbers from the following **text** string:

```
string text =
  "(800) 555-1211\n" +
  "(212) 555-1212\n" +
  "(506) 555-1213\n" +
  "(650) 555-1214\n" +
  "(888) 555-1215\n";
```

Next, the following **areaCodeRegExp** string contains a regular expression that matches an area code. This is a group of three numbers within parentheses—(800), for example. This group is named **areaCodeGroup** within the regular expression:

```
string areaCodeRegExp = @"(?<areaCode>\(\d\d\d\))";
```

You'll notice that group name **areaCodeGroup** is specified within < and > characters. As you'll see, you can use this name to get the matches for this group. Also, \d matches a number, and the subexpression (\d\d\d\) matches three consecutive numbers.

Similarly, the following **phoneRegExp** string contains a regular expression that matches a phone number. This is a group of seven numbers with a hyphen after the first three numbers—555-1212, for example. This group is named **phoneGroup** within the regular expression:

```
string phoneRegExp = @"(?<phoneGroup>\d\d\d\-\d\d\d\d)";
```

Next, the following example creates a **MatchCollection** object to store the matches:

```
MatchCollection myMatchCollection =
  Regex.Matches(text, areaCodeRegExp + " " + phoneRegExp);
```

To get the matches in **myMatchCollection**, you first start a **foreach** loop:

```
foreach (Match myMatch in myMatchCollection)
{
```

Within this **foreach** loop, you can display the matches using one of two techniques. The easiest and shortest is to display the matches in **areaCodeGroup** directly using **myMatch.Groups["areaCodeGroup"]**.

Groups is a property of a Match object and gets the GroupCollections object. Therefore, myMatch .Groups["areaCodeGroup"] gets the match for areaCodeGroup. For example:

```
Console.WriteLine("Area code = " + myMatch.Groups["areaCodeGroup"]);
```

In the first iteration of the foreach loop, this will display the following line:

```
Area code = (800)
```

As you can see, this is the area code of the first number in the text string.
Similarly, the next example displays phoneGroup using myMatch.Groups["phoneGroup"]:

```
Console.WriteLine("Phone = " + myMatch.Groups["phoneGroup"]);
```

In the first iteration of the foreach loop, this will display the following line:

```
Phone = 555-1212
```

The second technique for displaying the matches is to use a foreach loop to iterate over the Group objects, along with a nested foreach loop to iterate over the Capture objects in the current Group object. For example:

```
// use a foreach loop to iterate over the Group objects in
// myMatch.Group
foreach (Group myGroup in myMatch.Groups)
{

  // use a foreach loop to iterate over the Capture objects in
  // myGroup.Captures
  foreach (Capture myCapture in myGroup.Captures)
  {
    Console.WriteLine("myCapture.Value = " + myCapture.Value);
  }

}
```

The first iteration of this code displays the following lines:

```
myCapture.Value = (800) 555-1211
myCapture.Value = (800)
myCapture.Value = 555-1211
```

As you can see, the first technique that displayed the groups directly is much simpler than this method that involves nested foreach loops. We only showed you this second technique so that you can see the relationship between the various objects.

Listing C.2 illustrates groups and captures.

LISTING C.2: USING GROUPS AND CAPTURES

```
/*
  ExampleC_2.cs illustrates the use of groups and captures
*/
```

```csharp
using System;
using System.Text.RegularExpressions;

class ExampleC_2
{

  public static void Main()
  {

    // create a string containing area codes and phone numbers
    string text =
      "(800) 555-1211\n" +
      "(212) 555-1212\n" +
      "(506) 555-1213\n" +
      "(650) 555-1214\n" +
      "(888) 555-1215\n";

    // create a string containing a regular expression to
    // match an area code; this is a group of three numbers within
    // parentheses, e.g. (800)
    // this group is named "areaCodeGroup"
    string areaCodeRegExp = @"(?<areaCodeGroup>\(\d\d\d\))";

    // create a string containing a regular expression to
    // match a phone number; this is a group of seven numbers
    // with a hyphen after the first three numbers, e.g. 555-1212
    // this group is named "phoneGroup"
    string phoneRegExp = @"(?<phoneGroup>\d\d\d\-\d\d\d\d)";

    // create a MatchCollection object to store the matches
    MatchCollection myMatchCollection =
      Regex.Matches(text, areaCodeRegExp + " " + phoneRegExp);

    // use a foreach loop to iterate over the Match objects in
    // the MatchCollection object
    foreach (Match myMatch in myMatchCollection)
    {

      // display the "areaCodeGroup" group match directly
      Console.WriteLine("Area code = " + myMatch.Groups["areaCodeGroup"]);

      // display the "phoneGroup" group match directly
      Console.WriteLine("Phone = " + myMatch.Groups["phoneGroup"]);

      // use a foreach loop to iterate over the Group objects in
      // myMatch.Group
      foreach (Group myGroup in myMatch.Groups)
      {
```

```
        // use a foreach loop to iterate over the Capture objects in
        // myGroup.Captures
        foreach (Capture myCapture in myGroup.Captures)
        {
          Console.WriteLine("myCapture.Value = " + myCapture.Value);
        }

      }

    }

  }

}
```

The output from this program is as follows:

```
Area code = (800)
Phone = 555-1211
myCapture.Value = (800) 555-1211
myCapture.Value = (800)
myCapture.Value = 555-1211
Area code = (212)
Phone = 555-1212
myCapture.Value = (212) 555-1212
myCapture.Value = (212)
myCapture.Value = 555-1212
Area code = (506)
Phone = 555-1213
myCapture.Value = (506) 555-1213
myCapture.Value = (506)
myCapture.Value = 555-1213
Area code = (650)
Phone = 555-1214
myCapture.Value = (650) 555-1214
myCapture.Value = (650)
myCapture.Value = 555-1214
Area code = (888)
Phone = 555-1215
myCapture.Value = (888) 555-1215
myCapture.Value = (888)
myCapture.Value = 555-1215
```

Index

Note to the reader: Throughout this index **boldfaced** page numbers indicate primary discussions of a topic. *Italicized* page numbers indicate illustrations.

S

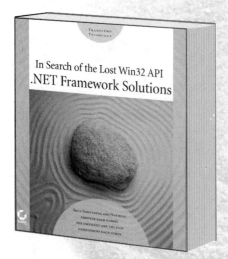

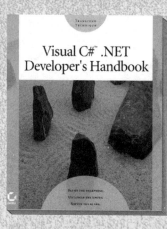